T0216768

Lecture Notes in Artificial Intelligence 727

Subseries of Lecture Notes in Computer Science
Edited by J. Siekmann

Lecture Notes in Computer Science

Edited by G. Goos and J. Hartmanis

Miguel Filgueiras   Luís Damas   (Eds.)

Progress in Artificial Intelligence

6th Portuguese Conference on AI, EPIA '93
Porto, Portugal, October 6-8, 1993
Proceedings

Springer-Verlag

Berlin Heidelberg New York
London Paris Tokyo
Hong Kong Barcelona
Budapest

Series Editor

Jörg Siekmann
University of Saarland
German Research Center for Artificial Intelligence (DFKI)
Stuhlsatzenhausweg 3,
D-66123 Saarbrücken, Germany

Volume Editors

Miguel Filgueiras
Luís Damas
LIACC, Universidade do Porto
R. do Campo Alegre 823, 4100 Porto, Portugal

CR Subject Classification (1991): I.2.3-6, I.2.7, I.2.11

ISBN 3-540-57287-2 Springer-Verlag Berlin Heidelberg New York
ISBN 0-387-57287-2 Springer-Verlag New York Berlin Heidelberg

This work is subject to copyright. All rights are reserved, whether the whole or part of
the material is concerned, specifically the rights of translation, reprinting, re-use of
illustrations, recitation, broadcasting, reproduction on microfilms or in any other way,
and storage in data banks. Duplication of this publication or parts thereof is permitted
only under the provisions of the German Copyright Law of September 9, 1965, in its
current version, and permission for use must always be obtained from Springer-Verlag.
Violations are liable for prosecution under the German Copyright Law.

© Springer-Verlag Berlin Heidelberg 1993
Printed in Germany

Typesetting: Camera ready by author
Printing and binding: Druckhaus Beltz, Hemsbach/Bergstr.
45/3140-543210 - Printed on acid-free paper

Preface

These are the proceedings of the 6th Portuguese Conference on Artificial Intelligence (EPIA'93) organised by the Portuguese Artificial Intelligence Association. Like the last two conferences in this series, this one was run as an international event with strict requirements as to the quality of accepted submissions. Fifty one submissions were received from 9 countries, the largest numbers coming from Portugal (18), Germany (10), and France (8).

With a few exceptions, submissions were evaluated by three referees, who were asked to comment on any reports where the overall evaluations did not agree. At the Programme Committee meeting, these cases as well as those in which only one or two reports were available were carefully examined. The Programme Committee decided on the acceptance of 25 out of the original 51 submissions. A further 8 were selected as posters, 7 of which have their abstracts included here. The members of the Programme Committee and the referees are listed below.

We had the honour to have as invited lecturers David H. D. Warren, Les Gasser, and Yoav Shoham, their presentations highly contributing to the interest and quality of the conference. Les Gasser prepared a written summary of his lecture for this volume. To all three our sincere thanks.

Our thanks also extend to all those who contributed in any form to make this conference possible namely, the Programme Committee members, the referees, the authors, the other members of the Organising Committee and the following institutions (in alphabetical order): Câmara Municipal do Porto, Centro de Informática da Universidade do Porto, Commission of the European Communities, Digital Equipment Portugal, Fundação António Almeida, Fundação Calouste Gulbenkian, Fundação Luso-Americana para o Desenvolvimento, IBM Portuguesa, and Junta Nacional de Investigação Científica e Tecnológica.

Porto, June 1993

Miguel Filgueiras
Luís Damas

Programme Chairmen

Miguel Filgueiras, Luís Damas

Programme Committee

António Porto, Universidade Nova de Lisboa
Armando Matos, Universidade do Porto
David Warren, University of Bristol
Ernesto Costa, Universidade de Coimbra
Eugénio Oliveira, Universidade do Porto
Jean-Louis Lassez, T. J. Watson Research Center, IBM
Luís Moniz Pereira, Universidade Nova de Lisboa

Organising Committee

Miguel Filgueiras, Nelma Moreira, Rogério Reis, Ana Paula Tomás

Referees

Alípio Jorge	Amílcar Cardoso	Ana Paula Tomás
António Mário Florido	António Porto	Armando Matos
Artur Miguel Dias	Carlos Bento	Claire Willis
Cristina Ribeiro	David H. D. Warren	Ernesto Costa
Eugénio Oliveira	Fernando Moura Pires	Fernando Silva
Francisco Menezes	Gabriel David	Joaquim Baptista
Joaquim Correia	John Galagher	John Lloyd
José C. Cunha	José Ferreira	José Júlio Alferes
José Paulo Leal	Giovanni Varile	Luís Caires
Luís Damas	Luís Moniz Pereira	Luís Monteiro
Luís Torgo	Margarida Mamede	Maria Benedita Malheiro
Michael Fisher	Michael Wooldridge	Michel Wermelinger
Miguel Filgueiras	Nelma Moreira	Nuno Mamede
Paulo Moura	Rogério Reis	Sabine Broda
Steve Gregory	Anonymous	

Table of Contents

Distributed Artificial Intelligence

Natural Language Processing

Knowledge Representation

Logic Programming

Non-standard Logics

Automated Reasoning

Constraints

Planning

Learning

Poster Abstracts

Organizations as Complex, Dynamic Design Problems

Les Gasser, Ingemar Hulthage, Brian Leverich,
Jon Lieb, and Ann Majchrzak
Computational Organization Design Lab
Institute of Safety and Systems Management
USC, Los Angeles, CA. 90089-0021 USA
(213) 740-8771
{<lastname> | majchrza}@usc.edu

Abstract. The ACTION organization design and analysis system is a research and development effort designed to assist business re-engineering and organizational or technology change by helping to improve the integration of technology, organizations, and people ("TOP-integration") in manufacturing enterprises. ACTION uses a multi-level constraint-based representation of organizational features including business objectives, unit structure, skills needed, performance monitoring/reward systems, decisionmaking discretion, employee values, coordination attributes, etc. to both evaluate existing organization designs and to help users develop new ones. ACTION's core software is domain-independent, theory-driven architecture designed for application to a wide range of design and analysis problems.

1 Introduction

The ACTION organization design and analysis system is a research and development effort designed to assist business re-engineering and organizational or technology change by helping to improve the integration of technology, organizations, and people ("TOP-integration") in manufacturing enterprises. ACTION helps analyze interactions among a wide range of technological and organizational features, and to design flexible and adaptive organizations that optimize a range of business-oriented objectives. The goal is to assure that the use of ACTION as part of a change management process will lead to

- Improved assessment of how/where organizations or technologies need to be changed to meet specific business objectives
- Increased confidence that fewer technology and business-process implementation issues are overlooked during planning
- More accurate assessment of technology plans in concurrent engineering processes
- Greater assurances that technology modernization plans will succeed
- Identifying the organizational and human costs of capital investment and business strategy decisions

- Increased awareness of alternatives through prior what if analyses
- Increased awareness of design options generated by ACTION
- Initiating discussions with technology planners and users
- Increased awareness of workforce (re)skilling and (re)training opportunities and needs.

1.1 Technology-Organization-People Integration

The ACTION project views TOP-integration as a problem of *matching and coordinating* numerous technological and organizational features (rather than optimizing just one of them), and of *optimizing this match to fit organizational business objectives and environmental circumstances*. ACTION's theory, methodology, and software efforts incorporate knowledge of technological and organizational features including

- Organizational objectives
- Values held by employees
- Performance management systems
- Customer involvement
- Decision-making discretion
- Skills and training needs and opportunities
- Information, tool, and technology resources
- Coordination among jobs and units
- Organizational unit structure
- Job design
- Variances (e.g., turnover, materials quality)
- Specific technical system characteristics

The core knowledge developed in the ACTION Project---a comprehensive model of positive and negative relationships among these key organizational features---is called the ACTION TOP-integration Theory. This theory is a general, domain-independent theoretical and conceptual framework.

The theory captures and represents a large number of manufacturing TOP features that trade-off with one another, in an *open-systems* (OS) model. The open-systems model is a structure that allows for dynamically matching and coordinating these features (rather than optimizing just one of them), and optimizing this match to fit a collection of selected objectives (see below) and circumstantial variances (such as materials quality, process variances, personnel turnover, attendance, etc.) The OS model treats each of these TOP factors as a variable in a large network of constraints. The OS theory specifies the variables, their potential values, and the mutually reinforcing or constraining relationships among them. The purpose of this model is to allow the designer/analyst 1) to capture and track a very large number of TOP features and their interactions, 2) to discover specific points of congruence and misalignment among features, as a basis for redesign or trade-off analysis for optimizing the environmental conservation objective, and 3) to flexibly revise and explore alternative model inputs and outputs and their impacts. ACTION also includes a set of domain-specific refinements to this framework that specialize ACTION's TOP-integration model to production areas of discrete-parts manufacturing organizations, and within this category, to four specific types of production context: short-life-cycle and general group technology cells, functional shops, and transfer lines.

The theory and tool have been developed as follows:

- Critical concepts and general statements of relationships were identified via a qualitative meta-analysis of empirical studies of successful and unsuccessful TOP integration in discrete parts manufacturing.
- To specify specific relationships for specific variables, a knowledge elicitation process was designed for use with industry TOP integration experts. The process included delphi, consensus-building, stable membership (over 1.5 years) in a technical development team, selection of team members to represent a wide diversity of industry contexts, explicit documentation and agreement on all terminology, use of matrices and decision trees to specify relationships, and iterations on theory and applications.
- The elicitation process proceeded over 1.5 years with team members from Digital Equipment Corporation, General Motors, Hewlett Packard, Hughes Aircraft Company, and Texas Instruments.
- The ACTION software decision support and analysis tool, designed for easy theory revision and enhancement, was developed with continuous industry review and input.
- The theory, structure, and usability features of ACTION are now being validated through pilot tests and via a study that incorporates detailed data from 100 sites.

ACTION supports four key functionalities:

- Summary-level analysis and design of TOP integration
- Detailed-level critique and evaluation of TOP integration
- Detailed-level design of TOP-integration
- Explanation of analysis/design concepts and results

ACTION represents the TOP-integration features in a design or evaluation problem as a set of business objectives (goals) to be optimized and a set of detailed, hierarchical constraints (called the theory minimodels) that describe how organizational features, such as above, interact to affect the level of optimization achieved for these objectives. Conversely, the mini-models describe how a required level of optimization, implies constraints on organizational features. ACTION's knowledgebase contains detailed constraint models of the possibility of achieving seven organizational objectives:

- Minimizing throughput time
- Maximizing product quality
- Maximizing employee flexibility
- Maximizing product responsiveness
- Maximizing process responsiveness
- Maximizing changeover responsiveness
- Maximizing manufacturability of designs

To guide the process of generating evaluations or design solutions, a user employs ACTION to select and manipulate constraints, trade-offs, and value-assignments for organization and technology variables that form the theory minimodels.

The ACTION project has built upon the knowledge and insights gained from two prior efforts: the HITOP (Highly-Integrated Technology, Organizations, and People) approach to analyzing human infrastructure impacts of advanced manufacturing technologies [Majchrzak 88; Majchrzak et al. 91], and the HITOP-A (HITOP-Automated) decision support system [Gasser and Majchrzak 92, Majchrzak and Gasser 92]. The HITOP-A system was initially developed at USC. Using decision rules and heuristics, this system predicted human infrastructure required for a particular state of organization, job design, and technology variables. The focus of HITOP-A was predictive decisionmaking and support for flexible manufacturing cells. Work on HITOP-A, completed in 1991, produced an operational prototype which was capable of developing the job and organizational designs that incorporate organizational and technological knowledge and input.

2 Overall System Strategies

The knowledge-based system software core of ACTION is a general, domain-independent tool that operationalizes ACTION domain-specific TOP theories or other theories, to create a combined analysis, design, and explanation/teaching system for a specific domain. This general modeling framework has been used to implement a software decision-support system that includes the ACTION discrete-parts manufacturing models. The overall strategy for ACTION has been to develop a core set of representation and knowledge structures which can be used as a single underlying theory and framework for accomplishing all of the key functionalities. These core knowledge structures are flexible and reconfigurable, so that they can be modified and improved without major software rebuilding. This unified approach leads to greater consistency, coherence, and integration across functionalities in the ACTION system, and improves maintainability. The core ACTION software is reconfigurable to incorporate new domain, control, or interface approaches. This means that the basic structure of the ACTION software and theory is directly applicable to a range of other problems (e.g. enterprise-level modeling), by "plugging in" new domain theories, design processes, and interface models.

This set of knowledge structures includes representations of

- Core ACTION domain theory (minimodels, theory matrices, business objectives/goal, user constraints, etc.)
- User interaction, exploration, explanation, and information facilities
- A constraint based reasoning system.

- Control knowledge such as design and analysis heuristics (e.g. priority rankings of goals or of minimodel elements), or system knowledge states (ACTION's record of what it has accomplished and what a user knows) and design process rules (ACTION's rules that capture recommendations about what ACTION steps to follow in what order, depending on a user's purpose).
- Theory abstractions such as matrices for summary-TOP analyses.

This set of representations is used simultaneously to achieve the four key ACTION functionalities. For example, design, evaluation, and explanation are all achieved by applying knowledge represented in the minimodels as constraints. For evaluation, a user specifies details of organizational unit structures and unit attributes, and the minimodels are applied unit-by-unit to derive information about what goals are achievable and what degree of match exists among an organizations attributes. For design, a user specifies a set of goals for an organization to meet, along with key design constraints, and ACTION uses the minimodels and unit design information to derive a unit structure and appropriate unit and technology attributes. For explanation, particular user-entered or system-derived values can be rationalized by reference to their place in the ACTION Domain Theory and prior minimodel-based conclusions.

ACTION allows for analysis and design of organizations at both summary and detailed levels. The strategy for accomplishing summary-level analyses that are coherent with detailed analyses is to use the same underlying knowledge and representation structures as a basis for both. Knowledge used for summary TOP analysis and design is simply abstracted from the knowledge used for detailed analysis and design. For example, the organizational goal **possibility of minimizing throughput** is linked to the detailed concept **percentage of technology that is reliable** through a dense network of concepts and relationships in the *throughput minimodel*. However, in the summary TOP analysis, this complex relationship has been simplified, and is represented as a pairwise constraint in the summary relationship matrix. In this way, summary relationships directly reflect underlying detailed theory, in abstracted form.

Summary TOP analyses focus on the relationships between organizational goals and key summary analytical variables. In addition, Summary TOP analysis provides high-level descriptions of basic unit design features, requirements, and strategies, taken from a small class of possibilities (rather than from a large class of detailed unit designs).

3 Data-Driven Approach to ACTION

Most routine knowledge-based systems development projects are based on capturing a well-understood (but possibly unarticulated) body of pre-existing knowledge. The ACTION development project has taken on an additional major challenge: the structure and the content of the theoretical and practical knowledge at the core of ACTION were not yet well understood at the outset of the project. Instead, these are under development concurrently with the structure and processing architecture of the ACTION software system. Thus ACTION is an exercise in a type of concurrent engineering, wherein a product (the theoretical and practical knowledge and methodology of ACTION) and a process (the set of tools, design and analysis algorithms, and usability features) are jointly and concurrently developed.

One challenge for ACTION development has been how to maintain the flexibility to accommodate revisions to both ACTION architecture and to ACTION knowledgebase content and structure throughout the development period and beyond, so that ACTION can be as responsive as possible to the needs of users and theory builders. One approach to such concurrent design is *design through abstraction*. Under this approach (which we are using), components of ACTION are being described, designed, and prototyped at successively finer levels of detail. Assumptions behind and interactions among components that arise along the way are refined iteratively as more and more knowledge becomes settled and codified, and more design commitments get made.

A complement to this iterative-abstraction-and-refinement approach to ACTION system development is the ability to remove and insert new component models and new functionalities as knowledge changes and as the level of detail increases. To do this, the ACTION system itself comprises a collection of replaceable and reconfigurable components. It is this replaceable and reconfigurable aspect that we term the *Data-Driven Model* approach to ACTION.

System architecture has been defined as a fixed, bounded, and static framework within which some variation in behavior and specification are possible [Erman 90]. Applying this viewpoint to ACTION, what needs to be defined is what parts of ACTION are static, fixed, and bounded, and what parts are flexible and allow for some variation in their behavior (see figure).

4 Organization Design

We treat organization design as a routine design problem (as vs. a creative design problem), with a well-defined space of possibilities and explicit evaluation criteria. Our approach is to model a designed artifact (in organization design this is an organization or *human infrastructure*) as a collection of variables with accompanying sets of possible values for each variable, at several interrelated levels of abstraction. These variables and values create a space of possible designs. For example, if we are designing chairs, we might use *strength-of-legs* as a design variable, with possible values being integers ranging from 10-100. A set of relations among these variables defines the hard evaluation criteria for designs, and divides the overall design space into acceptable designs (those in which the relations hold) and unacceptable designs (those in which the relations do not hold). The relations may be viewed as 1) constraints among variable values, 2) desired levels of correlation between variable values, or 3) desired levels of congruence (qualitative match) among variable values. For chairs, one such constraint might be *weight of chair + weight of heaviest*

7

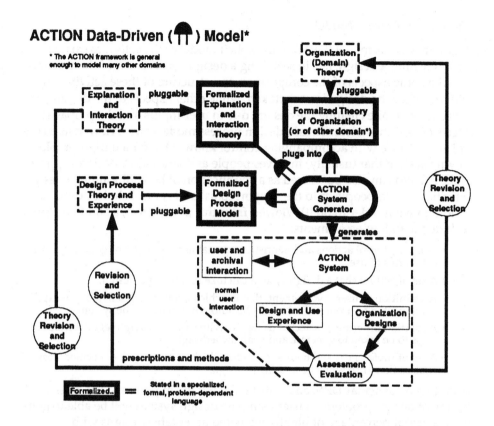

ACTION Data-Driven ( ) Model*

* The ACTION framework is general enough to model many other domains

Organization (Domain) Theory

Explanation and Interaction Theory — pluggable → Formalized Explanation and Interaction Theory

pluggable

Formalized Theory of Organization (or of other domain*)

plugs into

Design Process Theory and Experience — pluggable → Formalized Design Process Model

ACTION System Generator

Theory Revision and Selection

generates

user and archival interaction ↔ ACTION System

Revision and Selection

normal user interaction

Theory Revision and Selection

Design and Use Experience   Organization Designs

prescriptions and methods

Assessment Evaluation

Formalized.. = Stated in a specialized, formal, problem-dependent language

occupant must be less than or equal to strength of legs. Finally, within the space of acceptable designs, there is a set of evaluation criteria that describes "better" and "worse" designs.

In the abstract, then, a design problem is the problem of searching the space of possible designs (i.e., possible value assignments to design variables) for acceptable, highly-evaluated designs. Operators in this search include narrowing the size of sets of possible variable values, e.g. by assigning particular values to variables and propagating/analyzing the effects of the narrowed value sets. Heuristics include domain-specific search-ordering knowledge and domain-independent ordering analyses that depend on structural characteristics of the search space. The set of design description variables together with the set of relations, evaluation criteria and domain-dependent heuristics, is called the *organization design domain theory*. We include provisions for revisions to the domain theory, creating, in effect, a higher-order (theory-level) and more open search space. This allows manual or automatic searches through alternative domain theories, to find design spaces that encompass more appropriate designs.

4.1 Design Process Models

A design process model (DPM) is an explicit model of the activities carried out while creating a design, i.e., in searching a design space. Some of these activities and some aspects of the composition and structure of these activities are known before the design is undertaken, while other aspects of the design process emerge while creating the design, due to user inputs and the propagated effects of design choices. Thus, a design process model can be viewed as a control architecture with accompanying control knowledge for a design-problem solving system that (usually) involves people and automated design support tools. A DPM can also be viewed as a specification of both allocation of design activities (e.g. to people or to the support tools) and control choices (what to do and in what order to do it). Viewed from this perspective, a DPM needs to include the following elements:

- A set of control actions and heuristics, to establish strategies or goals for different modes of use.
- A set of actions that a design system can take in refining a design.
- A definition of user involvement, that is, which choices and activities are explicitly allocated to users and which to the automated parts of the system.
- A (partial) ordering of selected design activities that prescriptively describes the steps to be taken to generate and evaluate a design.
- A set of preferences and heuristics under which to make under-specified design choices that arise while generating a design.

Adopting a particular DPM amounts to making the hypothesis that, over a collection of design problems, a user using the design system will be able to generate a useful percentage of highly-evaluated acceptable designs with acceptable levels of effort.

4.2 Design as the Inverse of Evaluation

Evaluation criteria themselves can be seen as variables, each of which has an associated set of possible values; i.e., there is a space of possible design evaluations, independent of any particular design. Each of these variables can be seen as a characteristic of the design—that is, a way of describing a design in terms useful for evaluation. For example, a chair might be evaluated using a characteristic that directly reflects a design variable, such as *strength-of-legs*, or using a characteristic that relates to the design variables only indirectly, such as *cost*. The evaluation characteristics might have different possible values than those of the corresponding design variables, (e.g. high-med-low vs. 10-100). Evaluation criteria may also be joined using relations, such as an ideal strength-to-cost relation for chairs.

In general, then, we can think of an evaluation as a mapping between a set of design descriptions and a set of evaluation criteria. (We might think of this as applying evaluation functions to designs.) The inverse of this is a mapping from points in the space of evaluations to sets of designs, and this is how we see the activity of design: iteratively choosing a set of evaluation criteria and then finding sets of designs that are elements of this inverse mapping. We call these inverse mappings *design relations*. (They are relations, rather than functions, because they are in general one-to-many mappings.) The general sources for such relations are:

- The domain theory, i.e., in addition to evaluation functions some design relations may be known.
- Deduction from evaluation functions; some evaluation functions may have such a form that it is possible to obtain the inverse relation mathematically.
- Through search; in the absence of complete knowledge, it may be necessary to heuristically search through a range of possible designs in a generate-and-test paradigm. This search is guided by the design process model.

Three situations can occur:

- The inverse mapping does not exist, i.e. the design problem is unsolvable because it is overconstrained;
- There are many possible inverse maps, i.e. the design problem is underconstrained;
- There is a unique inverse, i.e the design problem has exactly one solution.

A basic design process, then, is to first find an estimated level of constraint, then to alternate between processes that

- adjust the degree of constraint (possibly using preferences) to moderate the ease or difficulty of finding solutions, and
- engage in search (or other methods of creating inverse mappings) to establish a set of acceptably-constrained design alternatives.

5 Unit Design

Unit design in ACTION is carried out as a highly-constrained search through a space of alternative unit designs. This is a heuristically guided exploratory search for several reasons. First, we have incomplete knowledge with which to design units algorithmically, and so unit design requires exploration, which must be to some extent a generate-and-test search process. Heuristics such as user priorities for goals or particular attributes, and user choice preferences are brought to bear during this search.

Second, the ability to explore and revise tentative conclusions opens the door to creative and possibly uniquely good, yet unforeseen, unit designs. This search through alternatives is thus important to maintain ACTION's capability to generate innovative and exploratory unit designs that nonetheless reflect solid, rational, and explainable design principles.

Search depends upon the ability efficiently to generate alternatives and the ability efficiently to test and differentiate promising avenues from unpromising ones. Thus search requires 1) good control (generation) heuristics, and 2) good evaluation heuristics---i.e., several good evaluation procedures graded in terms of resources required and solution quality, so that good and poor solutions can be differentiated rapidly, and so that greater effort can be put into detailed evaluation of highly promising solutions.

Overall unit design in ACTION requires designing two aspects: individual units themselves, and the set of relationships among units which, taken together, we call *unit structure*. There is no necessary commitment to which of these aspects is designed first. In ACTION Phase I, however, unit structure is constrained to be a hierarchy. This unit structure constraint means that at each hierarchical level, unit design can be seen as a problem of partitioning the collection of all activities at that level into a set of separate, disjoint units

5.1 Equivalence Relations as a Foundation for Unit Design

Unit design is based on the notion of equivalence classes, where units comprise activities that are found to be equivalent with respect to some equivalence criterium. The idea is that activities are put together in units because they are 'equivalent' in some sense, e.g. they may require the same resources or skills. By changing and composing the criterium for equivalence, ACTION can change the classification of activities into equivalence classes, and thus can manipulate the membership of activities in units. Since there is a number of different criteria, choices about *how* to construct an equivalence relation effectively yield a search through a space of alternative unit designs. The basis of this procedure is the fact that equivalence relations between objects in a set mathematically define a clustering into disjunctive clusters.

Using this approach, the issue becomes how to utilize several types of relations present in the ACTION domain theory to produce the "right" definition of equivalence and hence the right clustering.

The relations needed by this approach are found in the ACTION domain theory as factors such as:

- Subdivisibility of goals
- Reciprocal dependencies among tasks
- Motivational completeness of jobs
- Complete variance control
- Similarity of Information and Resource Needs
- Preference for job broadening
- Workload
- Needed vs. available skills
- Preference for single person jobs

These factors define relations between activities, but do not necessarily define equivalence. However, it turns out that even if a factor does not define an equivalence relation, it is usually possible to redefine the factor slightly, in a way that is inconsequential from the domain theory point of view, to make it an equivalence.

5.2 Unit Design Heuristics

There are two kinds of failure modes for a test evaluation, corresponding to the two dimensions of organizational evaluation used in ACTION; sociotechnical match and achievement of organizational goals. In the first case, a unit design may lead to an overconstrained set of organizational attributes (no sociotechnical match is possible among organizational features). In the second, the organizational feature matches may be underconstrained, but it may not be possible to fully meet organizational goals.

Unit design generation heuristics correspond to the failure modes of evaluations used in ACTION. For overconstrained attribute matches, these include ranking of equivalence criteria, (impacting what criteria are included or eliminated first, and thus which activities appear in which units) ranking of organizational goals (e.g., impacting core work scopes), and ranking of importance of organizational attributes (e.g., impacting what gets compromised first) for productive revision in overconstrained situations. For inability to meet organizational goals, these include ranking organizational attributes to manipulate criteria of acceptability.

6 Implementation Status

ACTION is implemented in Common Lisp, Garnet (a GUI tool), and X-Windows, and comprises approximately 2MB of application source code. As of this writing (May 1993) the ACTION software has gone through 6 major versions and over 40 minor versions in a development span of approximately 11 months, as part of its current design and development process. The software has been integrated and operational since August 1992, and has been in use and under pilot test on analyses of real manufacturing organizations since February 1993, and is being used in three manufacturing organizations.

7 Conclusions

The ACTION theory that forms the core of the knowledge in the ACTION decision support tool is based on an innovative open-systems approach to modeling the interactions among a wide array of TOP features in organizations. In addition, several innovative and theoretically strong approaches for knowledge representation, evaluation, design, explanation, and system generation. These include:

- Shared, replaceable knowledge representations for many system functionalities at several abstraction levels
- Constraint propagation for unit design and evaluation
- The use of equivalence relations as a foundation for unit design
- Direct representation of domain theory as a foundation for explanation
- System generation through incremental translation and aggregation of replaceable parts.

Overall, the ACTION project is an attempt to meld state-of-the-art knowledge representation, reasoning, control, and user-interaction structures into a usable and useful system for analysis and design of real human organizations. A second focus of ACTION is the development and synthesis of a robust and general theory of organization, with special attention to the integration of technological, organization-level, and human-level features. We expect that this theory will generalize to 1) other organizational contexts beyond production areas of discrete parts manufacturing (we are currently exploring applications in environmentally-conscious manufacturing and in software development organizations), and 2) non-human organizations, including distributed AI and multi-agent software systems. Finally, ACTION aims to provide a flexible and domain independent constraint-based modeling and reasoning structure that can be of significant value for development of many types on flexible theory-driven knowledge systems.

8 Acknowledgment

This paper was produced as a result of a program sponsored by the National Center for Manufacturing Sciences (NCMS).

9 References

[Erman 90] Lee D. Erman, ed. "Intelligent Real-Time Problem-Solving Workshop Report." Technical Report, TTR-ISE-90-101, Cimflex Teknowledge Corp., 1810 Embarcadero Road, P.O. Box 10119, Palo Alto, CA. 94303, 1990.

[Gasser and Majchrzak 92] Les Gasser and Ann Majchrzak, "HITOP-A: Coordination, Infrastructure and Enterprise Integration," in *Proceedings of the First International Conference on Enterprise Integration*, MIT Press, June, 1992.

[Majchrzak et al. 91] Ann Majchrzak, Mitchell Fleischer, Dave Roitman, and Joan Mokray, *Reference Manual for Performing the HITOP Analysis*. Industrial Technology Institute, Ann Arbor, MI, 1991.

[Majchrzak 88] Ann Majchrzak, *The Human Side of Factory Automation*, Jossey-Bass, San Francisco, 1988.

[Majchrzak and Gasser 92] Ann Majchrzak and Les Gasser, "HITOP-A: A Tool to Facilitate Interdisciplinary Manufacturing Systems Design," *International Journal of Human Factors in Manufacturing*, 2:3, 1992.

Specifying and Verifying Distributed Intelligent Systems

Michael Fisher and Michael Wooldridge

Department of Computing
Manchester Metropolitan University
Chester Street
Manchester M1 5GD
United Kingdom

Abstract. This paper describes first steps towards the formal specification and verification of Distributed Artificial Intelligence (DAI) systems, through the use of temporal belief logics. The paper first describes Concurrent METATEM, a programming language for DAI, and then develops a logic that may be used to reason about Concurrent METATEM systems. The utility of this logic for specifying and verifying Concurrent METATEM systems is demonstrated through a number of examples. The paper concludes with a brief discussion of the wider implications of the work, and in particular on the use of similar logics for reasoning about DAI systems in general.

1   Introduction

In the past decade, the discipline of DAI has moved from being a somewhat obscure relation of mainstream AI to being a major research area in its own right. DAI techniques have been applied to domains as diverse as archaeology and economics, as well as more mundane problems such as distributed sensing and manufacturing control [7]. Many testbeds for building and experimenting with DAI systems have been reported [2, 19, 21, 10, 26, 9, 24, 12]. And yet almost no research has considered the important problems of *specifying* and *verifying* DAI systems. In short, the purpose of this paper is to address these issues: we present preliminary results on specifying and verifying systems implemented using Concurrent METATEM, a novel new programming language for DAI [14, 13, 16]. A Concurrent METATEM system contains a number of concurrently executing *objects*, which are able to communicate via message passing; each object executes a temporal logic specification representing its desired behaviour. In this paper, we describe Concurrent METATEM in more detail, and then develop a *temporal belief logic* that can be used to reason about Concurrent METATEM systems. We show how this logic may be used to specify and verify the properties of Concurrent METATEM systems. Additionally, the paper discusses the wider issues involved in reasoning about DAI systems.

The remainder of the paper is structured as follows. In the following section, we outline the background to, and motivation for, our work. In §2, we describe Concurrent METATEM in more detail. In §3, we develop a Temporal Belief Logic (TBL), which is used, in §4, to axiomatize the properties of Concurrent METATEM systems. Examples of the use of the logic for specifying and verifying Concurrent METATEM systems are presented in §5. Some comments and conclusions are presented in §6; in particular, we discuss the implications of our work for reasoning about DAI systems in general.

1.1 Background and Motivation

Distributed AI is a subfield of AI whose loose focus is the study of cooperative activity in systems composed of multiple intelligent computational objects (or *agents*, as they are often called). Over the past decade, many frameworks for building and experimenting with DAI systems have been reported. Probably the best-known is MACE, a LISP-based fully instrumented testbed for building DAI systems at a range of sizes and complexity [19]. Other testbeds include Georgeff and Lanksy's procedural reasoning system [21], [20] (aspects of which have been formalised [25]), and the MCS/IPEM platform described by Doran *at al.*, (in which each agent has virtual access to a sophisticated non-linear planner) [10]. More recently, Shoham has described AGENT0, an interpreted programming language for DAI which represents a first step towards the ideal of an 'agent-oriented programming' paradigm [26]. Several actor-style languages for DAI have been developed [2]: Bouron *et al.* describe MAGES, a system based on the ACTALK actor language [9]; Ferber and Carle describe MERING IV, a reflexive concurrent object language [12]; Maruichi *et al.* describe an 'autonomous agent' model (similar in some respects to the computational model underlying Concurrent METATEM), in which autonomous, continually executing actor-like objects communicate through asynchronous message passing [24].

One aspect of DAI missing from all the above accounts is the notion of objects/agents as *reactive systems*, in the following sense: a reactive system is one which cannot adequately be described in terms of 'initial' and 'final' states. Any non-terminating system is therefore a reactive system. The purpose of a reactive system is to *maintain an interaction* with an environment [22]. Any concurrent system is a reactive system, since the objects/agents in a concurrent system must maintain an interaction with other objects/agents: DAI systems are therefore reactive. (The term 'reactive system' has recently been used in AI to describe systems that respond rapidly to the world, without reasoning explicitly about it: we do *not* use the term in this sense; we use it only in the sense we have just described.)

How is one to reason about reactive systems? *Temporal logic* has long been considered a viable tool for this purpose (see, for example, [11] for a good introduction to the extensive literature in this area). This is because temporal logic allows one to describe the ongoing behaviour of a system, which cannot be easily expressed in other formalisms (such as those based on pre- and post-conditions). We take it as axiomatic that the notion of a reactive system is a valuable one for DAI, and that temporal logic is appropriate for reasoning about DAI systems (these issues are examined in more detail in [16]).

Concurrent METATEM is a programming language for DAI in which the notion of reactivity is central. A Concurrent METATEM system contains a number of concurrently executing objects (a.k.a. agents), which are able to communicate through message passing. Each object executes a temporal logic specification of its desired behaviour. The move from specification to implementation in Concurrent METATEM is therefore a small one (since the specification and implementation languages have much in common). However, 'standard' temporal logic cannot simply be used to describe Concurrent METATEM systems (although see [13] for a semantics of Concurrent METATEM based on *dense* temporal logic [5]). This is because each object in a Concurrent METATEM system is a symbolic AI system in its own right: it contains a set of explicitly represented (temporal logic) formulae which it manipulates in order to decide what to do. Thus, to reason about the behaviour of Concurrent METATEM systems, we require some description of the formulae that each agent is manipulating at each moment in time. One way of doing this would be to use a first-order temporal meta-language (as in [4]). However, meta-languages are notationally cumbersome, and can be confusing. What we propose instead is to use a multi-modal language, which contain both temporal connectives and an indexed set of modal *belief* operators, one for each object. These belief operators will be used to describe the formulae that each agent manipulates (see [23] for a detailed exposition on the use of belief logics without a temporal component for describing AI systems).

We have now set the scene for the remainder of the paper. In the next section, we describe Concurrent METATEM in more detail. We then develop a temporal belief logic, and show how it can be used to reason about Concurrent METATEM systems.

2 Concurrent METATEM

In this section we introduce Concurrent METATEM, and present a short example to illustrate its use; in §2.3 we describe the temporal logic that is used for Concurrent METATEM program rules. Although first-order temporal logic is used to represent an object's behaviour in METATEM [15], we will, for the sake of simplicity, restrict our examples to the propositional case.

2.1 Objects and Object Execution

A Concurrent METATEM system contains a number of concurrently executing *objects*, which are able to communicate through asynchronous broadcast message passing. Each object directly executes a temporal logic specification, given to it as a set of 'rules'. In this section, we describe objects and their execution in more detail. Each object has two main components:

- an *interface*, which defines how the object may interact with its environment (i.e., other objects);
- a *computational engine*, which defines how the object may act.

An object interface consists of three components:

- a unique *object identifier* (or just object id), which names the object;
- a set of symbols defining what messages will be accepted by the object — these are called *environment propositions*;
- a set of symbols defining messages that the object may send — these are called *component propositions*.

For example, the interface definition of a 'stack' object might be [13]:

$$stack(pop, push)[popped, stackfull]$$

Here, *stack* is the object id that names the object, {*pop*, *push*} are the environment propositions, and {*popped*, *stackfull*} are the component propositions. Whenever a message headed by the symbol *pop* is broadcast, the *stack* object will *accept* the message; we describe what this means below. If a message is broadcast which is not declared in the *stack* object's interface, then *stack* ignores it. Similarly, the only messages which can be sent by the *stack* object are headed by the symbols *popped* and *stackfull*. (All other propositions used within the object are *internal* propositions, which have no external correspondence.)

The computational engine of an object is based on the METATEM paradigm of executable temporal logics. The idea which informs this approach is that of directly executing a declarative object specification, where this specification is given as a set of *program rules*, which are temporal logic formulae of the form:

$$\text{antecedent about past} \Rightarrow \text{consequent about future.}$$

The past-time antecedent is a temporal logic formula referring strictly to the past, whereas the future time consequent is a temporal logic formula referring either to the present or future. The intuitive interpretation of such a rule is 'on the basis of the past, do the future', which gives rise to the name of the paradigm: *declarative past and imperative future* [17]. The actual execution of an object is, superficially at least, very simple to understand. Each object obeys a cycle of trying to match the past time antecedents of its rules against a *history*, and executing the consequents of those rules that 'fire'[1].

To make the above discussion more concrete, we will now informally introduce a propositional temporal logic, called Propositional METATEM Logic (PML), in which the individual METATEM rules will be given. (A complete definition of PML is given in §2.3.)

PML is essentially classical propositional logic augmented by a set of modal connectives for referring to the *temporal ordering* of actions. PML is based on a model of time that is *linear* (i.e., each moment in time has a unique successor), *bounded in the past* (i.e., there was a moment that was the 'beginning of time'), and *infinite in the future* (i.e., there are an infinite number of moments in the future). The temporal connectives of PML can be divided into two categories, as follows.

1. Strict past time connectives: '●' (weak last), '❍' (strong last), '◆' (was), '■' (heretofore), '$\mathcal{S}$' (since) and '$\mathcal{Z}$' (zince, or weak since).
2. Present and future time connectives: '○' (next), '◇' (sometime), '□' (always), '$\mathcal{U}$' (until) and '$\mathcal{W}$' (unless).

The connectives { ❍, ●, ◆, ■, ○, ◇, □} are unary; the rest are binary. In addition to these temporal connectives, PML contains the usual classical logic connectives.

The meaning of the temporal connectives is quite straightforward, with formulae being interpreted at a particular moment in time. Let ϕ and ψ be formulae of PML. Then $\bigcirc\phi$ is true (satisfied), at the current moment in time if ϕ is true at the next moment in time; $\Diamond\phi$ is true now if ϕ is true now or at some future moment in time;

---

[1] There are obvious similarities between the execution cycle of an object and production systems — but there are also significant differences. The reader is cautioned against taking the analogy too seriously.

$\Box\phi$ is true now if ϕ is true now and at all future moments; $\phi\,\mathcal{U}\,\psi$ is true now if ψ is true at some future moment, and ϕ is true until then — $\mathcal{W}$ is a binary connective similar to $\mathcal{U}$, allowing for the possibility that the second argument never becomes true.

The past-time connectives are similar: $\mathbf{O}$ and $\bullet$ are true now if their arguments were true at the previous moment in time — the difference between them is that, since the model of time underlying the logic is bounded in the past, the beginning of time is a special case: $\mathbf{O}\phi$ will always be false when interpreted at the beginning of time, whereas $\bullet\phi$ will always be true at the beginning of time; $\spadesuit\,\phi$ will be true now if ϕ was true at some previous moment in time; $\blacksquare\phi$ will be true now if ϕ was true at all previous moments in time; $\phi\,\mathcal{S}\,\psi$ will be true now if ψ was true at some previous moment in time, and ϕ has been true since then; $\mathcal{Z}$ is the same, but allowing for the possibility that the second argument was never true. Finally, a temporal operator that takes no arguments can be defined which is true only at the first moment in time: this useful operator is called 'start'.

Any formula of PML which refers strictly to the past is called a *history formula*; any formula referring to the present or future is called a *commitment formula*; any formula of the form

$$history\ formula \Rightarrow commitment\ formula$$

is called a *rule*; an object specification is a set of such rules.

A more precise definition of object execution will now be given. Objects continually execute the following cycle:

1. Update the *history* of the object by receiving messages from other objects and adding them to their history. (This process is described in more detail below.)
2. Check which rules *fire*, by comparing past-time antecedents of each rule against the current history to see which are satisfied.
3. *Jointly execute* the fired rules together with any commitments carried over from previous cycles. This is done by first collecting consequents of newly fired rules and old commitments, which become *commitments*. It may not be possible to satisfy *all* the commitments on the current cycle, in which case unsatisfied commitments are carried over to the next cycle. An object will then have to choose between a number of execution possibilities.
4. Goto (1).

Clearly, step (3) is the heart of the execution process. Making a bad choice at this step may mean that the object specification cannot subsequently be satisfied (see [3, 15]).

A natural question to ask is: how do objects do things? How do they send messages and perform actions? When a proposition in an object becomes *true*, it is compared against that object's interface (see above); if it is one of the object's *component* propositions, then that proposition is broadcast as a message to all other objects. On receipt of a message, each object attempts to match the proposition against the environment propositions in their interface. If there is a match then they add the proposition to their history, prefixed by a ' $\mathbf{O}$ ' operator, indicating that the message has just been received.

The reader should note that although the use of only broadcast message-passing may seem restrictive, standard point-to-point message-passing can easily be simulated by adding an extra 'destination' argument to each message; the use of broadcast message-passing as the communication mechanism gives the language the ability to define more adaptable and flexible systems. We will not develop this argument further; the interested reader is urged to either consult our earlier work on Concurrent METATEM [13, 16], or relevant work showing the utility of broadcast and multicast mechanisms [8, 6, 24].

2.2 A Simple Concurrent METATEM System

To illustrate Concurrent METATEM in more detail, we present in Fig. 1 an example system (outlined originally in [3] and extended in [13])[2]. The system contains three objects: *rp*, *rc*1 and *rc*2. The object *rp* is a 'resource producer': it can '*give*' to only one object at a time (rule 3), and will commit to eventually *give* to any object that '*ask*'s' (rules 1 and 2). Object *rp* will only accept messages *ask*1 and *ask*2, and can only send *give*1 and *give*2 messages.

$$
\begin{aligned}
&rp(ask1, ask2)[give1, give2]: \\
&\quad 1.\ \bullet ask1 \Rightarrow \Diamond give1; \\
&\quad 2.\ \bullet ask2 \Rightarrow \Diamond give2; \\
&\quad 3.\ \text{start} \Rightarrow \Box\neg(give1 \wedge give2). \\
\\
&rc1(give1)[ask1]: \\
&\quad 1.\ \text{start} \Rightarrow ask1; \\
&\quad 2.\ \bullet ask1 \Rightarrow ask1. \\
\\
&rc2(ask1, give2)[ask2]: \\
&\quad 1.\ \bullet(ask1 \wedge \neg ask2) \Rightarrow ask2.
\end{aligned}
$$

Fig. 1. A Simple Concurrent METATEM System

The object *rc*1 will send an *ask*1 message on every cycle: this is because **start** is satisfied at the beginning of time, thus firing rule 1, while ● *ask*1 will then be true on the next cycle, thus firing rule 2, and so on. Thus *rc*1 asks for the message on every cycle, using an *ask*1 message. Object *rc*1 will only accept a *give*1 message, and can only send an *ask*1 message.

The object *rc*2 will send an *ask*2 message on every cycle where, on its previous cycle, it did not send an *ask*2 message, but *rc*1 sent an *ask*1 message. Object *rc*2 will only accept messages *ask*1 and *give*2, and can only send an *ask*2 message.

---

[2] Note that in the interests of readability, this program has been 'pretty printed' using the symbolic form of temporal connectives, rather than the plain-text form that the implementation actually requires; additionally, rule numbers have been introduced to facilitate easy reference — these are *not* part of the language!

To conclude, the system in Fig. 1 has the following properties:

1. Objects $rc1$ and $rc2$ will ask rp for the resource infinitely often;
2. Every time rp is 'asked', it must eventually 'give' to the corresponding asker.

From which we can informally deduce that:

3. Object rp will give the resource to both objects infinitely often.

In §5, we will show formally that the system does indeed have this behaviour.

2.3 A Propositional Temporal Logic (PML)

We now give a complete definition of the propositional temporal logic used for program rules (PML); for a fuller account of propositional temporal logic see, for example, [11].

Syntax

Definition 1 *The language of PML contains the following symbols:*

1. *a countable set,* Prop, *of proposition symbols;*
2. *the symbol* **true***;*
3. *the* unary propositional connective '¬' *and* binary propositional connective '∨';
4. *the* unary temporal connectives $\{\, \bullet, \bigcirc \,\}$;
5. *the* binary temporal connectives $\{\, \mathcal{U}, \mathcal{S} \,\}$;
6. *the punctuation symbols* $\{), (\}$.

All the remaining propositional and temporal connectives are introduced as abbreviations (see below). The syntax of PML is defined as follows.

Definition 2 *Well-formed formulae of PML, WFF(PML), are defined by the following rules.*

1. *All proposition symbols are PML formulae;*
2. *If ϕ is a PML formula then so are $\neg\phi$, $\bigcirc\phi$ and $\bullet\phi$;*
3. *If ϕ and ψ are PML formulae then so are $\phi \lor \psi$, $\phi\,\mathcal{U}\,\psi$, and $\phi\,\mathcal{S}\,\psi$;*
4. *If ϕ is a PML formula, then (ϕ) is a PML formula.*

Semantics The semantics of well-formed formulae of PML is given in the obvious way, with formulae being interpreted in a model, at a particular moment in time.

Definition 3 *A model, M, for PML is a structure $\langle \sigma, \pi_p \rangle$ where*

- *σ is the ordered set of states $s_0, s_1, s_2, \ldots$ representing 'moments' in time, and*
- *$\pi_p : \mathbb{N} \times \text{Prop} \rightarrow \{T, F\}$ is a function assigning T or F to each atomic proposition at each moment in time.*

$$\langle M, u \rangle \models \text{true}$$

$$\langle M, u \rangle \models p \quad \text{iff } \pi_p(u, p) = T$$

$$\langle M, u \rangle \models \neg\phi \quad \text{iff } \langle M, u \rangle \not\models \phi$$

$$\langle M, u \rangle \models \phi \vee \psi \text{ iff } \langle M, u \rangle \models \phi \text{ or } \langle M, u \rangle \models \psi$$

$$\langle M, u \rangle \models \bigcirc\phi \quad \text{iff } \langle M, u+1 \rangle \models \phi$$

$$\langle M, u \rangle \models \bullet\phi \quad \text{iff } u > 0 \text{ and } \langle M, u-1 \rangle \models \phi$$

$$\langle M, u \rangle \models \phi \, \mathcal{U} \, \psi \text{ iff } \exists v \in \mathbb{N} \cdot (u \leq v) \text{ and } \langle M, v \rangle \models \psi$$
$$\text{and } \forall w \in \{u, \ldots, v-1\} \cdot \langle M, w \rangle \models \phi$$

$$\langle M, u \rangle \models \phi \, \mathcal{S} \, \psi \text{ iff } \exists v \in \mathbb{N} \cdot (v < u) \text{ and } \langle M, v \rangle \models \psi$$
$$\text{and } \forall w \in \{v+1, \ldots, u-1\} \cdot \langle M, w \rangle \models \phi$$

Fig. 2. Semantics of PML

As usual, we use the relation '$\models$' to give the truth value of a formula in a model M, at a particular moment in time u. This relation is defined for formulae of PML in Fig. 2. Note that these rules only define the semantics of the basic propositional and temporal connectives; the remainder are introduced as abbreviations (we omit the propositional connectives, as these are standard):

$$\bullet\phi \stackrel{\text{def}}{=} \neg \bullet \neg\phi \qquad \phi \, \mathcal{W} \, \psi \stackrel{\text{def}}{=} \Box\phi \vee \phi \, \mathcal{U} \, \psi$$

$$\text{start} \stackrel{\text{def}}{=} \bullet\text{false} \qquad \blacklozenge \phi \stackrel{\text{def}}{=} \text{true} \, \mathcal{S} \, \phi$$

$$\Diamond\phi \stackrel{\text{def}}{=} \text{true} \, \mathcal{U} \, \phi \qquad \blacksquare\phi \stackrel{\text{def}}{=} \neg \blacklozenge \neg\phi$$

$$\Box\phi \stackrel{\text{def}}{=} \neg\Diamond\neg\phi \qquad \phi \, \mathcal{Z} \, \psi \stackrel{\text{def}}{=} \blacksquare\phi \vee \phi \, \mathcal{S} \, \psi$$

Proof Theory The proof theory of PML has been examined exhaustively elsewhere (see, for example, [18, 27, 1]). Here, we identify some axioms and inference rules that are later used in our proofs.

$$\vdash \Box(\phi \Rightarrow \psi) \Rightarrow (\Box\phi \Rightarrow \Box\psi) \tag{1}$$

$$\vdash \Box(\phi \Rightarrow \psi) \Rightarrow (\Diamond\phi \Rightarrow \Diamond\psi) \tag{2}$$

$$\vdash \bigcirc(\phi \Rightarrow \psi) \Rightarrow (\bigcirc\phi \Rightarrow \bigcirc\psi) \tag{3}$$

$$\vdash \Diamond\Diamond\phi \Leftrightarrow \Diamond\phi \tag{4}$$

$$\vdash (\text{start} \Rightarrow \Box\phi) \Rightarrow \Box\phi \tag{5}$$

$$\vdash \Box(\phi \Rightarrow \bigcirc\phi) \Rightarrow (\phi \Rightarrow \Box\phi) \tag{6}$$

$$\vdash \Box\phi \Rightarrow \phi \tag{7}$$

$$\vdash (\bigcirc\bullet\phi \Rightarrow \psi) \Leftrightarrow (\phi \Rightarrow \psi) \tag{8}$$

$$\vdash (\bullet\bigcirc\phi \Rightarrow \psi) \Rightarrow (\phi \Rightarrow \psi) \tag{9}$$

$$\text{From } \vdash \phi \text{ infer } \vdash \Box\phi \tag{10}$$

$$\text{From } \vdash \phi \text{ infer } \vdash \Diamond\phi \tag{11}$$

$$\text{From } \vdash \phi \text{ infer } \vdash \bigcirc\phi \tag{12}$$

3 A Temporal Belief Logic

This section introduces a Temporal Belief Logic (TBL), that can be used to reason about Concurrent METATEM systems. Like PML, it is a linear discrete temporal logic, with bounded past and infinite future. TBL is similar to the logic L^B that Konolige developed for his deduction model of belief [23]; it was derived from Wooldridge's work on reasoning about multi-agent systems [28, 29].

Syntax Syntactically, TBL can be thought of as PML augmented by an indexed set of unary modal operators $[i]$, (applied to formulae of PML), and closed under the propositional and temporal connectives of PML. The 'i' in $[i]$ is an object id. A TBL formula of the form $[i]\phi$ should be read "ϕ is in i's current state." Thus if ϕ is a history formula, this would say that ϕ was in i's history; if ϕ was a rule, this would say that ϕ was one of i's rules, and if ϕ were a commitment, it would say that i was committed to ϕ.

Definition 4 *The language of TBL contains all the symbols of PML, and in addition the square brackets {], [} and a countable set obj of object ids.*

Definition 5 *Well-formed formulae of TBL are defined by the following rules:*

1. *TBL contains all formulae of PML;*
2. *If ϕ is a formula of PML and $i \in obj$ then $[i]\phi$ is a formula of TBL;*
3. *TBL is closed under the propositional and temporal connectives of PML.*

Semantics One obtains a model for TBL by taking a PML model and adding a function mapping each object id and each moment in time to a set of PML formulae representing the object's state at that moment in time.

Definition 6 *A model $\mathcal{M}$ for TBL is a structure $\langle \sigma, \pi_p, \mathcal{O} \rangle$ where*

$$\mathcal{O} : obj \times \mathbb{N} \to \text{powerset } \mathrm{WFF(PML)}$$

and σ and π_p are as in PML.

The formula $[i]\phi$ will be satisfied if ϕ is in i's state at the appropriate time. This gives the following additional semantic rule, for formulae of the form $[i]\phi$.

$$\langle \mathcal{M}, u \rangle \models [i]\phi \quad \text{iff} \quad \phi \in \mathcal{O}(i, u)$$

Other formulae are interpreted using the same rules as before.

3.1 Proof Theory

TBL inherits all the axioms and inference rules of PML. Further, since there is no direct interaction between the temporal connectives and the '[i]' operators in the basic TBL system, then the only extra axiom that we add is the following.

$$\vdash [i](P \Rightarrow F) \Rightarrow (([i]P) \Rightarrow ([i]F)) \tag{13}$$

This characterises the fact that the '$\Rightarrow$' operator in Concurrent METATEM follows the same logical rules as standard implication.

4 Axiomatizing Concurrent METATEM

In this section, we use TBL to *axiomatize* the properties of Concurrent METATEM systems. This involves extending the basic TBL proof system outlined above to account for the particular properties of the Concurrent METATEM systems that we intend to verify properties of.

The first axiom we add describes the conditions under which an object will send a message: if a proposition becomes 'true' inside an object, and the proposition symbol appears in the object's component propositions, then the proposition is broadcast. (Note the use of ordinary PML propositions to describe messages.) So if P is one of i's component propositions, then the following axiom holds.

$$\vdash ([i]P) \Rightarrow \Diamond P \tag{14}$$

The second axiom deals with how objects *receive* messages: if a message is broadcast, and the proposition symbol of that message appears in an object's environment proposition list, then that message is accepted by the object, which subsequently 'believes' that the proposition was true. So if P is one of i's environment propositions, then the following axiom holds.

$$\vdash P \Rightarrow \Diamond [i] \bullet P \tag{15}$$

The third axiom states that objects maintain accurate histories.

$$\vdash ([i]\phi) \Rightarrow [i] \bigcirc \bullet \phi \tag{16}$$

To simplify the proofs, we will assume that all objects in a Concurrent METATEM system execute synchronously, i.e., the 'execution steps' of each object match. This simplification allows us to add the following *synchronisation axioms*. (Note that, without this simplification, each object would be executing under a distinct local clock, and so proving properties of such a system becomes *much* more difficult, though possible [13].)

$$\vdash (\bigcirc [i]\phi \Rightarrow \psi) \Leftrightarrow ([i]\bigcirc \phi \Rightarrow \psi) \tag{17}$$

$$\vdash (\bullet [i]\phi \Rightarrow \psi) \Leftrightarrow ([i]\bullet \phi \Rightarrow \psi) \tag{18}$$

Now, for every rule, R, in an object, i, we add the following axiom showing that once the object has started executing, the rule is always applicable.

$$\vdash [i]\mathbf{start} \Rightarrow \Box [i]R \tag{19}$$

Finally, to simplify the proofs still further, we will assume that all objects commence execution at the same moment, denoted by the global 'start' operator. Thus, for every object, i, we add the following axiom.

$$\vdash \; start \; \Rightarrow \; [i]start \tag{20}$$

5 Examples

In this section, we show how TBL can be used to reason about Concurrent METATEM systems. We begin by proving some properties of the system presented earlier. In the proofs that follow, we will use the notation $\{S\} \vdash \phi$ to represent the statement '*system S satisfies property ϕ*'. Also, as the majority of the proof steps involve applications of the *Modus Ponens* inference rule, we will omit reference to the particular rule used at each step. As we refer to the axioms and theorems used, the rule used will be clear at each step.

5.1 Resource Controller

Let the system given in Fig. 1 be called S1. This system contains three objects: a resource producer (rp), and two resource consumers ($rc1$ and $rc2$). The first property we prove is that the object $rc1$, once it has commenced execution, satisfies the commitment $ask1$ on every cycle.

Lemma 1. $\{S1\} \vdash \; start \; \Rightarrow \; \Box[rc1]ask1$.

Proof See Fig. 3.

Using this result, it is not difficult to establish that the message $ask1$ is then sent infinitely often.

Lemma 2. $\{S1\} \vdash \; \Box\Diamond ask1$.

Proof This, and all remaining proofs, are omitted due to space restrictions.

Similarly, we can show that any object that is *listening* for $ask1$ messages, in particular rp, will receive them infinitely often.

Lemma 3. $\{S1\} \vdash \; start \; \Rightarrow \; \Box\Diamond[rp]\mathbf{\bullet}\, ask1$.

Now, since we know that $ask1$ is one of rp's environment propositions, then we can show that once both rp and $rc1$ have started, the resource will be given to $rc1$ infinitely often.

Lemma 4. $\{S1\} \vdash \; start \; \Rightarrow \; \Box\Diamond give1$.

Similar properties can be shown for $rc2$. Note, however, that we require knowledge about $rc1$'s behaviour in order to reason about $rc2$'s behaviour.

Lemma 5. $\{S1\} \vdash \; start \; \Rightarrow \; \Box\Diamond[rp]\mathbf{\bullet}\, ask2$.

1. $[rc1]start \Rightarrow \Box[rc1](start \Rightarrow ask1)$ (rule 1 in $rc1$)
2. $start \Rightarrow \Box[rc1](start \Rightarrow ask1)$ (axiom 19, 1)
3. $\Box[rc1](start \Rightarrow ask1)$ (axiom 5, 2)
4. $[rc1](start \Rightarrow ask1)$ (axiom 7, 3)
5. $[rc1]start \Rightarrow [rc1]ask1$ (axiom 13, 4)
6. $start \Rightarrow [rc1]ask1$ (axiom 19, 5)
7. $[rc1]start \Rightarrow \Box[rc1](\bullet ask1 \Rightarrow ask1)$ (rule 2 in $rc1$)
8. $start \Rightarrow \Box[rc1](\bullet ask1 \Rightarrow ask1)$ (axiom 19, 7)
9. $\Box[rc1](\bullet ask1 \Rightarrow ask1)$ (axiom 5, 8)
10. $[rc1](\bullet ask1 \Rightarrow ask1)$ (axiom 7, 9)
11. $[rc1]\bullet ask1 \Rightarrow [rc1]ask1$ (axiom 13, 10)
12. $\bigcirc([rc1]\bullet ask1 \Rightarrow [rc1]ask1)$ (inf. rule 12, 11)
13. $\bigcirc[rc1]\bullet ask1 \Rightarrow \bigcirc[rc1]ask1$ (axiom 3, 12)
14. $\bigcirc\bullet[rc1]ask1 \Rightarrow \bigcirc[rc1]ask1$ (axiom 18, 13)
15. $[rc1]ask1 \Rightarrow \bigcirc[rc1]ask1$ (axiom 8, 14)
16. $\Box([rc1]ask1 \Rightarrow \bigcirc[rc1]ask1)$ (inf. rule 10, 15)
17. $[rc1]ask1 \Rightarrow \Box[rc1]ask1$ (axiom 6, 16)
18. $start \Rightarrow \Box[rc1]ask1$ (6, 17)

Fig. 3. Proof of Lemma 1

Given this, we can derive the following result.

Lemma 6. $\{S1\} \vdash start \Rightarrow \Box\Diamond give2$.

Finally, we can show the desired behaviour of the system; compare this to result (3) that we informally deduced in §2.2.

Theorem 7. $\{S1\} \vdash start \Rightarrow (\Box\Diamond give1 \land \Box\Diamond give2)$.

5.2 Distributed Problem Solving

We now consider a distributed problem solving system. Here, a single object, called *executive*, broadcasts a problem to a group of problem solvers. Some of these problem solvers can solve the particular problem completely, and some will reply with a solution.

We define such a Concurrent METATEM system in Fig. 4. Here, *solvera* can solve a different problem from the one *executive* poses, while *solverb* can solve the desired problem, but doesn't announce the fact (as *solution1* is not a component proposition

$$
\begin{aligned}
&executive(solution1)[problem1, solved1]:\\
&\quad 1.\ \mathbf{start} \Rightarrow \Diamond problem1;\\
&\quad 2.\ \bullet solution1 \Rightarrow solved1.\\
\\
&solvera(problem2)[solution2]:\\
&\quad 1.\ \bullet problem2 \Rightarrow solution2.\\
\\
&solverb(problem1)[solution2]:\\
&\quad 1.\ \bullet problem1 \Rightarrow \Diamond solution1.\\
\\
&solverc(problem1)[solution1]:\\
&\quad 1.\ \bullet problem1 \Rightarrow \Diamond solution1.
\end{aligned}
$$

Fig. 4. A Distributed Problem Solving System

$$
\begin{aligned}
&solverd(problem1, solution1.2)[solution1]:\\
&\quad 1.\ (\bullet solution1.2 \wedge \text{\ding{171}}\, problem1) \Rightarrow \Diamond solution1.\\
\\
&solvere(problem1)[solution1.2]:\\
&\quad 1.\ \bullet problem1 \Rightarrow \Diamond solution1.2.
\end{aligned}
$$

Fig. 5. Additional Problem Solving Agents

for *solverb*); *solverc* can solve the problem posed by *executive*, and will *eventually* reply with the solution.

If we call this system S2, then we can prove the following.

Theorem 8. $\{S2\} \vdash \mathbf{start} \Rightarrow \Diamond solved1.$

We now remove *solverc* and replace it by two objects who together can solve *problem*1, but can not manage this individually. These objects, called *solverd* and *solvere* are defined in Fig. 5.

Thus, when *solverd* receives the problem it cannot do anything until it has heard from *solvere*. When *solvere* receives the problem, it broadcasts the fact that it can some of the problem (i.e., it broadcasts *solution*1.2). When *solverd* sees this, it knows it can solve the other part of the problem and broadcasts the whole solution.

Thus, given these new objects we can prove the following (the system is now called S3).

Theorem 9. $\{S3\} \vdash \mathbf{start} \Rightarrow \Diamond solved1.$

6   Concluding Remarks

In this paper, we have described Concurrent METATEM, a programming language for DAI, and developed a Temporal Belief Logic for reasoning about Concurrent METATEM systems. In effect, we used the logic to develop a crude semantics for the language; this approach did not leave us with a complete proof system for Concurrent METATEM, (since we made the assumption of synchronous action). However, it has the advantage of simplicity when compared to other methods for defining the semantics of the language (such as those based on dense temporal logic [13], or first-order temporal meta-languages [4]).

More generally, logics similar to that developed herein can be used to reason about a wise class of DAI systems: those in which agents/objects have a classic 'symbolic AI' architecture. Such systems typically employ explicit symbolic representations, which are manipulated in order to plan and execute actions. A belief logic such as that described in this paper seems appropriate for describing these representations (see also [23]). A temporal component to the logic seems to be suitable for describing reactive systems, of which DAI systems are an example. In other work, we have developed a family of temporal belief logics, augmented by modalities for describing the actions and messages of individual agents, and demonstrated how these logics can be used to specify a wide range of cooperative structures [28, 29].

In future work we will concentrate on refining the axiomatisation of Concurrent METATEM, and on developing (semi-)mechanical proof procedures for logics such as TBL, based upon either multi-modal tableaux or multi-modal resolution.

Acknowledgements Michael Fisher was partially supported by the SERC under research grant GR/H/18449. Michael Wooldridge was partially supported by an SERC PhD award.

References

1. M. Abadi. *Temporal-Logic Theorem Proving.* PhD thesis, Department of Computer Science, Stanford University, March 1987.

2. G. Agha. *Actors - A Model for Concurrent Computation in Distributed Systems.* MIT Press, 1986.

3. H. Barringer, M. Fisher, D. Gabbay, G. Gough, and R. Owens. METATEM: A Framework for Programming in Temporal Logic. In *Proceedings of REX Workshop on Stepwise Refinement of Distributed Systems: Models, Formalisms, Correctness*, Mook, Netherlands, June 1989. (Published in *Lecture Notes in Computer Science*, volume 430, Springer Verlag).

4. H. Barringer, M. Fisher, D. Gabbay, and A. Hunter. Meta-Reasoning in Executable Temporal Logic. In J. Allen, R. Fikes, and E. Sandewall, editors, *Proceedings of the International Conference on Principles of Knowledge Representation and Reasoning (KR)*, Cambridge, Massachusetts, April 1991. Morgan Kaufmann.

5. H. Barringer, R. Kuiper, and A. Pnueli. A Really Abstract Concurrent Model and its Temporal Logic. In *Proceedings of the Thirteenth ACM Symposium on the Principles of Programming Languages (POPL)*, St. Petersberg Beach, Florida, January 1986.

6. K. Birman. The Process Group Approach to Reliable Distributed Computing. Techanical Report TR91-1216, Department of Computer Science, Cornell University, USA, July 1991.

7. A. H. Bond and L. Gasser, editors. *Readings in Distributed Artificial Intelligence*. Morgan Kaufmann, 1988.

8. A. Borg, J. Baumbach, and S. Glazer. A Message System Supporting Fault Tolerance. In *Proceedings of the Ninth ACM Symposium on Operating System Principles*, pages 90–99, New Hampshire, October 1983. ACM. (In ACM Operating Systems Review, vol. 17, no. 5).

9. T. Bouron, J. Ferber, and F. Samuel. MAGES: A Multi-Agent Testbed for Heterogeneous Agents. In Y. Demazeau and J. P. Muller, editors, *Decentralized AI 2 - Proceedings of the Second European Workshop on Modelling Autonomous Agents and Multi-Agent Worlds (MAAMAW)*. Elsevier/North Holland, 1991.

10. J. Doran, H. Carvajal, Y. J. Choo, and Y. Li. The MCS Multi Agent Testbed: Developments and Experiments. In S. M. Deen, editor, *Proceedings of the International Working Conference on Cooperating Knowledge Based Systems (CKBS)*. Springer-Verlag, 1991.

11. E. A. Emerson. Temporal and Modal Logic. In J. van Leeuwen, editor, *Handbook of Theoretical Computer Science*, pages 996–1072. Elsevier, 1990.

12. J. Ferber and P. Carle. Actors and Agents as Reflective Concurrent Objects: a MERING IV Perspective. *IEEE Transactions on Systems, Man and Cybernetics*, December 1991.

13. M. Fisher. Concurrent METATEM — A Language for Modeling Reactive Systems. In *Parallel Architectures and Languages, Europe (PARLE)*, Munich, Germany, June 1993. Springer-Verlag.

14. M. Fisher and H. Barringer. Concurrent METATEM Processes — A Language for Distributed AI. In *Proceedings of the European Simulation Multiconference*, Copenhagen, Denmark, June 1991.

15. M. Fisher and R. Owens. From the Past to the Future: Executing Temporal Logic Programs. In *Proceedings of Logic Programming and Automated Reasoning (LPAR)*, St. Petersberg, Russia, July 1992. (Published in *Lecture Notes in Computer Science*, volume 624, Springer Verlag).

16. M. Fisher and M. Wooldridge. Executable Temporal Logic for Distributed A.I. In *Proceedings of the Twelfth International Workshop on Distributed Artificial Intelligence*, Hidden Valley, Pennsylvania, May 1993.

17. D. Gabbay. Declarative Past and Imperative Future: Executable Temporal Logic for Interactive Systems. In B. Banieqbal, H. Barringer, and A. Pnueli, editors, *Proceedings of Colloquium on Temporal Logic in Specification*, pages 402–450, Altrincham, U.K., 1987. (Published in *Lecture Notes in Computer Science*, volume 398, Springer Verlag).

18. D. Gabbay, A. Pnueli, S. Shelah, and J. Stavi. The Temporal Analysis of Fairness. In *Proceedings of the Seventh ACM Symposium on the Principles of Programming Languages (POPL)*, pages 163–173, Las Vegas, Nevada, January 1980.

19. L. Gasser, C. Braganza, and N. Hermann. MACE: A Flexible Testbed for Distributed AI Research. In M. Huhns, editor, *Distributed Artificial Intelligence*. Pitman/Morgan Kaufmann, 1987.

20. M. P. Georgeff and F. F. Ingrand. Decision-Making in an Embedded Reasoning System. In *Proceedings of the Eleventh International Joint Conference on Artificial Intelligence (IJCAI)*, Detroit, USA, 1989. Morgan Kaufmann.

21. M. P. Georgeff and A. L. Lansky. Reactive Reasoning and Planning. In *Proceedings of the American Association for Artificial Intelligence (AAAI)*. Morgan Kaufmann, 1987.

22. D. Harel and A. Pnueli. On the Development of Reactive Systems. Technical Report CS85-02, Department of Applied Mathematics, The Weizmann Institute of Science, Revohot, Israel, January 1985.

23. K. Konolige. *A Deduction Model of Belief.* Pitman/Morgan Kaufmann, 1986.
24. T. Maruichi, M. Ichikawa, and M. Tokoro. Modelling Autonomous Agents and their Groups. In Y. Demazeau and J. P. Muller, editors, *Decentralized AI – Proceedings of the First European Workshop on Modelling Autonomous Agents and Multi-Agent Worlds (MAAMAW).* Elsevier/North Holland, 1990.
25. A. S. Rao and M. P. Georgeff. Modeling Agents within a BDI-Architecture. In R. Fikes and E. Sandewall, editors, *International Conference on Principles of Knowledge Representation and Reasoning (KR)*, Cambridge, Massachusetts, April 1991. Morgan Kaufmann.
26. Y. Shoham. Agent Oriented Programming. Technical Report STAN–CS–1335–90, Department of Computer Science, Stanford University, California, USA, 1990.
27. P. Wolper. The Tableau Method for Temporal Logic: An overview. *Logique et Analyse*, 110–111:119–136, June-Sept 1985.
28. M. Wooldridge. *The Logical Modelling of Computational Multi-Agent Systems.* PhD thesis, Department of Computation, UMIST, Manchester, UK, 1992.
29. M. Wooldridge and M. Fisher. A First-Order Branching Time Logic of Multi-Agent Systems. In *Proceedings of the Tenth European Conference on Artificial Intelligence (ECAI '92)*, Vienna, Austria, August 1992. Wiley and Sons.

A Logical Approach for
Distributed Truth Maintenance

Thilo C. Horstmann

German National Research Center for Computer Science (GMD)
I3.CSCW
P.O. Box 1316
D-53731 Sankt Augustin
Germany
e-mail: *t.horstmann@gmd.de*

Abstract. Distributed AI systems are intended to fill the gap between classical AI and distributed computer science. Such networks of different problem solvers are required for naturally distributed problems, and for tasks which exhaust the resource of an individual node. To guarantee a certain degree of consistency in a distributed AI system, it is necessary to inspect the beliefs of both single nodes and the whole net. This task is performed by Distributed Truth Maintenance Systems. Based on classical TMS theories, distributed truth maintenance extends the conventional case to incorporate reason maintenance in DAI scenarios.

Key words: Distributed AI, Logic Programming, TMS, Agent Model

Introduction

Recent research in the field of Distributed Artificial Intelligence (DAI) has led to a broad variety of applications characterized by autonomous, loosely connected problem solving nodes. Each single node, or *agent*, is capable of individual task processing and able to coordinate its actions in combination with those of other agents in the net. DAI applications span a large field ranging from cooperating expert systems, distributed planning and control to human computer cooperative work. In order to establish a domain-independent theory of interacting autonomous agents, current DAI research focuses on defining an abstract agent model, which allows the formalization of cooperation strategies and multi-agent reasoning mechanisms.

The requirements of multi-agent reasoning algorithms are manifold. In most cases, it is *not* desirable to constrain the autonomy of agents by building a 'superstrate reasoner' managing all inferences or rules of a set of different agents. The reasons are discussed fully in [5]. Instead, we want the agents to be able to reason autonomously; in particular, a single agent must deal with beliefs, which have probably been created in a complex cooperation process.

This requirement is best fulfilled by providing an agent with a Distributed Truth Maintenance System (DTMS). Based on classical TMS theories, distributed truth maintenance extends the conventional case to make reason maintenance suitable for multi-agent scenarios. A DTMS has to represent and manage inferences and rules of interacting agents in a way that ensures a specified degree of consistency. The various degrees of consistency will be defined in this paper. Furthermore, other modules of an agent should be able to use information stored by the DTMS. For instance, a problem solving unit may avoid recomputation or a cooperation process might be based on the current context of the consistent knowledge base.

We believe that using a JTMS as the basis for the DTMS is more advantageous than using an ATMS (e.g [11]). The domain of an agent, that is its assumptions, premises and rules, can be expected to increase greatly in a multi-agent cooperation process. An ATMS has to compute *all* newly arisen contexts. Fast query response time is overshadowed by the exponential cost of the ATMS labeling algorithm when maintaining a large domain.

In this paper we extend and modify the DTMS as presented in [2]. In that, data dependencies are recorded in propositional logic. It is based on the complete relabeling algorithm of [13]. The authors of [2] define *shared* beliefs and introduce four levels of consistency in a multi-agent context. But as we will see later, this approach allows a DTMS for dominating other DTMS, *even though it has less information*. In many cases, important information acquired by a single agent does not have consequences for the multi-agent inference process.

Our definition of consistency guarantees the propagation of information to all relevant agents. This is due to the fact, that our definition takes count of · beliefs *and* their foundations. If an agent later invalidates the foundation of an acquired belief, it might reconsult the agent from which the belief was originally acquired.

We use first-order logic to represent data dependencies. The rules and beliefs that have already been inferred are evaluated by a Prolog Meta Interpreter. This allows for more flexible and convenient data representation.

The key features of the DTMS are summarized below:

- maintenance of a consistent state of beliefs. Because we record data dependencies, checking consistency involves little recomputation when the knowledge base is modified.
- data dependencies are recorded in the Horn subset of first-order predicate logic instead of propositional logic.
- explicit representation of proofs allows for easier generation of explanations.
- interface for exchanging beliefs, data and proofs among agents.
- meta level predicates aiding the design of clearly specified autonomous agents. In addition, it simplifies the classification of goals into those upon which reason maintenance should be performed and those which remain static.
- the DTMS is designed as a generalization of a TMS. As a result, the application domain is not restricted to the field of DAI.

We start off by introducing the basic terminology and discussing the DTMS in a sample scenario. Finally, we show how the DTMS fits in an abstract agent model.

Basic Terminology

Querying the DTMS invokes the interpretation of a finite set of Horn clauses.[1] We divide this set into two disjunct sets: the set of (dynamic) justifications $\mathcal{J}$,[2] and the set of static and system predicates $\mathcal{S}$. When called, the DTMS will create or modify *beliefs*. Informally, a belief is an atomic formula to which is assigned four fields:

- *status:* one of the symbols in or out
- *constraint:* a first-order formula in conjunctive normal form
- *support:* a list of atomic formulas
- *consequences:* a list of atomic formulas

The *status* field designates belief (if in) or lack of belief (if out). The formula in *constraint* can be regarded as the reason for assigning this status. Furthermore, the fields *support* and *consequences* denote the dependencies of the atom according to the current set of beliefs. That is, *consequences* represents those beliefs which might have to be recomputed if the status changes. In the other direction, the elements of *support* are those beliefs, upon which the status of the atom is dependent.

We define these notions precisely in the following:

Definition 1. Let $\mathcal{A}$ be a finite set of positive literals, $\mathcal{L}(\mathcal{A})$ the set of all subsets of elements of $\mathcal{A}$ and $\mathcal{F}(\mathcal{A})$ the set of all formulas constructed of elements of $\mathcal{A}$. A **state** Ψ is a 4-tuple $\Psi = (\lambda, \mu, \nu, \xi)$ such that

1. $\lambda : \mathcal{A} \rightarrow \{\text{in, out}\}$
2. $\mu : \mathcal{A} \rightarrow \mathcal{F}(\mathcal{A})$
3. $\nu : \mathcal{A} \rightarrow \mathcal{L}(\mathcal{A})$
4. $\xi : \mathcal{A} \rightarrow \mathcal{L}(\mathcal{A})$

Definition 2. Let $\theta = \{v_1/t_1, \cdots, v_n/t_n\}$ be a substitution and j be a justification. Then j_θ is an **instance** of j, if each occurrence of variable v_i in j is simultaneously replaced by the term $t_i (i = 1, \cdots, n)$.

Definition 3. Let $\Psi = (\lambda, \mu, \nu, \xi)$ be a state and let j_θ be an instance of a justification with head h_θ and body b_θ. Furthermore, let $\mathcal{P}$ be a set of program clauses. Then j_θ is

---

[1] Throughout this paper we use the terminology of logic programming as introduced in [9].

[2] A justification must be a clause with non empty body. A justification with the symbol *true* as its body is called a *premise* justification.

1. **valid** (wrt Ψ), if θ is a correct answer substitution for $\mathcal{P} \cup \{b\}$[3]. In this case, for each positive literal p of b_θ, $\lambda(p) = $ **in** and for each positive counterpart of a negative literal n of j_θ, $\lambda(n) = $ **out**. We say, j_θ justifies h_θ.
2. **invalid** (wrt Ψ), if θ is not a correct answer substitution for $\mathcal{P} \cup \{b\}$. In this case, there is either a positive literal l of b_θ with $\lambda(l) = $ **out**, or a positive counterpart of a negative literal l of b_θ with $\lambda(l) = $ **in**. We say, l invalidates j_θ.

Example 1. Let $\mathcal{A} = \{a(2), b(2), c(2), d(2)\}$ with $\lambda(a(2)) = \lambda(d(2)) = $ **in** and $\lambda(b(2)) = \lambda(c(2)) = $ **out**. Furthermore, we have three justifications j1: $d(X) \leftarrow a(X), \neg b(X)$, j2: $d(X) \leftarrow a(X), b(X)$ and j3: $c(X) \leftarrow d(X)$. Then the instance of $j1_{\{X/2\}}$ is valid, but $b(2)$ invalidates $j2_{\{X/2\}}$.

Definition 3 generalizes the notion of propositional justifications to the first order case. In these terms, a justification in a first-order logic TMS represents the set of all instances of the justification. To introduce the central term *consistency*, we need some further definitions.

Definition 4. Let $\Psi = (\lambda, \mu, \nu, \xi)$ be a state and let $j_1, \cdots, j_n$ be a set of justifications with the same predicate a in the head. If each justification j_i is invalidated by a b_i, we will denote the set $\{b_1, \cdots, b_n\}$ by **inval (a)**.

Definition 5. Let p be a predicate and $\mathcal{J}$ be a set of justifications. The **definition of a justification** (written *def (p)*) is the disjunction of all bodies of clauses of $\mathcal{J}$ with the same predicate p in the head.

Definition 6. Let c be a conjunction of atomic formulas $a_1, \cdots, a_n$. Then [c] denotes the set of atoms $a_1, \cdots, a_n$.

Definition 7. Let $\Psi = (\lambda, \mu, \nu, \xi)$ be a state. *con (a)* is the set of atoms whose members are those atoms $c \in \mathcal{A}$, such that a is a member of $\nu(c)$.

Definition 8. Let $\Psi = (\lambda, \mu, \nu, \xi)$ be a state, and $\mathcal{P} = \mathcal{J} \cup \mathcal{S}$ be a union of disjunct sets of program clauses. Ψ is **consistent**, if the following conditions hold:

1. if $\lambda(a_\theta) = $ **in**, then either
   (a) there is a $j \in \mathcal{J}$ such that j_θ justifies a_θ. In this case, $\mu = b_\theta, \nu = [b_\theta], \xi = con(a_\theta)$ or
   (b) θ is a correct answer substitution of $\mathcal{S} \cup \{a\}$. In this case, $\mu = system$[4]$, \nu = [system], \xi = con(a_\theta)$.
2. if $\lambda(a_\theta) = $ **out**, then θ is not a correct answer substitution of $\mathcal{P} \cup \{a\}$. If there is a definition for a, then $\mu = cnf(not(def(a)))$[5]$, \nu = inval(a), \xi = con(a_\theta)$. In each other case $\mu = system, \nu = [system], \xi = con(a_\theta)$.

---

[3] That is, $\forall(b\theta)$ is a logical consequence of $\mathcal{P}$.

[4] In these terms, the symbol *system* denotes the support for a belief that is inferred from predicates on which we do not want to perform truth maintenance.

[5] cnf denotes the conjunctive normal form of a given formula.

3. there is no sequence $(a_0, \cdots, a_n)$ of elements of $\mathcal{A}$, such that $a_0 = a_n$ and for $i = 1, \cdots, n$, $\lambda(a_i) = $ **in** and a_{i-1} is in $\mu(a_i)$.

Definition 8 implies some notable points. Condition 3 prohibits circularities in the support of **in** beliefs in order to establish a well founded set of atomic formulas (see also Definition 13). Furthermore, a consistent state of beliefs guarantees a correct assignment of logical states to atomic formulas *and* a correct linkage of all beliefs in accordance to their logical dependencies.

Example 2. The state in the example of Definition 3 is *inconsistent*: the belief $c(2)$ is **out** but the instance $j3_{\{x/2\}}$ is valid. Thus, Condition 2 of Definition 8 is violated.

In order to represent a consistent state of beliefs, the DTMS stores for an atom **datum** the corresponding values of λ, μ, ν, ξ in the arguments **status**, **constraint**, **support** and **consequences** of dtms_node/6[6]:

> dtms_node(datum,status,constraint, support,consequences,rule_id)

We say, **datum** is in, or **datum** is *believed*, if the status field of **datum** has the value **in**.

Note, the symbol **true** can occur in the support field of **datum** in two cases: **datum** is **in** and justified with a premise justification, or **datum** is **out** and the justifications matching with **datum** contain no further subgoals. For instance, the justification $p \leftarrow fail$, is invalidated by the symbol **fail**.[7] Because $cnf(not(def(p))) = true$, the support field of a belief p would be the symbol **true**.

In addition, the argument **rule_id** denotes a unique identifier of the justification supporting a believed datum. The general representation of justifications in the DTMS is

> dtms_rule (justification, rule_id)

The heads of justifications define the atoms on which truth maintenance is performed. This is a notable difference from classical TMSs, in which these atoms have to be declared explicitly.

Beliefs in a DTMS

In the following, we consider a set of DTMSs, each identified by an unique DTMS identifier. Each DTMS contains static predicates, local justifications and its own set of beliefs. Additionally, a DTMS can *acquire* beliefs from other DTMSs, or it can *transmit* beliefs to other DTMSs. The next definitions make these notions more precise.

---

[6] The abstract mathematical object *set* is represented by the Prolog object *list*.

[7] The beliefs *true* and *fail* are in and out but not explicitly represented in the DTMS.

Definition 9. Let $\mathcal{P}$ be a set of program clauses, $\mathcal{B}$ be a set of beliefs and $\Psi = (\lambda, \mu, \nu, \xi)$ the state of $\mathcal{B}$. Then we call the triple $\delta = (\mathcal{P}, \mathcal{B}, \Psi)$ a **DTMS**. The DTMS identifier δ is logically equivalent to the symbol *true*.

Definition 10. Let $\mathcal{D} = \{\delta_1 = (\mathcal{P}_1, \mathcal{B}_1, \Psi_1), \cdots, \delta_n = (\mathcal{P}_n, \mathcal{B}_n, \Psi_n)\}$ be a set of DTMSs. A **positive dtms-rule** of $\mathcal{P}_j$ is a justification of the form

$$a \leftarrow \delta_i$$

and a **negative dtms-rule** is of the form

$$a \leftarrow \neg\delta_i$$

where a denotes an ordinary atomic formula and $i \in \{1, \cdots, n\}, (i \neq j)$.

Note, Definitions 9 and 10 imply that the positive dtms-rule $a \leftarrow \delta_i$ is valid, if $\lambda(a) = \mathbf{in}$ and the negative rule $a \leftarrow \neg\delta_i$ is valid, if $\lambda(a) = \mathbf{out}$ (with respect to the current state of beliefs of δ_j).

This is what a dtms-rule is intended to do: A belief a that is inferred by a DTMS with a positive dtms-rule might be interpreted as "I believe in a, because DTMS δ_i told me so" and a negative one as "I do not believe in a because neither I nor DTMS δ_i can prove a"[8]. In these terms, a dtms-rule *represents an inference in another DTMS*.

Thus, the beliefs of a DTMS may categorized according to the following definitions.

Definition 11. Let $\mathcal{D} = \{\delta_1 = (\mathcal{P}_1, \mathcal{B}_1, \Psi_1), \cdots, \delta_n = (\mathcal{P}_n, \mathcal{B}_n, \Psi_n)\}$ be a set of DTMSs. We say a belief $b_i \in \mathcal{B}_i$, denoting the atom l_i, is

1. **private** to δ_i, if there is no belief b_j in $\mathcal{B}_j$, such that l_i can be unified with l_j, $(i \neq j)$.
2. **common** to δ_i and δ_j, if there is a belief b_j in $\mathcal{B}_j$, such that l_i can be unified with l_j, $(i \neq j)$. The status of b_i might be different from the status of b_j.
3. **transmitted** to DTMS δ_j, if $\mathcal{P}_j$ contains either a positive dtms-rule of the form $l_i \leftarrow \delta_i$ or a negative dtms-rule of the form $l_i \leftarrow \neg\delta_i$ $(i \neq j)$.
4. **acquired** from DTMS δ_j, if $\mathcal{P}_i$ contains either a positive dtms-rule of the form $l_i \leftarrow \delta_j$ or a negative dtms-rule of the form $l_i \leftarrow \neg\delta_j$, $(i \neq j)$.
5. **mutual** to δ_i and δ_j, if b_i is transmitted to δ_j.

Transmitting a belief means passing a dtms-rule. Thus, a DTMS acquiring the dtms-rule is able to do its own, local, inferences based on this rule. In particular, the acquiring of a positive dtms-rule allows a DTMS to create a belief with the the same atom and status as in the transmitting DTMS. This is why we speak of transmitting beliefs rather than justifications.

Figure 1 shows an example for beliefs in which belief Q is private to DTMS I, belief S is common to DTMSs II and III and belief R is mutual to I, II and III.

Many questions arise, when considering that DTMSs can transmit their beliefs. We discuss them in the next section by defining terms for consistency.

---

[8] Assuming, of course, the DTMS does not have its own valid justification for a.

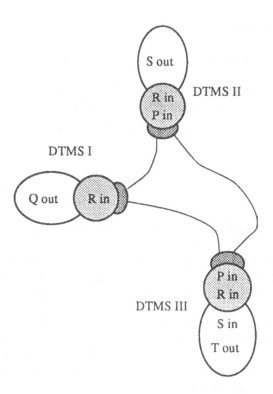

Fig. 1. Common and mutual beliefs

Consistency

Definition 10, in connection with Definition 8, allows us to define a DTMS's consistency. Informally, a DTMS is locally consistent if its own and acquired beliefs are consistent in accordance to its own set of program clauses.

Definition 12. Let $\{\delta_1, \cdots, \delta_n\}$ be a set of DTMSs. The DTMS $\delta_i = (\mathcal{P}, \mathcal{B}, \Psi)$ is **locally consistent**, if its state Ψ is consistent.

Definition 13. Let $\mathcal{D} = \{\delta_1 = (\mathcal{P}_1, \mathcal{B}_1, \Psi_1), \cdots, \delta_n = (\mathcal{P}_n, \mathcal{B}_n, \Psi_n)\}$ be a set of DTMSs. $\mathcal{D}$ is **proof consistent**, if the following conditions hold:

1. Each DTMS $\delta_i \in \mathcal{D}$ is locally consistent.
2. If a belief $b \in \mathcal{B}_i$ is transmitted to DTMS $\delta_j (i \neq j)$, then each ancestor $f_1, \cdots, f_m$ of b is either transmitted to DTMS δ_j or acquired. b and the acquired counterpart in DTMS δ_j are either both **in** or both **out**.
3. a belief $b_i \in \mathcal{B}_i$ that is acquired is not transmitted.
4. there is no set of beliefs $(b_0, \cdots, b_n) \in \mathcal{B}_1 \cup \cdots \cup \mathcal{B}_n$, such that $b_0 = b_n$ and for $i = 1, \cdots, n$, either

(a) $\lambda(b_i) = $ **in** and b_{i-1} is in $\mu(b_i)$

or

(b) there is a k such that $b_{i-1} \in \mathcal{B}_k$ and $\delta_k \in \mu(b_i)$.

Definition 13 implies that we allow common beliefs to be labeled differently. Condition 4 guarantees a well founded set of mutual beliefs.

Example 3. Let $\mathcal{D} = \{\delta_1 = (\mathcal{P}_1, \mathcal{B}_1, \Psi_1), \delta_2 = (\mathcal{P}_2, \mathcal{B}_2, \Psi_2)\}$ be two DTMSs with

$$\mathcal{P}_1 = \{b \leftarrow a, a \leftarrow \delta_2\}$$
$$\mathcal{B}_1 = \{b, a\} \text{ with } \lambda(b) = \lambda(a) = \text{in}, \nu(b) = a, \xi(b) = \{\} \text{ and } \nu(a) = \delta_2, \xi(a) = b.$$

$$\mathcal{P}_2 = \{a \leftarrow b, b \leftarrow \delta_1\}$$
$$\mathcal{B}_2 = \{b, a\} \text{ with } \lambda(b) = \lambda(a) = \text{in}, \nu(a) = b, \xi(a) = \{\} \text{ and } \nu(b) = \delta_1, \xi(b) = a.$$

We assume that belief b is transmitted from δ_1 to δ_2 and a from δ_2 to δ_1. $\{\delta_1, \delta_2\}$ is *not* proof consistent, because the well-foundedness condition is violated. But, each single DTMS is locally consistent (see also Footnote 11).

Note that a belief is only transmitted once in the net. That is, a DTMS cannot transmit a belief that it has already acquired. On the other hand, the number of DTMSs that can acquire another DTMS's belief is not constrained.

This concept clearly defines a state of consistency of mutually dependent beliefs across different DTMSs. This state is characterized by exchanging inferences *and* their foundations. Information, lost in former approaches, will now be propagated to all relevant DTMSs: Because one DTMS knows the foundations of an acquired inference of another DTMS, it can inform this DTMS when a foundation becomes invalid. Thereby, the DTMSs will not be overwhelmed with information. It is sufficient to exchange only a special, minimal representation of inferences between DTMSs.

Example of Using the DTMS

To motivate and explain our definition of consistency, we discuss a sample distributed scenario.

dynamic clauses of DTMS I:

```
dtms_node(engine_ok, in, (valve1_open , not 'temp>90'),
          [valve1_open, 'temp>90'], [], j1).
dtms_node(valve1_open, in, true, [true], [engine_ok], j2).
dtms_node('temp>90', out, true, [true], [engine_ok], _g55).

dtms_rule(engine_ok :- (valve1_open , not 'temp>90'), j1).
dtms_rule(valve1_open :- true, j2).
```

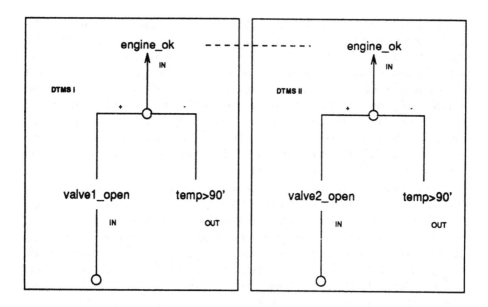

Fig. 2. Sample scenario

dynamic clauses of DTMS II:

```
dtms_node(engine_ok, in, (valve2_open , not 'temp>90'),
        [valve2_open, 'temp>90'], [], j1).
dtms_node(valve2_open, in, true, [true], [engine_ok], j2).
dtms_node('temp>90', out, true, [true], [engine_ok], _g55).

dtms_rule(engine_ok :- (valve2_open , not 'temp>90'), j1).
dtms_rule(valve2_open :- true, j2).
```

Consider Figure 2. DTMS I and DTMS II are two autonomous control systems controlling the correct behavior of an engine. They reason that the engine works correctly, if either valve 1 or valve 2 is open but the temperature of the engine does not exceed $90°C$. Because the temperature is so important, we decide to use two autonomous sensors connected to DTMSs, each able to detect a high temperature on its own. Furthermore, they each control a different valve. We want the DTMSs to reason cooperatively about the belief **engine_ok** (represented by the dashed line in Figure 2), that is, we don't want the DTMSs to have different statuses of **engine_ok**. Initially, querying the DTMSs about **engine_ok** would yield the solution **engine_ok** is **in**, in accordance with both DTMSs. Now, suppose DTMS II acquires a new justification for the belief **temp>90** because its sensor detects a temperature of more than $90°C$. This would cause DTMS II to relabel the beliefs **temp>90** and **engine_ok** in and out, respectively, in contradiction to the corresponding labels of DTMS I.

The distributed labeling algorithm [2], would now create the symbol in[9] for belief **engine_ok** of DTMS II, because DTMS I still has a valid justification for **engine_ok**. (DTMS I's temperature sensor did not recognize the high temperature for some reason.) However, we do not want the system to believe that the engine is still functioning. The reason for this undesired behavior is: In the scenario, only the *result* of an inference is shared between DTMSs, but not the *reasons* for it. DTMS II does not 'know' that DTMS I continues to believe the engine is ok because it has no reason to believe the temperature is higher than $90°C$. Thus, DTMS II does not inform DTMS I about its recognition of the high temperature and DTMS I will dominate, even though it has less information.

In our terms, the created state above would *not* be proof consistent, because Condition 2 of Definition 13 is violated. We require the transmission of all ancestors of a transmitted belief as well. If we want the DTMSs to yield a cooperative solution about a belief b in our system, the following will happen. Via a cooperation process, the DTMSs will select one single proof for b of one single DTMS. We say, this DTMS is *logically responsible* for b.[10] In this DTMS, *all* ancestors $f_1 \cdots f_n$ of b will be marked as transmitted. Furthermore, all of the DTMSs involved in the cooperation process will acquire DTMS rules represented as
dtms_rule $((f_i$ **:- responsible_dtms)**, $id_i)$.
or
dtms_rule $((f_i$ **:- not responsible_dtms)**, $id_i)$.
for each ancestor $f_1 \cdots f_n$. The positive dtms-rule is added if the corresponding ancestor in the logically responsible DTMS is in, otherwise the negative one is added.[11]

We will now assume that DTMS I is logically responsible for the belief **engine_ok**. DTMS I transmitted its beliefs **engine_ok**, **valve1_open**, **temp>90** to DTMS II. For each transmitted belief, there is an entry of the form **transmitted_node (node, dtms_list)** representing, in its second argument, all DTMSs

---

[9] In particular, the labeling algorithm as described in [2] will create the symbol **external**. It is logically equivalent to the symbol in, but denotes that the valid justification for the belief is in another DTMS.

[10] At this point, sophisticated cooperation methods might select the logically responsible DTMS. In our example it is sufficient to select the logically responsible DTMS randomly.

[11] Thus, we could represent the example of Definition 13 in Prolog code as follows:
DTMS I:
```
dtms_rule((b:-a), j1).
dtms_rule((a:-dtms_2), j2).
dtms_node(b, in, a, [a], [], j1).
dtms_node(a, in, dtms_2, [dtms_2], [b], j2).
```
DTMS II:
```
dtms_rule((a:-b), r1).
dtms_rule((b:-dtms_1), r2).
dtms_node(a, in, b, [b], [], r1).
dtms_node(b, in, dtms_1, [dtms_1], [a], r2).
```

to which the belief has been transmitted. The three DTMS-nodes represents its current set of beliefs, just as described above. DTMS II, however, acquired three dtms-rules from DTMS I:

```
dtms_rule('temp>90' :- not dtms_1, j5).
dtms_rule(valve1_open :- dtms_1, j4).
dtms_rule(engine_ok :- dtms_1, j3).
```

and created the following nodes:

```
dtms_node(valve2_open, in, true, [true], [], j2).
dtms_node(engine_ok, in, dtms_1, [dtms_1], [], j3).
dtms_node(valve1_open, in, dtms_1, [dtms_1], [], j4).
dtms_node('temp>90', out, dtms_1, [dtms_1], [], _g55).
```

We see from the current set of beliefs of DTMS II that the belief **engine_ok** is now supported by DTMS I and not by its own justification j1 (cf. the 4th argument of the second dtms_node). Nevertheless, j1 of DTMS II is still valid.

The DTMSs are *proof consistent*: Each DTMS Is locally consistent, all mutual beliefs have the same status and all ancestors of transmitted beliefs are also transmitted. Furthermore, the set of **in** beliefs is well founded wrt Condition 4 of Definition 13.

Now suppose DTMS II acquires a new valid justification **dtms_rule** (**'temp > 90'** :- **true, j6**) which disrupts proof consistency. Because **temp>90** changes its status originally supported by DTMS I, DTMS II 'tells', that is transmits, its new belief to DTMS I via passing the DTMS rule **temp>90 :- dtms_2**. Acquiring a new valid justification from DTMS II for its belief **temp>90**, DTMS I relabels downstream its belief **engine_ok** to status **out**. This involves belief **engine_ok** in DTMS II again, because **engine_ok** had been transmitted from DTMS I to DTMS II. In these terms, we get the labeling of **engine_ok** to **out** in both DTMSs:

Nodes of DTMS I:

```
dtms_node(valve1_open, in, true, [true], [], j2).
dtms_node('temp>90', in, dtms_2, [dtms_2], [engine_ok], j3).
dtms_node(engine_ok, out, not valve1_open ; 'temp>90',
        ['temp>90'], [], _g55).
```

Nodes of DTMS II:

```
dtms_node(valve2_open, in, true, [true], [], j2).
dtms_node(valve1_open, in, dtms_1, [dtms_1], [], j3).
dtms_node('temp>90', in, true, [true], [engine_ok], j6).
dtms_node(engine_ok, out, ((not valve2_open ; 'temp>90') , dtms_1),
        ['temp>90', dtms_1], [], _g55).
```

As we see in this example, *both* DTMSs are logically responsible for the status of **engine_ok** being out: DTMS I inferred **valve1_open** and transmitted it to DTMS II, while vice versa DTMS II inferred **temp>90** and transmitted it to DTMS I.

Our concept allows a DTMS to reason about its own justifications and rules acquired by other DTMSs while guaranteeing a defined degree of consistency. This degree of consistency ensures solutions to queries that are correct and consistent with all DTMSs involved in the reasoning process with a minimal exchange of knowledge. Thus, our definition of *proof consistency* can be seen as a trade-off between exchanging as little knowledge as possible and guaranteeing consistent solutions with respect to all involved DTMSs.

Furthermore, a DTMS does not have to know about the structure and the dependencies of another DTMS's proof; only the ancestors and the statuses of the ancestors has to be transmitted. This allows a DTMS to store and access knowledge of other DTMSs in a very efficient way.

The DTMS in an Abstract Agent Model

As the basis for designing real machine agents, we use the abstract agent model presented in [15], [10]. This model decomposes an agent into three main parts (Figure 3): The *agent mouth* realizes the communication functionality of an

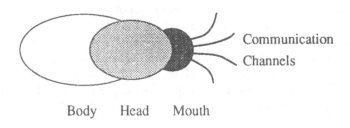

Fig. 3. Parts of an agent.

agent. Via communication channels, it receives and passes messages to the agents head, and in the other direction, it is able to post agent's messages coming from its head. The agent's mouth has to be provided with sufficient network knowledge, such as physical addresses of agents or knowledge about how to get these addresses. Furthermore, a sophisticated design of an agent's mouth would be able to deal with a variety of communication formats (natural language, graphical representations, bit streams ...) characterized by several different attributes. The authors of [15] distinguish, for instance, the priority of a message, its type and the type of expected answer.

The *agent's head* incorporates mechanisms for cooperation and inference control. Thus, the head of an agent contains both meta knowledge of its own capabilities (autoepistemic knowledge), as well as meta knowledge of capabilities, status and behavior of other agents (epistemic knowledge). Designing the agents' head is a complex task. The following items are some additional features an agent's head should be provided with:

- knowledge about the state of the current task
- task decomposition algorithms
- facilities for inter-agent communication
- methods to change its cooperation behavior depending on globally available cooperation structures

We might regard the agent's head as the "mediator between the agent's individual functionality and the overall problem solving context."

Finally, the *agent body* realizes the basic problem solving functionality of an agent. Following [15], the complexity of a body's functionality is not constrained: A sensor as well as whole expert systems or humans can be subsumed under the notion of 'agent body'.

The DTMS presented here provides meta-logic control (located in the agent's head) and basic functionality (located in the agent's body), Figure 4. This is

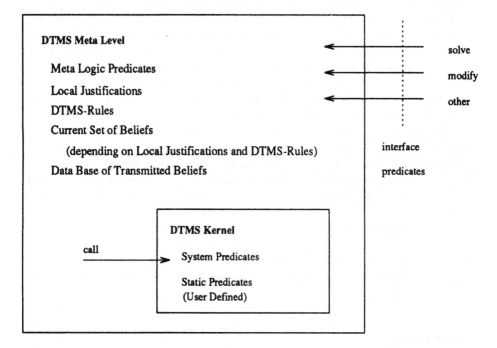

Fig. 4. DTMS architecture.

due to the fact that the DTMS is designed as a Prolog meta interpreter. The DTMS *Meta Level* includes meta-logic predicates, user defined justifications, the current state of beliefs, the DTMS *Kernel* system predicates and user defined static predicates. The meta level controls the evaluation of all goals, performs the bookkeeping of results and defines the DTMS interface while the kernel defines low level predicates: predicates, which might be evaluated through a meta call, but whose proof is not significant for the DTMS bookkeeping mechanism (cf. Definition 8).

The meta-logic predicate `dtms_solve/5` plays a central role in the meta level. The definition of `dtms_solve/5` realizes a modification of a standard Prolog meta interpreter. At first sight, this interpreter takes as an argument a Prolog query *g* and tries to find a proof for *g* in accordance with clauses of the kernel, the meta level and with the current set of beliefs. In the course of doing this, all data dependencies are stored or updated as necessary.

Justifications are defined in the meta level. These are dynamic program clauses defining the atomic formulas, on which truth maintenance will be performed. In former JTMSs, justifications are –in a different form– the only kind of rules. But we will see when considering DTMS applications that the combination of a TMS with a Prolog problem solver increases the TMS functionality by allowing for system predicates. As mentioned before, these predicates are also evaluated by `dtms_solve/5`. Furthermore, we will see that there is a whole class of predicates that should be evaluated in the same manner as system predicates. These are predicates that are never be altered such as `member/3` or `append/3`. Obviously, there is no point in performing truth maintenance on those predicates. Because of these reasons, we define the DTMS Kernel. In the kernel all predicates of the meta level are invisible, but the meta level can evaluate predicates defined here. The proof tree of the result of a kernel call will not be stored. In other words, you may regard the kernel may be regarded as the 'static true world' and the meta level as the 'dynamic changing world'.

Modifications to justifications must be done through the meta-level predicates. This means in particular, the kernel predicates may not assert or retract justifications. Violating this principle would result in a undefined behavior of the DTMS, because each modification of the justification database invokes the meta level `dtms_solve/5` predicate and possibly a call to the initial kernel predicate again.

The `dtms_solve/5` predicate allows other agents, i.e users, for querying an agent about its own knowledge. The DTMSs communicate with each other via the agents' mouth. It transfers prolog queries in low-level communication protocols, schedules outgoing and incoming messages, realizes single-, multi- and broadcasts, etc.

Conclusion

We presented a new concept supporting reasoning among autonomous interacting DTMSs in distributed scenarios and demonstrated its usefulness in a concrete implementation. Central to this concept is the new term *proof consistency* which clearly defines a state of consistency of mutually dependent beliefs across different DTMSs. This state is characterized by exchanging inferences *and* their foundations. We showed that in contrast to previous approaches, our definition of consistency allows agents to reason in a more complex way. Information, lost in former approaches, will now be propagated to all relevant DTMSs: Because one DTMS knows the foundations of an acquired inference of another DTMS, it can inform this DTMS when a foundation becomes invalid. In order to minimize the number of the foundations to be exchanged between the agents, we could establish what is relevant for each agent in his model. This has to be done *before* the reasoning process starts and the domain of relevance must not change. However, in general other matters become relevant for an agent later on, e.g. in a cooperation process, and so proof consistency might be disrupted.

Instead we have shown that the DTMSs will not be overwhelmed with information when transmitting beliefs and its foundations. It is sufficient only to exchange a special, minimal representation of inferences between DTMSs, that is for each belief of the proof to be exchanged a string (the atomic formula) and a boolean (the state of the atomic formula).

Our algorithm for establishing proof consistency in a multi-agent scenario is based on a first-order truth maintenance system. In contrast to propositional based TMSs, a first order representation of beliefs provides for more expressive interaction between DTMSs while simultaneously guaranteeing a precise theoretical background. Furthermore, our approach of defining a TMS as a variant of a Prolog meta interpreter relieves the application designer from evaluation control tasks; this is delegated to meta evaluation by the DTMS. In addition, meta logic control allows the application designer to distinguish between goals on which truth maintenance will be performed and goals which remain static. This yields higher performance and avoids unnecessary exchange of information between DTMS's.

Nevertheless, meta-logic control of goal evaluation incurs additional costs that can overshadow the performance of the DTMS in some cases. The DTMS is used to best advantage on asynchronous distributed applications, in which the message passing time dominate the computation time of the DTMS (group calendars, schedulers, task managers, etc, ...). For single DTMS contexts, the DTMS is used on applications where certain goals can be expected to be selected frequently. We are still confronted with the *lemma generation problem* ([14], [12]) that is not solved in the current version of the DTMS.

The use of our DTMS will constrain the autonomy of an agent in one important aspect: Only one DTMS is allowed to be active at one time. There is no provision for two DTMSs to change their beliefs simultaneously. This is due to fact that there is no synchronisation of messages between the DTMS. A message sent by a DTMS can recieve another DTMS before a previously sent message. We think of defining a causal ordering of message sends and deliveries as discussed in [3]. Although this is mainly a matter for designing an agent's head, it influences the design of an agent's head and body: e.g. the agents must be able to undo previous actions. Nevertheless, handling such cases is not trivial and is a subject for further research.

I would like to thank Project KIK of the DFKI and I3.CSCW of GMD for providing the environment conducive to this research. D. Steiner and A. Burt read numerous drafts and made valuable comments.

References

1. P. Barahona, L. Moniz Pereira, and A. Porto, editors. *EPIA 91: Proc. of the 5th Portuguese Conference on Artificial Intelligence.* Springer, Berlin, Heidelberg, 1991.
2. D. M. Bridgeland and M. N. Huhns. Distributed truth maintenance. In *Proc. of AAAI-90*, pages 72–77, Boston, MA, 1990.
3. B. Charron-Bost, F. Mattern, and G. Tel. Synchronous and asynchronous communication in distributed computations. Technical Report TR 91.55, Institut Blaise Pascal, University Paris, Paris, 1991. (revised version).
4. S. Costantini and G. A. Lanzarone. Metalevel representation of analogical inference. In E. Ardizzone, S. Gaglio, and F. Sorbello, editors, *Trends in Artificial Intelligence: Proc. of the 2nd Congress of the Italian Association for Artificial Intelligence, AI*IA*, pages 460–464. Springer, Berlin, Heidelberg, 1991.
5. Edmund H. Durfee, Victor R. Lesser, and Daniel D. Corkill. Trends in cooperative distributed problem solving. In *Transactions on Knowledge and Data Engineering*, 1989.
6. J. R. Galliers. The positive role of conflict in cooperative multi-agent systems. In Y. Demazeau and J.-P. Müller, editors, *Decentralized A.I. : Proc. of the First European Workshop on Modelling Autonomous Agents in a Multi-Agent World, Cambridge, England*, pages 33–46. North-Holland, Amsterdam, 1990.
7. J. R. Galliers. Cooperative interaction as strategic belief revision. In S. M. Deen, editor, *CKBS'90: Proc. of the International Working Conference on Cooperating Knowledge Based Systems*, pages 148–163. Springer, Berlin, Heidelberg, 1991.
8. T. C. Horstmann. Distributed truth maintenance. Technical Report D-91-11, German Center for Artificial Intelligence (DFKI), Kaiserslautern, Germany, 1991.
9. John W. Lloyd. *Foundations of Logic Programming.* Symbolic computation: Artificial Intelligence. Springer, 2nd edition, 1987.
10. Dirk Mahling, Thilo Horstmann, Astrid Scheller-Houy, Andreas Lux, Donald Steiner, and Hans Haugeneder. Wissensbasierte unterstuetzung von gruppenarbeit oder: Die emanzipation der maschinellen agenten. In J. Friedrich and K. H. Roediger, editors, *German Chapter of the ACM: Computergestuetzte Gruppenarbeit (CSCW)*, volume 34, pages 297–294. B. G. Teubner, Stuttgart, 1991. (in German).
11. Cindy L. Mason and Rowland R. Johnson. DATMS: A Framework for Distributed Assumption-Based Reasoning. In L. Gasser and M. N. Huhns, editors, *Distributed Artificial Intelligence, Volume II*, pages 293–318. Pitman/Morgan Kaufmann, London, 1989.
12. L. M. Pereira and A. Porto. Selective backtracking. In K. L. Clark and S.-A. Tärnlund, editors, *Logic Programming*, pages 107–114. Academic Press, London, 1982.
13. D. Russinoff. An algorithm for truth maintenance. Technical Report AI-062-85, MCC, 1985.
14. R. W. Southwick. The lemma generation problem. Technical report, Imperial College, London, 1990.
15. Donald Steiner, Dirk Mahling, and Hans Haugeneder. Human computer cooperative work. In M. Huhns, editor, *Proc. of the 10th International Workshop on Distributed Artificial Intelligence*, 1990.

Building Text Temporal Structure *

Irene Pimenta Rodrigues and José Gabriel Lopes

CRIA, UNINOVA,
Quinta da Torre,
2825 Monte da Caparica,
Portugal
email: ipr,gpl@fct.unl.pt

Abstract. In this paper we present a framework for the interpretation of the tense and aspect of each sentence of a text using the context provided by the previously interpreted sentences. In the proposed interpretation process the text temporal structure is captured. Each eventuality introduced by a new text sentence is temporally anchored relatively to the previously interpreted eventualities. Whenever it is possible it is structurally[2] related with some of those eventualities.

The interpretation process is driven by querying a knowledge base with the temporal predication of the new sentence's main eventuality. The answer to that query is the semantic interpretation of the sentence. It provides the additional knowledge that was not explicitly conveyed by the sentence, and the update of the text temporal structure.

1 Introduction

In this paper we present a framework for the interpretation of the tense and aspect of each sentence of a text. This is done in the context provided by the previously interpreted sentences. In the proposed interpretation process the text temporal structure is captured and is used to provide the interpretation context of each sentence.

In order to build the text temporal structure we need a clear criterion to group text sentences. In our approach sentences are grouped by constructors called segments. The criterion we use is based on the maintenance of temporal coherence between segments[16]. It relies on the inference of temporal relations between segments. These relations should be supported either by world knowledge about action and change or by linguistic knowledge. The inference of temporal relations between segments is a feasible and precise method for discourse segmentation[16, 17].

Discourse segmentation is accomplished in order to address temporal anaphora resolution. Our criterion uses the result of temporal anaphora resolution and supplies the information necessary for further anaphora resolution.

---

* This work has been supported by JNICT, FCT/UNL and Gabinete de Filosofia do Conhecimento.

[2] The word *structurally* is used in the sense that we need to describe the structure of events and the relation between events and states.

The anchoring of the eventuality time relative to previously introduced eventualities (temporal anaphora resolution) depends on syntactic constraints (sentence tense and aspect) and on the relations that can be assumed between the newly introduced eventuality and the previously interpreted eventualities [20, 6, 12, 3, 7, 2]. These relations are what some authors call contingency relations [10]. They reflect the internal structure of events an states.

Consider the texts:

Max opened the door. The room was pitch dark. (1)
Max switched off the light. The room was pitch dark. (2)
Max switched on the light. The room was pitch dark. (3)

The above three texts are similar in their syntactic forms. The first sentence describes an event and simple past tense is used. The second sentence introduces a state description. However, the tense and aspect interpretation of the above texts give different temporal relations between the event and the state. Namely, for text 1 $t_{open} \subset t_{darkroom}$, for text 2 $t_{switchoff} < t_{darkroom}$ and for text 3 $t_{switchon} > t_{darkroom}$.

In order to obtain these interpretations we must take into account more then the syntactic forms of the sentences. We need knowledge about the structure of events and states.

It is by considering that *"switching off the light has a dark room as consequence"* that we are able to give text 2 the interpretation $t_{switchoff} < t_{darkroom}$.

The accommodation of an eventuality described by a text sentence involves the recognition of the structure of the events and states already described by the text.

So we need an explicit representation for the event structure. We use predicates such as *consq, part, etc* that explicitly represent that an event has a state as a consequence, or that an event is in the preparatory phase of another event. With such predicates we are representing the structure of an *individual* of sort "event", not the structure of event types.

Regarding the interpretation process, we follow Hobbs' idea [4] and take interpretation as abduction. The interpretation of a text sentence is the set of assumptions that if true make that sentence true. We will only describe the process of interpretation of a sentence tense and aspect. And we claim that this process could be integrated in a more general process of text processing as a subprocess of tense and aspect interpretation.

So, our general strategy for tense and aspect interpretation is to query a knowledge base with the temporal predication of the sentence's main eventuality. The answer to this query is the set of assumptions (abductions) that make the eventuality a logic consequence of the interpretation knowledge base.

In [4], the discourse structure is captured by building rhetorical relations between sentences, but there is no concern in constraining sentence interpretation by the context defined by the previous discourse structure. In our approach we use the text temporal structure to provide an interpretation context for each sentence. This way we have a notion of *temporal focus* [20] or *temporal reference* [6] for the interpretation of tense and aspect.

In section 2, we present the definition of text segments and the semantic representation of text sentences. In section 3, the knowledge bases used in the interpretation process are briefly presented. In section 4, the interpretation knowledge base is explained in some detail, giving special relevance to the abduction process. In section 5, we describe the algorithms used for introducing a new segment into the discourse segment, and for checking if the resulting discourse structure is kept consistent. It is shown how a sentences' interpretation is constrained by the discourse structure. Finally in section 6, a detailed example is explained and some conclusions are presented in section 7.

2 Text Temporal Structure

In our approach a text is represented by a structure that captures the temporal properties of the text: the segment. A segment is a feature matrix (a term) that can represent a single clause sentence[3] or a group of such sentences. $\mathcal{L}_t$ is the language for describing segments. Later in this section we will introduce language $\mathcal{L}_s$ that will be necessary for the semantic representation of single sentences. This representation will be rewritten as a consequence of the interpretation process.

Language $\mathcal{L}_t$: A well formed formula of $\mathcal{L}_t$ is a term (a segment) with the following features-value pairs:
- — segment referent: s_i.
- — sort: $sort_i \in \{\text{none}, \text{bef}, \text{aft}, \text{cont}, \text{icont}, \text{over}, \text{basic}\}$.
- — tense: a verb tense.
- — time: t_i.
- — eventuality: e_i.
- — temporal predicate: $occurs(e_i, t_i)$ or $holds(e_i, t_i)$.
- — expression: $E : P$, where E is a set of discourse referents, P is an expression of language $\mathcal{L}_s$(described later).
- — subsegments: a (possibly empty) ordered list of segment referents.

A segment in a subsegment list must verify the restrictions imposed by its parent sort[16]. Given segment s, consider $subsegments(s) = \{s_1, s_2, \ldots, s_n\}$, let $t_{s_k} \equiv time(s_k)$, the meaning of $sort(s)$[4] is:

bef - $\forall i < k, t_{s_i} < t_{s_k}$.

aft - $t_{s_1} > t_{s_2}$.

cont- $t_{s_1} \subset t_{s_2}$.

icont- $t_{s_1} \supset t_{s_2}$.

over - $\forall i, k t_{s_i} \propto t_{s_k}$ (the intersection of t_{s_i} and t_{s_k} is non empty).

none - $\forall t_{s_j}, t_{s_k}$ there is no plausible temporal relation that they must obey.

basic - $n = 0$ i.e. $subsegments(s) = \emptyset$

A text is represented by a segment, sentences and groups of sentences are represented by segments. Two consecutive text sentences each represented by

---

[3] In order to represent multiclause sentences the segment must represent the eventuality of the main clause.

[4] Segments of sort *aft*, *cont* and *icont* have only 2 subsegments.

a segment of sort basic, may be represented by a nonbasic segment having the basic segments as subsegments, the sort of the segment will be one of the above depending on the temporal relation that the two segments obey (see section 5).

The features of a nonbasic segments are inherited from its subsegment features[5].

A segment of sort **none, bef** or **over** inherits the features:

— tense -   from its last subsegment tense.

— time referent: is the union of its subsegments' time referents.

— eventuality referent: is the union of its subsegments' eventuality referents.

A segment of sort **aft, cont** or **icont** (having only 2 subsegments) inherits the features *tense, time referent, eventuality referent, temporal predicate* from its first subsegment.

Visibility: the last subsegment of a visible segment is defined to be a *visible* segment. The discourse segment (the root) is visible.

Language $\mathcal{L}_s$: Well formed formulas of the Language $\mathcal{L}_s$ are:

- holds(e_i, t_i).
- occurs(e_i, t_i).
- eventuality(e_i,R) — with R $\in \mathcal{E}$ and $\mathcal{E}$ is a set of eventuality types (events or states). An eventuality type is a relation of arity n (e.g. *eat(X,Y), run(X), buy(X,Y), dead(X))*.
- t_i *int_rel* t_j, — with t_i, t_j time intervals and *int_rel* $\in \{<, >, \subset, \supset, \propto\}$[6]
- P — with P $\in \mathcal{P}$ and $\mathcal{P}$ is a set of nontemporal relations (e.g. *cat(X), men(X))*.
- bind(e_i, L_{rest}, S_{rest}) — [15] this predicate is used to mean that referent e_i is anaphoric. L_{rest} is a set of linguistic restrictions (e.g. gender and number for individuals, tense and aspect for the main sentence eventuality time).S_{rest} is a set of semantic restrictions (e.g the kind of individual for individuals, the eventuality referent for the main sentence eventuality time).
- $p_i = p_j$ — which means that p_i and p_j are two coreferring discourse referents of the same sort.
- $p_i \neq p_j$ — where p_i and p_j are two discourse referents of the same sort that do not corefer.
- C, — a contingency relation between two eventuality referents (cause, consq, terminates, part).
- ϕ, ψ — if ϕ and ψ are wffs.

Natural Language sentences are processed and translated into expressions (formulas) of this Language $\mathcal{L}_s$[7][5]. By further semantic interpretation (the process of introducing the new sentence segment in the discourse structure), the expression can grow by adding new valid formulas of this language.

A sentence is represented by a segment of sort *basic*. For instance the sentence "John shot a turkey with a gun" gives rise to the segment depicted in figure 1.

---

[5] See [16] where linguistic evidence is presented for segment inheritance rules.

[6] time interval relations

[7] This process will not be analyzed here.

s1 :basic		past
e1	t1	occurs(e1,t1)
e1,t1,x1,x2,x3:man(x1), name(x1,John), turkey(x2),gun(x3), eventuality(e1,shot(x1,x2,x3)), occurs(e1,t1), bind(t1,X^tense(X,past),Y^time(e1,Y)).		
NIL		

Fig. 1. Segment representing the sentence "John shot a turkey with a gun".

3 Knowledge Bases for the Interpretation of a Sentence

We briefly describe the knowledge bases that we use in the interpretation process.

• $kb_{visible}$ contains the values of the temporal predicate feature of any visible segment in the discourse structure. So, $kb_{visible} \models holds(e_i, t_i)$ and $kb_{visible} \models occurs(e_j, t_j)$ for every eventuality e_i or e_j such that $holds(e_i, t_i)$ or $occurs(e_j, t_j)$.

• kb_{text} is used to prove of $\mathcal{P}_i$, i.e. $kb_{text} \models \mathcal{P}_i$, if either $\mathcal{P}_i$ is a condition on discourse referents (an expression of $\mathcal{L}_s$) from the previous discourse, or if $\mathcal{P}_i$ is is a condition on discourse referents of the the new segment.

This knowledge base has a set of integrity constraints associated with it (I_{text}).

• kb_{time} is such that: $kb_{time} \models t_i \mathcal{R}_t t_j$ if t_i and t_j are discourse referents or temporal constants; and $\mathcal{R}_t \in \{<, >, \supset, \subset, \propto\}$; and there is a mapping $\mathcal{I}$ for all t_i, t_j in intervals $[t_a, t_b]$ with t_a, t_b reals such that $t_a < t_b$, and the obtained intervals can be a solution of the set of equations obtained by translating all the temporal relations that are in kb_{text}, giving the usual interpretation for the $\mathcal{R}_t$s, and in all possible mappings $\mathcal{I}$, $\mathcal{I}(t_i)\mathcal{R}_t\mathcal{I}(t_j)$ is satisfied.

• $kb_{interrogation}$ is such that: $kb_{interrogation} \models \mathcal{P}$, if $kb_{text} \models \mathcal{P}$ or if $\mathcal{P}$ is of the form $holds\_at(T_i, R)$[8], with T_i a temporal referent in the discourse structure or in the new segment, and R a relation that should hold at that time interval.

4 The Knowledge Base for the Semantic Interpretation

Additionally to the above mentioned knowledge bases we still need another one, the so called interpretation knowledge base. This knowledge base attempts to derive the temporal predication of the next sentence's main eventuality, in the text being interpreted.

The interpretation of a sentence's main eventuality is constrained by the discourse temporal structure, world knowledge about eventualities and the interpreted eventualities already stated in the text.

The local constraints upon the sentence's main eventuality are the tense and aspect of the sentence verb, the type of eventuality (the type of relation

---

[8] $holds\_at(t_i, R)$, means that the state type R holds at the time interval t_i. t_i is not required to be a maximal interval for the eventuality type R. For the predications $holds(e_i, t_i)$ and $occurs(e_j, t_j)$ time intervals t_i and t_j must be maximal[17].

used to represent it) the eventuality arguments (the arguments of the relation, representing verb arguments).

The new eventuality temporal predication (if it holds or occurs) is inferred by creating links between the new sentence referents and existing discourse referents. The binding of the new referents to early introduced referents is a result of the semantic interpretation of the new sentence.

The links between referents are represented by relations that are abducted.

Given α, the temporal predication of the main eventuality of the ith text sentence (it is always a predicate holds or occurs); given $D_{s_{i-1}}$, the discourse structure resulting from the interpretation of the first $i-1$ sentences in the given text, then the answer to the query α is derived from the interpretation knowledge base ($kb_{interpretation}$) together with $D_{s_{i-1}}$. This answer (the interpretation) is Δ together with the temporal discourse structure of the first i sentences of the text, D_{s_i}. This process can be represented by:

$$kb_{interpretation} + D_{s_{i-1}} \models (\Delta + D_{s_i}) \implies \alpha$$

Δ is a set of relations that are abducted, i.e. $kb_{interpretation} \cup \Delta \models \alpha$

Δ only has relations that relate discourse referents with the new sentence referents, so an answer to query α is a set of constraints on the discourse referents such that α can be a logic consequence of $kb_{interpretation}$.

Δ is not unique as there may exist several sets of abductions that can support α. Each such Δ gives rise to a different semantic interpretation of the new text sentence.

Let Δ_i and Δ_j be such sets (possible semantic interpretations), and if $\Delta_j \subset \Delta_i$, then Δ_i is not a minimal solution. We don't need to take into account non minimal solutions. The minimal solutions Δ_j, may have a preference relation associated with them. We may choose to maximize the number of abductions in minimal solutions in order to prefer more cohesive interpretations, those that anchor more referents in the previous discourse.

We shall fix the set of relations that can be abducted, and consider only the following three kinds of abductible relations.

Temporal relations between time referents. Consider the relations $\mathcal{R}_t \in \{<, >, \supset, \subset, \propto\}$. A temporal relation $t_i \, \mathcal{R}_t \, t_j$ is abductible if $kb_{time} \models \Diamond \, t_i \, \mathcal{R}_t \, t_j$[9].

The relation equal and not_equal between discourse referents. Given two discourse referents x_i, x_j the relation $x_i = x_j$ is abductible if $kb_{text} \models bind(x_j, \lambda X.\mathcal{C}_{sint}, \lambda Y.\mathcal{C}_{sem})$[10] and $kb_{interrogation} \models \lambda X.\mathcal{C}_{sint}(x_i), \lambda Y.\mathcal{C}_{sem}(x_i)$[11].

---

[9] This means that $kb_{time} \cup \{t_i \, \mathcal{R}_t \, t_j\}$ is consistent. The $\Diamond$ should be read as "it is possible that".

[10] $\lambda X.\mathcal{C}_{sint}$ is the relations that the referent x_j must obey, these relations are of syntactic sort, eg. number(sing,X), person(3,X), gen(masc,X), for a x_j resulting from the translation of "he". $\lambda Y.\mathcal{C}_{sem}$ is the set of relations that the referent x_j must obey, these are semantic constraints, eg. person(X) for a x_j.

[11] This means that a referent may refer to another one if it can satisfy its syntactic and semantic constraints. This is a simplification of the conditions for anaphora resolution.

The relation $x_i \neq x_j$ is abductible if $kb_{text} \not\models x_i = x_j$.

Relations between eventuality referents. Taking into account the internal structure of eventualities[10] and causal relations between events and states it is possible to define contingency relations between eventuality referents such as *consequence, terminates, part* (is in the preparatory phase of) and *cause*[12].

A contingency relation between two eventualities e_i and e_j can be abducted iff:

- the eventuality types of e_i and e_j can be in that contingency relation.

The check for compatibility of the eventuality types may involve assumptions on the referents that are arguments of the eventualities, enabling some anaphora (nominal and pronominal) and ellipsis resolution.

For instance, a shot can have a death as consequence if the shot was against the entity that died. This will be encoded by the $kb_{interpretation}$ rule[13]:

$$\text{gen\_consq}(e_i, e_j) \text{ if } (kb_{text} \models \text{eventuality}(e_i, \text{shoot}(X_1, X_2, X_3))),$$
$$(kb_{text} \models \text{eventuality}(e_j, \text{dead}(X_4))),$$
$$X_2 = X_4.$$

In this rule $X_2 = X_4$ is a relation between two discourse referents. It may have to be abducted. This rule can be read as: if there is textual evidence that some X_1 shot X_2 with a gun X_3 and that someone, X_4, died, and there is no evidence against the identity $X_2 = X_4$ then it is plausible that the death is a consequence of the shot.

- it is possible to assume the preconditions of the eventuality e_i at $time(e_i)$ $\equiv t_i$.

For instance, in order to assume that a shot had a death as consequence, it must be possible to assume that the gun was loaded at the time of the shot. This is encoded by the $kb_{interpretation}$ fact.

$$\text{precond\_consq}(\text{shoot}(\_,\_,X_3), \text{dead}(\_), \lambda \text{ T.holds\_at}(T, \text{loaded}(X_3))).$$

For ease of implementation we shall consider that the predicate $consq(e_i, e_j)$ can be abducted if the predicate not_consq can not be proved. The general definition of not_consq in $kb_{interpretation}$ will be:

$$\text{not\_consq}(E_1, E_2) \text{ if } (kb_{text} \models \text{eventuality}(E_1, R_1)),$$
$$(kb_{text} \models \text{eventuality}(E_2, R_2)),$$
$$(kb_{text} \models \text{occurs}(E_1, T_1),)$$
$$\text{precond\_consq}(R_1, R_2, \lambda \text{T.P}),$$
$$(kb_{interrogation} \models \text{not } \lambda \text{T.P}(T_1)).$$

The need for this rule will be more apparent when the rules of the interpretation knowledge base are described in the next section.

The *not* is interpreted as negation by failure. This means[14] that:

---

[12] In this paper we mainly focus upon the consequence relation.

[13] This rule can be read as "eventualities of type e_i can have eventualities of type e_j as consequence".

[14] In all interpretations of the interrogation knowledge base the conjunction of the preconditions is false.

$kb_{interrogation} \models \Box \neg \lambda T.P(T_1)$.

If the predicate $consq(e_i, e_j)$ is abducted, then the integrity constraint:

$$\leftarrow consq(e_i, e_j),\ not\_consq(e_i, e_j)$$

should be added to the set I_{text} of integrity constraints of the knowledge base kb_{text}. This way we don't need to make assertions about eventuality preconditions, as the integrity constraints will subsequently prevent the addition of knowledge to the kb_{text} that would violate those constraints. The integrity constraints will force the $kb_{interrogation}$ to entail the preconditions, preserving the monotonicity on these, allowing us to use nonmonotonic theories to model the world in $kb_{interrogation}$.

• the temporal relation between the eventuality times defined by the abducted contingency relation, can hold. eg. a contingency relation as $consq(e_i, e_j)$ implies that the relation $e_i < e_j$ holds.

A temporal relation $\mathcal{R}_t \in \{<, >, \supset, \subset, \propto\}$ between two eventuality referents E_i and E_j is a logic consequence of the interpretation theory if:

$E_i \mathcal{R}_t E_j$ if time(E_i, T_i), time(E_j, T_j),

   $T_i \mathcal{R}_t T_j$,

   insert$(E_i, E_j, \mathcal{R}_t)$.

the relation $T_i \mathcal{R}_t T_j$ may have to be abducted.

The predicate "insert" should succeed if the eventuality segment is already in the discourse structure or if the eventuality segment is successfully inserted in the discourse structure (see section 5).

A consistent semantic interpretation of a new sentence is a Δ such that:
$kb_{interrogation} \cup \Delta \models \alpha$ and $kb_{text} \cup \Delta$ verifies I_{text}, the integrity constraints of kb_{text}.

4.1   Rules of the Interpretation Knowledge Base

The rules of $kb_{interpretation}$ will model two sources of knowledge, world knowledge and linguistic knowledge.

Rules based on World Knowledge These rules allow the prediction of an eventuality predication "holds or occurs" by assuming a contingency relation between the new eventuality and some visible eventualities.

The knowledge base $kb_{visible}$ has all the facts $holds(e_i, t_i)$ or $occurs(e_i, t_i)$ that are in the temporal predication feature of visible segments.

The following axiom states that for every holding state E_1 in $kb_{visible}$ (the visible context) there is a rule in $kb_{interpretation}$ stating that every occurrence of an event that has E_1 as consequence is a logic consequence of this knowledge base.

$$\text{consequence}(E_2, E_1) \Longrightarrow \text{occurs}(E_2, T_2) \text{ if } kb_{visible} \models \text{holds}(E_1, T_1)\ (1)$$

The following axiom states that for every visible occurrence E_1 there is a rule in $kb_{interpretation}$ stating that every holding state, E_2, that is a consequence of E_1 is a logical consequence of $kb_{interpretation}$.

$$\text{consequence}(E_1, E_2) \Longrightarrow \text{holds}(E_2, T_2) \text{ if } kb_{visible} \models \text{occurs}(E_1, T_1) \ (2)$$

The following rule describes that the relation *consequence(E_1, E_2)* is a logic consequence when *gen_consq(E_1, E_2)* is a logic consequence of $kb_{interpretation}$ and *consq(E_1, E_2)* is abducted, and the segments of E_1 and E_2 are in the discourse structure and their times obey the temporal relation $T_1 < T_2$.

$$\text{gen\_consq}(E_1, E_2), \text{consq}(E_1, E_2), E_1 < E_2 \Longrightarrow \text{consequence}(E_2, E_1) \ (3)$$

Axiom (1) does not state that from the effect we predict the cause. It rather says that from the effect and assuming it was caused by a particular event then the cause must have occurred.

Rules based on Linguistic Knowledge The following axioms state what happens when we don't take into account world knowledge to relate the new sentence eventuality with visible eventualities.

They take into account eventualities' temporal predication and the verb tense of the sentences that originated the eventualities. It should be stressed that the translation of an eventuality by a predicate "holds" or "occurs" depends upon the sentence's aspectual modifiers and the eventuality's basic signature. These axioms follow from work on the interpretation of tense and aspect [10, 13, 14, 9, 12, 1, 6]

$\text{tense}(T_1,\text{past})$, $\quad \Longrightarrow \text{occurs}(E_2, T_2) \text{ if } kb_{visible} \models \text{holds}(E_1, T_1) \ (5)$
$\text{tense}(T_2,\text{past})$,
$T_1 \supset T_2$

$\text{tense}(T_1,\text{past})$, $\quad \Longrightarrow \text{occurs}(E_2, T_2) \text{ if } kb_{visible} \models \text{occurs}(E_1, T_1) \ (6)$
$\text{tense}(T_2,\text{past})$,
$T_1 < T_2$

$\text{tense}(T_1,\text{past})$, $\quad \Longrightarrow \text{holds}(E_2, T_2) \text{ if } kb_{visible} \models \text{occurs}(E_1, T_1) \ (7)$
$\text{tense}(T_2,\text{past})$,
$T_1 \subset T_2$

$\text{tense}(T_1,\text{past})$, $\quad \Longrightarrow \text{holds}(E_2, T_2) \text{ if } kb_{visible} \models \text{holds}(E_1, T_1) \ (8)$
$\text{tense}(T_2,\text{past})$,
$T_1 \propto T_2$

$\text{tense}(T_1,\text{past})$, $\quad \Longrightarrow \text{occurs}(E_2, T_2) \text{ if } kb_{visible} \models \text{occurs}(E_1, T_1) \ (9)$
$\text{tense}(T_2,\text{pastpast})$,
$T_1 > T_2$

Tense pastpast is used to portrait the past perfect or *plus-que-parfait*.

Linguistic Integrity constraints In order to take into account more linguistic restrictions that are not easily expressed by rules, we shall have integrity constraints in the set associated with kb_{text}, I_{text}. Let $Last_i$ be the last eventuality introduced in the discourse structure before the eventuality E_i. The following linguistic integrity constraint will be considered:

$$\leftarrow \text{time}(E_i, T_i), \text{tense}(T_i, \text{pastpast}), \text{time}(Last_i, T_{Last_i}), \text{tense}(T_{Last_i}, \text{past}),$$
$$T_{Last_i} < T_i.$$

This constraint reflects that an eventuality introduced by a sentence using the *plus-que-parfait* should not be temporally inserted after the previously interpreted eventuality that was introduced in the discourse by a sentence in the simple past.

The constraints in I_{text} must not be violated. For instance given the text:

John shot a turkey. It had been dead.

One of the interpretations for the second sentence using rule (2) is:
$$\Delta_1 = \{\text{consq}(e_{shot}, e_{death}), t_{shot} < t_{death}, x_{turkey} = x_{it}\}$$
This solution will not be accepted as a semantic interpretation of the second sentence because $kb_{text} \cup \Delta_1$ will contain the facts $\{$ time(e_{death}, t_{death}), tense$(t_{death}, \text{pastpast})$, time$(e_{shot}, t_{shot})$, tense$(t_{shot}, \text{past})$, $t_{shot} < t_{death}$ $\}$ that violate the above linguistic integrity constraint.

5 Building the Text Temporal Structure

The insertion of a new segment in the discourse structure is achieved by proving the predicate *insert(E_1, E_2, R)*. This predicate succeeds if the eventualities E_1 and E_2 are already in the discourse structure. Otherwise if the new eventuality referent is not in the discourse structure one must insert it there.

The procedure to insert an eventuality referent E_2 in the discourse segment D_p using E_1 as a referent obeying the temporal relation R is:

1. obtain the visible segment S_1 containing E_1 as eventuality referent.
2. obtain the new sentence segment S_2.
3.   – *if* $R \in \{none, \propto, <\}$ and the parent of S_1 is a segment S_p of kind *none, over, bef*, respectively, *then*
     (a) Add S_2 to the subsegments list of S_p.
     (b) • *If* consistent(D_p)[15] *then* the segment S_2 is inserted and the abductions that result from predicate consistent should be a result of the predicate insert.
          • *else* the predicate insert fails and the segment S_2 can not be inserted at this point.

---

[15] This predicate succeeds if D_p is consistent. See how it is defined in this section after the presentation of this algorithm.

- *else if* R is one of $\{\subset, \supset, >\}$ and the segment S_1 is of kind *cont, icont, aft*, respectively, *then*
  (a) obtain S_{second} the second subsegment of S_1.
  (b) push the visible context, $kb_{visible}$, and build a new one just with the temporal predicate of segment S_{second}.
  (c) • *if* $kb_{interpretation} \cup \Delta \models P_2$, P_2 is the temporal predication of segment S_2 *then*, pop $kb\_visible$, S_2 is inserted, and the relations in Δ should be a result of the predicate insert.
       • *else* the predicate insert fails and the segment S_2 can not be inserted at this point.
- *else*
  (a) build a new segment S_3 with sort defined by the relation R, with S_1 as first subsegment and S_2 as last subsegment.
  (b) substitute the segment S_2 in the discourse structure D_p by the segment S_3.
  (c) • *If* consistent(D_p) *then* the segment S_2 is inserted and the abductions that result from predicate consistent should be a result of the predicate insert.
       • *else* the predicate insert fails and the segment S_2 can not be inserted at this point.

Predicate *consistent(D_p)* succeeds if the segment D_p is consistent. Checking the consistency of discourse segment D_p consists in verifying if its right subsegments obey the temporal relations that its parent imposes. The consistency checking procedure is:

1. Let D_i be the last subsegment of D_p.
2. *if* D_i is a non-basic segment *then*
   if consistent(D_i) then goto 3 else consistent(D_p) fails.
3. Let t_i be the temporal referent of D_i, t_{i-1} be the temporal referent of the segment D_{i-1} which is the segment before D_i in D_p subsegment list, R be the temporal relation imposed by the sort of D_p.
   - *if* $kb_{time} \models t_{i-1}Rt_i$ *then* D_p is consistent.
   - *else*
     (a) push the visible context $kb_{visible}$ and build a new one just with the temporal predicate of segment D_{i-1}.
     (b) • *if* $kb_{interpretation} \cup \Delta \models P_i$, P_i is the temporal predication of segment D_i *and* $t_{i-1}Rt_i \in \Delta$ *then*, D_p is consistent. Pop $kb_{visible}$, Δ should be a result of the predicate consistent.
          • *else* the predicate consistent fails.

6   Detailed example

John was dead (s_1). Mary shot him with a gun(s_2). The gun was unloaded(s_3).

This text will have the following interpretations:

1. John was dead because Mary killed him with a shot. The gun was unloaded when john was dead.
2. John was dead. After he died Mary shot him. The gun was unloaded when john was dead.

The discourse structure and the temporal mappings that correspond to these interpretations are depicted in fig 2.

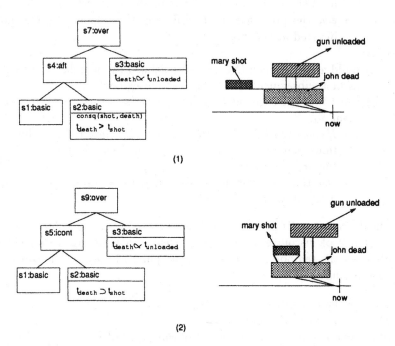

Fig. 2. Discourse segments and temporal mappings.

The first text sentence (s_1) gives rise to a basic segment s_1 with the expression feature:
$$l_1 \equiv \exists \, e_1, t_1, x_1 : person(x_1), name(x_1, john), eventuality(e_1, dead(x_1)),$$
$$holds(e_1, t_1), bind(t_1, \lambda X.tense(X, past), \lambda Y.time(e_1, Y)).$$

As it is the first text sentence, s_1 is the discourse segment and there is no further semantic interpretation.

The second sentence s_2 gives rise to a basic segment s_2 with the expression feature:
$$l_2 \equiv \exists \, e_2, t_2, x_2, x_3, x_4 :$$
$$person(x_2), name(x_2, mary), eventuality(e_2, shot(x_2, x_3, x_4)),$$
$$occurs(e_2, t_2), gun(x_4),$$
$$bind(x_3, \lambda X.(number(sing, X), gen(masc, X)), \lambda Y.person(Y)),$$
$$bind(t_2, \lambda X.tense(X, past), \lambda Y.time(e_2, Y)).$$

The query "$\leftarrow occurs(e_2, t_2)$" is launched in the interpretation kb, with $kb_{text} = l_1 + l_2$, the integrity constraints of kb_{text} in I_{text} are just the linguistic ones, $kb_{visible} = \{\text{holds}(e_1,t_1)\}$, $kb_{time} = \{\}$.

There are two possible answers to this query:

- $\Delta_1 = \{x_1 = x_3, \text{consq}(e_2,e_1), t_1 > t_2\}$[16] (using rule (1)) with the discourse structure $s_4 = aft(s_1,s_2)$[17], and the integrity constraint $I_1 = \{\leftarrow \text{consq}(e_2,e_1), \text{not\_consq}(e_2,e_1)\}$.
- $\Delta_2 = \{t_1 \supset t_2\}$[18] (using rule (5)), discourse structure $s_5 = icont(s_1,s_2)$[19].

Both answers are consistent because $kb_{text} \cup \Delta_1$ verifies the integrity constraints $I_{text} \cup I_1$, and $kb_{text} \cup \Delta_2$ verifies the integrity constraints of I_{text}.

To interpret sentence s_3 one of the previous interpretations must be chosen in order to have the interpretation context for this sentence. The basic segment s_3 representing sentence s_3 has the expression feature:

$$l_3 \equiv \exists\, e_3, t_3, x_5 : gun(x_5)eventuality(e_3, unloaded(x_5)), holds(e_3, t_3),$$
$$bind(x_5, \lambda X.(number(sing, X), gen(masc, X)), \lambda Y.gun(Y)),$$
$$bind(t_3, \lambda X.tense(X, past), \lambda Y.time(e_3, Y)).$$

Choosing Δ_1, the query "$\leftarrow holds(e_3,t_3)$" is launched in $kb_{interpretation}$, with $kb_{text} = l_1 + l_2 + l_3 + \Delta_1$, the integrity constraints $I_{text} = I_1 \cup I_{text}$, $kb_{visible} = \{\text{occurs}(e_2,t_2), \text{holds}(e_1,t_1)\}$, and $kb_{time} = \{t_1 > t_2\}$, the discourse structure is s_4.

The answers to the query are:

- $\Delta_3 = \{t_2 \subset t_3\}$, (using rule 7), discourse structure $s_6 = aft(s_1, cont(s_2,s_3))$.
- $\Delta_4 = \{t_1 \propto t_3\}$, (using rule 8), discourse structure $s_7 = over(aft(s_1,s_2), s_3)$.

The answer that could be obtained using rule (2) is blocked when $\Delta_{3_1} = \{x_4 = x_5, \text{consq}(e_2,e_3), t_2 < t_3\}$ as the consistency of the discourse segment obtained by the insertion of s_3 in the discourse structure s_4 fails. It fails because the insertion of s_3 in s_4 gives rise to the segment $aft(s_1, bef(s_2,s_3))$. In order to test for the consistency[20] of this segment the temporal relation $t_1 > t_3$ should be implied by the constraints $\{t_1 > t_2, t_2 < t_3\}$[21] or should be in an answer to the query "$\leftarrow holds(e_3,t_3)$", with $kb_{visible} = \{\text{holds}(e_1,t_1)\}$. But the only answer to that query is $\Delta = \{t_1 \propto t_3\}$ by rule (8). So the insertion fails and rule (2) cannot be used.

The answer Δ_3 is not a consistent semantic interpretation because the integrity constraint I_1 is no longer satisfied by $kb_{text} \cup \Delta_3$. $not\_consq(e_2,e_1)$ succeeds because $kb_{interrogation}$ should be such that:

$kb_{interrogation} \models not\ holds\_at(t_2, loaded)$ if $kb_{interrogation} \models holds\_at(t_3, unloaded)$, $t_2 \subset t_3$.

---

[16] This abduction set corresponds to the interpretation "Mary killed john".

[17] Δ_1 is added to l_2.

[18] This set of abduction corresponds to the interpretation "Mary shoot john who was already dead".

[19] Δ_2 is added to l_2.

[20] In the previous section this procedure is described.

[21] $t_1 > t_3$ is not a temporal relation implied by the constraints $\{t_1 > t_2, t_2 < t_3\}$.

So the final semantic interpretation of the text is the discourse segment of fig 2.1. The abductions made to obtain this interpretation are:

1. $\Delta_{t_1} = \Delta_1 \cup \Delta_4 = \{x_1 = x_3, consq(e_2, e_1), t_1 > t_2, t_1 \propto t_3\}$ with discourse structure $s_7 = over(aft(s_1, s_2), s_3)$.

The other semantic interpretations of the text are obtained choosing the alternative answer Δ_2 to the first query. The query "$\leftarrow holds(e_3, t_3)$" is launched in $kb_{interpretation}$, with $kb_{text} = l_1 + l_2 + l_3 + \Delta_2$, the integrity constraints $I_{text} = the$ linguistic ones, $kb_{visible} = \{occurs(e_2, t_2), holds(e_1, t_1)\}$, and $kb_{time} = \{t_1 \supset t_2\}$, the discourse structure is s_5.

The answers to the query are:

- $\Delta_5 = \{t_2 \sqsubset t_3\}$, (using rule 7), discourse structure $s_8 = icont(s_1, cont(s_2, s_3))$.
- $\Delta_6 = \{t_1 \propto t_3\}$, (using rule 8), discourse structure $s_9 = over(aft(s_1, s_2), s_3)$.

The answer $\Delta_{5_1} = \{x_4 = x_5, consq(e_2, e_3), t_2 < t_3\}$ is not obtained because when segment s_3 is inserted in the discourse structure, the resulting discourse structure $s = icont(s_1, bef(s_2, s_3))$, is not a consistent discourse structure. The relation $t_1 \supset t_3$ can not be inferred in $kb_{interpretation}$ with $kb_{visible} = \{holds(e_1, t_1)\}$[22] and current $kb_{time} \not\models t_1 \supset t_3$.

As $\Delta_5 \cup \Delta_2 \supset \Delta_6 \cup \Delta_2$, if we choose minimal solutions, we ignore Δ_5 and the second interpretation of the text is:

2. $\Delta_{t_2} = \Delta_2 \cup \Delta_6 = \{t_1 \supset t_2, t_1 \propto t_3\}$ with the discourse structure $s_9 = over(aft(s_1, s_2), s_3)$ in fig 2.2.

However by ignoring Δ_5 we are also ignoring the discourse structure s_8. This may not be a good option. Maybe the best is to choose minimal solutions just when the obtained discourse structures are the same.

7 Conclusions

We presented a framework for the interpretation of text sentences. This framework takes into account the temporal structure of discourse and uses it to constrain sentence interpretation. The interpretation knowledge base can easily be implemented with an abductive mechanism such as the one presented in [18], using the mechanism of contextual logic programing [11] in order to work with all the knowledge bases. The explosion of the abductive inference is controlled by the small number of temporal predications that are visible for each sentence interpretation.

A notion of consistent text interpretation is given by using integrity constraints that allow us to eliminate solutions that don't obey linguistic and specific world knowledge constraints; it is possible to build integrity constraints that

---

[22] We are assuming that we don't have world knowledge stating that the state of death ends after the state of unloaded.

block particular discourse structure configurations. The integrity constraints are checked using an interrogation theory that builds reasonable models from the acquired text facts. The interrogation knowledge base can be implemented using the same mechanism as the interpretation knowledge base, but the axioms about events and states should be more realistic,[23] and model notions such as "state persistence", "state and event prediction" and "event and state explanation" that are fundamental in commonsense temporal reasoning [19, 18].

In the second interpretation of the example discussed in section 6, Δ_{t_2}, the nominal anaphora of sentence (s_3) "the gun" was not solved. This is so because our approach is mainly concerned with the temporal anaphora resolution. But it is possible to complete this framework by defining processes of anaphora resolution, and by defining further criteria of segmentation on the obtained segments. This approach only deals with the temporal structure of the discourse. The abduction of a temporal relation is only made when there is world knowledge or linguistic knowledge about the eventualities that may support the abduction of the temporal relation between the eventualities' time referents.

Our approach to tense interpretation is close to that of [7, 8], except for the criterion used to perform segmentation. Ours is exclusively temporal while theirs is based in some rhetorical relations that have temporal properties. So they obtain a rhetorical discourse structure and we just obtain the discourse temporal structure. We try to isolate the contribution of the tense and aspect interpretation from other discourse phenomena, considering more then one interpretation for each sentence and giving a criterion to prefer one of them (the more cohesive). We will just obtain text interpretations that are temporally consistent, we are not able and don't try to evaluate text coherency. The temporal reasoning necessary to interpret a sentence tense is the focus of our work.

We define the discourse structure precisely, and our interpretation theory is built in such a way that it enables the interpretation of each sentence, taking into account the previous text structure. There is no explicit notion of update in our interpretation theory, however it implicitly embedded in the proposed framework. The abductive answer obtained from the interpretation knowledge base also includes a new temporal discourse structure.

References

1. Mary Dalrymple. The interpretatin of tense and aspect in english. In 26th Annual Meeting of the ACL, pages 68–74, June 1988.
2. Kurt Eberle. On representing the temporal structure of a natural language text. In Proceedings of the COLING'92, pages 288–294, 1992.
3. Kurt Eberle and Walter Kasper. Tenses as anaphora. In Proceedings of the 4th European Chapter of the ACL, pages 43–50, 1989.
4. Jerry Hobbs, Mark Stickel, Douglas Appelt, and Paul Martin. Interpretation as abduction. Technical Report 499, SRI International, December 1990.

---

[23] Linguistic rules make no sense in this knowledge base.

5. Hans Kamp and Uwe Reyle. *From Discourse to Logic: An Introduction to Modeltheoretic Semantics of Natural Language, Formal Logic and Discourse Representation Theory*. Institute for Computational Linguistics, University of Stuttgart, 1990.

6. Hans Kamp and Christian Rohrer. Tense in texts. In C. Bauerle, R. Schwarze and A. von Stechow, editors, *Use and Interpretation of Language*. de Gruyter, 1983.

7. Alex Lascarides and Nicholas Asher. Discourse relations and defeasible knowledge. In *Proceedings of the 29th Annual Meeting of ACL*, pages 55–62, 1991.

8. Alex Lascarides, Nicholas Asher, and Jon Oberlander. Inferring discourse relations in context. In *Proceedings of the 30th Annual Meeting of ACL*, pages 55–62, 1992.

9. Alex Lascarides and Jon Oberlander. Temporal coherence and defeasible knowledge. In *Workshop on Discourse Coherence*, April, 1991. University of Edinburgh.

10. Mark Moens and Mark Steedman. Temporal ontology and temporal reference. *Computational Linguistics*, 14(2):15–28, june 1988.

11. Luis Monteiro and Antonio Porto. Contextual logic programming. In Giorgio Levi and Maurizio Martelli, editors, *Logic Programming: Proc. 6th International Conference*, Cambridge, MA, 1989. MIT Press.

12. Alexander Nakhimovsky. Aspect, aspectual class, and temporal structure of narrative. *Computational Linguistics*, 14(2):29–43, june 1988.

13. Barbara H. Partee. Nominal and temporal anaphora. *Linguistics and Phylosophy*, 7:243–286, 1984.

14. Rebecca J. Passonneau. A computational model of the semantics of tense and aspect. *Computational Linguistics*, 14(2):44–60, june 1988.

15. F. Pereira and M. Pollack. Incremental interpretation. *Artificial Intelligence*, (50):40–82, 1991.

16. Irene Pimenta Rodrigues and José Gabriel Pereira Lopes. Discourse temporal structure. In *Proceedings of the COLING'92*, 1992.

17. Irene Pimenta Rodrigues and José Gabriel Pereira Lopes. A framework for text interpretation. In B. du Buley and V. Sgurev, editors, *Artificial Intelligence V — methodology, systems and applications*, pages 181–190. North Holland, 1992.

18. Murray Shanahan. Prediction is deduction but explanation is abduction. In *Proceedings of IJCAI'89*, pages 1055–1060, 1989.

19. Yoav Shoham. *Reasoning about Change*. The MIT Press, 1988.

20. Boonie Lynn Webber. Tense as discourse anaphor. *Computational Linguistics*, 14(2):61–73, june 1988.

Resolution of Constraints in Algebras of Rational Trees

Luis Damas, Nelma Moreira, Sabine Broda
{luis,nam,sbb}@ncc.up.pt

LIACC,Universidade do Porto
Rua do Campo Alegre, 823, 4100 Porto
Portugal

Abstract. This work presents a constraint solver for the domain of rational trees. Since the problem is NP-hard the strategy used by the solver is to reduce as much as possible, in polynomial time, the size of the constraints using a rewriting system before applying a complete algorithm. This rewriting system works essentially by rewriting constraints using the information in a partial model. An efficient C implementation of the rewriting system is described and an algorithm for factoring complex constraints is also presented.

1   Introduction

The topic of constraints over syntactic domains has raised a considerable interest in the Computational Linguistics community. As a matter of fact constraints over the algebra of rational trees can significantly contribute to the reduction of the search space of problems in NLP while increasing the expressive power of formalisms for NLP [DMV91, DV89].

Unification-based grammar formalisms ([SUP+83], [Usz86],[KB82], [PS87], etc.) describe linguistic information by means of constraints over *feature structures*, which are basically sets of attribute-value pairs, where values can be atomic symbols or embedded feature structures, e.g.

$$[cat = np, agr = [num = sg, pers = 3rd]]$$

These structures and their combination can be seen as conjunctions of equality constraints which satisfiability can be tested by efficient unification algorithms. But the extension of these formalisms to express complex constraints involving negation and disjunction of equality constraints, besides arising formal theoretical problems leads to a NP-hard satisfiability problem.

From a formal point of view the problem is well understood after the foundational works of [RK86, Smo89] establishing Feature Logics. It turns out that the standard model for feature logics, namely rational trees, has a close relationship with the standard algebra of rational trees in Logic Programming and with its complete axiomatization presented in [Mah88]. As a matter of fact it can be proved [DMV92] that the satisfiability problem for the complete axiomatization of feature logics can be reduced to the satisfiability problem for Maher complete axiomatization of the algebra of rational trees.

From a practical point of view the fact that the satisfiability problem is NP-hard tends to manifest itself in a dramatic way in practical applications motivated several specialized algorithms to minimize this problem [Kas87, ED88, MK91].

In [DV92] it was argued that any practical approach to the satisfiability problem should use factorization techniques to reduce the size of the input formulae to which any complete algorithm for satisfiability is applied, since such factorization can reduce by an exponential factor the overall computational cost of the process. In that work a rewrite system, working in polynomial time, was used to factor out deterministic information contained in a complex constraint and simplify the remaining formula using that deterministic information. In [DMV92] that rewrite system was extended to a complete rewrite system for satisfiability which avoided as much as possible the multiplication of disjunctions which is the origin of the NP-hardness of the satisfiability problem.

In this work we present a solver for constraints over the domain of rational trees using the rewrite system mentioned above.

The rest of this paper proceeds as follows. We start by defining our constraint language, which was designed to enable the introduction of equality constraints on terms or rational trees without using any quantifiers, in section 2. In section 3 we define a complete rewrite system for expressions in the constraint language. In section 4 we present in some detail the low-level implementation of part of the rewrite system. In section 5 we will present an algorithm for factoring out of two constraints any deterministic information which is common to both.

2 The Constraint Language

Consider the first order language $\mathcal{L}$ built from the countable sets of variables $Vars = \{x, y, z, \ldots\}$, function symbols $F = \{f, g, h, \ldots\}$ and equality as the only predicate symbol. As usual, the functional symbols of arity 0 will be denoted by a, b, ... and will be referred to as atoms. For this language Maher presented a complete axiomatization of the algebra of rational trees, $\mathcal{RT}$, [Mah88]. This theory of $\mathcal{RT}$ is complete in the sense that a sentence is valid in $\mathcal{RT}$ if and only if it is a logical consequence of the theory. We now introduce a quantifier free constraint language, in which the formulae of $\mathcal{L}$ will be encoded. Here function symbols appear, whenever necessary, with their arities and are then denoted by f^n, while f_i^n stands for the ith projection of a function symbol f of arity n. The letters s and t will always denote variables or atoms. Expressions of the form $x.f_i^n$ will be called *slots*. We define the *constraints* of the language by:

$$c ::= t.f^n \mid t = t \mid t.f_i^n \doteq t,\ 1 \leq i \leq n \mid$$
$$false \mid true \mid \neg c \mid c \wedge c \mid c \vee c$$

Note that one can look at each constraint c as an abbreviation for a formula of $\mathcal{L}$, interpreting $t.f^n$ as $\exists z_1 \ldots \exists z_n\ t = f(z_1, \ldots, z_n)$ and $t.f_i^n \doteq s$ as $\exists z_1 \ldots \exists z_n\ t = f(z_1, \ldots, z_n) \wedge z_i = s$. On the other hand there exists an equivalent constraint c for every formula of $\mathcal{L}$. To see this, recall that Maher proves in [Mah88] that any of these formulae is equivalent to a boolean combination of *rational basic* formulae, for which it is easy to find an equivalent constraint. Finally notice the similarity of this constraint language and the Smolka's Feature Logics [Smo89] with f_i^n playing the role of features. More recently Smolka and others [ST92] introduced a Feature Tree Logic which includes sort and arity constraints much similar to our $x.f^n$ constraint.

We call the first five types of constraints defined above atomic constraints and say that a set of atomic constraints $\mathcal{M}$, denoting their conjunction, is in *solved form* if and only if it satisfies the following conditions:

1. every constraint in $\mathcal{M}$ is of one of the forms $x.f^n$, $x.f_i^n \doteq t$ or $x = t$;
2. if $x = t$ is in $\mathcal{M}$, then x occurs exactly once in $\mathcal{M}$;
3. if $x.f_i^n \doteq t$ and $x.f_i^n \doteq s$ are in $\mathcal{M}$, then t is equal to s;
4. if $x.f_i^n \doteq t$ is in $\mathcal{M}$, then $x.f^n$ is also in $\mathcal{M}$;
5. if $x.f^n$ is in $\mathcal{M}$, then there is no constraint in $\mathcal{M}$ of the form $x.g^m$;
6. if for some x, y and t, both $x.f_i^n \doteq t$ and $y.f_i^n \doteq t$ are in $\mathcal{M}$, then for some j between 1 and n, there is no s, such that $x.f_j^n \doteq s$ and $y.f_j^n \doteq s$ are both in $\mathcal{M}$.

The purpose of the last clause in the previous definition is to force solved forms to contain $x = y$, whenever for some f^n and every i between 1 and n, there is s_i, such that $x.f_i^n \doteq s_i$ and $y.f_i^n \doteq s_i$ hold.

It is easy to prove that solved forms are satisfiable and that every set of atomic constraints $\mathcal{M}$ can be reduced in quadratic time to an equivalent set, which is either in solved form or equal to $\perp$, using the following set of simplification rules, that correspond to the Herbrand rules for solving equations in a first order logic.

1. $\{true\} \cup \mathcal{M} \to \mathcal{M}$
2. $\{false\} \cup \mathcal{M} \to \perp$
3. $\{t = t\} \cup \mathcal{M} \to \mathcal{M}$
4. $\{a = b\} \cup \mathcal{M} \to \perp$
5. $\{x = t\} \cup \mathcal{M} \to \{x = t\} \cup [t/x]\mathcal{M}$ if x is not equal to t and x occurs in $\mathcal{M}$
6. $\{a = x\} \cup \mathcal{M} \to \{x = a\} \cup \mathcal{M}$
7. $\{x.f_i^n \doteq t, x.f_i^n \doteq s\} \cup \mathcal{M} \to \{x.f_i^n \doteq t, t \doteq s\} \cup \mathcal{M}$
8. $\{a.f_i^n \doteq t\} \cup \mathcal{M} \to \perp$
9. $\{a.f^n\} \cup \mathcal{M} \to \perp$
10. $\{x.f_i^n \doteq t\} \cup \mathcal{M} \to \{x.f^n, x.f_i^n \doteq t\} \cup \mathcal{M}$ if $x.f^n \notin \mathcal{M}$
11. $\{x.f^n, x.g^m\} \cup \mathcal{M} \to \perp$
12. if $x = y \notin \mathcal{M}$, but for all $1 \le i \le n$ there exists t_i such that $x.f_i^n \doteq t_i \in \mathcal{M}$ and $y.f_i^n \doteq t_i \in \mathcal{M}$, then $\mathcal{M} \to \{x = y\} \cup \mathcal{M}$.

3 Rewriting System

From now on let $\mathcal{M}$ be a solved form and $\mathcal{C}$ a finite set of constraints representing their conjunction. We say that $\mathcal{M}$ is a *partial model* of $\mathcal{C}$ if and only if every model of $\mathcal{C}$ is a model of $\mathcal{M}$. When every model of $\mathcal{M}$ is a model of $\mathcal{C}$, but no proper subset of $\mathcal{M}$ satisfies this condition, we will say that $\mathcal{M}$ is a *minimal* model of $\mathcal{C}$. By using disjunctive forms it can be proved that any set of constraints $\mathcal{C}$ admits at most a finite number of minimal models.

Our rewriting system produces from a set of constraints $\mathcal{C}_0$ a partial model $\mathcal{M}$ and a smaller set of constraints $\mathcal{C}$, such that any minimal model of $\mathcal{C}_0$ can be obtained by conjoining (i.e. "unifying") a minimal model of $\mathcal{C}$ with $\mathcal{M}$ and moreover for any minimal model of $\mathcal{C}$ the union $\mathcal{M} \cup \mathcal{C}$ is satisfiable. The rewriting system for pairs $\langle \mathcal{M}, \mathcal{C} \rangle$ is defined by the following rules:

$$\langle \mathcal{M}, \mathcal{C} \cup \{false\} \rangle \rightarrow \langle \bot, \emptyset \rangle$$
$$\langle \mathcal{M}, \mathcal{C} \cup \{true\} \rangle \rightarrow \langle \mathcal{M}, \mathcal{C} \rangle$$
$$\langle \mathcal{M}, \mathcal{C} \cup \{x = t\} \rangle \rightarrow \langle \mathcal{M} \cup \{x = t\}, \mathcal{C} \rangle$$
$$\langle \mathcal{M}, \mathcal{C} \cup \{x.f^n\} \rangle \rightarrow \langle \mathcal{M} \cup \{x.f^n\}, \mathcal{C} \rangle$$
$$\langle \mathcal{M}, \mathcal{C} \cup \{x.f_i^n \dot{=} t\} \rangle \rightarrow \langle \mathcal{M} \cup \{x.f_i^n \dot{=} t\}, \mathcal{C} \rangle$$

with the convention that after each application of one of the rewrite rules the new partial model is reduced to solved form and the resulting set of constraints is closed under $\longrightarrow_{\mathcal{M}}$ as defined below.

The complete set of rewrite rules $\longrightarrow_{\mathcal{M}}$ for terms and constraints follows:

$x \longrightarrow_{\mathcal{M}} t$	if $x = t \in \mathcal{M}$
$x.f_i^n \longrightarrow_{\mathcal{M}} t$	if $x.f_i^n \dot{=} t \in \mathcal{M}$
$c \longrightarrow_{\bot} false$	
$\neg true \longrightarrow_{\mathcal{M}} false$	
$\neg false \longrightarrow_{\mathcal{M}} true$	
$\neg\neg c \longrightarrow_{\mathcal{M}} c$	
$\neg(c_1 \wedge c_2) \longrightarrow_{\mathcal{M}} \neg c_1 \vee \neg c_2$	
$\neg(c_1 \vee c_2) \longrightarrow_{\mathcal{M}} \neg c_1 \wedge \neg c_2$	
$true \wedge c \longrightarrow_{\mathcal{M}} c$	
$false \wedge c \longrightarrow_{\mathcal{M}} false$	
$c \wedge true \longrightarrow_{\mathcal{M}} c$	
$c \wedge false \longrightarrow_{\mathcal{M}} false$	
$true \vee c \longrightarrow_{\mathcal{M}} true$	
$false \vee c \longrightarrow_{\mathcal{M}} c$	
$c \vee true \longrightarrow_{\mathcal{M}} true$	
$c \vee false \longrightarrow_{\mathcal{M}} c$	
$(c_1 \wedge c_2) \wedge c_3 \longrightarrow_{\mathcal{M}} c_1 \wedge (c_2 \wedge c_3)$	
$a = b \longrightarrow_{\mathcal{M}} false$	if a and b are distinct atoms
$a = x \longrightarrow_{\mathcal{M}} x = a$	
$t = t \longrightarrow_{\mathcal{M}} true$	
$x.f^n \longrightarrow_{\mathcal{M}} true$	if $x.f^n \in \mathcal{M}$

$$x.f^n \longrightarrow_{\mathcal{M}} false \qquad\qquad\qquad \text{if } x.g^m \in \mathcal{M}$$
$$a.f^n \longrightarrow_{\mathcal{M}} false$$
$$a.f_i^n \doteq t \longrightarrow_{\mathcal{M}} false$$
$$x = t \longrightarrow_{\mathcal{M}} false \qquad\qquad\qquad \text{if } \mathcal{M} \cup \{x = t\} \to \bot$$
$$x = t \wedge c \longrightarrow_{\mathcal{M}} x = t \wedge c' \qquad\quad \text{if } c \longrightarrow^{*}_{\mathcal{M}\cup\{x=t\}} c'$$
$$x.f_i^n \doteq t \longrightarrow_{\mathcal{M}} false \qquad\qquad \text{if } \mathcal{M} \cup \{x.f_i^n \doteq t\} \to \bot$$
$$x.f_i^n \doteq t \wedge c \longrightarrow_{\mathcal{M}} x.f_i^n \doteq t \wedge c' \quad \text{if } c \longrightarrow^{*}_{\mathcal{M}\cup\{x.f_i^n\doteq t\}} c'$$
$$x.f^n \wedge c \longrightarrow_{\mathcal{M}} x.f^n \wedge c' \qquad\quad \text{if } c \longrightarrow^{*}_{\mathcal{M}\cup\{x.f^n\}} c'$$
$$x \neq t \wedge c \longrightarrow_{\mathcal{M}} c \wedge x \neq t \qquad\quad \text{if any non-negated equality occurs in } c$$
$$x.f_i^n \neq t \wedge c \longrightarrow_{\mathcal{M}} c \wedge x.f_i^n \neq t \quad \text{if any non-negated equality occurs in } c$$
$$\neg x.f^n \wedge c \longrightarrow_{\mathcal{M}} c \wedge \neg x.f^n \qquad \text{if any non-negated equality occurs in } c$$
$$(c_1 \vee c_2) \wedge c_3 \longrightarrow_{\mathcal{M}} (c_1 \wedge c_3) \vee (c_2 \wedge c_3) \text{ if both } c_1 \text{ and } c_2$$
$$\text{are } \mathcal{M}\text{-dependent with } c_3.$$

Note that in the rules above $\mathcal{M} \cup \mathcal{C}$ denotes the solved form of the union of $\mathcal{M}$ and $\mathcal{C}$, if one exists, or $\bot$ if that union is not satisfiable. The last rule must apply only when both c_1 and c_2 have variables in common with c_3, eventually through "bindings" in $\mathcal{M}$. In order to formalize this notion we need the following definition. Given two constraints c_1 and c_2 and a model $\mathcal{M}$, c_1 and c_2 are $\mathcal{M}$-dependent if and only if $Var_{\mathcal{M}}(c_1) \cap Var_{\mathcal{M}}(c_2) \neq \emptyset$, where $Var_{\mathcal{M}}(c)$ is the smallest set satisfying:

if $x \in c$, then $x \in Var_{\mathcal{M}}(c)$;
if $x \in Var_{\mathcal{M}}(c)$ and $x.f_i^n \doteq z \in \mathcal{M}$, then $z \in Var_{\mathcal{M}}(c)$.

Given an initial set of constraints $\mathcal{C}_0$ we apply the rewriting system to $\langle \emptyset, \mathcal{C}_0 \rangle$ to obtain $\langle \mathcal{M}, \mathcal{C} \rangle$. It is easy to prove that $\mathcal{C}_0$ (more precisely the conjunct of all the constraints in $\mathcal{C}_0$) is equivalent to $\mathcal{M} \cup \mathcal{C}$. As a matter of fact this follows from the fact that each rewrite rule is associated with a similar meta-theorem of First Order Logic and/or the axioms of $\mathcal{RT}$.

A proof that all the minimal models of $\mathcal{C}_0$ are obtained by conjoining $\mathcal{M}$ with those of $\mathcal{C}$ follows along similar lines as the proof in [DV92] for feature logics.

The other interesting property of the rewriting system above is that it is complete in the sense that $\langle \mathcal{M}, \mathcal{C} \rangle$ is satisfiable, unless it produces $\bot$ as the final model. The simple (but tedious) proof of this result uses induction. Completeness is achieved mainly by the last rule above for $\longrightarrow_{\mathcal{M}}$. However, even if this rule attempts to limit the number of cases where it applies to an essential minimum, it causes NP-completeness of the rewriting process since it can lead to an exponential growth of the constraints. If we omit this rule, then the rewrite process becomes polynomial, although incomplete. As a technique to decrease the number of times the rule is used, one can treat disjunctions $C_0^1 \vee C_0^2$ in the following way: First apply the rewrite system to each C_0^i obtaining partial models $\mathcal{M}_i$ and smaller sets of constraints C^i. Then push redundancies out of $\mathcal{M}_1$ and $\mathcal{M}_2$ using the algorithm described in the section 5 and obtain sets COM, $\tilde{\mathcal{M}}_1$ and $\tilde{\mathcal{M}}_1$, such that each $\mathcal{M}_i$ is equivalent to $COM \wedge \tilde{\mathcal{M}}_i$. Finally substitute $C_0^1 \vee C_0^2$ by $COM \wedge (\tilde{\mathcal{M}}_1 \cup C^1 \vee \tilde{\mathcal{M}}_2 \cup C^2)$.

4 Implementation

In this section we present a constraint solver based on the rewriting system described above. Note that given a solved form $\mathcal{M}$, and considering that the equality is a equivalence relation, $\mathcal{M}$ can be partitioned into equivalence classes. Given an order $<_T$ on terms[1] we can induce an order in these classes and so, to each set of satisfiable atomic constraints corresponds a set of normalized classes. A set $\mathcal{N} = \{l_1, \ldots, l_n\}$, is a normalized solved form iff:

1. each l_i is of the form $v_1 = \ldots = v_k$, where each v_i is a variable, an atom or a slot and $v_i <_T v_j$, for $i < j \in \{1, \ldots, k\}$, or l_i is $x.f_i^n$.
2. each l_i has at most an atom and in that case it is the first element.
3. if $v \in l_i$ then v occurs exactly once in $\mathcal{M}$.
4. if l_i is $x.f^n$, x does not occur in other l_j of this form.
5. if x is in l_i and the first element of l_i is an atom then there is no l_j of the form $x.f^n$, for any f and n.
6. if $x.f_i^n \in l_k$ then there is a l_j of the form $x.f^n$.

With a slight modification of rule 5 in section 2 to deal with ordered variables, it is easy to see that each satisfiable constraint can be reduced to an unique equivalent normalized solved form. We will describe an algorithm that given a set of atomic constraints returns a solved form as a set of equality classes or *false* if the set is not satisfiable. The main features of the algorithm are implemented in C but an interface to Prolog is provided via a set of basic predicates. The complete rewrite system was written in Prolog using these predicates. The C component of the solver implements essentially the unification of solved forms in a way which is very similar to the Prolog implementation of unification. The main reason for a detailed presentation is the novel use we made of the trail mechanism which is not only used to recover a previous state but also to produce, as a solved form, the "differences" between the current state and the previous state (see subsection 4.3).

4.1 Rational Tree Representation

The representation of rational trees to be used, allows not only an efficient implementation of unification but also provides an incremental way of obtaining partial models, which is suitable for the contexted rewrite of inner disjunctions of a complex constraint. Given a set of atomic constraints, a destructive unification algorithm is used, while producing a trail, and then undoing unification, by also using the trail, we retrieve the associated solved form (partial model).

---

[1] Let *Vars* and F be provided with the lexicographical order and let variables, atoms and slots be terms. Then consider the following order $<_T$ on terms: atoms are less than variables, and variables less than slots; two atoms or two variables are compared lexicographically; two slots are first compared by their variables, if equal then by their functor and arity and finally if every thing else is identical by their projections.

Besides variables and atoms, the notion of term is extended to objects of the form f^n, denoting a functor (function symbol) f with arity n, and to *slots* of the form $x.f_i^n$ [2]. Terms will be stored in a table where each one is a structure with the following fields:

kind which can have the values *AtomS*, *VarS*, *FuncS* or *SlotS* indicating that the term is an *atom*, a *variable*, a *functor* or a *slot* respectively. These values are sorted by increasing order.

name if the term corresponds to an atom or a variable this field is their identifier (a Prolog atom in the actual implementation); if the term is a slot, it is the projection identifier.

value a link to the terms in the same equality class or NIL.

daughters if the term is a variable or a slot this field is a link to its subtrees; otherwise its value is NIL.

base if the term is a slot $x.f_i^n$ this is a pointer to the entry corresponding to the variable x; if the term is a variable, it can be a pointer to a functor term.

next link to the next term in the table.

A partial model is represented on the **trail**. The **trail** is a stack that contains pointers to the terms which **value** have changed during the rewrite process. Two pointers **TrailOld** and **TrailPtr** will mark the beginning and the ending of the portion of stack currently in use.

4.2 Solved Form Algorithm

The basic algorithm for the unification of two terms is given in figure 2. As usual substitutions are replaced by a bind/dereference mechanism, so before any two terms are unified they must be dereferenced, see figure 1. In the unification procedure whenever the **value** of a term is bounded, its pointer is added to the top of the **trail**, see figure 1, and in this way the active model is extended. Whenever two variables $v1$ and $v2$ (or a variable and a slot) are unified we must ensure that all subtrees of $v2$ share with subtrees of $v1$. This is done by the procedure **UnifySubTrees**, figure 3. As new terms maybe added to the trail, this can lead to some redundancies which will be eliminated when the solved form will be retrieved. The rest of the algorithm is basically the implementation of the simplification rules given in section 2.

The following Prolog predicates are provided to rewrite atomic constraints (the number after the slash indicates its arity).

add_ac_va/2 add a constraint of the form $x = a$
add_ac_vv/2 add a constraint of the form $x = x$
add_ac_fa/5 add a constraint of the form $x.f_i^n \doteq a$
add_ac_fv/5 add a constraint of the form $x.f_i^n \doteq x$
add_ac_f/3 add a constraint of the form $x.f^n$

---

[2] Recall that it represents the ith projection of x which main functor is f of arity n

```
Deref(Term v)
{   while(v->value) v=v->value;
    return v;
}
Bind(Term v1,Term v2)
{   v1->value=v2;
    *TrailPtr++=v1;
}
```

Fig. 1. *Dereference of a term and bind of two terms.*

```
Unify(Term v1,Term v2)
{   if(v1->kind>v2->kind) { /* exchange v1 with v2 */
        Term t=v1; v1=v2; v2=t; }
    if(v1->kind==AtomS)
        if(v2->kind==AtomS) return v1==v2;
        if(v2->kind==VarS) {
            /* test if v2 is not bounded to a functor */
            if(IsFunctor(v2)) return 0;
                Bind(v2,v1);
                return 1;
            }
        if(v2->kind==SlotS) {
            /* test if v2 is not of the form a.f_i^n */
            if(!IsProper(v2)) return 0;
            Bind(v2,v1);
            return 1;
        }
    if(v1->kind==VarS) {
        /* v2 is a variable or slot */
        if(v1==v2) return 1;
        if(!SameFunctor(v1,v2))return 0;
        if(!IsProper(v2)) return 0;
        /* sort variables */
        if(Compare(v2,v1)) { exchange v1 with v2 */
            Term t=v1; v1=v2; v2=t; }
        Bind(v2,v1);
        return UnifySubTrees(v1,v2);
    }
}
```

Fig. 2. *Unification algorithm.*

```
UnifySubTrees(Term u, Term v)
{   Term du ,dv;
    if(!SameFunctor(v,u))return 0;
    /* ensure all daughters of v share with daughters of u */
    du =u;
    dv = v->daughters;
    while(dv!=NIL) {
        while(du->daughters!=NIL
                && du->daughters->name < dv->name)
            du = du->daughters;
        /* if u does not have that subtree it will be create */
        if(du->daughters==NIL ||du->daughters->name!=dv->name) {
            Term t = (Term) tmp_alloc(sizeof(*t));
            t->kind = SlotS;
            t->name=dv->name;
            t->base = u;
            t->value = NIL;
            t->daughters= du->daughters;
            du->daughters= t;
        }
        /* unify correspondent daughters of u and v */
        if(!Unify(Deref(du->daughters),Deref(dv)) return 0;
        dv=dv->daughters;
    }
    return 1;
    }
}
```

Fig. 3. *Unification of subtrees.*

For each argument the associated term is looked up in the **term table** and if not found, is created and added to the table [3]. Then the **Unify** procedure is called and if it fails, the predicate will fail. The last predicate **add_ac_f** is a bit different because instead of binding the **value** of x with the term representing f^n we just bind it to the **base** of x[4]. The reason is that two different terms can have the same functor. In this case they will be equal only if all their subtrees are defined and equal.

When no more constraints are to be added (and no failure has occurred) a call to the predicate **undo_ac/1**, see figure 4, returns a solved form as a set of equality

---

[3] In this stage some clashes can be detected, namely if a variable earlier bounded to an atom is now to be bound to a functor or to a different functor. This avoids some tests done later in the **Unify** procedure.

[4] In the algorithms presented in this paper it is omitted the code concerning the treatment of these constraints.

classes. According to the rule 12 in section 2, every two terms that agree in all their subtrees (slots) are unified. Then, beginning at the top of the **trail** each term is dereferenced and all the terms that dereference to the same **value** are removed from the **trail** and, joined in the same class. If a term is a slot, its **base** must be dereferenced[5] and the slot associated to the new **base** is added to the class. That is so, because that term could have been inserted in the trail before its **base** was bounded to another term. This step can also eliminate redundancies created by **UnifySubTrees**, see example below. Finally the values of all terms are zeroed and the **trail** is emptied. To illustrated, let $\mathcal{M}$ be a satisfiable set of atomic constraints: $\{z.f_1^4 \doteq b, z = y, z = x, w = b, x.f_1^4 \doteq u, x.f_1^4 \doteq b\}$. After adding these constraints, the **trail** contains pointers to the terms described in the following table:

term	term.value
$z.f_1^4$	b
z	y
$y.f_1^4$	b
y	x
$x.f_1^4$	b
w	b
u	b

where the third and fifth elements are due to unification of subtrees and the last one is due to the dereference of $x.f_1^4$. The last conjunct in $\mathcal{M}$ was trivially true, so no more elements were added. This leads to the following normalized solved form: $\{b = u = w = x.f_1^4, x.f^4, x = y = z\}$. Note that if the first two constraints in $\mathcal{M}$ were swapped, then the first element will not appear in the **trail**.

The claim that **undo_ac** returns a normalized solved form of $\mathcal{M}$ follows from the fact that:

- the unification algorithm ensures that $\mathcal{M}$ is satisfiable.
- every term in the **trail** occurred in an equation of $\mathcal{M}$ or results from the unification of subtrees (akin to application of a substitution); and its value is the other element of the equation or corresponds to one or more applications of rules 5 and 7 of section 2, which preserve equivalence.
- by construction the result of **undo_ac** is a normalized solved form.

The solved form algorithm for a set of atomic constraints can be summarized as follows:

```
solve(C,M):-
        clean_ac,
        add_constraints(C,C1),
        (C1==false -> M=false; undo_ac(M)).
```

---

[5] Function **DerefSlot** accomplishes that.

```
undo_ac()
{   Term *p,r0,r1;
    SolvForm classes=NIL;
    /* apply rule 12 */
    check_eq_terms();
    while(1){
        *p=TrailPtr;
        r0=*--p;
        /* find first thing left in the trail;
        if a term r has been removed from the
        trail marked(r) will succeed */
        while(p!=TrailOld && marked(r0)) r0=*--p;
        if(p==TrailOld) break; /* nothing left */
        r0=Deref(r0);
        ++p; /* r0 back to the trail */
        StartClass();
        AddToClass(r0);
        /* find another term in the same class */
        while(p!=TrailOld){
            r1=*--p;
            if(marked(r1)) continue;
            if(Deref(r1)!=r0) continue;
            mark(r1); /* remove r1 from the trail */
            /* check slot base */
            r1=DerefSlot(r1);
            AddToClass(r1);
        }
        classes=MkClasses(MkAtomicClass(),classes);
    }
    /* clean trail and term values */
    while(TrailPtr!=TrailOld)(*--TrailPtr)->value=NIL;
    TrailPtr=TrailOld;
}
```

Fig. 4. *Retrieve of a solved form.*

where C is a list of atomic constraints, clean_ac initializes the term table and the trail[6] and add_constraints for each atomic constraint calls the appropriate predicate and returns *false* if any of them fails.

4.3 General Algorithm

The above algorithm can be efficiently extended to deal with general constraints and implement the complete rewriting system. The basic idea is to mark the

---

[6] The active model is the empty model.

model whenever a disjunction or a negation occurs. In this way all conjunctions of atomic constraints can be treated in a similar manner. Whenever a disjunct is rewritten the solved form corresponding to its atomic part (set of atomic constraints) is extracted, if it is satisfiable. Otherwise the model constructed so far (back to the last mark) must be erased, a new mark must be set and *false* is produced (for that disjunct or negation). This mechanism is achieved by having a stack of **choice points** which are the trail bounds. To set a **choice** point the current beginning of the trail is added to the top of the **choice point stack** and the current beginning of the trail is reset to be the current ending. The inverse operation is done whenever a model is extracted (**undo_ac** only extracts a model between two **trail** bounds) or a failure occurs, see figure 5. The following Prolog predicates are provided:

clean_ac/0 set the active model to be the empty model

mark_ac/0 set a choice point for the model

undo_ac/1 restore previously marked model and returns a solved form

fail_ac/0 restore previously marked model

```
clean_ac()
{   if(TrailBase==0)
        TrailBase = (Term *) malloc(sizeof(Term)*TRAIL_SIZE);
    TermTable= 0;
    TrailPtr = TrailOld = TrailBase;
    ChoicePtr = ChoicePointBase ;
    return 1;
}

mark_ac()
{   *ChoicePtr++ = TrailOld;
    TrailOld = TrailPtr;
    return 1;
}

fail_ac()
{   while(TrailPtr!=TrailOld) (*--TrailPtr)->value = NIL;
    TrailOld = *--ChoicePtr;
    return 1;
}
```

Fig. 5. *Set and remove choice points.*

Now the complete rewriting system can be easily implemented in Prolog. Here we just present a small fragment of the program[7].

```
solve(C,C1):-
        clean_ac,
        rewrite(C,C0)
        (C0==C-> C1=C0; solve(C0,C1)).
rewrite(C,C1):-
        rewrite_atomic(C,C0),
        rewrite_m(C0,C1),
        undo_ac(M),and(M,C1,C2).
        ⋮

rewrite_m(and(A,B),C):-
        rewrite_m(A,A1),
        rewrite_m(B,B1).
        and(A1,B1,C).
rewrite_m(or(A,B),C):-
        mark_ac,
        rewrite(A,A1),
        rewrite_tail_or(B,B1),
        or(A1,B1,C).
rewrite_m(not(A),C):-
        mark_ac,
        rewrite(A,A1),
        not(A1,C).
        ⋮
```

The predicate rewrite_atomic is similar to add_constraints but scans a general constraint and looks for atomic constraints in the "top conjunction". The last rule of the rewrite system $\longrightarrow_\mathcal{M}$ in section 3, is applied only when nothing else applies.

5 Common Factor Detection

We now present an algorithm that, given two partial models A and B, constructs models COM, $\tilde{A}$ and $\tilde{B}$ such that $A \vee B$ is equivalent to $COM \wedge (\tilde{A} \vee \tilde{B})$, and such that $\tilde{A}$ and $\tilde{B}$ have no common factors. Remember that every partial model is in particular a solved form. For a solved form $\mathcal{M}$ we define the set of equivalence classes of $\mathcal{M}$ by

$$EQ(\mathcal{M}) = \{[s] : x = s \in \mathcal{M}\},$$

---

[7] Negations have been pushed down atomic constraints and the elimination of trivial constraints and earlier detection of failures have been omitted as well as other control features.

where

$$[s] = \{s\} \cup \{x : x = s \in \mathcal{M}\}.$$

We also define

$$Proj(\mathcal{M}) = \{class(x).f_i^n = class(t) : x.f_i^n \doteq t \in \mathcal{M}\},$$

and

$$Funct(\mathcal{M}) = \{class(x).f^n : x.f^n \in \mathcal{M}\},$$

where

$$class(u) = \begin{cases} [s] & \text{if } u \in [s] \text{ for some } [s] \in EQ(\mathcal{M}) \\ \{u\} & \text{otherwise.} \end{cases}$$

After computing $EQ(A)$, $EQ(B)$, $Proj(A)$, $Proj(B)$, $Funct(A)$ and $Funct(B)$ the algorithm consists of four steps:

(1) First let $COM = \emptyset$ and apply as long as possible the following simplification rule to $EQ(A)$, $EQ(B)$ and COM:

$$\begin{cases} EQ(A) := \{\{s_1, \ldots, u, \ldots, v, \ldots, s_n\}\} \cup Rest(A) \\ EQ(B) := \{\{t_1, \ldots, u, \ldots, v, \ldots, t_m\}\} \cup Rest(B) \\ COM \end{cases}$$

$$\Longrightarrow$$

$$\begin{cases} EQ(A) := \{\{s_1, \ldots, v, \ldots, s_n\}\} \cup Rest(A) \\ EQ(B) := \{\{t_1, \ldots, v, \ldots, t_m\}\} \cup Rest(B) \\ COM := COM \cup \{u = v\} \end{cases}$$

(2) Now apply as long as possible the next rule to $Proj(A)$, $Proj(B)$ and COM:

$$\begin{cases} Proj(A) := \{\{x_1, \ldots, z, \ldots, x_l\}.f_i^n = \{s_1, \ldots, u, \ldots, s_n\}\} \cup Rest\_Proj(A) \\ Proj(B) := \{\{y_1, \ldots, z, \ldots, y_k\}.f_i^n = \{t_1, \ldots, u, \ldots, t_m\}\} \cup Rest\_Proj(B) \\ COM \end{cases}$$

$$\Longrightarrow$$

$$\begin{cases} Proj(A) := Rest\_Proj(A) \\ Proj(B) := Rest\_Proj(B) \\ COM := COM \cup \{z.f_i^n \doteq u\} \end{cases}$$

(3) Apply the next rule to $Funct(A)$, $Funct(B)$ and COM:

$$\begin{cases} Funct(A) := \{\{x_1, \ldots, z, \ldots, x_l\}.f^n\} \cup Rest\_Funct(A) \\ Funct(B) := \{\{y_1, \ldots, z, \ldots, y_k\}.f^n\} \cup Rest\_Funct(B) \\ COM \end{cases}$$

$$\Longrightarrow$$

$$\begin{cases} Funct(A) := Rest\_Funct(A) \\ Funct(B) := Rest\_Funct(B) \\ COM := COM \cup \{z.f^n\} \end{cases}$$

(4) Finally compute $\tilde{A}$ and $\tilde{B}$ by

$$\begin{aligned} \tilde{X} = \{&x.f_i^n \doteq t : class(x).f_i^n = class(t) \in Proj(X)\} \cup \\ &\{x.f^n : class(x).f^n \in Funct(X)\} \cup \\ &\{x = s : x \in [s] \in EQ(X) \text{ and } x \text{ is different from } s\}. \end{aligned}$$

Applying this algorithm to

$$\begin{aligned} A &= \{x_2 = x_1, x_1.f_2^2 \doteq x_4, x_1.f^2, x_5 = x_4, x_6 = x_4, x_4.g^1\} \\ B &= \{x_2 = x_3, x_3.f_2^2 \doteq x_7, x_3.f^2, x_5 = x_7, x_6 = x_7, x_7.g^1\} \end{aligned}$$

we conclude that $A \vee B$ is equivalent to

$$\{x_2.f^2, x_2.f_2^2 \doteq x_5, x_6 = x_5, x_5.g^1\} \wedge (\{x_1 = x_2, x_4 = x_5\} \vee \{x_3 = x_2, x_7 = x_5\}).$$

Proposition 1 *Let A and B be two solved forms. Then the algorithm computes the sets COM, $\tilde{A}$ and $\tilde{B}$, such that there is no common factor in $\tilde{A}$ and $\tilde{B}$ and such that $A \vee B$ is equivalent to $COM \wedge (\tilde{A} \vee \tilde{B})$.*

Proof. Note that it is quite obvious that $A \vee B$ is equivalent to $COM \wedge (\tilde{A} \vee \tilde{B})$, since A is equivalent to $COM \wedge \tilde{A}$ and B is equivalent to $COM \wedge \tilde{B}$. To prove that there is no common factor left in $\tilde{A}$ and $\tilde{B}$ note that the set $\tilde{A}$, computed by the sets $EQ(A)$, $Proj(A)$ and $Funct(A)$ is such that:

(i) for every $\tilde{X} \in EQ(\tilde{A})$ exists $X \in EQ(A)$ such that $\tilde{X} \subseteq X$;

(ii) if $\tilde{X}.f_j^n = \tilde{Y} \in Proj(\tilde{A})$ then there is $X.f_i^n = Y \in Proj(A)$, such that $\tilde{X} \subseteq X$ and $\tilde{Y} \subseteq Y$;

(iii) if $\tilde{X}.f^n \in Funct(\tilde{A})$ then there is $X.f^n \in Proj(A)$, such that $\tilde{X} \subseteq X$.

Obviously $\tilde{B}$ has the same properties. Now suppose that there is $\tilde{A} \models s = t$ and $\tilde{B} \models s = t$ for some variables or atoms s and t. This means that both have to be in the same equivalence class in $EQ(\tilde{A})$ and in $EQ(\tilde{B})$. But this is impossible by (i) and since simplification step (1) doesn't apply to $EQ(A)$ and $EQ(B)$. In a similar way condition (ii) and the fact that simplification step (2) doesn't apply to $Proj(A)$ and to $Proj(B)$, make it impossible to have $\tilde{A} \models x.f_i^n \doteq s$ and $\tilde{B} \models x.f_i^n \doteq s$. The same reasoning goes for factors of the form $x.f^n$. •

6 Final Remarks

The constraint rewriting system and the low-level implementation presented in this paper have been successfully used in the implementation of a number of grammar formalisms (called Constraint Logic Grammars). Also they were easily modified to deal with feature structures, instead of rational trees. Some improvements in the efficiency of the implementation can be achieved if atomic negated constraints are considered in the solved form (c.f. [DMV92]). We are currently studying the extension of the constraint language to cover constraints over *lists* and *sets*.

References

[DMV91] Luis Damas, Nelma Moreira, and Giovanni B. Varile. The formal and processing models of CLG. In *Fiifth Conference of the European Chapter of the Association for Computational Linguistics*, pages 173–178, Berlin, 1991.

[DMV92] Luis Damas, Nelma Moreira, and Giovanni B. Varile. The formal and computational theory of constraint logic grammars. In *Proceedings of the Workshop on Constraint Propagation and Linguistic Description*, Lugano, 1992.

[DV89] Luis Damas and Giovanni B. Varile. CLG: A grammar formalism based on constraint resolution. In E.M.Morgado and J.P.Martins, editors, *EPIA 89*, volume 390 of *Lecture Notes in Artificial Intelligence*, pages 175–186. Springer Verlag, 1989.

[DV92] Luis Damas and Giovanni B. Varile. On the satisfiability of complex constraints. In *Proceedings of the 14th International Conference on Computational Linguistics (COLING)*, Nantes, France, 1992.

[ED88] A. Eisele and J. Dörre. Unification of disjunctive feature descriptions. In *26th Annual Meeting of the Association for Computational Linguistics*, Buffalo, New York, 1988.

[Kas87] R. T. Kasper. Unification method for disjunctive feature descriptions. In *25th Annual Meeting of the Association for Computational Linguistics*, Standford, CA, 1987.

[KB82] R. Kaplan and J. Bresnan. Lexical functional grammar: A formal system for grammatical representation. In Joan Bresnan, editor, *The Mental Representation of Grammatical Relations*. MIT Press, 1982.

[Mah88] Michael J. Maher. Complete axiomatizations of the algebras of finite, rational and infinite trees. Technical report, IBM Thomas J. Watson Research Center, P.O. Box 704, Yorktown Heights, NY 10598, U.S.A., 1988.

[MK91] John T. Maxwell and Ronald M. Kaplan. A method for disjunctive constraint satisfaction. In Massaru Tomita, editor, *Current Issues in Parsing Technology*. Kluwer Academic Publishers, 1991.

[PS87] Carl Pollard and Ivan Sag. *Information Based Syntax and Semantics, Volume 1, Fundamentals*, volume 13. Center for the Study of Language and Information Stanford, 1987.

[RK86] W.C. Rounds and R.T. Kasper. A complete logical calculus for record structures representing linguistic information. In *Symposium on Logic in Computer Science*, IEEE Computer Society, 1986.

[Smo89] Gert Smolka. Feature logic with subsorts. Technical report, IBM Wissenschafliches Zentrum, Institut für Wissensbasierte Systeme, 1989. LILOG Report 33.

[ST92] Gert Smolka and Ralf Treinen. Records for logic programming. In Krzysztof Apt, editor, *ICLP92*. MIT, 1992.

[SUP+83] Stuart M. Shieber, Hans Uszkoreit, Fernando C.N. Pereira, J. Robinson, and M. Tyson. The formalism and implementation of PATR-II. In B. J. Grosz and M. E. Stickel, editors, *Research on Interactive Acquisition and Use of Knowledge*. SRI report, 1983.

[Usz86] Hans Uszkoreit. Categorial unification grammar. In *Proceedings of the 11th International Conference on Computational Linguistics (COLING)*, Bonn, 1986.

Inheritance in a Hierarchy of Theories

Gabriel David and António Porto

Departamento de Informática
Universidade Nova de Lisboa
P-2825 Monte da Caparica
Portugal
e-mail: {gtd,ap}@fct.unl.pt
phone: 351(1)2953270

Abstract. This paper[1] contains a proposal for a knowledge representation formalism based on a taxonomy of theories. It aims at clarifying the notions of inheritance and dependency among properties and classes, which are mixed together in the "inheritance networks" formalism, while also providing more expressiveness.

A model-theoretic semantics in terms of sets of individuals is presented, which is parametric on the characterization of specificity. The case most thoroughly presented is rule inheritance which builds on the assumption that only facts have the force to impose overriding. A double denotation for classes, corresponding to two nested sets, is the key for interpreting defaults and exceptions.

The problem of ambiguity propagation in the resulting system is addressed in the context of a discussion of the relationship between it and inheritance nets.

1 Introduction

The scope of this work is the characterization of the set of consequences which should be expected of a knowledge base structured as a taxonomy of classes with associated theories. We have developed a corresponding inference system and proved it is sound w.r.t. the rule inheritance semantics, but we will not present it here. The work is inspired by the problems addressed by inheritance reasoning and makes use of the techniques developed in logic programming.

The main trend in inheritance reasoning is the inheritance network proposal, where the basic elements are nodes and links. Nodes represent individuals and defeasible properties. Links are of two kinds, positive (interpreted as IS-A) and negative (meaning IS-NOT-A). In these systems, there is no ontological distinction between classes and properties. However, in natural languages there is always a fundamental distinction between nouns (classes) and adjectives/verbs (properties), which seems to be an important characteristic that a knowledge representation system should possess in order to be natural. Inheritance of properties is related to the existence of paths along positive links (except, may be,

---

[1] Work done under partial support of JNICT project PEROLA.

the last), with certain characteristics determined by the way specificity is understood (contradiction, preemption, on-path, off-path, upwards, double chaining). Negative links express both the inheritance of a negative property and the blocking of further reasoning along that path. So, negative links have a different status and are mainly used to express exceptions. This induces a bias in the choice of which properties are to be presented in a positive way and which will be exceptions. This lack of symmetry may be unpleasant from a knowledge representation viewpoint.

In our proposal, a system is a taxonomic structure of classes. Class inclusion is strict and has a definitional flavor [Bra85]. This is the non-defeasible part of the system. Each class has a local associated theory from which its specific properties are obtained. The superclasses' theories provide properties which are inherited by the class, when they do not clash with more specific information. Properties constitute the defeasible part of the system. They behave as defaults which may be overridden by a contradictory property asserted in a subclass. Rules' heads in the theory may be positive or negative literals and these have the same status. Negation is not used to block reasoning but only to assert the non-property. Exceptions are obtained directly from the notion of contradiction[2], favoring the conclusion stated in the more specific class, no matter whether positive or negative. Heads are not disjunctive to allow for a constructive inference directed to the heads' literals. So rules are seen as defining properties.

A negative conclusion explicitly asserts the corresponding atomic property to be false. Failure to prove a literal and its opposite assigns the value undefined to the corresponding atom, and so does a contradiction (proving both) originated in two non-comparable classes. In order to get a symmetric treatment of both positive and negative information, it is also needed that reasoning may proceed from a negative conclusion. This arises naturally by allowing negative literals in rules' bodies.

Example 1 Reasoning from negative properties. Consider the following assertions:

1. Bats are mammals.
2. Mammals are animals.
3. Non-flying mammals are quadruped.
4. Flying animals are light.
5. Mammals do not fly.
6. Bats fly.

Taking the first two assertions as definitions and the other four as normative but allowing for exceptions, a possible representation, in our formalism, is displayed on the left of Fig. 1. The two rules in *mammal* support the conclusion *quadruped* there, whereas in *bat* what is inherited is the **rule** for *quadruped* which has no consequences since its premise is false.

The inheritance network on the right represents the same situation, but suffers from two problems. To represent assertion 3 we need a positive property for

---

[2] In Logic Programming, nonmonotonicity is based on failure to prove, instead.

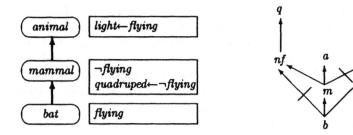

Fig. 1. Two representations of the *bat* world

non-flying (*nf*), allowing a path to *quadruped*. This node has no relationship with the node *f*, inside the system, so an external integrity constraint must be added insuring that both properties are interpreted as the negation of each other, i.e. they are not simultaneously true for any individual. To enforce such a constraint redundant links are needed, creating a potential problem of inconsistency. Two links are used to represent assertion 5, saying that *mammals* aren't *flying* and are *non-flying*. △

We argue that, from a knowledge representation viewpoint, the separation into a strict and a defeasible part provides greater expressiveness because it allows perennial (definitional) truths to be stated in a non-revisable form, as a hierarchy of classes. We also have the power to represent natural kinds, which admit exceptions, through defeasible properties. There is however, a certain duality between a class and its defining property, which is patent in the semantics of the system. Both classes and properties denote sets of individuals. But while every individual in a class must belong to all its superclasses, it is not forced to enjoy all the properties associated with them, i.e. to belong to the intersection of all such properties. What is then the meaning of saying that a set of properties characterizes a class? The answer involves the definition of a second denotation for classes, again a set of individuals, included in the previous one, which contains the **typical** individuals for the class, those individuals which do verify all the classes' properties. So, the order relation in the taxonomy imposes the inclusion of the classes, but the associated theories support conclusions which have to be true only for the corresponding typical subsets. Atypical individuals which are exceptions w.r.t. certain properties enjoyed by the class may still belong to it.

The problem of finding which properties hold for each class is previous to the interpretation in terms of sets of individuals. This account of the semantics is a framework where several inheritance mechanisms may be plugged in, shaping the system in different ways. We will briefly discuss predicate inheritance and present in a detailed way the more powerful rule inheritance.

Another advantage of our system is its ability to deal with dependencies on multiple premises, through conjunction in the bodies. In the example, assertion 3 becomes more accurate if rephrased as *non-flying and non-swimming mammals are quadruped*, with the obvious representation *quadruped ← ¬flying, ¬swimming*. Inheritance networks are not able to directly represent conjunction.

Assertion 4 establishes a generic dependency between *flying* and being *light* which is meaningful for animals, in general. This dependency is stated in the theory for class *animal*, accurately representing the expressed knowledge. It produces no result at that level, but becomes effective wherever *flying* is true in the corresponding subclasses and an explicit *¬light* isn't in force. In inheritance nets, adding an intermediate node between *bat* and *mammal* with a negative link to *light* would render the net ambiguous, because the new node cannot be considered more specific than *flying* on the grounds that the path *< bat, new, mammal, flying >* is negative. This unfortunate result stems from the double role negative links play, by simultaneously stating an exception and blocking further reasoning. This problem becomes even clearer in the following extension to the previous example.

Example 2 Globality of links. Add the following assertions to example 1.

7. Planes are aircrafts.
8. Aircrafts fly.
9. Planes are not light.

A representation in our proposal will have two classes, *aircraft* and *plane* as a subclass. The latter's local theory is *¬light* and the former's is just *flying*. In terms of the semantics we previously mentioned, omitting information about weight may mean that, among the typical individuals of *aircraft* some are *light* and other *¬light*. The corresponding inheritance net also adds the two nodes, a link from *aircraft* to *flying* and a negative link between *plane* and *light*. As a result, *aircraft* and *plane* are inheriting a dependency which was stated in the completely unrelated context of *animal*. If *plane* escapes the problem by contradicting conclusion *light*, *aircraft* has no way to do the same thing while staying inside the formulation of knowledge. Nothing is said about the weight of generic aircrafts (think of balloons, delta-wings and inter-continental jets) but it is forced to inherit the conclusion established for *animal* or to negate it. Eliminating the problematic link *< flying, light >* is not a solution because then every flying animal should have a second link to *light* therefore loosing the advantages of inheritance. △

The problem in the previous example is that a link in a net has an implicit universal quantification, because any node linked to its origin will inherit the corresponding target. This again is related to the links' double role of reasoning path and statement of properties. We think that a better result is achieved by using a different factorization of primitives, (IS-A, ←, ¬) meaning (inheritance, dependency, negation), instead of (IS-A, IS-NOT-A). The IS-A supports, at the semantic level, the taxonomic notion of subset inclusion of classes. The pair (←, ¬) is related to the notion of subset of typical elements of a class. There is a single notion of dependency ($\leftarrow$) and overriding is obtained through contradiction ($\neg$) and specificity, instead of being based on negative (asymmetric) links.

Negation by failure has been used [KS90] to model defaults, through the definition of abnormality predicates. This method suffers from non-locality [Tou87], because the representation of a single assertion may involve several different rules. Like inheritance networks it also relies on a preference for negative literals, understood as exceptions. Although negation by failure is used for other purposes too, we restrict ourselves to the use of strong negation. The hierarchy of classes forms a backbone around which theories defining properties and dependencies among them are organized and serves to guide the overriding process. This is the kind of default supporting mechanism we are studying.

The intended use of this formalism is not to represent general knowledge, but only its taxonomic fragment. So, the system presented can be considered part of a larger knowledge base offering other knowledge representation methods. The interconnection between the taxonomic module and the rest of the system can be defined in the following way: the taxonomic module acts as a server for special goals $c{:}p$ which are true if class c enjoys property p.

In the following sections we will present a semantics in terms of sets of individuals for the hierarchic system, the rule inheritance mechanism, and a comparison with the inheritance nets formalism.

2 Semantics of Hierarchically Structured Theories

In this section we will introduce the language of Hierarchically Structured Theories (HST, for short), define interpretation and model, and finally establish the semantics. A more detailed presentation of it can be found in [DP91].

Definition 1. A Hierarchically Structured Theory is a 4-tuple $\langle \mathcal{C}, \mathcal{P}, \prec, \mathcal{D} \rangle$ where

- $\mathcal{C}$ is the set of *class names*;
- $\mathcal{P}$ is the set of *properties*;
- $\prec$ is the *hierarchic relation*, which must be an acyclic relation on $\mathcal{C}$;
- $\mathcal{D}$ is a total function called *class definition* mapping each class name to a set of property definitions.

The hierarchic relation $\prec$ states just the direct sub/superclass relation. It will also be used $<$ and $\leq$ for its transitive and, resp. reflexive transitive closures. As no restriction is put on $\prec$ other than being acyclic, a class may have several direct superclasses, thus supporting **multiple inheritance**.

The set of **properties** is $\mathcal{P} = \mathcal{P}^+ \cup \mathcal{P}^-$. An atomic property $p \in \mathcal{P}^+$ is of the form $n(t_1, \ldots, t_m)$, where n is a property name (equipped with the arity m) and each t_i is a ground term. Terms are defined in the usual way out of a vocabulary of constants and function symbols used in the HST. The vocabulary is unique for the whole system to give a common language to all classes. The set $\mathcal{P}^- = \{\neg p \mid p \in \mathcal{P}^+\}$ contains the negations of atomic properties.

Definition 2. Complementation is defined for properties and sets of properties

$$p \in \mathcal{P}^+ \Rightarrow {\sim}p = \neg p$$
$$p = \neg r \Rightarrow {\sim}p = r$$
$$Q \in \wp(\mathcal{P}) \Rightarrow {\sim}Q = \{{\sim}p \mid p \in Q\}.$$

A property definition is a rule or conditional expression between properties. The set of all rules is

$$\mathcal{R}(\mathcal{P}) = \{p \leftarrow Q \mid p \in \mathcal{P}, Q \in \wp(\mathcal{P})\}.$$

So, $\mathcal{D} : \mathcal{C} \longrightarrow \wp(\mathcal{R}(\mathcal{P}))$ maps each class name a to the set of rules $\mathcal{D}_a$ locally defined in a. A definition $p \leftarrow \emptyset$ is the same as asserting p and will be called a **fact**.

As stated above, rules in definitions $\mathcal{D}$ consist of (ground) properties. However, uninstantiated terms may be allowed in property arguments. Rules containing such terms are considered universally quantified and taken as a short hand for their full instantiation over the vocabulary of constants and function symbols appearing in the rules of the HST.

In order to relate classes and properties a new entity is needed. The **characterization** of a class c (written $<c>$) is the set of properties which hold for that class. This set is built out of the definitions by an appropriate inheritance mechanism to be introduced later.

An interpretation $\mathcal{I}$ of a HST is defined over a domain of individuals $\mathcal{U}_\mathcal{I}$. The denotation functions are:

(taxonomic)	$c \in \mathcal{C} \Rightarrow [c]_\mathcal{I} \in \wp(\mathcal{U}_\mathcal{I})$
(property)	$p \in \mathcal{P} \Rightarrow [p]_\mathcal{I} \in \wp(\mathcal{U}_\mathcal{I})$
(typical)	$c \in \mathcal{C} \Rightarrow \ll c \gg_\mathcal{I} \in \wp(\mathcal{U}_\mathcal{I})$.

As said before, both classes and properties denote sets of individuals. The third interpretation function associates with each class name the set of **typical** individuals of that class. Sets of properties are interpreted conjunctively:

$$[\{p_1, \ldots, p_n\}]_\mathcal{I} = \bigcap_{i=1,\ldots,n} [p_i]_\mathcal{I}.$$

Interpretations are arbitrary provided they respect two basic pre-conditions: typical individuals of a class must belong to it; no individual may enjoy two contradictory properties.

$$c \in \mathcal{C} \Rightarrow \ll c \gg_\mathcal{I} \subseteq [c]_\mathcal{I}$$
$$p \in \mathcal{P} \Rightarrow [p]_\mathcal{I} \cap [{\sim}p]_\mathcal{I} = \emptyset$$

Individuals either belong or do not belong to a class, but the treatment of properties is 3-valued. A property p may hold for an individual, it may not hold, or it may be undefined. Our basic intuition is to deal with p and ${\sim}p$ in a totally symmetric way, as if they were different properties, although strongly connected by a sort of built-in integrity constraint forcing them to be disjoint.

Definition 3. An interpretation I is a **model** of a HST H ($I \in mod(H)$) iff, for any two class names c and b,

$$c \prec b \Rightarrow [c]_I \subseteq [b]_I$$

$$[c]_I - \bigcup_{b \prec c} [b]_I \subseteq \ll c \gg_I$$

$$\ll c \gg_I \subseteq [<c>]_I.$$

The first condition forces a model to obey a strict class inclusion policy as expected in a taxonomy. The second states that individuals in class c which do not belong to any of its subclasses must be typical individuals of c, with the consequence that knowledge is only expressed at the class level. The only way to distinguish between two individuals is by including them in different classes. The third condition assures that the typical subset of a class really collects individuals for whom all the properties in its characterization hold.

Exceptions are stated, basically, by defining in a lower class a a property contradictory with another defined above in the hierarchy, in b. As the individuals of $[a]$ belong also to $[b]$ the taxonomic denotation is not able to express this nonmonotonic behavior. The typical denotation establishes the connection between classes and their own characterizations.

Literals in the semantics are expressions of the form $c:p$ where c is a class name and p is a property. They denote boolean values **t, u, f** standing respectively for **true**, **undefined**, and **false**. **u** is meant to cater both for situations where a given property is not defined and situations where a conflicting pair exists.

Definition 4. Valuation in an interpretation I.

$$[c:p]_I = \begin{cases} \mathbf{t} & \ll c \gg_I \subseteq [p]_I \\ \mathbf{f} & \ll c \gg_I \subseteq [\sim p]_I \\ \mathbf{u} & otherwise \end{cases}$$

Though this definition is stated in terms of properties, it can be generalized to formulas including conjunction, constructive disjunction and negation, along the lines of the logic of strong negation [Wag90].

Definition 5. A literal $c:p$ is valid in a HST H iff its value is **t** in every model of H,

$$H \models c:p \Leftrightarrow \forall I \in mod(H) \ [c:p]_I = \mathbf{t} \ .$$

This definition coincides with what is intuitively expected from the common notion of inheritance as expressed in the next proposition. It stresses the importance of the characterization by establishing a relationship between this syntactic entity and the validity of certain formulas.

Proposition 6. *A literal $c:p$ is valid in a HST H iff the property p belongs to the characterization of the class c,*

$$H \models c:p \Leftrightarrow p \in <c> \ .$$

The proposed semantics for a HST is the set of valid literals,

$$sem(H) = \{c:p \mid H \models c:p\} \ .$$

3 Rule inheritance

In the previous section we left as an open problem the specification of the inheritance mechanism. In [DP91] we presented **predicate inheritance**. This method is based on the idea that the set of properties holding for a class a includes the properties inherited from its superclasses which are not overridden, plus the consequences of the rules in $\mathcal{D}_a$ itself. The resultant characterization $<a>$ is then passed to the subclasses of a as a set of defaults. If a consequence contradicts one of the defaults, the latter must be overridden. If a pair of contradictory consequences is obtained, a minimal set of defaults supporting them must be overridden. Provided that the class definition is consistent, i.e. does not imply a contradiction by itself, a suitable set of defaults can be found.

Predicate inheritance is a top-down iterative procedure, implementing the property flow metaphor [HTT87], where properties are viewed as percolating through the hierarchy from the most general to the most specific classes. Each class definition is compiled out with respect to the inherited properties before passing the updated set to its subclasses. This kind of inheritance is similar to the definition in [MP91] of **predicate inheritance**, as opposed to **clause inheritance**.

The main problem with this approach is that inheriting just (sets of) properties does not keep track of the dependencies among them, and this may result in retaining in subclasses conclusions whose support has been overridden, or in failing to reach some conclusions because of the corresponding rule being not active in the class where it is defined. For example, in Figure 1, the characterization of *animal* is empty because nothing is stated about the flying abilities of animals in general, $<mammal>= \{\neg flying, quadruped\}$ and *bat*, although *flying*, is still thought of as being *quadruped*, by predicate inheritance. The knowledge expressed in the theories would be better preserved if the rule defining *quadruped* itself were inherited instead of just its consequence. This is the main motivation behind **rule inheritance**.

Taking into consideration the inheritance of rules involves a deep change in the way specificity is seen. A generic rule contained in a theory high in the hierarchy may become active only in a distant subclass, where it may be compared with other conflicting rules for specificity. So, to find out the characterization of a class, its whole superstructure is needed in order to establish the overriding precedence. Predicate inheritance is more local, in the sense that it uses directly only the immediate superclasses' characterizations. Notice that specificity is taken relatively to a **target** class, for which a characterization is sought. The principle we will follow is to consider class b more **specific** than c w.r.t. a target class a if there is a path $a \leq b < c$, even if there is another alternative path $a \leq d < c$.

A property stated in a class is overridden by its opposite if stated in a more specific class. This strategy, first suggested by [San86], corresponds to off-path preemption [HTT87]. But, if the colliding properties originate in two incomparable classes ($d \not< b, b \not< d$), then specificity is of no help. It is general understanding that no one should prevail and **neutralization** (mutual annihilation) of the pair is recommended.

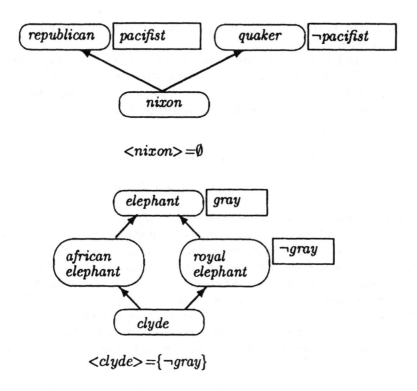

$$<nixon>=\emptyset$$

$$<clyde>=\{\neg gray\}$$

Fig. 2. Nixon dilemma and Clyde, the elephant

Example 3 Overriding and neutralization (adapted from [San86]). The overriding principle imposes that *clyde* is ¬*gray* though *elephant* and *african-elephant* are *gray*. By neutralization, *nixon* is neither *pacifist* nor ¬*pacifist*. △

Inheriting rules carries along a further difficulty. The specificity criterion, applied to the rules for a given property, is able to select the more specific. But the corresponding bodies may refer to rules with the inverse ordering. Classifying one of the overall arguments as more specific than the other seems not to be intuitively founded. It is even possible that the more specific rule never becomes active, rendering any overriding only apparent. So, the following condition is added to the notion of specificity to mitigate overriding: **only facts have the power to do overriding**. Rules are not considered reliable enough. This principle points to a bottom-up approach to the computation of the characterizations, closer in spirit to the argument construction paradigm [HTT87] than to the property flow metaphor.

We see the rules in theories as definitions for the properties in the respective heads, expressing dependencies between properties. It is not necessary to search inside the bodies in order to check that a property cannot be overridden. It is enough to note that there are no rules for its opposite. This view is consistent with seeing the arrow as an inference rule and not as a classical implication

[Wag90, GL90]. In classical logic, using the contrapositive, from $\neg p$ and $p \leftarrow r$, it could be inferred $\neg r$.

Next we define the **rule inheritance** mechanism for the computation, in the context of a given HST, of the characterization $<c>$ of a target class c. The system and the target class will be implicit in the following definitions. A class can inherit only from its superclasses. So, the **program** for a class c is the family of definitions $D = (D_a)_{c \leq a}$.

Definition 7. Immediate consequence operator,

$$T_D(I) = \{p \mid \exists a : p \leftarrow Q \in D_a, Q \subseteq I, \neg \exists b < a : \sim p \in D_b\}.$$

In the definition, I is a set of positive and negative properties. The operator produces the immediate consequences of all the superclasses' definitions, except that **facts** override upper definitions. As negative properties behave as independent atoms, D corresponds to a positive program. As only the facts are able to override, their action is independent of the set I. The operator $T_D(I)$ is monotonic and has a least fixpoint obtainable in w steps $T^*(D) = T_D \uparrow w$.

The set of consequences of D contained in $T^*(D)$ consists of all properties which can be obtained from the program, including contradictions and their consequences. Nothing else can be derived. This puts an upper bound on the set $<c>$.

Definition 8. Restriction operator,

$$(D\lceil I)_a = \{p \leftarrow Q \in D_a \mid \sim p \notin I\}.$$

The restricted program $D\lceil I$, w.r.t. a set of properties I, is void of conflicting rules. All the properties derived from it can't be opposed and must be kept. But it is not enough to remove all the generated contradictions. A second application of $T^*(D)$ is necessary to wipe out the consequences which become unsupported after such removal:

$$\Delta_D = T^*(D\lceil T^*(D)).$$

The set Δ_D contains the safe conclusions which can be obtained from the current program and imposes a lower bound on $<c>$. The intended set lies between these two extremes. Δ_D is used next to simplify the program.

Definition 9. Division operator,

$$(D/J)_a = \{p \leftarrow (Q \setminus J) \mid p, \sim p \notin J, p \leftarrow Q \in D_a, \sim Q \cap J = \emptyset\}.$$

The quotient of a program D by a set of properties J is the part of the program which is able to generate new conclusions beyond that set. Everything else is deleted. The crucial point here is that some rules may become facts after the division and then be enabled to do some overriding. The whole procedure may be iterated.

Definition 10. Safe conclusions operator,

$$S_D(J) = J \cup \Delta_{(D/J)}.$$

As Δ_D can only contain new literals, it eventually becomes empty and operator S_D reaches a fixpoint, which contains the intended set of properties holding for the class in the given HST. So the characterization of class c in the HST $\langle \mathcal{C}, \mathcal{P}, \prec, \mathcal{D} \rangle$ is

$$<c> = S_{(\mathcal{D}_a)_{c \leq a}} \uparrow w.$$

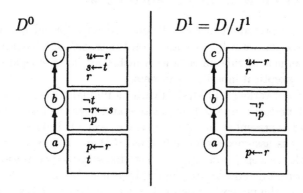

Fig. 3. A convoluted example

Example 4 Rule inheritance[3]. For target class a the program is $D = \{\mathcal{D}_a, \mathcal{D}_b, \mathcal{D}_c\}$. The two bounds on $<a>$, starting with $J^0 = \emptyset$ and $D^0 = D$, are

$$T^*(D^0) = \{t, \neg p, r, p, u, s, \neg r\}$$
$$\Delta_{D^0} = T^*(D^0 \lceil T^*(D^0)) = \{t, s\}.$$

Notice that $\neg t$ is not generated by $T^*(D^0)$ because it is blocked by t, and that $u \notin \Delta_{D^0}$, although there are no rules for $\neg u$, because it depends on r, a conflicting property. Taking $J^1 = J^0 \cup \Delta_{D^0}$ for granted, the program can be simplified:

$$D^1 = D/J^1$$
$$T^*(D^1) = \{\neg p, \neg r\} = \Delta_{D^1}.$$

The transformation of $\neg r \leftarrow s$ in class b into a fact $\neg r$ forces the overriding of r in c, leaving the rule $p \leftarrow r$ inactive in class a. As no contradictions were generated in $T^*(D^1)$ the increment Δ_{D^1} coincides with it, subsequently reaching the fixpoint

$$<a> = J^2 = J^1 \cup \Delta_{D^1} = \{t, s, \neg p, \neg r\}.$$

Repeating the same procedure for the other classes, $<b> = \{\neg t, u, \neg p, r\}$ and $<c> = \{u, r\}$. In this example, there are more exceptions than defaults (compare $<a>$ and $<b>$). △

The compilation of the conclusions for c's superclasses is not useful to obtain $<c>$, if dependencies among properties expressed in the rules are to be captured. The method works as if the rules were pulled to the target class and then used, instead of producing effects in their own original classes. Fetching the rules may be blocked if a contradictory fact is found in the set of paths between the rule's class and the target class.

4 Comparison with inheritance networks

We have already presented in the introduction an informal discussion of this topic. In this section we will concentrate on the translation from nets into HST and on a refinement of rule inheritance which does not propagate ambiguities, in the spirit of skeptical inheritance in nets.

Inheritance networks [THT87] deal with individuals (the leaves) and properties (the other nodes) connected by positive and negative links (meaning IS-A, IS-NOT-A and represented by $<n, +m>, <n, -m>$). Inference is path-based and a property is assigned to an individual if there is a path, consisting only of positive links (except, possibly, the last) between the corresponding nodes, which is not contradicted nor pre-empted by other paths.

Each node in the network is defeasible, so it is translated into the HST formalism as a property. Positive links represent inheritance flow paths and are kept in the hierarchic relation. Negative links aren't because they block inheritance. As class membership is strict, there is no correspondence between nodes and classes, except for the leaves, and new names must be created for them. Pruning a net and its HST translation in a similar way enables a correspondence between intermediate entities. Finally, the dependency between nodes, expressed by the links, is represented by rules in the HST.

Definition 11. Translation of inheritance network N into hierarchic system H.

$$a^* \prec b^* \in H \iff <a, +b> \in N$$
$$p \leftarrow n \in \mathcal{D}_{n^*} \iff <n, +p> \in N$$
$$\neg p \leftarrow n \in \mathcal{D}_{n^*} \iff <n, -p> \in N$$

A query $<a, p> \in conclusions(N)$? is translated into $p \in <a^*>$? and put to the HST obtained from H by adding property a to the class a^*. Adding property a as a fact will ground the HST, otherwise unable to provide any answer, by asserting that typical a^*'s must enjoy the property of being a. The translation is uniform for all nodes and a single translation is enough for each network.

Conclusions obtained from the HST coincide with those derived from the net in several common examples in the literature, when using the **skeptical, upwards, off-path** variant [HTT87] of inheritance reasoning. However this is not always the case, as will be seen in example 5.

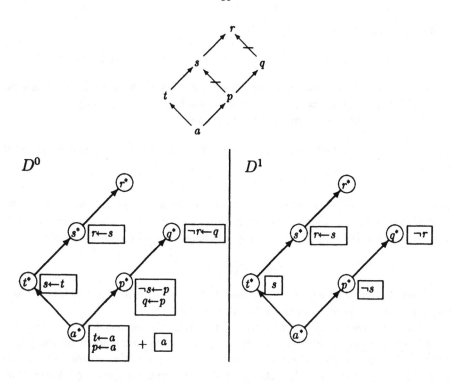

Fig. 4. Propagating ambiguities

Example 5 Double diamond (adapted from [THT87]). For this net the skeptical reasoner would say that $\neg r$ holds. However, considering the symmetries in the net, $\neg r$ results more from an opportunism of the path $<a, p, q, \neg r>$, which profits from the fact that $<a, t, s, r>$ is neutralized by $<a, p, \neg s>$, than from being a desirable consequence of the net. If we insist on propagating ambiguities, then $\neg r$ should not show up. In this example, the proposed formalism for HST agrees with this view. The ambiguity is propagated along the **zombie path** [MS91] $<a, t, s, r>$, neutralizing $<a, p, q, \neg r>$, although the path itself is killed by $<a, p, \neg s>$. Notice that $S_D \uparrow w = S_D(\emptyset) = J^1 = \{a, t, p, q\}$. Despite the simplified program for a^*, D^1, is not empty, $\Delta_{D^1} = \emptyset$ because only contradictions can be derived. △

In some more complex and also ambiguous nets, the skeptical algorithm mentioned produces some desirable conclusions which the HST formalism does not obtain (cf. **floating conclusions** and **floating path** [MS91]). So we propose a refined version of rule inheritance which does not propagate ambiguities in order to obtain a closer approximation of that algorithm.

The idea is to extend to **pairs of contradictory facts** the principle that only facts are allowed to do overriding. If one can not override the other, then there is no way to avoid mutual neutralization.

Definition 12. Neutralization.

$$N(D) = \{r \mid r \in D_a, \sim r \in D_b, \neg \exists d < a : \sim r \leftarrow Q' \in D_d, \neg \exists e < b : r \leftarrow Q'' \in D_e\}.$$

The set $N(D)$ contains the pairs of contradictory facts for which there are no rules with opposing heads below. This set is used to further simplify the program in conjunction with the current safe conclusions set.

Definition 13. Refined rule inheritance. The refined safe conclusions operator is

$$S'_D(J) = J \cup \Delta_{D/J'}$$

where $J' = J \cup N(D/J)$ is the extension of the set of properties J with the neutralized facts which arise in the simplified program D/J. The characterization of a class c in a HST $\langle C, P, \prec, D \rangle$, under refined rule inheritance, is then

$$<c> = S'_{(D_a)_{c \leq a}} \uparrow w.$$

Example 5 now produces $\neg r$ because r was conditional on s which is deleted together with its pair $\neg s$ in the refined procedure.

Although closer to the algorithm in [HTT87], this version does not match it completely because in HST the notion of specificity is independent of properties while in the nets they are mixed together. So, any translation must settle on a fixed hierarchic relation. In nets, specificity depends on the target node, thus producing different (and sometimes unintuitive) results when complex patterns of interaction among defeaters arise [TTH91].

5 Conclusion

We finish by reminding a few characteristics of HST.

- Symmetric treatment of properties presented in a positive and negative way.
- Dependencies on multiple premises.
- Enhanced modularity.
- Separation between inheritance paths and the statement of dependencies among properties.

The resulting compositionality of theories is complex, but the simpler approach of predicate inheritance cannot capture the dependencies expressed by the rules.

There is a lack of incrementality, because no property in a superclass is a priori enjoyed by the subclasses.

The hierarchy of classes with its strict inclusion acts as a backbone around which defeasible properties are grouped. This is a different view from the one expressed in [HT88] where strict and defeasible links are mixable in a more liberal way giving rise to reasoning methods which are essentially an extension to those used with totally defeasible nets, in order to enforce backward propagation of negation along strict paths.

Although sharing with our work a similar starting point, that of structuring a logic program as a hierarchy of modules, [McC93] follows a different approach. It is based on predicate inheritance rather than rule inheritance, although extended with a *self* construct, which enables the evaluation of annotated goals in a different module. As the language does not contain negative heads, exceptions must be explicitly programmed, instead of being based on a generic logic criterium using the notion of contradiction.

We have been essentially dealing with a propositional version of the language but the door to a lifting to first order languages is left open. For instance, shared variables in a conjunction are local to the corresponding rule. Such lifting is hard to conceive in inheritance networks because of its lack of locality. Terms denote individuals in an universe disjoint from the domain U_T where classes and properties have their denotations. An interesting topic for future work is to allow terms denote also sets of individuals in U_T.

The overall result is to clarify the IS-A primitive, and the characterization of classes in terms of sets of properties they enjoy, leaving obscure just the nesting of sets of typical individuals, precisely the part where exceptions are manifest. In inheritance nets all the notions are mixed, in a framework where everything is defeasible.

References

[Bra85] Ronald J. Brachman. I lied about the trees or, defaults and definitions in knowledge representation. *AI Magazine*, 1985.

[DP91] Gabriel David and António Porto. Semantics of property inheritance in a hierarchic system with explicit negation. In Luís Moniz Pereira and António Porto, editors, *EPIA '91 5th Portuguese Conference on Artificial Intelligence*, Berlin, 1991. Springer-Verlag.

[DP92] Gabriel David and António Porto. Rule-based inheritance in structured logic programming. In Edson Carvalho Filho, editor, *IX Simpósio Brasileiro de Inteligência Artificial*, page 144, Rio de Janeiro, 1992. Sociedade Brasileira de Computação.

[GL90] Michael Gelfond and Vladimir Lifschitz. Logic programs with classical negation. In David H. D. Warren and Peter Szeredi, editors, *Logic Programming*, Cambridge, MA, 1990. MIT Press.

[HT88] John F. Horty and Richmond H. Thomason. Mixing strict and defeasible inheritance. In *Proc. Seventh National Conference on Artificial Intelligence*, Los Altos CA, 1988. Morgan Kaufmann Publishers.

[HTT87] John F. Horty, Richmond H. Thomason, and David S. Touretzky. A skeptical theory of inheritance in nonmonotonic semantic networks. In *Proc. Sixth National Conference on Artificial Intelligence*, Los Altos CA, 1987. Morgan Kaufmann Publishers.

[KS90] Robert Kowalski and Fariba Sadri. Logic programs with exceptions. In David H. D. Warren and Peter Szeredi, editors, *Logic Programming*, Cambridge, MA, 1990. MIT Press.

[McC93] Francis G. McCabe. An introduction to *L&O*. In K. R. Apt, J. W. de Bakker, and J. J. M. M. Rutten, editors, *Logic Programming Languages: Constraints, Functions and Objects*, page 204, Cambridge, MA, 1993. The MIT Press.

[MP91] Luís Monteiro and António Porto. Syntactic and semantic inheritance in logic programming. In J. Darlington and R. Dietrich, editors, *Proc. Phoenix Workshop and Seminar on Declarative Programming*, 1991.

[MS91] David Makinson and Karl Schlechta. Floating conclusions and zombie paths: Two deep difficulties in the directly skeptical approach to defeasible inheritance nets. *Artificial Intelligence*, 1991.

[San86] Erik Sandewall. Nonmonotonic inference rules for multiple inheritance with exceptions. *IEEE Proceedings*, 10/86.

[THT87] David S. Touretzky, John F. Horty, and Richmond H. Thomason. A clash of intuitions: the current state of nonmonotonic multiple inheritance systems. In Drew McDermott, editor, *Proc. Tenth International Joint Conference on Artificial Intelligence*, Los Altos CA, 1987. Morgan Kaufmann Publishers.

[Tou87] David S. Touretzky. Implicit ordering of defaults in inheritance systems. In Matthew L. Ginsberg, editor, *Readings in Nonmonotonic Reasoning*, Los Altos, CA, 1987. Morgan Kaufmann Publishers.

[TTH91] David S. Touretzky, Richmond H. Thomason, and John F. Horty. A skeptic's menagerie: Conflictors, preemptors, reinstaters, and zombies in nonmonotonic inheritance. In *Proc. Twelfth International Joint Conference on Artificial Intelligence*, Los Altos CA, 1991. Morgan Kaufmann Publishers.

[Wag90] Gerd Wagner. Logic programming with strong negation and inexact predicates. *Journal of Logic and Computation*, 1990.

Semantics of
Interworking Knowledge Based Systems

Georg Reichwein and José Fiadeiro

INESC / DMIST
Apartado 10105, 1017 Lisboa Codex, Portugal
{ger,llf}@inesc.pt

Abstract. Mixed institutions are proposed as a semantic framework for interworking heterogeneous knowledge based systems, where heterogeneity means that the components of a knowledge base may be based on different logical systems. Using deductive databases as an example, we illustrate the use of this framework for extending relational databases with inference capabilities in first order and temporal logic. Taking institutions as the formal notion of a logical system, a novel institution of relational algebra is introduced together with an institution morphism which formally relates it to first-order logic. Reasoning about dynamics is encompassed by a general construction of a temporal logic institution over an arbitrary base institution. The results are relevant for a declarative semantics of interoperable knowledge bases and multi-agent systems.

1 Introduction

Database theory has more and more approached Artificial Intelligence in its shift from merely relational to "intelligent" and deductive databases. These are systems which incorporate advanced integrity checking mechanisms and/or the ability to deduce derived information from the stored relations (henceforth called *knowledge bases*). Such systems are based on some logic, where a knowledge base is considered as a set of formulae in the logic. Within this logical database paradigm, query evaluation treats also queries as formulae, usually with free variables whose bindings resulting from the evaluation phase define the answers to the query [3, 17, 18].

Reasoning in specific application domains has pushed the definition of different logics. Hence, it is likely that big knowledge based systems will grow out of components each of which uses a specialised logic, making it necessary to develop mechanisms via which these components may interwork. For instance, there are huge fact (data) bases around, and new systems have to interwork with them. They cannot just be re-engineered into the formalism of the knowledge based application which wants to use them, because the "original" functions of the database must not be interrupted. Thus we arrive at systems where, for example, the query language of a knowledge base is relational algebra, whereas the deduction rules are given in Horn clause logic. This can be solved by taking advantage of the well-known correspondence between relational algebra and relational calculus, the embedding of the latter into richer predicate logics being obvious.

Another example is reasoning about temporal properties. The problem with properties about the dynamic evolution of a knowledge base is that, to check them, at least two different states of the same (evolving) knowledge base have to be considered. First-order logic as it is does not provide the proper means to specify and reason about dynamics. Temporal logic is much more adequate for this purpose. Building on the concepts introduced using the simple example of relating relational algebra to first-order logic, we provide a general construction of a temporal logic on top of some given other logic. The construction is such that theories (i.e., databases) specified in the "base" logic are incorporated as modules into a temporal theory (i.e., the dynamic integrity constraints).

These are two applications of a framework for heterogeneity which is based on the categorial theory of institutions [Goguen & Burstall 92]. The notion of *institution* provides a precise definition of what constitutes a logical system, and how theories (deductive databases, integrity constraints) from different logical systems can be combined using morphisms between institutions. This framework has already been successfully applied to define *ex post* the semantics of the interaction primitives of *Epsilon* ([15] and [16]). The distributed KBMS Epsilon has been developed by an ESPRIT project targeted at the integration of data and knowledge bases from various logics [2, 11].

Some authors argue that integrity constraints and other meta-knowledge should be expressed in an epistemic logic (cf. [5, 17]). This gives rise to another situation where the constraints are expressed in a different logic as the database they talk about. Since epistemic logic is, like temporal logic, a special kind of modal logic, our construction applies to this case as well. This further confirms our claim that the framework presented in this paper is a strong basis for a semantical, model-theoretic theory of interworking knowledge bases.

The paper is organized as follows. First we introduce a novel institution of relational algebra, and an institution morphism from an institution of first-order logic to this new institution. These basic constructions already explain the composition of relational databases from independent components, which is relevant for the declarative semantics of distributed, federated and interoperating databases, and the imposition of first-order static integrity constraints onto a database whose query language is based on relational algebra. We can thus "re-engineer" and integrate existing relational databases into knowledge bases. Having illustrated our technical means, namely mixed institutions, by means of this rather simple case, we proceed by introducing a family of mixed institutions which model theories about the dynamic evolution of a knowledge base. We show how from an arbitrary institution (i.e., logical system) a temporal (mixed) institution can be obtained. A similar construction can be defined for epistemic logic.

2 An Institution of Relational Databases

We assume that the reader has some basic familiarity with the concepts of category theory as they are defined in e.g. [1]. Building on these concepts we introduce the notion of *institution* as presented in [9]. It provides a precise generalization of the informal notion of a "logical system".

Definition 1 (institution) An *institution* consists of
- a category SIG of signatures
- a functor Sen: SIG→SET giving the sentences over a given signature

- a functor Mod: SIG→CAT^{op} giving the category of interpretation structures for a given signature.
- a satisfaction relation $\vDash_\Sigma\ \subseteq\ |Mod(\Sigma)|\times Sen(\Sigma)$ for each Σ in $|SIG|$

such that for each arrow f: $\Sigma\to\Sigma'$ in SIG and each m' in $|Mod(\Sigma')|$ and each e in $Sen(\Sigma)$ the following *satisfaction condition* holds:

$$m' \vDash_{f(\Sigma)} Sen(f)(e) \text{ iff } Mod(f)(m') \vDash_\Sigma e \qquad\qquad \square$$

Signatures provide the specific vocabulary over which theories can be built. The functor Sen introduces the grammar of the logic, i.e. it specifies the syntactically well-formed formulae. The satisfaction relation states that when the signature is changed (by a signature morphism) the satisfaction relation between sentences and models changes consistently. [9] prove that any institution whose syntax is rich enough to support gluing together signatures also supports gluing together theories (i.e. collections of sentences) to form larger theories.

Relational databases provide one of the most simple examples of an institution.

Definition 2 (relational signature) A *relational signature* is a quintuple $\Sigma = (S,C,R,A,T)$ where

- S   is a finite set of sort symbols
- $C = \{C_s\}_{s\in S}$ is a finite, non-empty S-indexed family of data symbols
- R   is a finite set of relation symbols
- $A = \{A_s\}_{s\in S}$ is a finite, non-empty S-indexed family of attribute symbols
- T: $R\to A^+$ maps each relation symbol to a non-empty sequence of attribute symbols $\qquad\qquad\square$

Relational signatures correspond to what is usually called a (relational) database schema, with T defining the tables. As already pointed out, sorted signatures enforce "syntactical" integrity constraints, i.e. those which in the proof-theoretic view correspond to type predicates (cf. [18]). Schemata can be related through morphisms, where intuitively a morphism $\sigma: \Sigma_1 \to \Sigma_2$ means that, under appropriate renaming, Σ_1 is a subschema of Σ_2.

Definition 3 (relational signature morphism) A *morphism* $\sigma: \Sigma_1 \to \Sigma_2$ of relational signatures from $\Sigma_1 = (S_1,C_1,R_1,A_1,T_1)$ to $\Sigma_2 = (S_2,C_2,R_2,A_2,T_2)$ is a quintuple $(\sigma_s, \sigma_c, \sigma_r, \sigma_a, \sigma_t)$ with

- $\sigma_s: S_1 \to S_2$ a map of sort symbols (a total function)
- $\sigma_c: C_1 \to C_2$ an S_1-indexed family of total functions
  $$(\sigma_c)_s: C_{1s} \to C_{2\sigma_s(s)}$$
- $\sigma_r: R_1 \to R_2$ a map of relation symbols (a total function)
- $\sigma_a: A_1 \to A_2$ an S_1-indexed family of total functions
  $$(\sigma_a)_s: A_{1s} \to A_{2\sigma_s(s)}$$
- $\sigma_t: T_1 \to T_2$ a total function $\sigma_t: (R_1 \to A_1^+) \to (R_2 \to A_2^+)$
  such that $\sigma_a^+(t(r)) \subseteq \sigma_t(t)(\sigma_r(r))$

where $a_1...a_n \subseteq a_1...a_m$ iff $\{a_1,...,a_n\} \subseteq \{a_1,...,a_m\}$ as multisets, and where $\sigma_a^+: A_1^+ \to A_2^+$ is the extension of σ_a to strings defined by $\sigma_s{}^*(a) = a$ and $\sigma_a^+(aw) = \sigma_a(a)\sigma_a^+(w)$. $\qquad\qquad\square$

The component σ_t of the morphism relates the sequence $T(r)$ of attributes of a relation r to the sequence $\sigma_t(T)(\sigma_r(r))$ of attributes of its image $\sigma_r(r)$. The condition on σ_t means that the image $\sigma_r(r)$ of a relation symbol r can have a "bigger" arity than r, meaning that morphisms may add columns to tables, and that columns may be re-ordered by the morphism.

Lemma 4 (category RSIG) Relational signatures and their signature morphisms form a category RSIG. This category is finitely co-complete. □

The general techniques of gluing together theories in institutions whose category of signatures is finitely co-complete can thus be applied to give declarative semantics to the interoperation of the components of a relational multidatabase, as is explained below.

Relational expressions (representing queries against a relational database) are constructed from the symbols provided by a relational signature. We consider only the basic operators projection, cartesian product, and selection, plus (set) union and difference. Other common operators, like join and quotient, can be defined in terms of these basic operators. The following definition introduces them along with their usual interpretation with respect to a relational database, where, given a relational signature Σ, a Σ-database gives a set of values D_s for each sort symbol s such that each data symbol d is mapped to a value $\mathcal{D}(d)$, and a relation $\mathcal{R}(r)$ over those sets for each relation symbol r. Moreover we define, for each relational expression, its arity as a string over the alphabet provided by A, i.e., as a sequence of attribute symbols. For primitive expressions consisting of only a single relation symbol the arity is the one given by the T component of the relational signature. In expressions, however, we label each attribute symbol with the relation it originates from. This is necessary to distinguish, in complex expressions, between attributes which happen to have the same name, but belong to different relations.

Definition 5 (relational expressions) Given a relational signature $\Sigma = (S,C,R,A,T)$, the set $R(\Sigma)$ of *relational expressions* over Σ and their *interpretation* by a Σ-database $\mathbb{D} = (D,\mathcal{D},\mathcal{R})$ is inductively defined as follows:

- if $r \in R$, then $r \in R(\Sigma)$; and r has *arity* $r.a_1...r.a_n$ if $T(r) = a_1...a_n$
  $$[\![\, r \,]\!]^{\mathbb{D}} = \mathcal{R}(r)$$
- if $r \in R(\Sigma)$ with arity u and $a \in A^+$ such that $r'.a$ is a substring of u for some $r' \in R$, then $\pi_{r'.a}(r) \in R(\Sigma)$ with arity $r'.a$
  $$[\![\, \pi_{r'.a}(r) \,]\!]^{\mathbb{D}} = \text{proj}_i\, ([\![\, r \,]\!]^{\mathbb{D}})\ \text{if } r'.a \text{ is the i-th entry in the arity of } r$$
- if $p \in R(\Sigma)$ with arity u and $r \in R(\Sigma)$ with arity v, then $p{\times}r \in R(\Sigma)$ with arity uv
  $$[\![\, p{\times}r \,]\!]^{\mathbb{D}} = [\![\, p \,]\!]^{\mathbb{D}} \times [\![\, r \,]\!]^{\mathbb{D}}$$
- if $p,r \in R(\Sigma)$ with arity u, then $p{+}r \in R(\Sigma)$ with arity u
  $$[\![\, p{+}r \,]\!]^{\mathbb{D}} = [\![\, p \,]\!]^{\mathbb{D}} \cup [\![\, r \,]\!]^{\mathbb{D}}$$
- if $p,r \in R(\Sigma)$ with arity u, then $p{-}r \in R(\Sigma)$ with arity u
  $$[\![\, p{-}r \,]\!]^{\mathbb{D}} = [\![\, p \,]\!]^{\mathbb{D}} \setminus [\![\, r \,]\!]^{\mathbb{D}}$$
- if $r \in R(\Sigma)$ and $sel \in E(\Sigma,r)$, then $r_{sel} \in R(\Sigma)$ and r_{sel} has the same arity as r
  $$[\![\, r_{sel} \,]\!]^{\mathbb{D}} = \{\, t \mid t \in \mathcal{R}(r) \text{ and } [\![\, sel \,]\!]^{\mathbb{D}}(t) = true \,\}$$

where, given a relational expression $r \in R(\Sigma)$ with arity $r_1.a_1...r_n.a_n$, the set $E(\Sigma,r)$ of *selections* on r is the set of all finite conjunctions of *atomic selections*, each of one of the forms

- $\pi_{r_i.a} = c$ or $\pi_{r_i.a} \neq c$ where $c \in C_S$ and $r_i.a \in A_S$
  $[\![\pi_{r'.a}=c]\!]^{\mathbb{D}} = \lambda t.(t_{|i}=\mathcal{D}(c))$ if r'.a is the i-th entry in the arity of r (the same for '$\neq$')

- $\pi_{r_i.a} = \pi_{r_j.b}$ or $\pi_{r_i.a} \neq \pi_{r_j.b}$ where $r_i.a \in A_S$ and $r_j.b \in A_S$
  $[\![\pi_{r'.a}=\pi_{r'.b}]\!]^{\mathbb{D}} = \lambda t.(t_{|i}=t_{|j})$ if r'.a is the i-th and b the j-th entry in the arity of r (the same for '$\neq$')

- $[\![s \wedge ss]\!]^{\mathbb{D}} = \lambda t.([\![s]\!]^{\mathbb{D}}(t) \wedge [\![ss]\!]^{\mathbb{D}}(t))$ where the empty conjunction is interpreted as the constant function *true* □

Relational signature morphisms σ extend to translations of relational expressions in the usual way. The language and model functors of our intended relational institution are obvious from the above definitions. To define satisfaction, relational expressions are considered to be making assertions about the existence of certain tuples in a database.

Definition 6 (satisfaction) A Σ-database $\mathbb{D}$ *satisfies* a relational expression, written $\mathbb{D} \vDash_\Sigma r$, iff $[\![r]\!]^{\mathbb{D}} \neq \varnothing$. □

It is easy to see that if $\sigma: \Sigma_1 \rightarrow \Sigma_2$ is a relational signature morphism, $r \in R(\Sigma)$ a relation and $\mathbb{D}_2$ a Σ_2-database, then $\mathbb{D}_2 \vDash_{\Sigma_2} Sen(\sigma)(r)$ iff $Mod(\sigma)(\mathbb{D}_2) \vDash_{\Sigma_1} r$. This is exactly the satisfaction condition required for an institution, and hence

Theorem 7 (institution $\mathcal{RDB}$) Relational databases form an institution $\mathcal{RDB}$. □

The following example shows how relational databases can be built from components which are linked through morphisms. The existence of a morphism from the signature of a relational database DB to the signature of another relational database DB' means that the schema of DB' subsumes that of DB. In other words, DB' is an extension of DB, with the morphism expressing the inclusion of DB as a part into DB'. The satisfaction condition simply states that the image of a DB-tuple T belongs to a DB'-relation R if and only if T belongs to the restriction of R to its DB-part.

For the example below, suppose that all data are either integers or strings. Then the signature of the (composed) database $DB1 \perp DB2$ is (S,C,R,A,T) with
— S = {Integer, String}
— $C_{integer}$ is the set of available numbers, and C_{String} the set of available strings
— R = {suppliers, parts}
— $A_{Integer}$ = {id, pnum} and A_{String} = {city, descr}
— T maps suppliers to <id,city> and parts to <pnum,descr>

If we regard a system of interoperating databases as one huge global database (this global database is a conceptual entity, we do not need an explicitly defined schema for it), then we can identify inclusion morphisms from the component databases to the global one. In the general case, the components may have relations in common which account for the interaction. This situation is treated through co-limits of categorial diagrams. In the simple example given below, which involves only two components, the co-limit reduces to a pushout.

From the satisfaction condition we can conclude that for example all tuples in companies of DB1 (see the figure below) have an image in suppliers of DB1⊥DB2. All tuples in products of DB2 have an image in parts of DB1⊥DB2. The most interesting case is the relation products which is common the both DB1 and DB2 (it could have been renamed in either one of them). The pushout effects that in DB1⊥DB2, where products appears as the second column of parts, these images of tuples in D' are identified. Data symbols may have different name in the different databases, the appropriate renaming is performed by the morphisms.

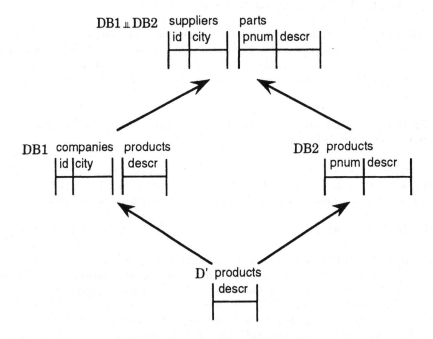

Fig.1. A pushout of databases

Since this work is about semantics, the example ignores the schema and data conflicts which make interoperability an re-engineering difficult in practice. Notice, however, that the above described is a general method which works for every institution whose category of signatures is at least finitely co-complete (this property ensures that every diagram has a co-limit).

Logical systems can be linked through institution morphisms, including theories of one system as sentences into the theories of another system. This gives rises to so called mixed institutions, our formal setting for explaining the semantics of heterogeneous integrity constraints.

3 Static Reasoning

A deductive database augments the relations (facts) with rules that allow to obtain derived information from them, which can be either previously implicit facts, or the satisfaction of (static) integrity constraints. According to the logical view a database is a model of its integrity constraints. As shown above, schemas in a many-sorted formalism already express type constraints, i.e. those integrity constraints which can be checked "syntactically". Other, "semantic" integrity constraints are usually expressed in some (subset of) first-order logic which allows to reason (make inferences) about the facts recorded in a relational database. A typical static integrity constraint for the above DB1⊥DB2 would be: "For every tuple (comp,part) in supplies there has to exist a tuple S in suppliers such that S.id = comp and a tuple P in parts such that P.pnum = part". We model integrity constraints enforced by some kind of first order theorem prover, as well as their enforcement itself, through institution morphisms. This captures the fact that integrity constraints need not be expressed in the same formalism that encompasses the query language. Therefore we now briefly introduce another institution, viz. first order clause logic.

Definition 8 (first-order signature) A *first-order signature* is a pair $\Omega = (F, P)$ where

- $F = \{F_n\}_{n \in \mathbb{N}_o}$ is an $\mathbb{N}_o$-indexed family of function symbols
- $P = \{P_n\}_{n \in \mathbb{N}_o}$ is an $\mathbb{N}_o$-indexed family of predicate symbols   □

Starting from this definition we build an institution along the lines described for the relational institution. We use an unsorted first-order logic, and therefore do not have sort symbols in our first-order signatures. Function and predicate symbols are instead indexed by a natural number, i.e., their arity is simply the number of arguments they take. Notice that in the first-order case we have function symbols which allow for the construction of more complex data terms than just the constants permitted in the relational case. Such terms, as well as literals and clauses, are defined in the usual way.

The definition of interpretation structures is similar to the relational case (using the symbols A, $\mathcal{F}$, and $\mathcal{P}$ to denote the carrier set and the interpretations of function and predicate symbols), only that now we have also functions interpreting the function symbols, with the relational data constants corresponding to the special case of 0-ary functions. Satisfaction is defined in the usual way. From [9] we take the following result:

Theorem 9 (institution $\mathcal{FOL}$) First-order logic is an institution $\mathcal{FOL}$.   □

Now, how can we (formally) let a first-order theorem prover use a relational database? Or, equivalently, how can we use an independently existing relational database as a "fact base" for a deductive knowledge base or expert system? The above described composition techniques using co-limits work within one single institution. To account for more general cases (like the two just mentioned) of interoperating databases where each one may employ a different logical system we need a means to incorporate into a theory in one institution a theory from another institution. This can be achieved through special sentences in so-called mixed institutions [9]. Their construction however presupposes the existence of an institution morphism between the involved institutions.

Definition 10 (institution morphism) Let $I_1 = (SIG_1, Sen_1, Mod_1, \vDash_1)$ and $I_2 = (SIG_2, Sen_2, Mod_2, \vDash_2)$ be institutions. Then an *institution morphism* $\Phi: I_1 \to I_2$ consists of

- a functor $\Phi: SIG_1 \to SIG_2$
- a natural transformation $\alpha: \Phi; Sen_2 \Rightarrow Sen_1$
- a natural transformation $\beta: Mod_1 \Rightarrow \Phi; Mod_2$

such that for each I_1-signature Σ in $|SIG_1|$, each interpretation structure $\mathbb{A}$ in $|Mod(\Sigma)|$, and each I_2-sentence e in $Sen_2(\Phi(\Sigma))$ the following *satisfaction condition* holds:

$$\mathbb{A} \vDash_\Sigma \alpha_\Sigma(e) \text{ iff } \beta_\Sigma(\mathbb{A}) \vDash_{\Phi(\Sigma)} e \qquad \square$$

In the present case of $\mathcal{FOL}$ and $\mathcal{RDB}$ such a construction amounts to providing a mapping of first-order signatures into relational signatures, plus a transformation of queries in relational algebra into first order sentences, such that the satisfaction condition holds (the transformation of the first order interpretation structures into relational ones is just forgetting the $\mathcal{F}$ component).

The basic idea of the signature mapping is to identify predicate symbols with relation symbols. To overcome the formal difficulty that first order logic is unsorted, while we have sorts in $\mathcal{RDB}$, we introduce in the relational signature a unique sort symbol, say s, and transform a predicate arity n into a string of n symbols s. For the set of data symbols we take the function symbols with arity 0, all other function symbols are "forgotten" by the functor. With this mapping of signatures, the transformation of queries is the same as in the standard proof that the relational calculus is as expressive as the relational algebra. Having omitted nearly all technical details, we only report the result (see [14] for details):

Theorem 11 (institution morphism) There is an institution morphism $\Phi: \mathcal{FOL} \to \mathcal{RDB}$. $\qquad \square$

The purpose of introducing institution morphisms like the above is the possibility to define mixed institutions whose sentences may belong to different logical systems. Recall that a theory in an institution is just a set of sentences.

Definition and Theorem 12 (mixed institution) Let $\Phi: I_1 \to I_2$ be an institution morphism. Then $\mathcal{M}(\Phi)$ is the *mixed institution* of I_1 and I_2 with

- its signatures Σ those from I_1
- its sentences either sentences from $Sen_1(\Sigma)$ or else pairs of the form $\langle T, \theta: Sign(T) \to \Phi(\Sigma) \rangle$
  where T is a theory in I_2 and θ is a signature morphism in I_2
- its interpretation structures those from I_1
- $m \vDash_\Sigma \langle T, \theta: Sign(T) \to \Phi(\Sigma) \rangle$ iff $Mod_2(\theta)(\beta_\Sigma(m)) \vDash_{\Phi(\Sigma)} T$ $\qquad \square$

See [9] for the proof that $\mathcal{M}(\Phi)$ is indeed an institution. The "mixed" sentence means that the I_2-theory T is interpreted in models translated from I_1. This sentence incorporates T into I_1-theories in the sense that, loosely speaking, every model of the combined theory has to be a model of T as well.

In our case of first order deduction rules expressing integrity constraints of relational databases we use mixed sentences to input the relational database as a set of "facts" into the deductive one. As an example consider the already mentioned integrity constraint for our suppliers-and-parts database (call it D): "For every tuple (comp,part) in supplies there has to exist a tuple S in suppliers such that S.id = comp and a tuple P in parts such that P.pnum = part". The constrained database can be expressed as the following first order theory T (in PROLOG-like notation):

```
suppliers (Comp,City)  :- supplies (Comp,Part).
parts (Part,Descr)  :- supplies (Comp,Part).
mix ('D', θ).
```

where the morphism θ specifies the renaming of symbols in D to the corresponding one in the image of T under the institution morphism Φ of theorem 14. As a tentative programming notation we use a predicate symbol `mix` for the mixed sentence $\langle D, \theta: \text{Sign}(D) \to \Phi(\Sigma) \rangle$, with Σ the signature of the logic program into which the theory D is imported. Of course there may be several mixed sentences in the same program, corresponding to the inclusion of various databases. See also [16] for more advanced applications of mixed institutions.

4 Dynamic Reasoning

Static reasoning refers to one single state of the knowledge base, and is well understood. Dynamic reasoning refers to the temporal evolution of the knowledge base, and hence to verify them at least two states of the knowledge base have to be considered. A typical example (a dynamic integrity constraint) is "the salary of an employee must never decrease". Dynamic integrity is still a field of active research [13]. There is a consensus, however, that some sort of temporal logic has to be employed for expressing and reasoning about dynamic integrity constraints [7]. This section applies the technique introduced in the previous ones to this new problem, namely applying temporal integrity constraints to a relational or deductive data- or knowledge base. Technically, we present a way to construct a "temporal" institution for an arbitrary "base" institution. Work in the same direction, though not involving institutions, is reported in [8].

Definition 13 (temporal formula) Given an institution $I = (\text{SIG}, \text{Sen}, \text{Mod}, \vDash)$ and an I-signature Σ, *atomic temporal Σ-formulae* are defined as follows:
- every $s \in \text{Sen}(\Sigma)$ is an atomic temporal Σ-formula
- if p is a temporal Σ-formula, then $\bigcirc$p is an atomic temporal Σ-formula
- if p is a temporal Σ-formula, then $\square$p is an atomic temporal Σ-formula

The language of *temporal Σ-formulae* is the propositional language over the atomic temporal Σ-formulae. □

This is to say that assertions like $\bigcirc$p (next time p) and $\square$p (always in the future p) can be combined using the propositional logic operators $\neg$, $\wedge$, and $\vee$. A common abreviation is $\diamond$p for $\neg(\square(\neg p))$ (eventually p). These symbols are interpreted below as the connectives of future temporal logic; it is easy to imagine the corresponding past temporal operators ● (previous time) and ■ (always in the past). Notice that there is no quantification allowed outside temporal operators; our temporal language is hence close to the one proposed in [12] for temporal integrity constraints. The above definition gives rise to a functor Temp which takes any category Sen(Σ) of atomic Σ-formulae to a category Temp;Sen(Σ) of temporal Σ-formulae.

Since they refer to (in this case) the evolution of a knowledge base, i.e. to a succession of states, temporal formulae have to be interpreted in more complex interpretation structures than relational queries or first-order clauses. The most simple approach is to take sequences of objects of the corresponding category Mod(Σ) of interpretation structures of the "underlying" institution. In the language of category theory this is the category of functors from the category ω of natural numbers to Mod(Σ). With Mod: SIG$\rightarrow$CAT^{op} also Mod$^\omega$: SIG$\rightarrow$CAT^{op}. The model functor of the intended temporal institution is Mod$^\omega$ composed with the functor $\times_\omega$ which takes a category C to the category $C \times \omega$ whose objects are pairs (c,i) with $c \in |C|$ and $i \in |\omega|$, and whose morphisms are defined componentwise. Satisfaction of temporal Σ-formulae by such structures is defined as follows:

Definition 14 (satisfaction) Let $I = (SIG, Sen, Mod, \vDash)$ be an institution and $\Sigma \in SIG$. The *satisfaction* of a temporal Σ-formula by an interpretation structure $(\mathbb{S},i) \in |Mod^\omega; \times_\omega|$, written $(\mathbb{S},i) \vDash_\Sigma p$, is defined as follows:

- if $p \in Sen(\Sigma)$, then $(\mathbb{S},i) \vDash_\Sigma p$ iff p is satisfied by the ith element of $\mathbb{S}$
- $(\mathbb{S},i) \vDash_\Sigma Op$ iff p is satisfied by the $(i+1)^{th}$ element of $\mathbb{S}$
- $(\mathbb{S},i) \vDash_\Sigma \Box p$ iff p is satisfied by all elements of $\mathbb{S}$ with index greater than i
- $\neg$, $\wedge$, and $\vee$ have their usual meanings ☐

The signatures of the temporal theories are the same as those of the underlying non-temporal ones, so the translations (by signature morphisms) of the respective languages carry over from the "underlying" institution through the functor Temp, and hence the satisfaction condition remains valid even after the introduction of the temporal operators. This is summarized into the following result:

Theorem 15 (temporal institutions) Let $I = (SIG, Sen, Mod, \vDash)$ be an institution. Then $T(I) = (SIG, Temp;Sen, Mod^\omega; \times_\omega, \vDash)$ is also an institution, the *temporal institution* over I. ☐

This construction immediately gives rise to morphisms $\Phi_I: T(I) \rightarrow I$ between institutions and their temporal extensions. The functor between the categories of signatures is the identity functor, and the natural transformation α between the sentences is also trivial because every I-sentence is also an (atomic) temporal formula in $T(I)$. Finally, given $(\mathbb{S},i)$, the reduced interpretation structure is $\mathbb{S}(i)$.

Corollary 16 (institution morphisms) Every pair I and $T(I)$ gives rise to an institution morphism $\Phi_I: T(I) \rightarrow I$. ☐

Such institution morphisms are the formal (logical) link between databases and their dynamic integrity constraints. The database (possibly together with some static constraints) can be incorporated as an argument into the constraint theory using a suitable mixed institution. Notice that institutions and their morphisms again form a category $I\mathcal{N}ST$, hence institution morphisms compose in an associative way. Hence establishing a few basic morphisms already gives a large variety of possible combinations of logical systems.

5 Concluding Remarks

We proposed mixed institutions as a semantic framework for static and dynamic heterogeneous integrity constraints, where heterogeneity means that the involved knowledge base and its constraint theories may be based on different logical systems. This is an example of interworking logical systems. Taking institutions as the formal notion of a logical system, we formalized the inclusion of knowledge bases as modules into constraint theories. Mixed institutions extend the "intra-logic" modularization techniques provided by institutions with finitely co-complete categories of signatures to "inter-logic" techniques. In this framework, reasoning about dynamics is encompassed by a general construction of a temporal logic institution over an arbitrary base institution.

Multidatabases are another important area of current research, as is evidenced by the number of both academic and industrial projects (see [10] and [4] for overviews). The theory presented herein also provides a semantic basis for interoperability of data and knowledge bases, a need that has by now been widely recognized (cf. [6]). This is because, besides the "usual" problems of defining a common semantics for heterogeneously coded data in disparate database systems (i.e. of resolving schema and data conflicts, or conflicts between global and local transaction management), interoperable *deductive* database systems have to provide ways to distribute deductions in a sound way, taking into account that the interoperating components may employ different logical systems.

Our presented framework is a good candidate for a declarative semantics of interoperability because mixed sentences reflect a basic requirement for multidatabases, namely that the federated components maintain full autonomy over their data and continue to provide their functionality as "stand-alone" systems, for security reasons and to preserve previous investments. Mixed institutions reflect this property in the semantics because mixed sentences completely encapsulate the theory they import, i.e., the importing logical system has no means to decompose the imported theory (knowledge base) and access single assertions (facts).

Acknowledgement

This work has been partly supported by JNICT under contract PBIC/C/TIT/1227/92 (Interoperability of Deductive Databases).

References

1. Barr, M.; Wells, C.: "Category Theory for Computing Science", Prentice Hall 1990

2. Bense, H.; Cremers, A.B.; Kouloumdjian, J.; Levi, G.; Modesti, M.; Rouault, J.: "The EPSILON Project", in CEC DG XIII (ed) Information Processing Systems: Results and Progress of ESPRIT Projects in 1989

3. Bibel, W.; Nicolas, J.-M.: "The Role of Logic for Data and Knowledge Bases: A Brief Survey", in Schmidt, J.W.; Thanos, C. (eds) Foundations of Knowledge Base Management, Springer Verlag 1989

4. Bright, M.W.; Hurson, A.R.; Pakzad, S.: "A Taxonomy and Current Issues in Multidatabase Systems", IEEE Computer 25(3), 1992, pp. 50-60

5. Boman, M.; Johannesson, P.: "Epistemic Logic as a Framework for Federated Information Systems", in [6], pp. 255-270

6. Deen, S.M. (ed): Proceedings of the International Working Conference on Cooperating Knowledge Based Systems, Springer Verlag 1990

7. Fiadeiro, J..; Sernadas, A.: "Specification and Verification of Database Dynamics", Acta Informatica 25, 1988, pp. 625-661

8. Finger, M.; Gabbay, D.M.: "Adding a Temporal Dimension to a Logic System", Journal of Logic, Language, and Information, 1992

9. Goguen, J.; Burstall, R.: "Institutions: Abstract Model Theory for Specification and Programming", Journal of the ACM 39, 1992, pp. 95-146 an earlier version appeared in Clarke, E.; Kozen D. (eds) Proc. Logics of Programming Workshop, LNCS 164, Springer Verlag 1984, pp. 221-256

10. Hsiao, D.; Kamel, M.: "Heterogeneous Databases: Proliferations, Issues and Solutions", IEEE Transactions on Data and Knowledge Engineering 3(1), 1989

11. Kniesel, G.; Rohen, M.; Cremers, A.B.: "A Management System for Distributed Knowledge Based Applications", in Proc. Int. GI-Kongreß Verteilte KI und kooperatives Arbeiten, Springer Verlag 1991, pp. 65-76

12. Lipeck, U.; Saake, G.: "Monitoring Dynamic Integrity Constraints Based on Temporal Logic", Information Systems 12(3), 1987, pp. 255-269

13. Lipeck, U.; Thalheim, W. (eds): "Modelling Database Dynamics", Springer Verlag, 1992

14. Reichwein, G.; Fiadeiro, J.: "A Semantic Framework for Interoperability", DMIST / INESC Technical Report, 1992

15. Reichwein, G.; Rohen, M.; Fiadeiro, J.: "Composed Modular Knowledge Bases in Duplex Institutions", COMPULOG Meeting on Programming Languages, University of Pisa, 1992

16. Reichwein, G.; Fiadeiro, J.; Rohen, M.: "Semantic Issues in Interoperable Deductive Databases", Proc. ICICIS'93, IEEE Computer Society Press 1993, pp. 291-299

17. Reiter, R.: "What should a Database Know?", Journal of Logic Programming 14 , 1992, pp. 127-153

18. Reiter, R.; "Towards a Logical Reconstruction of Relational Database Theory", in Brodie, M.; Mylopoulos, J.; Schmidt, J. (eds) On Conceptual Modelling, Springer Verlag 1984, pp. 191-233

Combining Terminological Logics with Tense Logic*

Klaus Schild

German Research Center for Artificial Intelligence (DFKI)
Stuhlsatzenhausweg 3, 66123 Saarbrücken, FRG
e-mail: schild@dfki.uni-sb.de

Abstract. We show how to add full first-order temporal expressiveness to terminological logics. This can be achieved by embedding point-based tense operators in propositionally closed concept languages like $\mathcal{ALC}$. The resulting temporal terminological logics are fully expressive over linear, Dedekind complete time such as $\mathbb{N}$ and $\mathbb{R}$ in the sense that all first-order temporal formulae over these time structures are expressible. We then prove that augmenting $\mathcal{ALC}$ by future-oriented tense operators interpreted over linear, discrete, unbounded time like $\mathbb{N}$ does not increase its computational complexity. To establish this complexity result we show that coherence in $\mathcal{ALC}$ augmented by functional roles and their transitive closure is computable in polynomial space. We finally show how to obtain directly an axiomatization and a tableau-based algorithm for the tense-logical extension of terminological logics.

1 Introduction

Terminological logics or *concept languages* have been designed for the logical reconstruction and specification of knowledge representation systems derivating from KL-ONE such as BACK, CLASSIC, $\mathcal{KRIS}$, and LOOM.[1] These systems are able to represent dictionary-like definitions, and their task is to arrange these definitions in a hierarchy according to semantic relations like subsumption and equivalence. Concept languages comprise two syntactic categories, namely *concepts* and *roles*. Concepts such as 'woman' or 'man' correspond to unary predicates whereas roles like 'parent of' correspond to binary ones. Concepts can be composed using logical connectives and restrictions on roles. Because of their variable-free notation terminological logics are well readable. Moreover, there are practical algorithms for computing the subsumption and equivalence relation with respect to a finite number of concept definitions. However, concept languages are often seriously restricted in their expressive power. They are in particular not able to represent temporal schemes occurring in most terms and most technical applications. Schmiedel [17] demonstrated how to incorporate temporal knowledge

---

* The author is currently under grant of the *Deutsche Forschungsgemeinschaft* (DFG).
[1] For a good overview of the 'KL-ONE family' the reader is referred to [22]. For KL-ONE itself see [2].

in concept languages in principle. In his interval-based *temporal terminological logic* a mortal being, for instance, can be defined as follows:

MortalBeing $\doteq$ *Being* and (sometime (X) (after X *Now*) (at X (not *Being*)))

This definition states that a mortal being is a being that will not be alive at an interval X sometime after the current interval *Now*. Unfortunately, his approach seems to sacrifice the main benefit of concept languages, viz. the fact that they give rise to practical inference algorithms or at least to *any* inference algorithm: Schmiedel's temporal terminological logic is neither decidable nor effectively axiomatizable in the presence of concept negation.[2] Moreover, his integration is hardly balanced since its temporal component is far more expressive than its terminological base.

The fact that Schmiedel's language is undecidable seems to be typical rather than exceptional as all nontrivial *interval-based* temporal logics involving quantification over time seem to be undecidable, even in the propositional case [10, 8]. Note that terms like 'mortal being' inherently involve quantification over time, so that Allen's [1] decidable interval calculus cannot serve for our purpose. We therefore suggest to enrich concept languages with the *point-based* temporal operators of the *propositional tense logic*. Propositional tense logic bears the same benefits as terminological logics, i.e., it is well readable and it gives rise to practical algorithms as well. In addition, it is well-understood in terms of expressiveness, model theory, axiomatizability, and computational complexity. Finally, it has been applied successfully to such different fields like linguistics [11], reasoning about concurrency [6] and planing.[3] For a thorough introduction into tense logic, the reader is referred to [18] and to [7].

2 The Tense-Logical Extension of Terminological Logics

The tense-logical extension to be presented will be based on various terminological logics. One terminological base will be the well-known propositionally closed language $\mathcal{ALC}$ considered by Schmidt-Schauß and Smolka [16] in their seminal paper. Concepts of $\mathcal{ALC}$ can be built up from the *universal concept* $\top$ and from *concept names* by applying logical connectives as well as *existential and universal value restrictions*. The latter take an arbitrary *role name* RN and an arbitrary concept C as their arguments and are written as $\exists RN{:}C$ and as $\forall RN{:}C$. The

---

[2] We proved that the propositional closed version of Schmiedel's [17] temporal terminological logic is neither decidable nor effectively axiomatizable, at least when considering unbounded, Dedekind complete time such as $\mathbb{N}$ or $\mathbb{R}$. The main observation is that Halpern and Shoham's [10] *propositional modal logic of time intervals* is a fragment of Schmiedel's language when augmented by concept negation. The former is known to be undecidable for unbounded time and it is even not effectively axiomatizable for unbounded, Dedekind complete time [10, Theorem 9 & 12]. Therefore, the same holds for Schmiedel's logic when closed under concept negation.

[3] We showed that full propositional STRIPS planning can be done within propositional linear tense logic.

universal concept $\top$ is to be paraphrased by "anything" and denotes the full domain whereas concept names represent not further specified subsets of this domain. Not very surprising, the logical connectives $\sqcap$, $\sqcup$ and $\neg$ denote the corresponding set operations on the domain. The universal value restriction $\forall R{:}C$ is to be read as "every R is a C" and denotes those objects d for which all objects that are related to d by R are members of the concept C. In contrast to this, the existential value restriction $\exists R{:}C$ should be read as "some R is a C" and denotes all those objects d for which there exists at least one object e related to d by R such that e is a member of C. Using these concept operators, we can define, for instance, a mother as a woman who is the parent of a woman or a man:

$$Mother \doteq Woman \sqcap \exists parent\_of{:}(Woman \sqcup Man)$$

When considering the tense-logical extension of $\mathcal{ALC}$, we have a number of additional temporal concept operators at our disposal. One of these is the *existential future operator* $\Diamond$ ("eventually") taking an arbitrary concept as its argument. Employing this operator, we can define, for example, a mortal being as a being that eventually will not be alive any more:

$$MortalBeing \doteq Being \sqcap \Diamond \neg Being$$

It should be clear that such temporal concepts no longer denote sets of objects but sets of ordered pairs of the form $\langle d, t \rangle$ such that d is an object of the domain and t is a time instant. The tuple $\langle d, t \rangle$ being in the denotation of a concept C then means that at time t the object d is a C. Clearly, the denotation of roles has to be modified by time points too. The denotation of the role *parent_of*, for instance, must be a set of ordered triples of the form $\langle d, d', t \rangle$ such that d and d' are objects of the domain and t is a time instant. For example, if $\langle d, d', t \rangle$ is in the denotation of *parent_of*, then d is a parent of d' at time t. In this framework value restrictions quantify over objects of the domain whereas temporal operators quantify over time instants. That is, at time t the existential value restriction $\exists R{:}C$ denotes all those objects d for which there exists at least one object e such that at time t e is related to d by R and e is a member of C. On the other hand, at time t the existential future operator $\Diamond C$ represents all those objects which are a C at some time $t' \geq t$. The concept $Being \sqcap \Diamond \neg Being$, for instance, denotes the set of object-time pairs $\langle d, t \rangle$ such that at time t the object d is a $Being$ and, moreover, there is a time instant $t' \geq t$ at which d is no $Being$ any more. In this particular case, however, t' cannot be equal to t since it is impossible that d is a $Being$ and no $Being$ at the same time.

In addition to the existential future operator, the tense-logical extension comprises also its universally quantifying counterpart $\Box$ ("henceforth"), called the *universal future operator*. At time t the concept $\Box C$ denotes all those objects which are a C at every time instant $t' \geq t$. With this tense operator on hand, we can precise the definition of a mortal being by saying that a mortal being is a being that eventually will not be alive any more and then will never be alive again. Of course, one can accept this definition only if not believing in rebirth.

$$MortalBeing \doteq Being \sqcap \Diamond\Box\neg Being$$

A closer look at this definition, however, reveals that it is still incomplete. The explanation is that at time t the concept $Being \sqcap \Diamond\Box\neg Being$ denotes all those beings that are alive at time t and that will not be alive any more at every time after some time instant $t' \geq t$. Note, however, this definition does not tell anything about the time *between* t and t'. At this time the being can be alive or not! The binary tense operator U ("until") due to Kamp [11] has been introduced to fill such gaps. Using this operator, we can redefine a mortal being as a being that is alive *until* never being alive any more:

$$MortalBeing \doteq Being \sqcap (Being\, U\, \Box\neg Being)$$

In general, at time t the concept $C\,U\,D$ denotes all those objects which are a D at some time instant $t' > t$ and which are a C at every time instant t'' with $t < t'' < t'$. It should be clear that even though the second definition of *MortalBeing* subsumes the third one, they are not equivalent. Kamp's until operator is rather strong in expressive power. It can express, for instance, even the so-called *next instant operator* $\bigcirc$. At time t the concept $\bigcirc C$ denotes all those objects which are a C at some time *immediately* succeeding t. In fact, this operator is definable in terms of Kamp's until operator:

$$\bigcirc C \stackrel{\text{def}}{=} \bot\, U\, C$$

In applications involving discrete time a slight variant of Kamp's until operator together with the next instant operator is more convenient. This variant is simply named $\mathcal{U}$ and at time t the concept $C\,\mathcal{U}\,D$ denotes all those objects which are a D at some time instant $t' \geq t$ and which are a C at every time instant t'' with $t \leq t'' < t'$. In this case, t and t' can be equal, so that the second condition is then trivially fulfilled. One can easily check that in the particular case of the last definition of *MortalBeing*, U can be replaced with $\mathcal{U}$ without changing its meaning.

Definition 1. Assume $\mathcal{N}$ is the union of two disjoint, countably infinite sets, $\mathcal{N}_C$ and $\mathcal{N}_\mathcal{R}$, the elements of which are called **concept names** and **role names** respectively. The concepts and roles of $\mathcal{ALCT}$ are inductively defined as follows:

1. Each concept name is a concept of $\mathcal{ALCT}$.
2. If C and D are concepts of $\mathcal{ALCT}$ and if RN is a role name, then $C \sqcap D$, $\neg C$, $\forall RN{:}C$, $\Box C$, $\Diamond C$, $C\,\mathcal{U}\,D$ and $C\,U\,D$ are concepts of $\mathcal{ALCT}$.
3. These are all concepts of $\mathcal{ALCT}$.

Of course, we may use parentheses to resolve ambiguities. As usual, we read the concepts $C \sqcup D$, $\bot$, $\top$ and $\exists R{:}C$ as abbreviations of $\neg(\neg C \sqcap \neg D)$, $CN \sqcap \neg CN$, $\neg(CN \sqcap \neg CN)$ and of $\neg\forall R{:}\neg C$ respectively.

The concepts of $\mathcal{ALCT}$ can be used to form so-called axioms which can be of the form $C \doteq D$ or $C \sqsubseteq D$. The axiom $C \doteq D$ forces the denotation of C and the denotation of D to be equal, whereas the $C \sqsubseteq D$ forces the denotation of C to be a subset of the denotation of D.

Definition 2. Assume $\mathcal{L}$ is an arbitrary concept language. If C and D are concepts of $\mathcal{L}$, then $C \doteq D$ is an **axiom** of $\mathcal{L}$. We treat $C \sqsubseteq D$ as an abbreviation of $C \doteq C \sqcap D$.

We shall consider not only the tense-logical extension of $\mathcal{ALC}$, but also the tense-logical extension of the rather expressive yet decidable concept language $\mathcal{ALCF}^*$ considered in [14]. The reason to do so is that the tense-logical extension of this language will turn out to be reducible to its base $\mathcal{ALCF}^*$— at least as far as discrete, unbounded time is concerned. $\mathcal{ALCF}^*$ extends $\mathcal{ALC}$ by the following role expressions: First of all, $\mathcal{ALCF}^*$ comprises regular role expressions, i.e., it comprises the disjunction $R \sqcup S$ and the composition $R \circ S$ of two roles, and it contains the reflexive-transitive closure R^* of a role. The role *parent_of* $\circ$ *parent_of*, for instance, denotes the relation 'grandparent of' whereas *parent_of* $\circ$ *parent_of** represents the relation 'is descendant of'. Furthermore, $\mathcal{ALCF}^*$ comprises the *range restriction* $R|C$ which restricts the range of a role to a concept. One can express, for example, the role 'is parent of a lawyer' by the range restriction *parent_of*$|$*Lawyer*. Last but not least, $\mathcal{ALCF}^*$ contains the *identity role id* as well as *feature names*. The latter are special role names which denote functions mapping objects of the domain to objects of the domain rather than binary relations.

Definition 3. Assume $\mathcal{N_F}$ is a designated subset of $\mathcal{N_R}$, where the elements of $\mathcal{N_F}$ are called **feature names**. The concepts and roles of $\mathcal{ALCF}^*\mathcal{T}$ are then inductively defined as follows:

1. Each concept name is a concept of $\mathcal{ALCF}^*\mathcal{T}$.
2. If C and D are concepts of $\mathcal{ALCF}^*\mathcal{T}$ and if R is a role of $\mathcal{ALCF}^*\mathcal{T}$, then $C \sqcap D$, $\neg C$ and $\forall R{:}C$ are concepts of $\mathcal{ALCF}^*\mathcal{T}$.
3. Each role name, each feature name and id is a role of $\mathcal{ALCF}^*\mathcal{T}$.
4. If R and S are roles of $\mathcal{ALCF}^*\mathcal{T}$ and if C is a concept of $\mathcal{ALCF}^*\mathcal{T}$, then $R \sqcup S$, $R \circ S$, R^* and $R|C$ are roles of $\mathcal{ALCF}^*\mathcal{T}$.
5. These are all concepts and roles of $\mathcal{ALCF}^*\mathcal{T}$.

3 Temporal Semantics

The model-theoretical semantics of the tense-logical extension will be given in terms of temporal interpretations and time structures. A **time structure** is a tuple $\langle \mathcal{T}, < \rangle$ such that $\mathcal{T}$ is a nonempty set and $<$ is a transitive binary relation over $\mathcal{T}$. The elements of $\mathcal{T}$ are called **time points** or **time instants** and the binary relation $<$ is to be thought of as the *precedence relation* on the set of time instants. We define $\leq$ to be $<$ closed under indentity over $\mathcal{T}$. Of course, we shall consider more concrete time structures such as discrete, branching, linear and unbounded time rather than general time structures with only transitivity imposed upon. These common time structures are given formally as follows:

- The time structure $\langle \mathcal{T}, < \rangle$ is **discrete** iff for all t and t' in $\mathcal{T}$ with $t < t'$ there is an immediate successor s of t such that $s \leq t'$ — where s is an *immediate successor* of t iff $t < s$ and there is no $s' \in \mathcal{T}$ with $s \neq s'$ such that $t < s' < s$.
- The time structure $\langle \mathcal{T}, < \rangle$ is **branching** iff for all t, t' and t'' in $\mathcal{T}$ with $t < t'$, $t < t''$ and $t' \neq t''$ there is no $s \in \mathcal{T}$ such that $t' < s$ and $t'' < s$ whenever neither $t' < t''$ nor $t'' < t'$ holds. That is to say, a time instant of a branching time structure may have two or more successors which are not related to each other by $<$, but only if these successors do not have any successor in common.
- The time structure $\langle \mathcal{T}, < \rangle$ is **linear** iff for all t, t' and t'' in $\mathcal{T}$ with $t < t'$, $t < t''$ and $t \neq t''$, it holds either $t' < t''$ or $t'' < t'$. Every linear time structure is clearly branching as well.
- The time structure $\langle \mathcal{T}, < \rangle$ is **unbounded** iff for every $t \in \mathcal{T}$ there is some $t' \in \mathcal{T}$ such that $t < t'$.

We denote the set of all discrete, branching, linear and unbounded time structures by **Dis**, **Bra**, **Lin** and by **Unb** respectively. It should be stressed that $Lin \cap Dis \cap Unb$ does contain 'nonstandard' time structures. Such a 'nonstandard' time structure is $\langle \{1\}, < \rangle$ with $1 < 1$. Another one is $\langle \{1, 2\}, < \rangle$ with $1 < 1$ and $2 < 2$ such that neither $1 < 2$ nor $2 < 1$ holds. For this reason, we shall investigate also the 'standard' linear, discrete, unbounded time structure $\langle \mathbb{N}, < \rangle$ with $<$ being the usual ordering on $\mathbb{N}$. In case of time structures like $\langle \mathbb{N}, < \rangle$ for which the precedence relation $<$ is obvious, we may omit $<$ and may simply write $\mathbb{N}$ instead of $\langle \mathbb{N}, < \rangle$.

The following operations on relations are introduced in order to ease the definition of a temporal interpretation. First of all, for any three-place relation R, $R(z)$ is defined to be $\{\langle x, y \rangle : \langle x, y, z \rangle \in R\}$. Second, for any binary relation R over some set Δ and for any natural number i, R^i is inductively defined as follows: If $i = 0$, then R^i is the identity over Δ, otherwise it is $R \circ R^{i-1}$. As usual, $\circ$ denotes the composition of two binary relations.

Definition 4. Assume $\langle \mathcal{T}, < \rangle$ is some time structure and assume $\Delta^\mathcal{I}$ is an arbitrary set. The tuple $\langle \Delta^\mathcal{I}, \cdot^\mathcal{I} \rangle$ is called to be a **temporal interpretation** if $\cdot^\mathcal{I}$ is some function which maps concepts to subsets of $\Delta^\mathcal{I} \times \mathcal{T}$ and roles to subsets of $\Delta^\mathcal{I} \times \Delta^\mathcal{I} \times \mathcal{T}$ such that:

$$(C \sqcap D)^\mathcal{I} = C^\mathcal{I} \cap D^\mathcal{I}$$
$$(\neg C)^\mathcal{I} = (\Delta^\mathcal{I} \times \mathcal{T}) \setminus C^\mathcal{I}$$
$$(\forall R{:}C)^\mathcal{I} = \{\langle d, t \rangle : \forall d'(\langle d, d', t \rangle \in R^\mathcal{I}), \langle d', t \rangle \in C^\mathcal{I}\}$$
$$(\Diamond C)^\mathcal{I} = \{\langle d, t \rangle : \exists t'(t \leq t'), \langle d, t' \rangle \in C^\mathcal{I}\}$$
$$(\Box C)^\mathcal{I} = \{\langle d, t \rangle : \forall t'(t \leq t'), \langle d, t' \rangle \in C^\mathcal{I}\}$$
$$(C \mathcal{U} D)^\mathcal{I} = \{\langle d, t \rangle : \exists t'(t \leq t'), \langle d, t' \rangle \in D^\mathcal{I} \; \& \; \forall t''(t \leq t'' < t'), \langle d, t'' \rangle \in C^\mathcal{I}\}$$
$$(C U D)^\mathcal{I} = \{\langle d, t \rangle : \exists t'(t < t'), \langle d, t' \rangle \in D^\mathcal{I} \; \& \; \forall t''(t < t'' < t'), \langle d, t'' \rangle \in C^\mathcal{I}\}$$
$$(R \sqcup S)^\mathcal{I} = R^\mathcal{I} \cup S^\mathcal{I}$$

$$(R \circ S)^{\mathcal{I}} = \{\langle d, d', t \rangle : \langle d, d' \rangle \in R^{\mathcal{I}}(t) \circ S^{\mathcal{I}}(t)\}$$
$$(R^*)^{\mathcal{I}} = \{\langle d, d', t \rangle : \langle d, d' \rangle \in \bigcup_{i \geq 0} R^{\mathcal{I}}(t)^i\}$$
$$(R|C)^{\mathcal{I}} = \{\langle d, d', t \rangle \in R^{\mathcal{I}} : \langle d', t \rangle \in C^{\mathcal{I}}\}$$
$$id^{\mathcal{I}} = \{\langle d, d, t \rangle : d \in \Delta^{\mathcal{I}}, t \in \mathcal{T}\}$$

In addition, for each feature name FN, d' and d'' must be identical if both $\langle d, d', t \rangle$ and $\langle d, d'', t \rangle$ are in $FN^{\mathcal{I}}$. That is, FN can be thought as denoting at any time a partial function mapping elements of $\Delta^{\mathcal{I}}$ to elements $\Delta^{\mathcal{I}}$. We call $\Delta^{\mathcal{I}}$ to be the **domain** of the temporal interpretation.

Definition 5. The temporal interpretation $\langle \Delta^{\mathcal{I}}, .^{\mathcal{I}} \rangle$ is a **model** of the axiom $C \doteq D$ iff $C^{\mathcal{I}} = D^{\mathcal{I}}$, and it is a model of a set of axioms iff it is a model of each axiom of the set.

Recall that $C \sqsubseteq D$ is treated as an abbreviation of $C \doteq C \sqcap D$. It should be stressed that the models of $C \sqsubseteq D$ are in fact all those temporal interpretations in which the denotation of C is a subset of the denotation of D. That is, a temporal interpretation $\langle \Delta^{\mathcal{I}}, .^{\mathcal{I}} \rangle$ is a model of $C \sqsubseteq D$ iff $C^{\mathcal{I}} \subseteq D^{\mathcal{I}}$.

Definition 6. Assume $\mathcal{A} \cup \{C \doteq D\}$ is an arbitrary *finite* set of axioms and assume Θ to be some set of time structures. We say that $\mathcal{A}$ **entails** $C \doteq D$ with respect to Θ, written $\mathcal{A} \models_\Theta C \doteq D$, iff for each time structure $\langle \mathcal{T}, < \rangle \in \Theta$ and for each temporal interpretation $\mathcal{I} = \langle \Delta^{\mathcal{I}}, .^{\mathcal{I}} \rangle$ over $\langle \mathcal{T}, < \rangle$, $\mathcal{I}$ is a model of $C \doteq D$ whenever $\mathcal{I}$ is a model of $\mathcal{A}$. If it is *not* the case that $\emptyset \models_\Theta C \doteq \bot$, then C is said to be **coherent** with respect to Θ.

Please, bear in mind that entailment is defined solely with respect to *finite* sets of axioms and that coherence is defined with respect to the *empty* set of axioms.

For the sake of simplicity, we introduce the following conventions. We may omit the curly brackets of sets, and empty sets can be omited altogether. This convention concerns both the set of axioms $\mathcal{A}$ and the set of time structures Θ. For example, we may write $\models_{\langle \mathcal{T}, < \rangle} C \doteq D$ instead of $\emptyset \models_{\{\langle \mathcal{T}, < \rangle\}} C \doteq D$. If we allow only a certain set of time structures, say Γ, we simply postfix '(Γ)'. $\mathcal{ALCT}(\mathbb{N})$, for instance, denotes $\mathcal{ALCT}$ when considering only temporal interpretations over $\langle \mathbb{N}, < \rangle$.

Its is easily seen that both the existential and the universal future operator is redundant since they can be eliminated in favor of $\mathcal{U}$ without increasing the length of concepts more than linearly:

$$\models \Diamond C \doteq \top \mathcal{U} C$$
$$\models \Box C \doteq \neg \Diamond \neg C$$

Therefore, we henceforth assume that the tense-logical extension comprises only $\mathcal{U}$ and U as temporal operators whereas $\bigcirc$, $\Diamond$ and $\Box$ are defined as abbreviations in terms of $\mathcal{U}$ and U. Moreover, the following equivalence proves $\mathcal{U}$ to be expressible in terms of U:

$$\models C \mathcal{U} D \doteq D \sqcup (C \sqcap (C U D))$$

Repeatedly replacing concepts of the form CUD with $D \sqcup (C \sqcap (CUD))$ can unfortunately cause an exponential blow up.

At this stage, a remark on the relation between the presented temporal semantics and the ordinary nontemporal semantics for terminological logics is in order. By 'ordinary semantics' we mean the semantics for $\mathcal{ALC}$ given, e.g., in [16] and the one for $\mathcal{ALCF}^*$ given in [14]. This semantics can be obtained from Definition 4 by simply ignoring the temporal index and by omitting the mapping for the tense operators. We call interpretations defined in this way to be *nontemporal*. It can easily be seen that entailment in this sense is equivalent to entailment with respect to an arbitrary set of time structures as far as only concepts not containing any tense operator are concerned. On the other hand, we get exactly the semantics for propositional tense logic by simply ignoring the object index. Therefore, we can directly carry over the lower complexity bounds and the expressiveness results proved for propositional tense logic. In particular, Gabbay *et al.* [6] proved propositional tense logic to be *fully expressive for future time* over linear, Dedekind complete time like $\mathbb{N}$ or $\mathbb{R}$ in the sense that each purely future first-order temporal formula over these structures is expressible. The latter are first-order formulae involving solely variables, unary predicates, as well as the binary predicates $<$ and $=$ as nonlogical symbols. In addition, each quantifier must be of the form $\exists y(x < y)$ or of the form $\forall y(x < y)$, i.e., each quantifier is restricted to the future. For details the reader is referred to Gabbay *et al.* [6]. Wolper [20], though, proved that second-order properties such as being true at all *even* time instants are not expressible by propositional tense logic interpreted over $\mathbb{N}$.

4 Representation Theorems

This section is devoted to two fundamental representation theorems which give rise to complexity results, axiomatizations, and complete algorithms. Representation Theorem 2 states that in case of branching, discrete, unbounded time, entailment in $\mathcal{ALCF}^*\mathcal{T}$ is log space reducible to entailment in its base $\mathcal{ALCF}^*$. An immediate consequence of this theorem is that in this case the addition of tense operators does not increase the computational complexity. To establish this representation theorem the following intermediate reduction is needed: Representation Theorem 1 states that in case of branching, discrete, unbounded time entailment in $\mathcal{ALCF}^*\mathcal{T}$ is log space reducible to entailment in the so-called *pseudo-temporal* version of $\mathcal{ALCF}^*\mathcal{T}$. This semantic variant interprets all concepts and roles nontemporally, i.e., as in $\mathcal{ALCF}^*$ they denote subsets of $\Delta^\mathcal{I}$ and subsets of $\Delta^\mathcal{I} \times \Delta^\mathcal{I}$ respectively. Consequently, the precedence relation $<$ has to be treated as a transitive relation over the *domain* $\Delta^\mathcal{I}$, hence the name *pseudo-temporal*. This means pseudo-temporal $\mathcal{ALCF}^*\mathcal{T}$ is the ordinary *union* of $\mathcal{ALCF}^*$ and tense logic rather than the two-dimensional combination of both. This reduction can be interpreted as stating that in case of branching, discrete, unbounded time there are no interactions between temporal and nontemporal operators. This is not the case for general time structures though. Consider, for instance, the concept $\exists R{:}\exists S{:}\bigcirc C$. It can easily be seen that this concept is subsumed by $\bigcirc\top$, i.e., $\models (\exists R{:}\exists S{:}\bigcirc C) \sqsubseteq \bigcirc\top$. This means, the temporal operator $\bigcirc C$ occurring inside an existential value restriction can affect the very surface of the latter. Note, however, in case of unbounded time *each* concept is subsumed by $\bigcirc\top$, so that $\models (\exists R{:}\exists S{:}\bigcirc C) \sqsubseteq \bigcirc\top$ holds trivially.

Representation Theorem 1 has a number of immediate far-reaching consequences. For linear, discrete, unbounded time, it yields, for instance, a sound and complete tableau algorithm for $\mathcal{ALCF}^*\mathcal{T}$ as we can simply *join* the tableau algorithm for $\mathcal{ALCF}^*$ [14] to the one for propositional linear tense logic [21]. As another consequence we directly obtain a sound and complete axiomatization for $\mathcal{ALCF}^*\mathcal{T}$. Again, we can simply *join* the axioms for $\mathcal{ALCF}^*$ [14] to the corresponding axioms for propositional linear tense logic [3].

In order to make clear what exactly is meant by pseudo-temporal $\mathcal{ALCF}^*\mathcal{T}$, we define pseudo-temporal interpretations which extend ordinary nontemporal interpretations to cope with tense operators.

Definition 7. A **pseudo-temporal interpretation** over some time structure $\langle \Delta^{\mathcal{I}}, < \rangle$ is a nontemporal interpretation $\langle \Delta^{\mathcal{I}}, < \rangle$ such that additionally:

$$(C\,\mathcal{U}\,D)^{\mathcal{I}} = \{d : \exists d'(d \leq d'), d' \in D^{\mathcal{I}} \ \& \ \forall d''(d \leq d'' < d'), d'' \in C^{\mathcal{I}}\}$$
$$(C\,U\,D)^{\mathcal{I}} = \{d : \exists d'(d < d'), d' \in D^{\mathcal{I}} \ \& \ \forall d''(d < d'' < d'), d'' \in C^{\mathcal{I}}\}$$

Recall that the definition of a nontemporal interpretation can be obtained from Definition 4 by simply omitting both the temporal index and the mapping for the tense operators. For the understanding of the representation theorems, it is crucial not to confuse nontemporal, pseudo-temporal, and temporal interpretations:

- *Nontemporal* interpretations map concepts and roles of $\mathcal{ALCF}^*$ to subsets of $\Delta^{\mathcal{I}}$ and to subsets of $\Delta^{\mathcal{I}} \times \Delta^{\mathcal{I}}$ respectively.
- *Pseudo-temporal* interpretations map concepts and roles of $\mathcal{ALCF}^*\mathcal{T}$ to subsets of $\Delta^{\mathcal{I}}$ and to subsets $\Delta^{\mathcal{I}} \times \Delta^{\mathcal{I}}$ respectively. The denotation of tense operators is the very same as in ordinary tense logic when viewing the elements of $\Delta^{\mathcal{I}}$ as time instants rather than objects. The concept $\Diamond C$, for instance, is mapped to $\{d : \exists d'(d < d'), d' \in C^{\mathcal{I}}\}$, where the precedence relation $<$ is a transitive binary relation over $\Delta^{\mathcal{I}}$, the domain of the pseudo-temporal interpretation.
- *Temporal* interpretations map concepts and roles of $\mathcal{ALCF}^*\mathcal{T}$ to subsets of $\Delta^{\mathcal{I}} \times \mathcal{T}$ and to subsets of $\Delta^{\mathcal{I}} \times \Delta^{\mathcal{I}} \times \mathcal{T}$ respectively. They map $\Diamond C$ to $\{\langle d, t\rangle : \exists t'(t < t'), \langle d, t'\rangle \in C^{\mathcal{I}}\}$, where the precedence relation $<$ is a transitive binary relation over $\mathcal{T}$, the set of time instants.

The definition of *pseudo-temporal entailment*, indicated by $\models^1_\Theta$, in terms of pseudo-temporal interpretations can be defined in the very analogous way as entailment is defined in terms of temporal interpretations.

It is a well-known fact that the tense operators $\mathcal{U}$ and U are expressible by the reflexive-transitive closure *, at least as far as tree-like time structures are concerned (e.g., see [9, Remark 5.4.2]). The following mapping performs this reduction.

Definition 8. Assume $succ$ is some fixed fresh role name. The mapping π maps concepts of $\mathcal{ALCF}^*\mathcal{T}$ to concepts of $\mathcal{ALCF}^*$. π applied to an arbitrary concept repeatedly replaces each occurrence of the form $C\,U\,D$ and $C\,\mathcal{U}\,D$ with $\exists(succ|C)^*{:}\exists succ{:}D$ and with $\exists(id|C \circ succ)^*{:}D$ until there is no more occurrence of U or $\mathcal{U}$. We extend π to sets of axioms in the sense that π applied to a set $\mathcal{A}$ of axioms of $\mathcal{ALCF}^*\mathcal{T}$ yields $\{\pi(C) \doteq \pi(D) : C \doteq D \in \mathcal{A}\}$.

Lemma 1. *Assume* $\mathcal{A} \cup \{C \doteq D\}$ *is some finite set of axioms of* $\mathcal{ALCF}^*\mathcal{T}$. *It then holds that:*

$$\mathcal{A} \models^1_{Bra \cap Dis} C \doteq D \text{ iff } \pi(\mathcal{A}) \models \pi(C) \doteq \pi(D)$$

Recall that $\models^1$ denotes pseudo-temporal entailment in $\mathcal{ALCF}^*\mathcal{T}$, whereas $\models$ denotes in this case entailment in $\mathcal{ALCF}^*$.

Representation Theorem 1. *Assume* $\mathcal{A} \cup \{C \doteq D\}$ *is any finite set of concepts of* $\mathcal{ALCF}^*\mathcal{T}$. *It then holds that:*

$$\mathcal{A} \models_{Bra \cap Dis \cap Unb} C \doteq D \text{ iff } \mathcal{A} \models^1_{Bra \cap Dis \cap Unb} C \doteq D$$

Proof. We prove both parts by contraposition. For the if-part suppose $\mathcal{A}$ does *not* entail $C \doteq D$ with respect to $Bra \cap Dis \cap Unb$. That is, there exists a *temporal* interpretation $\mathcal{I} = \langle \Delta^{\mathcal{I}}, \cdot^{\mathcal{I}} \rangle$ over a branching, discrete, unbounded time structure $\langle \mathcal{T}, < \rangle$ which is a model of $\mathcal{A}$ but which is no model of $C \doteq D$. Because of the discreteness of $\langle \mathcal{T}, < \rangle$ there must be a minimal base $\prec$ of $<$. We define the *pseudo-temporal* interpretation $\mathcal{J} = \langle \Delta^{\mathcal{J}}, \cdot^{\mathcal{J}} \rangle$ over the time structure $\langle \Delta^{\mathcal{J}}, \tilde{<} \rangle$ as follows:

$$\Delta^{\mathcal{J}} = \Delta^{\mathcal{I}} \times \mathcal{T}$$
$$\tilde{<} = \{\langle\langle d,t\rangle,\langle d,t'\rangle\rangle : d \in \Delta^{\mathcal{I}}, t < t'\}$$
$$CN^{\mathcal{J}} = CN^{\mathcal{I}}, \text{ for all } CN \in \mathcal{N}_C$$
$$RN^{\mathcal{J}} = \{\langle\langle d,t\rangle,\langle d',t\rangle\rangle : \langle d,d',t\rangle \in RN^{\mathcal{I}}\}, \text{ for all } RN \in \mathcal{N}_{\mathcal{R}}$$

The time structure $\langle \Delta^{\mathcal{J}}, \tilde{<} \rangle$ can be thought of as consisting of n copies of the time structure $\langle \mathcal{T}, < \rangle$, where n is the cardinality of $\Delta^{\mathcal{I}}$. That is, $\langle \Delta^{\mathcal{J}}, \tilde{<} \rangle$ is the disjoint union of time structures which are isomorphic to $\langle \mathcal{T}, < \rangle$. Inspection of the definitions of branching, discrete and unbounded time shows that $Bra \cap Dis \cap Unb$ is closed under disjoint union. The time structure $\langle \Delta^{\mathcal{J}}, \tilde{<} \rangle$ is therefore also a member of $Bra \cap Dis \cap Unb$. Induction on the complexity of concepts and roles of $\mathcal{ALCF}^*\mathcal{T}$ prove that for every concept C of $\mathcal{ALCF}^*\mathcal{T}$ and for every role R of $\mathcal{ALCF}^*\mathcal{T}$, $C^{\mathcal{J}}$ is $C^{\mathcal{I}}$ and that $R^{\mathcal{J}}$ is $\{\langle\langle d,t\rangle,\langle d',t\rangle\rangle : \langle d,d',t\rangle \in R^{\mathcal{I}}\}$. As $\mathcal{I}$ is a model of $\mathcal{A}$ but no model of $C \doteq D$, the same must apply to $\mathcal{J}$ as well, so that it cannot be the case that $\mathcal{A} \models^1_{Bra \cap Dis \cap Unb} C \doteq D$.

For the only-if-part suppose it is *not* the case that $\mathcal{A} \models^1_{Bra \cap Dis \cap Unb} C \doteq D$. This clearly implies that $\mathcal{A} \cup \{\top \doteq \bigcirc\top\} \models^1_{Bra \cap Dis} C \doteq D$ does not hold either.

According to Lemma 1, this amounts to saying that $\pi(\mathcal{A} \cup \{\mathsf{T} \doteq \bigcirc \mathsf{T}\})$ does not entail $\pi(C) \doteq \pi(D)$. That is, there must be a *nontemporal* interpretation $\mathcal{I} = \langle \Delta^{\mathcal{I}}, \cdot^{\mathcal{I}} \rangle$ which is a model of $\pi(\mathcal{A} \cup \{\mathsf{T} \doteq \bigcirc \mathsf{T}\})$ but which is no model of $\pi(C) \doteq \pi(D)$. According to [19, Section 3], we may assume without loss of generality that $\mathcal{I}$ is tree-structured (with a fixed branching factor). We therefore may also assume that there are sets, $\mathcal{D}$ and $\mathcal{T}$, such that:

$$\Delta^{\mathcal{I}} = \mathcal{D} \times \mathcal{T}$$
$$RN^{\mathcal{I}} \subseteq \{\langle \langle d, t \rangle, \langle d', t \rangle \rangle : d, d' \in \mathcal{D},\ t \in \mathcal{T}\},\ \textit{if } RN \in \mathcal{N}_{\mathcal{R}}\ \&\ RN \neq succ$$
$$succ^{\mathcal{I}} \subseteq \{\langle \langle d, t \rangle, \langle d, t' \rangle \rangle : d \in \mathcal{D},\ t, t' \in \mathcal{T}\}$$

This can be achieved by simply *renaming* the elements of $\Delta^{\mathcal{I}}$. This renaming is in fact possible because $\mathcal{I}$ is tree-structured and therefore $RN^{\mathcal{I}} \cap succ^{\mathcal{I}} = \emptyset$, for each role name $RN \neq succ$. Now recall, $\mathcal{I}$ is not only tree-structured (with a fixed branching factor), but it is also a model of $\pi(\mathsf{T} \doteq \bigcirc \mathsf{T})$ which is defined to be $\mathsf{T} \doteq \exists succ : \mathsf{T}$. Hence, for each $d \in \Delta^{\mathcal{I}}$ there is a fixed number of distinct $d_i \in \Delta^{\mathcal{I}}$ such that $\langle d, d_i \rangle \in succ^{\mathcal{I}}$. This means, there must be a binary relation $<$ over $\mathcal{T}$ such that:

$$succ^{\mathcal{I}} = \{\langle \langle d, t \rangle, \langle d, t' \rangle \rangle : d \in \mathcal{D},\ t < t'\}$$

We now define the *temporal* interpretation $\mathcal{J} = \langle \Delta^{\mathcal{J}}, \cdot^{\mathcal{J}} \rangle$ over the branching, discrete and unbounded time structure $\langle \mathcal{T}, < \rangle$ as follows:

$$\Delta^{\mathcal{J}} = \mathcal{D}$$
$$CN^{\mathcal{J}} = CN^{\mathcal{I}},\ \textit{for all } CN \in \mathcal{N}_C$$
$$RN^{\mathcal{J}} = \{\langle d, d', t \rangle : \langle \langle d, t \rangle, \langle d', t \rangle \rangle \in RN^{\mathcal{I}}\},\ \textit{for all } RN \in \mathcal{N}_{\mathcal{R}}$$

Induction on the complexity of concepts and roles of $\mathcal{ALCF}^*\mathcal{T}$ proves that for every concept C of $\mathcal{ALCF}^*\mathcal{T}$ and for every role R of $\mathcal{ALCF}^*\mathcal{T}$, $C^{\mathcal{J}}$ is $C^{\mathcal{I}}$ and that $R^{\mathcal{J}}$ is $\{\langle d, d', t \rangle : \langle \langle d, t \rangle, \langle d', t \rangle \rangle \in R^{\mathcal{I}}\}$. As $\mathcal{I}$ is a model of $\mathcal{A}$ but no model of $C \doteq D$, the same applies to $\mathcal{J}$, so that $\mathcal{A}$ does not entail $C \doteq D$ with respect to $Bra \cap Dis \cap Unb$. $\qquad\square$

Representation Theorem 2. *Assume $\mathcal{A} \cup \{C \doteq D\}$ is a finite set of concepts of $\mathcal{ALCF}^*\mathcal{T}$. It then holds that:*

$$\mathcal{A} \models_{Bra \cap Dis \cap Unb} C \doteq D \textit{ iff } \pi(\mathcal{A} \cup \{\mathsf{T} \doteq \bigcirc \mathsf{T}\}) \models \pi(C) \doteq \pi(D)$$

Proof. Suppose $\pi(\mathcal{A} \cup \{\mathsf{T} \doteq \bigcirc \mathsf{T}\}) \models \pi(C) \doteq \pi(D)$. According to Lemma 1, this holds iff $\mathcal{A} \cup \{\mathsf{T} \doteq \bigcirc \mathsf{T}\} \models^1_{Bra \cap Dis} C \doteq D$. The latter in turn holds clearly iff $\mathcal{A} \models^1_{Bra \cap Dis \cap Unb} C \doteq D$. Representation Theorem 1 states that this amounts to saying that $\mathcal{A} \models_{Bra \cap Dis \cap Unb} C \doteq D$. $\qquad\square$

There are two important comments concerning the two representation theorems. First of all, it is a well known fact from modal logic that $\mathcal{A} \models_{Unb} C \doteq D$ iff $\mathcal{A} \models_{Bra \cap Dis \cap Unb} C \doteq D$ provided $\mathcal{A}$, C and D contain only tense operators of the form $\Diamond$ and of the form $\mathsf{T} U$ [7, Section 3]. Both representation theorems therefore also hold in case of unbounded time if only tense operators of this form are involved. Interestingly, $\Diamond$ and $\top U$ are nothing but *serial, transitive modalities (KD4)* which are in case of $\Diamond$ also *reflexive (KT4)*. On the other hand, both representation theorems can easily be generalized to deal with many other serial or reflexive modalities such as *KD, KT, KDB, KTB* and *S5*. These modalities can be mapped to concepts of $\mathcal{ALCF}^*$ as well, where for symmetric modalities the inverse R^{-1} of a role R is also needed. The reflexive, transitive and symmetric modality (S5), for instance, would be mapped to the concept $(succ \sqcup succ^{-1})^*$.

On the other hand, both representation theorems are obviously also valid for *Bra* replaced with *Lin* provided that *succ* is a feature name. The latter observation will be important in the next section.

5 Computational Complexity

In this section the following complexity results will be presented: First of all, we prove that the addition of tense operators does *not* increase the computational complexity of entailment in $\mathcal{ALCF}^*$, at least as far as branching, discrete, unbounded time or linear, discrete, unbounded time is concerned. This complexity result is just an immediate consequence of Representation Theorem 2. We then show that in case of linear, discrete, unbounded time, the addition of tense operators does *not* increase the complexity of coherence in $\mathcal{ALC}$ which is known to be complete for polynomial space. In order to prove this, we have to observe that reducing $\mathcal{ALCT}$ to $\mathcal{ALCF}^*$ via π yields concepts in which the reflexive-transitive closure * is only applied to *functional* roles. This restricted use of * does not cause hardness for exponential time, even though its unrestricted use does cause hardness for exponential time. In fact, we shall prove that coherence in $\mathcal{ALCF}^\times$ is computable in polynomial space, where $\mathcal{ALCF}^\times$ extends $\mathcal{ALC}$ by *functional* roles and their reflexive-transitive closure. This is a new and rather surprising result as coherence in $\mathcal{ALC}$ augmented by the reflexive-transitive closure of a single role name is hard for exponential time [14]. Last but not least, we shall see that in contrast to linear, discrete, unbounded time, in case of branching, discrete, unbounded time, the addition of tense operators does cause hardness for exponential time.

Complexity Theorem 1. *With respect to $Bra \cap Dis \cap Unb$ and with respect to $Lin \cap Dis \cap Unb$ entailment in $\mathcal{ALCF}^*\mathcal{T}$ is decidable in exponential time.*

Proof. According to Representation Theorem 2 entailment in $\mathcal{ALCF}^*\mathcal{T}$ is in both cases reducible to entailment in $\mathcal{ALCF}^*$ via π. The mapping π is computable in logarithmic space and yields concepts the length of which is linearly bounded in the length of the original concepts. Hence, as entailment in $\mathcal{ALCF}^*$ is decidable in exponential time [14], so is entailment in $\mathcal{ALCF}^*\mathcal{T}$ in both cases. $\square$

To determine the computational complexity of $\mathcal{ALCT}$, we first consider a language named *strict deterministic propositional dynamic logic, SDPDL* for short, investigated by Halpern and Reif [9]. In analogy to the correspondence between $\mathcal{ALCF}^*$ and the *deterministic propositional dynamic logic DPDL* [14], SDPDL can be viewed as the corresponding sublanguage of $\mathcal{ALCF}^*$. This sublanguage is inductively defined as follows:

1. Each concept name is a concept of SDPDL.
2. If C and D are concepts of SDPDL and if R is a role of SDPDL, then $C \sqcap D$, $\neg C$ and $\forall RN{:}C$ are concepts of SDPDL.
3. Each role name, each feature name and id is a role of SDPDL.
4. If F and G are roles of SDPDL and if C is a concept of $\mathcal{ALCF}^*$, then $F \circ G$, $F|C$, **while** C **do** F, and **if** C **then** F **else** G are roles of SDPDL.
5. These are all concepts and roles of SDPDL.

The roles **while** C **do** F and **if** C **then** F **else** G are treated as abbreviations of $(C? \circ F)^* | \neg C$ and of $(C? \circ F) \sqcup (\neg C? \circ G)$ respectively, where $C?$ is a shorthand for the role $id|C$. In contrast to the roles of $\mathcal{ALCF}^*$, all roles of SDPDL are functional, i.e., they denote partial functions mapping elements of the domain to elements of the domain [9, Lemma 2.8(3)]. Halpern and Reif [9] proved coherence in SDPDL to be complete for polynomial space [9, Theorem 5.1 & 5.5]. SDPDL is yet quite expressive since the transitive closure of *functional* roles can be expressed as the following equivalences due to Halpern and Reif [9, Remark 6.2] prove:

$$\models \exists F^*{:}C \doteq \exists \textbf{while } \neg C \textbf{ do } F{:}\top \tag{1}$$

$$\models \forall F^*{:}C \doteq \forall \textbf{while } C \textbf{ do } F{:}\bot \tag{2}$$

Please bear in mind that the right hand sides of these equivalences are linearly bounded in the length of their left hand sides. However, these equivalences do *not* show that iterated applications of the transitive-reflexive closure are expressible in SDPDL. Furthermore, Parikh [13, Theorem 7.1] showed that replacing each occurrence of a role name RN by $(FN_{RN} \circ FN_{new})^*$ preserves coherence, provided FN_{RN} and FN_{new} are fixed new feature names. This result together with the equivalences (1) and (2) implies that SDPDL can simulate role names as well. It is worth mentioning that the restriction to express solely noniterated transitive closures prevents SDPDL from simulating the transitive closure of role names which would cause hardness for exponential time [5, Theorem 4.4]. Now, it should be obvious that coherence in $\mathcal{ALC}$ augmented by feature names and the transitive-reflexive closure of functional roles is log space reducible to coherence in SDPDL.

Definition 9. The concepts, roles, and functional roles of $\mathcal{ALCF}^\times$ are inductively defined as follows:

1. Each concept name is a concept of $\mathcal{ALCF}^\times$.
2. If C and D are concepts of $\mathcal{ALCF}^\times$ and if R is a role of $\mathcal{ALCF}^\times$, then $C \sqcap D$, $\neg C$ and $\forall R{:}C$ are concepts of $\mathcal{ALCF}^\times$.
3. Each role name is a role of $\mathcal{ALCF}^\times$.
4. If F is a functional role of $\mathcal{ALCF}^\times$, then F and F^* are roles of $\mathcal{ALCF}^\times$.

5. Each feature name and id is a functional role of $\mathcal{ALCF}^\times$.

6. If F and G are both functional roles of $\mathcal{ALCF}^\times$ and if C is a concept of $\mathcal{ALCF}^\times$, then $F \circ G$ and $F|C$ are functional roles of $\mathcal{ALCF}^\times$.

7. These are all concepts, roles and functional roles of $\mathcal{ALCF}^\times$.

Complexity Theorem 2. *Coherence in $\mathcal{ALCF}^\times$ is log space reducible to coherence in SDPDL and, therefore, it is complete for polynomial space.*

Complexity Theorem 3. *With respect to $Lin \cap Dis \cap Unb$ coherence in $\mathcal{ALCT}$ is log space reducible to coherence in $\mathcal{ALCF}^\times$ and, therefore, it is complete for polynomial space.*

Proof. According to Representation Theorem 2, we know that if $succ$ is the feature name used in the mapping π, then $\models_{Lin \cap Dis \cap Unb} C \doteq D$ holds iff the axiom $\top \doteq \exists succ{:}\top$ entails $\pi(C) \doteq \pi(D)$. Inspection of the definition of π shows that $\pi(C)$ and $\pi(D)$ are concepts of $\mathcal{ALCF}^\times$. Moreover, we can get rid of the axiom $\top \doteq \exists succ{:}\top$ since it comprises no concept name.[4] The reason for this is that, for every axiom $C \doteq D$, $\top \doteq \exists succ{:}\top$ entails $C \doteq D$ holds iff $\models \tilde{C} \doteq \tilde{D}$. The concepts $\tilde{C}$ and $\tilde{D}$ are obtained from their negation normal form[5] by conjoining $\exists succ{:}\top$ to each subconcept not being in the scope of $\neg$. The described abstraction from the axiom $\top \doteq \exists succ{:}\top$ is (as the mapping π) computable in logarithmic space. □

Notice that coherence in $\mathcal{ALC}$ alone is complete for polynomial space [16], so that the addition of tense operators to $\mathcal{ALC}$ does not increase its computational complexity in case of linear, discrete, unbounded time. However, this is not the case for branching, discrete, unbounded time as the next theorem states:

Complexity Theorem 4. *With respect to $Bra \cap Dis \cap Unb$ and with respect to $Bra \cap Dis$ coherence in $\mathcal{ALCT}$ is hard for exponential time.*

Proof. The corresponding lower complexity bounds for propositional tense logic [4] directly carry over to $\mathcal{ALCT}$. □

We have so far determined the computational complexity of $\mathcal{ALCT}$ with respect to the set of linear, discrete, unbounded time structures. As we have already mentioned, $Lin \cap Dis \cap Unb$ does contain 'nonstandard' time structures which are not isomorphic to $\langle \mathbb{N}, < \rangle$. Nevertheless, it is well known that the presented tense operators are not able to distinguish between such 'nonstandard' time structures and $\mathbb{N}$ [7, Section 9], so that the following theorem is evident:

Complexity Theorem 5. *Coherence in $\mathcal{ALCT}(\mathbb{N})$ is complete for polynomial space.*

---

[4] Note, however, Nebel [12] showed that this would not be the possible for arbitrary axioms.

[5] The *negation normal form* of a concept is an equivalent concept such that no compound is negated. It can be obtained by introducing $\sqcup$ and $\exists{:}$ into the language rather than treating them as abbreviations and then exploiting de Morgan's Laws as well as the equivalence $\models \forall R{:}C \doteq \neg(\exists R{:}\neg C)$.

6 Conclusion

We considered the temporal terminological logic $\mathcal{ALCT}$ combining the propositional closed concept language $\mathcal{ALC}$ with tense logic. It turned out that if based on the time structure $\mathbb{N}$, $\mathcal{ALCT}$ can express each purely future first-order temporal formula over $\mathbb{N}$ although it has the very same computational complexity as its base $\mathcal{ALC}$. We also briefly described how to obtain an axiomatization as well as a tableau-based algorithm for this language. Finally, we mentioned that the *modal extension* of terminological logics is nothing but a special case of our tense-logical extension, at least for most serial or reflexive modalities.

Another point worth considering is that there are also *interval-based* tense logics which can serve as temporal extensions of terminological logics as well. In particular, Halpern and Shoham's [10] *propositional modal logic of time intervals* seems to be quite promising since it is both elegant and rather expressive: Employing six basic temporal operators quantifying over intervals all 13 basic relations between two time intervals and all point-based tense operators are expressible. Furthermore, all common time structures such as linear, unbounded, discrete, dense, and even Dedekind complete time can be distinguished within the logic itself. This means that we can distinguish even real time from rational time which is not possible within first-order logic. This language is unfortunately undecidable for unbounded time and is even not effectively axiomatizable for unbounded, Dedekind complete time such as $\mathbb{N}$ or $\mathbb{R}$. There are similar discouraging results for the logic proposed by Halpern *et al.* [8] which is based on the so-called *chop operator*. This binary operator denotes the composition of two time intervals. Employing this chop operator, we can express all possible relations between *three* time intervals which cannot be done in Halpern and Shoham's [10] logic of time intervals. Unfortunately, this logic is undecidable as well [8, §4]. All this shows that the presented temporal extension of terminological logics is a rather good choice since it adds sufficient temporal expressiveness while not increasing the computational complexity of its terminological base.

References

1. James F. Allen. Maintaining knowledge about temporal intervals. *Communications of the ACM*, 26(11):832–843, 1983.
2. Ronald J. Brachman and James G. Schmolze. An overview of the KL-ONE knowledge representation system. *Cognitive Science*, 9(2):171–216, 1985.
3. John P. Burgess. Axioms for tense logic: I. "since" and "until". *Notre Dame Journal of Formal Logic*, 23(4):367–374, 1982.
4. E. Allen Emerson and Joseph Y. Halpern. Decision procedures and expressiveness in the temporal logic of branching time. *Journal of Computer and System Science*, 30:1–24, 1985.
5. Michael J. Fischer and Richard E. Ladner. Propositional dynamic logic of regular programs. *Journal of Computer and System Science*, 18:194–211, 1979.
6. Dov Gabbay, Amir Pnueli, Saharon Shela, and Jonathan Stavi. On the temporal analysis of fairness. In *Proceedings of the 7th Symposium on Principles of Programming Languages*, Las Vegas, Nevada, 1980.

7. Robert Goldblatt. *Logics of Time and Computation*, volume 7 of *CSLI Lecture Notes*. Chicago University Press, Chicago, Ill., 1987.

8. Joseph Y. Halpern, Zohar Manna, and Ben Moszkowski. A hardware semantics based on temporal intervals. In *Proceedings of 10th International Colloquium on Automata, Languages and Programming*, pages 278–291, Barcelona, Spain, 1983.

9. Joseph Y. Halpern and John Reif. The propositional dynamic logic of deterministic, well-structured programs. *Theoretical Computer Science*, 27:127–165, 1983.

10. Joseph Y. Halpern and Yoav Shoham. A propositional modal logic of time intervals. In D. Gabbay and F. Guenther, editors, *Proceedings of the Symposium on Logic in Computer Science, IEEE*, Boston, 1986.

11. Hans Kamp. *Tense Logic and the Theory of Linear Order*. PhD thesis, University of California, Los Angeles, 1968.

12. Bernhard Nebel. Terminological Reasoning is Inherently Intractable. *Artificial Intelligence*, 43:235–249, 1990.

13. Rohit Parikh. Propositional dynamic logics of programs: A survey. In *Proceedings of the Workshop on Logic of Programs*, pages 102–144, Zürich, Switzerland, 1979.

14. Klaus Schild. A correspondence theory for terminological logics: Preliminary report. In *Proceedings of the 12th International Joint Conference on Artificial Intelligence*, pages 466–471, Sydney, Australia, 1991.

15. Klaus Schild. A tense-logical extension of terminological logics. KIT Report 92, Department of Computer Science, Technische Universität Berlin, Berlin, FRG, 1991.

16. Manfred Schmidt-Schauß and Gert Smolka. Attributive concept descriptions with complements. *Artificial Intelligence*, 48(1):1–26, 1991.

17. Albrecht Schmiedel. A Temporal Terminological Logic. In *Proceedings of the 9th National Conference of the American Association for Artificial Intelligence*, pages 640–645, Boston, Mass., 1990.

18. Johan van Benthem. *The Logic of Time*. Reidel, Dordrecht, Holland, 1984.

19. Moshe Y. Vardi and Pierre Wolper. Automata theoretic techniques for modal logics of programs (extended abstract). In *Proceedings of the 16th ACM Annual Symposium on Theory of Computing*, pages 446–456, Washington, D.C., 1984.

20. Pierre Wolper. Temporal logic can be more expressive. *Information & Control*, 56:72–99, 1983.

21. Pierre Wolper. The tableau method for temporal logic: An overview. *Logique et Analyse*, 110-111:119–136, 1985.

22. William A. Woods and James G. Schmolze. The KL-ONE family. In F.W. Lehmann, editor, *Semantic Networks in Artificial Intelligence*, pages 133–178. Pergamon Press, 1992.

Towards Complete Answers
in Concept Languages

Margarida Mamede and Luís Monteiro

Departamento de Informática
Universidade Nova de Lisboa
2825 Monte da Caparica, Portugal
{mm,lm}@fct.unl.pt

Abstract. In recent years, much attention has been given to concept-based knowledge bases. In spite of the fact that there are several well-known distinct problems, like consistency, coherence, subsumption, instantiation, realization and retrieval, they have been reduced to each other, whenever possible, in order to prove (in)tractability and (un)decidability results. Only for the first three problems, however, have efficient algorithms been studied. In particular, little attention has been given to the retrieval problem which computes the set of individuals that belong to a given concept in all models of the knowledge base.

Lenzerini and Schaerf studied the retrieval problem in [10, 11] and proposed using two concept languages: one for expressing the knowledge in the base and the other for making queries. However, their algorithm works by generate-and-test in the sense that it tests, for every individual i that occurs in the knowledge base, if a certain concept $C(i)$ (built from those concepts of the knowledge base associated with i) subsumes a subconcept of the query. The authors show that their query-answering algorithm is complete and tractable.

Our paper describes a similar system, but differs from the work of Lenzerini and Schaerf in two important respects. First, our query-answering algorithm is syntax-directed rather than of the generate-and-test sort, hence more efficient. This point is important in connection with actual implementations of the system. Second, we can provide answers that may refer to individuals whose existence may be deduced but have no explicit representation in the knowledge base. Thus, our answers are more complete, hence more informative to the user. We prove that our algorithm is also complete and tractable.

Keywords: Knowledge representation, concept languages, query answering, tractable reasoning.

1 Introduction

In recent years, much attention has been given to concept-based knowledge bases and several systems have been proposed: $\mathcal{KRIS}$ [2, 3, 7], KRIPTON [4], LOOM [12], BACK [16, 20], NIKL [18] and CLASSIC [19]. In spite of the fact that there are several well-known distinct problems, like consistency (or satisfiability), coherence, subsumption, instantiation, realization and retrieval (see [2, 3, 7, 17]), they have been reduced to each other, whenever possible, in order to prove (in)tractability and (un)decidability results. Only for the first three problems, however, have efficient algorithms been studied [6, 8, 9, 22]. In particular, little attention has been given to the retrieval problem which computes the set of individuals that belong to a given concept in all models of the knowledge base.

In those concept languages that allow negation of arbitrary concepts, such as $\mathcal{ALC}$ [1, 22] or $\mathcal{KRIS}$ [2, 3, 7], the retrieval problem is reduced to the satisfiability problem as follows. Given the concept C, we look for every individual i that occurs in the knowledge base Kb and conclude that i belongs to C if and only if $Kb \cup \{i : \neg C\}$ is inconsistent.

Recently, Schaerf [21] showed that retrieval can be strictly harder than satisfiability in $\mathcal{ALE}$, a language that does not allow negation of arbitrary concepts and in which satisfiability had been proved to be nondeterministic polynomial time [5].

Lenzerini and Schaerf studied the retrieval problem in [10, 11] and proposed using two concept languages: one for expressing the knowledge in the base and the other for making queries. Since the first language is not closed for negation of concepts of the second language, i.e., if Q is a query $\neg Q$ might not be a concept allowed in the knowledge base, the previous type of reasoning cannot be performed. However, their algorithm works also by generate-and-test in the sense that it tests, for every individual i that occurs in the knowledge base, if a certain concept $C(i)$ (built from those concepts of the knowledge base associated with i) subsumes a subconcept of the query. The authors show that their query-answering algorithm is complete and tractable.

Our paper describes a similar system, but differs from the work of Lenzerini and Schaerf in two important respects. First, our query-answering algorithm is syntax-directed rather than of generate-and-test sort, hence more efficient. This point is important in connection with actual implementations of the system. Second, we can provide answers that may refer to individuals whose existence may be deduced but have no explicit representation in the knowledge base. Thus, our answers are more complete, hence more informative to the user. We prove that our algorithm is also complete and tractable.

The rest of the paper is organized as follows. Section 2 describes the language in which the knowledge is expressed and presents a tractable algorithm for testing satisfiability of a knowlegde base. This algorithm works by computing the completion of the knowledge base. Several examples are included, as in all subsequent Sections, to explain the motivation of some notions or to illustrate some definitions.

Section 3 introduces the query language and the definition of answer, and describes an abstract query-answering algorithm which is sound, complete and polynomial with respect to the size of the knowledge base and the length of the query. This abstract algorithm is based on the completion of the knowledge base. An example illustrating in which sense our approach provides more complete answers than the existing frameworks is also presented.

Section 4 describes the main points of an existing implementation of the system. While the abstract query-answering algorithm, introduced in the previous Section, is based on the completion of the knowledge base whose size is polynomial in the size of the knowledge base, the prototype works directly on the knowledge base, a set that is significantly smaller than its completion. In Section 4.1 we define the notion of "empty expression", which is needed to simplify the most difficult case of the abstract algorithm, show how to compute the set of empty expressions in polynomial time and how to use it in the query-answering process. Then, in Section 4.2, we describe the main points of the prototype that deal with all the other cases.

Finally, Section 5 includes some comments on the research done in the paper and some directions of future work. Complete proofs of all stated results can be found in [15].

2 Knowledge Base

The assertional language in which the knowledge can be expressed is a tuple $\mathcal{AL} = (\text{Prim}, \text{Rel}, \text{Ind})$ of pairwise disjoint sets of *primitive concepts* $P \in \text{Prim}$, binary *relation* names $r \in \text{Rel}$ and *individuals* $i \in \text{Ind}$. A *concept* C is defined by the grammar

$$C \longrightarrow P \mid \neg P \mid C_1 \sqcap C_2 \mid \forall r.C' \mid \exists r$$

and an $\mathcal{AL}$-*assertion* is an expression of the form $i : C$ or $r(i_1, i_2)$. A *knowledge base* is a finite set of $\mathcal{AL}$-assertions.

Intuitively, a concept C denotes the set of individuals that belong to a primitive concept (P) or to its complement $(\neg P)$, those that are in the intersection of two concepts $(C_1 \sqcap C_2)$, or those whose image by the relation r is contained in C' $(\forall r.C')$ or is not empty $(\exists r)$. $\mathcal{AL}$-assertions state that "the individual i belongs to the concept C" or that "the pair of individuals (i_1, i_2) belongs to the relation r".

Let us give the intuitive meaning of the following knowledge base, Kb_1, assuming that **animal** is a primitive concept, **hunts** and **eats** are relation names and **lion** and **deer** are individuals:

hunts(lion,deer)	Lions hunt deers.
lion:∀hunts.animal	Lions hunt only animals.
lion:∀hunts.∃eats	Everything lions hunt eats something.
deer:∀eats.plant	Everything deers eat is a plant.

An *interpretation* of $\mathcal{AL} = (\text{Prim}, \text{Rel}, \text{Ind})$ is a pair $I = (\Delta^I, \cdot^I)$, where Δ^I is a nonempty set, called the *interpretation domain*, and $\cdot^I$ is the *interpretation function* which associates $P^I \subseteq \Delta^I$ with every $P \in \text{Prim}$, $r^I \subseteq \Delta^I \times \Delta^I$ with every $r \in \text{Rel}$ and $i^I \in \Delta^I$ with every $i \in \text{Ind}$ such that $i_1^I = i_2^I$ implies $i_1 = i_2$.

We denote by $r^I(a)$, with $a \in \Delta^I$, the set $\{b \mid (a, b) \in r^I\}$ and if $X \subseteq \Delta^I$, $r^I(X) = \bigcup_{a \in X} r^I(a)$. The interpretation function can be extended to arbitrary concepts in the following way:

- $(\neg P)^I = \Delta^I \setminus P^I$;
- $(C_1 \sqcap C_2)^I = C_1^I \cap C_2^I$;
- $(\forall r.C)^I = \{a \in \Delta^I \mid r^I(a) \subseteq C^I\}$;
- $(\exists r)^I = \{a \in \Delta^I \mid r^I(a) \neq \emptyset\}$.

Note that any concept is equivalent to a concept, called its *standard form*, that is a conjunction of concepts in the form $\forall r_1.\forall r_2 \ldots \forall r_n.C$ ($n \geq 0$), where C is a primitive concept, its complement, or an existential concept. Indeed, this follows from the equivalence of $\forall r.(C_1 \sqcap C_2)$ and $(\forall r.C_1) \sqcap (\forall r.C_2)$.

An interpretation I *satisfies* $i : C$ or $r(i_1, i_2)$ if $i^I \in C^I$ or $(i_1^I, i_2^I) \in r^I$, respectively. A knowledge base Kb is *satisfiable* if there is an interpretation I that satisfies all of its $\mathcal{AL}$-assertions. In this case, I is said to be a *model* of Kb. An $\mathcal{AL}$-assertion α is a *logical consequence* of the knowledge base Kb, and we write $Kb \models \alpha$, if every model of Kb satisfies α.

It is possible to check if a knowledge base Kb is satisfiable by generation of "propositions" that are logical consequences of Kb. For example, any model of Kb_1 satisfies both **deer:animal** and **deer:∃eats**. This last assertion states that in every model M of Kb_1 there is an element $a_M \in \Delta^M$ such that $(\mathbf{deer}^M, a_M) \in \mathbf{eats}^M$. It is useful to have denotations for such elements whose existence is guaranteed by existential assertions. In order to represent this kind of information, we define another language of assertions, $\mathcal{L}$, which accepts *terms* t of the form $i/r_1/ \cdots /r_n$, with $i \in \text{Ind}$, $r_1, \ldots, r_n \in \text{Rel}$ and $n \geq 0$. $\mathcal{L}$-*assertions* are either $t : C$ or $r(i_1, i_2)$.

In our previous example, the term **deer/eats** is used to represent "anything eaten by deers". More formally, the *denotation* of the term t by an interpretation I is defined as follows:

$$[i]^I = \{i^I\} \quad \text{and} \quad [t/r]^I = r^I([t]^I).$$

I *satisfies* $t : C$ if $\emptyset \neq [t]^I \subseteq C^I$ and, as before, satisfies $r(i_1, i_2)$ if $(i_1^I, i_2^I) \in r^I$.

Note that an $\mathcal{AL}$-assertion is an $\mathcal{L}$-assertion and that the two definitions of satisfiability coincide. When the distinction is not important or when it is clear from the context we will use only the word "assertion".

The abstract algorithm that tests the satisfiability of a knowledge base Kb starts with the set Kb to which it adds new $\mathcal{L}$-assertions by applying the four following rules until no more information can be generated. The final set is called the *completion* of Kb and is denoted by $\overline{Kb}$.

Precisely, $\overline{Kb}$ is the least set containing Kb such that:

(⊓-rule) If $t : C_1 \sqcap C_2 \in \overline{Kb}$ then $t : C_1 \in \overline{Kb}$ and $t : C_2 \in \overline{Kb}$.
(r∃-rule) If $r(i, i') \in \overline{Kb}$ then $i : \exists r \in \overline{Kb}$.
(∀r-rule) If $i : \forall r.C \in \overline{Kb}$ and $r(i, i') \in \overline{Kb}$ then $i' : C \in \overline{Kb}$.
(∀∃-rule) If $t : \forall r.C \in \overline{Kb}$ and $t : \exists r \in \overline{Kb}$ then $t/r : C \in \overline{Kb}$.

For example, the completion of Kb_1 comprises the following $\mathcal{L}$-assertions:

(1) `hunts(lion,deer)`
(2) `lion:∀hunts.animal`
(3) `lion:∀hunts.∃eats`
(4) `deer:∀eats.plant`
(5) `deer:animal`   by (1), (2) and (∀r-rule).
(6) `deer:∃eats`   by (1), (3) and (∀r-rule).
(7) `deer/eats:plant`   by (4), (6) and (∀∃-rule).
(8) `lion:∃hunts`   by (1) and (r∃-rule).
(9) `lion/hunts:animal` by (2), (8) and (∀∃-rule).
(10) `lion/hunts:∃eats` by (3), (8) and (∀∃-rule).

The next two propositions show that if the completion does not contain an obvious contradiction, the knowledge base is satisfiable, and that the completion process is always tractable. In fact, to state and prove these propositions, (r∃-rule) is not needed and its inclusion gives rise to useless assertions — from (8) to (10) in the example — from the point of view of the satisfiability of the knowledge base. However, since the abstract query-answering algorithm presented in the next Section is based on this completion of the knowledge base and (r∃-rule) does not affect the tractability result, we decided to include also this rule here to avoid future repetition of the rules.

Proposition 1. *A knowledge base Kb is satisfiable iff there do not exist a term t and a primitive concept P such that $\{t : P, t : \neg P\} \subseteq \overline{Kb}$.*

The *length* of an assertion $r(i_1, i_2)$ is 1 and the length of $t : C$ is equal to the number of subconcepts of C. For instance, `lion:∀hunts.∃eats` is of length 2. The *size* of a set of assertions X is a pair (N, D), where N is the cardinal of X and D is the maximum length of the assertions in X. For example, the size of Kb_1 is $(4, 2)$.

Proposition 2. *The completion of a knowledge base can be computed in polynomial time in the size of the knowledge base.*

3 Queries and Answers

The *query language* $\mathcal{Q_L}$, also defined over (Prim, Rel, Ind), is the following (with $n \geq 0$):

$$Q \longrightarrow P \mid \neg P \mid Q_1 \sqcap Q_2 \mid \forall r.Q' \mid \exists r.Q' \mid \{i_1, \ldots, i_n\}$$

If I is an interpretation of (Prim, Rel, Ind) we define (the other cases are defined as previously):

– $(\exists r.Q)^I = \{a \in \Delta^I \mid r^I(a) \cap Q^I \neq \emptyset\}$;
– $(\{i_1, \ldots, i_n\})^I = \{i_1^I, \ldots, i_n^I\}$.

We say that I *satisfies* $t : Q$ if $\emptyset \neq [t]^I \subseteq Q^I$.

From now on, let Kb be a satisfiable knowledge base whose $\mathcal{AL}$-assertions are in standard form. A *query* to Kb is a concept Q that satisfies the following property. If $\exists r.Q'$ is a subconcept of Q that is not in the scope of a universal quantifier, there is no subconcept of Q' of the form $\exists r'.Q''$[1]. The *answer* to Q is the set Answer(Kb, Q) of all terms t such that $Kb \models t : Q$.

Function CompAns(Kb, Q) =
    case Q of:

P	: return $\{t \mid t : P \in \overline{Kb}\}$
$\neg P$	: return $\{t \mid t : \neg P \in \overline{Kb}\}$
$\{i_1, \ldots, i_n\}$	: return $\{i_1, \ldots, i_n\}$
$Q_1 \sqcap Q_2$	: return CompAns(Kb, Q_1) $\cap$ CompAns(Kb, Q_2)
$\forall r.Q'$	: Decompose($Q, Q_1 \sqcap \ldots \sqcap Q_m$)
	return $\bigcap_{i=1}^{m}$ AnsUniv(Kb, Q_i)
$\exists r.Q'$	: return $\{t \mid t/r \in$ CompAns(Kb, Q') or
	$(\exists i)\ r(t, i) \in Kb, i \in$ CompAns(Kb, Q')$\}$

Function AnsUniv($Kb, \forall r_1 \ldots q_k r_k.C$) =
  return $\{t \mid$ condition (1) or condition (2) holds $\}$

(1) $\begin{cases} t : \forall r_1 \ldots \forall r_k.C \in \overline{Kb}; \\ t : \forall r_1 \ldots \forall r_{j-1}.\exists r_j \in \overline{Kb} \text{ whenever } q_j = \exists \text{ and } 2 \le j \le k. \end{cases}$

(2) $\begin{cases} \text{For some } 1 \le u \le k : \\ t : \forall r_1 \ldots \forall r_u.\bot \in \text{Null}(\overline{Kb}); \\ t : \forall r_1 \ldots \forall r_{j-1}.\exists r_j \in \overline{Kb} \text{ whenever } q_j = \exists \text{ and } 2 \le j \le u. \end{cases}$

Fig. 1. The Query-answering Algorithm.

The query-answering algorithm is presented in Figure 1. It can be easily seen by the code of CompAns(Kb, Q), the function that computes the answer to the query Q, that the most difficult queries begin with the universal quantifier. In this case, the procedure

$$\text{Decompose}(Q, Q_1 \sqcap \ldots \sqcap Q_m)$$

transforms the query Q into a conjunction of $m = n + 1$ queries Q_i where the symbol "$\sqcap$" does not occur (if n is the number of these symbols in Q) by applying the rules[2]:

- $\forall r.(Q_1' \sqcap Q_2') = (\forall r.Q_1') \sqcap (\forall r.Q_2')$;
- $\exists r.(Q_1' \sqcap Q_2') = (\exists r.Q_1') \sqcap (\exists r.Q_2')$.

---

[1] This restriction, similar to the ones imposed in [10, 11], is necessary to prove the completeness result.

[2] If concepts of the form $\exists r.C$ were allowed in $\mathcal{AL}$, the last rule would not be valid.

For example, if $Q = \forall r_1.\exists r_2.(P_1 \sqcap \neg P_2)$, the query $(\forall r_1.\exists r_2.P_1) \sqcap (\forall r_1.\exists r_2.\neg P_2)$ is returned. Then the function AnsUniv computes the answer to each

$$Q_i = \forall r_1 \ldots q_k r_k.Q',$$

with $q_j \in \{\forall, \exists\}$ for $2 \leq j \leq k$ and $k \geq 1$, and Q' a query of type P, $\neg P$ or $\{i_1, \ldots, i_p\}$. Finally, the answer to Q comprises the terms that are in the answer to all Q_i.

Before explaining AnsUniv(Kb, Q), let us introduce intuitively the kind of reasoning we perform. Suppose Kb_2 is the following knowledge base:

`lion:∀hunts.∃eats`	Everything lions hunt eats something.
`lion:∀hunts.∀eats.plant`	Everything eaten by what lions hunt is a plant.
`deer:∀hunts.animal`	Everything deers hunt is an animal.
`deer:∀hunts.¬animal`	Nothing deers hunt is an animal.

Suppose also that the query is $Q = $ `∀hunts.∃eats.plant` which asks for "the individuals such that everything they hunt eats plants". By the easiest case of AnsUniv — case (1) — `lion` belongs to the answer due to the first two assertions. However, it is also true that "everything deers hunt eats plants" because "there is nothing hunted by deers" in all models of Kb_2 — case (2) — due to the last two assertions.

To compute AnsUniv we need the notion of *null assertion* $t : \forall r_1 \ldots \forall r_u.\bot$ ($u \geq 1$) where $\bot$ is the *null concept* with $\bot^I = \emptyset$ for all interpretations I. Note that $t : \forall r_1 \ldots \forall r_k.C$ is true if $t : \forall r_1 \ldots \forall r_u.\bot$ is true for some $u \leq k$. We also need the set Null($\overline{Kb}$) of null assertions derived from $\overline{Kb}$, characterized as follows:

- If $t : \forall r_1 \ldots \forall r_u.P \in \overline{Kb}$ and $t : \forall r_1 \ldots \forall r_u.\neg P \in \overline{Kb}$
  then $t : \forall r_1 \ldots \forall r_u.\bot \in$ Null($\overline{Kb}$).
- If $t : \forall r_1 \ldots \forall r_u.\forall r_{u+1}.\bot \in$ Null($\overline{Kb}$) and $t : \forall r_1 \ldots \forall r_u.\exists r_{u+1} \in \overline{Kb}$
  then $t : \forall r_1 \ldots \forall r_u.\bot \in$ Null($\overline{Kb}$).

The justification of these rules is that $P \sqcap \neg P = \bot$ and $(\forall r.\bot) \sqcap \exists r = \bot$.

Let us explain case (2) of AnsUniv(Kb_3, Q) when $Q = \forall r_1.\exists r_2.\forall r_3.\exists r_4.P'$ and $\overline{Kb_3}$ is:

$$t : \forall r_1.\forall r_2.\forall r_3.\forall s_1.P$$
$$t : \forall r_1.\forall r_2.\forall r_3.\forall s_1.\neg P$$
$$t : \forall r_1.\forall r_2.\forall r_3.\exists s_1$$
$$t : \forall r_1.\exists r_2$$

Since $t : \forall r_1.\forall r_2.\forall r_3.\bot \in$ Null($\overline{Kb_3}$) by the first three assertions, we conclude that $[t]^M \subseteq [\forall r_1.\forall r_2.\forall r_3.Q']^M$ in all models M of Kb_3, for all queries Q'. Taking into account the last assertion, $[t]^M \subseteq [\forall r_1.\exists r_2.\forall r_3.Q']^M$ and, in particular, $[t]^M \subseteq [Q]^M$. To conclude that $t \in$ Answer(Kb, Q) we must have $[t]^M \neq \emptyset$, which follows from the fact that every term that occurs in the completion of a knowledge base has nonempty denotation in any model of the knowledge base.

It might seem that this query-answering algorithm is more complicated than the classical ones but this is due to the formalization of case (2) of AnsUniv.

However, there is another formalization of this function, which will be presented in Section 4.1.

The next proposition states the soundness and completeness of the query-answering algorithm.

Proposition 3. [Soundness/Completeness] CompAns(Kb, Q) = Answer(Kb, Q).

The *length of a query* Q is also the number of subconcepts of Q.

Proposition 4. *The query-answering algorithm has polynomial complexity with respect to the size of the knowledge base and the length of the query.*

Now we present an example illustrating in which sense our approach provides more complete answers than the existing frameworks. Suppose that we ask the following knowledge base Kb_4 what are the animals:

> hunts(lion,deer)
> lion:∀hunts.animal
> lion:∃eats
> lion:∀eats.animal
> deer:∀hunts.animal

The answer is {deer, lion/hunts, lion/eats}, interpreted as "deers" and "anything hunted or eaten by lions". Note that in any model of Kb_4 lions hunt (and eat) something and everything they hunt (eat) is an animal. Even though it is also true that everything deers hunt is an animal, the term deer/hunts does not belong to the answer because there are models of Kb_4 in which deers hunt nothing and we consider that informative answers should only comprise terms whose denotation is not empty (in all models).

At this level, the difference between our approach and all the other frameworks we know of is that we do not restrict ourselves to individuals. If we had defined Answer(Kb, Q) as the set of all individuals i such that $Kb \models i : Q$, like the other authors do [2, 3, 7, 10, 11, 17, 21], the answer to the previous example would be just {deer}.

4 Implementation

The abstract query-answering algorithm, presented in Figure 1, is based on the completion of the knowledge base, $\overline{Kb}$, and on the set of null assertions derived from it, Null($\overline{Kb}$). Although these sets have polynomial cardinality with respect to the size of the knowledge base (and our prototype could work on them), we developed a propotype that is based on two other sets: the knowledge base, Kb, and the set of "empty expressions" derived from Kb, EmptyExp(Kb). The idea behind the latter is to collect all the information needed in case (2) of AnsUniv(Kb, Q), namely, null assertions and (some) existential assertions.

In Section 4.1 we define "empty expression" and show how to compute the set EmptyExp(Kb) and how to use it in the query-answering algorithm. Then, in Section 4.2, we describe the main points of the prototype.

4.1 Empty Expressions

Let us introduce by examples the notion of "empty expression" and its use in the computation of case (2) of $\text{AnsUniv}(Kb, Q)$. By the definition of null assertion, given in Section 3, if Kb_5 $(= \overline{Kb_5})$ is:

$$i : \forall r_1.\forall r_2.\forall r_3.\forall s_1.P$$
$$i : \forall r_1.\forall r_2.\forall r_3.\forall s_1.\neg P$$
$$i : \forall r_1.\forall r_2.\forall r_3.\exists s_1$$
$$i : \forall r_1.\exists r_2$$

$\text{Null}(\overline{Kb_5})$ is the set with the following null assertions:

$$i : \forall r_1.\forall r_2.\forall r_3.\forall s_1.\bot$$
$$i : \forall r_1.\forall r_2.\forall r_3.\bot$$

As a consequence, the terms $i/r_1/r_2/r_3/s_1$ and $i/r_1/r_2/r_3$, obtained by concatenating the term on the left hand side of a null assertion with all the relations on the right hand side of that null assertion, and called *empty terms* of Kb_5, verify:

$$[i/r_1/r_2/r_3/s_1]^M = \emptyset \quad \text{and} \quad [i/r_1/r_2/r_3]^M = \emptyset$$

for any model M of Kb_5. The advantage of using this term notation is that it is often more compact. For example, if Kb_6 was $Kb_5 \cup \{i : \exists r_1\}$, its completion, $\overline{Kb_6}$, would be:

$$
\begin{array}{lll}
i : \forall r_1.\forall r_2.\forall r_3.\forall s_1.P & i/r_1 : \forall r_2.\forall r_3.\forall s_1.P & i/r_1/r_2 : \forall r_3.\forall s_1.P \\
i : \forall r_1.\forall r_2.\forall r_3.\forall s_1.\neg P & i/r_1 : \forall r_2.\forall r_3.\forall s_1.\neg P & i/r_1/r_2 : \forall r_3.\forall s_1.\neg P \\
i : \forall r_1.\forall r_2.\forall r_3.\exists s_1 & i/r_1 : \forall r_2.\forall r_3.\exists s_1 & i/r_1/r_2 : \forall r_3.\exists s_1 \\
i : \forall r_1.\exists r_2 & i/r_1 : \exists r_2 & \\
i : \exists r_1 & &
\end{array}
$$

and the set $\text{Null}(\overline{Kb_6})$ would comprise:

$$
\begin{array}{lll}
i : \forall r_1.\forall r_2.\forall r_3.\forall s_1.\bot & i/r_1 : \forall r_2.\forall r_3.\forall s_1.\bot & i/r_1/r_2 : \forall r_3.\forall s_1.\bot \\
i : \forall r_1.\forall r_2.\forall r_3.\bot & i/r_1 : \forall r_2.\forall r_3.\bot & i/r_1/r_2 : \forall r_3.\bot
\end{array}
$$

while the empty terms of Kb_6 would be exactly the same, i.e., $i/r_1/r_2/r_3/s_1$ and $i/r_1/r_2/r_3$.

On the other hand, empty terms (and null assertions) do not contain all the information needed to compute case (2) of $\text{AnsUniv}(Kb, Q)$ and the existential information that is missing is integrated as follows. If there is an existential assertion concerning relation r_j, the symbol before r_j is "/", as previously, otherwise, the symbol is "?". More precisely, an *empty expression* of Kb has the form $t|_1 r_1 \cdots |_u r_u$ where $|_j \in \{/, ?\}$ for $1 \leq j \leq u$ and $u \geq 1$, such that:

- $t/r_1 \cdots /r_u$ is an empty term of Kb
  (that is, $t : \forall r_1 \ldots \forall r_u.\bot$ is a null assertion derived for $\overline{Kb}$);
- $|_j = /$ if and only if $t : \forall r_1 \ldots \forall r_{j-1}.\exists r_j \in \overline{Kb}$.

For example, $i?r_1/r_2?r_3/s_1$ and $i?r_1/r_2?r_3$ are empty expressions of Kb_5, and $i/r_1/r_2?r_3/s_1$ and $i/r_1/r_2?r_3$ are empty expressions of Kb_6.

Finally, since some empty expressions (e.g. $i?r_1/r_2?r_3/s_1$) can be seen as particular cases of the others (e.g. $i?r_1/r_2?r_3$), and we are interested in reducing space, the information stored in EmptyExp(Kb) concerns only the most general empty expressions, i.e., those for which there is no proper prefix that is also an empty expression.

Function EmptyExp(Kb) =
    $X \leftarrow Kb$ $Y \leftarrow \emptyset$
    repeat
        $X \leftarrow \overline{X \cup Y}$
        $Y \leftarrow \{e?r : C \mid e : \forall r.C \in X,\ e : \exists r \notin X\}$
    until $Y = \emptyset$
    return $\{e?r \mid (\exists e', P)\ e' : P, e' : \neg P \in X, e' = e?r/s_1/\cdots/s_n\ (n \geq 0)\}$

Function AnsUniv2($Kb, \forall r_1 \ldots q_k r_k.C$) =
    return $\{t \mid$ condition (1) or condition (2) holds $\}$
        (1) (As in Figure 1.)
        (2) $\begin{cases} \text{For some } t|_1 r_1 \cdots |_u r_u \in \text{EmptyExp}(Kb) : \\ r_1, \ldots, r_u \text{ is a prefix of } r_1, \ldots, r_k; \\ |_j = /\ \text{whenever } q_j = \exists \text{ and } 2 \leq j \leq u. \end{cases}$

Fig. 2. The Second Version of AnsUniv(Kb, Q).

The algorithm that computes the set EmptyExp(Kb), presented in Figure 2, makes use of the completion algorithm. Instead of the letter "t" that stands for terms, we used the letter "e" for representing expressions, which can be seen as terms where some symbols "/" were possibly replaced by "?". Note that the set returned by the algorithm could be simply written $\{e?r \mid e?r :\perp\in \text{Null}(X)\}$, but we have chosen the displayed form because it is algorithmically simpler.

The second version of the function AnsUniv(Kb, Q) is also in Figure 2. Now, case (2) reduces to find out empty expressions $t|_1 r_1 \cdots |_u r_u$ such that t is a term (that will belong to the answer), the sequence of relations $r_1, \ldots, r_u$ is a prefix of the sequence of relations of the query, and whenever the symbol "$\exists$" occurs in the query prefix, there is a corresponding "/" in the expression.

For instance, CompAns($Kb_6, \forall r_1.\exists r_2.\forall r_3.\exists r_4.P'$) = $\{i\}$ due to the empty expression $i/r_1/r_2?r_3$ of Kb_6, CompAns($Kb_6, \forall r_2.\forall r_3.\exists r_4.P'$) = $\{i/r_1\}$ for the same reason and CompAns($Kb_5, \forall r_2.\forall r_3.\exists r_4.P'$) = $\emptyset$ because $i?r_1$ is not a term (and this implies that there is a model in which its denotation is empty, so it cannot belong to any answer).

The next proposition shows that AnsUniv2(Kb, Q) works fine, as expected.

Proposition 5. AnsUniv(Kb, Q) = AnsUniv2(Kb, Q).

Proposition 6. *Let Kb be any satisfiable knowledge base.*
The set EmptyExp(Kb) *can be computed in polynomial time in the size of Kb.*
Moreover, the second version of the query-answering algorithm has polynomial
complexity with respect to the size of Kb and the length of the query.

4.2 Prototype

We developed a prototype in Prolog that works directly on the knowledge base
Kb and on the set EmptyExp(Kb). Since the query-answering algorithm is based
on $\overline{Kb}$, except the second case of AnsUniv2(Kb, Q) which requires EmptyExp(Kb),
the idea is to "compute" the subset of the completion that is needed to answer a
query, only when the query is asked. If the query begins with a universal quantifier, the set EmptyExp(Kb) is then used to find out more terms that belong to
the answer, as described previously. Note that the algorithm that computes this
set should run after each update of the knowledge base as the one that checks
its satisfiability.

Let us begin with the way $\mathcal{AL}$-assertions are stored:

- Each primitive concept P is a predicate of arity two. The first argument
  concerns the assertions that end with P and the second argument concerns
  those ending with $\neg P$. We omit the symbols "$\forall$" in coded assertions.
  E.g., $\{i : P, i' : \forall r.P, i'' : \forall r.\forall r'.\neg P\}$ is translated into $P([i, i' : r], [i'' : r.r'])$;
- Assertions ending with an existential quantifier, $i : \forall r_1 \ldots \forall r_n.\exists r_{n+1}$ $(n \geq 0)$,
  are transformed in unary predicates, $r_{n+1}(i : r_1 \ldots r_n)$;
- Relations $r(i, i')$ remain unchanged.

The kernel of our prototype is an algorithm that, given an entity of the form
$i : s_1 \ldots s_m$, computes an appropriate set of terms t which are nonempty in all
models. As a first example, suppose we ask the query $\forall$eats.plant to Kb_7:

Assertions	Coded Assertions
hunts(lion,deer)	hunts(lion,deer)
lion:∀hunts.∀eats.plant	plant([lion:hunts.eats],[])

The terms t that belong to the answer must verify $t : \forall$eats.plant$\in \overline{Kb_7}$ so
they must be obtained by applying the rules ($\forall r$-rule) or ($\forall\exists$-rule) to the second
assertion, meaning that they are obtained from the individual lion and the
relation hunts, which we call being generated by lion:hunts. In this case, the
answer is {deer,lion/hunts}.

More generally, to answer queries Q of type $\forall r_1.q_2 r_2 \ldots q_n r_n.(\neg)P$ $(n \geq 0)$,
the system has to find out the terms t such that $t : \forall r_1.\forall r_2 \ldots \forall r_n.(\neg)P$ belongs
to the completion of the knowledge base but these terms are somehow generated
by $i : s_1 \ldots s_m$ such that $i : s_1 \ldots s_m.r_1.r_2 \ldots r_n$ belongs to the first (second) list
associated with P.

It can be proved that all terms that belong to the answer to a query that
begins with the universal quantifier and ends with a set of individuals come

from the second case of AnsUniv2(Kb, Q). On the other hand, conjunctions and queries that begin with an existential quantifier are treated recursively, so the previous cases also apply.

Let us see the main idea behind the algorithm that computes the terms t generated by $i : s_1.s_2 \ldots s_m$. To begin with, let $S \leftarrow \{i\}$ and $j \leftarrow 1$. While $S \neq \emptyset$ and $j \leq m$, the image of t by the relation s_j, written $s_j[t]$, is computed for every $t \in S$, and $j \leftarrow j + 1$. When this loop ends, the result is in S. Now, there are three cases:

1. In case t is an individual, $s_j[t] = \{i' \mid s_j(t, i') \in Kb\}$ if this set is not empty.
2. In case t is not an individual or the previous set is empty, $s_j[t] = \{t/s_j\}$ if there is an existential assertion $s_j(x) \in Kb$ and t is generated by x.
3. Otherwise, $s_j[t] = \emptyset$.

Note that we conclude that $t = j/r_1/\cdots/r_n$, $(n \geq 0)$, is generated by x when:

- $x = j' : r'_1 \ldots r'_k.r_1 \ldots r_n$, $(k \geq 0)$, and
- j is generated by $j' : r'_1 \ldots r'_k$, which can be computed by an algorithm equal to the one we are presenting, except that $s_j[t]$ is always $\{i' \mid s_j(t, i') \in Kb\}$.

We conclude with an example. Suppose Kb_8 is the following knowledge base:

Assertions	Coded Assertions
hunts(lion,deer)	hunts(lion,deer)
hunts(lion,antelope)	hunts(lion,antelope)
hunts(lion,zebra)	hunts(lion,zebra)
eats(deer,grass)	eats(deer,grass)
antelope:∃eats	eats(antelope)
stripes:∀hairPatternOf.∃eats	eats(stripes:hairPatternOf)
hairPatternOf(stripes,zebra)	hairPatternOf(stripes,zebra)
hairPatternOf(stripes,tiger)	hairPatternOf(stripes,tiger)
lion:∀hunts.∀eats.plant	plant([lion:hunts.eats],[])

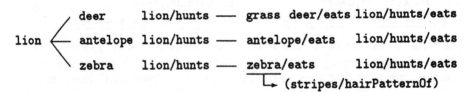

Fig. 3. The Terms Generated by lion:hunts.eats.

Figure 3 shows the logical dependencies that are established to compute the terms generated by lion:hunts.eats. First, by case (1.), hunts[lion] is the set {deer, antelope, zebra} and, again by (1.), eats[deer] = {grass}. We also reach antelope/eats and zebra/eats by applying case (2.) with the assertions eats(antelope), in the first case, and eats(stripes:hairPatternOf) and `hairPatternOf(stripes,zebra)`, in the second one. All the other terms are generated automatically. For instance, the term `lion/hunts` is generated three times due to the assertions `hunts(lion,deer)`, `hunts(lion,antelope)` and `hunts(lion,zebra)`.

If we ask Kb_8 for the plants, the system is able to give the structured answer:

"Those that are eaten by what lions hunt, which comprise:
>the elements eaten by deers,
>>like grass;
>the elements eaten by antelopes;
>the elements eaten by zebras."

5 Conclusion and Future Work

The purpose of the work described in this paper was twofold. On the one hand, we wanted to extend the definition of answer in order to provide information that in spite of being available in the knowledge base is not expressible in terms of individuals only. To this end, we introduced the notion of term, which extends that of individual, and defined answer as the set of all terms whose nonempty denotation is contained in the denotation of the query. In addition, we developed a prototype that is able to structure the answer. Since these nonempty terms can be seen as descriptions of some elements that exist in all models of the knowledge base, some descriptions are given as particular cases of the others. So, our answers are more complete and more informative than the usual ones. Note that we do not consider that they are more concise. Actually we admit that our answers are more complex, mainly because the enumeration of individuals is still given, not to mention that the same individual may occur more than once. Nevertheless, this work shows that answers in concept languages may refer to structured terms and need not be restricted to individuals only. A partially order relation defined over these terms and reflecting denotation containment, and a new definition of answers that filters the maximal elements (of the current answer), are required to achieve conciseness. But this has been left for future work.

On the other hand, we wanted to develop an efficient query-answering algorithm. Although the classical procedures are also tractable when applied to this simple languages (see [10, 11]), they generate all individuals of the knowledge base and test, for each one, if its denotation is an element of the query denotation, either by subsumption of concepts or by inconsistency of a set of assertions. In our case, since we have established the relationship between the syntax of the query and the syntax of the assertions of the completion of the knowledge base that produce terms to the answer, the algorithm fetches directly these relevant assertions and selects the corresponding terms. Besides, once this step has been taken we were able to reduce space and the prototype works on the knowledge base instead of on its completion.

Concerning future work, there are two topics we are interested in investigating. First, we are studying a more powerful language that will take the place of both $\mathcal{AL}$ and $\mathcal{Q_L}$, which are obviously insufficient to specify and query practical knowledge bases. As an example, it will be possible to state that lions eat every herbivore they attack. The main drawback we are aware of is that tractability will not be preserved. Second, we want to be able to give concise answers. Besides solving the problem mentioned previously, we would like to extend this framework in order to deal with a taxonomy of atomic types (like the ones presented in [13, 14]) instead of just with a set of individuals. This integration will give rise to more concise answers, in the sense that, for instance, the atomic type **human** will be returned instead of **man** and **woman**. On the other hand, the assertion **human:∃motherOf.female** will state that every man and every woman have a (female) mother.

Acknowledgements

This work was partially supported by JNICT and BRA 6810 COMPULOG II. Margarida Mamede owns a scholarship from JNICT. We would like to thank the referees for their comments and suggestions.

References

1. F. Baader, H.-J. Bürckert, B. Hollunder, W. Nutt, J. Siekmann. Concept Logics. In *Proc. Symposium on Computational Logic*. J. W. Lloyd (ed.), ESPRIT Basic Research Series, DG XIII, Springer-Verlag, 1990.
2. F. Baader, B. Hollunder. KRIS: Knowledge Representation and Inference System. *SIGART Bulletin*, 2(3):8-14, 1991.
3. F. Baader, B. Hollunder. A Terminological Knowledge Representation System with Complete Inference Algorithms. Em *Proc. International Workshop PDK'91*, Kaiserslautern, H. Boley and M. M. Richter (eds.), LNAI 567, Springer-Verlag, 1991.
4. R. Brachman, R. Fikes, H. Levesque. KRYPTON: A Functional Approach to Knowledge Representation. In *Readings in Knowledge Representation*, R. Brachman and H. Levesque (eds.), Morgan Kaufmann, 1985.
5. F. Donini, M. Lenzerini, D. Nardi, B. Hollunder, W. Nutt, A. Spaccamela. The complexity of existential quantification in concept languages. *Artificial Intelligence*, 53(2-3):309-327, 1992.
6. F. Donini, M. Lenzerini, D. Nardi, W. Nutt. Tractable Concept Languages. In *Proc. 12th International Joint Conference on Artificial Intelligence*, Sidney, 1991.
7. B. Hollunder. *Hybrid Inferences in KL-ONE-based Knowledge Representation Systems*. DFKI Research Report RR-90-06, DFKI, Postfach 2080, D-6750 Kaiserslautern, Germany, 1990.
8. B. Hollunder, W. Nutt. *Subsumption Algorithms for Concept Languages*. DFKI Research Report RR-90-04, DFKI, Postfach 2080, D-6750 Kaiserslautern, Germany, 1990.
9. H. Levesque, R. Brachman. A Fundamental Tradeoff in Knowledge Representation and Reasoning. In *Readings in Knowledge Representation*, R. Brachman and H. Levesque (eds.), Morgan Kaufmann, 1985.

10. M. Lenzerini, A. Schaerf. Concept Languages as Query Languages. In *Proc. 9th National Conference of the American Association for Artificial Intelligence*, AAAI, 1991.

11. M. Lenzerini, A. Schaerf. Querying Concept-based Knowledge Bases. In *Proc. International Workshop PDK'91*, Kaiserslautern, H. Boley and M. M. Richter (eds.), LNAI 567, Springer-Verlag, 1991.

12. R. MacGregor. Inside the LOOM Description Classifier. *SIGART Bulletin*, 2(3):88-92, 1991.

13. M. Mamede, L. Monteiro. A Constraint-Based Language for Querying Taxonomic Systems. In *Proc. 5th Portuguese Conference on Artificial Intelligence*, P. Barahona, L. Moniz Pereira and A. Porto (eds.), LNAI 541, Springer-Verlag, 1991.

14. M. Mamede, L. Monteiro. A Constraint Logic Programming Scheme for Taxonomic Reasoning. In *Logic Programming: Proc. Joint International Conference and Symposium on Logic Programming*, K. Apt (ed.), MIT Press, 1992.

15. M. Mamede, L. Monteiro. *Bases de Conhecimento Baseadas em Conceitos com Algoritmos de Resposta Completos e Tratáveis*. Technical Report RT 11/92-DI/UNL, Universidade Nova de Lisboa, 1992.

16. B. Nebel. Computational Complexity of Terminological Reasoning in BACK. *Artificial Intelligence*, 34(3):371-383, 1988.

17. B. Nebel. *Reasoning and Revision in Hybrid Representation Systems*. LNAI 422, Springer-Verlag, 1990.

18. P. F. Patel-Schneider. Undecidability of Subsumption in NIKL. *Artificial Intelligence*, 39(2):263-272, 1989.

19. P. Patel-Schneider, D. McGuinness, R. Brachman, L. Resnick, A. Borgida. The CLASSIC Knowledge Representation System: Guiding Principles and Implementation Rationale. *SIGART Bulletin*, 2(3):108-113, 1991.

20. C. Peltason. The BACK System – An Overview. *SIGART Bulletin*, 2(3):114-119, 1991.

21. A. Schaerf. On the Role of Subsumption Algorithms in Concept Languages. To appear in *Proc. 7th International Symposium on Methodologies for Intelligence Systems*, Trondheim, Norway, June 1993.

22. M. Schmidt-Schauß, G. Smolka. Attributive Concept Descriptions with Complements. *Artificial Intelligence*, 48(1):1-26, 1991.

Version Space Algorithms on Hierarchies with Exceptions

Grigoris Antoniou

University of Osnabrück
Dept. of Mathematics and Computer Science
Albrechtstrasse 28, D-4500 Osnabrück, Germany
e-mail: ga@informatik.uni-osnabrueck.de

Abstract. In this paper, we present version space algorithms working on hierarchies with exceptions, exceptions meaning that some nodes may not be covered by some of their predecessors. Such representations are known from nonmonotonic reasoning. We give formal definitions and correctness results for the algorithms. Then we discuss what happens when the background knowledge is slightly modified by introduction of a new exception. Here lies the major advantage of our approach: when the knowledge is dynamically (nonmonotonically) modified, it is still possible to save almost all of the learned information instead of having to restart the version space learning method from scratch. Finally, we discuss the version space method in case several hierarchy trees (with or without exceptions) are combined to form a conjunctive concept.

1 Motivation

Knowledge representation is an issue increasingly gaining attention in machine learning. Interest is turning away from simple representation methods like propositional taxonomies (for example [5,8]) to more expressive representations like predicate logic ([1,6,7]). In the present paper, we shall take another way by considering *hierarchies with exceptions* that are more general than taxonomies, while not being too far from them. Hierarchies with exceptions are known from *nonmonotonic reasoning*. Whereas attention in knowledge representation and machine learning has been focussed on monotonic methods and logics, it is our belief that nonmonotonic reasoning is a crucial issue for modeling intelligent behavior, and must therefore be taken into account. Thus our work is also a contribution to combining learning with nonmonotonicity.

We present a family of version space algorithms, depending on the definition of the 'covers' relation, and present correctness results. The variety of algorithms is due to the several possibilities of interpreting exceptions (see subsection 3.2 for details).

The main reason for choosing a nonmonotonic representation is the ability to deal with dynamic modifications of knowledge in a proper manner. We analyze what may happen when the background knowledge is slightly modified in form of new exceptions. This is a main advantage of our approach: if the hierarchy must only be slightly modified (in form of new exceptions) the information learned so far is further usable (in a modified form) and does not have to be learned from scratch.

Finally, we combine several hierarchies with exceptions (one for each characteristic of the concept to be learned) to form a directed graph, and show how the new version space method works on this extended representation.

2 Hierarchies with Exceptions

Consider a hierarchy of flying creatures including relations like

> Birds are flying creatures.
> Insects are flying creatures.
> Ostriches are birds.
> etc.

and suppose that we learn about penguins that they are birds but cannot fly. This situation is especially usual in changing environments, or during multi- strategy learning, when the results of a learning method have consequences for learning in another context. In our case, if the background knowledge stems from a learning process using other learning methods, a nonmonotonic revision of parts of the background knowledge should not be surprising.

Therefore, more flexible knowledge representations should be considered that are not only more expressive but also give a possibility to add new knowledge of specific kinds without having to reorganize the whole knowledge. Such a representation method is *hierarchies with exceptions*. In order to take advantage of this flexibility, learning methods running on strict hierarchies should be extended to deal with the new knowledge without having to start from the beginning. In the present paper we show how this can be done for version spaces.

The representation method for background knowledge

For hierarchies with exceptions, knowledge is given as a tree with nodes denoting properties or individuals, and positive links connecting such nodes; this hierarchy relation is denoted by < ('direct predecessor'). Note that paths of this tree represent reasoning chains. Classical hierarchies would regard links of the tree as being strict. Here we introduce a means for nonmonotonic behavior by allowing *exceptions* to links (which are thus interpreted as being revisable). Any node n can be an exception to a link placed 'above' n. Consider for example the following knowledge items:

> Generally, molluscs are shell-bearers.
> Cephalopods are molluscs.
> Cephalopods are not shell-bearers.
> Nautiluses are cephalopods.

Note that the interpretation of exceptions has not been laid down yet: we know that *shell-bearer* will neither include *cephalopod* nor *nautilus*, but we do not know how concepts above *shell-bearer* are affected by the exception. There are several possibilities of exception interpretation leading to different notions of the 'covers' relation (see subsection 3.2 for more details).

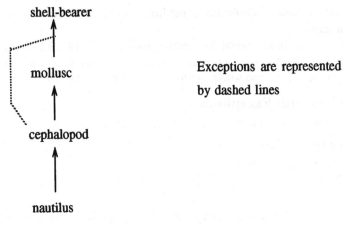

Figure 1

Also note that addition of new exceptions into a hierarchy changes its meaning by invalidating some conclusions that were formerly possible; it is the sort of nonmonotonic, dynamic behavior we shall discuss in section 4.

Why are new version space algorithms needed?

The classical version space algorithm is working only on strict hierarchies (stated another way, the syntactic concept 'above' is equivalent to the semantic concept 'includes'). Therefore, it cannot deal with exceptions in a reasonable way. The theme of this paper is to show how the classical algorithm can be extended to the expanded class of problems described above.

3 Version Space for Hierarchies with Exceptions

3.1 The Classical Version Space Algorithm

Given are
- the background knowledge in form of one or several hierarchies; the nodes of this hierarchy are taken from a language L (we use the same language for expressing concepts and examples; the language of examples consists of the terminal nodes in the hierarchy).

- a set of positive examples $P \subseteq L$

- a set of negative examples $N \subseteq L$.

We are looking for a concept $c \in L$ such that c covers all positive examples from P and no negative example from N (in this case we say that c *is consistent with* P *and* N).

The version space algorithm maintains sets G and S of most general resp. most specific concepts compatible with the examples presented so far. In case T consists of only one hierarchy (tree) and the first example presented is positive, G and S are singletons.

The update of G and S, given a new example, can be easily realized by operations on trees (see [3] for details). Here is a simple example (a fragment of geographic knowledge):

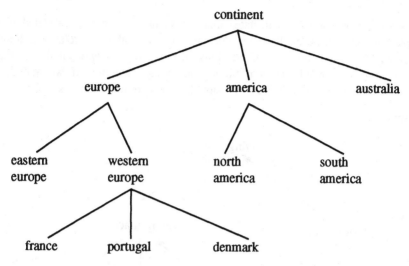

Figure 2

First positive example: france

G={continent}, S={france}

2. example:australia negative

G={europe}, S={france}

3. example: portugal negative

G={europe}, S={western europe}

3.2 Variants of the 'covers' Relation

The relation 'covers' is central in the classical version space algorithm. Here, it has to be modified to take exceptions into account (e.g. in the example above *shell-bearer* does not cover *nautilus*). There are several possibilities for doing so, leading to different algorithms. So seen, we shall present a *family of version space algorithms* for hierarchies with exceptions. The choice of the appropriate definition of 'covers' *is a question of knowledge representation* and depends on the problem considered. Let us give some natural possibilities for such definitions.

Variant 1 Node n *covers* node n' iff there is a path $n_0 n_1 \ldots n_k$ in the hierarchy tree with $n_0 = n'$, $n_k = n$, and for no $i \in \{1, \ldots, k\}$ exists a $j < i$ such that n_j is an exception to the link connecting n_{i-1} with n_i. n is called *more general than* n', n' *more specific than* n.

Variant 2 Node n *covers* node n' iff there is a path $n_0 n_1 \ldots n_k$ in the hierarchy tree with $n_0 = n'$, $n_k = n$, and n_0 is not an exception to the link connecting n_{k-1} with n_k.

Variant 1 is natural, as it states that a reasoning chain is invalidated if interrupted by an exception. Whereas this view is reasonable for relational logical reasoning, it is often too strict if we think in terms of concepts: In the example from section 2, it would prevent birds from being creatures, if we added the rule 'Flying creatures are creatures'. Version 2 is far more liberal in this sense.

Example

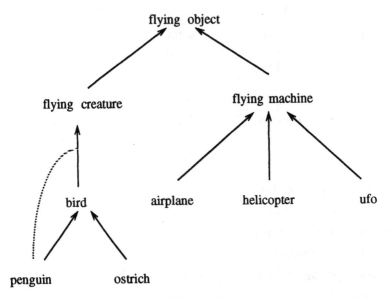

Figure 3

According to variant 1, *flying object* does not cover *penguin*, whereas according to variant 2 it does. So, in this case variant 1 is preferable. Note though that in other cases variant 2 can be more suitable, for example if we replace *flying object* by *creature*, which should include *penguin*.

Other variants are also conceivable, whose strength lies between the both definitions above. For example, the following:

Variant 3 Node n *covers* node n' iff there is a path $n_0 n_1 \ldots n_k$ in the hierarchy tree with $n_0 = n'$, $n_k = n$, and no n_j with $j < k$ is an exception to the link connecting n_{k-1} with n_k.

We would like to point out the distinction between the syntactic concept of 'above' (the reflexive and transitive closure of the hierarchy relation $<$) and the semantic concept of 'includes' or 'covers' once again: whereas they are equivalent

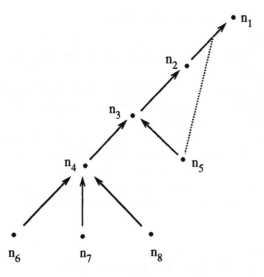

Figure 4

in (monotonic) hierarchies, they are no longer identical once exceptions are added, since 'above' does no longer imply 'covers'. In the following, the version space algorithms are defined in terms of the semantic-oriented 'covers' relation.

3.3 The new version space algorithms

Given are

- the background knowledge in form of a hierarchy with exceptions; the nodes of this hierarchy are taken from a language L (we use the same language for expressing concepts and examples; the language of examples consists of the terminal nodes in the hierarchy).
- a set of positive examples $P \subseteq L$
- a set of negative examples $N \subseteq L$.

We are looking for a concept $c \in L$ such that c covers all positive examples from P and no negative example from N (in this case we say that c *is consistent with* P *and* N).

The main problem in defining a version space method on hierarchies with exceptions is that, in the presence of exceptions, the relation 'covers' is no longer transitive, thus allowing gaps between s and g (the most specific resp. general concept compatible with P and N). Consider, for example, the hierarchy in Figure 4.

Suppose the positive examples $P = \{n_6, n_7\}$ and the negative example $N = \{n_5\}$ have been presented so far. Then, n_1 and n_4 are consistent with this set of examples, but not n_2 and n_3 (as they cover n_5).

So, there is not much sense in maintaining and manipulating the boundaries (as in the classical algorithm). We should rather *maintain the version space itself.*

Based on this idea, the algorithm (family) looks as follows:

- The first positive example lays down the *'main path'*, along which the rest of the algorithm works (note that this is so because we are working on hierarchy *trees* with exceptions).
- The nodes along the main path are marked as *consistent* or *inconsistent*, depending on whether they cover the first positive example or not (according to the appropriate definition of 'covers').
- For each new example, we work up from the example towards the root, and change, if necessary, the marking of some nodes on the main path to *inconsistent*. Note that according to all discussed variants of 'covers', the relevant exceptions and their target links are found on the way from the example to the root, so no additional computational effort is necessary.

Example

Consider the hierarchy with exceptions in the following figure.

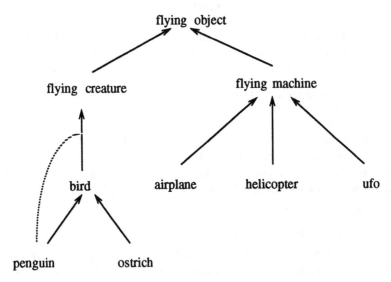

Figure 5

Let *ostrich* be the first positive example. Then, the path from *ostrich* to *flying object* is the main path, and all nodes in this path are marked consistent as they cover *ostrich*. Let *airplane* be a negative example given next. Then, *flying object* is marked as inconsistent, as it covers the negative example. Let *penguin* be a positive example given next. On the way towards the root, *bird* is the first node on the main path found. All nodes beneath it, in our case *ostrich*, are marked as inconsistent since they do not cover the new positive example. Also, *flying creature* becomes inconsistent, as it does not cover *penguin* due to the existing exception (this follows by the exception with origin *penguin*; the relevant information was collected on our way from *penguin* towards the root). The only consistent concept on the main path after this example is *bird*, so the algorithm terminates with success.

Now we give a formal concretization of the above informal description for the first variant of 'covers'.

Initialization Phase
Let p be the first positive example.

> Let x:=p; Exc:= set of exceptions with origin p;
> Found:=false; mark(p):= consistent;
> WHILE x≠Root DO
> > x:=up(x);
> > IF Found OR there is an exception in Exc
> > with target the last link we went up
> > THEN mark(x):=inconsistent; Found:=true
> > ELSE mark(x):=consistent;
> > > Exc:=Exc∪{exceptions with origin x}
> > END
> END

Running Phase
Let n be a new negative example.

> Let x:=n; Exc:= set of exceptions of n; Found:=false;
> WHILE NOT Found AND x not on the main path DO
> > x:=up(x); Exc:=Exc∪{exceptions with origin x};
> > IF there is an exception in Exc with target the
> > last link we went up
> > THEN Found:=true
> > END
> END;
> (∗ x is the lowest common node of the main path
> and the path from n to the root ∗)
> IF Found THEN terminate END;
> WHILE x≠Root DO
> > mark(x):=inconsistent;
> > x:=up(x);
> > IF there is an exception in Exc with target the
> > last link we went up
> > THEN terminate
> > ELSE Exc:=Exc∪{exceptions with origin x}
> > END
> END

A new positive example is treated in an analogous way.

The following correctness result states that the algorithm above maintains the version space (space of concepts consistent with the examples presented so far) in a correct manner.

Theorem *After the Initialization Phase and after each execution of the Running Phase, a node on the main path is marked consistent if and only if it is consistent with all examples presented so far.*

Proof outline

We give the loop invariants for the loops in the Initialization and Running Phase. The rest follows directly by the definition of the first variant of *covers*. The invariant for the loop in the Initialization Phase is the following:

Found=false $\Rightarrow$ Exc = {set of exceptions with origin y between p and x}

Found=true $\Leftrightarrow$ there is an exception in Exc with target a link below x

For all y between p and x: marked(y)=consistent $\Leftrightarrow$ y covers p

The invariant for the first loop in the Running Phase is the following:

All y below x are not on the main path

Found=true $\Leftrightarrow$

there is a y$\leq$*x such that for all z between y and x
z does not cover n (in variant 1).

The invariant for the second loop is as follows:

Exc = {set of exceptions with origin y, where y lies between n and x}

For all y$\leq$*x on the main path, y covers n (in variant 1)

For all y$\leq$*x on the main path, mark(y)=inconsistent

(note that $\leq$* is the syntactic 'above' relation, not to be confused with 'covers') In case the second loop is stopped in the THEN case, all concepts from x to the root remain unaffected since they do not cover n. By induction hypothesis (induction on the number of executions of the Running Phase, i.e. on the number of presented examples), their marking are correct. The same applies in case the second loop is not executed at all. ∎

One remark concerning combination of several versions of the covers relation is in order: it is possible that in one hierarchy, some exceptions are interpreted according to one variant, whereas other exceptions are interpreted according to another variant. 'Mixed handling' of exceptions can be integrated into the version space algorithm running on such hierarchies. We hope we have made clear that the information needed to interpret exceptions correctly can in any case be collected when working from the new example presented towards the root. We restricted discussion to variant 1 because of space limitations, but would like to point out that it is the hardest variant to be treated. For more details, please refer to [2].

4 Dynamic Behavior

Now we discuss how to save as much of the learned information as possible when the background knowledge is modified by the introduction of a new exception. Clearly, the set of concepts consistent with the examples presented so far may be changed. This is even possible if a concept was learned before (i.e. $g=s=c$). To see this, consider the example in Figure 6.

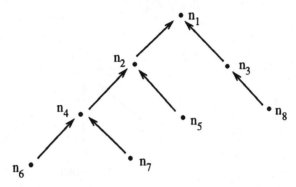

Before: $P=\{n_6, n_5\}$, $N=\{n_8\}$, $s=g=n_2$

New exception: n_8 to link $n_3 \rightarrow n_1$

After: $g=n_1$, $s=n_2$

Figure 6

Apparently, the examples presented before the introduction of the new exception have to be reconsidered. Fortunately, only some of them, if any, must be really treated again:

- In variants 1 and 3 of 'covers', only old examples beneath the new exception are affected.

- In variant 2 it is far easier: if the new exception is an example given so far, we have to reanalyze it (and only it).

The real challenge comes from another fact: suppose some concept c covers some negative example n and is thus marked inconsistent. If a new exception prevents c from covering n, then c *may* become consistent with all examples. But in order to decide this, we have to reconsider the other examples as well. Of course, this is not what we want to do.

The reason for our problem is that our consistency information is too weak. Therefore, we should refine the representation in our version space algorithms as follows: attach to each node c on the main path a set of examples with which c is inconsistent (an empty set corresponds to the marking *consistent* in subsection 3.2, a nonempty set with *inconsistent*). When adding a new exception to the background knowledge, the local modification of information regards only the affected examples and leads to correct results.

Example

Consider the hierarchy in Figure 7. Suppose *ostrich* has been presented as positive example, *penguin* and *helicopter* as negative. Then *ostrich* is the only consistent concept, *bird* and *flying creature* are associated with the inconsistency set {penguin}, and *flying object* is associated with the set {penguin, helicopter}.

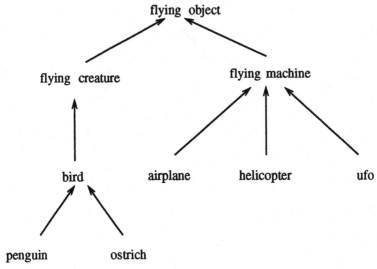

Figure 7

Now suppose that a new exception is added, namely that penguins do not fly (i.e. *penguin* is an exception to the link connecting *bird* and *flying creature*). The only example affected by this new exception is *penguin* itself. Working up towards the root, *bird* remains unchanged, but *penguin* must be deleted from the inconsistency sets of *flying creature* and *flying object* as they cover *penguin* no more (assuming variant 1 of covers). The set for *flying creature* becomes empty, thus indicating that it is now consistent with the presented examples, while *flying object* has the set {helicopter}, as it still covers a negative example. The modifications to the algorithms from subsection 3.3 are simple and obvious.

5 Conjunctive Concepts

In this section we discuss the version space method in case several hierarchies with (or without) exceptions dealing with different aspects of the concept to be learned are combined to form conjunctive concepts. For example, we can combine a hierarchy T_1 of colors

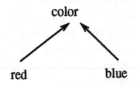

and the hierarchy T_2 of flying objects from Figure 3. In this example, concepts are of the form *(red, flying machine)*.

The general situation is as follows: given are k hierarchies with exceptions $T_1,...,T_k$ in languages $L_1,...,L_k$. We say that a concept $(c_1,...,c_k) \in L_1 \times ... \times L_k$ covers a concept $(d_1,...,d_k)$ iff each c_i covers d_i. Note that the version of the 'covers' relation used may vary from hierarchy to hierarchy according to representational necessities.

Our idea of defining a version space algorithm on such representations is to make direct use of the algorithms presented in section 3. At first sight we might think that the compound version space (set of compatible concepts) is the Cartesian product of version spaces $VS_1 \times ... \times VS_k$ corresponding to hierarchies $T_1,...,T_k$. This will turn out to be insufficient.

- Given a positive example $p=(p_1,...,p_k)$, $VS_1,...,VS_k$ must be updated with $p_1,...,p_k$ respectively as a new positive example, using the algorithm from section 3. The compound result is the new version space.

- Given a negative example $n=(n_1,...,n_k)$, it would be wrong to update all $VS_1,...,VS_k$ simultaneously, since it is sufficient for one n_i to be covered to prevent the entire n from being covered by a compound concept.

The consequence is that we have to maintain *a set* of compound version spaces. The version space is thus represented as the union of several *partial version spaces*. Each of them is built up as the Cartesian product $VS_1 \times ... \times VS_k$, where each VS_i is a (standard) version space for hierarchy with exceptions T_i. Given a new example, the version space is updated in the following way:

- In case of a positive example
  $p=(p_1,...,p_k)$, replace each partial version space $VS_{i1} \times ... \times VS_{ik}$ by $VS'_{i1} \times ... \times VS'_{ik}$, where VS'_{ij} is obtained from VS_{ij} by using p_j as a new positive example on hierarchy T_j.

- In case of a positive example
  $n=(n_1,...,n_k)$, replace each partial version space by (maximally k) partial version spaces obtained in the following way: use each n_i as a new negative example in VS_i, while leaving the other components VS_j $(j \neq i)$ unaffected

In both cases, treatment of a new example in VS_i is done according to section 3. Also, if one version space component VS_i becomes empty, then delete the entire partial version space from the set. The main advantages of this approach are the following:

- usage of the algorithms presented in section 3
- avoidance of explicit (exponential) representation of the entire Cartesian product

Example

Consider the 'color - flying object' example $T_1 \times T_2$ from the beginning of this section. Here is an exemplary run of the version space method:

First positive example: (red, airplane)

VS={red,color}×{airplane,flying machine,flying object}

2. example: (blue, ostrich) negative

VS= {red}×{airplane,flying machine,flying object}∪
{red,color}×{airplane,flying machine}

3. example: (red, ufo) negative

VS= ∅×{airplane,flying machine,flying object}∪
{red}×{airplane}∪
∅×{airplane,flying machine}∪
{red,color}×{airplane}=
{red,color}×{airplane}

4. example: (blue, airplane) negative

VS={red}×{airplane}

Concept learned!

Obviously, choice of good examples is essential for efficient learning. Also, we should take care to avoid multiple occurrences in different partial version spaces (i.e. the partial version spaces should be kept disjoint). In the example above, this is done after the third example).

6 Conclusion and Further Research

In the present paper we introduced hierarchies with exceptions as representation methods more flexible than hierarchies, discussed the version space learning method on hierarchies with exceptions, and gave correctness results about the method. The main advantage is: when knowledge has to be slightly modified (in form of additional exceptions), the learning method needs not start from scratch, but can make use of information obtained so far. The algorithms we presented are being implemented in Prolog (a report [2] will be published soon). When the implementation is finished, we shall be able to apply the algorithm to realistic applications.

One aspect we have not treated in this paper is the realization of dynamic behavior when hierarchies are combined as in section 5. We intend to discuss this issue in the near future.

Open questions remain also concerning the efficiency of the approach. For example, the algorithm in section 5 may require an exponential number of partial version spaces. Complexity investigations seem to be interesting. Also, we shall work on dropping the restriction to propositional representations used in this paper. There are two possibilities of expanding the background knowledge towards first order representations: either directly using a nonmonotonic formalism like default logic [5], or using logic programs with exceptions [4]; the latter seems to us more promising.

References

1. Buntine, W.: Generalized Subsumption and its Application to Induction and Redundancy. Artificial Intelligence 36, 149-176 (1988)

2. Grothaus, M.: Version Space Algorithmen auf Hierarchien mit Ausnahmen. Diplomarbeit, Universität Osnabrück 1993 (in German)

3. Kodratoff, Y.: Introduction to Machine Learning. Pitman 1988

4. Kowalski, R.A. and Sadri, F.: Logic Programs with Exceptions. New Generation Computing 9, 387-400 (1991)

5. Mitchell, T.M.: Generalization as Search. Artificial Intelligence 18, 203-226 (1982)

6. Muggleton, S. and Buntine, W.: Machine invention of first-order predicates by inverting resolution. In Proc. 5th International Conference on Machine Learning, Morgan Kaufmann 1988

7. Muggleton, S. and Feng, C.: Efficient induction of logic programs. In Proc. 1st Conference on Algorithmic Learning Theory, Tokyo 1990. Ohmsha Publishers

8. Quinlan, J.R.: Induction of Decision Trees. Machine Learning Journal 1, 81-106 (1986)

9. Reiter, R.: A Logic for Default Reasoning. Artificial Intelligence 13 (1980)

Regular Languages
and a Class of Logic Programs

Armando B. Matos

LIACC, Universidade do Porto
Rua do Campo Alegre 823, 4100 Porto, Portugal

Abstract. We show that the success set of a specific family of logic programs (having only monadic functors and monadic predicates) can be characterized by a regular language with star-height 0 or 1 and reciprocally that for every such set S there is a logic program belonging to the family whose success set is characterized by S.

1 Introduction and Definitions

Several languages weaker than (*i.e.* properly included in) Prolog are used in practice, namely in the areas of Deductive Databases and Type Theory, so that it is important to characterize their expressiveness. This paper deals with the theoretical power of a few of these languages; in particular, we study the case where all predicates and functional symbols are monadic.

The power of restricted classical languages was studied before; for instance the interesting paper [HA72] by Hoare and Allison studies the relationship between the structure of a programming language and the possibility of programming a boolean function that decides if a computation halts.

There has been a large amount of research in the area of "loop programs". Meyer and Ritchie ([MR67]) defined a hierarchy of functions $\mathcal{L}_0, \mathcal{L}_1, \ldots$ where $\mathcal{L}_i$ is the class of functions computable by loop programs with a nesting of at most i loops; this class of programs is called L_i. It has been proved that for all integers $n \geq 0$ we have $\mathcal{L}_n \subseteq \mathcal{L}_{n+1}$ and $\mathcal{L}_n \neq \mathcal{L}_{n+1}$; moreover $\bigcup_{i \geq 0} \mathcal{L}_i$ is the class of primitive recursive functions ([Rog67]). Cherniavsky ([Che76]) characterized another sub-recursive class L_+ of languages that essentially lies between L_1 and L_2 and that realizes exactly Presburger formulas ([Men66]). In [KA80] and [AC81] the time complexity of computations in sub-recursive languages is studied.

Let us now describe an important decision problem in logic programming. Given a class C of Prolog programs all of them including the definition of a predicate p — the *starting* predicate — and an instance program $P \in C$ we ask: does the query " $: - p(\cdots)$ " have a SLD–refutation? We call this the *SUCCESS* problem for class C. The exact form of the query must of course be specified.

We now define the Predicate Dependence Graph and characterize some restrictions on Prolog programs. These restrictions are characterized by the structure of that graph that and by the complexity of terms and atoms.

Definition 1 *Let P be a Prolog program, let V be the set of predicates defined in P and let E be the set of all pairs (p, q) such that $p \in V$, $q \in V$ and at least one clause defining p has a body containing a literal on q (we say that p "calls" q). The* Predicate Dependence Graph *of P is the directed graph (V, E).*

We define the classes of programs used in this work.

Definition 2

- *A program is called* dag *if its Predicate Dependence Graph is acyclic.*
- *A program is called* almost acyclic *if all the cycles of its Predicate Dependence have length 1 (they are loops (p, p) where p is a node).*
- *A program is called* monadic *if it has only monadic predicates and monadic functors.*
  Moreover, in order to simplify the discussion, we require that monadic programs contain only one constant a, that all unit clauses are ground and that all non unit clauses contain only one logical variable.
- *A program is called* simple *if it is monadic, almost acyclic and if every non unit clause has the form*

$$p(f_1(f_2(\cdots f_k(X) \cdots))) :- q(X)$$

(where q may be identical to p).

The class of monadic programs should not be confused with the class of formulas of the monadic predicate calculus. The later is much simpler for it does not contain functional symbols.

This paper deals with monadic and simple programs. In order to give an idea of the equivalence studied consider the logic program

$$p(g(a)).$$
$$p(f(X)) :- p(X).$$
$$p(h(X)) :- r(X).$$
$$r(a).$$
$$r(h(X)) :- r(X)$$

The goal " $:- p(X)$" may be refuted with all substitutions Θ such that $p(X)\Theta$ belongs to set

$$\{p(f^n(g(a))) : n \geq 0\} \cup \{p(f^n(h^m(a))) : n \geq 0, m \geq 1\}$$

This language can also be characterized by the following regular expression

$$f^* g + f^* h h^*$$

We define the star-height of a regular expression and of a regular language.

Definition 3 *The star-height $h(E)$ of a regular expression E is defined by the rules*

$$
\begin{aligned}
h(\lambda) &= 0 \\
h(\emptyset) &= 0 \\
h(a) &= 0 \qquad\qquad for\ a \in \Sigma \\
h(E + F) &= max(h(E), h(F)) \\
h(EF) &= max(h(E), h(F)) \\
h(E^*) &= h(E) + 1
\end{aligned}
$$

The star-height of a regular language is the __minimum__ star-height of a regular expression denoting that language.

For example the expression $(fg^*)^*$ has a star-height 2 but denotes a language which has a star-height 1 because it is equivalent to the expression $f(f+g)^* + \lambda$ and it is not equivalent to any regular expression not using "$*$".

The study of the star-height of regular languages is an active area of research; for instance only recently it has been proved that there is an algorithm to compute the star-height of a given regular language ([Has87]).

In the next section we prove the main result of this paper which says that for simple programs the success set can always be characterized by a regular expression with star-height 0 or 1. We close with some open questions and suggestions for further work.

2 Monadic Programs

2.1 Decidability of the SUCCESS problem

Before dealing with the complexity of the success set for monadic programs we make a few remarks about the decidability of the SUCCESS problem. The following theorem states that for logic program containing only monadic functors (but with no restriction on the arity of the predicates) the problem may be undecidable.

Theorem 1. *There are classes of programs having only monadic functors for which the SUCCESS problem is recursively unsolvable.*

Proof. Every instance of PCP (Post Correspondence Problem) can be "programmed" using only monadic functors. The details can be found in [Mat92] □

To our knowledge it is not known whether the problem is solvable when all predicates are also monadic.

Question 2. Is the SUCCESS problem solvable for all classes whose programs have only monadic functors and monadic predicates?

2.2 Monadic and Simple Programs

Recall that monadic programs have only monadic predicates and functors and a unique constant a; moreover all unit clauses are ground and all non unit clauses have only one logical variable, say X. A consequence of this definition is that a goal $p(X)$ can only succeed with X instantiated as

$$T = f_1(f_2(\cdots f_k(a)\cdots))$$

where $k \geq 0$ and $f_1,\ldots,f_k$ are (monadic) functional symbols. If $p(X)$ succeeds with this instantiation we say that the program with the starting predicate p *realizes* the word $f_1 f_2 \cdots f_k$. Given a finite set of functional symbols

$$\Sigma = \{f_1, f_2, \cdots, f_n\}$$

we say that a program P *realizes* the language $L \subseteq \Sigma^*$ if it realizes exactly the words of L.

Before studying realizable sets it is interesting to notice that we can restrict somewhat the form the monadic programs without reducing their expressive power.

Theorem 3. *For every monadic program P there is an equivalent monadic program P' satisfying the following conditions.*

1. *The argument of all unit clauses is a.*
2. *The body of every clause consists of at most 2 literals.*
3. *The body of every clause consists of non ground literals i.e. literals with the form*
$$p(f_1(f_2(\cdots f_k(X)\cdots)))$$

Proof. We prove separately each condition; the symbol F represents a sequence of functors

$$f_1(f_2(\cdots f_k()\cdots))$$

which corresponds to the word $f_1 f_2 \cdots f_k$; if t is a term, Ft will denote the term

$$f_1(f_2(\cdots f_k(t)\cdots))$$

1. Replace a unit clause $p(Fa)$ with $F \neq \lambda$ by the clauses

$$p(FX) :- q(X)$$
$$q(a)$$

where q is a new predicate name.

2. Use iteratively the following folding ([BD77]) transformation in the bodies of clauses containing 3 or more literals: replace

$$\cdots, p(F_1X), q(F_2X), \cdots$$

by $\cdots, s(X), \cdots$ where s is a new predicate defined by the clause

$$s(X) :- p(F_1X), q(F_2X)$$

3. A ground literal either succeeds or fails. In the first case delete it from the clause body; in the second case delete the clause. □

2.3 The Success Set for Monadic Programs

We now characterize some sets realizable by monadic programs. We use the standard notation for regular expressions ([HU79]) augmented with the operators $\cap$ (set intersection) and $\ominus$; the latter denotes (note that L is a set and w is a word)

$$L \ominus w = \{x | wx \in L\}$$

Lemma 4. *Suppose that L, L_1 and L_2 are sets realizable by monadic programs and that w, w_1, ... are words realizable by monadic programs; then the following are also realizable by monadic programs.*

1. *The word λ.*
2. *All words $f \in \Sigma$.*
3. *The set $\emptyset$.*
4. *The set $L_1 + L_2$.*
5. *The set wL.*
6. *The set $L \ominus w$.*
7. *The set $(w_1 + \cdots + w_k)^* L$.*
8. *The set $L_1 \cap L_2$.*

A brief justification for each case follows.

1. The word λ is realized by the one clause program $p(a)$.
2. The word $f \in \Sigma$ is realized by the one clause program $p(f(a))$.
3. The set $\emptyset$ is realized by the empty program.
4. If L_1 and L_2 are realized by two disjoint programs whose starting predicates are respectively q and r, then $L_1 + L_2$ is realized by predicate p in a program consisting of the clauses of the two programs and

$$p(X) :- q(X)$$
$$p(X) :- r(X)$$

   defining the new starting predicate p.
5. Suppose that L is realized by the predicate q. The set wL is realized by the new predicate p defined by the clause $p(wX) :- q(X)$.
6. The set $L \ominus w$ can be obtained by adding the new clause $p(X) :- q(wX)$ where q realizes L.
7. The set $(w_1 + \cdots + w_k)^* L$ is realized by the following program where q realizes L

$$p(X) \quad :- q(X)$$
$$p(w_1 X) :- p(X)$$
$$\cdots \quad \cdots \cdots$$
$$p(w_k X) :- p(X)$$

8. If L_1 and L_2 are realized by two disjoint programs whose starting predicates are respectively q and r, then $L_1 \cap L_2$ is realized by a program consisting of the clauses of the two programs and the new clause

$$p(X) :- q(X), r(X)$$

We now study the class of regular languages that are realizable by monadic almost acyclic programs.

Theorem 5. *A regular language with a star-height 0 or 1 is realizable by a simple program.*

Proof. Obvious for star-height 0 (the language is finite). A language with star-height 1 can be represented by a regular expression E with star-height 1. Let F^* be a starred subexpression of E; as F is finite we can write

$$F^* = (w_1 + w_2 + \cdots + w_k)^*$$

where all the w_i are words. Using the properties of regular expressions, we can reduce the complete expression E to

$$E = x_1 + x_2 + \cdots + x_n$$

where each x is a concatenation

$$x = y_1 y_2 \cdots y_m$$

Here y_i is either a word or a reduced expression like F^*. The result follows if we use induction on m and numbers 4, 5 and 7 of Lemma 4.

Note that cycles of the Program Dependence Graph are only introduced by the use of number 7 of Lemma 4 which shows that the graph is almost acyclic; moreover only 1 literal clause bodies are used. $\square$

We now show that the class of languages realizable by simple programs is exactly the subclass of the regular languages that have star-height 0 or 1. Denote by S_n where $n \geq 0$ the class of the regular languages that have star-height not exceeding n. The class S_1 has a number of interesting properties; for example the following closure properties holds: if L, L_1 and L_2 are in S_1 and w, $w_1, \ldots,$ and w_k are fixed words then the following languages are also in S_1

- $L_1 + L_2$
- wL
- $(w_1 + \cdots + w_k)^* L$
- $w \ominus L$ (Use induction on $|w|$)

Theorem 6. *A language realized by a simple program belongs to S_1.*

Proof. Let the clauses which define the starting predicate p be

$$p(u_1 a).$$
$$\ldots$$
$$p(u_k a).$$
$$p(v_1 X) \quad :- \quad q_1(X)$$
$$\ldots \quad\quad \ldots \ldots$$
$$p(v_m X) \quad :- \quad q_m(X)$$
$$p(w_1 X) \quad :- \quad p(X)$$
$$\ldots \quad\quad \ldots \ldots$$
$$p(w_n X) \quad :- \quad p(X)$$

where the u's, the v's and the w's are fixed words and the q_i's are predicates distinct from p not necessarily all distinct. By induction we may assume that for $1 \leq i \leq m$ the language L_i which corresponds to q_i is in S_1 (recall that the Predicate Dependence Graph is almost acyclic). The first $k + m$ clauses realize the language

$$L_a = (u_1 + \ldots + u_k) + (v_1 L_1 + \ldots + v_m L_m)$$

which is in S_1. It is not difficult to see that the language L realized by p is

$$L = (w_1 + \cdots + w_n)^* L_a$$

This language is also in S_1. This result includes several particular cases; for example, if $n = 0$, we get $L = \emptyset^* L_a = \lambda L_a = L_a$ and, if $k = m = 0$, we have $L = \emptyset^*(\emptyset + \emptyset) = \emptyset$ □

Theorems 5 and 6 show that the languages realizable by simple programs are exactly the regular languages having a star-height of 0 or 1. Once this is the most important result of this paper and we state it as a theorem.

Theorem 7. *The class of languages realizable by simple programs coincides with S_1.*

We close this Section with a decidability result for simple programs.

Corollary 8. *The SUCCESS Problem for simple programs is recursively solvable.*

Proof. The Proof of Theorem 6 allows us to define a regular expression denoting the set realized by a simple program and it is recursively decidable whether a regular expression denotes the empty set. □

3 Conclusions and Open Problems

In this paper we have discussed the theoretical properties of a few languages obtained by restricting Prolog. A large number of problems remain (to our knowledge) open; these include the following related questions (a positive answer to the second implies a positive answer to the first)

1. Is the SUCCESS problem recursively solvable for the class of monadic programs?
2. Is the SUCCESS problem recursively solvable for the class of logic programs containing only monadic functors and monadic predicates (this is Question 2)?
3. Theorem 7 provides a characterization of the language realized by simple programs. Do monadic programs correspond to some interesting family of languages?
   Notice that Lemma 4 is also valid for the class containing only monadic functors and monadic predicates, so that both classes are closed under intersection. This implies that no one of them is the class of context free languages.

4. Does the functional complexity of some families of logic programs with no restriction on the arity of functors correspond to known classes of languages?

Clearly, much research on the relationship between restricted forms of logic programming languages and the theoretical structure of the corresponding success sets is needed. The benefits of establishing a simple relation would be twofold. First, it would be possible to give a theoretical basis for the selection of the restrictions on the language used in a particular application. Second, it would give a more unified view of the relationship between the theoretical complexity of the success set and the form of the language used.

References

[AC81]   A. Amihud and Y. Choueka. Loop programs and polinomially computable functions. *International Journal of Computer Mathematics, Section A*, 9:195–205, 1981.

[BD77]   R. M. Burstall and John Darlington. A transformation system for developing recursive programs. *Journal of the Association for Computing Machinery*, 24(1):44–67, 1977.

[BMNR92] Howard Blair, Wiktor Marek, Anil Nerode, and Jeffrey Remmel, editors. *Informal Proceedings of the Workshop on Structural Complexity and Recursion-Theoretic Methods in Logic programming*, Washigton DC, 1992.

[Che76] John C. Cherniavsky. Simple programs realize exactly Presburger formulas. *SIAM Journal on Computing*, 5:666–677, 1976.

[HA72]   C. A. R. Hoare and D. C. S. Allison. Incomputability. *Computing Surveys*, 4:169–178, 1972.

[Has87] K. Hashigushi. Algorithms for determining relative star height. *Information and Control*, 78:124–169, 1987.

[HU79]   John E. Hopcroft and Jeffrey D. Ullman. *Introduction to Automata Theory, Languages, and Computation*. Addison–Wesley, Reading, MA, 1979.

[KA80]   Takumi Kasai and Akeo Adachi. A characterization of time complexity by simple loop programs. *Journal of Computer and System Sciences*, 20:1–17, 1980.

[Mat92] Armando B. Matos. Some results on the complexity and decidability of restricted logic programs. Technical report, Centro de Informática, Universidade do Porto, 1992.

[Men66] Elliot Mendelson. *Introduction to Mathematical Logic*. Van Nostrand, Princeton, 1966.

[MR67]   A. Meyer and D. Ritchie. The complexity of loop programs. In *Proceedings of the 22nd National Conference of the ACM*, pages 465–469, Washington, 1967.

[Rog67] Hartley Jr. Rogers. *Theory of Recursive Functions and Effective Computation*. McGraw Hill., New York, 1967.

Some Results on the Complexity of SLD-Derivations

Armando B. Matos

LIACC, Universidade do Porto
Rua do Campo Alegre 823, 4100 Porto, Portugal

Abstract. In this paper we consider a few simple classes of definite programs and goals and study the problem of deciding whether a given goal has a successful SLD-derivation (the SUCCESS problem). Although the problem is always decidable for the classes studied, it turns out to be NP-complete even for some very simple classes.

The transition between two specific classes of pairs of logic programs and goals (classes C_2 and C_3) is studied in detail by considering a number of intermediate classes. Some of these belong to the complexity class P while others are NP-Complete. This transition seems to be quite "erratic" in the sense that there is apparently no simple property of the class in consideration that corresponds to NP-hardness.

1 Introduction

Many problems related to imperative programming languages are either undecidable or NP-hard. For instance, unless very restricted forms of language are used, the "halting" problem is undecidable (see [7]) and the computed functions are not "simple". (see for instance [1, 2, 8]) A similar situation happens in logic programming: many questions in different areas such as semantics [10, 9, 4] or parallelism [3], turn out to be undecidable or NP-hard.

In this paper we consider very simple classes of definite programs (consisting only of ground unit clauses) and goals and study the problem of deciding whether a given goal has a successful SLD-derivation (we call this the SUCCESS problem). This problem is related (but not identical) to the question mentioned in [10] of inferring ground literals in some semantics. Although the problem is always decidable for the classes studied, it is NP-complete even for some very simple classes.

We define some classes consisting of pairs of logic programs and goals and study in detail the transition between two specific classes by considering a number of intermediate classes. Logic programming provides a rich source of problems whose study may help to characterize the border between some complexity classes (such as P and NP-complete).

The importance of establishing that some simple class C of programs and goals is NP-hard can not be overestimated. It implies that, *for every class containing* C, the SUCCESS problem can not be solved efficiently (i.e. in polynomial time) *by any algorithm* (unless P=NP). This fact has implications for such areas as optimization and abstract interpretation of programs. It should be mentioned however that these implications are far from being straightforward. For instance, the basic theory of NP-hardness deals exclusively with worst-case behavior.

Definition 1. The *unit SUCCESS problem* is a decision problem characterized by

INSTANCE: A definite program P consisting only of ground unit clauses and a definite goal G consisting of literals defined in P with arguments that are logical variables.

QUESTION: Is there a SLD-derivation of $P \cup \{G\}$?

Clearly, the unit SUCCESS problem is always decidable. We will study the complexity of the SUCCESS problem in classes of programs and goals which are even more restricted. These sub-classes are characterized in next section. Can we find the exact border between the classes for which the SUCCESS problem has a polynomial solution and those that are sufficiently expressive so as to have a NP-complete problem? Although some steps in this direction are given in this paper, the question remains largely unsolved.

We now define a more general form of SUCCESS problem that will be only considered in section 4.

Definition 2. The *general SUCCESS problem* is a decision problem characterized by

INSTANCE: A definite program P and a definite goal G consisting of literals defined in P. The program and goal must belong to a class such that

1. It is decidable whether there is a SLD-derivation.
2. If there is a derivation, the goal succeeds with a substitution Θ such that $G\Theta$ is ground.

QUESTION: Is there a SLD-derivation of $P \cup \{G\}$?

The rest of this paper is organized as follows. In the next section the complexity of four simple families of programs and goals (called C_2, C_3, C_{S2} and C_{S3}) is considered. In section 3 the transition from C_2 — for which the SUCCESS problem is polynomial — to C_3 —where the problem is NP-complete — is studied. In section 4 other problems in the polynomial hierarchy are considered. We conclude with some general comments about the problems studied in this paper.

2 Some Families

A NP-hardness result is stronger if the corresponding class of problems is more restricted. That is why, for instance, asserting that 3-SATISFIABILITY is NP-complete is stronger than asserting that SATISFIABILITY is NP-complete. In this work we consider a particular class (C_3) of goal-program pairs and prove that

1. The corresponding SUCCESS problem is NP-complete.
2. If the class is slightly restricted the SUCCESS problem can be solved in polynomial time (this is considered in more detail in next section).

We now characterize some classes of pairs. Each class somewhat reflects the problem (such as 3-COLOURABILITY or 3-SATISFIABILITY) that we will use to prove its complexity. In a sense, it is the possibility of "programming" some NP-problem within the restrictions of a certain class that makes that class "hard".

Definition 3. The following classes consist of pairs

$$(program, goal)$$

Within each class the *program* is the same for all pairs (only the *goal* varies).

- Class C_2 is characterized in Figure 1. The program consist of 2 clauses defining a predicate.
- Class C_3 (Figure 2) is similar to class C_2 but the predicate is defined by 6 clauses.
- Class C_{S2} of programs is characterized in Figure 3. The program in this class defines four binary predicates $p_0,\ldots,p_3$ each through three clauses (a total of 12 clauses).
- Class C_{S3} of programs is characterized in Figure 4. The program of this class defines eight ternary predicates $p_0,\ldots,p_7$ each through seven clauses (a total of 56 clauses).

As an example consider a pair *(program, goal)* of class C_2. The program is given in Figure 1. The goal part may be, for instance

$$s(A, B), s(A, C), s(B, D), s(C, D), s(C, E), s(E, D)$$

The answer for this instance of the SUCCESS problem is <u>no</u>.

Given a class C the corresponding SUCCESS problem will be denoted by C-SUCCESS.

Theorem 4. *The problem C_3-SUCCESS (described in Figure 2) is NP-complete.*

Proof. The proof is based on the reduction

$$3\text{-COLOURABILITY} \propto C_3\text{-SUCCESS}$$

The 3-COLOURABILITY problem (see [5]) can be described as follows: Given a graph $G = (V, E)$ we ask "Is there a function $f : V \to \{1, 2, 3\}$ such that $f(u) \neq f(v)$ whenever $(u, v) \in E$?"; this problem is NP-complete. Every instance of the 3-COLOURABILITY can easily be mapped — i.e. *programmed* — into a program of C_3 in such a way that the graph can be 3-coloured if and only if the goal succeeds. Moreover this transformation can be made in polynomial time. □

Theorem 5. *The C_2-SUCCESS problem (described in Figure 1) is solvable in polynomial time.*

Proof. Follows from two facts

1. C_2-SUCCESS can be polynomially reduced to 2-COLOURABILITY.
2. 2-COLOURABILITY is solvable in polynomial time. □

At this point we should perhaps make a comment about the *practical* consequences of this Theorem. If we use some simple computation rule and search strategy (for instance those of standard Prolog) a refutation in class C_2 will probably take (in the worst case) exponential time. What Theorem 5 says is that *there is some* algorithm that decides in polynomial time if there is a refutation to a given goal. Similarly, Theorem 6 states that no algorithm can make such decision for the class C_3 in polynomial time. Complexity theory deals only with the *possibility* of solving problems efficiently.

Theorem 6. *The SUCCESS problem for class C_{S3} (described in Figure 4) is NP-complete.*

Proof. Use the polynomial reduction

$$3\text{-SATISFIABILITY} \propto C_{S3}\text{-SUCCESS}$$

Note that if T, U and V are either f, t or a logical variable then the goal $c0(T, U, V)$ always succeeds except if $T = t$, $U = t$ and $V = t$, $c1(T, U, V)$ always succeeds except if $T = t$, $U = t$ and $V = f$, ... and $c7(T, U, V)$ always succeeds except if $T = f$, $U = f$ and $V = f$. These predicates allows the translation of any 3 literal clause into an appropriate literal in the body of the clause for p. For example the clause

$$(\overline{u_1}, u_2, \overline{u_3})$$

is translated into

$$c2(U1, U2, U3)$$

Notice that the only "missing clause" for $c2$ is $c2(t, f, t)$. □

Theorem 7. *The C_{S2}-SUCCESS problem (described in Figure 3) is solvable in polynomial time.*

Proof. Follows from

1. C_{S2}-SUCCESS can be polynomially reduced to 2-SATISFIABILITY.
2. 2-SATISFIABILITY is solvable in polynomial time. □

The two previous theorems show that even for programs belonging to very simple classes there is no polynomial algorithm to solve the SUCCESS problem (assuming that $P \neq NP$). Obviously the problem is either NP-hard or undecidable for every class containing C_3 or C_{S3}.

```
:− <goal>.
s(a, b).
s(b, a).
```

Fig. 1. The class C_2. By $<goal>$ we denote a sequence of 0 or more literals of the type $s(X, Y)$ where X and Y are variables.

```
:− <goal>.
s(a, b). s(b, c). s(c, a).
s(b, a). s(c, b). s(a, c).
```

Fig. 2. The class C_3. By $<goal>$ we denote a sequence of 0 or more literals of the type $s(X, Y)$ where X and Y are variables.

```
:− <goal>.
c0(f, f). c0(f, t). c0(t, f).
c1(f, f). c1(f, t).          c0(t, t).
c2(f, f).          c2(t, f). c2(t, t).
          c3(f, t). c3(t, f). c3(t, t).
```

Fig. 3. The class C_{S2} where $<goal>$ denotes a sequence of 0 or more literals $ci(X, Y)$ where X and Y are variables and $0 \leq i \leq 3$.

```
:− <goal>.
c0(f, f, f). c0(f, f, t). c0(f, t, f). c0(f, t, t).
c0(t, f, f). c0(t, f, t). c0(t, t, f).

c1(f, f, f). c1(f, f, t). c1(f, t, f). c0(f, t, t).
c1(t, f, f). c1(t, f, t).               c1(t, t, t).

c2(f, f, f). c2(f, f, t). c2(f, t, f). c2(f, t, t).
c2(t, f, f).               c2(t, t, f). c2(t, t, t).

c3(f, f, f). c3(f, f, t). c3(f, t, f). c3(f, t, t).
              c3(t, f, t). c3(t, t, f). c3(t, t, t).

c4(f, f, f). c4(f, f, t). c4(f, t, f).
c4(t, f, f). c4(t, f, t). c4(t, t, f). c4(t, t, t).

c5(f, f, f). c5(f, f, t).               c5(f, t, t).
c5(t, f, f). c5(t, f, t). c5(t, t, f). c5(t, t, t).

c6(f, f, f).               c6(f, t, f). c6(f, t, t).
c6(t, f, f). c6(t, f, t). c6(t, t, f). c6(t, t, t).

              c7(f, f, t). c7(f, t, f). c7(f, t, t).
c7(t, f, f). c7(t, f, t). c7(t, t, f). c7(t, t, t).
```

Fig. 4. The class C_{S3}. By $<goal>$ we denote a sequence of 0 or more literals $ci(X, Y, Z)$ where X, Y and Z are variables and $0 \leq i \leq 7$.

3 From C_2 to C_3. Where Does NP-Completeness Begin?

In this section we consider classes from C_2 "up to" C_3 to find out when the SUCCESS problem becomes NP-Complete.

The classes considered to be between C_2 and C_3 are those which have the following characteristics (inspired by the colourability problem)

1. Number L of atomic constants between 0 and 3.
2. Only one predicate s is defined by the program.
3. All clauses are unit having as arguments *distinct* constants.
4. A goal literal has the form $s(X, Y)$ where X and Y are distinct logical variables.

In Table 1 the 16 essentially distinct forms of programs are listed. These forms correspond to the 16 directed graphs with 3 nodes (see Appendix 2 of [6]). Each form is numbered and the complexity of the corresponding complexity problem is given.

Table 1. One predicate programs defined by clauses which are binary (2 distinct arguments) ground, function free and unit.

L	no.	Clauses	Complexity
0	0.1		P (Succeeds only for empty goal)
1	1.1	$s(a,b)$	P (No paths with length > 1)
2	2.1	$s(a,b)$, $s(b,a)$	P (Class C_2)
2	2.2	$s(a,b)$, $s(a,c)$	P (No paths with length > 1)
2	2.3	$s(c,a)$, $s(a,b)$	P (See note)
2	2.4	$s(a,b)$, $s(c,b)$	P (No paths with length > 1)
3	3.1	$s(a,b)$, $s(b,a)$, $s(a,c)$	P (See note)
3	3.2	$s(a,b)$, $s(b,a)$, $s(c,a)$	P (See note)
3	3.3	$s(a,b)$, $s(a,c)$, $s(c,b)$	P (No paths with length > 2)
3	3.4	$s(a,b)$, $s(b,c)$, $s(c,a)$	P (See note)
4	4.1	$s(a,c)$, $s(c,a)$, $s(b,c)$, $s(c,b)$	P (See note)
4	4.2	$s(b,a)$, $s(c,a)$, $s(b,c)$, $s(c,b)$	P (See note)
4	4.3	$s(b,a)$, $s(a,c)$, $s(b,c)$, $s(c,b)$	NP-Complete (See note)
4	4.4	$s(b,a)$, $s(b,c)$, $s(a,c)$, $s(c,a)$	P (See note)
5	5.1	$s(b,a)$, $s(a,c)$ $s(c,a)$, $s(b,c)$, $s(c,b)$	NP-Complete (See note)
6	6.1	$s(a,b)$, $s(b,a)$ $s(a,c)$, $s(c,a)$, $s(b,c)$, $s(c,b)$	NP-Complete (C_3)

Notes: For some of the classes in Table 1 we give either a property that can be checked in polynomial time or a proof (in the Appendix) of NP-completeness.

- $\boxed{2.3}$ Acyclic graphs with no paths with length greater than 2, and such that whenever (X, Y, Z) is a path there is no edge (X, Z).
- $\boxed{3.1 \text{ and } 3.2}$ Similar to class C_2; nodes coloured with c can also be coloured with b.
- $\boxed{3.4}$ All (simple) cycles have a length which is multiple of 3.
- $\boxed{4.1}$ Like C_2. Use colour a instead of colour b.
- $\boxed{4.2}$ Let $G = (V, E)$ be the graph to be "coloured" by a program 4.2 and let U be the following subset of V (the "sinks")

$$U = \{X \mid \forall Y \in V, \; (X, Y) \notin E\}$$

All the vertices in U (and only these) can be painted a so that the subgraph with vertices $V - U$ can be coloured with 2 colours if and only if G can be "coloured" by class 4.2.

- $\boxed{4.3}$ Transformation from 3-SATISFIABILITY. An outline of the proof is given in the Appendix.
- $\boxed{4.4}$ Similar to 4.2; if we consider instead the set of "source" vertices

$$\{X \mid \forall Y \in V, \; (Y, X) \notin E\}$$

we can also reduce this problem to colouring with 2 colours.

- $\boxed{5.1}$ Transformation from 3-SATISFIABILITY. An outline of the proof is given in the Appendix.

We close this section with some comments on the requirements that the programs of a class (as characterized in the definition of the unit SUCCESS problem) must have in order that the SUCCESS problem may be NP-complete.

Denote by A the number of atomic constants (as before) and by A the (maximum) predicate arity.

1. The literals of the goal must share logical variables (easy to establish).
2. If $L \geq 3$ we must have $A \geq 2$ (this results from the comparison of C_2 to C_3; in these cases the atoms correspond to the 3 colours).
3. If $L = 2$ we must have $A \geq 3$ (from two facts: 2-SATISFIABILITY belongs to class P and 3-SATISFIABILITY belongs to class NP-complete.

4 Beyond NP-Completeness

The number of instances of a NP-complete problem is infinite so that a polynomial reduction to a SUCCESS problem requires an infinite class of program-goal pairs; it follows that there can be no upper bound for the size of the pairs within such a class; either the program size or the goal size (or both) must be unbounded.

Classes C_3, C_2 and C_{S3} consist of pairs with fixed programs and varying goals. Other problems may be more naturally transformed into pairs having non fixed programs.

In this section we consider the general SUCCESS problem as defined earlier.

The SUCCESS problem for such a class may well be not NP because SLD-refutations may have an exponential size (although the height of SLD trees is obviously linear).

Problems which are co-NP-complete can also be transformed into certain classes of logic programs and goals. But unless NP=co-NP (a very unlikely possibility, see [5]) one of the following must be true (otherwise the problem would belong to NP)

1. The class includes recursive programs.
2. The transformation does not take polynomial time.

EXAMPLE—A problem co-NP-Complete. As an example consider the complement of the 3-COLOURABILITY problem. Every instance can be transformed in a program of the class outlined in Figure 5.

In order to clarify this transformation we should make a few remarks about this class. The goal is p. The number of occurrences of "$s(s(0))$" in the first clause is equal to the number of occurrences of "0" in the second and to the number of vertices. A list like

$$[X - C_X, Y - C_Y, \cdots, Z - C_Z]$$

where C_X, $C_Y \ldots, C_Z$ are either 0 or $s(0)$ or $s(s(0))$, represents a colour assignment to the vertices of the graph. Consider the predicate

$$decrement(L, Ld)$$

If the list L is the base 3 representation (in reverse order) of the integer n then Ld is the base 3 representation (in reverse order) of $n - 1$. For instance, the following goal succeeds

$$decrement([0, s(s(0)), 0], [0, s(0), s(s(0))])$$

The predicate $tryall(L)$ succeeds if, for all colour assignments from L down to $[0, ..., 0]$, the graph is not 3-colourable (predicate $wrong\_colours$). Although this translation can easily be made in polynomial time the class is recursive ($tryall$ and $decrement$ call themselves). It is easy to see that the "execution" of goal p takes exponential time for there are 3^n possible colour assignments where n is the number of vertices. $\square$

The previous example shows that for some classes of definite logic programs and goals the (general) SUCCESS problem may belong to the co-NP-Complete class. Although we have not studied this problem in detail, we conjecture that the same is true for all the classes in the polynomial hierarchy ([11]).

Conjecture 8. *For every nonnegative integer k there are sub-problems P_1, P_2 and P_3 of the general SUCCESS problem such that P_1 is in Σ_k^p, P_2 is in Π_k^p and P_3 is in Δ_k^p.*

$$p \; :- \; tryall([X - s(s(0)), Y - s(s(0)), \cdots, z - s(s(0))]).$$
$$tryall([X - 0, Y - 0, \cdots, Z - 0]) \; :-$$
$$wrong\_colours([X - 0, Y - 0, \cdots, Z - 0]).$$
$$tryall(L) \; :-$$
$$wrong\_colours(L),$$
$$decrement(L, L1),$$
$$tryall(L1).$$
$$wrong\_colours(L) \; :-$$
$$edge(A, B),$$
$$member(A - C, L),$$
$$member(B - C, L).$$
$$decrement([A - s(X)|L], [A - X|L]).$$
$$decrement([A - 0|L], [A - s(s(0))|Ld]) \; :-$$
$$decrement(L, Ld).$$

$\cdots$

Fig. 5. A class suitable for mapping instances of co-3-COLOURABILITY.

5 Conclusions

In this work we have studied in some detail the transition between the classes C_2 and C_3 by considering a number of intermediate classes. Some of these (like C_2) belong to the complexity class P while the others (including C_3) are NP-Complete.

This transition seems to be quite "erratic" in the sense that no simple property of the class in consideration expresses its NP-hardness. In fact this is not a new phenomena: for instance, in [5] there are some examples of pairs of slightly different problems which belong to completely distinct classes of complexity.

Similar studies for other transitions — for instance, between the classes C_{S2} and C_{S3} — may, on the one hand, help to characterize the intrinsic difficulty of the SUCCESS problem and, on the other hand, contribute to the knowledge of the "quality" of the separation between P and NP-Complete problems.

The consideration of other restricted classes may elucidate the relationship between program structure and the location of the SUCCESS problem in the polynomial hierarchy.

A Appendix: Two Proofs of NP-Completeness

A.1 Case 4.3

We show that the SUCCESS problem is NP-Complete for the case 4.3. The proof is by reduction of 3-SATISFIABILITY to the SUCCESS problem.

In the following, when we talk about the colourability problem of a graph what we really mean is the SUCCESS problem for the class 4.3; clearly, an edge of the graph corresponds directly to a literal of the goal.

Let U be the set of variables and C the set of clauses of an instance of 3-SATISFIABILITY. We define the following graph

1. For each variable X in U define two nodes x and x' and two edges (x, x') and (x', x). Clearly, these two vertices must be coloured with b and c. In the correspondence between the instances of the two problems, if x has colour c (and x' has colour b), X has the logical value *true*; otherwise it has the value *false*.

2. For each clause (L_1, L_2, L_3) in C we associate 3 vertices l_1, l_2 and l_3 in a "loop" (edges (l_1, l_2), (l_2, l_3) and (l_3, l_1)). One of them must be coloured a, other b and the other c.

3. Every clause literal is connected (in a way to be explained later) to the corresponding variable. A positive literal, say X, is connected to x and a negative literal, say $\overline{X}$, is connected to x'.

The connections between literals and variables (or primed variables) are made through "connectors" (see Figure 6) sharing two vertices (w and r) with the rest of the graph. If vertex w (which corresponds to a clause literal) has colour a then vertex r (corresponding to a variable or to a primed variable) must have colour c; otherwise (if w has colour b or c) it may have any colour.

If the graph is colourable (by some pair (P, G) in class 4.3) we may assign *true* to the logical variables X if the colour of x is c and *false* otherwise. Reciprocally, if the clauses are satisfiable by some assignment of logical values to the variables it is not difficult to see that the corresponding graph is colourable.

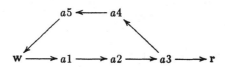

Fig. 6. A "connector" for the case 4.3.

A.2   Case 5.1

We provide a proof that in the case 5.1 the SUCCESS problem is NP-Complete. We reduce 3-SATISFIABILITY to the SUCCESS problem. The proof is similar to the previous one (case 4.3) so that we only state the differences.

As in the previous case, for each instance of 3-SATISFIABILITY we characterize a graph. The only differences are

1. For each variable X in U define the nodes x, O_X and x' and the edges (x, x'), (x', x), (x, O_X) and (x', O_X) (Figure 7). Clearly, one of the vertices x and x' must have colour b and the other color c.

2. The structure of the connectors is different (see figure 8). The correspondence between the colours of w (which as before corresponds to a clause literal) and r (corresponding to a variable or to a primed variable) is

w	r
a	a or c
b	a or b or c
c	b or c

Note however that colour a in vertex r is not possible so that the reasoning may proceed exactly as before.

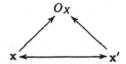

Fig. 7. Subgraph corresponding to a logical variable in case 5.1.

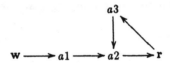

Fig. 8. A "connector" for the case 5.1.

References

1. A. Amihud and Y. Choueka. Loop programs and polinomially computable functions. *International Journal of Computer Mathematics, Section A*, 9:195–205, 1981.

2. John C. Cherniavsky. Simple programs realize exactly Presburger formulas. *SIAM Journal on Computing*, 5:666–677, 1976.

3. Arthur Delcher and Simon Kasif. Some results on the complexity of exploiting data dependency in parallel logic programs. *Journal of Logic Programming*, 6:229–241, 1989.

4. Thomas Eiter and Georg Gottob. Complexity results for logic-based abdunction. In *Informal Proceedings of the Workshop on Structural Complexity and Recursion-Theoretic Methods in Logic programming*, pages 438–449, Washigton DC, 1992.

5. Michael Garey and David S. Johnson. *Computers and Intractability: A Guide to the Theory of NP-Completeness*. Freeman, San Francisco, 1979.

6. Frank Harary. *Graph Theory*. Addison–Wesley, Reading, MA, 1969.

7. C. A. R. Hoare and D. C. S. Allison. Incomputability. *Computing Surveys*, 4:169–178, 1972.

8. A. Meyer and D. Ritchie. The complexity of loop programs. In *Proceedings of the 22nd National Conference of the ACM*, pages 465–469, Washington, 1967.

9. John Schlipf. The expressive power of the logic programming semantics. Technical Report CIS-TR-90-3, Computer Science Departement, University of Cincinnati, 1990.

10. John Schlipf. A survey of complexity and undecidability results in logic programming. Technical Report CIS-TR-92-4, Computer Science Departement, University of Cincinnati, 1992.

11. L. J. Stockmeyer. The polynomial hierarchy. *Theoretical Computer Science*, 3:1–22, 1976.

An Or-Parallel Prolog Execution Model for a Distributed Shared Memory Machine

Fernando M. A. Silva

LIACC, Universidade do Porto,
R. do Campo Alegre 823, 4100 Porto, Portugal
(Email: fds@ncc.up.pt)

Abstract. Recently, new parallel architectures, namely distributed shared memory architectures, have been proposed and built. These combine the ease-of-use of shared memory architectures with the scalability of the message-passing architectures. These architectures provide software and hardware support for shared virtual address space on physically distributed memory.

This paper describes Dorpp, an execution model that supports or-parallelism for these machine architectures, namely for the EDS parallel machine. Dorpp uses a shared memory model for or-parallelism. It attempts, however, at exploiting locality and at reducing communication overheads through scheduling and by caching accesses to remote shared data. The problem of memory coherency of cached data is discussed and solutions are proposed. Preliminary evaluation results of the execution model through simulation are presented.

Keywords: Languages for AI, Or-parallel Prolog, Distributed Shared Memory, Memory Choerency, Scheduling.

1 Introduction

Prolog is a popular programming language that is particularly important in Artificial Intelligence applications. Traditionally, Prolog has been implemented in the common, sequential general-purpose computers. More recently, Prolog implementations have also been proposed for parallel architectures where several processors work together to speedup the execution of a program. By giving better speedups, parallel implementations of Prolog should enable better performance for current problems, and expand the range of applications we can solve with Prolog.

One way to take advantage of parallel architectures for Prolog programs is by exploiting the implicit parallelism in the logic programs. Two main sources of implicit parallelism can be identified in Prolog programs: *or-parallelism* and *and-parallelism*. Or-parallelism arises from the parallel execution of multiple clauses capable of solving a goal, that is from exploring the non-determinism present in logic programs. And-parallelism arises from the parallel execution of multiple subgoals in a clause body.

Or-parallelism is particularly attractive because (i) Prolog's generality and simplicity can be preserved[LWH88]; (ii) it "offers good potential for large-scale, large-granularity parallelism across a wide range of applications" [War87a]. In particular, applications in the area of artificial intelligence involving detection of all solutions or large searches such as expert systems, natural language processing, theorem proving or answering a database query, contain large amounts of or-parallelism [She86]; (iii) the efficient implementation techniques developed for Prolog can be easily extended to cope with or-parallelism [LWH88, Car90, AK90].

Indeed, the Aurora and Muse systems are examples of two successful or-parallel Prolog systems. Such systems support full Prolog, and have obtained good speedups for a wide range of applications. These systems were designed for bus-based shared-memory machines, where the several processors can access a common store via a bus. Unfortunately, current (bus-based) shared memory machines fail to scale over a few tens of processors due to the limited communication bandwidth of the shared bus. This restricts the maximum parallelism a parallel Prolog system can extract.

To attain more parallelism, traditionally one would use distributed memory machines which are scalable to very large numbers (thousands) of processors [AG89]. In these parallel machines, each processor has its own local memory. Access to remote memory, as well as communication and synchronisation between processors, is accomplished through a message passing mechanism. This approach is rather inflexible and expensive for the implementation of Prolog, as any shared datum must be explicitly copied between the processors.

Recently, new parallel architectures, namely distributed shared memory architectures, have been proposed and built. These architectures contain no physically shared memory, although they provide software and hardware support for shared virtual memory. Fundamentally, this is implemented by making each local memory to work as a cache for the shared virtual memory. One example of such architecture is the EDS machine[WTW90]. In this machine, whenever a processor accesses a remote memory location, a page containing that location is copied and stored in the processor's cache. This localises subsequent accesses to cached pages, hence reducing overall communication overheads. Note that a mechanism is required to ensure memory coherency (a similar requirement exists for shared memory architectures using caches). The shared virtual memory simplifies the programming process as it allows complex structures to be passed by reference and hides the remote communication mechanism from the processes.

By combining the advantages of large number of processors with the advantages of a shared memory programming model, distributed shared memory architectures are an ideal target for the execution of Prolog programs with much parallelism. In this paper, we describe Dorpp, an execution model that supports or-parallelism for these architectures, and particularly for the EDS machine.

The main problem for Dorpp to solve, in order to use a distributed shared machine efficiently, is to reduce the number of remote memory accesses, or in other words, to cache data as much as possible. In practice, read-only data is easier to cache, and to obtain the best results, we were interested in making the shared memory as much read-only as possible. This is supported by Warren's SRI model [War87b], and we base Dorpp on this model. Our model thus supports the important notion of Binding Array, and further addresses the important issues of memory coherency characteristic of a distributed shared memory architecture.

This paper is organised as follows. First, we detail the fundamental issues in the design of the model, and discuss what should be the most important efficient considerations. Secondly, we discuss the memory coherency issues introduced by the EDS architecture, and propose efficient solutions. Thirdly, we discuss how scheduling should be performed for this architecture, and present a scheduling strategy. We then present some initial performance results obtained through simulation, and discuss these results.

2   The Execution Model

In Dorpp, a set of workers, one per PE, executes a Prolog program by traversing an or-search tree. Each worker executes Prolog sequentially in a depth-first left-to-right order with backtracking and performs scheduling duties when necessary.

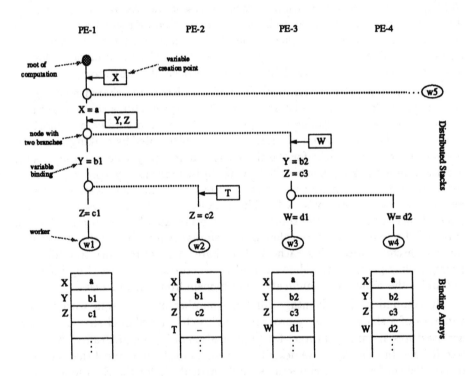

Fig. 1. A distributed stack corresponding to the search tree of some program.

The WAM-stacks, local, global and trail stacks, are now generalised to *distributed stacks* mirroring the shape of the computation tree, and are physically distributed among the different store units although a global logical structure is implicitly preserved. Each worker physically owns part of each stack, together with a private binding array to keep record of conditional bindings. Figure 1 illustrates a distributed stack corresponding to the search tree of some program. It shows the worker that is working at the top of a branch of the distributed stack. The arrows point to the part of the stack where the variables were created. The conditional bindings made to shared variables by the various workers are also shown.

When a worker starts a new task, that is starts executing an alternative branch of an or-node of the computation tree, it inherits an environment from the parent worker. This inherited environment, which corresponds to parts of stacks owned by other workers, has the property of being read-only. If a worker needs to modify the shared environment, for example, to bind a shared variable it does so through its local binding array. Therefore, each worker always writes to its local store and grows its own stacks (these are linked to other workers' stacks forming a logical stack).

The computation tree is not only physically distributed, it is also implicitly divided into shared and private parts, with corresponding shared and private or-nodes. A Node is created as private and it becomes shared when a remote worker starts working on one of its branches. Nodes with untried alternatives are termed *live-nodes*, and those with no untried alternatives *dead-nodes*. A path from the root node to a certain node, *n*, below in the tree, is said to be *shared*, if and only if there are two or more workers working below node *n*, on alternative branches. Obviously, a shared environment corresponds to a shared path. Figure 2 shows the shared parts of a computation tree.

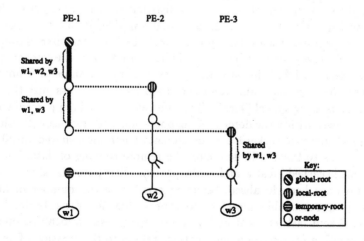

Fig. 2. Shared environments in a computation tree.

The computation tree can, simplistically, be seen as a tree of or-nodes. To this abstract view three types of root nodes have been added: *global-root*, *local-root*, and *temporary-root*. A global-root is defined by the worker that starts executing the initial query, the *root-worker*, and marks the root of the computation tree. A local-root is defined by each of the remote workers to indicate the root of their sub-tree. A temporary-root is defined whenever a worker suspends its current task and switches to a new temporary task; it marks the root of the sub-tree corresponding to the temporary task. Figure 2 illustrates these three types of root nodes. When a worker backtracks to a root node, it indicates that the current task has just terminated. Root nodes are also used to save the state of suspended tasks so that they can be re-activated later.

Contrary to other shared environment schemes, such as the one adopted by Aurora, workers can only access shared nodes lying on their shared path. However, shared nodes may be held on remote stores, therefore allowing a worker to "walk" throughout its shared path is not an appealing idea on a distributed memory machine where remote accesses are always costly. In Dorpp, a worker accesses the shared environment mainly when it has to dereference a non-local shared variable for the first time.

2.1 Efficiency considerations

Variable access and binding is a constant-time operation for shared environment models based on the Binding Arrays method [GJ90], therefore it is a constant-time operation within the proposed model. Variable dereferencing is not a constant-time operation and therefore deserves special attention on any or-parallel model design.

Variable dereferencing, in a shared environment, often implies following a chain of pointers, possibly throughout the parent's frames. This chain of pointers might lead to various remote stores in a distributed memory machine. If, every time a worker tries to dereference a shared variable, it has to make various remote store accesses, then this operation would be a major source of overhead in our model. However, simulation studies indicate that when dereferencing shared variables, less than 1% of them require access to 2 or more ancestor frames, about 1/3 access one ancestor frame, and the majority, 2/3, access just the current frame which is always local [Tic87]. This indicates a very high percentage of the variable accesses within the dereferencing operation to be localised. Furthermore, in Dorpp, whenever a worker has to dereference a non-local shared variable, only the first access to that variable incurs the remote copying of data. Thereafter, the variable is cached locally, and in the process other potential shared variables might also have been localised, reducing even more the number of non-local accesses. It is reasonable therefore to expect that the variable dereferencing operation is kept fast, efficient and, in most of the cases, a localised operation.

Task creation (or environment creation) relates to the creation of new nodes in the search tree and allocation of space for variables. This is a constant-time operation (as in the SRI model) since space for new variables is automatically allocated in the BA when a variable is created (even though its binding may turn out to be unconditional later.

A third operation which has to be done efficiently is task-switching (often named as task-migration). A worker is said to switch tasks when it leaves its current task at a certain node and moves to another task at another node in the search tree. This occurs when a worker terminates its current task or when it backtracks to a dead node with still active workers below the node. In both situations there is no local work left, therefore the worker has to search for a new task and if it succeeds in finding one then it performs a task-switch. The cost of task switching is the time taken by the worker to change its current environment to that at the new node.

In Dorpp, a task-switch involves copying all the conditional variables corresponding to the path from the new node up to the root of the search tree from the BA of the worker owning the new node, and copying all WAM registers stored in that node.

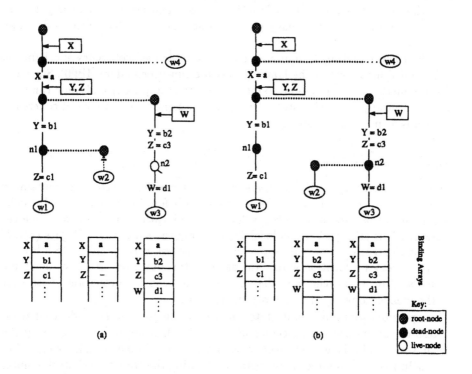

Fig. 3. Contents of the Binding Arrays of a worker before and after a task-switch: a) worker w2 has completed its task at node n1; and, b) w2 is starting a new task at node n2.

When a worker switches from a task at node n1 to a task at node n2 it copies all the conditional bindings up to n2 from the BA of the worker owning n2 as well as the WAM registers stored in n2 (figure 3 illustrates the conditional bindings copied by worker, w2, when it moved from n1 to n2). It shares the environment (that is, the WAM stacks) defined by the path from n2 up to the root of the search tree. The computation state (defined by WAM registers and conditional bindings) for the new task is determined, locally, where the new node is physically located and copied eagerly by the worker switching tasks.

2.2 Memory Coherency

The sector copying mechanism and the caching of remote sectors of data contribute to achieve high locality of reference in Dorpp's binding scheme. There is, however, one major problem arising from the caching of remote data and that is *memory coherency*. For example, suppose that a worker accesses twice the same remote sector, and suppose that in between those accesses the sector is overwritten by its owner. In a simple, but incorrect implementation this would cause problems. At the second access, the copying mechanism detects that the sector is in the local cache, as result of the first access, and accesses it locally, hence, resulting in a memory coherency problem since the sector has been modified at its origin.

The EDS operating system allows for user-controlled-coherency mechanisms to be added in as part of the language specific run time system [IB90]. Since coherence mechanisms are bound to introduce extra complexity and some run time overhead in any parallel system, Dorpp was designed so as to avoid coherence problems as much as possible.

First coherency issue

Figure 4 illustrates a memory coherency issue. Consider a sector, s1, containing a choice point, cp1, and part of the environment before the choice point. It might well happen that a remote worker, w2, accesses a location within s1, while a local worker, w1, is still growing its local stack within the same sector (figure (a)). If at a later stage, w2, now working on a different task corresponding to a branch of cp2, accesses a location within the same sector, but after cp1, and the sector s1 is found in w2's cache then the value returned can be inconsistent with that of the master copy in w1's memory (figure (b)).

A possible solution would be to impose on remote workers a delayed read-access to sectors containing choice points and still being write-accessed by the local worker. This is not, however, an easy solution to implement. Instead, a simpler solution was adopted, it consists of adjusting the top-of-local-stack pointer to point to the beginning of the next sector whenever a choice point is created in the local stack. This gap left in a stack-sector, after each choice point creation, ensures that when the sector is remotely accessed, any copy being sent across will not contain any locations which might be later modified by the worker owning the sector.

This measure by itself is not sufficient to avoid all memory coherency problems. It still requires a scheduling strategy which makes it impossible for remote

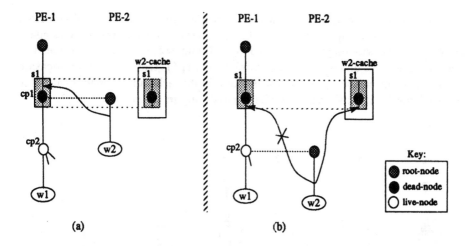

Fig. 4. First memory coherency issue: a)a sector is being copied into the cache of worker w2 after it tried to access a remote location for the first time; b) worker w2 is accessing a remote location within a sector that has been copied earlier into its cache and is now out of date.

copied sectors from a shared path between two workers to be modified by the worker physically owning the sector. In Dorpp this is ensured by the scheduling mechanism in which a worker always grabs work from the topmost node in another worker's sub-tree which still has some alternatives left. Furthermore, it prevents a worker from backtracking past a node below which there are still active workers, hence preserving the integrity of the environment being shared with these workers.

Second coherency issue

There is another situation which without being careful could lead to a memory coherency fault. It occurs when a worker suspends its current task, and after backtracking through a previously shared address space, switches to a new task and starts re-using the same previously shared address space. Suppose that a sector location within the shared space had been accessed by a remote worker. If this worker, now working on a different task, tries to access a location within the same sector, the sector is found in its cache and, therefore, it is accessed locally. However, since the sector has been re-written at its origin, it is now out of date.

Figure 5 illustrates the above situation. Suppose that worker w2 is working on a branch of cp2 and accesses a remote location within s2. The sector s2 is copied by the remote sector copy mechanism into the cache of w2 (figure (a)). Consider now that w2 terminates its current task and that w1 backtracks up to cp1. Since cp1 is a dead-node with still active workers below, w1 suspends its current task and switches to a new one corresponding to a branch of cp3 from worker w3. When computing the new task, w1 starts re-using the address space below cp1 that was previously shared by w1 and w2. If at a later stage, w2, now working on a different task from w1 (node cp4), tries to access a location within the same sector s2, the sector is found in its cache and therefore the value returned can be inconsistent with the master copy in the memory of w1.

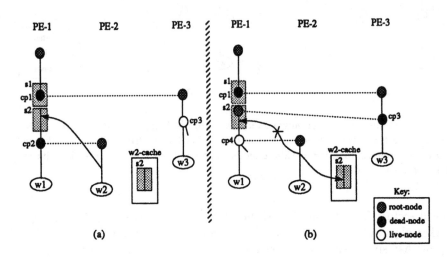

Fig. 5. A memory coherency fault resulting from the re-use of memory space: a) a sector is being copied into the cache of worker w2 as a result of a remote memory access; b) worker w2 is accessing a remote address within the space being re-used. Since the sector containing that address has been cached earlier, the local value is accessed and therefore it may be now out of date.

A solution for this problem can be achieved by invalidating all remote copies of sectors corresponding to previously shared space that is about to be re-used. A worker backtracking from a previously shared node to a shared dead-node with active workers below, has to suspend its current task, look for another task, and switch to the new task when found. This worker would trigger the invalidation mechanism when initialising the new task, that is, before it starts executing it. This is the scheme chosen for Dorpp.

This mechanism is not expected to be activated very frequently and since it is confined to just one previously shared chunk of a workers' sub-tree, it should not impose any major run time overhead on our scheme.

3 Distributed Scheduling

The aim of a scheduling strategy is to improve the performance of a multiprocessor system by appropriately transfering work from heavily loaded processors to idle or lightly loaded processors. It normally involves two important decisions, one is to determine which tasks can be executed in parallel, and the other is to determine where to execute the parallel tasks [SK90].

Dorpp emploies a distributed and receiver-initiated scheduling strategy. In Dorpp there is a scheduler per worker (i.e. processor) making independent and localised decisions related to work-sharing without incurring in extra interprocessor communications. The work-sharing decisions are receiver-initiated in that a worker chooses to search for busy workers from which work may be transferred, only when it becomes idle after completing its current task.

Each worker has a local work-queue and it adds to the back of queue entries to every node (or parallel choice-point) it creates during execution. Remote workers looking for work take the node entry from the front of the queue as it corresponds to the topmost node in the sub-tree of the local worker. The local worker consumes work from the back of the queue whenever it tries to get more local work. This strategy, called dispatching on the topmost [CS89], is hopped to induce large grain tasks which contribute to reduce task-switching and communication overheads. The fact that each worker executes preferentially its locally produced work will contribute to better locality.

Whenever a worker runs out of local work, it searches for more work from work-queues of other workers. To avoid the obvious inefficiencies of a blind search, each worker has a work-load bitmap that indicates which other workers have shareable work (i.e. high work-load) in their work-queues. Furthermore, two threshold values, a *lower threshold* and an *upper threshold*, are associated to each work-queue. The idea behind this scheme is that, initially, the workers build up a reserve of local work until the upper threshold is reached. At this point the worker informs the other workers that its work-load is high, hence allowing for idle workers to steal work from its work-queue. When the amount of work in the work-queue falls to the lower threshold, the worker informs the other workers that its work-load is low hence stopping them from stealing work from its work-queue.

A Dorpp worker can be found in any of three states. It is in the **active** stage when it is executing a task. It is in the **idle** stage when in transition from the active to the scheduling state, when suspended waiting on a remote store access, or when preempted by a higher priority instance being executed in the same PE; and a worker is in the **scheduling** stage when looking for work. A worker in the active state proceeds in the computation tree in a depth-first left-to-right manner with normal backtracking. When an active worker fails to get local work through normal backtracking, it becomes idle. This failure to get local work happens when it completes its current task or when it backtracks to a shared dead-node with child workers working below it. Whenever a worker becomes idle as a result of either situation, it transits to the scheduling state and starts looking for work.

The work-search strategy followed by a worker in the scheduling state is decided within the backtracking algorithm. When a worker backtracks to a root-node, case in which it has completely exhausted the task it was working on, then it directs the work search to the parent worker from which it got the just exhausted task. Failing to get work from the parent, then any other worker known to have shareable work will be targeted, except if the root-node was a temporary-root in which case a previously suspended task will be reactivated. If, however, the worker backtracks to a node with no parallel work left but still with child workers below it, then the worker directs the work search to one of the child workers. Failing to get work from any child, then any other worker with shareable work will be targeted.

This work-search strategy in which a worker tries to get a new task from the same worker (the parent) as the just terminated task has two advantages. Firstly, it helps to reduce task creation/switching costs, since it may well happen that the new task is found off the same node as the previous task, in which case no conditional bindings need to be copied. Secondly, there will be a maximum overlapping environment between the previous task and the new task, which helps to increase locality of reference.

4 Results

Initial results of Dorpp's performance were obtained by running it through a parallel simulator for the EDS machine [Sar91]. The following benchmark programs were used:

Chat this program represents a database search type application. The program uses part of the database from Warren and Pereira's Chat-80 natural language query system. It finds all the possible solutions to the query "Which Western-European country borders a country in Eastern-Europe?".

Atlas this program is also related to the Chat-80 system. It finds the countries in the database which have approximately the same population densities.

Houses this is the "who owns the zebra" puzzle, using constraint directed search [Sze89].

Map this solves the problem of colouring a map with four colours, such that no two neighbours have the same colour.

Queens8 this is a generate and test solution for the problem of placing 8 queens on a chess-board such that no two queens attack each other.

Cubes4, Cubes5 these programs, from [Tic91], solve the N-cubes (also called Instant Insanity) problem, with $N = 4$ and $N = 5$. It consists of stacking N colored cubes in a column, so that no color appears twice within any given side of the column.

All benchmarks find all the solutions for the problem. Multiple solutions are computed through "automatic backtracking on failure" after a solution has been found. Table 1 shows the performance of Dorpp configured with multiple workers. It presents the execution times in miliseconds, for the benchmark programs, with speedups (relative to the 1 worker case) given in parentheses. The benchmarks are divided in three groups according to the speedup shown: group H (high speed-up), group M (medium speedup) and group L (low speedup).

Table 1. The execution times for the benchmark programs.

Group	Programs	Dorpp - Workers (msecs)					SICStus v0.6
		1	2	4	8	16	
H	Cubes5	9874.8	4938.9 (2.00)	2495.7 (3.97)	1288.0 (7.67)	700.6 (14.09)	3610.0 (2.7)
	Cubes4	2549.2	1278.9 (1.99)	657.8 (3.88)	358.5 (7.11)	209.1 (12.19)	870.0 (2.9)
	Queens8	5678.0	2855.6 (1.99)	1454.6 (3.90)	768.1 (7.40)	494.8 (11.48)	2639.0 (2.2)
M	Atlas	127.3	67.2 (1.89)	36.8 (3.46)	21.1 (6.03)	15.5 (8.21)	59.0 (2.2)
	Map	779.2	395.8 (1.97)	230.4 (3.38)	140.0 (5.57)	112.0 (6.96)	335.0 (2.3)
L	Chat	91.1	51.7 (1.76)	33.8 (2.70)	23.0 (3.96)	23.4 (3.89)	20.0 (4.5)
	Houses	186.0	100.1 (1.86)	64.8 (2.87)	58.9 (3.16)	51.1 (3.64)	49.0 (3.8)

The results show the ability of Dorpp to exploit or-parallelism, providing effective speedups over execution on one PE. The quality of the speedups achieved depends significantly on the amount of parallelism in the program being executed. The programs in group H have rather large search spaces, and are therefore amenable to the execution of coarse-grained tasks. This group shows good speedups up to 16 workers. A striking result here is the increase in speedup for **Cubes5** relatively to **Cubes4**, which is mainly due to the increase in granularity. **Atlas** and **Map** are in an intermediate performance group, group M, with relatively good speedups up to 8 workers. **Chat** and **Houses**, group L, show poor results with speedups leveling off very quickly.

The table also compares Dorpp's performance, when configured with a single worker, with the performance of SICStus Prolog version 0.7 on a sparc-480 server (nominally the same speed as the EDS processor). It shows that Dorpp is between 2 and 4 times slower than SICStus. The main factors contributing to this difference are (i) Dorpp is a parallel version and therefore its results incorporate parallel overheads, (ii) Dorpp does not have yet shallow backtracking optimisation, (iii) SICStus compiler is already a mature, high speed and commercial implementation of Prolog.

Further results and statistics are reported in [Sil93]. These results indicate, among other things, that the Dorpp execution model is successful in achieving very high locality of reference and in keeping communication overheads to a level where they are not significant, except at very low granularities.

Acknowledgements

The author is grateful to Vítor Santos Costa for his valuables comments on drafts of this paper. The author also wishes to thank the following institutions, Universidade do Porto, JNICT (Portugal) and EEC-ESPRIT project, for their finantial support during his postgraduate studies at Manchester University, Department of Computer Science.

References

[AK90]   Ali, K., Karlsson, R.: The Muse Or-parallel Prolog Model and its Performance, *In Proc. of NACLP'90*. The MIT Press, 757–776, Oct., (1990)

[AG89]   Almasi, G., Gottlieb, A.: *Highly Parallel Computing*. Benjamin/Cummings Inc. (1989)

[Car90]   Carlsson, M.: Design and Implementation of an OR-Parallel Prolog Engine. Ph. D. Thesis, SICS, Sweden, (1990)

[CS89]   Calderwood, A. and Szeredi, P.: Scheduling Or-parallelism in Aurora – the Manchester Scheduler. *In Proc. of 6th ICLP*, The MIT Press, Lisbon, 419–435, June, (1989)

[GJ90]   Gupta, G. and Jayaraman, B.: On Criteria for Or-parallel Execution of Logic Programs. *In Proc. of NACLP'90*. The MIT Press, Oct., (1990)

[IB90]   Istavrinos, P. and Borrmann, L.: A process and memory model for a distributed-memory machine. *In Proc. of CONPAR'90*, LNCS – 457, Springer-Verlag, 479–488, Zurich, Sept., (1990)

[LWH88]   Lusk, E., Warren, D.H.D., Haridi, S., et al.: The Aurora Or-Parallel Prolog System. *In Proc. of FGCS'88*, 819–830, ICOT, Tokyo, Japan, Nov. (1988)

[Sar91]   Sargeant, J.: EDS Parallel Machine Simulator: version 2. Tech. Report EDS.UD.3I.M016, EDS Group, Univ. Manchester, Nov., (1991)

[She86]   Shen, K.: An Investigation of the Argonne Model of Or-Parallel Prolog. M.Sc. Thesis, Dep. of Comp. Science, Univ. of Manchester, (1986)

[SK90]   Shivaratri, N.G. and Krueger, P.: Two Adaptative Location Policies for Global Scheduling Algorithms. *In Proc. of 10th Int. Conf. on Distributed Computing Systems*, Paris, IEEE, 502–509, May, (1990)

[Sil93]   Silva, F.M.A.: An Implementation of Or-Parallel Prolog on a Distributed Shared Memory Architecture. Ph.D. Thesis, Dept. of Comp. Science, Univ. of Manchester, (1993)

[Sze89]   Szeredi, P.: Performance Analysis of the Aurora Or-parallel Prolog System. *In Proc. of NACLP'89*, The MIT Press, 713–732, Oct., (1989)

[Tic87]   Tick, E.: *Memory Performance of Prolog Architectures*. Kluwer Academic Publishers, (1987)

[Tic91]   Tick, E.: *Parallel Logic Programming*. The MIT Press, (1991)

[WTW90]   Ward, M., Townsend, P., and Watzlawik, G.: EDS Hardware Architecture. *In Proc. of CONPAR'90*. Springer-Verlag, LNCS–457, 816–827, Zurich, Sept. (1990)

[War87a] Warren, D.H.D.: Or-Parallel Execution Models of Prolog. *In Proc. of TAPSOFT'87*. Springer-Verlag, LNCS, 243–259, Pisa, March, (1987)

[War87b] Warren, D.H.D.: The SRI Model for Or-Parallel Execution of Prolog – Abstract Design and Implementation Issues. *In Proc. of ISLP'87*, IEEE, San Francisco, California, 92–102, (1987)

Diagnosis and Debugging as Contradiction Removal in Logic Programs

Luís Moniz Pereira, Carlos Viegas Damásio, José Júlio Alferes

CRIA, Uninova and DCS, U. Nova de Lisboa*
2825 Monte da Caparica, Portugal
{lmp | cd | jja}@fct.unl.pt

Abstract. We apply to normal logic programs with integrity rules a contradiction removal approach, and use it to uniformly treat diagnosis and debugging, and as a matter of fact envisage programs as artifacts and fault-finding as debugging. Our originality resides in applying to such programs the principle that if an assumption leads to contradiction then it should be revised: assumptions are **not A** literals with no rules for A; contradiction is violation of an integrity rule; and revision consists in assuming A instead. Since revised assumptions may introduce fresh contradictions the revision process must be iterated. To do so we've devised an algorithm which is sound and complete.

Our use of normal logic programs extends that of Horn programs made by Konolige, and so adds expressiveness to the causal part of his framework. Non-abnormalities are assumed rather than abduced, and are revised only if they result in contradiction; simple logic programming techniques achieve it.

Keywords: Diagnosis, Debugging, Non-monotonic Reasoning, Logic Programming

1 Introduction

There is evidence that non-monotonic reasoning problems can be solved with recourse to contradiction removal techniques in logic programs extended with a second (explicit) negation [10, 11, 12]. Here we adapt to normal logic programs with integrity rules the contradiction removal approach, and use it to uniformly treat diagnosis and debugging, in fact envisaging programs as artifacts, and fault-finding as debugging.

Our originality resides in applying to normal logic programs the principle that if an assumption leads to a contradiction then it should be revised: assumptions are **not A** literals with no rules for A; contradiction is violation of an integrity rule; and revision consists in assuming A instead. Since revised assumptions may introduce fresh contradictions, the revision process must be iterated.

* We thank JNICT and Esprit BR project Compulog 2 (no 6810) for their support.

We also set forth a novel simple method to debug logic programs [9], showing how debugging can be envisaged as contradiction removal. Thus, exactly the same technique can be employed to first debug the blueprint specification of an artifact, and used next to perform diagnoses with the debugged specification.

Because [16] relies on Generalised Stable Models [7] to define diagnoses, they are at odds to produce an algorithm to compute minimal ones, as they themselves acknowledge (p. 520). Instead of requiring a new semantics we view diagnoses as an iterative program update process.

Our use of normal logic programs extends that of Horn programs made by [8], and so adds expressiveness to the causal part of his framework. Non-abnormalities are assumed rather than abduced, and are revised only if they result in contradiction; simple logic programming techniques achieve it.

All examples and algorithms were implemented and tested using Prolog.

2 Revising Contradictory Logic Programs

A logic program is a normal logic program plus integrity rules. A logic program is a set of rules and integrity rules having the form

$$H \leftarrow B_1, \ldots, B_n, not\, C_1, \ldots, not\, C_m \quad (m \geq 0, n \geq 0)^2$$

where $H, B_1, \ldots, B_n, C_1, \ldots, C_m$ are atoms (or positive literals), and in integrity rules H is the symbol $\perp$ (*contradiction*). **not L** is called a default or negative literal. Literals are either positive or default ones. A set of rules stands for all its ground instances. Contradictory programs are those where $\perp$ belongs to the program model M_P. Programs with integrity rules are liable to be contradictory.

Example 1. Consider $P = \{a \leftarrow not\, b; \perp \leftarrow a\}$. Since we have no rules for b, **not b** is true by Closed World Assumption (CWA) on b. Hence, by the second rule, we have a contradiction. We argue the CWA may not be held of atom b as it leads to contradiction.

To remove contradiction the first issue is defining which default literals **not A**, true by CWA, may be **revised** to false, i.e. by adding A. Contradiction removal is achieved by adding to the original program the complements of some revisables.

Definition 1 (Revisables). The revisable literals of a program P are a subset of $Rev(P)$, the set of all default literals **not A** with no rules for A in P.

Definition 2 (Positive assumptions of a program). A set S of positive literals is a set of positive assumptions of program P iff

$$\forall L \in S \Rightarrow not\, L \in Rev(P)$$

---

[2] When $n = m = 0$, H is an alternative representation for rule $H \leftarrow$.

Definition 3 (Revised program wrt positive assumptions). Let A be a set of positive assumptions of P. The revised P wrt A, $Rev(P, A)$, is the program $P \cup A$.

Definition 4 (Revising assumptions of a program). A set of positive assumptions S of P is a set of revising assumptions (or a **revision**) iff $\perp \notin Con(Rev(P, S))^3$

Next we identify which subsets of the revisables support contradiction via some integrity rule. The revision of elements from each subset, i.e. adding the corresponding positive assumptions, can eliminate the introduction of contradiction (i.e. $\perp$) via that rule, by withdrawing the support given to the rule body by such CWA elements. But the revision wrt those assumptions may also introduce fresh contradiction via some other integrity rule. If that is the case then the revision process is simply iterated. Finally, we are interested in the minimal revisions after iteration, i.e. the minimal sets of revising assumptions.

First we define support:

Definition 5 (Support set of a literal). Support sets of any literal L true in the model M_P of a normal program P, are denoted by $SS(L)$, always exist and are obtained as follows:

1. If L is a positive literal, then for each rule $L \leftarrow \mathcal{B}^4$ in P such that $\mathcal{B}$ is true in M_P, each $SS(L)$ is formed by the union of $\{L\}$ with some $SS(B_i)$ for each $B_i \in \mathcal{B}$. i.e. there are as many $SS(L)$ as ways of making true some rule body for L.
2. If L is a default literal $not\ A$:
   (a) if no rules exist for A in P then the single support set of L is $\{not\ A\}$.
   (b) if rules for A exist in P then choose from each rule with non-empty body a single literal whose complement[5] is true in M_P. For each such multiple choice there are several $SS(not\ A)$, each formed by the union of $\{not\ A\}$ with a SS of the complement of every chosen literal. i.e. there are as many $SS(not\ A)$ as minimal ways of making false all rule bodies for A.

The revisables on which contradiction rests are those in supports of $\perp$:

Definition 6 (Assumption set of $\perp$ wrt revisables). An assumption set of $\perp$ wrt revisables R is any set $AS(\perp, R) = SS(\perp) \cap R$, for some $SS(\perp)$.

We define a spectrum of possible revisions with the known notion of hitting set:

Definition 7 (Hitting set). A hitting set of a collection of sets C is a set formed by the union of one non-empty subset from each $S \in C$. A hitting set is minimal iff no proper subset is a hitting set for C. If $\{\} \in C$ then C has no hitting sets.

---

[3] A literal $L \notin Con(P)$ iff $P \not\models L$

[4] $H \leftarrow \mathcal{B}$ is alternative rule notation where $\mathcal{B}$ is the set of literals in its body.

[5] The complement of a positive literal L is $not\ L$, and of a default literal $not\ L$ is L.

We revise programs by revising the literals of candidate removal sets:

Definition 8 (Candidate removal set). A candidate removal set of P wrt revisables R is a minimal hitting set of the collection of all assumption sets $AS(\perp, R)$.

A program is not revisable if $\perp$ has a support set without revisable literals.

Based on the above, we have devised an iterative algorithm to compute the minimal sets of revising assumptions of a program P wrt to revisables R, and shown its soundness and completeness for finite R. The algorithm is a repeated application of an algorithm to compute candidate removal sets.[6]

The algorithm starts by finding out the $CRSs$ of the original program plus the empty set of positive assumptions (assuming the original program is revisable, otherwise the algorithm stops after the first step). To each CRS there corresponds a set of positive assumptions obtained by taking the complement of their elements. The algorithm then adds, non-deterministically, one at a time, each of these sets of assumptions to the original program. One of three cases occurs: (1) the program thus obtained is non-contradictory and we are in the presence of one minimal revising set of assumptions; (2) the new program is contradictory and non-revisable (and this fact is recorded by the algorithm to prune out other contradictory programs obtained by it); (3) the new program is contradictory but revisable and this very same algorithm is iterated until we finitely attain one of the two other cases.

The sets of assumptions used to obtain the revised non-contradictory programs are the minimal revising sets of assumptions of the original program. The algorithm can terminate after executing only one step when the program is either non-contradictory or contradictory and non-revisable, i.e., it has no $CRSs$. For a precise description of the algorithm the reader is refered to [15]. It can be shown this algorithm is NP-Hard [3].

3 Application to Declarative Debugging

In this section we apply contradiction removal to perform debugging of terminating normal logic programs. Besides looping there are only two other kinds of error, cf. [9]: wrong solutions and missing solutions.

3.1 Debugging Wrong Solutions

Consider the following buggy program P:

$$a(1) \qquad\qquad b(2) \quad c(1,X)$$
$$a(X) \leftarrow b(X), c(Y,Y) \quad b(3) \quad c(2,2)$$

---

[6] [17] gives an "algorithm" for computing minimal diagnoses, called DIAGNOSE (with a bug corrected in [4]). DIAGNOSE can be used to compute $CRSs$, needing only the definition of the function Tp refered there. Our Tp was built from a top-down derivation procedure adapted from [14, 13].

As you can check, goal $a(2)$ succeeds in the above program. Suppose now that $a(2)$ should not be a conclusion of P, so that $a(2)$ is a wrong solution. What are the minimal causes of this bug? There are three. First, the obvious one, the second rule for a has a bug; the second is that $b(2)$ should not hold in P; and, finally, that neither $c(1,X)$ nor $c(2,2)$ should hold in P.

This type of error (and its causes) is easily detected using contradiction removal by means of a simple transformation applied to the original program:

- Add default literal $not\ ab(i, [X_1, X_2, \ldots, X_n])$ to the body of each i-th rule of P, where n is its arity and $X_1, X_2, \ldots, X_n$ its head arguments.

Applying this to P we get program P_1:

$$a(1) \leftarrow not\ ab(1,[]) \qquad a(X) \leftarrow b(X),\ c(Y,Y),\ not\ ab(2,[X])$$
$$b(2) \leftarrow not\ ab(3,[2]) \qquad b(3) \leftarrow not\ ab(4,[3])$$
$$c(1,X) \leftarrow not\ ab(5,[1,X]) \quad c(2,2) \leftarrow not\ ab(6,[2,2])$$

Now, if we have wrong solution $p(X_1, X_2, \ldots, X_n)$ in P just add to P_1 integrity rule $\perp \leftarrow p(X_1, X_2, \ldots, X_n)$, and revise it to find the possible causes of the wrong solution, using as revisables the ab literals.

Since $a(2)$ is a wrong solution, by adding $\perp \leftarrow a(2)$ to P_1 we obtain the minimal revisions $\{ab(2,[2])\}$, $\{ab(3,[2])\}$ and $\{ab(5,[1,1]), ab(6,[2,2])\}$, as expected.

3.2 Debugging Missing Solutions

Suppose now the program should not finitely fail on some goal but does so. This is the missing solution problem. Say, for instance, $a(4)$ should succeed in program P above. Which are the minimal sets of rules that added to P make $a(4)$ succeed ? There are two minimal solutions: either add rule $a(4)$ or rule $b(4)$.

To find this type of bug it suffices to add for each predicate p with arity n the rule to P_1:

- $p(X_1, X_2, \ldots, X_n) \leftarrow missing(p(X_1, X_2, \ldots, X_n))$.

All that's necessary to state that if some predicate q has a missing solution $q(X_1, X_2, \ldots, X_n)$ then a contradiction arises, is to add to the program the integrity rule $\perp \leftarrow not\ q(X_1, X_2, \ldots, X_n)$, and revise the transformed program using as revisables $not\ missing(A)$, for all atoms A. The transformed program obtained is P plus the rules:

$$a(X) \leftarrow missing(\ a(X)\ )$$
$$b(X) \leftarrow missing(\ b(X)\ )$$
$$c(X,Y) \leftarrow missing(\ c(X,Y)\ )$$

If we want to find the possible causes of the missing solution to $a(4)$ then we add the integrity rule $\perp \leftarrow not\ a(4)$ and obtain, as expected, the two minimal revisions $\{missing(a(4))\}$ and $\{missing(b(4))\}$.

In the case of definite programs only one at a time of the two previous transformations suffices to detect the possible causes of an error. In the case of normal logic programs both transformations must be applied simultaneously in order to achieve complete detection of the both types of error, as the type of error revisables which are relevant change from *ab* to *missing* and vice-versa, at each body rule *not* (cf [9]):

Example 2. Consider program

$$a \leftarrow not\ b \quad a \leftarrow c \quad b \leftarrow$$

The two transformations result in:

$$a \leftarrow not\ b,\ not\ ab(1) \quad a \leftarrow c,\ not\ ab(2) \quad b \leftarrow not\ ab(3)$$
$$a \leftarrow missing(a) \quad\quad b \leftarrow missing(b) \quad\quad c \leftarrow missing(c)$$

When a is considered a missing solution the integrity rule $\perp \leftarrow not\ a$ is added to the transformed program, thereby generating contradiction. The minimal revisions of the program are:

$$\{missing(a)\},\ \{missing(c)\},\ \{ab(3)\}$$

If just the missing solution transformation were applied then the third minimal, intuitive, revision would be left out.

4 Updating Knowledge Bases

In this section we exhibit a program transformation to solve the problem of updating knowledge bases. Remember that a logic program stands for all its ground instances.

As stated in [5, 6] the problem of updating knowledge bases is a generalisation of the view update problem of relational databases. Given a knowledge base, represented by a logic program, an integrity constraint theory and a first order formula the updating problem consists in updating the program such that:

- It continues to satisfy the integrity constraint theory;
- When the existential closure of the first-order formula is not (resp., is) a logical consequence of the program then, after the update, it becomes (resp., no longer) so.

Here, we restrict the integrity constraint theory to sets of integrity rules (c.f. Sect. 2) and the first-order formula to a single ground literal. The method can be generalised as in [6], with possible floundering problems, in order to cope with first-order formulae.

We assume there are just two primitive ways of updating a program: retracting a rule (or fact) from the program or asserting a fact. A transaction is a set of such retractions and assertions.

Next, we define a program transformation in all respects similar to the one used to perform declarative debugging:

Definition 9. The transformation T_{upd} that maps a logic program P into a logic program P' is obtained by applying to P the following two operations:

- Add to the body of each rule $H \leftarrow B_1, \ldots, B_n, not\, C_1, \ldots, not\, C_m$ in P the literal $not\, retract\_inst((H \leftarrow B_1, \ldots, B_n, not\, C_1, \ldots, not\, C_m))$.
- Add the rule $p(X_1, X_2, \ldots, X_n) \leftarrow assert\_inst(p(X_1, X_2, \ldots, X_n))$ for each predicate p with arity n in the language of P.

It is assumed predicate symbols *retract_inst* and *assert_inst* don't belong to the language of P. The revisables of the program P' are the *retract_inst* and *assert_inst* literals.

If an atom A is to be inserted in the database P, then the integrity rule $\bot \leftarrow not\, A$ is added to $T_{\text{upd}}(P)$. The minimal revisions of the latter program and integrity rule are the minimal transactions ensuring that A is a logical consequence of P. If an atom A is to be deleted, then add the integrity rule $\bot \leftarrow A$ instead. With this method the resulting transactions are more "intuitive" than the ones obtained by [6]:

Example 3 [6]. Consider the following logic program and the request to make pleasant(fred) a logical consequence of it (insertion problem):

pleasant(X)←not old(X), likes_fun(X)
pleasant(X)←sports_person(X), loves_nature(X)
sports_person(X)←swimmer(X)
sports_person(X)←not sedentary(X)
old(X)←age(X,Y), Y > 55
swimmer(fred)
age(fred,60)

The transactions returned by Guessoum and LLoyd's method are:

1. { assert(pleasant(fred)) }
2. { assert(likes_fun(fred)),retract((old(X) ← age(X,Y),Y>55)) }
3. { assert(likes_fun(fred)),retract(age(fred,60)) }
4. { assert(sports_person(fred)),assert(loves_nature(fred)) }
5. { assert(swimmer(fred)),assert(loves_nature(fred)) }
6. { assert(loves_nature(fred)) }

Notice that transactions 4 and 5 are asserting facts (sports_person(fred), resp. swimmer(fred)) that are already conclusions of the program ! Also remark that in transaction 2 the whole rule is being retracted from the program, rather than just the appropriate instance. On the contrary, our method returns the transactions:

1. { assert_inst(pleasant(fred)) }
2. { assert_inst(likes_fun(fred)),retract_inst((old(fred)←age(fred,60),60>55)) }

3. { assert_inst(likes_fun(fred)),retract_inst(age(fred,60)) }
4. { assert_inst(loves_nature(fred)) }

If the second transistion is added to the program then it is not necessary to remove the rule old(X)←age(X,Y), Y > 55 from it. Only an instance of the rule is virtually retracted via assertion of the fact retract_inst(age(fred,60))[7].

Another advantage of our technique is that the user can express which predicates are liable to retraction of rules and addition of facts by only partially transforming the program, i.e. by selecting to which rules the *not retract* is added or to which predicates the second rule in the transformation is applied.

In [5] is argued that the updating procedures should desirably return minimal transactions, capturing the sense of making "least" changes to the program. These authors point out a situation where minimal transactions don't obey the integrity constraint theory:

Example 4 [5]. Consider the definite logic program from where $r(a)$ must not be a logical consequence of it (the deletion problem):

$$
\begin{array}{ll}
r(X)\leftarrow p(X) & p(a) \\
r(X)\leftarrow p(X),q(X) & q(a)
\end{array}
$$

and the integrity constraint theory $\forall_X (p(x) \leftarrow q(x))$. Two of the possible transactions that delete $r(a)$ are:

$$T_1 = \{retract(p(a))\} \text{ and } T_2 = \{retract(p(a)), retract(q(a))\}$$

Transaction T_1 is minimal but the updated program does not satisfy the integrity contrainst theory. On the contrary, the updated program using T_2 does satisfy the integrity constraint theory.

With our method we firstly apply T_{upd} to the program obtaining (notice how the integrity constraint theory is coded):

r(X)←p(X), not retract_inst((r(X) ← p(X)))
r(X)←p(X), q(X), not retract_inst((r(X) ← p(X), q(X)))
p(a) ←not retract_inst(p(a))
q(a) ←not retract_inst(q(a))

p(X)←assert_inst(p(X))
q(X)←assert_inst(q(X))
r(X)←assert_inst(r(X))

⊥ ←not p(X), q(X)

---

[7] It may be argued that we obtain this result because we consider only ground instances. In fact, we have devised a sound implementation of the contradiction removal algorithm that is capable of dealing with non-ground logic programs such as this one. For the above example the transactions obtained are the ones listed.

The request to delete $r(a)$ is converted in the integrity rule $\perp \leftarrow r(a)$ which is added to the previous program. As the reader can check, this program is contradictory. By computing its minimal revisions, the minimal transactions that *satisfy* the integrity theory are obtained:

1. $\{retract\_inst(p(a)), retract\_inst(q(a))\}$
2. $\{retract\_inst(r(a) \leftarrow p(a)), retract\_inst((r(a) \leftarrow p(a), q(a)))\}$
3. $\{retract\_inst(q(a)), retract\_inst((r(a) \leftarrow p(a)))\}$

Remark that transaction T_1 is not a minimal revision of the previous program.

Due to the uniformity of the method, i.e. insert and delete requests are translated to integrity rules, the iterative contradiction removal algorithm ensures that the minimal transactions thus obtained, when enacted, do satisfy the integrity constraints.

5 Application to Diagnosis

In this section we show diagnostic problems in the sense of [1] can be expressed in normal logic programs with integrity rules. By revising the program to remove contradiction we obtain the diagnostic problem's minimal solutions, i.e. the diagnoses. The unifying approach of abductive and consistency-based diagnosis presented by these authors enables us to represent easily, and solve, a major class of diagnostic problems using contradiction removal. Similar work has been done by [16] using Generalised Stable Models [7].

We start by making a short description of a diagnostic problem as defined in [1, 2]. A **DP** is a triple consisting of a system description, inputs and observations. The system is modeled by a Horn theory describing the devices, their behaviours and relationships. In this diagnosis setting, each component of the system to be diagnosed has a description of its possible behaviours with the additional restriction that a given device can only be in a single mode of a set of possible ones. There is a mandatory mode in each component model, the correct mode, that describes correct device behaviour; the other mutually exclusive behaviour modes represent possible faulty behaviours.

Having this static model of the system we can submit to it a given set of inputs (contextual data) and compare the results obtained with the observations predicted by our conceptualized model. Following [1] the contextual data and observation part of the diagnostic problem are sets of parameters of the form *parameter(value)* with the restriction that a given parameter can only have one observed valued.

With these introductory definitions, [1] present a general diagnosis framework unifying the consistency-based and abductive approaches. These authors translate the diagnostic problem into abduction problems where the abducibles are the behaviour modes of the various system components. From the observations of the **DP** two sets are constructed: Ψ^+, the subset of the observations that must be explained, and $\Psi^- = \{\neg f(X) : f(Y) \text{ is an observation, for each}$

admissible value X of parameter f other than Y}. A diagnosis is a minimal consistent set of abnormality hypotheses, with additional assumptions of correct behaviour of the other devices, that consistently explain some of the observed outputs: the program plus the hypotheses must derive (cover) all the observations in Ψ^+ consistent with Ψ^-. By varying the set Ψ^+ a spectrum of different types of diagnosis is obtained.

Theorem 1. *Given an abduction problem corresponding to a diagnostic problem, its minimal solutions are the minimal revising assumptions of the modeling program plus contextual data, and the following rules:*

1. $\perp \leftarrow not\ obs(v)$ for each $obs(v) \in \Psi^+$
2. $\perp \leftarrow obs(v)$ for each $obs(v) \in \Psi^-$

and for each component c_i with distinct abnormal behaviour modes b_j and b_k:

3. $correct(c_i) \leftarrow not\ ab(c_i)$
4. $b_j(ci) \leftarrow ab(c_i), fault\_mode(c_i, b_j)$
5. $\perp \leftarrow fault\_mode(c_i, b_j), fault\_mode(c_i, b_k)$ for each b_j, b_k

with revisables $fault\_mode(c_i, b_j)$ and $ab(c_i)$.

We don't give here a proof of this result but take into consideration that:

- Rule 1 ensures that in each consistent set of assumptions $obs(v) \in \Psi^+$ must be entailed by the program
- Rule 2 guarantees the consistency of the sets of assumptions with Ψ^-
- Rules 4 and 5 deal with and generate all the possible mutually exclusive behaviours of a component

Finally, note that in no revision there appears the literal $fault\_mode(c, correct)$, thus guaranteeing that minimal revising assumptions are indeed minimal solutions to the diagnostic problem.

5.1   Examples

Example 5 [8].
    Three bulbs are set in parallel with a source via connecting wires and a switch, as specified in the first three rules (where ok is used instead of $correct$). Normality is assumed by default in the rule for ok. The two integrity rules enforce that the switch is always either $open$ or $closed$. Since both cannot be assumed simultaneously, this program has two minimal revisions, with $ab, open, closed$ being the revisables: one obtained by revising the CWA on $open$ (i.e. adding $open$); the other by revising the CWA on $closed$ (i.e. adding $closed$). In the first $open, not\ on(b1), not\ on(b2), not\ on(b3)$ are true in the model; in the second $closed, on(b1), on(b2), on(b3)$ do.

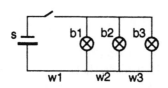

on(b1) ← closed, ok(s), ok(w1), ok(b1)   ⊥ ← not open, not closed
on(b2) ← closed, ok(s), ok(w1), ok(w2), ok(b2)   ⊥ ← open, closed
on(b3) ← closed, ok(s), ok(w1), ok(w2), ok(w3), ok(b3)   ok(X) ← not ab(X)

Further integrity rules specify observed behaviour to be explained. For instance, to explain that bulb 1 is on it is only necessary to add ⊥ ← *not on(b1)* to obtain the single, intuitive, minimal revision {*closed*}.

Suppose instead we wish to explain that bulb 2 is off (i.e. not on). Adding ⊥ ← *on(b2)*, five minimal revisions explain it, four of which express faults:

$$\{closed, not\ ab(s)\} \quad \{closed, not\ ab(w_1)\}$$
$$\{closed, not\ ab(b_2)\} \quad \{closed, not\ ab(w_2)\}$$
$$\{open\}$$

Adding now both integrity rules, only two of the previous revisions remain: both with the switch closed, but one stating that bulb 2 is abnormal and the other that wire 2 is.

Example 6. Two inverters are connected in series. Rules 1-2 model normal inverter behaviour, where *correct* has been replaced by *not ab*. Rules 6-7 specify the circuit topology. Rules 3-4 model two fault modes: one expresses the output is stuck at 0, and the other that it is stuck at 1, whatever the input may be (although it must exist). According to rule 8 the two fault modes are mutually exclusive. Rule 9 establishes the input as 0. Rule 11 specifies the observed output is 1, and that it must be explained (i.e. proved) on pain of contradiction. Rule 10 specifies that the expected output 0 does not obtain, and so is not to be proven. The revisables are *ab* and *fault_mode*.

0 —— a —|g1|>o—— b —|g2|>o—— c —— 1

Explanation is to be provided by finding the revisions of revisables that added to the program avoid contradiction. Indeed, contradiction ensues if all CWAs are assumed.[8]

---

[8] Comments: In rules 3-4, not ab(G) is absent (but could be added) because we presuppose, for simplicity, that the revision of a *fault_mode* to true implicitly signals an abnormality. Rule 8 is not strictly necessary since fault model rules 3-4 already make the fault modes incompatible.

inv(G,I,1) ← node(I,0), not ab(G)		1
inv(G,I,0) ← node(I,1), not ab(G)		2
inv(G,I,0) ← node(I,_), fault_mode(G,s0)		3
inv(G,I,1) ← node(I,_), fault_mode(G,s1)		4
node(b,B) ← inv(g1, a, B)		6
node(c,C) ← inv(g2, b, C)		7

⊥	← fault_mode(G, s0), fault_mode(G, s1)	8
node(a,0) ←		9
⊥	← node(c,0)	10
⊥	← not node(c,1)	11

The following expected minimal revisions are produced by our algorithm:

$$\{ab(g1), fault\_mode(g1, s0)\} \ \{ab(g2), fault\_mode(g2, s1)\}$$

To see this, note that the above program entails ⊥. In order to find the minimal revisions we apply our iterative algorithm. In the first iteration, the sets of positive assumptions:

$$A_1 = \{ab(g1), fault\_mode(g1, s0)\} \ A_2 = \{ab(g2), fault\_mode(g2, s1)\}$$
$$A_3 = \{ab(g2), fault\_mode(g1, s0)\} \ A_4 = \{ab(g1), fault\_mode(g2, s1)\}$$

are generated from the complements of the candidate removal sets. $Rev(P, A_3)$ and $Rev(P, A_4)$ are contradictory. In the second iteration new sets of positive assumptions are computed:

$$A_5 = \{ab(g2), fault\_mode(g1, s0), fault\_mode(g2, s1)\}$$
$$A_6 = \{ab(g1), fault\_mode(g1, s0), fault\_mode(g2, s1)\}$$
$$A_7 = \{ab(g1), fault\_mode(g1, s1), fault\_mode(g2, s1)\}$$

The set of positive assumptions A_5 is originated by $Rev(P, A_3)$ and the last two by $Rev(P, A_4)$. $Rev(P, A_7)$ is still contradictory and a further iteration is required, producing $A_8 = \{ab(g1), ab(g2), fault\_mode(g1, s1), fault\_mode(g2, s1)\}$. The algorithm thus computes the sets of revising assumptions A_1, A_2, A_5, A_6 and A_8, with A_1 and A_2 being the minimal ones, i.e. the minimal revisions of the original program.

Consider next that we make the fault model only partial by, withdrawing rule 4. So that we can still explain all observations, we "complete" the fault model by introducing rule 5 below, which expresses that in the presence of input to the inverter, and if the value to be explained is not equal to 0 (since that is explained by rule 3), then there is a missing fault mode for value V. Of course, *missing* has to be considered a revisable too.

inv(G,I,V) ← node(I,_), not equal(V,0), missing(G,V)	5
equal(V,V)	12

Now the following expected minimal revisions are produced:

$$\{ab(g1), fault\_mode(g1, s0)\} \; \{ab(g2), missing(g2, 1)\}$$

The above fault model "completion" is a general technique for explaining all observations, with the advantage, with respect to [8]'s lenient explanations, that missing fault modes are actually reported. In fact, we are simply debugging the fault model according to the methods of the previous section: we've added a rule that detects and provides desired solutions not found by the normal rules, just as in debugging. But also solutions not explained by other fault rules: hence the $not\,equal(V,0)$ condition. The debugging equivalent of the latter would be adding a rule to "explain" that a bug (i.e. fault mode) has already been detected (though not corrected). Furthermore, the reason $node(I, \_)$ is included in 5 is that there is a missing fault mode only if the inverter actually receives input. The analogous situation in debugging would be that of requiring that a predicate must actually ensure some predication about goals for it (eg. type checking) before it is deemed incomplete.

The analogy with debugging allows us to debug artifact specifications. Indeed, it suffices to employ the techniques of the previous section. By adding $not\,ab(G, R, HeadArguments)$ instead of $not\,ab(G)$ in rules, where R is the rule number, revisions will now inform us of which rules possibly produce wrong solutions that would explain bugs. Of course, we now need to add $not\,ab(G, R)$ to all other rules, but during diagnosis they will not interfere if we restrict the revisables to just those with the appropriate rule numbers. With regard to missing solutions, we've seen in the previous paragraph that it would be enough to add an extra rule for each predicate. Moreover the same rule numbering technique is also applicable.

We now come full circle and may rightly envisage a program as just another artifact, to which diagnostic problems, concepts, and solutions, can profitably apply:

Example 7. The (buggy) model of an inverter gate below entails $node(b,0)$, and also (wrongly) $node(b,1)$, when its input is 1.

```
inv(G,I,0)←node(I,1), not ab(G)
inv(G,I,1)←node(I,1), not ab(G) % bug: node(I,0)
node(b,V)←inv(g1,a,V)
node(a,1)
```

After the debugging transformation:

$$inv(G,I,0) \leftarrow node(I,1), not\ ab(G,1,[G,I,0])$$
$$inv(G,I,1) \leftarrow node(I,1), not\ ab(G,2,[G,I,1])$$
$$node(b,V) \leftarrow inv(g1,a,V),\ not\ ab(3,[b,V])$$
$$node(a,1) \leftarrow not\ ab(4,[a,V])$$

Now, adding to it $\perp \leftarrow node(b,1)$, and revising the now contradictory program the following minimal revisions are obtained:

$$\{ab(g1,2,[g1,a,1])\}\ \{ab(3,[b,1])\}\ \{ab(4,[a,1])\}$$

The minimal revision $\{ab(g1,2,[g1,a,1])\}$ states that either the inverter model is correct and therefore gate 1 is behaving abnormally or that rule 2 has a bug.

References

1. L. Console and P. Torasso. A spectrum of logical definitions of model-based diagnosis. *Computational Intelligence*, 7:133–141, 1991.
2. J. de Kleer and B.C. Williams. Diagnosis with behavioral modes. In *Proc. IJCAI'89*, pages 1329–1330, 1989.
3. M. R. Garey and D. S. Johnson. *Computers and Intractability*. Freeman and Co., 1979.
4. R. Greiner, B. A. Smith, and R. W. Wilkerson. A correction to the algorithm in reiter's theory of diagnosis. *Artificial Intelligence*, 41:79–88, 1989.
5. A. Guessoum and J. W. Lloyd. Updating knowledge bases. *New Generation Computing*, 8(1):71–89, 1990.
6. A. Guessoum and J. W. Lloyd. Updating knowledge bases II. *New Generation Computing*, 10(1):73–100, 1991.
7. A. C. Kakas and P. Mancarella. Generalised stable models: A semantics for abduction. In *Proc. ECAI'90*, pages 401–405, 1990.
8. K. Konolige. Using default and causal reasoning in diagnosis. In C. Rich B. Nebel and W. Swartout, editors, *Proc. KR'92*, pages 509–520. Morgan Kaufmann, 1992.
9. J. W. Lloyd. Declarative error diagnosis. *New Generation Computing*, 5(2):133–154, 1987.
10. L. M. Pereira, J. J. Alferes, and J.N. Aparício. Contradiction removal within well founded semantics. In W. Marek A. Nerode and V.S. Subrahmanian, editors, *Proc. Logic Programming and NonMonotonic Reasoning'91*, pages 105–119. MIT press, 1991.
11. L. M. Pereira, J. J. Alferes, and J.N. Aparício. Contradiction removal semantics with explicit negation. In *Proc. Applied Logic Conf.*, Amsterdam, 1992. ILLC.
12. L. M. Pereira, J. J. Alferes, and J.N. Aparício. Logic programming for nonmonotonic reasoning. In *Proc. Applied Logic Conf.*, Amsterdam, 1992. ILLC.
13. L. M. Pereira, J. J. Alferes, and C. Damásio. The sidetracking principle applied to well founded semantics. In *Proc. Simpósio Brasileiro de Inteligência Artificial SBIA'92*, pages 229–242, 1992.
14. L. M. Pereira, J.N. Aparício, and J. J. Alferes. Derivation procedures for extended stable models. In *Proc. IJCAI-91*. Morgan Kaufmann, 1991.

15. L. M. Pereira, C. Damásio, and J. J. Alferes. Diagnosis and debugging as contradiction removal. In L. M. Pereira and A. Nerode, editors, *2nd Int. Ws. on Logic Programming and NonMonotonic Reasoning*, pages 316–330. MIT Press, 1993.
16. C. Preist and K. Eshghi. Consistency-based and abductive diagnoses as generalised stable models. In *Proc. Fifth Generation Computer Systems '92*. ICOT, 1992.
17. R. Reiter. A theory of diagnosis from first principles. *Artificial Intelligence*, 32:57–96, 1987.

Well-Founded Approximations of Autoepistemic Logic

Jürgen Kalinski

University of Bonn
Institute of Computer Science III
Römerstr. 164, 53117 Bonn, Germany

Abstract. Autoepistemic Logic is used as a unifying principle for the introduction of stable states for disjunctive logic programs and programs with strong negation. But as stable states are a generalization of stable models, their computational complexity prevents them from being implemented in knowledge representation systems. It is therefore shown that the well-founded semantics for normal programs can be viewed as an approximate superset of all stable models. The same idea can also be applied to the other program classes, thus yielding efficient and semantically characterizable approximations of stable states. In each case the immediate consequence operator for the corresponding class of positive programs is combined with the Gelfond-Lifschitz transformation and semi-operationalizations are derived from structural observations.

1 Introduction

This paper is written from the perspective of autoepistemic reasoning. It shows that Autoepistemic Logic (originally proposed by Moore in [8]) can be used as a unifying principle for the treatment of negation in logic programs. The stable model semantics for normal programs is thereby generalized to disjunctive programs and programs with strong negation. Unfortunately, Autoepistemic Logic is a useful conceptual framework, but due to its computational complexity its practical value must be esteemed low. We will therefore show that the significantly more efficient well-founded semantics can be regarded as an approximation of the stable model semantics and that analogous well-founded approximations can be given for the other program classes. It is not our objective to offer yet another logic program semantics or non-monotonic logic. To the opposite, we prefer to discuss structural relationships between existing approaches.

2 Preliminaries

2.1 Logic Programs

A logic program is a set of rules

$$A_1 \vee \ldots \vee A_m \leftarrow B_1, \ldots, B_n$$

where every A_i is an atom and every B_i an atom or an atom negated by '$\sim$'. Function symbols are not allowed. When $m = 1$, the program is called *normal*, otherwise *disjunctive*. Programs without any occurrence of '$\sim$' are *positive*. Positive, normal programs are also called *definite*. For the following semantical discussion we assume that a logic program has been substituted by the finite set of all its ground instantiations in the Herbrand universe. Hence, the terms 'atom' and 'literal' will subsequently always refer to ground instances. As this whole paper is about the close relationship between autoepistemic knowledge bases and logic programs, both terms will be used interchangeably.

The semantics of definite programs have been studied by van Emden and Kowalski in [13]. On the model-theoretic side an atom is implied by a program if and only if it is in its smallest Herbrand model. On the procedural side SLD-resolution is sound and complete. The link between both viewpoints has been provided with the *immediate consequence operator*. For a definite program P this operator is a function on Herbrand interpretations:

$$T_P(I) = \{\, p \mid p \text{ an atom, there is some } p \leftarrow q_1, \ldots, q_n \in P$$
$$\text{with } q_i \in I \text{ for all } 1 \leq i \leq n \,\}$$

The least fixpoint of p consists of all atomic consequences of P.

2.2 Autoepistemic Logic

Autoepistemic Logic as proposed by Moore in [8] is one of the major Artificial Intelligence formalisms which aim at a union of declarative, logic-based knowledge representation with the non-monotonicity of human reasoning.

For illustration let us assume that you attend your doctor. She diagnoses some disease and also knows that a drug called Medsan has proved rather effective in such cases. Unfortunately, Medsan may cause harmless side-effects, such that it is only prescribed, *as long as it is not known* that the patient is allergic to the drug. Moore's Autoepistemic Logic (cf. [8]) is a formalization of this proper distinction between not-knowing whether some fact holds and the firm belief that it does not hold. The notion of 'not to know something' can only be given meaning when it is understood as a relative term, i.e. as 'not to know in a certain belief state'. So, as a first step the concept of a 'belief state' will have to be specified.

Our scenario consists of a knowledge-based system which is provided with a set of formulas (the knowledge base). User queries are queries about the belief state determined by the knowledge base. The reasonable belief states derivable from the knowledge base will be called 'stable models' or 'stable states'[1]. Statements about the system's belief state are represented by a belief operator '$\sim$'. An expression '$\sim$allergic' is true, if it is not believed or known that the patient is allergic to a drug, i.e. if the belief state does not incorporate a fact about the patient's allergy. Then the doctor's inference can be represented by the implication 'Medsan $\leftarrow$ disease, $\sim$allergic'.

---

[1] They correspond to Moore's 'expansions' (see [8]).

3 Autoepistemic Logic Program Semantics

3.1 Normal Programs: Stable Models

A belief state models a human's or knowledge-based system's beliefs about the world, i.e. about facts that he, she or it believes to be true. When the knowledge base consists of normal rules, its belief states are composed of atoms and of disjunctions of atoms in the context of disjunctive rules. The belief states which will be dealt with in the sequel of this paper are sets of atoms, closed sets of disjunctions of atoms, sets of literals and closed sets of disjunctions of literals.

Not to know a statement means not to know it with respect to some belief state. The Gelfond-Lifschitz transformation is a syntactic program transformation which enforces the interpretation of belief expressions '$\sim p$' relative to a given belief state.

Definition 1. Let P be a set of rules and I a belief state. The *Gelfond-Lifschitz transformation* P/I of P modulo I is defined by the following procedure:

- Delete all rules of P which have an expression $\sim p$ in the body and $p \in I$.
- Delete every expression $\sim p$ in the bodies of all remaining clauses.

As P/I is definite, its atomic consequences can be determined by the least fixpoint of the immediate consequence operator. Let us introduce some more notation:

$$S_P(I) := \text{lfp } T_{P/I}$$

The 'reasonable' belief states derivable from a knowledge base satisfy the following condition.

Definition 2. Let P be a normal logic program. A Herbrand interpretation I is called a *stable model* of P if and only if

$$I = S_P(I)$$

The *stable model semantics* ascribes a normal logic program the set of all its stable models.

Example 1. The program

$$p_1 \leftarrow \sim q_1 \qquad q_1 \leftarrow \sim p_1$$
$$\vdots \qquad\qquad \vdots$$
$$p_n \leftarrow \sim q_n \qquad q_n \leftarrow \sim p_n$$

has 2^n stable models, namely $\{A_1, \ldots, A_n\}$ where every A_i is either p_i or q_i. □

3.2 Disjunctive Programs: Stable States

For a positive disjunctive program P the *Minker consequence operator* is the counterpart of van Emden's and Kowalski's immediate consequence operator. It is defined on sets of disjunctions of atoms:

$$T_P^\vee(I) = \{\, \delta \mid \delta \text{ a disjunction of atoms, } \beta \leftarrow p_1, \ldots, p_n \in P,$$
$$p_i \vee \delta_i \in I \text{ for } 1 \le i \le n,\, \delta = \beta \vee \delta_1 \vee \ldots \vee \delta_n \,\}$$

Disjunctions are regarded as sets of atoms, although we hold on to write 'p ∨ q'. Hence no such disjunction contains the same atom twice. The Minker consequence operator (cf. [7]) is monotonic. In the same way as the least fixpoint of van Emden and Kowalski's consequence operator coincides with the smallest Herbrand model, the disjunctions of atoms which are implied by a positive disjunctive program are determined by the least fixpoint of Minker's consequence operator.

Theorem 3 (Minker/Rajasekar [7]). *Let P be a positive disjunctive program and δ a disjunction of atoms. Then the following are equivalent:*

1. *δ is a logical consequence of P.*
2. *$M \models \delta$ for every minimal model M of P.*
3. *$\delta' \in \operatorname{lfp}(T_P^\vee)$ for some subclause δ' of δ.*

Example 2. For the program $P = \{\, s, p \vee q \leftarrow s, t \leftarrow p, t \leftarrow q \,\}$ the least fixpoint of the Minker consequence operator is:

$$\operatorname{lfp}(T_P^\vee) = \{\, s, p \vee q, q \vee t, p \vee t, t \,\}$$

The disjunction $p \vee q \vee t$ contains the subclause $p \vee q \in \operatorname{lfp}(T_P^\vee)$. □

Although the $T_P^\vee$-operator is defined on sets of disjunctions, Minker and Rajasekar correlate it with the concept of models (see Theorem 3). Interestingly, belief states more directly mirror the operational concept on the declarative side. They also consist of disjunctions of atoms with the only additional condition that they are to be 'closed': Whenever a disjunction is included in the state, the same holds for every weaker disjunction. Thus the belief state induced by the foregoing example also contains $p \vee q \vee t$, whereas $\operatorname{lfp} T_P^\vee$ does not. Let us therefore introduce an operator for 'closing-off' a set of disjunctions.

Definition 4. The *disjunctive closure* of a set I of disjunctions of atoms is defined as:

$$\operatorname{cl}(I) := \{\, \delta \mid \delta \text{ a disjunction of atoms and there exists}$$
$$\delta' \in I \text{ such that } \delta' \text{ is a subclause of } \delta \,\}$$

We can now define the counterpart of stable models for disjunctive programs. Obviously, Definition 1 can be generalized to the case where I is a set of disjunctions of atoms. Let $S_P^\vee(I)$ denote the set of all disjunctions implied by P/I. By Theorem 3 we have

$$S_P^\vee(I) := \operatorname{cl}(\operatorname{lfp} T_{P/I}^\vee)$$

Definition 5. Let P be a disjunctive program. A set of disjunctions of atoms I is called a *stable state* for P if and only if

$$I = S_P^\vee(I)$$

Example 3. If P is positive, then $P/I = I$ for every I. Hence, the only stable state of a positive disjunctive program is the smallest fixpoint of the Minker-operator blown up, i.e. $\mathrm{cl}\,(\mathrm{lfp}\,T_P^\vee)$. □

The *stable state semantics* ascribes a disjunctive logic program the set of all its stable states. It generalizes the stable model semantics.

Theorem 6. *Let P be a normal program.*

1. *If I is a stable model, then $\mathrm{cl}\,(I)$ is a stable state.*
2. *The atomic subset of a stable state is a stable model.*

Example 4. The program

```
penguin(b1) ∨ ostrich(b1)
sparrow(b2)
sparrow(b3) ∨ ostrich(b3)
bird(X) ← sparrow(X)
bird(X) ← penguin(X)
bird(X) ← ostrich(X)
non-flyer(X) ← penguin(X)
non-flyer(X) ← ostrich(X)
flies(X) ← bird(X), ∼non-flyer(X)
```

has exactly one stable state, namely the closure of

```
{ penguin(b1) ∨ ostrich(b1), bird(b1), non-flyer(b1),
  sparrow(b2), bird(b2), flies(b2),
  sparrow(b3) ∨ ostrich(b3), bird(b3), flies(b3) }
```

Note that in the presence of the disjunction `sparrow(b3) ∨ ostrich(b3)` it is not known for sure that `b3` is a non-flyer. Hence, the last rule derives that it can fly.

The example also illustrates the basic difference between semantics based on interpretations (which distinguish between truth and falsity) and autoepistemic reasoning based on belief states (which talk about beliefs and non-beliefs). In the presence of the disjunction `penguin(b1) ∨ ostrich(b1)` it is not known that `b1` is a penguin, nor is it known that it is an ostrich. Hence, both belief expressions `∼penguin(b1)` and `∼ostrich(b1)` are true. In terms of belief states this is not in contradiction with the disjunction, whereas the disjunction together with `¬penguin(b1)` and `¬ostrich(b1)` would certainly be inconsistent. □

3.3 Drawbacks of Autoepistemic Logic

The problem with the stable model semantics is that it does not offer any constructive method for the computation of its models. The operator S_P is not monotonic. One can just 'guess' a model and check whether it satisfies the equation of Definition 2. Although the stable model semantics is conceptually elegant, its practical value must be esteemed low.

1. Programs do no longer have a canonical model. Indeed, Example 1 gives a program with an exponential number of stable models.
2. A program may fail to have any stable model at all (e.g. $P = \{ \mathbf{r} \leftarrow \sim \mathbf{r} \}$). Of course, this program does not make much sense. But conceive a knowledge base consisting of thousands of useful facts. It is hardly acceptable to let such a knowledge base become invalidated by a single 'junk rule'.
3. Even for the simple case of propositional programs the decision whether a stable model exists is NP-complete (cf. [5])!

Especially the last item is a knock-out for the stable model semantics (and for stable states as a generalization of stable models). But we regard its basic concepts of a grounded belief state as important and intelligible enough that we will try to save as much as possible of this framework. Especially what regards the treatment of disjunction (and strong negation later on), we think that Autoepistemic Logic provides one of the most intelligible conceptualizations available.

4 Well-Founded Approximations of Normal Programs

4.1 Definitions

The Gelfond-Lifschitz transformation formalizes the interpretation of belief expressions relative to a belief state. As long as we do not know which states a given knowledge base specifies, every belief state I is a candidate for the transformation. But if some atom is implied by every P/I, it is certainly a belief enforced by the knowledge base. Likewise, if it is not implied by any P/I, it is a disbelief. This argument provides additional constraints about the possible belief states. While the initial set contains every state, we can now focus on the collection of all states which include every belief but none of the disbeliefs.

Alternatively, the construction process can be regarded as an approximation of the set of all stable models. Take any such superset $\mathcal{I}$ for given — say the set of all Herbrand interpretations as an admittedly bad guess. The following observations follow from Definition 2:

- If $\mathbf{p} \in S_P(I)$ for all $I \in \mathcal{I}$, then $\mathbf{p}$ must be believed in every stable model.
- If $\mathbf{p} \notin S_P(I)$ for all $I \in \mathcal{I}$, then $\mathbf{p}$ must be disbelieved in every stable model.

Again we obtain additional information about the superset of stable models. Every stable model must subsume $\bigcap_{I \in \mathcal{I}} S_P(I)$. Furthermore, it must be disjoint from $\bigcap_{I \in \mathcal{I}} \overline{S_P(I)}$, i.e. it must not exceed $\bigcup_{I \in \mathcal{I}} S_P(I)$.

Definition 7 (Stable model operator). Let P be a normal logic program. Then $\mathcal{S}_P$ is an operator on sets of Herbrand interpretations defined by

$$\mathcal{S}_P(\mathcal{I}) := \{\, J \mid J \text{ a Herbrand interpretation,} $$
$$\bigcap_{I \in \mathcal{I}} S_P(I) \subseteq J \subseteq \bigcup_{I \in \mathcal{I}} S_P(I) \,\}$$

Proposition 8. *The operator $\mathcal{S}_P$ is monotonic.*

We regard the complete lattice of all sets of Herbrand interpretations to be partially ordered by the superset relation. The smallest element with respect this order is the set of all interpretations and iterative applications of the stable state operator starting from this set will end up in its least fixpoint $\mathrm{lfp}\,(\mathcal{S}_P)$. An atom is believed with respect to a set of belief states if it is included in all of its members, and disbelieved if it is included in none. Otherwise its belief status remains undetermined. So, the least fixpoint stands out by the fact that it is the least informative one, i.e. the one with the greatest number of undefined atoms or the one which specifies the smallest number of beliefs and disbeliefs about the world.

Example 5. The atom p is believed in $\{\{p\}, \{p, q\}\}$, whereas the status of q is left undefined. In $\{\emptyset, \{q\}\}$ the atom p is disbelieved. □

The next theorem states a one-to-one correspondence between singleton fixpoints and stable models.

Theorem 9. *Let P be a normal program. Then I is a stable model of P if and only if $\{I\}$ is a fixpoint of $\mathcal{S}_P$.*

Corollary 10. *Let P be a normal program and p an atom.*

1. *If p is in every member of $\mathrm{lfp}\,(\mathcal{S}_P)$, then it is in every stable model.*
2. *If p is in no member of $\mathrm{lfp}\,(\mathcal{S}_P)$, then it is in no stable model.*

The preceding corollary justifies our denotation of the $\mathrm{lfp}\,(\mathcal{S}_P)$-construction as an approximate superset of all stable models, i.e. as an approximation of the stable model semantics.

4.2 Operationalization

Of course, we cannot seriously propose to operate on sets of interpretations. As it turns out things can be simplified a lot due to some structural properties of the approximation. It will first be shown that iterative applications of $\mathcal{S}_P(\mathcal{I})$ exclusively generate lattices of interpretations. Second, it will be proved that it is not necessary to take an entire lattice into account. The smallest fixpoint of the stable model operator can alternatively be computed by an operator on single belief states. Iterative applications of this operator will result in the smallest and greatest elements of the lattices.

Proposition 11. *Let P be a normal logic program and $\mathcal{I}$ a set of Herbrand interpretations. Then $\mathcal{S}_P(\mathcal{I})$ is closed under union and intersection.*

Proposition 12. *Let P be a normal program.*

1. *$\mathcal{S}_P$ is anti-monotonic.*
2. *$\mathcal{S}_P^2$ is monotonic.*

Let $\mathcal{I}$ be closed under intersection and union. From all its members, the top element $\mathrm{lub}(\mathcal{I})$ is the one with the most atoms believed and the bottom element $\mathrm{glb}(\mathcal{I})$ the one with the most atoms disbelieved. From all the possible Gelfond-Lifschitz transformations of P it is $P/\mathrm{glb}(\mathcal{I})$, where a maximal number of negative body literals is true, whereas in $P/\mathrm{lub}(\mathcal{I})$ a minimal number is true and a maximal number of clauses of P removed instead. In the same way as the consequence relation for definite programs can be reduced to membership in the canonical smallest Herbrand model, the above construction originally based on sets of interpretations can always be reduced to two canonical models, namely the bottom and top elements of intermediate states. This is in sharp contrast to the possibly exponential number of stable models[2].

Lemma 13. *Let P be a normal program and $\mathcal{I}$ a set of Herbrand interpretations closed under union and intersection.*

1. *$\mathcal{S}_P(\mathcal{I}) = \mathcal{S}_P(\{\mathrm{glb}(\mathcal{I}), \mathrm{lub}(\mathcal{I})\})$*
2. *$\mathrm{glb}(\mathcal{S}_P(\mathcal{I})) = \mathcal{S}_P(\mathrm{lub}(\mathcal{I}))$ and $\mathrm{lub}(\mathcal{S}_P(\mathcal{I})) = \mathcal{S}_P(\mathrm{glb}(\mathcal{I}))$*

The preceding theorem has two important consequences. First, the believed and disbelieved atoms of $\mathcal{S}_P^n(\wp(B_P))$ can be determined on the basis of its bottom and top element[3]: Every member of the bottom element must be included in every other member, and what is not contained in the top element cannot be in any other member. Second, it is not necessary to completely compute any intermediate state. The bottom and top elements of any intermediate state can be computed on the basis of the top and bottom element of its predecessor. Fig. 1 depicts the sequence of lattices as computed by $\mathcal{S}_P$ and the results of $\mathcal{S}_P$-applications to their bottom and top elements.

Lemma 14. *Let P be a normal program. For every $n \geq 0$ the following holds:*

$$\mathrm{glb}\,\mathcal{S}_P^{2n}(\wp(B_P)) = \mathcal{S}_P^{2n}(\emptyset) \quad and \quad \mathrm{lub}\,\mathcal{S}_P^{2n}(\wp(B_P)) = \mathcal{S}_P^{2n}(B_P)$$

Theorem 15 (Main Theorem for Normal Programs). *Let P be a normal program and p an atom.*

$$\mathbf{p} \in \mathrm{lfp}\,\mathcal{S}_P^2 \iff \forall I \in \mathrm{lfp}\,\mathcal{S}_P : \mathbf{p} \in I$$
$$\implies \mathbf{p} \text{ is in every stable model of } P$$
$$and \quad \mathbf{p} \notin \mathrm{gfp}\,\mathcal{S}_P^2 \iff \forall I \in \mathrm{lfp}\,\mathcal{S}_P : \mathbf{p} \notin I$$
$$\implies \mathbf{p} \text{ is in no stable model of } P$$

---

[2] Proofs are deferred the more general section on Disjunctive Programs.
[3] $\wp(B_P)$ denotes the powerset of the Herbrand base.

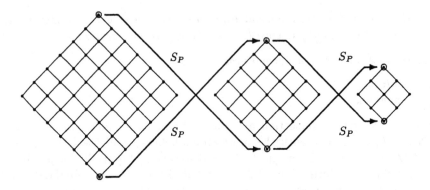

Fig. 1. Operators at work: $\mathcal{S}_P$ and S_P

The postulation of a least and greatest fixpoint of $S_P{}^2$ is justified by Proposition 12 and the fact that we operate in the complete powerset lattice of the Herbrand base. By now we have an approximation of the set of stable models. But we did not say anything about how expressive or how 'good' the approximation is.

Theorem 16. *Let P be a normal program and $\langle T, F \rangle$ its well-founded model. Then:*

$$\mathbf{p} \in I \text{ for all } I \in \text{lfp}\, \mathcal{S}_P \iff \mathbf{p} \in T$$
$$\text{and} \quad \mathbf{p} \notin I \text{ for all } I \in \text{lfp}\, \mathcal{S}_P \iff \mathbf{p} \in F$$

Furthermore, computation of the beliefs and disbeliefs of $\text{lfp}\,(\mathcal{S}_P)$ *is quadratic in the size of P.*

Proof. It has already been stated in [1] that the true atoms of the well-founded model coincide with what is contained in both $\text{lfp}\, S_P^2$ and $\text{gfp}\, S_P^2$ and its false atoms with what is contained in none of them. The claim then follows from Theorem 15. □

Hence, the approximation is significantly more efficient than the stable model semantics. Examples for the expressiveness of normal programs under the well-founded semantics and applications for knowledge representation problems can be found in [14] and [10].

4.3 Related Work

Let us first of all say in how far our approach differs from and coincides with Baral's and Subrahmanian's stable model classes in [1] and Van Gelder's alternating fixpoint procedure in [15]. Although originally formulated in a somewhat different notation, Allen Van Gelder's alternating fixpoint procedure (v. [15]) computes the greatest fixpoint of S_P^2. Its complement consists of all the atoms which are false in the well-founded model. In order to obtain the true atoms, S_P must be applied one more time as already stated in Lemma 13. Therefore Van Gelder can write the well-founded model of P as $\langle S_P(\text{gfp } S_P^2), \text{gfp } S_P^2 \rangle$. In [1] Baral and Subrahmanian rephrase it as $\langle \text{lfp } S_P^2, \overline{\text{gfp } S_P^2} \rangle$.

The basic notion of Baral's and Subrahmanian's approach is that of a *stable model class* which is a set $\mathcal{I}$ of interpretations such that

$$\mathcal{I} = \{ S_P(I) \mid I \in \mathcal{I} \}$$

It is only a technical result that the smallest stable model class — when imposing an adequate partial order — coincides with $\{\text{lfp } S_P^2, \text{gfp } S_P^2\}$. In our eyes neither the concept of a stable model class nor the idea of iterative applications of an anti-monotonic operator as in Van Gelder's approach are satisfyingly intuitive. We once again stress that the two canonical models are only a convenient representation of the idea to approximate the set of stable models by an appropriate superset.

5 Well-Founded Approximations of Disjunctive Programs

5.1 Definitions

While in the case of normal programs it suffices to consider the lattice of interpretations partially ordered by set inclusion, it will for disjunctive programs be necessary to consider all closed sets of disjunctions.

$$\mathcal{D}_P := \{ I \mid I \text{ a set of disjunctions of atoms with } \text{cl}(I) = I \}$$

Proposition 17. *The set $\langle \mathcal{D}_P, \subseteq \rangle$ is a complete lattice with set intersection and union. The bottom and top elements are the disjunctive closures of the empty set and the Herbrand base.*

The whole argument and procedure is now completely analogous to that of normal programs. We will therefore confine ourselves to a listing of the main results.

Definition 18 (Stable state operator). Let P be a disjunctive program and $\mathcal{I}$ a set of sets of disjunctions. Then $S_P^\vee$ is the operator defined by

$$S_P^\vee(\mathcal{I}) := \{ J \mid J \in \mathcal{D}_P, \bigcap_{I \in \mathcal{I}} S_P^\vee(I) \subseteq J \subseteq \bigcup_{I \in \mathcal{I}} S_P^\vee(I) \}$$

Theorem 19. *Let P be a disjunctive program. Then I is a stable state of P if and only if $\{I\}$ is a fixpoint of $S_P^\vee$.*

Corollary 20. *Let P be a normal program and δ a disjunction of atoms.*

1. *If δ is in every member of $\text{lfp}(S_P^\vee)$, then it is in every stable state of P.*
2. *If δ is in no member of $\text{lfp}(S_P^\vee)$, then it is in no stable state of P.*

5.2 Operationalization

We can now once again reduce the construction process from sets of closed sets of disjunctions to single members of $\mathcal{D}_P$.

Proposition 21. *Let P be a disjunctive program and $\mathcal{I} \subseteq \mathcal{D}_P$. Then $S_P^\vee(\mathcal{I})$ is closed under union and intersection.*

Proposition 22. *Let P be a disjunctive program.*

1. *$S_P^\vee$ is anti-monotonic.*
2. *$S_P^{\vee^2}$ is monotonic.*

Lemma 23. *Let P be a disjunctive program and $\mathcal{I} \subseteq \mathcal{D}_P$ closed under union and intersection.*

1. *$S_P^\vee(\mathcal{I}) = S_P^\vee(\{\mathrm{glb}\,(\mathcal{I}), \mathrm{lub}\,(\mathcal{I})\})$*
2. *$\mathrm{glb}\,(S_P^\vee(\mathcal{I})) = S_P^\vee(\mathrm{lub}\,(\mathcal{I}))$ and $\mathrm{lub}\,(S_P^\vee(\mathcal{I})) = S_P^\vee(\mathrm{glb}\,(\mathcal{I}))$*

Proof. For every $I \in \mathcal{I}$ we have $\mathrm{lub}\,(\mathcal{I}) \supseteq I \supseteq \mathrm{glb}\,(\mathcal{I})$ which implies

$$S_P^\vee(\mathrm{lub}\,(\mathcal{I})) \subseteq S_P^\vee(I) \subseteq S_P^\vee(\mathrm{glb}\,(\mathcal{I}))$$

by Definition 1 and Proposition 22. Hence:

$$S_P^\vee(\mathcal{I}) = \{\, J \mid J \in \mathcal{D}_P, \bigcap_{I \in \mathcal{I}} S_P^\vee(I) \subseteq J \subseteq \bigcup_{I \in \mathcal{I}} S_P^\vee(I)\,\}$$
$$= \{\, J \mid J \in \mathcal{D}_P,$$
$$\mathrm{glb}\,(\{S_P^\vee(I) \mid I \in \mathcal{I}\}) \subseteq J \subseteq \mathrm{lub}\,(\{S_P^\vee(I) \mid I \in \mathcal{I}\})\,\}$$
$$= \{\, J \mid J \in \mathcal{D}_P, S_P^\vee(\mathrm{lub}\,(\mathcal{I})) \subseteq J \subseteq S_P^\vee(\mathrm{glb}\,(\mathcal{I}))\,\}$$
$$= S_P^\vee(\{\mathrm{glb}\,(\mathcal{I}), \mathrm{lub}\,(\mathcal{I})\})$$

Obviously, the greatest lower bound of this set is $S_P^\vee(\mathrm{lub}\,(\mathcal{I}))$ and $S_P^\vee(\mathrm{glb}\,(\mathcal{I}))$ the least upper bound. $\qquad\square$

Lemma 24. *Let P be a disjunctive program with Herbrand base B_P. For every disjunction δ and every $n \geq 0$ the following holds:*

$$\mathrm{glb}\, S_P^{\vee^{2n}}(\mathcal{D}_P) = S_P^{\vee^{2n}}(\mathrm{cl}\,(\emptyset))   \text{ and }   \mathrm{lub}\, S_P^{\vee^{2n}}(\mathcal{D}_P) = S_P^{\vee^{2n}}(\mathrm{cl}\,(B_P))$$

Proof. For $n = 0$ the claim is fairly obvious. Assume it has been proved up to some n.

$$\mathrm{glb}\, S_P^{2(n+1)}(\mathcal{D}_P) = S_P^\vee\big(\mathrm{lub}\, S_P^{2n+1}(\mathcal{D}_P)\big)   \text{(by Lemma 23)}$$
$$= S_P^\vee\big(S_P^\vee(\mathrm{glb}\, S_P^{2n}(\mathcal{D}_P))\big)   \text{(by Lemma 23)}$$
$$= S_P^\vee\big(S_P^\vee(S_P^{\vee^{2n}}(\mathrm{cl}\,(\emptyset)))   \text{(induction hypothesis)}$$
$$= S_P^{\vee^{2(n+1)}}(\mathrm{cl}\,(\emptyset))$$

$$\operatorname{lub} S_P^{\vee\, 2(n+1)}(\mathcal{D}_P) = S_P^{\vee}\left(\operatorname{glb} S_P^{2n+1}(\mathcal{D}_P)\right) \qquad \text{(by Lemma 23)}$$
$$= S_P^{\vee}\left(S_P^{\vee}(\operatorname{lub} S_P^{2n}(\mathcal{D}_P))\right) \quad \text{(by Lemma 23)}$$
$$= S_P^{\vee}\left(S_P^{\vee}(S_P^{\vee\, 2n}(\operatorname{cl}(B_P)))\right) \quad \text{(induction hypothesis)}$$
$$= S_P^{\vee\, 2(n+1)}(\operatorname{cl}(B_P))$$

The claim then follows from the induction hypothesis. □

Theorem 25 (Main Theorem for Disjunctive Programs). *For every disjunctive program P and every disjunction of atoms δ the following holds:*

$$\delta \in \operatorname{lfp} S_P^{\vee\, 2} \iff \forall I \in \operatorname{lfp} S_P^{\vee} : \delta \in I$$
$$\implies \delta \text{ is in every stable state of } P$$

$$\text{and} \quad \delta \notin \operatorname{gfp} S_P^{\vee\, 2} \iff \forall I \in \operatorname{lfp} S_P^{\vee} : \delta \notin I$$
$$\implies \delta \text{ is in no stable state of } P$$

Proof. Let δ be a disjunction of atoms:

$$\delta \in \operatorname{lfp} S_P^{\vee\, 2} \iff \delta \in \operatorname{glb}(\operatorname{lfp} \mathcal{S}_P) \qquad \text{(by Lemma 24)}$$
$$\iff \delta \in I \text{ for all } I \in \operatorname{lfp} \mathcal{S}_P \quad \text{(by Proposition 21)}$$
$$\implies \delta \text{ is in every stable state of } P \quad \text{(by Theorem 19)}$$

Let I be a stable state of P:

$$\delta \in I \implies \delta \in I \text{ for some } I \in \operatorname{lfp} \mathcal{S}_P \quad \text{(by Theorem 19)}$$
$$\iff \delta \in \operatorname{lub}(\operatorname{lfp} \mathcal{S}_P^2) \qquad \text{(by Proposition 21)}$$
$$\iff \delta \in \operatorname{gfp} S_P^{\vee\, 2} \qquad \text{(by Lemma 24)}$$

□

Example 6. For the knowledge base of Example 4 the approximation $\operatorname{lfp} S_P^{\vee\, 2} = \operatorname{gfp} S_P^{\vee\, 2}$ coincides with the unique stable state. □

5.3 Related Work

There have been several proposals in the logic programming community to extend the stable model as well as the well-founded semantics from normal to disjunctive programs (e.g. [12], [3], [11]). It is a common feature of all these approaches that they hold on to a model-based perspective when changing from normal to disjunctive programs. Literals '$\sim$p' are not interpreted with respect to belief states but with respect to certain models of the program where they are identified with '$\neg$p'. As a basic difference, it cannot be the case that both $\neg$p and $\neg$q are true, when the disjunction of the two atoms is true. In an autoepistemic setting literals are interpreted with respect to belief states and '$\sim$p' is read as 'p is not known'. It has already been pointed out in Example 4 that $\sim$p and $\sim$q are consistent with the disjunction.

We believe that there are three advantages of the autoepistemic viewpoint. First, the formulation of stable states provides an intuitive reading of 'negations' in rule bodies. The model-based viewpoint blurs the differences between '$\sim$' and '$\neg$' which makes it impossible to incorporate the concept of strong negation in addition to negation as failure. Second, stable states can be given a well-founded approximation which combines the immediate consequence operator for the corresponding class of positive programs with the Gelfond-Lifschitz transformation. Finally, we regard the uniformity of the semantic background, the approximations and the semi-operational formulations as the highest recommendation of the autoepistemic viewpoint.

6 Strong Negation

It is by now fairly obvious how to extend this idea to incorporate strong negation '$\neg$'. One just has to base the above formalisms on ground literals instead of atoms. Thus in a rule

$$A_1 \vee \ldots \vee A_m \leftarrow B_1, \ldots, B_n$$

every A_i is a literal and every B_i a literal or a literal negated by '$\sim$'. For efficiency reasons this framework does not and should treat strong negation in the classical sense: The interpretation of a negated atom is completely decoupled from the interpretation of the atom itself. Thus $p \leftarrow q$ and $\neg p$ does not imply $\neg q$ and $\{p, \neg p\}$ is not inconsistent. This viewpoint is more in the spirit of [2] and in contrast to contradiction removal as done by [9]. To prevent the derivation of both an atom and its negation would be the task of integrity constraints. Belief states are sets of literals or closed sets of disjunctions of literals.

$$T_P^\neg(I) = \{ A \mid A \text{ a literal, there is some } A \leftarrow B_1, \ldots, B_n \in P$$
$$\text{with } B_i \in I \text{ for all } 1 \leq i \leq n \}$$

$$S_P^\neg(I) := \text{lfp}\, T_{P/I}^\neg$$

$$T_P^{\neg\vee}(I) = \{ \delta \mid \delta \text{ a disjunction of literals, } \beta \leftarrow B_1, \ldots, B_n \in P,$$
$$B_i \vee \delta_i \in I \text{ for } 1 \leq i \leq n, \delta = \beta \vee \delta_1 \vee \ldots \vee \delta_n \}$$

$$\text{cl}^\neg(I) := \{ \delta \mid \delta \text{ a disjunction of literals and there exists}$$
$$\delta' \in I \text{ such that } \delta' \text{ is a subclause of } \delta \}$$

$$S_P^{\neg\vee}(I) := \text{cl}^\neg(\text{lfp}\, T_{P/I}^{\neg\vee})$$

One can now proceed in complete analogy to the cases of normal and disjunctive programs. A set of literals I (resp. set of disjunctions of atoms) is called *stable* if and only if $I = S_P^\neg(I)$ (resp. $I = S_P^{\neg\vee}(I)$). One can specify their well-founded approximations and reduce them to the smallest and greatest fixpoint of $S_P^{\neg 2}$ and $S_P^{\neg\vee 2}$. We will not go into details here, but just illustrate strong negation by an example.

Example 7. Part of the ornithological knowledge of Example 4 can more adequately be modeled as:

```
¬flies(X) ← penguin(X)
¬flies(X) ← ostrich(X)
flies(X) ← bird(X),∼¬flies(X)
```

The approximation yields:

$$\text{lfp } S_P^{\neg\vee^2} = \text{cl}(\{\text{penguin(b1)} \vee \text{ostrich(b1)}, \text{sparrow(b2)},$$
$$\text{sparrow(b3)} \vee \text{ostrich(b3)}, \text{bird(b1)},$$
$$\text{bird(b2)}, \text{bird(b3)}, \neg\text{flies(b1)},$$
$$\text{flies(b2)}, \text{flies(b3)}\})$$
$$= \text{gfp } S_P^{\neg\vee^2}$$

The two canonical states are identical and correspond to our intuitive understanding of the knowledge base. ☐

In contrast to [3] or [6] which are based on the notion of stable models our approach adopts the nice complexity results of the well-founded semantics.

7 Conclusion

Strictly following the guideline given by Autoepistemic Logic, we have proposed the notion of stable states as a generalization of stable models. The autoepistemic perspective provides an intuitive conceptual background for the reading of normal and disjunctive knowledge bases. While its computational complexity rules it out for practical purposes, we have shown that the well-founded semantics can be regarded as an approximation of the stable model semantics. We have also introduced a completely analogous approximation procedure for stable states. Hence, from the viewpoint of logic programming the autoepistemic perspective provides a uniform frame for semantic modeling, for semantically characterizable approximations and for semi-operational formulations in terms of immediate consequence operators. From the viewpoint of non-monotonic reasoning the reduction of Autoepistemic Logic to logic programs paves the way for its implementation in a knowledge representation system.

In [4] we have taken a converse approach defining a well-founded approximation for Moore's autoepistemic expansions. The logic programming perspective of this paper seems to be more relevant for practical applications. From a formal viewpoint both approaches follow the same line of reasoning. We are currently investigating an algebraic formulation of their common core which supports an extension of the concept of well-founded approximations from logic programs to object-oriented logic programs.

References

1. Chitta R. Baral and V. S. Subrahmanian. Stable and extension class theory for logic programs and default logics. *Journal of Automated Reasoning*, 8:345–366, 1992.
2. Nuel D. Belnap. How a computer should think. In Gilbert Ryle, editor, *Contemporary Aspects of Philosophy*, pages 30–56. Oriel Press, 1976.
3. Michael Gelfond and Vladimir Lifschitz. Classical negation in logic programs and disjunctive databases. *New Generation Computing*, 9:365–385, 1991.
4. Jürgen Kalinski. Weak autoepistemic reasoning and well-founded semantics. In *Proc. of the Workshop on Theoretical Foundations of Knowledge Representation and Reasoning (to be published)*, 1992.
5. H. A. Kautz and B. Selman. Hard problems for simple default logics. In *Proc. of the 1st Int. Conf. on Principles of Knowledge Representation and Reasoning*, pages 189–197. Morgan Kaufmann, 1989.
6. Robert A. Kowalski and Fariba Sadri. Logic programs with exceptions. In *Proc. of the 7th Int. Conf. on Logic Programming*, pages 598–613. MIT Press, 1990.
7. Jack Minker and Arcot Rajasekar. A fixpoint semantics for disjunctive logic programs. *Journal of Logic Programming*, 9:45–74, 1990.
8. Robert C. Moore. Semantical considerations on nonmonotonic logic. *Artificial Intelligence*, 25(4):75–94, 1985.
9. L. M. Pereira, J. N. Aparício, and J. J. Alferes. Contradiction removal within well-founded semantics. In *Proc. of the 1st Int. Workshop on Logic Programming and Non-monotonic Reasoning*, pages 105–119. MIT Press, 1991.
10. L. M. Pereira, J. N. Aparício, and J. J. Alferes. Non-monotonic reasoning with well founded semantics. In *Proc. of the 8th Int. Conf. on Logic Programming*, pages 475–489. MIT Press, 1991.
11. Teodor C. Przymusinski. Stable semantics for disjunctive programs. *New Generation Computing*, 9:401–424, 1991.
12. Kenneth A. Ross. The well founded semantics for disjunctive logic programs. In *Proc. of the 1st Int. Conf. on Deductive and Object-Oriented Databases*, pages 385–402. North-Holland, 1990.
13. M. H. van Emden and R. A. Kowalski. The semantics of predicate logic as a programming language. *Journal of the ACM*, 23(4):733–742, 1976.
14. A. Van Gelder, K. A. Ross, and J. S. Schlipf. The well-founded semantics for general logic programs. *Journal of the ACM*, 38(3):620–650, 1991.
15. Allen Van Gelder. The alternating fixpoint of logic programs with negation. In *Proc. of the 8th Symp. on Principles of Database Systems*, pages 1–10, 1989.

A Process Model for Default Logic and Its Realization in Logic Programming

Grigoris Antoniou
Elmar Langetepe

Dept. of Mathematics and Computer Science
Albrechtstrasse 28, D-4500 Osnabrück, Germany
e-mail: ga@informatik.uni-osnabrueck.de

Abstract. One of the main themes of making logics applicable in computer science and artificial intelligence is to provide mechanisms for dealing with them operationally. In this paper we introduce processes as a procedural interpretation of the usual fixed-point definition of extensions. Processes allow to compute the extensions of simple default theories by hand. Then we give a prototypical Prolog implementation of our model in Prolog. We do not claim that the program is very efficient, but it is able to compute the extensions of the usual examples found in literature. Finally, we give a more efficient implementation by translating default theories (with some restrictions) to logic programs and making direct use of Prolog's reasoning capacities.

1 Motivation

Many concrete nonmonotonic logics like default [1,2,8] or autoepistemic logic [7] are based on the notion of *extension* which describes a possible 'view of the world'. Extensions are traditionally defined in form of fixed-point equations. Though mathematically precise, such definitions tell nothing about how to practically find out the extensions of a theory. In fact, nonmonotonic logic suffers since its beginnings from deficiencies concerning the easy applicability of its concepts to concrete examples. Even for small theories, it seems to be difficult to calculate extensions. In order to show that this is not only a problem for novices, we cite Moore [6]: '*One of the problems with our original presentation of autoepistemic logic was that, since both the logic and its semantics were defined nonconstructively, we were unable to easily prove the existence of stable expansions of nontrivial sets of premises*'.

In the present paper we address the problem of operationality by giving an operational model for Reiter's default logic [1,8] based on processes. With it, we may compute extensions of many theories by hand. Another advantage of processes is that they can also be used as *theoretical tools*, leading to simpler and clearer proofs; the reader can find in [9] many new proofs for well-known results on default logic based on the process concept.

A further advantage of our approach is that it can be implemented in Prolog in a natural manner. Though straightforward, the first implementation given in section 4 is unsatisfactory from the efficiency viewpoint. Therefore, we show how default theories of a special kind (for details see section 5) can be translated into Prolog programs that compute exactly the default extensions. The idea is to make direct use of the reasoning capabilities of Prolog, instead of interacting with a separate theorem prover. Throughout the paper, we assume familiarity with the basics of predicate logic and logic programming (see, for example, [5,10]).

2 Basics of Default Logic

1. Definition A default δ *is a string* $\varphi:\psi_1,...,\psi_n/\chi$ *with closed first-order formulas* $\varphi,\psi_1,...,\psi_n$ *and* χ *(n>0). We call* φ *the prerequisite,* $\psi_1,...,\psi_n$ *the justifications, and* χ *the consequent of* δ. *A default schema is a string of the form* $\varphi:\psi_1,...,\psi_n/\chi$ *with arbitrary formulas. Such a schema defines a set of defaults, namely the set of all ground instances* $\varphi\sigma:\psi_1\sigma,...,\psi_n\sigma/\chi\sigma$ *of* $\varphi:\psi_1,...,\psi_n/\chi$, *where* σ *is an arbitrary ground substitution.*

2. Definition A default theory T is a pair (W,D) consisting of a set of closed formulas W (the set of truths) and a denumerable set of defaults D. The default set D may be defined using default schemata.

The purpose of a default theory T is to lay down what an agent may believe in. The current belief of an agent forms a set E of closed formulas, called an *extension* for T. Usually, there will be several concurring (perhaps mutually excluding) extensions.

3. Definition Let $\delta=\varphi:\psi_1,...,\psi_n/\chi$ *be a default, and E and F sets of formulas. We say that* δ *is applicable to F with respect to belief set E iff* $\varphi\in F$, $\neg\psi_1\notin E,...,\neg\psi_n\notin E$. *For a set D of defaults, we say that F is closed under D with respect to E iff, for every default* $\varphi:\psi_1,...,\psi_n/\chi$ *in D that is applicable to F with respect to belief set E, its consequent* χ *is also contained in F.*

4. Definition Given a default theory T=(W,D) and a set of closed formulas E, let $\Lambda_T(E)$ *be the least set of closed formulas that contains W, is closed under logical conclusion and closed under D with respect to E.*

5. Definition Let T be a default theory. A set of closed formulas E is called an extension of T iff $\Lambda_T(E)=E$.

6. Example

Consider the default theory $T=(\varnothing,\{\delta_0=\text{true}:B/B,\ \delta_1=\text{true}:\neg B/\neg B\})$. $E_1=\text{Th}(\{B\})$ is an extension of T: It trivially includes the truths of T, $\text{Th}(E_1)=E_1$, and E_1 is closed under the default set w.r.t. E_1. Furthermore, E_1 is a minimal such set:

the only deductively closed proper subset of E_1 is $Th(\emptyset)$, but $Th(\emptyset)$ is not closed under D w.r.t. E_1.

This shows that $\Lambda_T(E_1)=E_1$, so E_1 is an extension of T. Likewise, $E_2=Th(\{\neg B\})$ is also an extension of T. Are there any more extensions? We feel quite sure that this is not the case (as δ_0 'blocks' application of δ_1 and vice versa) but how could we prove our claim? And if we have such difficulties in this trivial example, what about really complicated theories? In the next section we shall present a method for obtaining an overview of all extensions of a default theory, thus giving an answer to these pessimistic questions.

3 A Process Concept for Default Logic

7. Definition Let $T=(W,D)$ be a default theory and $\Pi=(\delta_0,\delta_1,\delta_2,...)$ a finite or infinite sequence of defaults from D not containing any repetitions (modelling an application order of defaults from D). We denote by $\Pi[k]$ the initial segment of Π of length k, provided the length of Π is at least k. Then we define the following concepts:

(a) $In(\Pi)$ is $Th(M)$, where M contains the formulas of W and all conclusions of defaults occurring in Π.

(b) $Out(\Pi)$ is the set of negations of all justifications of defaults occurring in Π.

(c) Π is called a **process** of T iff δ_k is applicable to $In(\Pi[k])$ w.r.t. belief set $In(\Pi[k])$, for every k such that δ_k occurs in Π.

(d) Π is called a **successful process** of T iff $In(\Pi)\cap Out(\Pi)=\emptyset$, otherwise it is called a **failed process**.

(e) Π is a **closed process** of T iff every $\delta\in D$ which is applicable to $In(\Pi)$ with respect to belief set $In(\Pi)$ already occurs in Π.

$In(\Pi)$ collects all formulas in which we believe after application of the defaults in Π, while $Out(\Pi)$ consists of all those formulas which we should avoid to believe for the sake of consistency.

The following theorem states the fundamental relationship between the extensions of a default theory T and the closed successful processes of T (its proof is found in Appendix A).

8. Theorem Let $T=(W,D)$ be a default theory. If Π is a closed successful process of T, then $In(\Pi)$ is an extension of T. Conversely, for every extension E of T there exists a closed, successful process Π of T with $E=In(\Pi)$.

The extensions of a default theory T are thus just the In-sets of closed, successful processes of T. So, to determine extensions, we may simply apply defaults in an arbitrary order hoping that never a failure occurs. Having arrived at a failure situation, we must give up the current knowledge base and trace back within our process. There is no reason why to control the selection of defaults in order to avoid failed processes.

The approach above is obviously inadequate in case that D contains an infinite number of defaults. The definition of closed processes seems to require a look ahead to the final extension In(Π) already while constructing Π. This problem is simply resolved by the following lemma.

9. Lemma *An infinite process* Π *of T is closed iff every* $\delta \in D$ *that is applicable to In(Π[k]) with respect to belief set In(Π[k]), for infinitely many numbers k, is already contained in* Π.

The simple proof is an application of the compactness theorem of predicate logic. So, to achieve closed processes we must eventually apply each default which is, from some stage on, constantly demanding for application. This is nothing more than *fairness,* a situation commonly known from various fields dealing with concurring processes. If a survey of all possible processes of a default theory T is aspired, we may arrange all possible processes in a canonical manner within the so-called process tree of T.

10. Definition *Let* $T=(W,D)$ *be a default theory. The* **process tree of** *T is a finite or infinite tree with edges labelled with defaults from D and nodes labelled with a theory I (the In-set built up so far) and a formula set O (the Out-set obtained so far) as follows:*

- *The root node is labelled with Th(W) and* $\emptyset$.

- *Consider a node N labelled with theory I and formula set O.*

  If $I \cap O \neq \emptyset$ *then N is a leaf. Else N possesses a successor node* $N(\delta)$ *for every default* $\delta = \varphi : \psi_1, \ldots, \psi_n / \chi$ *such that* δ *does not already occur along the path from the root to the considered node and* δ *is applicable to I with respect to belief set I. The edge from N to* $N(\delta)$ *is labelled with* δ, *and* $N(\delta)$ *is labelled with* $Th(I \cup \{\chi\})$ *and* $O \cup \{\neg\psi_1, \ldots, \neg\psi_n\}$.

A **path** *is any maximal sequence of nodes starting at the root of T.*

Note that the process tree of T may contain four types of paths with respect to the sequence Π of defaults along it:

- failed (thus finite) paths
- successful paths of finite length (these are automatically closed)
- successful paths of infinite length which are closed
- successful paths of infinite length which are not closed

11. Example

Consider $T=(\emptyset,\{\text{true}:A/\neg A,\})$. The process tree of T is found in Figure 1. T has no extensions. This is an example of a default application that a posteriori invalidates a previously successful consistency check.

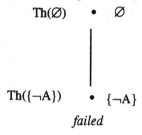

$$\text{Th}(\emptyset) \quad \bullet \quad \emptyset$$

$$\text{Th}(\{\neg A\}) \quad \bullet \quad \{\neg A\}$$

failed

Figure 1

12. Example

Consider $T=(\emptyset,D)$ with $D=\{\delta_0=\text{true}:P/\neg Q,\ \delta_1=\text{true}:Q/R\}$. The process tree of T looks as shown in Figure 2.

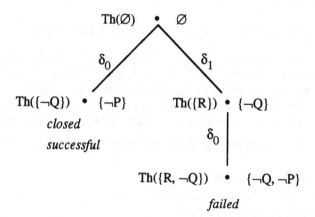

$$\text{Th}(\emptyset) \quad \bullet \quad \emptyset$$

$\delta_0 \qquad \delta_1$

$$\text{Th}(\{\neg Q\}) \quad \bullet \quad \{\neg P\} \qquad \text{Th}(\{R\}) \quad \bullet \quad \{\neg Q\}$$

closed

successful

δ_0

$$\text{Th}(\{R, \neg Q\}) \quad \bullet \quad \{\neg Q, \neg P\}$$

failed

Figure 2

13. Example

Consider the default theory $T=(\emptyset,\{\delta_0,\delta_1\})$ with $\delta_0=\text{true}:P/P$ and $\delta_1=\text{true}:Q/\neg P$. It has exactly one extension, $\text{Th}(\{\neg P\})$, as seen from its process tree in Figure 3.

We close the discussion of the process model by a brief complexity analysis. Given a default theory with n defaults, the worst case is that all permutations of defaults must be considered, leading to complexity n! This is very unsatisfactory, since there are at most 2^n extensions. In fact, all extensions of a theory can be determined in exponential time (at most $n*4^n$) by systematically

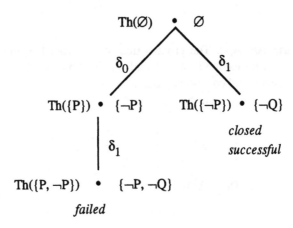

Figure 3

checking whether one of the 2^n potential extensions is indeed one. The latter approach is, of cource, extremely inefficient in practice, whereas most default sequences usually do not form processes, so the efficiency of the process model is not as bad as it seems.

4 A Prototypical Prolog Implementation of Processes

Though our process model can be easily used for small examples, calculating extensions by hand can be uncomfortable for larger or complicated default theories. As we have already stated in the introduction, it is possible to give a simple Prolog implementation of our model in a straightforward way. For the sake of simplicity, we restrict ourselves to defaults with one justification. Defaults A:B/C are represented as default(A,B,C), the negation symbol $\neg$ by ~.

```
extension(W,D,E) :- process(D,[ ],W,[ ],_,E,_).
process(D,Pcurrent,InCurrent,OutCurrent,P,In,Out) :-
        element(default(A,B,C),D),
        not element(default(A,B,C),Pcurrent),
        sequent(InCurrent,[A]),
        not sequent(InCurrent, [~B]),
        % default A:B/C is applicable to InCurrent w.r.t. InCurrent
        process(D, [default(A,B,C) I Pcurrent],
                   [C I InCurrent],
                   [~B I OutCurrent],P,In,Out).
process(D,P,In,Out,P,In,Out) :-  % P is a closed and successful process
        closed(D,P,In),
        success(In,Out).
```

```
closed(D,P,In) :-   % P is closed under D w.r.t. In
       not (  element(default(A,B,C),D),
              not element(default(A,B,C),P),
              sequent(In,[A]),
              not sequent(In,[~B])).
```

```
success(In,Out) :- not (element(B,Out), sequent(In,[B])). %Th(In)∩Out=∅
```

Predicate extension computes extensions E of default theory (W,D). Predicate process computes a new path P with In-set In and Out-set Out from a current path Pcurrent.

Missing are an input component for default theories, and a (classical) theorem prover (it is predicate sequent in the program text above; it could be Wang's algorithm for theories in pure propositional logic).

This implementation is, of course, far from being efficient for application in practice. An obvious improvement would be to make direct use of Prolog's deductive capabilities instead of requiring an external theorem prover. This is the starting point for the approach to be presented in the next section.

5 Translation of Default Theories into Prolog Programs

Our aim is to replace the calls of the external prover sequent in the program of section 4 by appropriate calls of equivalent Prolog goals. This already implies a first restriction on default theories: the set of truths W should form a Horn logic program.

A default $\varphi{:}\psi/\chi$ can be operationally read as follows: 'In order to derive χ, derive φ, and show that $\neg\psi$ does not follow from the current knowledge. The first idea for 'encoding' default theories in Prolog is to make use of Prolog's negation operator 'not', but a straightforward, naive approach would lead to errors. Consider, for example, the Nixon diamond; we would be tempted to express the theory in Prolog as follows:

```
pac :- qua, not no-pac.
no-pac :- rep, not pac.
rep.
qua.
```

where no-pac is a new predicate symbol denoting ¬pac. This representation obviously leads to an infinite loop. The main problem can be formulated as follows in a general setting: When testing applicability of a default, only the current knowledge must be taken into consideration (i.e. In(Π) for the process Π built so far) instead of the entire knowledge. In our concrete example, if we decide to start with the first default, then the second default may not be used when checking consistency of the justification (i.e. when calling not no-pac).

We solve this problem by numbering the defaults and introducing a list L which keeps track of the defaults that have been applied so far (L represents thus the process that has been built so far). A default may be used at this stage only if its number occurs in L.

Our approach works only on finite default theories satisfying the following conditions:

- All truths are Horn logic formulas.
- Only one justification per default is allowed (for the sake of simplicity only).
- The prerequisite, justification, and conclusion of each default is a literal (i.e. no compound formulas occur in the defaults).

This restriction may seem quite strong, but includes on the other side wellp-known classes of default theories like taxonomic default theories [3] that have applications in practice [4].

From each default theory T=(W,D) we construct a logic program that computes exactly the extensions of T. The logic program consists of three parts: A (problem independent) extension generator, a representation of the defaults, and a representation of the truths.

Defaults An occurrence of a negative fact $\neg p(t_1,\ldots,t_n)$ in a default is replaced by 'no $p(t_1,\ldots,t_n)$', where 'no' is an 1-ary prefix operator.

- Given a default p:q/r (with 0-ary predicate symbols p,q,r), we add to the Prolog program the clauses

    default(p(L), no q(L), r(L), i, L).

    r(L) :- member(i,L).

  where i is the number of the default (according to a chosen numbering). The first fact represents the default (note that not(no q(L)) is the consistency check to be executed when the defaults in L have been applied). The second clause expresses the inclusion of the default's conclusion in the In-set in case that i∈ L, i.e. the default has been 'executed'.

- Double occurrences of 'no' are deleted; so, p:¬q/r is represented by

    default(p(L), q(L), r(L), j, L).

    r(L) :- member(j,L).

Truths They are always applicable (i.e. in any In-set), so they should not depend on the current list L. Therefore, a rule $p(\underline{t})$:- $q_1(\underline{s}_1),\ldots,q_k(\underline{s}_k)$ is represented by

$p(\underline{t},L)$:- $q_1(\underline{s}_1,L),\ldots,q_k(\underline{s}_k,L)$.

Extension generator For each chosen default default(A, NoB, C, I, Lold) check whether A is provable with Lold, I∉ Lold, and not NoB is provable with Lold. In this case, extend Lold by adding I.

Program ExtGen
process(Lold,L) :- default(A,NoB,C,I,Lold),
                A,

```
                    not member(I,Lold),
                    not NoB,
                    process([I | Lold],L).
process(L,L) :- closed(L), successful(L).
closed(L) :- not (default(A,NoB,C,I,Lold),A,
                  not member(I,Lold),not NoB).
successful(L) :- not (member(I,L),default(_,NoB,_,I,L),NoB).
```

The relationship between the extensions of a default theory and the computed answers of the corresponding logic program is as follows. First, it is possible to prove a soundness result as follows:

Every answer substitution Lσ of goal ?- process([ ],L) *for the logic program above corresponds to an extension E=In(Π) of the default theory in the following way: i∈Lσ iff the default i occurs in the closed, successful process Π.*

For the completeness result we must take care that the operational nature of the logic program constructed is not destroyed by the truths W (if, for example, W includes the formula p:-p, then the logic program may not terminate). Under the condition that W forms a hierarchical program [5] we may prove the following:

In the opposite direction, for each closed, successful process Π of the default theory exists an answer substitution Lσ of goal ?- process([ ],L) *such that i∈Lσ iff the default i occurs in Π.*

Now let us look at some examples. It should be noted that the Prolog program corresponding to a default theory can be *automatically generated*.

14. Example

Consider T=({rep, qua},{rep:¬pac/¬pac,qua:pac/pac}). It has exactly two extensions, Th({¬pac,rep,qua}) and Th({pac,rep,qua}). T is translated to the following logic program:

```
default(qua(L),no pac(L), pac(L),1,L).
default(rep(L),pac(L),no pac(L),2,L).
pac(L) :- member(1,L).
no pac(L) :- member(2,L).
rep(_).
qua(_).
+ ExtGen
```

The goal ?- process([ ],L) leads to the two solutions L=[1] and L=[2] corresponding to the two extensions of the default theory.

Defaults are often given in form of a *default schema* that represents all ground instances of the schema. In this case, L does not consist of numbers solely, but contains also the ground substitution used.

15. Example

Let T=(W,$\{\delta_1,\delta_2,\delta_3,\delta_4\}$) with

W={bearded(peter), veryold(peter), veryold(jim),
      adult(X):-student(X)}

δ_1=student(X):¬married(X)/¬married(X)

δ_2=adult(X):married(X)/married(X)

δ_3=bearded(X):student(X)/student(X)

δ_4=veryold(X):¬student(X)/¬student(X)

The corresponding program looks as follows:

default(student(X,L),married(X,L),no married(X,L),[X,1],L).
default(adult(X,L),no married(X,L),married(X,L),[X,2],L).
default(bearded(X,L),no student(X,L),student(X,L),[X,3],L).
default(veryold(X,L),student(X,L), no student(X,L),[X,4],L).
no married(X,L) :- member([X,1],L).
married(X,L) :- member([X,2],L).
student(X,L) :- member([X,3],L).
no student(X,L) :- member([X,4],L).
bearded(peter,_).
veryold(peter,_).
veryold(jim,_).
adult(X,L) :- student(X,L).
+ ExtGen

The program computes three answers:

L=[[jim,4],[peter,1],[peter,3]]
L=[[jim,4],[peter,2],[peter,3]], and
L=[[jim,4],[peter,4]]

(as well as the permutations thereof; they could be avoided by additional checks, if required)

that correspond to the three extensions of the default theory.

Th(W∪{¬student(jim),student(peter),¬married(peter)})

Th(W∪{¬student(jim),student(peter),married(peter)})

Th(W∪{¬student(jim),¬student(peter)})

16. Example

We give a solution to the N-Queens-Problem. It can be represented in default logic by the schema

    field(I,J):blocked(I,J)/setQueen(I,J)

plus a truth set W containing an appropriate definition of the predicates field and block. The corresponding Prolog program looks as follows:

```
default(field(I,J), blocked(I,J,L), setQueen(I,J,L), [ [I,J],1],L).
setQueen(I,J,L) :- member([ [I,J],1],L).
blocked(I,J,L) :- setQueen(I,N,L), N =\= J.
blocked(I,J,L) :- setQueen(M,J,L), M =\= I.
blocked(I,J,L) :- setQueen(M,N,L), N-J =:= M-I, M =\= I.
blocked(I,J,L) :- setQueen(M,N,L), N-J =:= I-M, M =\= I.
field(I,J,L) :-   member(I,[1,2,3,4,5,6,7,8,]),
                  member(J,[1,2,3,4,5,6,7,8,]).
```

6 Conclusion

In this paper we introduced processes as a procedural interpretation of the usual fixed-point definition of extensions. Processes allow to compute the extensions of simple default theories by hand. Then we gave a prototypical Prolog implementation of our model in Prolog. We do not claim that the program is very efficient, but it is able to compute the extensions of the usual examples found in literature.

We consider this program as starting point and fundament for further implementations. In section 5, we showed how we can make direct use of Prolog's reasoning capacities by translating default theories (with some restrictions) to logic programs.

Topics of further work are dropping the condition that defaults may contain only literals. Other interesting question are usage of more intelligence in the traversal of the process tree (perhaps using some control information provided by the user), a comparison with truth maintenance implementations of default logic, and a direct Prolog implementation of a goal-oriented approach (the so-called 'proof theory') of normal default theories.

Literature

1. Besnard, P.: An Introduction to Default Logic. Springer 1989
2. Brewka, G.: Nonmonotonic Reasoning. Cambridge University Press 1991
3. Froidevaux, C.: Taxonomic Default Theory. In Proc. ECAI-86, Brighton 1986
4. Garlati, S.: Default Logic Models of Certain Inheritance Systems with Exceptions. Fundamenta Informaticae 18: 129-149 (1993)
5. Lloyd, J.W.: Foundations of Logic Programming 2. edition. Springer 1987

6. Moore, R.C.: Possible-world semantics for autoepistemic logic. In Proc. Non-monotonic Reasoning Workshop, New Paltz 1984

7. Moore, R.C.: Semantical Considerations on Nonmonotonic Logic. Artificial Intelligence 25 (1985)

8. Reiter, R.: A Logic for Default Reasoning. Artificial Intelligence 13 (1980)

9. Sperschneider, V.: Default Logic - Autoepistemic Logic. OSM P143, Fachbereich 6, Universität Osnabrück 1991

10. Sperschneider, V. and Antoniou, G.: Logic: A Foundation for Computer Science. Addison-Wesley 1991

Appendix A: Proof of Theorem 8

Let Π be a closed, successful process of T and $E=\text{In}(\Pi)$. This means that $\text{In}(\Pi) \cap \text{Out}(\Pi)=\varnothing$ and every $\delta \in D$ which is applicable to $\text{In}(\Pi)=E$ with respect to belief set E already occurs within Π. We show that $\Lambda_T(E) \subseteq E$ (where $\Lambda_T(E)$ is the smallest deductively closed set of formulas that contains W and is closed under application of defaults in D with respect to belief set E). First, $W \subseteq E$ and $\text{Th}(E)=E$ by definition of the In-operator. Also, E is closed under D with respect to E, since Π was assumed to be closed. This shows $\Lambda_T(E) \subseteq E$.

Next we show $E \subseteq \Lambda_T(E)$. By induction on k we show that $\text{In}(\Pi[k]) \subseteq \Lambda_T(E)$, for all k such that $\Pi[k]$ exists. For k=0 we have $\text{Th}(W) \subseteq \Lambda_T(E)$, since $\Lambda_T(E)$ is deductively closed and contains W. Assume we have already shown $\text{In}(\Pi[k]) \subseteq \Lambda_T(E)$ and $\varphi:\psi_1,...,\psi_n/\chi$ is the k-th element of Π. By definition of a process, $\varphi \in \text{In}(\Pi[k])$, and thus $\varphi \in E$. Also $\neg\psi_1,...,\neg\psi_n \in \text{Out}(\Pi[k]) \subseteq \text{Out}(\Pi)$. Thus, $\neg\psi_1,...,\neg\psi_n \notin \text{In}(\Pi)=E$. This shows that $\varphi:\psi_1,...,\psi_n/\chi$ is applicable to E with respect to belief set E. The definition of $\Lambda_T(E)$ implies that $\chi \in \Lambda_T(E)$. Thus $\text{In}(\Pi[k+1])=\text{Th}(\text{In}(\Pi[k]) \cup \{\chi\}) \subseteq \Lambda_T(E)$. Altogether, we have shown $E=\Lambda_T(E)$, i.e. E is an extension of T.

Conversely, consider an extension E of T. We choose an enumeration $\{\delta^0,...,\delta^k,....\}$ of the set of defaults D. Then we define a process Π of T such that $\text{In}(\Pi[i]) \subseteq E$ and $\text{Out}(\Pi[i]) \cap E=\varnothing$ for all i such that $\Pi[i]$ is defined. The definition is as follows (note that case 2 preserves the above property):

Let $\Pi[i]$ be already defined such that $\text{In}(\Pi[i]) \subseteq E$ (*) and $\text{Out}(\Pi[i]) \cap E=\varnothing$ (for i=0, this is trivially true).

Case 1 Every $\delta \in D$ which is applicable to $\text{In}(\Pi[i])$ with respect to belief set E already occurs in $\Pi[i]$. Then terminate the construction of Π.

Case 2 There exists some $\delta \in D$ which is applicable to $\text{In}(\Pi[i])$ with respect to E and does not occur in $\Pi[i]$. In the fixed enumeration of D choose the first such δ and append δ to $\Pi[i]$ to obtain $\Pi[i+1]$.

For case 1, we show that $E \subseteq In(\Pi[i])$. Since $E = \Lambda_T(E)$ it suffices to show that $In(\Pi[i])$ is a deductively closed set that contains W and is closed under D with respect to belief set E. The former properties are clear, the latter property by definition of case 1. Together with (*) we have $E = In(\Pi[i])$. Altogether we have shown that, in case 1, $\Pi[i]$ is a closed, successful process of T with $E = In(\Pi[i])$.

Now we consider the case that the construction above yields a process Π of infinite length. We show that Π is a closed process of T. By construction, $In(\Pi) \cap Out(\Pi) = \varnothing$ since $In(\Pi[i]) \subseteq E$ and $Out(\Pi[i]) \cap E = \varnothing$ for all i. So Π is a successful process of T. Next we show that $In(\Pi) = E$. One inclusion, namely $In(\Pi) \subseteq E$, holds by construction. For the reversed inclusion, namely $E \subseteq In(\Pi)$, we note that $In(\Pi)$ is a deductively closed set that contains W and show that it is closed under D with respect to belief set E. For this, consider an arbitrary default $\delta = \varphi : \psi_1, \ldots, \psi_n / \chi$ in D with $\varphi \in In(\Pi) \subseteq E$ and $\neg \psi_1, \ldots, \neg \psi_n \notin E$. Now we choose a number i such that $\varphi \in In(\Pi[i])$ and every $\delta' \in \Pi$ that appears before δ in the fixed enumeration of D is already contained in $\Pi[i]$. By definition of case 2, δ is the default chosen in stage i+1. Thus, its conclusion χ is contained in $In(\Pi)$.

The argument above together with the just proved equation $E = In(\Pi)$ also shows that Π is closed. ∎

A Unified Approach to Default Reasoning and Belief Revision*

Maria R. Cravo and João P. Martins

Instituto Superior Técnico
Av. Rovisco Pais
1000 Lisboa, Portugal
351-1-847 34 21-x1265
JMartins@interg.pt

Abstract. We present a unified approach to three important areas of AI: nonmonotonic logics, belief revision theories, and belief revision systems. The nonmonotonic logic we present, SWMC, is appropriate to support belief revision systems, because it keeps a track of dependencies between formulas. Another distinguishing feature of SWMC is the distinction between what follows soundly from a set of premises, and what can plausibly be concluded. In what concerns belief revision theories, we present a theory based on a nonmonotonic logic, SWMC, which, to the best of our knowledge, is a novel approach. Finally, we use an implementation of a belief revision system based on the logic and the belief revision theory, to illustrate these formalisms.

1 Introduction

Very little of what we believe about the world is absolute and certain. The large majority of our reasoning is dictated by commonsense rules whose conclusions may be invalidated in face of further information. For this reason, it should not be suprising that since the early beginnings, AI researchers have been concerned with the development of commonsense reasoning programs.

The formalization of commonsense reasoning raises two questions: (1) how to characterize the mechanism that allows "jumping to conclusions" in face of incomplete information; and (2) how to define what to do when we find out that the conclusions that we have reached turned out to be wrong, in the sense that they clash with previously held conclusions or beliefs.

Since AI is concerned with the development of working programs, the two aspects discussed in the previous paragraph have somehow to be included into programs. When attention is shifted from theories to programs, the concerns for efficiency and economy of work become important.

AI researchers have actively addressed these three issues for the last 15 years: the mechanisms that allow jumping to conclusions have been studied in the

* This work was partially supported by Junta Nacional de Investigação Científica e Tecnológica (JNICT), under Grants 87-107, 90/167, and 1243/92.

area of *nonmonotonic logics*; the concern about how to revise what one believes has been studied in the area of *belief revision theories*; and the concern for implementing efficient systems that are capable of changing what they believe has been addressed by *belief revision systems*.[2]

Despite their close interconnections, these areas have been studied in isolation, that is, the work performed in each one of them bears little or no concern about the problems and issues involved in the other areas. For example, the work in belief revision theories is based on classical logic, thus ignoring the problems that should be addressed when a nonmonotonic logic is considered.

In the last years, the formalisms developed in these areas have been compared, but to the best of our knowledge, no work has been done towards the integration of the formalisms of different areas, in the sense of developing a unified formalism that benefits from the work done in these areas. To achieve this goal it is not enough to put together a nonmonotonic logic, a belief revision theory, and a belief revision system. It is necessary, once the logic is chosen, that the belief revision theory considers it as the underlying logic, and that the belief revision system not only is adequate to the logic, but also incorporates the belief revision theory, for instance, that it can resolve contradictions in the way dictated by the belief revision theory.

In this paper we present a unified approach to these three areas: we developed a nonmonotonic logic, keeping in mind that it would be used to dictate the reasoning of a belief revision system; we studied a belief revision theory that considers the inferences produced by the logic; and we defined and implemented a belief revision system that embodies the logic and the belief revision theory.

In the next section we discuss the problems that we addressed and the main contributions in each of these areas. We then discuss in some detail the work that has been developed regarding the logic, and the belief revision theory. Finally we present an example that shows the features of our work.

2 Problems Addressed and Contributions

In discussing the problems that have been addressed by our work it is important to consider the three areas that it covers.

2.1 Nonmonotonic Logics

We developed a nonmonotonic logic, SWMC,[3] that provides a way of keeping records of dependencies among propositions.[4] Although these records were introduced to keep track of the dependencies needed in a belief revision system, they turned out to be very useful in allowing the distinction between what follows soundly from what is believed, and what it is only plausible to believe. This is

---

[2] Also known as *truth maintenance systems* and *reason maintenance systems*.

[3] After Shapiro, Wand, Martins, and Cravo.

[4] SWMC is an extension of SWM (Martins and Shapiro, 1983, 1988), a monotonic logic that supports belief revision systems.

crucial in situations where we cannot afford to act based upon less than certain conclusions, for the risks involved are too high, should the conclusion be proved wrong after all.

2.2 Belief Revision Theories

We developed a belief revision theory that is based on a nonmonotonic logic, SWMC. This aspect allows new alternatives for getting rid of beliefs (by the addition of hypotheses, rather than by their removal) and challenges some of the well established axioms that govern the changes in beliefs (Gärdenfors, 1988).

In addition, in comparison with other theories (Gärdenfors, 1988; Nebel, 1989, 1990; Fuhrmann, 1991), our theory allows some extra functionality in the specification of preferences between beliefs: we contemplate the existence of several partial orders between beliefs as well as a partial order between these partial orders.

2.3 Belief Revision Systems

Based on SWMC and on the belief revision theory, we specified the behaviour of a nonmonotonic ATMS-like system (de Kleer, 1986; Dressler, 1989; Junker, 1989) with reasoning capabilities. This system has been implemented in SNePS, giving rise to SNePSwD (Cravo, 1992; Cravo and Martins, 1993). The reason for using SNePS is that this is the knowledge representation system available to the authors, and it would be quite a waste to start an implementation from scratch. There is no reason however, why all the theoretical work presented here could not be implemented using any other knowledge representation formalism.

The integrated use of formalisms allowed the proper specification of a non-monotonic ATMS, which has been a problem for researchers in this field (Cravo, 1992) and the inclusion of revision capabilities within the system.

3 The Logic SWMC

To allow for the support of belief revision systems, SWMC deals with supported wffs. A *supported wff* is of the form $<A, \tau, \alpha>$, where A is a wff, τ an origin tag and α an origin set. The supported wff $<A, \tau, \alpha>$ corresponds to a particular derivation of the wff A.

The *origin tag* indicates how the supported wff was generated. It is an element of the set $\{hyp, asp, der\}$: *hyp* identifies hypotheses, *asp* identifies assumptions, and *der* identifies derived wffs. Hypotheses and assumptions sould be distinguished. *Hypotheses* represent the available information, ¿from which we want to draw conclusions. *Assumptions*, on the other hand, *do not* represent any kind of information, they are used in the recording of dependencies, when we draw a defeasible conclusion by applying a default rule to a particular individual; assumptions are used to record the fact that the defeasible conclusion depends, among other things, on the *assumption* or *supposition* that the default rule is applicable to that particular individual.

The *origin set* indicates the dependencies of the supported wff on other wffs. It is a set of hypotheses and/or assumptions and contains those hypotheses and assumptions that were used in that particular derivation of the wff.

3.1 The Language of SWMC

The language of SWMC, $\mathcal{L}$, is the union of four sets: (1) The set of *standard wffs*, $\mathcal{L}_{FOL}$, which corresponds to the language of First Order Logic; (2) The set of *default rules*, $\mathcal{L}_D$, which are of the form $\bigtriangledown(x) \, A(x) \rightarrow B(x)$, where $A(x)$ and $B(x)$, are standard wffs; For example, $\bigtriangledown(x)Bird(x) \rightarrow Flies(x)$ is a default rule, whose intended meaning is *Typically birds fly*; (3) The set of *assumptions*, $\mathcal{L}_A$, which are of the form $Applicable(D, c)$ where D is a default rule and c is an individual symbol. This wff represents the assumption that the default rule D is applicable to the particular individual c; and (4) The set of *exceptions*, $\mathcal{L}_E$, which are of the form $\forall(x) \, E(x) \rightarrow \neg Applicable \, (D, \, x)$, where D is a default rule. These wffs are used to express exceptions to default rules.

3.2 Rules of Inference

SWMC is a natural deduction system. It has two distinct sets of inference rules: (1) *Standard rules*, which include a rule of hypothesis, and basically two rules for each connective ($\wedge, \vee, \rightarrow, \neg$) and quantifier ($\forall, \exists$); (2) *Extended rules*, which deal with default rules. The following is a condensed version of the extended rules:[5]

Assumption and Default Elimination. From $<D, hyp, \{D\}>$, $<A(c), \tau,$ $\alpha >$ (where $D = \bigtriangledown(x) \, A(x) \rightarrow B(x)$, and c is an individual symbol), infer $<Applicable(D, \, c), asp, \{Applicable(D, \, c)\} \cup \{D\} \cup \alpha >$ and $<B(c), der,$ $\{Applicable(D, \, c)\} \cup \{D\} \cup \alpha >$.

Assumptions are necessary to record the fact that when $B(c)$ is inferred ¿from $\bigtriangledown(x) \, A(x) \rightarrow B(x)$, and $A(c)$, the inferred wff depends not only on these two wffs, but also on the *assumption* that the default rule is applicable to the individual c, i.e., $Applicable(\bigtriangledown(x) \, A(x) \rightarrow B(x), c)$.

The set of all supported wffs that can be generated by the rules of inference of SWMC is denoted by $\overline{\Sigma}$.

Given a set of wffs α and a wff A, we say that A is *derivable* from α, written $\alpha \vdash_{SWMC} A$, iff there is a supported wff $\mathcal{A} \in \overline{\Sigma}$ whose wff is A and whose origin set is contained in α. This notion of derivability is monotonic: if $\alpha \vdash_{SWMC} A$, and $\alpha \subseteq \beta$, then $\beta \vdash_{SWMC} A$. The nonmonotonic character of SWMC will become apparent when we define the notion of consequence.

---

[5] The standard rules can be found in (Cravo and Martins, 1990a; Cravo, 1992).

3.3 The Notion of Consequence

SWMC's notion of derivability is not enough for an agent using SWMC, to know what wffs it should believe, given a set of wffs. Suppose that the agent believes that *Tweety is a bird*, and is given the default rule *By default birds fly*. How do we express the fact that the agent should believe that *Tweety flies*? Using the notion of derivability, the best we can do is to write $\{Bird(Tweety),$ $\bigtriangledown(x)\ Bird(x) \rightarrow Flies(x), Applicable(\bigtriangledown(x)\ Bird(x) \rightarrow Flies(x), Tweety)\}$ $\vdash_{SWMC} Flies(Tweety)$. Furthermore, if the agent now came to believe that *Tweety doesn't fly*, we could still write

$$\{Bird(Tweety),$$
$$\bigtriangledown(x)\ Bird(x) \rightarrow Flies(x),$$
$$Applicable(\bigtriangledown(x)Bird(x) \rightarrow Flies(x), Tweety),$$
$$\neg Flies(Tweety)\}\ \vdash_{SWMC}\ Flies(Tweety).$$

We need a notion of consequence that, given the information available to an agent, tells it what it should believe. This notion is based on two concepts, context and belief space determined by a context. A *context* is any set of hypotheses, $\beta \subset \mathcal{L}$.[6] Given a consistent context,[7] a *belief space* determined by this context is a consistent set of wffs in $\mathcal{L}_{FOL}$, which are derivable ¿from the hypotheses in the context, and eventually some assumptions. If we think of a context as representing the information available to the agent, a belief space defined by this context will correspond to an acceptable set of beliefs of the agent.

Determining the belief spaces defined by a context β is not a single step process. It involves the construction of three intermediate sets of supported wffs: (1) The extended context of β, (2) the primitive cores of β, and (3) the cores of β. We now define each of these concepts.

Given a consistent context β, the *extended context* determined by this context, $EC(\beta)$, is a set of *supported wffs* whose origin tags are either *hyp* or *asp*: the hypotheses are all the hypotheses in the context, and the assumptions correspond to the assumptions which can consistently be added to the context.

Given a context β, a default rule $D \in \beta$, and an individual symbol c, we define $Implicit(D, c, \beta) = \{\neg E(c) : \forall(x)\ E(x) \rightarrow \neg Applicable(D, x) \in \beta\}$. When we apply a default rule D to an individual c, the set $Implicit(D, c, \beta)$ can be seen as the set of implicit assumptions we are making. For instance, when we assume that *Tweety flies*, based on the information that *Tweety is a bird, By default birds fly, Penguins and ostriches are an exception to this rule*, and the assumption that *The default rule is applicable to Tweety*, we are also implicitly assuming that *Tweety is not a penguin* and *Tweety is not an ostrich*. For this

---

[6] A hypothesis is any wff A in a supported wff of the form $<A,\ hyp,\ \{A\}>$. The rule of Hypothesis restricts the possible hypotheses to the union of the sets $\mathcal{L}_{FOL}$, $\mathcal{L}_D$, and $\mathcal{L}_E$.

[7] An *inconsistent* set of wffs γ is a set of wffs such that a contradiction is derivable from γ, i.e., $\gamma \vdash_{SWMC} (A \wedge \neg A)$. A *consistent* set of wffs is a set of wffs which is not inconsistent.

reason, the set $Implicit(D, c, \beta)$ is called *the set of implicit assumptions* of assumption $Applicable(D, c)$ in β. We use the expression $Implicit(\alpha, \beta)$, where α is a set of wffs, to represent the union of the sets of implicit assumptions of all the assumptions in α.

Given a consistent context, β, the extended context it determines, represented by $EC(\beta)$, is defined as:[8]

$$EC(\beta) = \{\mathcal{A} \in \overline{\Sigma} : (ot(\mathcal{A}) = hyp \ and \ wff(\mathcal{A}) \in \beta) \ or$$
$$(ot(\mathcal{A}) = asp, \ and \ hyps(os(\mathcal{A})) \subseteq \beta$$
$$and \ os(\mathcal{A}) \cup \beta \cup Implicit(os(\mathcal{A}), \beta) \ is \ consistent)\}.$$

Since the extended context may contain assumptions which are mutually incompatible, or whose implicit assumptions are mutually incompatible, the next step is to split the extended context into maximal subsets, that only contain assumptions which are mutually compatible, and so are their implicit assumptions. These maximal subsets of the extended context of a context β are called the primitive cores of context β. Each of these primitive cores will be a potential basis for constructing an acceptable state of beliefs. Formally, given a consistent context β, the *primitive cores* it determines are defined to be the maximal subsets Σ of the extended context that satisfy the following conditions:[9]

- $\beta \subseteq wffs(\Sigma)$
- $\forall \mathcal{A} \in \Sigma : os(\mathcal{A}) \subseteq wffs(\Sigma)$
- $wffs(\Sigma) \cup Implicit(wffs(\Sigma), \beta)$ is consistent

The set of all primitive cores determined by a context β is denoted $Pcores(\beta)$.

Each of the primitive cores is a potential basis for constructing an acceptable set of beliefs, or belief space. Although the definition of a belief space from each of the primitive cores will produce reasonable belief spaces in many cases, there are some situations in which the belief spaces corresponding to some of the primitive cores cannot be considered acceptable sets of beliefs. Such situations occur when one primitive core Σ does not contain an assumption $\mathcal{A}$ that belongs to the extended context, simply because the presence of $\mathcal{A}$ in Σ (or, which is the same, the presence of the conclusion,[10] $B(c)$, of that assumption in Σ) would contradict the implicit assumptions of the assumptions in Σ.

The next step is to discard those primitive cores that would correspond to unacceptable belief spaces. The remaining are called the cores of the context, and each of them will define an acceptable set of beliefs. Formally, given a primitive core Σ of a consistent context β, we say that Σ is a *core* of β, written $\Sigma \in Cores(\beta)$, if for every assumption $Applicable(D, c)$ $(D = \bigtriangledown(x) \ A(x) \rightarrow B(x))$ that belongs to the wffs of some primitive core of β, and does not belong to the wffs of Σ, one of the following conditions is verified:

---

[8] The function $hyps$ takes as argument a set of wffs and selects from them those that correspond to hypotheses.

[9] The function $wffs$ takes as argument a set of supported wffs, and returns a set of wffs, and is defined as follows: $wffs(\Phi) = \{A : (\exists \mathcal{A} \in \Phi : wff(\mathcal{A}) = A)\}$.

[10] Given an assumption $Applicable(\bigtriangledown(x) \ A(x) \rightarrow B(x), c)$, its conclusion is the wff $B(c)$.

- $wffs(\Sigma) \not\vdash_{SWMC} A(c)$.
- $wffs(\Sigma) \cup \{B(c)\} \cup Implicit(wffs(\Sigma), \beta)$ is consistent.
- $wffs(\Sigma) \cup \{B(c)\} \cup Implicit(D, c, \beta)$ is inconsistent.

Finally, we can define the belief spaces determined by a context β. There will be one belief space for each core Σ determined by β. That belief space consists of all the *standard wffs* derivable from $wffs(\Sigma)$. Given $\Sigma \in Cores(\beta)$, the corresponding belief space is defined by:

$$BS(\Sigma) = \{A \in \mathcal{L}_{FOL} : wffs(\Sigma) \vdash_{SWMC} A\}.$$

In summary, given a context, i.e., a set of hypotheses, the goal is to compute the belief spaces it determines. However, to go from a context to the belief spaces it determines, we need to go through several intermediate steps, namely the construction of the extended context, the primitive cores, and the cores.

Having defined belief space we can now define the notion of consequence, between a context and a wff in $\mathcal{L}_{FOL}$.[11] In SWMC, when we say that a wff $A \in \mathcal{L}_{FOL}$ is a consequence of a set of wffs β, we may mean one of three things: (1) Only the hypotheses in β were used in the derivation of A. In this case, the wff A will be in every belief space determined by β, and will be in every belief space determined by any consistent superset of β. In this case we say that A is a *sound consequence* of β and write $\beta \vdash A$; (2) The wff A was derived using not only the hypotheses in β, but also possibly some assumptions, and A belongs to every belief space determined by β. In this case, there may be consistent supersets of β such that A is no longer in all, or even in any, of the belief spaces they determine. In this case we say that A is a *plausible consequence* of β and write $\beta \vdash_P A$; (3) Finally, we may just mean that there is at least one belief space determined by β that contains A. In this case we say that A is a *conceivable consequence* of β and write $\beta \vdash_C A$.

Intuitively, these notions correspond to: Given β then A *must* follow; Given β *there are reasons to suppose A, and no reasons against it*; Given β, *there are reasons to suppose A, but there are also reasons against supposing A*. The notion of sound consequence is monotonic, i.e., if $\alpha \vdash A$, and $\alpha \subseteq \beta$, then $\beta \vdash A$, for any consistent contexts α and β. The nonmonotonicity of the logic is reflected by the notions of plausible and conceivable consequence. The following theorem states that a restricted form of monotonicity, semi-monotonicity, is verified in some cases.

Theorem Semi-monotonicity *Let β_1 and β_2 be two consistent contexts, containing only standard wffs and default rules, and such that $\beta_1 \subseteq \beta_2$ and $\beta_2 - \beta_1 \subset \mathcal{L}_D$. Let γ_1 be a belief space defined by β_1. Then there exists a belief space, γ_2, defined by β_2, such that $\gamma_1 \subseteq \gamma_2$.*

Proof: See Cravo (1992, p. 311).

---

[11] We are only interested in wffs ¿from $\mathcal{L}_{FOL}$ because only these will correspond to beliefs of an agent using SWMC.

4 The Belief Revision Theory

In this section we describe a belief revision theory which considers SWMC as the underlying logic. Like Nebel (1989, 1990) and Fuhrmann (1991) we represent the beliefs of an agent by a finite set of wffs, or, in SWMC's terminology, a context (set of hypotheses). Unlike all other theories (to the best of our knowledge) we allow the specification of any number (including zero) of partial orders among the hypotheses in a context, as well as a preference (another partial order) among these orders. The result of a change in beliefs is either unique or consists of several equally acceptable alternatives, depending on the amount of available information (expressed by the orders) to guide the change.

We consider three different belief changes: 1) *Addition* which consists in adding a wff to a context; 2) *Removal* which consists in removing a wff from a context; 3) *Revision* which consists in adding a wff to a context, with the request that the resulting context is consistent and contains the added wff.

4.1 Addition

This operation is traditionally designated by expansion. However, since the underlying logic is nonmonotonic, the addition of a wff to a context may invalidate consequences of the initial context. Thus, in what concerns the set of consequences of the context which suffers the addition of a wff there is not necessarily an expansion.

Given a context β and a wff A,[12] the *addition* of A to β, represented by $(\beta + A)$, is trivially defined by $(\beta + A) = \beta \cup \{A\}$.

4.2 Removal

The removal of a wff A from a context β, represented by $(\beta - A)$, consists in changing β in such a way that A is no longer a consequence of β. Since there are in general several ways of obtaining this result, $(\beta - A)$ will be a set of contexts, such that A is not a consequence of any of them. Due to the nonmonotonic nature of SWMC the removal of a wff may simultaneously add some consequences to the modified context(s). For this reason, we call this operation removal instead of contraction, as is usual.

It is obvious that, given a context β and a wff A, to change β in such a way that A is no longer a consequence of the modified context(s), we must invalidate all the ways of deriving A from β. We define the *set of valid derivations* of A in β as[13]

$$ValDer(A, \beta) = \{\alpha : \alpha \vdash_{SWMC} A, \exists \Sigma \in Cores(\beta) : \alpha \subseteq wffs(\Sigma) \text{ and}$$
$$(\gamma \subset \alpha) \rightarrow (\gamma \nvdash_{SWMC} A)\}$$

Given $ValDer(A, \beta)$, we have to invalidate each derivation α in this set.[14] The way to invalidate a derivation α depends on the contents of α:

---

[12] $A \in (\mathcal{L}_{FOL} \cup \mathcal{L}_D \cup \mathcal{L}_E)$.

[13] It is sufficient to consider minimal sets of wffs from which A is derivable.

[14] If $ValDer(A, \beta) = \{\}$, this means that A is not a consequence of β and no change needs to be made.

- If $\alpha = \{\}$, then A is a consequence of every consistent context, i.e., it cannot be removed from any context. In this case $(\beta - A) = \{\beta\}$.
- If α only contains hypotheses (i.e., no assumptions) the only way to invalidate it is to remove from β at least one of the hypotheses in α.
- If α also contains assumptions, then α can be invalidated either by removing or adding hypotheses to β.[15]

The last case is the interesting one: the presence of assumptions in α means that one or more default rules were used in this derivation of the wff A. Since default rules are rules with exceptions, the most natural way to invalidate α is to add information which reflects that we are in presence of an exception to some default rule used in α. Suppose that we know that *typically birds fly, except for ostriches and penguins*, and that *Tweety is a bird*. From this we may plausibly conclude that *Tweety flies*. Suppose now that we have reasons to doubt that *Tweety flies*, although we are not sure that it doesn't. In this situation, we will want to abandon the conclusion that *Tweety flies*. Surely, the most natural way to achieve this is to believe that Tweety is some kind of exception to the default rule, i.e., that it is either an ostrich, or a penguin, or that it simply doesn't fly (which includes all possible exceptions). Surely too, we would not reject the information that *typically birds fly* or that *Tweety is a bird*. This small example shows that the way to remove wffs that correspond to reasonable (but not sound) conclusions should be radically different from the way to remove sound conclusions, which is the only one considered in all other theories, because they all consider a monotonic underlying logic.

Given this, let's now look at the technical details. To invalidate, in a context β, a derivation α which contains assumptions, we will augment β in such a way that some assumption in α will not belong to any of the cores defined by the modified β; in this case we say that we invalidate this assumption. Since α may contain more than one assumption, the first decision concerns which assumption to invalidate. To keep the change as small as possible, we must choose an assumption in α such that no other assumption in α depends on it. We call *maximal assumptions in α* to such assumptions,[16] and represent their set by $Max(\alpha)$. The next question is which hypothesis should be added to β to invalidate the chosen assumption. Let this be $Applicable(D, c)$, where $D = \nabla(x) \, A(x) \rightarrow B(x)$, and $Implicit(D, c, \beta) = \{\neg E_1(c), \ldots, \neg E_n(c)\}$. Then, the addition of any of $E_1(c), \ldots, E_n(c), \neg B(c)$ to β will invalidate the assumption. Since we want to keep the change as small as possible, we will add to β the disjunction of these wffs, i.e., $E_1(c) \vee \ldots \vee E_n(c) \vee \neg B(c)$; this wff is called the *absorbing hypothesis* of the assumption $Applicable(D, c)$ in β.[17] Given a set of

---

[15] The fact that α relies on assumptions means that it can be invalidated by additional information.

[16] This notion is closely related to the notion of maximal assumption in Doyle's TMS.

[17] The absorbing hypothesis corresponds to the most modest hypothesis, in the sense of Quine and Ullian (1978), which say that a hypothesis adopted to explain observed facts should, besides having other qualities, be as modest as possible (a hypothesis H_1 is more modest than a hypothesis H_2 if it is logically weaker, i.e., if H_1 is implied by

wffs γ, and a context β, we define $\perp(\gamma, \beta) = \{H : H$ is the absorbing hypothesis in β of an assumption in $\gamma\}$.

In summary, to invalidate in a context β a derivation α which contains assumptions we will add to β the absorbing hypothesis in β of a maximal assumption in α.

We now turn to the problem of invalidating not one, but a set of derivations in a context. Recall that, in the general case, there will be more than one alternative to achieve this. We represent an alternative to invalidate a set of derivations in a context β by a pair of sets of hypotheses, (ϵ, δ). This means that we must add to β all the hypotheses in ϵ, and remove from β all the hypotheses in δ. Formally, given a context β, and a wff A, we say that (ϵ, δ) is an alternative to remove A from β iff

$$\forall \alpha \in ValDer(A, \beta) : \epsilon \cap \alpha \neq \{\} \text{ or } \delta \cap \perp(\alpha, \beta) \neq \{\}.$$

To keep the change as small as possible, we introduce the notion of minimal alternative, which needs the notion of minimal change. Given (ϵ_1, δ_1) and (ϵ_2, δ_2) we say that (ϵ_1, δ_1) represents a *smaller change* than (ϵ_2, δ_2) iff $\epsilon_1 \subset \epsilon_2$ or $(\epsilon_1 = \epsilon_2$ and $\delta_1 \subset \delta_2)$. Intuitivelly "smaller change" means that we keep as many hypotheses as possible, i.e., that we retain as many of our previous beliefs as possible. This is reflected by the condition $\epsilon_1 \subset \epsilon_2$, which disregards the relation between δ_1 and δ_2. In other words, even if $\delta_2 \subset \delta_1$, i.e., if the alternative (ϵ_2, δ_2) adds less hypotheses than (ϵ_1, δ_1), we will consider the last alternative a smaller change, as long as $\epsilon_1 \subset \epsilon_2$. This means that we'd rather change a context by adding hypotheses than by removing hypotheses. This preference is justified in two ways. (1) On the one hand there is the question of naturalness as illustrated by the example in the previous page: we typically invalidate reasonable consequences by admitting the presence of some kind of exception, rather than by abandoning some of our previous beliefs. (2) On the other hand, and still referring to the same example, our beliefs change less if we choose to believe that *Tweety is either an ostrich, a penguin, or that is doesn't fly* (note that this belief doesn't add much to our previous knowledge), than if we had chosen to give up the belief that *Tweety is a bird* or that *Typically birds fly*. These two aspects, the naturalness of the process, and the minimization of change, are not unrelated, since it is well known from psychological studies that humans are very reluctant to let go of their beliefs. In what concerns the second condition in the definition of smaller change, $(\epsilon_1 = \epsilon_2$ and $\delta_1 \subset \delta_2)$, we think that it is quite obvious: we add exactly the hypotheses necessary to invalidate the derivations of a wff, and no more.

H_2, but not vice-versa). In the present case, we may say that the absorbing hypothesis is adopted, not to explain observed facts, but to explain unobserved facts: when we add to a context β the absorbing hypothesis of an assumption $Applicable(D, c)$, we are giving an explanation for the non-observation of the fact corresponding to the wff $B(c)$; this explanation consist in admitting that the individual c is an exception to the default rule D.

Given an alternative (ϵ, δ) to remove a wff A from a context β, we say that it is a *minimal alternative*, iff given any (ϵ', δ') which represents a smaller change than (ϵ, δ), (ϵ', δ') is not an alternative to remove A from β.

Let's now see how, if available, the partial orders among the hypotheses in a context, as well as a partial order among these orders, can be used to induce a preference among alternatives. Suppose that we have n partial orders, $\leq_1, \ldots,$ $\leq_n$, among the hypotheses of a context β. Given $H_1, H_2 \in \beta$, $H_1 \leq_i H_2$ means that, according to $\leq_i$, H_2 is at least as valuable as H_1. Let's also suppose that there is a partial order $\preceq$ among the orders $\leq_1, \ldots, \leq_n$. Intuitively, $\leq_i \preceq \leq_j$ means that in case of disagreement between $\leq_i$ and $\leq_j$, $\leq_j$ should prevail over $\leq_i$. The first step is to combine all these orders to obtain a single partial order, $\leq_\beta$, among the hypotheses in β:

$$\forall H_1, H_2 \in \beta : H_1 \leq_\beta H_2 \text{ iff } \exists i : H_1 \leq_i H_2 \text{ e } \forall j \neq i (H_2 \leq_j H_1 \rightarrow \leq_j \preceq \leq_i)$$
$$\text{or } \exists H_3 \in \beta : H_1 \leq_\beta H_3 \text{ and } H_3 \leq_\beta H_2.$$

Now that we have defined $\leq_\beta$, the question is how to use it to define a preference among alternatives. Given a minimal alternative (ϵ, δ), and an order $\leq_\beta$ among the hypotheses in β, we say that (ϵ, δ) *respects the order* $\leq_\beta$, iff, given any minimal alternative (ϵ', δ'), we have:

$$(\exists H \in (\epsilon - \epsilon') \, \exists H' \in (\epsilon' - \epsilon) : H' <_\beta H) \rightarrow$$
$$(\exists H \in (\epsilon - \epsilon') \, \exists H' \in (\epsilon' - \epsilon) : H <_\beta H').$$

To use the order $\leq_\beta$ to select the maximal assumptions which correspond to default rules of lesser value according to $\leq_\beta$, we define:

$$MaxMin_{\leq_\beta}(\alpha) = \{Applicable(D, c) \in Max(\alpha) :$$
$$(\forall Applicable(D', c') \in Max(\alpha) : D' \not<_\beta D)\}.$$

Finally we define the set of minimal alternatives, which respect the order $\leq_\beta$, to remove a wff A from a context β as:

$$MinAlt_{\leq_\beta}(A, \beta) = \{(\epsilon, \delta) : (\epsilon, \delta) \text{ is a minimal alternative to remove } A \text{ from } \beta,$$
$$(\epsilon, \delta) \text{ respects the order } \leq_\beta, \text{ and}$$
$$\delta \subseteq \bigcup_{\alpha_i \in DerVal(A, \beta)} \perp(MaxMin_{\leq_\beta}(\alpha_i), \beta)\}.$$

Given this definition, it is now trivial to define the removal of a wff A from a context β:

$$(\beta - A) = \begin{cases} \{\beta\} & if \, \{\} \in DerVal(A, \beta) \\ \{((\beta - \epsilon) \cup \delta) : \\ \quad (\epsilon, \delta) \in AltMin_{\leq_\beta}(A, \beta)\} \, otherwise \end{cases}$$

4.3 Revision

The revision of a consistent context β with a wff A, represented by $(\beta * A)$, consists in changing β in such a way that it contains A and is consistent. The case of interest is when $\beta \cup \{A\}$ is inconsistent, otherwise we can just add A to β. When $\beta \cup \{A\}$ is inconsistent, we will have to remove $\neg A$ from β, before we can add A. Since, in general, there will be several ways of removing $\neg A$ from β, the result of the revision is a set of contexts. Note that if $\neg A$ is only a plausible or conceivable (but not sound) consequence of β, we can just add A to β; SWMC ensures that $\neg A$ is no longer a consequence of $\beta \cup \{A\}$. In other words, when removing $\neg A$ from β, we only have to invalidate those derivations of $\neg A$ that do not rely on assumptions, i.e., the derivations of $\neg A$ in $(\beta \cap \mathcal{L}_{FOL})$. Given this, we define (in this definition, $\beta_{FOL} = \beta \cap \mathcal{L}_{FOL}$, $\beta_D = \beta \cap \mathcal{L}_D$, and $\beta_E = \beta \cap \mathcal{L}_E$):

$$(\beta * A) = \begin{cases} \{\beta' \cup \beta_D \cup \beta_E \cup \{A\} : \beta' \in (\beta_{FOL} - \neg A)\} & \text{if } A \in \mathcal{L}_{FOL} \\ \{\beta \cup \{A\}\} & \text{if } A \in \mathcal{L}_D \cup \mathcal{L}_E \end{cases}$$

4.4 Properties

It is usual to assess the rationality of a belief revision theory by checking whether its operations verify the Gärdenfors' postulates (Gärdenfors, 1988). We do not present here in detail the results of the application of these postulates to our theory (for a detailed presentation and proofs, see (Cravo, 1992)). However, we can say that all the operations we defined satisfy Gärdenfors' postulates when we restrict ourselves to contexts containing only standard wffs.[18] In the general case, some postulates are not verified.

We will briefly discuss which postulates are not verified, and the reasons for that. We will start by considering the removal operation. Three of Gärdenfors' postulates are not verified. The first one, corresponding to Gärdenfors' postulate $K^- 2$, can be stated in our theory as:[19]

$$\forall \beta' \in (\beta - A) : CN(\beta') \subseteq CN(\beta).$$

This postulate is not verified because of the nonmonotonicity of the underlying logic. When we remove a wff from a context (whether this is done by withdrawing or adding hypotheses to the context) we may end up with some new consequences. Recall that this was the reason why we decided to change the designation of this operation from "contraction" to "removal". So, we didn't expect our theory to verify this postulate from the very beginning.

The second postulate for removal that is not verified, corresponding to Gärdenfors' postulate $K^- 4$, is much more important, because it concerns the success of this operation:

$$\text{If } A \notin CN(\{\}), \text{ then } \forall \beta' \in (\beta - A) : A \notin CN(\beta').$$

The failure of this postulate implies that we cannot guarantee the success of the removal operation. This happens because when we discard one hypothesis H ¿from a context to invalidate a derivation of a wff A, we may be allowing some new derivation(s) for A, due to the nonmonotonicity of the logic. Although we were disappointed, at first, with this result, we now think that it isn't as

---

[18] In this case, SWMC is "equivalent" to First Order Logic.

[19] $CN(\beta)$ is the set of consequences (sound, plausible or conceivable) of β.

bad as it seems. In fact, this situation only occurs in pathological cases: note that what we said implies that our beliefs are such that the same hypothesis H is simultaneously a reason to believe A (that's why we removed H from the context), and a reason against believing A (that's why the withdrawal of H allowed some new derivation(s) for A). For an example of such a pathological case see (Cravo, 1992, pp.152–153).

Finally, the last postulate that is not verified by our removal operation, corresponding to Gärdenfors' postulate K^-5, is:

$$If\ A \in CN(\beta),\ then\ \forall \beta' \in (\beta - A):\ CN(\beta) \subseteq CN(\beta' \cup \{A\}).$$

The same happens with the theory of Fuhrmann (1991), and this is due to the fact that we are dealing with finite sets of wffs (contexts). Thus, to remove a wff A from a context, we may withdraw a hypothesis which will not be recovered even if we now add A to the context(s) resulting from the removal.

As for the operation of revision, only one postulate is not verified, corresponding to G

$$\forall \beta' \in (\beta * A):\ CN(\beta') \subseteq CN(\beta + A).$$

This is not verified in precisely the interesting case, i.e., when $(\beta + A)$ $(= \beta \cup \{A\})$ is inconsistent, for a technical reason, concerning the underlying logic: the set of consequences of an inconsistent context is the empty set.

It may seem stange at first sight that we can guarantee the success of the revision operation, since it was defined in terms of the removal operation, and we could not guarantee the success of this operation in all situations. This can be explained by the fact that in the definition of revision, the removal operation is only used in the particular case of contexts that only contain standard wffs, in which case its success can be guaranteed.

To summarize, we can say that the failure of some postulates is due to the characteristics of the logic, namely its nonmonotonicity. This leads us to think that when we consider a nonmonotonic logic as underlying a belief revision theory, different criteria of rationality are necessary.

5   Example

In this section we present an example that illustrates the formalisms we described. This presentation is an edited version of the interaction with a belief revision system, SNePSwD (Cravo, 1992; Cravo and Martins, 1993). SNePSwD performs nonmonotonic reasoning based on SWMC, and also incorporates the belief revision theory we described.[20]

In the example below, we start by introducing the hypotheses that define the context we want to consider: {wff1, ..., wff6}. After that, we ask the system to infer a given wff. Finally, we ask the system to remove this wff from the context under consideration. Since there is only alternative to do so, the system

---

[20] It has other interesting and distinguishing features, which we do not mention in this paper.

performs the removal automatically, i.e., without consulting the user (comments are preceded by a semicolon).

```
: A(p)
  WFF1:  A(P)


: B(p)
  WFF2:  B(P)


: all(x) (A(x) or B(x) => C(x))
  WFF3:  all(X) (A(X) or B(X) => C(X))


: default(x) (A(x) => C(x))
  WFF4:  default(X) (A(X) => C(X))


: all(x) (E1(x) => ~Applicable(wff4,x))
  WFF5:  all(X) (E1(X) =>
                   ~APPLICABLE(default(x) (A(x) => C(x)),X))


: all(x) (E2(x) => ~Applicable(wff4,x))
  WFF6:  all(X) (E2(X) =>
                   ~APPLICABLE(default(x) (A(x) => C(x)),X))


: C(p)?  ;try to infer C(p)
  WFF7:  C(P) {<DER,{WFF3,WFF1}>,<DER,{WFF8,WFF4,WFF1}>,
                <DER,{WFF3,WFF2}>}
;C(p) derived in 3 different ways


:WFF8   ;describe wff8
  WFF8:  APPLICABLE(default(x) (A(x) => C(x)),P)
         {<DER,{WFF8,WFF4,WFF1}>}


:add-order o1 (wff1 wff3)
;according to o1, wff3 is at least as valuable as wff1


:add-order o2 (wff2 wff4) (wff3 wff1)
;according to o2, wff4 is at least as valuable as wff2,
;and wff1 is at least as valuable as wff3


:add-order-of-orders (o1 o2)
;in case of conflict o2 should prevail over o1


:remove-wff wff7
Removed:
   WFF3:  all(X) (A(X) or B(X) => C(X))
Added:
   WFF14:  E1(P) or E2(P) or ~C(P)
```

To remove wff7 from the context {wff1, ..., wff6}, the system had to invalidate three derivations: {wff3, wff1}, {wff3, wff2}, {wff8, wff4, wff1}. The first two only contain hypotheses, so at least one hypothesis from each of them must be removed. Given the available orders, the system chooses to remove wff3. The third one contains an assumption, wff8, so it is invalidated by the addition of its absorbing hypothesis, wff14.

6   Concluding Remarks

We presented SWMC, a nonmonotonic logic that allows for default reasoning. SWMC is suitable for supporting belief revision systems in the sense that it associates with each proposition the reasons that lead to its derivation. The logic allows the distinction between what must follow from a set of premises, what is a plausible conclusion and what is a conceivable conclusion.

A semantics has been developed for SWMC, based on the notion of classical model, and on an ordering of sets of models (Cravo and Martins, 1990b; Cravo, 1992). In relation to this semantics, the logic is sound and complete.

We also presented a belief revision theory based on SWMC. The nomonotonicity of the logic had drastic consequences on the theory. In addition, our theory makes weaker assumptions than all other theories concerning the available information to guide the changes in belief: it allows for the specifictation of any number (including zero) of partial orders among beliefs.

Finally, we presented the result of the interaction with an implementation of a belief revision system based on the logic and the belief revision theory.

These contributions are a result from our unified approach to the areas of nonmonotonic logics, belief revision theories, and belief revision systems. The main achievement in the logic, the possibility of distinguishing between different types of consequences, results from the use of the dependency records that are needed by the belief revision system. The main achievements in the belief revision theory stem ¿from the fact that it is based on a nonmonotonic logic and that it was developed having in mind its use by a belief revision system that could, as much as possible select the change that had to be made to a set of beliefs. The main achievement in the area of belief revision systems, a definition of a nonmonotonic ATMS, is due to the use of an underlying nonmonotonic logic that guides the reasoning of the system.

Although the work presented here was not developed keeping in mind the resolution of any kind of particular problem, but rather as a contribution to the incorporation of some aspects of commonsense in computer programs, we were pleasantly surprised with the way our system is capable of solving problems in different domains such as as inheritance hierarquies, diagnosis, counterfactual reasoning, hypothetical reasoning, and reasoning about actions. This confirms the well known fact that, even when solving problems of a very specific nature, we use a great deal of commonsense knowledge.

References

Cravo M.R.: *Raciocínio por Omissão e Revisão de Crenças: Dois Aspectos do Senso Comum*. PhD Thesis, Instituto Superior Técnico, Lisbon, Portugal, 1992.

Cravo M.R. and Martins J.P.: Defaults and Belief Revision, A Syntactical Approach. Technical Report GIA 90/02, Instituto Superior Técnico, Lisbon, Portugal, 1990a.

Cravo M.R. and Martins J.P.: A Semantics for SWMC. Technical Report GIA 90/03, Instituto Superior Técnico, Lisbon, Portugal, 1990b.

Cravo M.R. and Martins J.P.: SNePSwD, A Newcomer to the SNePS Family. *Journal of Experimental and Theoretical Artificial Intelligence*, 5, 1993.

de Kleer J.: Extending the ATMS. *Artificial Intelligence*, 28 (2), 163–196, 1986.

Dressler O.: An Extended Basic ATMS. In Reinfrank, de Kleer, Ginsberg e Sandewall (eds), *Proc. Second International Workshop on Non-Monotonic Reasoning*, Lecture Notes in Artificial Intelligence 346, 143–163, Springer-Verlag, Heidelberg, Germany, 1989.

Fuhrmann A.: Theory Contraction through Base Contraction. *Journal of Philosophical Logic*, 20 (2), 175–203, 1991.

Gärdenfors P.: *Knowledge in Flux: Modeling the Dynamics of Epistemic States*, The MIT Press, Cambridge, MA, 1988.

Junker U.: A Correct Non-Monotonic ATMS. *Proc. IJCAI-89*, 1049–1054, 1989.

Martins J.P. and Shapiro S.C.: Reasoning in Multiple Belief Spaces. *Proc. IJCAI-83*, 370–373, 1983.

Martins J.P. and Shapiro S.C.: A Model for Belief Revision. *Artificial Intelligence* 35, 25–79, 1988.

Nebel B.: A Knowledge Level Analysis of Belief Revision. In Brachman, Levesque e Reiter (eds), Proc. First International Conference on Principles of Knowledge Representation and Reasoning, 301–311, Morgan Kaufmann Inc., San Mateo, CA, 1989.

Nebel B.: *Reasoning and Revision in Hybrid Representation Systems*. Springer-Verlag, Heidelberg, Germany, 1990.

Quine W. and Ullian J.: *The Web of Belief*. Random House, New York, NY, 2nd Edition, 1978.

Second Order E-Matching as a Tool for Automated Theorem Proving

Régis Curien

CRIN and INRIA-Lorraine

BP239, 54506 Vandoeuvre-les-Nancy Cedex, France*

Abstract

We describe a second order matching algorithm which takes account of algebraic properties of functions. Higher order allows us the use of function variables and is relevant in many applications concerning functional or logical schemes. To add algebraic properties significantly increases the expressiveness of the matching process and extends the set of problems having solutions. This higher order E-matching works for a set of algebraic theories E which have to satisfy some properties. It has been implemented for the Associative Commutative case and adapted for similar theories like AC1 which do not fulfill the previous requirements.

Keywords : Automated reasoning, pattern recognition, higher-order logic, equational theories.

1   Introduction

Pattern matching is one of the most basic tools in A.I. and computer science and is used in many applications. The expressiveness of pattern matching has been widely enhanced by performing this process modulo a set of first order axioms (called an equational theory). The most common ones are Associativity Commutativity axioms (for short AC). $AC = \{f(x, f(y, z)) \sim f(f(x, y), z); f(x, y) \sim f(y, x)\}$ (for instance $\wedge$ and $\vee$ connectives are AC). Another useful pattern matching process deals with higher order pattern matching and is required when we are dealing with schemes instead of first order terms. There has been a growing interest in higher order topics since researchers have realized that they can be handled much more easily than it seemed at first glance. The decidability of higher order matching is still an open question (for orders greater than three [Dow92]), but if one restricts oneself to second order terms, there exists an algorithm due to Huet and Lang [HL78]. In many applications, second order matching is all that we need.

In this paper, we consider second order pattern matching modulo a first order equational theory as a tool needed in a higher order toolbox which can be used in

---

*email : curien@loria.fr

applications like higher order theorem proving, first order theorem proving or higher order rewriting.

Indeed, formula simplification is a useful process to carry out, before performing the automated deduction, in order to simplify the search for a proof. Therefore, the main difference between our second order E-matching and current work on E-unification is that we must obtain a termination property. We shall provide examples which show how second order E-matching can be used to find recurrence patterns in a logic program and make simplifications in a first order logic formula in order to prove this formula.

We have implemented the method and give examples. Then, we present the algorithm mechanism on a simple example in section 2. Section 3 contains useful definitions and notations. In section 4, we produce the rules and the strategy for using them, defining the algorithm. We give in section 5 the main properties of the algorithm (we give proofs in an appendix) and section 6 shows some applications of the method. We give our conclusions in section 7.

2 Example

We shall describe the main features of our algorithm on a simple example : how to recognize a classical tautology like '$x \vee \neg x$' in some formula φ.

This pattern recognition process is an heuristic used in some theorem provers in order to simplify the formulae to prove, using $x \vee \neg x \ \rightarrow \ \top$ and this is repeated until all such tautologies are eliminated.

Let φ be $((d \Rightarrow \neg c) \wedge ((a \vee (b \wedge d)) \vee (e \Leftrightarrow f) \vee \neg((d \wedge b) \vee a))) \Leftrightarrow g$. We are looking for some context F such that $\varphi = F[x \vee \neg x]$. Hence, we can see this pattern recognition process as a higher order pattern matching algorithm. Therefore, second order pattern matching works fine for this goal when first order would not perform well[1]. Unfortunately, syntactic higher order matching is too weak for this purpose. The algebraic properties of the boolean operators '$\wedge$' and '$\vee$' are necessary in order to get a successful match.

Higher order matching works on typed λ-terms. The given problem is described as *the rigid term* $\varphi = ((d \Rightarrow \neg c) \wedge ((a \vee (b \wedge d)) \vee (e \Leftrightarrow f) \vee \neg((d \wedge b) \vee a))) \Leftrightarrow g$ *is an instance of* $\psi = F[x \vee \neg x]$ *if and only if there exists a substitution* σ *such that* $\sigma\psi =_{\beta\eta E} \varphi$ where F, the context, is a function variable of type $Bool \rightarrow Bool$. The relation '$=_{\beta\eta E}$' is an equivalence relation modulo β-abstraction, η-conversion, and the theory E. The solution will have the form : $\sigma = \{x \leftarrow t \; ; \; F \leftarrow s\}$ where t and s are closed terms.

An algorithm to perform second order E-matching will rely on two existing tools which are the second order matching algorithm developed by Huet and Lang [HL78] and first order E-matching algorithms for the theories we are interested in. Our algo-

---

[1]A possible way is to test the matching at each position of φ. Anyway, in some examples, we have predicate variables in φ. We should then try each possible predicate at each occurrence in φ.

rithm, based on the combination of second order matching and first order E-matching is proved sound, complete and terminating. Termination is necessary for our purpose, since our E-matching algorithm is used in a pre-processing step to simplify formulae before invoking the actual automated theorem prover. This is the main difference with previous works on the combination of E-unification algorithm and higher order (see [NQ91] and [QW92]). It has allowed us to implement our algorithm for Associative Commutative axioms (in short AC). But we are able to deal with Associative Commutative axioms with a neutral element (AC1), AC and an idempotent axiom (ACI) because these algebraic theories also enjoy some good properties which are defined in the next section.

Let us see how this works on our example. All the symbols $a, b, \ldots$ represent boolean constants except x and z which are first order variables. We give only one solution computed by our algorithm.

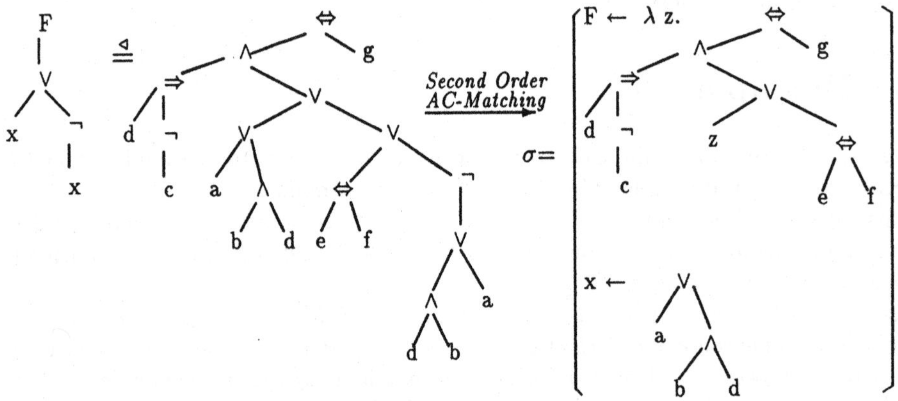

Figure 1: Recognition of a tautology

This example, shows how successful is the combination of first order AC-matching and second order matching for finding the tautological scheme in a logical term. The result in F is the term which contains the tautology. We can read the result as *the given rigid term is a function $F = \lambda z \cdot ((d \Rightarrow \neg c) \wedge (z \vee (e \Leftrightarrow f))) \Leftrightarrow g$ applied to a formula AC equivalent to $a \vee (b \wedge d)$.* Then, φ can be simplified modulo associativity and commutativity into $(d \Rightarrow \neg c) \Leftrightarrow g$.

3 Terms and theories

This section contains all the definitions, conventions and notations used in the sequel.

3.1 Terms

The reader is assumed to be familiar with typed λ-calculus [HS86] and first order matching. Then, we shall give the definitions and notions that we actually need.

The set of the types T is inductively defined by : $\tau \in T_0 \Rightarrow \tau \in T$ where T_0 is the set of base types, and $\alpha, \beta \in T \Rightarrow \alpha \to \beta \in T$.

Note that $\to$ associates to the right and in the sequel, we shall write $\alpha_1 \times \alpha_2 \times \cdots \times \alpha_n \to \beta$ for $(\alpha_1 \to \cdots (\alpha_n \to \beta) \cdots)$ or $\overline{\alpha_n} \to \beta$ which is a more convenient notation.

The **order** of a type $O(\tau)$ is 1 if $\tau \in T_0$, and $O(\overline{\alpha_n} \to \beta) = max\{O(\alpha_i) \mid 1 \le i \le n\} + 1$ otherwise.

Signature : for each type $\tau \in T$, there is a denumerable set $\mathcal{V}_\tau$ of variable symbols of type τ. The set of all variable symbols is $\mathcal{V}$, and for each type $\tau \in T$, there is a denumerable set $\mathcal{C}_\tau$ of constant symbols of type τ. The set of all constant symbols is $\mathcal{C}$.

The set of **atoms** is $\mathcal{A} = \mathcal{V} \cup \mathcal{C}$, and the set $\mathcal{T}$ of terms is defined by $\mathcal{T} = \bigcup_{\alpha \in T} \mathcal{T}_\alpha$ with

Application : $(\phi\, t) \in \mathcal{T}_\beta$ if $\phi \in \mathcal{T}_{\alpha \to \beta}$ and $t \in \mathcal{T}_\alpha$

Abstraction : $\lambda x.t \in \mathcal{T}_{\tau_1 \to \beta}$ if $t \in \mathcal{T}_\beta$ and $x \in \mathcal{V}_{\tau_1}$

The **order of a term** is the order of its type. We shall note $(\cdots (\phi\, t_1) \cdots t_n)$ as $\phi(t_1, t_2, \ldots, t_n)$ or $\phi(\overline{t_n})$. t and s will denote terms. **A language of order** n contains constants of order at most $n + 1$, and variables of order at most n. We study here a language of order two.

Convention : In the following, we shall use (unless stated otherwise) α, β and *Bool* for base types and τ for any type; f and g for constants of higher order; F and H for second order variables; x, y and z for variables of any order and ϕ for any function symbol.

As usual, in the term $\lambda \overline{x_n} \cdot t$, $\overline{x_n}$ is called the **binder**, t is the **matrix** and the occurrences of the variable x_i in t are called **bound**. $BV(t)$ is the set of all the variables which are bound in t and $FV(t)$ is the set of all the variables which occur free in t. For each term $t = \lambda \overline{x_m} \cdot \phi(\overline{t_n})$, ϕ is the **head** of the term. We denote it by $\mathcal{H}(t) = \phi$. The term t is said to be **rigid** if its head is a constant or a bound variable and **flexible** otherwise. In the sequel, $[x \leftarrow t_2]t_1$ will be the result of replacing each free occurrence of x in t_1 by t_2. We consider terms modulo α-conversion. i.e. if two terms are equivalent modulo bound variable renaming, they are considered syntactically equivalent.

long-$\beta\eta$-normal form : a term $\lambda \overline{x_m} \cdot \phi(\overline{t_n})$ is in long-$\beta\eta$-normal form if it is in β-normal form, $\tau(\phi(\overline{t_n})) \in T_0$ and each t_i is in long-$\beta\eta$-normal form (in short l$\beta\eta$-nf). l$\beta\eta$-nf is unique. Therefore, we consider terms in l$\beta\eta$-nf.

A substitution σ is **normalized** iff $\forall x \in Dom(\sigma)$, $\sigma(x)$ is in l$\beta\eta$-nf.

Order on substitutions : let W be a set of variables. If $\forall x \in W \sigma(x) = \theta(x)$, σ and θ are equal over W and we write $\sigma = \theta[W]$. β-*equality* is defined by $\sigma =_\beta \theta[W]$ iff $\forall x \in W \sigma(x) \leftrightarrow^*_\beta \theta(x)$. So, σ is more general than θ over W (denoted by $\sigma \le_\beta \theta[W]$ iff there exists a substitution γ such that $\theta =_\beta \sigma \circ \gamma[W]$. σ is said to be **idempotent** when $\sigma \circ \sigma = \sigma$. Snyder [Sny88] has shown that for any substitution σ and a set of variables W containing $Dom(\sigma)$, there exists σ' idempotent such that $Dom(\sigma) = Dom(\sigma')$, $\sigma' \le_{\beta\eta} \sigma[W]$. Thus, without loss of generality [NQ91], we shall only use idempotent substitutions.

3.2 Theories

We give here the useful definitions for the theories and the properties of the theories we are manipulating. Let A_0 be $\bigcup_{\alpha \in T_0} A_\alpha$. The set of the **algebraic terms** T^E [NQ91] is the smallest set such that if $f \in C_{\overline{\alpha_n} \to \beta}$ with $\alpha_i \in T_0$ $1 \leq i \leq n$ and $s_i \in T^E \cap T_{\alpha_i}$, $1 \leq i \leq n$ then $f(\overline{s_n}) \in T^E$. An **equation** (or axiom) is an unordered pair $t \sim s$ with $\tau(t) = \tau(s)$ and t and s are algebraic terms. A set E of equations is an **algebraic theory**. E is **regular** if $\{\mathcal{V}(l)\} = \{\mathcal{V}(r)\}$ where $\{\mathcal{V}(l)\}$ is the set of variables in l. For a given theory E, T^E denotes its terms and C^E the constants appearing in it. The **equivalence modulo E** denoted by $=_E$ is the smallest equivalence relation on the terms such that $t[\sigma(l)] =_E t[\sigma(r)]$ $\forall t, \sigma$ and $l \sim r \in E$. So, we define the $\beta\eta E$-equivalence (in short $=_{\beta\eta E}$) by the reflexive, transitive and symmetric closure of $=_E \cup \to_{\beta\eta}$. A useful result [BT88] is that for any pair of terms $< t_1, t_2 >$, $t_1 =_{\beta\eta E} t_2$ iff $t_1 \downarrow_{l\beta\eta} =_E t_2 \downarrow_{l\beta\eta}$ ($t \downarrow_{l\beta\eta}$ is the $l\beta\eta$-nf of t).

We now define the size of terms :

$$\text{the size } \mid t \mid \text{ is defined by } \left\{ \begin{array}{l} \mid x \mid = 1 \\ \mid \lambda \overline{x_m} \cdot \phi(\overline{t_n}) \mid = 1 + \sum_{i=1}^{n} \mid t_i \mid. \end{array} \right.$$

We say that a theory is **size preserving** if :

- $\{\{\mathcal{V}(l)\}\} = \{\{\mathcal{V}(r)\}\}$ for each equation $l \sim r \in E$ (where $\{\{\mathcal{V}(l)\}\}$ is the multiset of the variables in l),

- $\mid l \mid = \mid r \mid$ for each equation $l \sim r \in E$.

Lemma 1 *If a theory E preserves size, then it is regular and if t_1 and t_2 are two terms with $t_1 =_E t_2$ then $\mid t_1 \mid = \mid t_2 \mid$.*

A size preserving theory will be called **root-preserving** if each axiom of this theory is such that $\mathcal{H}(l) = \mathcal{H}(r)$ for each $l \sim r \in E$. For instance, AC is such a theory.

An axiom $l \sim r$ is said **regular collapsing** if it is regular, and collapsing, i.e. $r = x$ where x is a variable. Then, a regular collapsing axiom has the form $l \sim x$ with $\mathcal{V}(l) = \{x\}$, but $l \neq x$. Note that it implies $\mid l \mid > 1$. We say that a term is in **collapsed form** if no collapsing axiom can be applied to it in the direction $l \to x$ at any occurrence. Because each term has a collapsed form, we shall assume we only have terms in collapsed form. By application of a collapsing rule, a term can only get smaller. Then a collapsed form t of a term is smaller than any element of the infinite equivalence class $\|t\|_E$ such that $t' \in \|t\|_E$ iff $t' \to^+_{l \to x} t$ (+ means at least one time) because $t' \to^+_{l \to x} t \Rightarrow \mid t' \mid > \mid t \mid$ is obvious. We say that t' is **more general** than t.

Collapsing size preserving theories : let E be the union of two theories E_1 and E_2. If E_1 is root and size preserving theory, and E_2 only made of regular collapsing axioms, then we say that E is a collapsing size preserving theory.

Remark: AC1 for $\vee$ is AC $\cup \{x \vee false \sim x\}$. Then, it is a collapsing size preserving theory.

4 Rules and strategy

We present here the rules and the strategy which define our second order E-matching algorithm. A preliminary assumption is that we have an algorithm for first order E-matching which gives a finite complete set of more general solutions in a finite time.

$t_1 \overset{\triangle}{=} t_2$ is a **matching pair** if t_1 and t_2 are two terms in $l\beta\eta$-nf, t_2 is rigid, and $\tau(t_1) = \tau(t_2)$. We assume that t_2 doesn't contain any free variable (otherwise, they can be frozen during the matching). The theory we shall use cannot introduce free variables in this term, since it is regular. Let S be a set of matching pairs, σ is an **E-matcher** of S iff for each pair $t_1 \overset{\triangle}{=} t_2$ of S, we have $\sigma t_1 =_{\beta\eta E} t_2$. $\mathcal{M}_E$ denotes the set of all such E-matchers. A matching pair $x \overset{\triangle}{=} t$ is said to be in **solved form** if x is a variable and $x \notin FV(S - \{x \overset{\triangle}{=} t\})$. S is solved if all its matching pairs are solved or if S is empty. Note that if x is of order two, x is not in $l\beta\eta$-nf in $x \overset{\triangle}{=} t$. In fact, a solved form $x \overset{\triangle}{=} t$ means $x \leftarrow t$. A **complete set of E-matchers** of a set of matching pairs S denoted by $CS\mathcal{M}_E(S)$ is a set of substitutions requiring **soundness** (i.e. $CS\mathcal{M}_E(S) \subseteq \mathcal{M}_E(S)$) and **completeness** (i.e. for each solution in $\mathcal{M}_E$ there exists a smaller one in $CS\mathcal{M}_E(S)$).

4.1 The rules

Let $t_1 \overset{\triangle}{=} t_2$ be a matching pair. Assume $\mathcal{H}(t_1)$ and $\mathcal{H}(t_2)$ are constants of the theory E. We then have to do first order matching in E. But before this, we have to abstract t_1 to make it pure in E. Therefore, we define the notion of **maximal alien subterms** :

$$MAS(\lambda\overline{x_m} \cdot \phi(\overline{t_n})) = \begin{cases} \{t_i\} \cup FV(\phi(\overline{t_n})) & \text{if } \mathcal{H}(t_i) \in \mathcal{C}^E \\ MAS(t_i) & \text{otherwise} \end{cases}$$

The E-matching rule is then :

$$\frac{\lambda\overline{x_m} \cdot \phi(\overline{s_n}) \overset{\triangle}{=} \lambda\overline{x'_m} \cdot \phi'(\overline{s'_{n'}})}{\lambda\overline{x_m}.t_i \overset{\triangle}{=} \lambda\overline{x'_m}.t'_i} \text{E--matching}$$

where

- $\{t_i\} = MAS(\lambda\overline{x_m} \cdot \phi(\overline{s_n}))$,

- t'_i are such that $X_i \overset{\triangle}{=} t'_i$ are solution of $\{\lambda\overline{x_m}.[t_i \leftarrow X_i]\overline{s_n} \overset{\triangle}{=} \lambda\overline{x'_m} \cdot \phi'(\overline{s'_{n'}})\}$ in E where X_i are new distinct variables of the appropriate type.

Remark:

$[t_i \leftarrow X_i]$ represents the abstraction. i.e we replace the maximum alien subterm t_i by the new variable X_i.

Decomp1

$$\frac{\lambda B_1.F(\overline{t_m}) \overset{\triangle}{=} \lambda B_2.G(\overline{t'_m})}{\lambda B_1.t_1 \overset{\triangle}{=} \lambda B_2.t'_1; \ldots; \lambda B_1.t_m \overset{\triangle}{=} \lambda B_2.t'_m}$$

Decomp2

$$\frac{\lambda\overline{x_m} \cdot f(\overline{t_n}) \overset{\triangle}{=} \lambda\overline{x'_m} \cdot f(\overline{t'_n})}{\lambda\overline{x_m}.t_1 \overset{\triangle}{=} \lambda\overline{x'_m}.t'_1; \cdots; \lambda\overline{x_m}.t_n \overset{\triangle}{=} \lambda\overline{x'_m}.t'_n}$$

where
$$B_1 = x_1 \ldots x_i \, F \, x_{i+1} \ldots x_n \text{ and } B_2 = x'_1 \ldots x'_i \, G \, x'_{i+1} \ldots x'_n.$$

	Imitation	Projection

$$\frac{\lambda\overline{x_n} \cdot F(\overline{t_m}) \stackrel{\triangle}{=} \lambda\overline{x'_n} \cdot f(\overline{t'_{m'}})}{[F \leftarrow \lambda\overline{x_m}.f(\overline{u_{m'}})]t_F \stackrel{\triangle}{=} \lambda\overline{x'_n} \cdot f(\overline{t'_{m'}}); \ F \stackrel{\triangle}{=} \lambda\overline{x_m}.f(\overline{u_{m'}})} \qquad \frac{\lambda\overline{x_m} \cdot F(\overline{t_p}) \stackrel{\triangle}{=} \lambda\overline{x'_m}.s}{\lambda\overline{x_m}.t_i \stackrel{\triangle}{=} \lambda\overline{x'_m}.s; \ F \stackrel{\triangle}{=} \lambda\overline{x_p}.x_i}$$

where

- t_F is $\lambda\overline{x_n} \cdot F(\overline{t_m})$, and $\overline{x_p}$ are new variables of the appropriate type

- with the following definition of u_i (due to Huet and Lang [HL78]) :

  if $\tau(t'_i) \in T_0$ then $u_i = H_i(\overline{x_m})$

  if $\tau(t'_i) = (\alpha_1 \times \cdots \times \alpha_n \to \beta)$ then $u_i = \lambda w_1, w_2, \ldots, w_s \cdot H_i(\overline{x_m}, \overline{w_s})$

                       and $\tau(w_j) = \alpha_j \ 1 \le j \le s$

  Where w_i and H_i are new variables of the appropriate type.

Remarks:

Decomposition denotes either Decomp1 or Decomp2. We are working with a second order language combined with a first order theory. Therefore, in the imitation rule, if f is in E, then the order of f is at most two (because E is of order 1). As a consequence, the case $\tau(t'_i) = (\alpha_1 \times \alpha_2 \times \cdots \times \alpha_n \to \beta)$ only appears for an imitation of a symbol f not in the theory.

4.2 The strategy

S is a **success case** if it is empty or solved. We can then build a substitution σ_S with all the pairs in solved form of S, and we have $\sigma_S t_1 =_{\beta\eta E} t_2$ for all $t_1 \stackrel{\triangle}{=} t_2$ in the initial set S_0. S is a **failure case** if it contains a pair such that :
$\lambda\overline{x_m} \cdot \phi(\overline{t_n}) \stackrel{\triangle}{=} \lambda\overline{x'_m} \cdot \phi'(\overline{t'_n})$ with ϕ and ϕ' two different constants not in E. To start the E-matching, we need a set S_0 of matching pairs such that all the terms in S_0 are in $1\beta\eta$-nf, and such that $\tau(t_1) = \tau(t_2)$ for each pair $t_1 \stackrel{\triangle}{=} t_2$ in S_0.
The strategy : if S is neither in solved form nor empty nor in a failure case, we select arbitrarily a pair.

- **a) If we have a rigid-rigid pair :**

  - if $\mathcal{H}(t_1) \in E$ and $\mathcal{H}(t_2) \in E$, then we apply E-matching,
  - if $\mathcal{H}(t_1) \notin E$ and $\mathcal{H}(t_2) \notin E$ and $\mathcal{H}(t_1) = \mathcal{H}(t_2)$, then use Decomp,
  - if $\mathcal{H}(t_1)$ and $\mathcal{H}(t_2)$ are bound variables, use Decomp,
  - it's a failure otherwise.

- **b) If we have a flexible-rigid pair :**

  - if $O(\mathcal{H}(t_1)) = 1$, then either the pair is in solved form, and we do not select it, or it is a failure case,

- if $\mathcal{H}(t_2) \notin E$, then if $\mathcal{H}(t_2) \in \mathcal{V}$, we apply the rule Projection as many times (at most the number of arguments of $\mathcal{H}(t_1)$) as the type constraints permit it, and each time, we shall try to find a different solution.

  i.e. when we have $t_1 = \lambda \overline{x_m} \cdot F(\overline{t_p})$, we shall try a new matching with each $\lambda \overline{x_m} . t_i$ such that $\tau(t_i) = \tau(F(\overline{t_p}))$.

  if $\mathcal{H}(t_2) \in \mathcal{C}$, we shall then apply the projections as in the previous case, and we shall add another solution which will be given by the application of the imitation followed by the decomposition.

- otherwise we have a matching pair $P = \{\lambda \overline{x_n} \cdot F(\overline{t_m}) \overset{\triangle}{=} \lambda \overline{x'_n} \cdot f(\overline{t'_{m'}})\}$ with $f \in E$. We apply the projection rule as in the previous cases, and we apply the imitation followed by E-matching. We continue with each matching pair of each solution of the E-matching except the ones which are of the form $\{\lambda \overline{x_n} \cdot H_i(\overline{t_m}) \overset{\triangle}{=} \lambda \overline{x'_n} \cdot f(\overline{t'_{m'}})\}$. The solutions of these pruned matching pairs are the solutions that we find for P.

To explain the last point, we give a small example. Suppose we try to compute the matching pair $F(x, y) \overset{\triangle}{=} a + b$. We shall compute the two possible projections ($[F \leftarrow \lambda x_1 x_2 \cdot x_1]$ and $[F \leftarrow \lambda x_1 x_2 \cdot x_2]$) and the imitation of '+' which is a symbol of the theory $AC1_+$. We then have the following scheme :

$$F(x, y) \overset{\triangle}{=} a + b$$

Imitation   *2 Projections*

$$F \leftarrow \lambda x_1 x_2 . + (H_1(x_1, x_2), H_2(x_1, x_2))$$
$$+ (H_1(x, y), H_2(x, y)) \overset{\triangle}{=} a + b$$

     . . .

E-matching gives 4 solutions

$\boxed{H_1(x, y) \overset{\triangle}{=} a + b}$	$H_1(x, y) \overset{\triangle}{=} 0$	$H_1(x, y) \overset{\triangle}{=} a$	$H_1(x, y) \overset{\triangle}{=} b$
$H_2(x, y) \overset{\triangle}{=} 0$	$\boxed{H_2(x, y) \overset{\triangle}{=} a + b}$	$H_2(x, y) \overset{\triangle}{=} b$	$H_2(x, y) \overset{\triangle}{=} a$

The framed new matching pairs are identical to $F(x, y) \overset{\triangle}{=} a + b$. Then, the idea is simply that two identical problems have the same solutions, and there is no need to compute them twice.

5   Soundness, termination and completeness

In this section, we give the three main properties of this algorithm for collapsing size preserving theories. We call ρ the set of rules. Let ρ_i be any of these rules.

5.1   Soundness

Soundness means that any computed solution is a solution of the initial problem. Therefore, it is the basic requirement for our algorithm and is stated as follows :

Lemma 2 *Let S and S' be sets of matching pairs, $\dfrac{S}{S'}\rho_i$ implies $CSM_E(S') \subseteq CSM_E(S)$.*

5.2 Completeness

Completeness means that for each solution of a given matching problem, our strategy generates a sequence of rules which gives an equivalent solution.

Lemma 3 *Let $t_1 \stackrel{?}{=} t_2$ be a matching pair not solved. If $\sigma \in CSM_E(\{t_1 \stackrel{?}{=} t_2\})$, then there exists a rule ρ_i in ρ such that $\dfrac{t_1 \stackrel{?}{=} t_2}{S}\rho_i$ and σ is solution of S.*

Theorem 1 *(Completeness) : Let S be a set of matching pairs not solved. If $\sigma \in CSM_E(S)$, then there exists a sequence of rules of ρ generated by the strategy which gives a set of solved matching pairs S_m such that $\sigma_{S_m} =_{\beta\eta E} \sigma[FV(S)]$.*

5.3 Termination

The termination property is proved, by showing that some complexity decreases when a rule is applied. Then, we give our definition of complexity.

The *Alternation* is defined for a term by (C^E is the set of constants appearing in E) :

$$IAST(\lambda\overline{x_m}\cdot\phi(\overline{t_n})) = \begin{cases} FV(\lambda\overline{x_m}\cdot\phi(\overline{t_n})) \cup \{t_i\} \mid \mathcal{H}(t_i) \in C^E & \text{if } \phi \notin C^E \\ FV(\lambda\overline{x_m}\cdot\phi(\overline{t_n})) \cup \{t_i\} \mid \mathcal{H}(t_i) \notin C^E & \text{if } \phi \in C^E \\ IAST(t_i) & \text{otherwise} \end{cases}$$

We denote the alternation of a term by $Alt(t)$ such that :
$Alt(t) = 1 + max_{s \in IAST(t)}Alt(s)$. For a set S of matching pairs, we define $Alt_1(S)$ by :

$$Alt_1(S) = \{\{Alt(t_1)\} \mid t_1 \stackrel{?}{=} t_2 \in S \text{ and not solved}\}$$

where $\{\{\}\}$ stands for multisets. Multisets of integers are compared using the multiset extension of $<$.

$$\xi_1(S) = \sum \mid t_1 \mid \text{ for all } t_1 \text{ such that } t_1 \stackrel{?}{=} t_2 \text{ not solved in } S$$
$$\xi_2(S) = \sum \mid t_2 \mid \text{ for all } t_2 \text{ such that } t_1 \stackrel{?}{=} t_2 \text{ not solved in } S$$

So, to prove the termination of the algorithm, we use the complexity triple

$$CT(S) =< Alt_1(S), \xi_2(S), \xi_1(S) >$$

by comparing $CT(S)$ and $CT(S')$ lexicographically.

The following lemma is used in the termination proof, and it justifies the use of collapsing size preserving theories.

Lemma 4 *For a theory E such that $E = E_1 \cup E_2$ with E_1 a root preserving and size preserving theory, and E_2 a set (possibly empty) of regular collapsing axioms, then the more general solutions $[x_i \leftarrow s_i]$ of a matching problem $f(\overline{x_m}) \stackrel{\triangle}{=} f(\overline{t_m})$ are such that $s_i =_E f(\overline{t_m})$, or $\mid s_i \mid < \mid f(\overline{t_m}) \mid$.*

Then we can give the termination lemma :

Lemma 5 *(Termination (for collapsing size preserving theories)) : for any derivation with the given set of rules, $\dfrac{S_1}{S_2}\rho_i$, either S_2 is a terminal case, or $CT(S_2) <_{lex} CT(S_1)$.*

The proofs are given in appendix.

Remark about complexity : We can see the search of solutions as a tree which has S_0 as root and inference rules as nodes. A leaf is then a success or a failure. Then, if we can find a binding of the height of this tree and a binding of the complexity of the rules, we shall be able to bind the complexity of the algorithm for finding a solution.

Let $T(n, a)$ be the height of the search tree for the matching pair $t_1 \stackrel{\triangle}{=} t_2$ where n is the number of symbols in the matrix of t_1 and a is an upper bound of the function symbol arities. One can see that for each inference rule, we have the tree height which is $O(n)$.

For instance, by decomposition, we obtain a new problems if a is the arity of the decomposed function. Then, $T(n, a) = T(n_1, a) + T(n_2, a) + \cdots + T(n_p, a)$ with $p \leq a$ and $\Sigma n_i = n - 1$. Then, if we assume that $T(n, a) \leq C.n$ for a constant C, by reccurence, we have $T(n, a) \leq C.\Sigma n_i = C(n - 1)$. Similar reasoning can be held for the other rules. We then have a height which is linear for the number of symbols in t_1.

In the other hand, the most complex rule is obviously the *E-matching* rule. For instance, if we take the AC theory, we know that the first order AC-matching is NP. Hence, the complexity for finding a solution to a second order AC-matching problem via our algorithm is NP.

6 Applications

There are many applications of second order E-matching. Each domain where one tries to recognize higher order patterns will be described more precisely if first order algebraic properties are taken into account. This enhances the expressiveness of the syntactical approach in many A.I. applications. We show in the next example how we can recognize a recurrent pattern in a logic program. But it can be applied also to automated reasoning, program transformation, higher order rewriting systems, ...

6.1 Logic programming and program transformation

Assuming we are working with Horn clauses, we know that a recurrence schema on the integers for any predicate P has the form : 'P(0) $\wedge$ P(suc(x)) : −P(x)'. Then, if we try to match a logic program with this pattern, the algorithm will return all the relations which can instantiate P. i.e. all the relations on which a recurrence is applied. For instance :

$$F(P(0) \wedge \qquad\qquad \overset{\triangleleft}{=} \qquad\qquad b : -a \wedge$$
$$(P(suc(x)) : -P(x))) \qquad\qquad\qquad p(suc(x_1)) : -p(x_1) \wedge$$
$$d : -c \wedge$$
$$p(0) \wedge$$
$$g : -e$$

will give the solutions[2] :

$x \leftarrow x_1$	$F \leftarrow \lambda y \cdot (g : -e \wedge$	$x \leftarrow x_1$
$P \leftarrow \lambda y \cdot p(y)$	$d : -c \wedge$	$P \leftarrow \lambda y \cdot p(y)$
$F \leftarrow \lambda y \cdot (g : -e \wedge$	$p(0) \wedge$	$F \leftarrow \lambda y \cdot (g : -e \wedge \quad [\cdots]$
$d : -c \wedge$	$b : -a \wedge$	$d : -c \wedge$
$b : -a \wedge$	$p(suc(x_1)) : -p(x_1))$	$y \wedge$
$y)$		$b : -a)$

Without considering the AC properties of '$\wedge$', we would not be able to produce this result. First order E-matching should try to match at each possible occurrence, but furthermore with each relation P occurring in the program. This pattern recognition is also useful in fold-unfold program transformation where the folding rule rapidly becomes unmanageable by hand and requires some mechanical tool.

6.2 Automated reasoning

As previously stated, looking for tautologies can be applied in a pre-processing step in order to simplify formulae before invoking a theorem prover. We shall illustrate here a new way for simplifying formulae using this method. Consider the following formula : $(p(x) \Rightarrow q(x)) \wedge (q(y) \Rightarrow r(y))$ where x and y are universally quantified. Trivially, by transitivity of the implication, we can simplify into $p(x) \Rightarrow r(x)$. In order to make such simplifications in the formulae, we perform some abstraction on this scheme to obtain the more general scheme : $\psi = F((P(x) \Rightarrow Q(x)) \wedge (Q(y) \Rightarrow R(y)))$ where P Q and R are second order variables. We can then match the pair $\psi \overset{\triangleleft}{=} \varphi$ with $\varphi = ((q(x) \Rightarrow r(x)) \wedge (p(a) \vee r(b)) \wedge (p(x) \Rightarrow q(x))) \Rightarrow (r(a) \vee r(b))$. The matching problem

$$F((P(x) \Rightarrow Q(x)) \wedge (Q(y) \Rightarrow R(y)))$$
$$\overset{\triangleleft}{=}$$
$$((q(x_1) \Rightarrow r(x_1)) \wedge (p(a) \vee r(b)) \wedge (p(x_1) \Rightarrow q(x_1))) \Rightarrow (r(a) \vee r(b))$$

has a solution :

---

[2]Note that x_1 is a frozen variable (other solutions do exist).

$F \leftarrow \lambda z \cdot (z \wedge (p(a) \vee r(b))) \Rightarrow (r(a) \vee r(b))$
$P \leftarrow \lambda z \cdot p(z)$
$Q \leftarrow \lambda z \cdot q(z)$
$R \leftarrow \lambda z \cdot r(z)$
$x \leftarrow x_1$
$y \leftarrow x_1$

Hence, we obtain : $\varphi' = ((p(x) \Rightarrow r(x)) \wedge (p(a) \vee r(b))) \Rightarrow (r(a) \vee r(b))$ after simplification. Again, this result could not be obtained without taking account of the AC properties of '$\wedge$'. To use first order, we should have tried all the combinations to instantiate P Q and R, and to try to match at each position in φ.

7 Discussion and conclusions

The main problem relating to the implementation, is the number of solutions and this has two essential reasons. First, we deal with second order. This produces a lot of useless solutions. In particular, solutions which assign closed functions (terms like $\lambda x.t$ with $x \notin t$) to second order variables. One can be easily convinced by looking at the presented examples. Secondly, we cannot avoid the number of solutions given by the first order E-matching. Furthermore, these two reasons can be combined. For example, if one solution is a closed function $\lambda \overline{x_n} \cdot s$ we shall have as other solutions, all the closed functions $\lambda \overline{x_n} \cdot s'$ such that s' is equivalent to s modulo the considered theory. These solutions are obviously useless. One solution could be to keep only one element of this class which would be the normal form. But we are not interested at all by these solutions and computing only one good solution is a much better way of improving the pattern recognition step in Automated Theorem Proving. We are convinced that for our purpose, the first solution which have no closed function in its range associated with a second order variable symbol is the one we need.
Note that experiments have shown that to use a term representation à la De Bruijn or a similar encoding will not provide a substantial improvement since the most important wasting of time is due to irrelevant solutions.

What we have presented is a second order matching algorithm which is able to take into account algebraic properties. The termination property is obtained for collapsing size preserving theories and an appropriate strategy. This algorithm is a first step toward a toolbox using higher order mechanisms in Automated Theorem Proving which is currently under development.

Acknowledgments : We are very grateful to Denis Lugiez for his help during this work, Eric Domenjoud for helpful discussions about theories and Adam Cichon for his comments on a previous version. We also thank referees for helpful remarks.

References

[BT88]   V. Breazu-Tannen. Combining algebra and higher-order types. In *Proceedings 3rd IEEE Symposium on Logic in Computer Science, Edinburgh (UK)*, pages 82–90, 1988.

[Dow92] G. Dowek. Third order matching is decidable. In *Proceedings of LICS'92*, Santa-Cruz (California, USA), June 1992.

[HL78]   G. Huet and B. Lang. Proving and applying program transformations expressed with second-order patterns. *Acta Informatica*, 11:31–55, 1978.

[HS86]   J. Roger Hindley and Johnathan P. Seldin. *Introduction to Combinators and Lambda-calculus*. Cambridge University, 1986.

[NQ91]   T. Nipkow and Z. Qian. Modular higher-order E-unification. In R. V. Book, editor, *Proceedings 4th Conference on Rewriting Techniques and Applications, Como (Italy)*, volume 488 of *Lecture Notes in Computer Science*, pages 200–214. Springer-Verlag, 1991.

[QW92]   Z. Qian and K. Wang. Higher-order E-unification for arbitrary theories. In K. Apt, editor, *LOGIC PROGRAMMING : Proceedings of 1992 joint international conference and symposium on logic programming*, 1992.

[Sny88] W.S. Snyder. *Complete Sets of Transformations for General Unification*. PhD thesis, University of Pennsylvania, 1988.

A Proofs

Proof: (of lemma 1). The regularity is trivial because $\{\{\mathcal{V}(l)\}\} = \{\{\mathcal{V}(r)\}\}$ implies $\{\mathcal{V}(l)\} = \{\mathcal{V}(r)\}$ which is the definition of regularity.

$=_E$ is the smallest equivalence relation on terms such that $[\sigma(l)]t =_E [\sigma(r)]t \; \forall t, \sigma$ and $l \sim r \in E$. The number of constant symbols is the same for l and r for each equation of the theory, (because the total number of symbols is constant and also the number of variables). The only way to make a term grow is to apply a substitution σ. But σ is applied to both sides and if $x \in Dom(\sigma)$, then $x \in \mathcal{V}(t_1) \Longleftrightarrow x \in \mathcal{V}(t_2)$ and so, each variable appears the same number of times in both sides. That means we preserve the property $\mid \sigma(t_1) \mid = \mid \sigma(t_2) \mid$.

$\square$

Proof: (of lemma 2).

E-matching : Let $[t_1 \leftarrow t_2]$ mean that we replace all the occurrences of t_1 by t_2, then we summarize the result of $E-matching$ by :

$$[t_i \leftarrow t_i']\lambda \overline{x_m} \cdot \phi(\overline{s_n}) =_E \lambda \overline{x'_m} \cdot \phi'(\overline{s'_{n'}}) \qquad (1)$$

because $[t_i \leftarrow X_i][X_i \leftarrow t_i'] \equiv [t_i \leftarrow t_i']$. Then, it is easy to see that if there is a σ such that $\sigma(\lambda \overline{x_m}.t_i) =_{\beta\eta E} \lambda \overline{x'_m}.t_i'$ for each i, from (1) we can conclude that $\sigma(\lambda \overline{x_m} \cdot \phi(\overline{s_n})) =_{\beta\eta E} \lambda \overline{x'_m} \cdot \phi'(\overline{s'_{n'}})$ (t_i' cannot contain variables).

Decomp : if we have a σ such that $\sigma(\lambda \overline{x_m}.t_i) =_{\beta\eta E} \lambda \overline{x'_m}.t_i'$, it is straightforward to say that $\sigma(\lambda\overline{x_m}\cdot\phi(\overline{t_n})) =_{\beta\eta E} \lambda\overline{x'_m}\cdot\phi'(\overline{t'_n})$ if ϕ and ϕ' are either the same constant or bound variables because we are working modulo α-conversion.

Projection : Let σ be such that $\sigma(\lambda\overline{x_m}.t_i) =_{\beta\eta E} \lambda\overline{x'_m}.s$. $[F \leftarrow \lambda\overline{x_p}.x_i]\lambda\overline{x_m}.F(\overline{t_p}) =_{\beta\eta}$ $\lambda\overline{x_m}.t_i$ where $[F \leftarrow \lambda\overline{x_p}.x_i]$ is a possible projection. Then, $(\sigma \cup [F \leftarrow \lambda\overline{x_p}.x_i])\lambda\overline{x_m}.F(\overline{t_p}) =_{\beta\eta E} \lambda\overline{x'_m}.s$ (with F and $x_1,\ldots,x_p$ of the appropriate type).

Imitation : We have σ such that

$$\sigma(\lambda\overline{x_n}.f(\lambda\overline{w_{k_1}}.H_1(\overline{t_m},\overline{w_{k_1}}),\ldots,\lambda\overline{w_{k_{m'}}}.H_{m'}(\overline{t_m},\overline{w_{k_{m'}}}))) =_{\beta\eta E} \lambda\overline{x'_n}\cdot f(\overline{t'_{m'}})$$

Then, if we note θ the imitation, $\theta = [F \leftarrow \lambda x^1\ldots x^m.f(\lambda\overline{w_{k_1}}.H_1(x^1,\ldots,x^m,\overline{w_{k_1}}),\ldots$ $,\lambda\overline{w_{k_{m'}}}.H_{m'}(x^1,\ldots,x^m,\overline{w_{k_{m'}}}))]$, $\theta(\lambda\overline{x_n}\cdot F(\overline{t_m})) =_{\beta\eta} \lambda\overline{x_n}.f(\lambda\overline{w_{k_1}}.H_1(\overline{t_m},\overline{w_{k_1}}),\ldots,\lambda\overline{w_{k_{m'}}}.H_{m'}(\overline{t_m},\overline{w_{k_{m'}}}))$ Hence, $(\sigma \cup \theta)(\lambda\overline{x_n}\cdot F(\overline{t_m})) =_{\beta\eta E} \lambda\overline{x'_n}\cdot f(\overline{t'_{m'}})$

$\Box$

Proof: (of lemma 3). Let us consider the different cases for the form of this pair and let $\sigma \in CSM_E(\{t_1 \overset{\triangle}{=} t_2\})$.

Rigid-rigid :
$\mathcal{H}(t_1) \in \mathcal{C}^E$ **and** $\mathcal{H}(t_2) \in \mathcal{C}^E$: if we consider the *abstracted* t_1 i.e. $t_1[t_i \leftarrow X_i]$ where t_i are the maximal alien subterms of t_1, then $Dom(\sigma) \cap FV(abstracted\ t_1) = \emptyset$ because *abstracted* t_1 is just made of constants of the theory and new variables.

$$\text{Hence, } \sigma t_1 = [t_i \leftarrow \sigma t_i]t_1 \quad (1)$$

Let $\theta \in CSM_E(\{abstracted\ t_1 \overset{\triangle}{=} t_2\})$ i.e. $\theta([t_i \leftarrow X_i]t_1) =_E t_2$. Then, θ will be of the form $\{[X_i \leftarrow t'_i]\}$.

$$\text{Therefore, } t_2 =_E [t_i \leftarrow X_i][X_i \leftarrow t'_i]t_1 \quad (2)$$

On the other hand, we assumed that $\sigma t_1 =_{\beta\eta E} t_2$. Then, by (1) and (2), we have (assuming that we have all the substitutions $\theta \mid \theta \in CSM_E(\{abstracted\ t_1 \overset{\triangle}{=} t_2\})$),

$$\sigma t_1 = [t_i \leftarrow \sigma t_i]t_1 =_{\beta\eta E} t_2 =_E [t_i \leftarrow t'_i]t_1$$

Therefore, $[t_i \leftarrow \sigma t_i]t_1 =_{\beta\eta E} [t_i \leftarrow t'_i]t_1$. Hence, $\sigma t_i =_{\beta\eta E} t'_i$ for each i, and this is the result of the E-matching rule. Remember that the E-matching algorithm considers the maximum alien subterms of the rigid term as constants not in the theory.
$\mathcal{H}(t_1) = \mathcal{H}(t_2) \in \mathcal{C}\backslash\mathcal{C}^E$: then $\mathcal{H}(t_1) \in \mathcal{C}$ implies $\mathcal{H}(t_1) \notin Dom(\sigma)$, therefore, $\sigma(\lambda\overline{x_m}\cdot f(\overline{t_n})) =_{\beta\eta E} \lambda\overline{x'_m}\cdot f(\overline{t'_n})$ implies $\lambda\overline{x_m}\cdot f(\overline{\sigma t_n}) =_{\beta\eta E} \lambda\overline{x'_m}\cdot f(\overline{t'_n})$.
Then, trivially, $\sigma t_i =_{\beta\eta E} t'_i$ which is the result of Decomp1.
$\mathcal{H}(t_1) \in BV(t_1)$ **and** $\mathcal{H}(t_2) \in BV(t_2)$: $\sigma(\lambda B_1.F(\overline{t_m})) =_{\beta\eta E} \lambda B_2.G(\overline{t'_m})$. With $\sigma(\lambda B_1.F(\overline{t_m})) = \lambda B_1.F(\overline{\sigma t_m})$ for the same reason as before. Then, $\sigma t_i = t'_i$ which is Decomp2.

Flexible-rigid : then, for the pair $\lambda\overline{x_m}\cdot F(\overline{t_p}) \overset{\triangle}{=} \lambda\overline{x'_m}\cdot f(\overline{t'_n})$, we have $\sigma \mid \sigma(\lambda\overline{x_m}\cdot F(\overline{t_p})) =_{\beta\eta E} \lambda\overline{x'_m}\cdot f(\overline{t'_n})$. Hence, $[F \leftarrow s] \in \sigma$ because $F \in FV(\lambda\overline{x_m}\cdot F(\overline{t_p}))$. s is in $l\beta\eta$-nf, and $\tau(s) = \tau(F) = \tau(t_1) \rightarrow (\tau(t_2) \rightarrow (\cdots \rightarrow (\tau(t_p) \rightarrow \tau_0)\cdots))$. For a term of this type in $l\beta\eta$-nf, there are only two cases :
$s = \lambda\overline{x_p}.x_i$: with $\tau(x_i) = \tau_0$ which is the case of application of the projection. Then, $[F \leftarrow s](\lambda\overline{x_m}\cdot F(\overline{t_p})) =_{\beta\eta} \lambda\overline{x_m}\cdot t_i$. And we know that σ is a solution of the matching pair $\lambda\overline{x_m}\cdot t_i \overset{\triangle}{=} \lambda\overline{x'_m}\cdot f(\overline{t'_m})$ which is the result of one of the projections.
$s = \lambda\overline{x_p}.s'$ with $s' \neq x_i$ We still have two subcases.

$f \notin E$ we then have $\mathcal{H}(s') = f$ and $s = \lambda \overline{x_p} \cdot f(\lambda \overline{w_{k_1}} . s_1(\overline{x_p}, \overline{w_{k_1}}), \ldots, \lambda \overline{w_{k_n}} . s_n(\overline{x_p}, \overline{w_{k_n}}))$
hence, $[F \leftarrow s] \lambda \overline{x_m} \cdot F(\overline{t_p}) =_{\beta \eta} \lambda \overline{x_p} \cdot f(\lambda \overline{w_{k_1}} . s_1(\overline{t_p}, \overline{w_{k_1}}), \ldots, \lambda \overline{w_{k_n}} . s_n(\overline{t_p}, \overline{w_{k_n}}))$ We
then have $\forall i \in 1 \ldots n$, $\sigma(\lambda \overline{x_m w_{k_i}} . s_i(\overline{t_p}, \overline{w_{k_i}})) =_{\beta \eta E} \lambda \overline{x'_m} \cdot t'_i$ which is the result of
the imitation and decomposition. Note that decomposition is the only rule we
can apply to the pair
$$\lambda \overline{x_m} \cdot f(\lambda \overline{w_{k_1}} . s_1(\overline{t_p}, \overline{w_{k_1}}), \ldots, \lambda \overline{w_{k_n}} . s_n(\overline{t_p}, \overline{w_{k_n}})) \stackrel{\triangle}{=} \lambda \overline{x'_m} \cdot f(\overline{t'_n}).$$

$f \in E$ We then have $s = \lambda \overline{x_p} \cdot f(s_1(\overline{x_p}), \ldots, s_n(\overline{x_p}))$
hence $[F \leftarrow s] \lambda \overline{x_m} \cdot F(\overline{t_p}) =_{\beta \eta} \lambda \overline{x_m} \cdot f(s_1(\overline{t_p}), \ldots, s_n(\overline{t_p}))$ We then know that σ
is solution of the matching problem
$\lambda \overline{x_m} \cdot f(s_1(\overline{t_p}), \ldots, s_n(\overline{t_p})) \stackrel{\triangle}{=} \lambda \overline{x'_m} \cdot f(\overline{t'_n})$ with $f \in E$ (1).
Hence, $\exists \theta \in CSM_E(f(x_1, \ldots, x_n) \stackrel{\triangle}{=} f(\overline{t'_n}))$ i.e. $\theta f(x_1, \ldots, x_n) =_E f(\overline{t'_n})$ s.t.
$(s_i(\overline{t_p}) = \theta x_i)$. This solution will be generated by imitation followed by E-
matching (assuming that the E-matching algorithm gives the complete set of
more general solutions).

□

Proof: (of theorem 1). By the previous lemma, we know that for each $\mathcal{S}$, if we have
$\sigma \in CSM_E(\mathcal{S})$, then $\exists \rho_i \in \rho$ s. t. $\dfrac{\mathcal{S}}{\mathcal{S}'} \rho_i$ with $\sigma \in CSM_E(\mathcal{S}')$. And such a sequence
of rule applications is finite (termination) and sound (soundness). Then $\mathcal{S}_0, \ldots, \mathcal{S}_m$
exists, $\sigma_{\mathcal{S}_m} \in CSM_E(\mathcal{S}_0)$ and $\sigma \in CSM_E(\mathcal{S}_m)$. Then $\sigma_{\mathcal{S}_m} =_{\beta \eta E} \sigma[FV(\mathcal{S})]$.

□

Proof: (of lemma 4). Assume s_i in collapsed form such that $[x_i \leftarrow s_i]$ is in the solution.
Then, $f(x_1, \ldots, s_i, \ldots, x_n) =_E f(\overline{t_m})$. There are two cases :
- $f(x_1, \ldots, x_i, \ldots, x_n) =_{E_2} x_i$ then, either $s_i =_{E_1} f(\overline{t_m})$ and $\mid s_i \mid = \mid f(\overline{t_m}) \mid$, or s_i is
not in collapsed form,
- or $f(x_1, \ldots, s_i, \ldots, x_n) =_{E_1} f(\overline{t_m})$ which implies by definition of size preserving
theories that $\mid s_i \mid < \mid f(\overline{t_m}) \mid$.

□

Proof: (of lemma 5). Note that the strategy cannot generate an infinite set of solutions
because E-matching is assumed to give a finite set of more general solutions. We have
to examine all the rules.
E-matching : in this rule, t_i is a maximal alien subterm of $\lambda \overline{x_m} \cdot \phi(\overline{s_n})$. It means that
ϕ is a constant of the theory, and the head of t_i is not in E. Therefore, the alternation
has decreased by 1 between $\lambda \overline{x_m} \cdot \phi(\overline{s_n})$ and each t_i. We then have $Alt_1(\mathcal{S}_2) < Alt_1(\mathcal{S}_1)$
which implies $CT(\mathcal{S}_2) <_{lex} CT(\mathcal{S}_1)$. It is clear here that regularity is required to avoid
free variables in terms t'_i.
Decomp : if $\mathcal{H}(t_1)$ and $\mathcal{H}(t_2)$ are constants, they are not in E, otherwise, we would
apply the E-matching rule. If they are variables, they are bound ones (otherwise, it's
a Flexible-Flexible case). For these two cases, the alternation cannot increase. $\xi_1(\mathcal{S})$
and $\xi_2(\mathcal{S})$ are decreasing because t_i and t'_i are strict subterms of respectively $(F(\overline{t_m})$
and $f(\overline{t_n}))$ or $(G(\overline{t'_m})$ and $f(\overline{t'_n}))$. Therefore $CT(\mathcal{S}_2) <_{lex} CT(\mathcal{S}_1)$.
Projection : Again, t_i is a strict subterm of $\lambda \overline{x_m} \cdot F(\overline{t_p})$, then Alt_1 cannot increase.
$F \stackrel{\triangle}{=} \lambda \overline{x_p} . x_i$ is in solved form. $\lambda \overline{x_m} . s$ doesn't change. So, ξ_2 doesn't increase. And ξ_1
is decreasing because t_i is a strict subterm of $\lambda \overline{x_m} \cdot F(\overline{t_p})$. Then, $CT(\mathcal{S}_2) <_{lex} CT(\mathcal{S}_1)$.

Imitation : We have to distinguish two cases :
1- imitation of a symbol f not in the theory.

$$\lambda \overline{x_n} \cdot F(\overline{t_m}) \stackrel{\triangleleft}{=} \lambda \overline{x'_n} \cdot f(\overline{t'_{m'}})$$

Imitation : $F \leftarrow \lambda x_1 \ldots x_m.f(\lambda w_1 \ldots w_{k_1} \cdot H_1(x_1, \ldots, x_m, w_1, \ldots, w_{k_1}), \ldots,$
$\lambda w_1 \ldots w_{k_{m'}} \cdot H_{m'}(x_1, \ldots, x_m, w_1, \ldots, w_{k_{m'}}))$
After application of imitation and β-reduction, we have the pair :

$$\lambda \overline{x_n}.f(\lambda w_1 \ldots w_{k_1}.H_1(\overline{t_m}, \overline{w_{k_1}}), \ldots, \lambda w_1 \ldots w_{k_{m'}}.H_{m'}(\overline{t_m}, \overline{w_{k_{m'}}})) \stackrel{\triangleleft}{=} \lambda \overline{x'_n} \cdot f(\overline{t'_{m'}})$$

In this case, the only rule we can apply is the decomposition. The result is the following set of matching pairs.

$$\{(\lambda \overline{x_n w_{k_1}}.H_1(\overline{t_m}, \overline{w_{k_1}}) \stackrel{\triangleleft}{=} \lambda \overline{x'_n}.t'_1), \ldots, (\lambda \overline{x_n w_{k_{m'}}}.H_{m'}(\overline{t_m}, \overline{w_{k_{m'}}})) \stackrel{\triangleleft}{=} \lambda \overline{x'_n}.t'_{m'})\}$$

We then have $Alt_1(S_1) = Alt(\lambda \overline{x_n} \cdot F(\overline{t_m}))$ with $\phi \notin E$ and $Alt_1(S_2) = Alt(\lambda \overline{x_n w_{k_i}}.H_i(\overline{t_m}, \overline{w_{k_i}})) = Alt_1(S_1)$ because $H_i \notin E$. But we have $\xi_2(S_2) = \sum_i |t'_i| = \xi_2(S_1) - 1$. therefore, $\xi_2(S_2) < \xi_2(S_1)$, and then $CT(S_2) <_{lex} CT(S_1)$.
2- imitation of a symbol f of the theory. After application of the imitation and β-reduction, we have the same pair :

$$\lambda \overline{x_n}.f(H_1(\overline{t_m}), \ldots, H_{m'}(\overline{t_m})) \stackrel{\triangleleft}{=} \lambda \overline{x'_n} \cdot f(\overline{t'_{m'}})$$

But $f \in E$ and $H_i \notin E$. Then, trivially $MAS(\lambda \overline{x_n}.f(H_1(\overline{t_m}), \ldots, H_{m'}(\overline{t_m}))) = \{H_1(\overline{t_m}); \ldots; H_{m'}(\overline{t_m})\}$. The E-matching rule is then applied on the pair $f(x_1, x_2, \ldots, x_{m'}) \stackrel{\triangleleft}{=} f(\overline{t'_{m'}})$ where the x_i's are the abstractions of the $(H_i(\overline{t_m}))$'s. The k (assumed finite) more general solutions will be :

		*sol.*1						*sol.k*
$H_1(\overline{t_m})$		x_1	$\leftarrow$	s_1^1	$\cdots$	$\cdots$	x_1	$\leftarrow$	s_1^k
$\vdots$			$\vdots$					$\vdots$	
$H_{m'}(\overline{t_m})$		$x_{m'}$	$\leftarrow$	$s_{m'}^1$	$\cdots$	$\cdots$	$x_{m'}$	$\leftarrow$	$s_{m'}^k$

We shall have then the k matching problems :
$$S_1 = \cup_{i \in 1 \ldots m'}(H_i(\overline{t_m}) \stackrel{\triangleleft}{=} s_i^1)$$
$$\vdots$$
$$S_k = \cup_{i \in 1 \ldots m'}(H_i(\overline{t_m}) \stackrel{\triangleleft}{=} s_i^k)$$

We note here that without collapsing axioms, we do not have to consider pairs like $\{\lambda \overline{x_n} \cdot H_i(\overline{t_m}) \stackrel{\triangleleft}{=} \lambda \overline{x'_n} \cdot f(\overline{t'_{m'}})\}$ because they do not exist. The rest of the proof is still valid. This comes down to showing the termination of the other branches.
The strategy says that we continue except for the case where we encounter matching pairs such that $\{\lambda \overline{x_n} \cdot H_i(\overline{t_m}) \stackrel{\triangleleft}{=} \lambda \overline{x'_n} \cdot f(\overline{t'_{m'}})\}$ for which we take the results of the other branches because $\{\lambda \overline{x_n} \cdot H_i(\overline{t_m}) \stackrel{\triangleleft}{=} \lambda \overline{x'_n} \cdot f(\overline{t'_{m'}})\}$ is the same matching problem as $P = \{\lambda \overline{x_n} \cdot F(\overline{t_m}) \stackrel{\triangleleft}{=} \lambda \overline{x'_n} \cdot f(\overline{t'_{m'}})\}$. We then just have to show that the other branches make the complexity triple decrease. We showed this for Projections. For the matching pairs different from $\{\lambda \overline{x_n} \cdot H_i(\overline{t_m}) \stackrel{\triangleleft}{=} \lambda \overline{x'_n} \cdot f(\overline{t'_{m'}})\}$, after E-matching, we have $Alt(H_i(\overline{t_m})) = Alt(F(\overline{t_m}))$, and $\xi(H_i(\overline{t_m})) = \xi(F(\overline{t_m}))$. Therefore, the only way to prove termination with this method is to assume $\xi(s_i^j) < \xi(f(\overline{t'_{m'}}))$, $\forall i \forall j$. i.e. for a matching problem $f(x_1, x_2, \ldots, x_{m'}) \stackrel{\triangleleft}{=} f(t'_{m'})$, solutions are of the form $\cup_i[x_i \leftarrow s_i]$, where each s_i is such that $|s_i| < |f(\overline{t'_{m'}})|$. This is shown by lemma 4 for collapsing size preserving theories (this is true for root and size preserving theories equally without collapsing axiom).

□

Attribute-Specific Interchangeability in Constraint Satisfaction Problems*

Alois Haselböck and Markus Stumptner

Institut für Informationssysteme, Technische Universität Wien
Paniglgasse 16, A-1040 Vienna, Austria

Abstract. Constraint satisfaction problems consist of finding a value assignment to a set of variables such that all constraints on these variables are satisfied. In various application areas (e.g., engineering domains), domain values are actually used to denote complex objects, whose structure then must be derived by additional constraints. Greater effectiveness and a shorter problem description can be achieved by a component-oriented constraint formalism that allows explicit specification of the relationship between a component and its fixed attributes. To this goal, we introduce attribute functions into constraint networks. We define a variant of interchangeability suitable for these extended problems, based on computing domain partitions depending on attribute function values of the constraint variables, and give an algorithm for computing these partitions. By a slight modification of the key constraint filtering and search procedures, the domain partitions can be used to increase efficiency of the majority of existing algorithms for such problems.

1 Introduction

Many application areas of constraint satisfaction have the characteristic that variable domains consist of elements that actually represent composite objects rather than atomic values. In engineering applications, complex systems are often modelled from a component-oriented point of view, where different units with predefined, intrinsic properties form a system (say, some technical device) and constraints describe the behavior of the overall system or express restrictions on the structure of the device. Such a representation is used for reasoning tasks such as configuration [MF89] or model-based diagnosis [Str88, GP87].

If the various components are treated as domain values, the relationships between components and their properties (e.g., the amount of power generated by an engine of a given type, or the access time of a hard disk) would be represented by introducing new variables and constraints to express the relationship. This leads to increased size of the constraint network. After a component has been chosen for assignment to a variable, values for the new variables that describe its properties need to be inferred even though they are actually determined *ab initio*

* This work was supported by Siemens Austria AG under project grant CSS (GR 21/96106/4).

for each component. Formally, such relationships are better expressed by functions defined on the components[2], because this explicitly expresses that attributes (function values) are actually dependent on the given component (function argument). The advantage of such a representation was pointed out in [MF87], where components are viewed as the result of compiling the constraints on a subset of the variables. We provide a scheme to define such *attribute functions* as a slight enhancement to conventional constraint systems. We argue that this results in advantages in terms of efficiency as well as naturalness of expression. The latter advantage has also been recognized in logic programming, where a number of authors have discussed ways in which properties can be attributed to values [KL89]. We present algorithms which exploit the additional information inherent in the use of attribute functions to arrive at improved search efficiency.

The paper is organized as follows: Section 2 introduces the constraint framework augmented with attribute functions. In Sect. 3, we prepare the theoretical basis for the use of attribute information by using it to determine partitions of variable domains. An algorithm for computing these partitions is given in Sect. 4. Section 5 shows how the main part of existing constraint filtering and search algorithms can be modified for exploitation of these domain partitions. Finally, in Sect. 6 we indicate the advantageous behaviour of the proposed mechanism on a small configuration example.

2 A Constraint Framework for Attributed Objects

A *constraint network*[3] in the traditional sense consists of a finite set V of variables, a set D_v of domain values that is associated with each variable v, and a set of constraints. A constraint c on the variables $var(c) \subseteq V$ restricts the valid variable assignments of the variables in $var(c)$. Hence, the relation $rel(c)$ denotes the extensional definition of c and is a subset of the Cartesian product of the corresponding domains $(rel(c) \subseteq \mathbf{X}_{v \in var(c)} D_v)$. An *assignment* of a value o to a variable v is denoted by $v \leftarrow o$. Searching for one or all variable assignments of the variables in V such that no constraint is violated are typical problem tasks in constraint satisfaction.

As discussed above, we intend to augment conventional constraint networks by the inclusion of attribute information.

Definition 1 Constraint Variables on Attributed Objects. Let R be a constraint network on the variables V. Associated with each domain D_v ($v \in V$) is a set of attribute functions A_v, where each function $\alpha \in A_v$ maps the domain values of D_v to constants from a set $\mathcal{K}_\alpha$:

$$\alpha : D_v \mapsto \mathcal{K}_\alpha, \quad \text{for all } \alpha \in A_v, v \in V.$$

---

[2] Note that we speak about *constant* properties, i.e., attributes whose values are fixed for each component.

[3] Our notation is similar to the one used in [Dec92].

Example 1. Let D_{slot_1} be $\{jumper\_a, jumper\_b, jumper\_c, switch\_a, switch\_b\}$. An attribute function *type* maps each component of the domain of variable $slot_1$ to *jumper* or *switch*, corresponding to its functionality. Thus,

$$type : \{jumper\_a, jumper\_b, \ldots, switch\_b\} \mapsto \{jumper, switch\}.$$

Let V be the set of variables, C the constraints, and A the set of all attribute functions. We define a function $attr : C \times V \mapsto 2^A$, where $attr(c,v)$ returns the exhaustive set of attribute functions from A_v that are used by constraint c.[4] A constraint then represents a relation $rel_{attr}(c)$ on the attribute values of variables it refers to, i.e., for each constraint c the following holds: $rel_{attr}(c) \subseteq \mathbf{X}_{v \in var(c), \alpha \in attr(c,v)} \alpha(v)$. (We assume a cardinal ordering on the sets V and A.) An assignment tuple to the variables $var(c)$ then satisfies c iff the following condition holds:

$$\langle \alpha(o) \mid v \in var(c), \alpha \in attr(c,v), v \leftarrow o \in t \rangle \in rel_{attr}(c).$$

Example 2. Let $slot_1$ and $slot_2$ be two variables with domains as variable $slot_1$ in the example above. If the constraint c is defined by $type(slot_1) \neq type(slot_2)$, then $attr(c, slot_1) = attr(c, slot_2) = \{type\}$. While $rel(c)$ consists of six tuples (one tuple for every combination of a jumper and a switch), $rel_{attr}(c) = \{\langle jumper, switch \rangle, \langle switch, jumper \rangle\}$.

This representation has several advantages. It allows a natural expression of component structure and properties. The one-to-one relationship expressed by attribute functions can be handled directly during search. Of course, the same expressiveness could be achieved by introducing separate variables for the function value and representing the function itself by a binary constraint. However, that will lead to the constraints having to compete with others instead of being checked on the spot whenever a constraint is influenced by a component assignment. In addition, this representation requires a separate variable for each function-variable combination appearing in the constraint network. Attribute function thus are a representation well adapted to component-oriented constraint reasoning. The advantages of such specialized representations are discussed in [vB92].

The exploitation of optimization techniques used with conventional constraint systems is in no way hindered by this extension. In [Fre91], the notion of *interchangeability* was introduced as a means of removing redundancy from CSPs. In [Has93], algorithms were introduced to compute interchangeability relationships at a lower level of granularity than that proposed in [Fre91], by partitioning variable domains according to their use in constraints. Small alterations to the traditional constraint search algorithms are sufficient to exploit these relationships during search.

---

[4] If a constraint refers to the value of the variable itself, the identity function *id* : $D_v \mapsto D_v$ is used.

3   Attribute-based Domain Partitions

The basic notion behind interchangeability lies in recognizing sets of domain values which behave in the same manner in a local or global environment of the constraint network, where local means that interchangeability is restricted to a certain subset of variables and/or constraints. All values which are proved to be interchangeable can be treated equally, which implies that instead of dealing with them separately, a whole group can be considered all at once, with specific representative being chosen later, either if extending the context makes a distinction necessary, or nondeterministically when all values from a group may occur in a solution. In effect, variable domains are partitioned along the lines of these groups. In the following, we use attribute function values as the deciding property in deriving such domain partitions, which we define in the usual manner.

Definition 2 Domain Partition. A domain partition π_v of the domain D_v is a set of non-empty subsets of D_v where the elements of π_v are mutually exclusive ($\forall s_1, s_2 \in \pi_v : s_1 \cap s_2 = \emptyset$) and the decomposition is exhaustive ($\bigcup_{s \in \pi_v} s = D_v$).

As usual, such a domain partition π_v induces an equivalence relation $\equiv_{\pi_v}$, i.e., for any two values $o_1, o_2 \in D_v$, $o_1 \equiv_{\pi_v} o_2$ iff there is some element $s \in \pi_v$ such that $\{o_1, o_2\} \subseteq s$. The set s is called the *equivalence class* of o_1 and o_2 (written $\overline{o_1}$ or $\overline{o_2}$).

We call two domain values o_1, o_2 from the domain of a variable v *interchangeable* with regard to a constraint c, iff (1) for every value assignment to $var(c)$ that satisfies c and which includes $v \leftarrow o_1$, c will also be satisfied if o_1 is replaced by o_2; (2) for every value assignment to $var(c)$ that satisfies c and which includes $v \leftarrow o_2$, c will also be satisfied if o_2 is replaced by o_1.[5] This definition is quite similar to that of Freuder [Fre91], except that it is defined with respect to a single constraint instead of a global solution.

Definition 3 Admissible Domain Partitions. A domain partition π_v^c is said to be admissible w.r.t. the constraint c, iff for each pair of domain values $o_1, o_2 \in D_v$ such that $o_1 \equiv_{\pi_v^c} o_2$, it holds that o_1 and o_2 are interchangeable with regard to c.

Example 3. Let $V = \{v_1, v_2\}$, $D_{v_1} = D_{v_2} = \{-3, -2, \ldots, 3\}$, and the constraint $c(v_1, v_2)$: $sign(v_1) \neq sign(v_2)$. The domain partition $\pi 1 = \{\{-3, -2, -1\}, \{0\}, \{1, 2, 3\}\}$ of D_{v_1} is admissible w.r.t. c. As a non-admissible example, consider the partition $\pi 2 = \{\{-3, -2, -1, 0, 1\}, \{2, 3\}\}$. Although the values -1 and 1 lie in the same class of $\pi 2$, the assignment tuple $\{v_1 \leftarrow -1, v_2 \leftarrow 3\}$ is valid, while the tuple $\{v_1 \leftarrow 1, v_2 \leftarrow 3\}$ violates the constraint c.

We now define how such domain partitions can be induced by attribute functions or sets of attribute functions on domain values.

---

[5] In terms of Codd's Relational Algebra, this condition can be expressed as
$$\pi_{var(c)-v}(\sigma_{v=o_1}(rel(c))) = \pi_{var(c)-v}(\sigma_{v=o_2}(rel(c))).$$

Definition 4 π_v^α and $\pi_v^{\{\alpha_1,...,\alpha_m\}}$. Let D_v be a variable domain and α an attribute function on the values of D_v. The set π_v^α consists of all value sets s, where s is a maximal, non-empty subset of D_v s.t. $\forall o_1, o_2 \in s : \alpha(o_1) = \alpha(o_2)$.

Of course, a partition can also be based on a set of attributes on a variable domain. Let $\alpha_1, \ldots, \alpha_m$ be attribute functions on the domain D_v. The set $\pi_v^{\{\alpha_1,...,\alpha_m\}}$ consists of all value sets s, where s is a maximal, non-empty subset of D_v s.t. $\forall o_1, o_2 \in s, \forall i \in \{1, \ldots, m\} : \alpha_i(o_1) = \alpha_i(o_2)$.

Lemma 5. *The sets π_v^α and $\pi_v^{\{\alpha_1,...,\alpha_m\}}$ as defined above are domain partitions of the domain D_v in the sense of Definition 2.*

Proof. It is a well-known fact in set theory that each function α on a set S induces an equivalence relation $\equiv_\alpha$: $a \equiv_\alpha b$ $(a, b \in S)$, iff $\alpha(a) = \alpha(b)$. Furthermore, each equivalence relation on S induces exactly one domain partition of S. Consequently, each vector of attributes can be seen as a multi-valued function and therefore induces a domain partition, too. $\square$

Example 4. In the example above, the domain partition $\pi 1$ constitutes $\pi_{v_1}^{sign}$.

Proposition 6. *Let D_v be the domain of variable v, c a constraint where $v \in var(c)$, and $attr(c, v)$ defined as above. The domain partition $\pi_v^{attr(c,v)}$ is an admissible partition of D_v w.r.t. the constraint c.*

Proof. Lemma 5 tells us that each decomposition of a domain induced by a set of attributes (here, $attr(c, v)$) is in fact a domain partition. The proposition is falsified, iff there exist two domain elements $o_1, o_2 \in D_v$ with $o_1 \equiv_{\pi_v^{attr(c,v)}} o_2$, but o_1 is not interchangeable with o_2 with regard to the constraint c. This can not be the case, because the constraint c only refers to the properties $attr(c, v)$ of the variable v, and the domain partition $\pi_v^{attr(c,v)}$ is constructed *along* this set of attributes $attr(c, v)$. $\square$

Of course, there is no guarantee of maximal utilization of constraint information. Consider the cases where a constraint handles a set of different attribute values equally. In that cases, the number of equivalence classes w.r.t. the attribute vector of a constraint is greater than the number of classes induced by full evaluation of all equivalences, i.e., the equivalence classes induces by the afflicted attribute functions are not *maximal*. In [Has93], a method is proposed how maximal domain partitions can be extracted from the constraint relations and exploited during constraint filtering and search. However, the computation of these partitions, which consider all local interchangeabilities, is quite resource consuming (in [Has93], we sketch an algorithm based on the construction of discrimination trees, which has worst-case time complexity $O(a^k)$ for one partition, where a is the domain size and k the constraint arity). As shown in the next section, domain partitions induced by attribute functions can be computed very efficiently.

Admissible domain partitions provide the possibility for handling groups of domain values equally in certain situations. As we will see in Sect. 5, these information can be integrated quite simply into conventional consistency and search procedures, and inference can be made more efficient by this kind of local problem reduction.

4 Computing Domain Partitions

Such decompositions can easily be computed by constructions of *discrimination trees* (the proposed algorithm is similar to Freuder's procedure for the computation of neighborhood interchangeabilities in [Fre91]). A discrimination tree is a tuple $\langle N, E, \phi, \psi \rangle$, where N is a set of nodes, E is a set of edges (each edge is a pair $\langle n1, n2 \rangle$, $n1, n2 \in N$), ϕ is a labeling function which assigns to each node of N a (possible empty) set of domain values, and where the edges are labeled by attribute values $\alpha(o)$ (α is an attribute function, o is a domain value). Each label of a leaf node picks up the domain objects with the same tuple of attribute values along the path from *root* to the leaf node. Figure 1 shows a procedure performing this task and therefore computing $\pi_v^{\{\alpha_1, \ldots, \alpha_m\}}$ for a variable v and the attribute functions $\alpha_1, \ldots, \alpha_m$ on v.

```
1    procedure partition(v, {α₁, ..., αₘ}):
2        DT ← root;
3        for each o ∈ Dᵥ do:
4            n ← root of DT;
5            for i ← 1 to m do:
6                if there exists an edge ⟨n, n_succ⟩ with ψ(⟨n, n_succ⟩) = αᵢ(o)
7                    then n ← n_succ;
8                    else create node n_succ; φ(n_succ) ← ∅;
9                        create edge ⟨n, n_succ⟩; ψ(⟨n, n_succ⟩) ← αᵢ(o);
10                       n ← n_succ;
11           φ(n) ← φ(n) ∪ {o};
12       return the set {φ(n) | n is leaf node of DT}.
```

Fig. 1. Computing domain partition induced by a set of attributes.

The complexity of this procedure can be evaluated by inspecting the two loops 3–11 and 5–10, and therefore it is $O(a.m)$, if a is the domain size and m the number of attributes taken into account. So we can see that these domain classifications can be computed efficiently in linear time to the size of a. Hence, if C is the set of all constraints of a constraint network, the overall cost for computing all domain partitions preliminary to the actual search is

$$\Sigma_{c \in C} \Sigma_{v \in var(c)} |D_v|.|attr(c, v)|.$$

5 Exploiting Domain Partitions

Now we are in the position to show how these domain partitions can be used to increase efficiency of various existing algorithms. We give a few modifications of the key procedures and show the advantages of the use of such techniques for certain problem types. We focus on *binary* CSPs.

5.1 Constraint Filtering

Constraints are most commonly used in a *destructive* manner. The critical and most time consuming task in network consistency procedures is to check if all values of a particular variable domain can potentially be member of a solution. These checks are done repetitively for singular variables w.r.t. singular constraints. In the case of binary constraints, usually the procedure *revise*(v_i, v_j) is used, which removes all values of D_{v_i} for which no value of the domain of v_j can be found such that the binary constraint c_{ij} between v_i and v_j is satisfied. Thus, the worst-case complexity of *revise* is $O(a^2)$ where a is the maximum domain size.

In Fig. 2, a modified procedure called *revise*^{dp} is depicted. This procedure makes use of partitioned domains, where each partition π_v^c is assumed to be *admissible* w.r.t. the constraint c. Here, the partitions $\pi_v^{attr(c,v)}$ can be used (this is justified by Proposition 6), which can be computed in an efficient manner as shown in the previous section. We use the expression $\overline{o}_v^c$ to denote the equivalence class of value o subject to π_v^c: $\overline{o}_v^c = \{o' \mid o' \equiv_{\pi_v^c} o\}$.

```
1    procedure revise^dp(v_i, v_j):
2        Δ_i := {};
3        do until D_{v_i} becomes empty:
4            x := an element of D_{v_i};
5            Δ_j := D_{v_j};
6            do until Δ_j becomes empty:
7                y := an element of Δ_j;
8                if ⟨x, y⟩ ∈ rel(c_{ij})
9                    then Δ_i := Δ_i ∪ (x̄_{v_i}^{c_{ij}} ∩ D_{v_i});  Δ_j := {};
10                   else Δ_j := Δ_j - ȳ_{v_j}^{c_{ij}};
11           D_{v_i} := D_{v_i} - x̄_{v_i}^{c_{ij}};
12       D_{v_i} := Δ_i.
```

Fig. 2. The revise procedure which uses domain partitions.

The main difference between the "classical" *revise* and *revise*^{dp} is that the former checks in the worst case all tuples from $D_{v_i} \times D_{v_j}$ and the latter treats groups of interchangeable values equally and therefore possibly saves checks by utilizing information included in the domain partitions. If we assume that the equivalence classes of the domain partitions are of size $a1$ $(1 \leq a1 \leq a)$, a worst case bound of algorithm $revise^{dp}$ is $O(a1^2)$.

It is easy to see that $revise$ and $revise^{dp}$ produce exactly the same outcome. In that way, algorithms which use $revise$ (such as arc- and path-consistency algorithms) simply have to replace each call to $revise$ by a call to $revise^{dp}$ and get effective use of reduced domain sizes. Also many backtrack procedures use $revise$ and therefore can benefit from $revise^{dp}$.

5.2 Backtrack Search

In the following we want to develop a slightly modified tree search scheme where interchangeable search branches are recognized by the use of domain partition information. The structure of the algorithm is basically the same as classical backtrack tree search (described, for instance, in [MN90]).

Each output of a traditional backtrack procedure is an assignment tuple representing a solution for the given CSP. Because we want to handle *groups* of interchangeable values, we have to modify the form of the output. Instead of single assignment values, sets are used. In that way, assignment tuples are shifted to assignment *bundles*, where an assignment bundle Δ is a set of cardinality n (n is the number of variables) and the ith element of Δ is a subset of D_{v_i}. Those $\Delta = \{\Delta_1, \ldots, \Delta_n\}$ are said to be *solution bundles*, where the Cartesian product $\Delta_1 \times \ldots \times \Delta_n$ is a subset of the solutions of the CSP.

```
1    procedure backtracking^{dp}(k,D):
2        revise^{dp}(k,p) for 1 ≤ p < k; % or do some kind of look ahead filtering
3        Δ^{rest} ← D[k];
4        do until Δ^{rest} becomes empty:
5            choose x from Δ^{rest};
6            C^f ← all constraints on v_k to future variables;
7            D[k] ← (∩_{c∈C^f} x̄^c_{v_k}) ∩ Δ^{rest};
8            Δ^{rest} ← Δ^{rest} − D[k];
9            if k = n then output(D) else backtracking^{dp}(k + 1,D).
```

Fig. 3. A backtrack procedure using domain partitions.

Figure 3 sketches the new algorithm $backtracking^{dp}$. At each cycle in the search process the set of variables can be partitioned into three groups: the *past* variables, the *current* variable, and the *future* variables. Since all the remaining domain values of the current variable are consistent to the assignments of the past variables (this is guaranteed by the $revise$ at line 2), they are interchangeable w.r.t. that partial solution (bundle). Now the domain of the current variable is going to be partitioned according to its occourence in constraints which refer to future variables. For each group of such interchangeable values a new search branch is opened. Clearly, each output of a call to that procedure is an assignment bundle. The procedure is sound and complete in the sense that each output is a solution bundle, and the set of all outputs covers all solutions.

The advantageous behavior of the search shell $backtracking^{dp}$ for certain problem types is obvious. Interchangeable search branches are bundled and visited once. If a dead-end occurs, all the partial assignments represented by the derived assignment bundle are proven to be conflicting. A solution bundle represents a group of valid assignments. In [Has93], a more detailed description of the above sketched algorithms, proofs of their correctness, and indications of their efficiency by theoretical considerations and experimental analysis is given.

The net effect is that the domain partitions derived from attribute function occurences in the constraint network can be used in a wide range of CSP algorithms (both filtering and search) with minimal change of procedures. Apart from a small amount of additional overhead of computing domain partitions in a preprocessing phase and managing groups of domain values instead of singular elements, the new worst-case complexities are not worse than those of the original algorithms. If the problem structures are adequate (i.e., if the cardinality of domain decompositions are really smaller than the original domain sizes), effective cost reductions can be achieved.

6 Solving an Example

In this section, we present a small example to demonstrate the behavior and advantages of the proposed formalism. Let the set of variables V be $\{s1, s2, s3\}$, where each of these variables represents a slot in a (physical) frame. Modules of certain types are to be inserted in these slots. Components of several different types are available, namely of types $\tau_1, \ldots, \tau_6$. Therefore, the domains of the three variables are

$$D_{s1} = D_{s2} = D_{s3} = \{\tau_1, \tau_2, \tau_3, \tau_4, \tau_5, \tau_6\}.$$

Each component type is described by a set of attributes, where the attributes *channel_capacity* and *modulation* are of interest in our exemplary problem. As previously described, these two attributes are represented in terms of functions:

channel_capacity: $\{\tau_1, \ldots, \tau_6\} \mapsto \{1, 2, 3\}$.
modulation: $\{\tau_1, \ldots, \tau_6\} \mapsto \{AM, FM\}$.

The table below summarizes the concrete attribute values for each of the component types.

modulation \ channel_capacity	1	2	3
AM	τ_1, τ_2	τ_4	
FM	τ_3	τ_5	τ_6

$channel\_capacity(s1) < channel\_capacity(s2)$

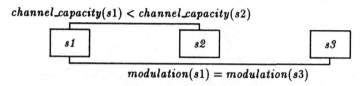

$modulation(s1) = modulation(s3)$

Fig. 4. The constraint graph of the example CSP.

For instance, the *modulation* of all components of type τ_1 is *AM*, while their *channel_capacity* is 1. Now valid constellations are restricted by the following two constraints: (c1) the channel capacity of the component mounted on slot $s1$ must be less than the channel capacity of the component mounted on slot $s2$; (c2) the modulation principle of the components mounted on slots $s1$ and $s3$ must be the same. This simple constraint network is depicted in Fig. 4.

action	$s1$	Δ^{rest}	$s2$	Δ^{rest}	$s3$	Δ^{rest}
assign($s1$)	$\{\tau_1,\tau_2\}$	$\{\tau_3,\tau_4,\tau_5,\tau_6\}$				
revise($s2,s1$)	$\{\tau_1,\tau_2\}$	$\{\tau_3,\tau_4,\tau_5,\tau_6\}$		$\{\tau_4,\tau_5,\tau_6\}$		
assign($s2$)	$\{\tau_1,\tau_2\}$	$\{\tau_3,\tau_4,\tau_5,\tau_6\}$	$\{\tau_4,\tau_5,\tau_6\}$	$\{\}$		
revise($s3,s1$)	$\{\tau_1,\tau_2\}$	$\{\tau_3,\tau_4,\tau_5,\tau_6\}$	$\{\tau_4,\tau_5,\tau_6\}$	$\{\}$		$\{\tau_1,\tau_2,\tau_4\}$
assign($s3$)	$\{\tau_1,\tau_2\}$	$\{\tau_3,\tau_4,\tau_5,\tau_6\}$	$\{\tau_4,\tau_5,\tau_6\}$	$\{\}$	$\{\tau_1,\tau_2,\tau_4\}$	$\{\}$
assign($s1$)	$\{\tau_3\}$	$\{\tau_4,\tau_5,\tau_6\}$				
revise($s2,s1$)	$\{\tau_3\}$	$\{\tau_4,\tau_5,\tau_6\}$		$\{\tau_4,\tau_5,\tau_6\}$		
assign($s2$)	$\{\tau_3\}$	$\{\tau_4,\tau_5,\tau_6\}$	$\{\tau_4,\tau_5,\tau_6\}$	$\{\}$		
revise($s3,s1$)	$\{\tau_3\}$	$\{\tau_4,\tau_5,\tau_6\}$	$\{\tau_4,\tau_5,\tau_6\}$	$\{\}$		$\{\tau_3,\tau_5,\tau_6\}$
assign($s3$)	$\{\tau_3\}$	$\{\tau_4,\tau_5,\tau_6\}$	$\{\tau_4,\tau_5,\tau_6\}$	$\{\}$	$\{\tau_3,\tau_5,\tau_6\}$	$\{\}$
assign($s1$)	$\{\tau_4\}$	$\{\tau_5,\tau_6\}$				
revise($s2,s1$)	$\{\tau_4\}$	$\{\tau_5,\tau_6\}$		$\{\tau_6\}$		
assign($s2$)	$\{\tau_4\}$	$\{\tau_5,\tau_6\}$	$\{\tau_6\}$	$\{\}$		
revise($s3,s1$)	$\{\tau_4\}$	$\{\tau_5,\tau_6\}$	$\{\tau_6\}$	$\{\}$		$\{\tau_1,\tau_2,\tau_4\}$
assign($s3$)	$\{\tau_4\}$	$\{\tau_5,\tau_6\}$	$\{\tau_6\}$	$\{\}$	$\{\tau_1,\tau_2,\tau_4\}$	$\{\}$
assign($s1$)	$\{\tau_5\}$	$\{\tau_6\}$				
revise($s2,s1$)	$\{\tau_5\}$	$\{\tau_6\}$		$\{\tau_6\}$		
assign($s2$)	$\{\tau_5\}$	$\{\tau_6\}$	$\{\tau_6\}$	$\{\}$		
revise($s3,s1$)	$\{\tau_5\}$	$\{\tau_6\}$	$\{\tau_6\}$	$\{\}$		$\{\tau_3,\tau_5,\tau_6\}$
assign($s3$)	$\{\tau_5\}$	$\{\tau_6\}$	$\{\tau_6\}$	$\{\}$	$\{\tau_3,\tau_5,\tau_6\}$	$\{\}$
assign($s1$)	$\{\tau_6\}$	$\{\}$				
revise($s2,s1$)	$\{\tau_6\}$	$\{\}$		$\{\}$		

Table 1. Trace of a call to *backtracking*[dp].

Solving this problem with a traditional backtracking procedure will result in a high number of constraint checks during search. However, because certain

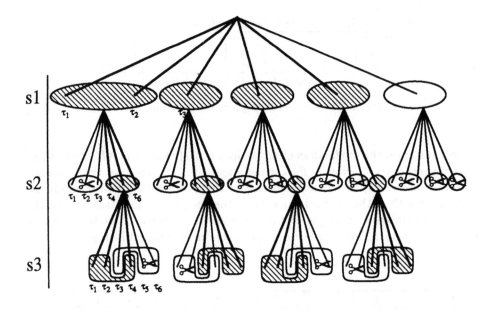

Fig. 5. A derivation tree for finding all solutions.

groups of component types are interchangeable w.r.t. the constraint $c1$ or $c2$, many of these checks are actually redundant. The admissible domain partitions are fairly obvious in this example, since constraint $c1$ refers to attribute *channel_capacity* only, while constraint $c2$ refers only to *modulation*. The resulting domain partitions are:

$$\pi_{s1}^{attr(c1,s1)} = \pi_{s2}^{attr(c1,s2)} = \{\{\tau_1, \tau_2, \tau_3\}\{\tau_4, \tau_5\}, \{\tau_6\}\}.$$
$$\pi_{s1}^{attr(c2,s1)} = \pi_{s3}^{attr(c2,s3)} = \{\tau_1, \tau_2, \tau_4\}, \{\tau_3, \tau_5, \tau_6\}\}.$$

Table 1 shows a trace through a run of the procedure *backtracking*^{dp}. For example, after assigning $\{\tau_1, \tau_2\}$ to $s1$, the call to *revise*^{dp} in the second line results in the elimination of 3 values ($\{\tau_1, \tau_2, \tau_3\}$) and the retention of $\{\tau_4, \tau_5, \tau_6\}$ at a total cost of 3 constraint checks.

The search for all solutions results in a total of 23 consistency checks (which are usually accepted as a good indicator of search complexity). The search tree of this derivation is depicted in Fig. 5. Shaded nodes represent bundles of consistent value assignments that will be part of a complete solution (e.g., all paths starting with the non-shaded rightmost node at the first level, representing assignment of τ_6 to $s1$, will eventually be filtered out).

Using identical variable and value orderings, conventional backtracking (i.e., without considering attribute equivalence) will result in 78 checks. Use of forward-checking[6] would reduce this to 66. Thus, even on that simple exam-

---

[6] Forward-checking is a backtrack procedure where at each level in the search process all future variables are filtered against the last-assigned variable. This method is known to behave in a very efficient manner [HE80].

ple it can be seen that many consistency checks are avoided by the proposed method. As shown in [Has93], the profit of the approach grows with the size of the problem.

7 Conclusion

The increase in efficiency engendered by using abstractions in constraint problems has been discussed in [MMH85]. Mackworth et.al. described a filtering algorithm that made use of hierarchical value groupings, without, however, discussing the origin of these hierarchies. Mittal and Frayman [MF87] discuss the use of structured components. Groupings of components with equivalent properties are either derived at the moment an assignment is decided upon, or again by use of user-defined taxonomies. Freuder [Fre91] uses interchangeability by comparing complete solutions, whereas we work on a constraint-by-constraint basis and then combine equivalence classes.

The mechanism as described is domain-independent, though a variety of possible application areas do exist. It should be noted that our example deals only with component types. However, in many application areas, for example configuration (i.e., the composition of parts to form complex technical systems), we will not deal only with multiple types, but also with multiple components of each type, where some component attributes will remain fixed and thus can be made subject to partioning. Since constraints are often the representation of choice for configuration [MF89, HS93], use of this technique during inferencing will be easy to achieve and help a great deal in coping with systems that consist of a multitude of smaller and often strongly similar parts.

In summary, we have presented a simple extension to constraint networks that allows natural expression of the component-oriented problem descriptions which are appropriate for a variety of application areas. We have defined a notion of interchangeability based on attribute function values and have provided for its use in backtracking search and the *revise* procedure which is the heart of constraint filtering algorithms.

References

[Dec92] Rina Dechter. From Local to Global Consistency. *Artificial Intelligence*, 55:87–107, 1992.

[Fre91] Eugene C. Freuder. Eliminating Interchangeable Values in Constraint Satisfaction Problems. In *Proc. AAAI Conf.*, pages 227–233, 1991.

[GP87] Hector Geffner and Judea Pearl. An Improved Constraint-Propagation Algorithm for Diagnosis. In *Proc. 10th IJCAI*, pages 1105–1111, 1987.

[HE80] Robert M. Haralick and Gordon L. Elliott. Increasing Tree Search Efficiency for Constraint Satisfaction Problems. *Artificial Intelligence*, 14:263–313, 1980.

[Has93]   Alois Haselböck. Exploiting Interchangeabilities in Constraint Satisfaction Problems. In *Proceedings of the International Joint Conference on Artificial Intelligence*, 1993. To appear.

[HS93]   Alois Haselböck and Markus Stumptner. A Constraint-Based Architecture for Assembling Large-Scale Technical Systems. In *Proc. IEA/AIE Conf.*, pages 18–25, Edinburgh, June 1993. Gordon and Breach Science Publishers. Also Tech. Report DBAI-CSP-TR 92/3.

[KL89]   Michael Kifer and Georg Lausen. F-Logic: A Higher-Order Language for Reasoning about Objects, Inheritance and Scheme. *Communications of the ACM*, pages 134–146, 1989.

[MF87]   Sanjay Mittal and Felix Frayman. Making Partial Choices in Constraint Reasoning Problems. In *Proceedings AAAI Conference*, pages 631–636, July 1987.

[MF89]   Sanjay Mittal and Felix Frayman. Towards a Generic Model of Configuration Tasks. In *Proc. 11th IJCAI*, pages 1395–1401. Morgan Kaufmann Publishers, Inc., August 1989.

[MMH85] Alan K. Mackworth, Jan A. Mulder, and William S. Havens. Hierarchical Arc Consistency: Exploiting Structured Domains in Constraint Satisfaction Problems. *Computational Intelligence*, 1(3):118–126, 1985.

[MN90]   Sanjay Mittal and Bernard Nadel. Constraint Reasoning: Theory and Applications. Tutorial SP4 of the AAAI-90, 1990.

[Str88]   Peter Struss. Extensions to ATMS-based Diagnosis. In J.S. Gero, editor, *Artificial Intelligence in Engineering: Diagnosis and Learning*, Southampton, 1988.

[vB92]   Jeffrey van Baalen. Automated Design of Specialized Representations. *Artificial Intelligence*, 54:121–198, 1992.

The Use and Interpretation
of Meta Level Constraints

Pierre Berlandier

SECOIA Project, INRIA-CERMICS,
2004, Route des Lucioles, B.P. 93, 06902 Sophia-Antipolis Cedex

Abstract. This paper introduces a model for dynamic constraint problems in which constraints and variables are comparable entities. This model provides a natural way to represent configuration or design problems wherein the set of objects and their constraints are bound to evolve during the solving process. Metaconstraints, i.e. constraints on constraint descriptions, are the central contribution of the model. Depending on which part of the description (the set of constrained variables or the relation that links them) they apply to, metaconstraints can be used to monitor the evolution of the problem's variables or constraints. The implications of metaconstraints on the consistency maintenance process are studied and an implementation within the PROSE constraint language is briefly described.

1 Introduction

Constraint languages are still young programming systems. So far, the major concerns in their design have been the improvement of the solvers efficiency and the cooperation of various solvers in a single interpreter. Now that techniques are known for handling a wide range of constraints with fair efficiency, more attention is paid to the expressive power of those languages. In particular, topics like partial constraint satisfaction [6, 5], integration into an object world [1] or the use of constraint combinators [9] are being investigated.

The work reported in this paper is born of the observation that constraint expression is usually restricted to a *fixed* set of attributes taken from a *flat* set of variables. Yet, there are domains such as computer aided design where:

- constrained variables follow a hierarchical decomposition (an artefact is recursively composed of subparts),
- constraint problems are subject to dynamic evolvement as the search progresses (parts are added or removed).

To support these needs, we propose a new model for constraint problems, namely *dynamic constraint problems*. In the remainder of the paper, we first present the regular and then the dynamic constraint problem model. We show that the latter allows the expression of metaconstraints which fulfill our needs as they enable the construction of both hierarchical and evolving constraint networks. Then, we present a method for interpreting these constraints for consistency maintenance and we briefly describe an implementation. Finally, we conclude with a comparison between our model and a closely-related work.

2 Constraint Problems

The regular constraint formalism derives from [15]. It presents a constraint problem as a tuple $\langle \mathcal{X}, \mathcal{D}, \mathcal{C}, \mathcal{R} \rangle$ where:

- $\mathcal{X} = \{x_1, \ldots, x_n\}$ is the finite set of variables of the problem.
- $\mathcal{D}$ is a finite set of domains and D is a bijection from $\mathcal{X}$ to $\mathcal{D}$ such that $D(x_i)$ is the domain attached to x_i. A domain may be finite or infinite, discrete or continuous.
- $\mathcal{C} = \{c_1, \ldots, c_m\}$ is the finite set of constraints where c_i is a tuple of variables $\langle x_{i_1}, \ldots, x_{i_p} \rangle$ from $\mathcal{X}^p$. The x_{i_j} are called the attributes of the constraint. The set of constraints forms a hypergraph, usually termed the constraint network.
- $\mathcal{R}$ is the finite set of relations and R is a bijection from $\mathcal{C}$ to $\mathcal{R}$ such that $R(c_i)$ is the relation attached to c_i defining (in extension or intention) the set of p-tuples allowed by this constraint.

The *constraint satisfaction* problem consists in finding one or more instanciations V of all the variables in $\mathcal{X}$ so that:

$$\begin{cases} \forall x_i \in \mathcal{X}, V(x_i) \in D(x_i) \\ \forall c_i \in \mathcal{C}, \ \langle V(x_{i_1}), \ldots, V(x_{i_p}) \rangle \in R(c_i) \end{cases}$$

The search for solutions can be achieved (quite efficiently in spite of the NP-completeness of the problem) for different types of domains such as discrete sets, real numbers, booleans or trees, using appropriate techniques [13, 4].

Another important problem is *consistency maintenance* where, given a solution V, a partial instanciation δ_V of a subset $\delta_\mathcal{X}$ of $\mathcal{X}$ (which stands for the modifications made to the given solution) and/or a set of added constraints $\delta_\mathcal{C}$, we want to find another solution V' so that:

$$\begin{cases} \forall x_i \in \delta_\mathcal{X}, V'(x_i) = \delta_V(x_i) \\ \forall c_i \in \delta_\mathcal{C}, \ \langle V'(x_{i_1}), \ldots, V'(x_{i_p}) \rangle \in R(c_i) \end{cases}$$

Moreover, it is generally desirable for V' to be close to V according to some semantics (for example, we may wish that the number of changed variables is as small as possible). This problem is usually solved by an incremental revision of the initial solution using techniques such as the propagation of known values [16]. Those techniques do not ensure completeness: there is no guarantee that a solution, if it exists, will be found. Nevertheless, they remain attractive because of their complexity which is linear in the number of variables.

3 Dynamic Constraint Problems

The simple idea behind dynamic constraint problems is to turn the sets of values $\mathcal{C}$ and $\mathcal{R}$ into sets of variables. Now, a dynamic constraint problem is again a tuple $\langle \mathcal{X}, \mathcal{D}, \mathcal{C}, \mathcal{R} \rangle$ where:

- $\mathcal{X}$ is again the finite set of variables we wish to determine and $\mathcal{D}$ the corresponding set of domains.
- $\mathcal{C} = \{c_1, \ldots, c_m\}$ is now a finite set of variables, each one ranging over a set of subtuples of $\mathcal{X} \cup \mathcal{C} \cup \mathcal{R}$, the whole set of the variables of the problem.
- $\mathcal{R}$ is a finite set of variables, each one ranging over a set of possible relations.

A dynamic constraint problem is an intensional representation of a space of regular constraint problems. A complete instanciation of the variables in $\mathcal{C} \cup \mathcal{R}$ defines *one* regular problem. A dynamic constraint problem is of no interest *per se*. What makes the model attractive is that constraints and constrained objects have the same status, thus opening a door on the creation of *metaconstraints*.

A metaconstraint is a constraint that involves one or more parts of a constraint description (i.e. the constraint itself or its relation) and ties them to a given relation. For example, if we let c_i and c_j be two constraints, then we can implement sentences such as "c_i and c_j involve the same attributes" or "the relation of c_i is not an equality".

While the interpretation of regular constraints deals with the value of the problem variables, the interpretation of metaconstraints builds or adjusts the structure or the semantics of the problem itself. When we try to satisfy metaconstraints, we design a problem inside a given world. An example is shown on figure 1 where $\mathcal{X} = \{x_1, x_2, x_3, x_4\}$, $\mathcal{C} = \{c_1, c_2, c_3\}$. At the meta-level, we have $c_3 = \{c_1, x_1, c_2\}$ (c_3 might mean here that c_1 and c_2 must share the x_1 same attributes). Solving this constraint leads to the instanciations $c_1 = \{x_2, x_3\}$ and $c_2 = \{x_2, x_3\}$ which now define a solution space.

Now, when we maintain the consistency with respect to metaconstraints, we adjust the structure of the problem to the change that occurred in this world. This adaptation process is crucial in computer aided design systems, especially during redesign phases. In the following two sections, we exhibit the use of two types of metaconstraints *in the framework of consistency maintenance*.

4 Metaconstraints on Constraints

Let us suppose that we are using constraints for an office design system. An office is composed of several pieces of furniture, each one being characterized by its price. The variables of the problem are the *office* the value of which is a set of components, the *components* which are characterized by their price and the total *cost* of the office, the value of which is also a price. The following equation links these variables:

$$cost = \sum_{component \, \in \, office} component$$

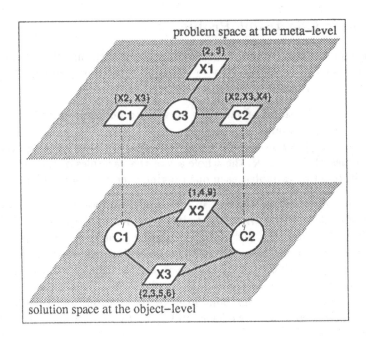

problem space at the meta-level

solution space at the object-level

Fig. 1.

To implement this constraint, the most intuitive solution is to set an n-ary sum constraint c_a between all the components of the office and the cost. Let us suppose that the office is currently furnished with a *desk*, a *lamp* and a *chair*. The constraint c_a could then be defined in the following way:

$$\begin{cases} c_a = \langle cost, desk, lamp, chair \rangle \\ R(c_a) = \{ \langle \langle s \rangle . V \rangle \mid s = \sum_{v_i \in V} v_i \} \end{cases}$$

Unfortunately, this implementation does not work properly when the instanciation of the office is modified by adding or removing components. The existing constraint no longer reflects the intended equation. Metaconstraints can help here. The key fact is that attributes of c_a must follow the value of the *office* variable and this can be translated into another constraint c_{ma} which acts at a metalevel. This constraint can be defined by:

$$\begin{cases} c_{ma} = \langle c_a, office \rangle \\ R(c_{ma}) = \{ \langle v_1, v_2 \rangle \mid v_1 = \langle cost \rangle \cup v_2 \} \end{cases}$$

Figure 2a shows how the c_a and c_{ma} constraint network is organized. When, for example, the value of the *office* variable is modified (by adding the *board*, figure 2b), constraint c_{ma} is waked up and updates the value of c_a which is triggered in its turn (figure 2c) and reinstates the constraint intended by the programmer.

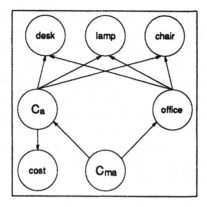

(a): the initial constraint network

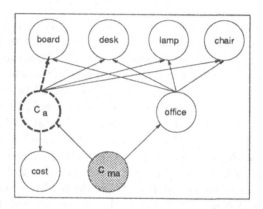

(b): the *office* modification wakes up c_{ma} and consequently updates c_a

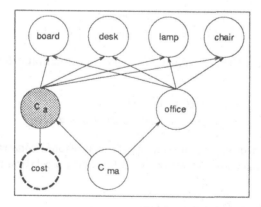

(c): the modification of c_a wakes it up, computing a consistent value for *cost*

Fig. 2.

Of course, the stacking level of metaconstraints is not limited. If we imagine that the *office* is an element of the *department* variable, another metaconstraint could link c_{ma} with *department* to monitor its possible evolution.

Generally speaking, this type of metaconstraint is useful when the constraint semantics is known but the variables to be constrained are not. They are subject to evolution and they can be computed by a functional link with other variables. Here, metaconstraints take the place of an external process that would continually and automatically withdraw obsolete constraints and add fresh ones. As emphasized in [14], such a role is beneficial as the separation between constraint creation and constraint solving is cumbersome and inefficient when the two processes have to interact to make their decisions.

5 Metaconstraints on Relations

It is often useful to modulate the applicability of a constraint according to the current configuration of the world. For example, let us suppose that the *budget* of the department ranges over the discrete set of values {low, average, high}. Furthermore, financial imperatives restrict the furniture of the office to a *maximum* number of components when the budget is low. We would like this restrictive relation to appear in the problem only when its condition is fulfilled and disappear in the opposite case. Now, removing a constraint from consideration is equivalent to associating the *universal relation* (i.e. the set of all possible tuples) to it. So, to implement a conditional constraint, we can resort to a metaconstraint that installs a functional link between the predicate representing the condition and the relation of the conditioned constraint. When the predicate is not verified, the universal relation is associated with the conditioned constraint. In our example, this constraint can be defined in the following way:

$$\begin{cases} c_c = \langle \textit{office}, \textit{maximum} \rangle \\ R(c_c) = \mathsf{r} = \{\langle v_1, v_2 \rangle \mid |v_1| < v_2\} \end{cases}$$

where $|v|$ denotes the cardinality of v. The metaconstraint on $R(c_c)$ has then this definition:

$$\begin{cases} c_{mc} = \langle R(c_c), \textit{budget} \rangle \\ R(c_{mc}) = \{\langle \mathsf{r}, \mathsf{low} \rangle, \langle \mathsf{universal}, v \neq \mathsf{low} \rangle\} \end{cases}$$

A straightforward way to implement the conditional constraint would have been to create a constraint on all the variables with a relation that embeds the condition such as:

$$\begin{cases} c = \langle \textit{budget}, \textit{office}, \textit{maximum} \rangle \\ R(c) = \{\langle \mathsf{low}, v_2, v_3 \rangle \mid |v_2| < v_3\} \cup \{\langle v_1, v_2, v_3 \rangle \mid v_1 \neq \mathsf{low}\} \end{cases}$$

This implementation works perfectly but is not flexible. No arbitrary condition can be added dynamically to a given constraint. Neither can the condition be changed nor removed at will. For instance, when the budget value has been fixed at a certain stage of the design, the "all-in-one" constraint becomes inadequate and cumbersome. Moreover, each time it is triggered, the condition part is reevaluated even when the attributes have not changed their value. These drawbacks are points in favor of our dynamic conditional constraints.

6 Consistency Maintenance

Monitoring the consistency of a constraint network usually involves a value propagation mechanism [16, 7]. It consists in triggering local recomputations of values in the network as long as needed, that is until the leaves of the network are reached or a contradiction is discovered. Unfortunately, this cannot work in a straightforward way for dynamic constraints. Indeed, the network they generate is subject to topological modification upon a mere variable instanciation. The problem that faces us is thus to build a plan for recomputations using a graph that evolves during its traversal. It is a bad idea to resort to the usual propagation method combined with backtracking to manage causal correctness. Of course, we are loosing the benefit of the linear complexity of propagation. But worse still is the termination matter which can no longer be guaranteed. The origin of the danger here is that dynamic constraints allow the expression of problems lacking clear semantics, leading propagation to a deadlock. For example, it is perfectly possible to express that we want $x_i + x_j = 0$ when $x_i + x_j \neq 0$.

Reactive synchronous languages are frequently confronted with similar problem. Nevertheless, they manage to reject nonsensical programs at compile time by determining the causal correctness of instructions [2]. In our case, the set of constrained variables is dynamic and therefore, any dependency analysis is useless. A system for change propagation in object dependency graphs presented in [17] also faces the same problem, but no solution is brought: it is presented as a natural counterpart of the gain in expressiveness. Therefore, the responsibility for the correctness is left to the user.

We have chosen to overcome the problem and, in order to do so, we simply disallow any metaconstraint on a constraint c_i or on its relation $R(c_i)$ to share attributes with the set of variables that are potentially influenced by c_i. As for the implementation, we are asking the programmer to define a strong partition among the variables according to their participating level in the meta hierarchy. Then, we use this partition to preclude the instanciation of constraints which attributes belong to different levels. Considering the constraints we have expressed in the previous two sections, such a partition would be:

$$\{cost, desk, lamp, chair\} \prec \{office, maximum\} \prec \{budget\}$$

The induced layers of the constraint network are presented on figure 3. The level of a constraint is implicitly defined as the level of its attributes plus one and the level of a relation is defined as the level of its corresponding constraint.

Whereas this trivial layering method narrows the expressive power of metaconstraints, it keeps low the complexity and ensures the correctness of the consistency maintenance process. Indeed, we now just have to organize propagation

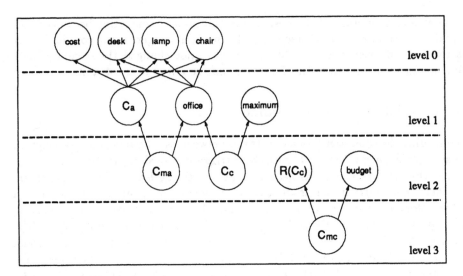

Fig. 3.

in successive steps, starting with the variables of the highest level and ending with the lowest ones as detailed below.

Let δ_C be the set of added constraints and δ_X the set of disturbed variables. propagate is a classical value propagation function as implemented, for example, in [16]. Its input is the set of constraint which consistency must be checked and reinforced; its output is the set of constraints which value (or the value of their corresponding relation) has been changed. Propagation through multiple levels acts as follows ($L(c)$ denotes the level of constraint c):

propagate-through-levels(δ_C, δ_X)
while $\delta_C \neq \emptyset$
    or $\delta_X \neq \emptyset$
do let $all = \delta_C \cup \{c_i \in C \mid \delta_X \cap V(c_i) \neq \emptyset\}$
   and then $ready = \{c_i \in all \mid L(c_i) = \max_{c_j \in all}(L(c_j))\}$
   $\delta_C \leftarrow (\delta_C \setminus ready) \cup \text{propagate}(ready)$
   $\delta_X \leftarrow \delta_X \setminus \bigcup_{c_i \in ready} V(c_i)$
end do

7 Implementation

Our work on metaconstraints is born of the hybridation of the PROSE [1] constraint language with the SMECI [11] knowledge representation system. As in many similar systems, part of the knowledge expression in SMECI relies on dynamic hierarchies of structured objects. This feature naturally imposed the dynamic constraint model.

Now, this model is implemented in TELOS, the object layer of LE_LISP V16 [12]. A variable is defined by a structure with the *value* and *domain* slot.

A constraint is also a structure with the *attributes* and *relation* slots, the value of which is of course a variable structure. To optimize the management of conditional constraints, we attached an *activity* slot to constraints. This slot holds a boolean value that tells whether any interpretation process has to consider the constraint or not. When a constraint has to be withdrawn, we simply assign its activity to false instead of assigning its relation the universal relation. This prevents from further unnecessary constraint checks.

8 Related Works

A constraint problem can be seen as composed of two parts: a syntactical one which is played by the variables and the constraints, and a semantic one which is played by the relations. To our knowledge, previous works on dynamic constraint problems have focused on either part but not both.

When they have been motivated by design applications, the dynamic aspect was generally dedicated to syntax. Dynamic constraints were then implementing the context-sensitive existence of objects, may it be constraints as in [10] or variables as in [14, 3].

A recent work presented in [8] is interested in the dynamic aspect of the semantical part of the problems. It proposes a dynamic constraint model which is close to ours. This model involves the same principle in the sense that all objects have the same status, but the point of view is reversed as all objects are constraints. In particular, variables of regular problems are mapped to 0-ary dynamic constraints with their domain acting as the relation.

Metaconstraints are used to supervise the relation associated with other constraints. Their interpretation in satisfaction allows to relax over-constrained problems while remaining in the framework of the satisfaction process. Backtracking on a metaconstraint during the enumeration phase of the satisfaction process will result in instanciating the object constraint with another possible relation, preferably weaker than the former. Antagonistic constraints are thus progressively relaxed until a solution can be found.

This use is complementary to ours. First, it falls in the domain of the constraint satisfaction problem when here, we only deal with the consistency maintenance problem. Second, it is in the vein of partial constraint satisfaction whereas we have focused on dynamic and hierarchical consistency maintenance.

References

1. P. Berlandier. *A Study of Constraint Interpretation Mechanisms and of their Integration in a Knowledge Representation Language*. PhD thesis, University of Nice, 1992. (in french).
2. G. Berry and G. Gonthier. The ESTEREL synchronous programming language: Design, semantics, implementation. Rapport de Recherche 842, INRIA Sophia Antipolis, 1988.

3. J. Bowen and D. Bahler. Conditional existence of variable in generalized constraint networks. In *Proc. AAAI*, 1991.

4. J. Cohen. Constraint logic programming languages. *Communications of the ACM*, 33(7), 1990.

5. A. Borning et al. Constraint hierarchies. In *Proc. OOPSLA*, 1987.

6. E. Freuder. Partial constraint satisfaction. In *Proc. IJCAI*, Detroit, Michigan, 1989.

7. J. Gosling. *Algebraic Constraints*. PhD thesis, Carnegie–Mellon University, 1983.

8. H. Güsgen and J. Hertzberg. *A Perspective of Constraint-Based Reasoning*, volume 597 of *Lecture Notes in Artificial Intelligence*. Springer–Verlag, 1992.

9. P. Van Hentenryck, H. Simonis, and M. Dincbas. Constraint satisfaction using constraint logic programming. *Artificial Intelligence*, 58:113–159, 1992.

10. K. Hua, B. Faltings, and D. Haroud. *Dynamic Constraint Satisfaction in a Bridge Design System*, volume 462 of *Lecture Notes in Artificial Intelligence*, pages 217–232. Springer–Verlag, 1990.

11. ILOG, 2 Av. Galliéni, F-94253 Gentilly. SMECI *Version 1.3, Users' Reference Manual*, 1988.

12. ILOG, 2 Av. Galliéni, F-94253 Gentilly. LE-LISP *Version 16, Users' Reference Manual*, 1992.

13. V. Kumar. Algorithms for constraint satisfaction problems: A survey. *AI Magazine*, 13(1):32–44, 1992.

14. S. Mittal and B. Falkenhainer. Dynamic constraint satisfaction problems. In *Proc. AAAI*, 1990.

15. U. Montanari. Networks of constraints: Fundamental properties and application to picture processing. *Information Science*, 7(3):95–132, 1974.

16. G. Steele. *The Definition and Implementation of a Computer Programming Language Based on Constraints*. PhD thesis, Massachusetts Institute of Technology, 1980.

17. M. Wilk. Change propagation in object dependency graphs. In *Proc. Technology of Object-Oriented Languages and Systems (TOOLS USA)*, 1991.

Preliminary Formalization of an Incremental Hierarchical Constraint Solver

Francisco Menezes and Pedro Barahona

Departamento de Informática, Universidade Nova de Lisboa,
2825 Monte da Caparica, PORTUGAL

Abstract. This paper presents a first formalization of an incremental method to solve hierarchies of constraints over finite domains, which borrows techniques developed in intelligent backtracking, and finds *locally-predicate-better* solutions. A prototype implementation of this method, IHCS, was written in C and can be integrated with different programming environments. In particular, with Prolog producing an instance of an HCLP language. Possible applications of IHCS are briefly illustrated with a time-tabling and a set covering problem.

Keywords: Incremental Constraint Solving, Hierarchical Constraints, CLP.

1 Introduction

Real problems are usually over constrained, and the best answer a constraint solver could give is a partial solution satisfying all but the least important constraints. Preferences among constraints may be declared explicitly by associating a strength denoting the degree of requirement to preferred or non-required constraints, in contrast with required constraints that are mandatory. In [2], a general scheme is proposed for Hierarchical Constraint Logic Programming (HCLP) languages, parameterized by $\mathcal{D}$, the domain of the constraints and by a comparator $\mathcal{C}$ that allows to compare different possible solutions and select the best ones.

A *constraint hierarchy* $\mathcal{H}$ is a set of *labelled constraints* c@*level* relating a set of variables ranging over finite domains where c is a constraint on some variables and *level* the strength of c in the hierarchy. Level 0 corresponds to the required constraints and the other levels to the non-required (or preferred) constraints. The higher the level, the weaker a constraint is.

A *valuation* to a constraint hierarchy $\mathcal{H}$, is a mapping of the free variables in $\mathcal{H}$ to elements in their respective domains, that satisfies all the required constraints (level 0). Given two valuations θ and σ, θ is *locally-predicate-better* than σ [2] if a) θ and σ both satisfy exactly the same number of constraints in each level until some level k, and b) in level $k+1$ θ satisfies more constraints than σ.

The Incremental Hierarchical Constraint Solver (IHCS) that we have developed is intended to be the kernel of a HCLP($\mathcal{FD}$, $\mathcal{LPB}$) instance of this scheme, where $\mathcal{FD}$ stand for finite domains and $\mathcal{LPB}$ is the *locally-predicate-better* comparator. Operationally, our approach diverges from the one presented in [2] because it is incremental. Instead of delaying the non-required constraints until the complete reduction of a goal, IHCS tries, in its forward phase, to satisfy constraints as soon as they appear. In case of inconsistency, a special backward algorithm is evoked.

This can be seen as an "optimistic" treatment of preferred constraints (i.e. we bet they will participate in the search for a solution), as opposed to the "pessimistic" view of [2] where non-required constraints (source of possible inconsistency) are delayed as long as possible. The advantage is to actively use these constraints for pruning the search space. This approach nevertheless requires a specialized backward phase where dependencies between constraints, caused by their handling of common variables, are exploited to identify pertinent causes of failure. This is done much in the same way as in intelligent backtracking [10,4], although instead of finding pertinent choice points, IHCS identifies pertinent non-required constraints to be relaxed.

Because of its portability and incremental nature, IHCS is well suited for reactive systems, allowing the interactive introduction and removal of preferred constraints. This is the case of many decision support systems that are usually concerned with supplying the decision maker with a set of alternative scenarios in which the most important constraints are satisfied [1].

The paper is organized as follows. The formal specification of IHCS is presented in Sect. 2 and its implementation in Sect. 3. Extensions to cope with disjunctions of constraints are described in Sect. 4.Two applications are presented in Sect. 5 and final remarks in Sect. 6.

2 Definitions and Formal Specification of IHCS

Given a constraint hierarchy $\mathcal{H}$ with n variables and m constraints, $\mathcal{V} = \{v_1, v_2, \ldots, v_n\}$ denotes the set of variables and $\mathcal{C} = \{c_1, c_2, \ldots, c_m\}$ the set of constraints. In our notation, c or c_i designates any constraint from $\mathcal{C}$. The index indicates the *introduction order* of the constraint in the hierarchy.

Definition 1 (Constraint Store). A *constraint store* S is a set of constraints ordered by *introduction order*, i.e., if c_i and c_j belong to S and $i < j$ then c_i precedes c_j in S. Any operation on constraint stores preserves this ordering.

Definition 2 (Configuration). A *configuration* Φ of hierarchy $\mathcal{H}$ is a triple of disjoint constraint stores $\langle \mathcal{AS} \bullet \mathcal{RS} \bullet \mathcal{US} \rangle$, such that $\mathcal{AS} \cup \mathcal{RS} \cup \mathcal{US} = \mathcal{C}$. $\mathcal{AS}$ is the *Active Store*, $\mathcal{RS}$ the *Relaxed Store* and $\mathcal{US}$ the *Unexplored Store*.

A configuration may be seen as a state of the evaluation of a hierarchy where the active store contains all the active constraints (i.e. those that might have reduced some domains of its variables), the relaxed store is composed by the relaxed constraints and the unexplored store is the set of candidates "queuing" for activation. We will denote that a store S is consistent by $S \not\vdash_X \perp$, where X designates a network consistency algorithm (e.g. $X = $ AC for Arc-Consistency [7]). S_i denotes the subset of S containing only constraints of level i. A store $S' = S \cup \{c\}$ may be expressed by $c.S$ if c is the element of S' with lower introduction order or by $S.c$ if c is the element of S' with higher introduction order.

Definition 3 (Final Configuration). A *configuration* $\langle AS \bullet RS \bullet US \rangle$ of hierarchy $\mathcal{H}$ is a *final configuration* if, given the initial domains of the variables the following conditions hold:

1. $AS \not\vdash_X \bot$;
2. $AS \cup \{c\} \vdash_X \bot \quad (\forall c \in RS)$;
3. $US = \emptyset$.

Definition 4 (Locally-Predicate-Better). $\langle AS \bullet RS \bullet US \rangle$ is *locally-predicate-better* than $\langle AS' \bullet RS' \bullet US' \rangle$, if and only if exists some level $k > 0$ such that:

1. $\#(AS_i \cup US_i) = \#(AS'_i \cup US'_i) \quad (\forall i < k)$;
2. $\#(AS_k \cup US_k) > \#(AS'_k \cup US'_k)$.

Definition 5 (Best Configuration). A final configuration Φ is a *best configuration* if there is no other final configuration Φ' which is locally-predicate-better than Φ.

Definition 6 (Promising Configuration). $\Phi = \langle AS \bullet RS \bullet US \rangle$ is a *promising configuration*, denoted PC(Φ), if i) $AS \not\vdash_X \bot$ and ii) there is no final configuration Φ' which is locally-predicate-better than Φ.

IHCS aims at computing best configurations incrementally: given an hierarchy $\mathcal{H}$ with a known best configuration $\langle AS \bullet RS \bullet \emptyset \rangle$, if a new constraint c is inserted into $\mathcal{H}$, then starting from the promising configuration $\langle AS \bullet RS \bullet \{c\} \rangle$ several transitions will be performed until a best configuration is reached undoing and redoing as little work as possible.

The following rules define the valid transitions for configurations. If we start with a promising configuration and a solution to the hierarchy exist, transitions will always stop at the base rule with a best configuration. While the active store is consistent and the unexplored store is not empty, the forward rule keeps activating a new constraint. If a conflict is raised (the active store becomes inconsistent) the backward rule searches for an alternative promising configuration for the hierarchy, relaxing some constraints and possibly reactivating other constraints previously relaxed. More formally,

Base rule

$$\frac{AS \not\vdash_X \bot}{\langle AS \bullet RS \bullet \emptyset \rangle}$$

Forward rule

$$\frac{AS \not\vdash_X \bot}{\langle AS \bullet RS \bullet c.US \rangle \to \langle AS.c \bullet RS \bullet US \rangle}$$

Backward rule

$$\frac{AS \vdash_X \perp \quad \mathcal{R}elax \subseteq AS \cup US \quad Activate \subseteq \mathcal{R}S \quad Reset \subseteq AS \setminus \mathcal{R}elax \quad PC(\Phi)}{\langle AS \bullet \mathcal{R}S \bullet US \rangle \to \Phi}$$

$$\text{where } \Phi = \langle AS' \bullet \mathcal{R}S' \bullet US' \rangle \quad \begin{cases} AS' = AS \setminus (\mathcal{R}elax \cup Reset) \\ \mathcal{R}S' = (\mathcal{R}S \setminus Activate) \cup \mathcal{R}elax \\ US' = (US \setminus \mathcal{R}elax) \cup Reset \cup Activate \end{cases}$$

The main idea of the backward rule is to find constraints pertinent to the conflict that should be relaxed (the $\mathcal{R}elax$ set). Since the relaxation of these constraints may also resolve previous conflicts, constraints previously relaxed may now be re-activated (the $Activate$ set). Constraints affected by the relaxed ones must be reset (temporary removed from the active store) in order to re-achieve maximum consistency (the $Reset$ set). The configuration obtained $\Phi = \langle AS' \bullet \mathcal{R}S' \bullet US' \rangle$ must be a promising configuration, since if no other conflict is found, future transitions performed by the forward rule will lead to the final configuration $\langle AS' \cup US' \bullet \mathcal{R}S' \bullet \emptyset \rangle$ which will then be a best configuration.

3 Implementation of IHCS

IHCS is divided in two phases: a forward phase corresponding to the forward rule where one constraint is activated using an incremental arc-consistency algorithm ($X = \text{AC}$) and a backward phase corresponding to the backward rule that is evoked to solve any conflict raised during the forward phase.

3.1 The Forward Algorithm

Since methods to verify strong K-consistency are exponential for $K > 2$, [6], usually other weaker consistency conditions, such as Arc-consistency ($K = 2$) [7], are better suited for real implementations.

The forward algorithm is an adaptation of an arc consistency algorithm based on constraint propagation, generalized for the case of constraints with an arbitrary number of variables. In our implementation we adapted the AC5 [11], but since arc consistency algorithms are not the main issue of this article, a simplified algorithm is described to keep this presentation clear.

Some notation must be introduced before proceeding. The domain of variable v is denoted by D_v and $\mathcal{C}_v$ ($\mathcal{C}_v \subseteq \mathcal{C}$) is the set of active constraints on v. For each constraint c, the set of its variables is designated by $\mathcal{V}_c$ ($\mathcal{V}_c \subseteq \mathcal{V}$) and the hierarchical level of c is expressed by $level_c$. During this phase we only have to be concerned with the active store. The current active store is defined implicitly by $AS = \bigcup_{v \in \mathcal{V}} \mathcal{C}_v$.

The forward rule is implemented with function Forward. A counter AO is increased any time a new constraint c is inserted in the active store, to update the *activation order* of that constraint (AO_c). This order will be needed in the backward phase, as will be seen later.

A set of trail stacks is also kept to undo work in the backward phase when constraints are deactivated. For each constraint c a trail stack $\mathcal{T}_c$ is kept to record any transformation made on data structures caused by the activation of c. The set of all trail stacks may be seen as a single partitioned trail stack. This partitioning allows to save work that is not related with the conflict raised, as it will be seen in the backward phase.

function Forward()
    while $\mathcal{US} = c_j.\mathcal{US}'$ **do**
        $\mathcal{US}$ $\leftarrow$ $\mathcal{US}'$
        $\mathcal{AS}$ $\leftarrow$ $\mathcal{AS} \cup \{c_j\}$
        AO $\leftarrow$ $AO + 1$
        $AO_{c_j} \leftarrow AO$
        Enqueue(c_j, Q)   % Q initially empty
        while Dequeue(Q, c_k) **do**
            if **not** Revise($c_k, \mathcal{T}_{c_j}, Q$) **then**
                if **not** Backward(c_k) **then**   **return** false
    return true

Function Revise($c, \mathcal{T}, Q$) performs the removal of inconsistent values from the domain of c variables and updates a dependency graph (as will be explained in Sect. 3.2). All these transformations are stacked in trail $\mathcal{T}$ and all active constraints over affected variables are enqueued in Q (the propagation queue). If there are no values to satisfy c then Revise($c, \mathcal{T}, Q$) returns "false", otherwise it returns "true".

3.2 The Dependency Graph

To cope with hierarchical constraints, a *dependency graph* ($\mathcal{DG}$) with information about the dependency between active constraints, must be kept and updated during the forward phase. When a conflict is raised, the backward algorithm is evoked, which will analyse $\mathcal{DG}$ to find out the pertinent causes of the failure and what will be affected by the relaxation of some constraints.

Definition 7 (Constrainer). c ($c \in \mathcal{AS}$) is a *constrainer* of v ($v \in \mathcal{V}_c$) if it actually caused the reduction of D_v, i.e., values where removed from the domain of v during some revision of c. We also designate c as a constrainer (without mentioning of which variable) if it is a constrainer of some variable.

Notice that a constraint may be redundant for some of its variables, i.e. it never becomes a constrainer of these variables.

Definition 8 (Immediate Dependency\Support). c_k is *immediately dependent* of c_j (conversely c_j is an *immediate supporter* of c_k), written $c_j \hookrightarrow c_k$, iff $\exists v \in \mathcal{V}_{c_k}$ s.t. c_j is a constrainer of v.

Proposition 1 $c \hookrightarrow c$ iff c is a constrainer.

This proposition is a trivial consequence of Definition 8.

Definition 9 ($\mathcal{DG}$). $\mathcal{DG}$ is a direct graph whose nodes are the constraints in $\mathcal{AS}$ and there is an arc from c_j to c_k ($\forall c_j, c_k \in \mathcal{C}$) iff $c_j \hookrightarrow c_k$.

Definition 10 (Dependent\Supporter). c_k is dependent of c_j (conversely c_j is a supporter of c_k) iff $c_j \overset{*}{\hookrightarrow} c_k$, i.e, there is a path from c_j to c_k in $\mathcal{DG}$.

Definition 11 (Immediate Relation). c_j is immediately related to c_k , written $c_j \leftrightharpoons c_k$, iff $c_j \hookrightarrow c_k$ or $c_k \hookrightarrow c_j$.

Definition 12 (Related). c_j is related to c_k iff $c_j \overset{*}{\leftrightharpoons} c_k$, i.e. there is a path between c_j and c_k in the underlying undirected graph of $\mathcal{DG}$.

The dependency relation is based on *local propagation* of constraints in the following way: whenever a constraint c_j ($c_j \in \mathcal{AS}$) makes a restriction on some v ($v \in \mathcal{V}_{c_j}$), any other constraint c_k ($c_k \in \mathcal{AS}$) such that $v \in \mathcal{V}_{c_k}$ will be reactivated and probably cause the reactivation of further constraints, even if they do not share any variable with c_j. The restrictions performed by c_j may consequently affect all those constraints and for this reason they all become dependent of c_j.

A simple way to implicitly maintain $\mathcal{DG}$ is to record for each variable v the set of its constrainers, $\mathcal{C}_v^*$ ($\mathcal{C}_v^* \subseteq \mathcal{C}_v$), and for each constraint c the set of its constrained variables, $\mathcal{V}_c^*$ ($\mathcal{V}_c^* \subseteq \mathcal{V}_c$). Observe that, following intelligent backtracking techniques, we record dependencies at the level of the constraint network, as opposed to [5] where a truth-maintenance system is coupled with a finite domains constraint solver. All necessary operations on $\mathcal{DG}$ will be made through the following functions:

$$
\begin{aligned}
\text{vars} &: \wp(\mathcal{C}) \longrightarrow \wp(\mathcal{V}), & \text{vars}(S) &= \bigcup_{c \in S} \mathcal{V}_c \\
\text{cvars} &: \wp(\mathcal{C}) \longrightarrow \wp(\mathcal{V}), & \text{cvars}(S) &= \bigcup_{c \in S} \mathcal{V}_c^* \\
\text{IS} &: \wp(\mathcal{C}) \longrightarrow \wp(\mathcal{C}), & \text{IS}(S) &= \bigcup_{v \in \text{vars}(S)} \mathcal{C}_v^* \\
\text{SUP} &: \wp(\mathcal{C}) \longrightarrow \wp(\mathcal{C}), & \text{SUP}(S) &= \text{IS}(S)\!\uparrow\!\omega \\
\text{ID} &: \wp(\mathcal{C}) \longrightarrow \wp(\mathcal{C}), & \text{ID}(S) &= \bigcup_{v \in \text{cvars}(S)} \mathcal{C}_v \\
\text{IR} &: \wp(\mathcal{C}) \longrightarrow \wp(\mathcal{C}), & \text{IR}(S) &= \text{IS}(S) \cup \text{ID}(S) \\
\text{REL} &: \wp(\mathcal{C}) \longrightarrow \wp(\mathcal{C}), & \text{REL}(S) &= \text{IR}(S)\!\uparrow\!\omega
\end{aligned}
$$

Proposition 2 Given $S \subseteq \mathcal{AS}$, $\text{IS}(S)$ returns the set of all immediate supporters of any constraint in S, i.e.

$$\text{IS}(S) = \{c_k \in \mathcal{AS} \mid (\exists c_j \in S)\, c_k \hookrightarrow c_j\}$$

Proposition 3 Given $S \subseteq \mathcal{AS}$, $\text{ID}(S)$ returns the set of all constraints wich are immediately dependent on any constraint in S, i.e.

$$\text{ID}(S) = \{c_k \in \mathcal{AS} \mid (\exists c_j \in S)\, c_j \hookrightarrow c_k\}$$

Proposition 4 *Given $S \subseteq AS$, IR(S) returns the set of all constraints wich are immediately related to any constraint in S, i.e.*

$$\mathrm{IR}(S) = \{c_k \in AS \mid (\exists c_j \in S)\ c_j \leftrightarrows c_k\}$$

Propositions 2 and 3 are trivial consequences of Definition 8, and Proposition 4 is a trivial consequence of Propositions 2 and 3 and Definition 11. It is also trivial to see that $\wp(C)$ (the powerset of C) is a complete partial order under the subset relation, and that functions IS, ID and IR are all monotonic and continuous. Therefore they all contain some fix points in their domains.

Definition 13 (Straight Path). A *straight path* of $\mathcal{DG}$ is a path without repeated nodes.

Proposition 5 *Given $S \subseteq AS$, SUP(S) is a fix point of IS which represents the set of all supporters of any constraint in S, i.e.*

$$\mathrm{SUP}(S) = \{c_k \in AS \mid (\exists c_j \in S)\ c_k \overset{*}{\hookrightarrow} c_j\}$$

Proof. Let $S_1 = \mathrm{IS}(S), S_2 = \mathrm{IS}(S_1) = \mathrm{IS}(S){\uparrow}2, \ldots, S_n = \mathrm{IS}(S_{n-1}) = \mathrm{IS}(S){\uparrow}n$. Suppose that S_n is the fix point reached by this iterations. Since S_i $(1 \leq i \leq n)$ only contains constrainers, by Proposition 1 $S_i \subseteq \mathrm{IS}(S_i)$, i.e, each iteration preserves the elements collected so far. S_1 is composed of the immediate supporters, that is, the supporters distanced by a single link in a straight path of $\mathcal{DG}$, from constraints in S. Applying IS to S_1, and thus obtaining S_2, will add all the supporters distanced by two links. This iterative process keeps adding new supporters with longer straight paths of $\mathcal{DG}$ leading to constraints in S. If n is the maximal length of a straight path of $\mathcal{DG}$ leading to some constraint in S, then $\mathrm{IS}(S_n) = S_n$ since there are no more new supporters to add. Consequently, $\mathrm{IS}(S){\uparrow}\omega = \mathrm{SUP}(S)$ is the set of all possible supporters of any constraint in S.

Proposition 6 *Given $S \subseteq AS$, REL(S) is a fix point of IR which represents the set of all constraints related to any constraint in S, i.e.*

$$\mathrm{REL}(S) = \{c_k \in AS \mid (\exists c_j \in S)\ c_j \overset{*}{\leftrightarrows} c_k\}$$

The proof for this proposition is similar to the one used for Proposition 5.

3.3 The Backward Algorithm

The backward phase is used to resolve any conflict raised during the forward phase, by relaxing some non-required constraints. The following properties must be satisfied: a) only constraints pertinent to the conflict should be changed (relaxed or reactivated) to avoid non useful search; b) a potentially best configuration must be re-achieved to obtain a sound behavior; c) no promising configuration should be repeated to avoid loops; d) no promising configuration should be skipped for completeness of the algorithm; e) global consistency of the new active store must be re-achieved, undoing as little work as possible.

The main steps of the backward algorithm are:

1. [Conflict configuration]   Pertinent constraints to the conflict.

2. [Relax and Activate sets] Constraints to be relaxed and re-activated.

3. [Reset set]   Constraints to be reset.

4. [Untrailing]   Untrail constraints.

5. [New configuration]   Updates the current configuration.

Step 1) Conflict configuration. Given the current configuration $\Phi = \langle AS \bullet RS \bullet US \rangle$ and the constraint $c_j \in AS$ that becomes un-satisfiable in the forward phase, this step will determine a simplified (a pair instead of a triple) sub-configuration $\Phi_{\text{conf}} = \langle AS_{\text{conf}} \bullet RS_{\text{conf}} \rangle$, the *conflict configuration*, including only constraints pertinent to the conflict ($AS_{\text{conf}} \subseteq (AS \cup US)$ and $RS_{\text{conf}} \subseteq RS$). Φ_{conf} represents the only portion of the whole configuration that should be changed to solve the conflict. AS_{conf} are the candidates for relaxation and RS_{conf} the candidates for re-activation. Note that, to ensure that all promising configurations will be tried, AS_{conf} might also contain non active constraints from US, since some of them may have to be relaxed (in this case, no longer activated).

Suppose that the current conflict is the n-th conflict ocurred so far. The current *conflict set* (CS_n), is composed of the supporters of c_j. Those supporters represent the constraints that directly or indirectly restricted the domains of the variables of c_j, leaving no consistent values to satisfy c_j. Since required constraints may not be relaxed, CS_n will only include the non-required supporters of the failing constraint and is defined by:

$$CS_n = \{c_k \in \text{SUP}(\{c_j\}) \mid level_{c_k} > 0\}$$

If CS_n is empty then there is no possible solution to the conflict and the constraint hierarchy is not satisfiable (function Backward fails).

Constraints from CS_n will be included in the conflict configuration Φ_{conf}. To ensure a complete enumeration of configurations, any constraint from a previous conflict set CS_i ($i < n$) that has common elements with CS_n (i.e. $CS_n \cap CS_i \neq \emptyset$), will also have to be included in Φ_{conf}. Constraints relaxed in previous conflicts will then be candidates for re-activation. This reflects the possibility that the relaxations to solve the current conflict might also solve those early conflicts, therefore allowing previously relaxed constraints to become active. Φ_{conf} is thus computed as follow:

$$TotalConflict = \bigcup_{\forall i \text{ s.t. } CS_n \cap CS_i \neq \emptyset} CS_i$$
$$AS_{\text{conf}} = (AS \cup US) \cap TotalConflict$$
$$RS_{\text{conf}} = RS \cap TotalConflict$$

Step 2) Activate and Relax sets. By analyzing the conflict configuration, this step determines which constraints from $\mathcal{AS}_{conf}$ should be relaxed (the $\mathcal{Relax}$ set), and which constraints from $\mathcal{RS}_{conf}$ should be re-activated (the $\mathcal{Activate}$ set) in order to obtain a promising configuration.

There is a complete process for enumerating simplified configurations by ascendent order relatively to $\mathcal{LPB}$ comparisons, respecting the introduction order (c.f. Sect. 2) of each constraint. Using this enumeration (described in [8]) it is possible to determine $\langle \mathcal{AS}_{next} \bullet \mathcal{RS}_{next} \rangle$, the successor of $\langle \mathcal{AS}_{conf} \bullet \mathcal{RS}_{conf} \rangle$.

$\mathcal{AS}_{next}$ should not contain any conflict set computed so far, otherwise the next configuration to be tested would reproduce a redundant conflict. In such cases the successor of $\langle \mathcal{AS}_{next} \bullet \mathcal{RS}_{next} \rangle$ is computed. The $\mathcal{Relax}$ and $\mathcal{Activate}$ sets are calculated as follow:

$$Activate = \mathcal{RS}_{conf} \setminus \mathcal{RS}_{next} \; (= \mathcal{RS}_{conf} \cap \mathcal{AS}_{next})$$
$$\mathcal{Relax} \;\;= \mathcal{AS}_{conf} \setminus \mathcal{AS}_{next} \; (= \mathcal{AS}_{conf} \cap \mathcal{RS}_{next})$$

Step 3) Reset Set. The $\mathcal{Reset}$ set is composed of all the constraints that will have to be reset, i.e. moved from the active store to the unexplored store, to re-achieve global consistency. If c_j is one of the constraints to be relaxed and c_k is a constraint inserted in the active store after c_j $(AO_{c_k} > AO_{c_j})$, then $\mathcal{DG}$ must be inspected to decide whether c_k needs to be reset.

If there is a path from c_j to c_k then c_k is dependent of c_j. In this case, either directly or indirectly by constraint propagation, c_j has caused the removal of some values from the domains of c_k variables, that otherwise c_k itself would be charged to remove. Therefore c_k will have to be reset to perform such removal.

If there is a path from c_k to c_j then, by local constraint propagation, c_j possibly made more restrictions after the activation of c_k. Therefore c_k will have to be reset, to be used in a context where such removals will not take place.

As explained before, resetting c_k means removing it from the active store and re-inserting it afterwards. Consequently, the same reasoning applies with respect to this removal, i.e. any other constraint activated after c_j that has a path either from c_k or to c_k must also be reset. This recursive procedure is repeated until no more such constraints are found. Taking into account all the constraints to be relaxed, $\mathcal{Reset}$ is defined by:

$$\mathcal{Reset} = \bigcup_{c_j \in \mathcal{Relax}} \{c_k \in \mathrm{REL}(\{c_j\}) \mid AO_{c_k} \geq AO_{c_j}\}$$

Remember that $\mathcal{Relax}$ is composed of active constraints (from $\mathcal{AS}_{conf}$) and unexplored constraints (from $\mathcal{US}_{conf}$). Since $\mathcal{AS}_{conf}$ only contains constrainers, by Proposition 1, all the active constraints from $\mathcal{Relax}$ will also be included in $\mathcal{Reset}$. This set is thus composed of all the active constraints that will be removed from the active store.

Step 4) Untrailing. Only the trails of the constraints in $\mathcal{Reset}$ will be used, saving the work made by other constraints not affected by the conflict:

$$\textbf{for each} \quad c \in \mathcal{R}eset \quad \textbf{do}$$
$$\text{untrail}(\mathcal{T}_c)$$
$$AO_c = 0$$

Step 5) New configuration. As explained in Sect. 3.1, the active store is maintained implicitly by $AS = \bigcup_{v \in \mathcal{V}} C_v$. The following assignments will perform the updating of the current configuration:

$$C_v = C_v \setminus \mathcal{R}eset \quad (\forall v \in \text{vars}(\mathcal{R}eset))$$
$$\mathcal{R}S = (\mathcal{R}S \setminus \mathcal{A}ctivate) \cup \mathcal{R}elax$$
$$US = (US \cup \mathcal{R}eset \cup \mathcal{A}ctivate) \setminus \mathcal{R}elax$$

Example 1. Given variables X and Y with initial domains $D_X = D_Y = 1..10$, consider the following constraints: $c_1 \equiv X + Y = 15@1$; $c_2 \equiv 3 \cdot X - Y < 5@1$; $c_3 \equiv X > Y + 1@2$; $c_4 \equiv X < 7@2$. The incremental insertion of each constraint is given by the following transitions:

Action	Configuration	D_X	D_Y	Relaxed @1	@2	Rule
insert c_1	$\langle \emptyset \bullet \emptyset \bullet \{c_1\} \rangle$	1..10	1..10	0	0	forward
	$\langle \{c_1\} \bullet \emptyset \bullet \emptyset \rangle$	5..10	5..10	0	0	base
insert c_2	$\langle \{c_1\} \bullet \emptyset \bullet \{c_2\} \rangle$	5..10	5..10	0	0	forward
	$\langle \{c_1, c_2\} \bullet \emptyset \bullet \emptyset \rangle$	$\emptyset$	$\emptyset$	0	0	backward
	$\langle \{c_1\} \bullet \{c_2\} \bullet \emptyset \rangle$	5..10	5..10	1	0	base
insert c_3	$\langle \{c_1\} \bullet \{c_2\} \bullet \{c_3\} \rangle$	5..10	5..10	1	0	forward
	$\langle \{c_1, c_3\} \bullet \{c_2\} \bullet \emptyset \rangle$	7..10	5..8	1	0	base
insert c_4	$\langle \{c_1, c_3\} \bullet \{c_2\} \bullet \{c_4\} \rangle$	7..10	5..8	1	0	forward
	$\langle \{c_1, c_3, c_4\} \bullet \{c_2\} \bullet \emptyset \rangle$	$\emptyset$	$\emptyset$	1	0	backward
	$\langle \{c_1, c_3\} \bullet \{c_2, c_4\} \bullet \emptyset \rangle$	7..10	5..8	1	1	base

3.4 Obtaining alternative solutions

Several best configurations to an hierarchy may exist since $\mathcal{LPB}$ ordering is not a total ordering. Given $\Phi = \langle AS \bullet \mathcal{R}S \bullet \emptyset \rangle$, the current best configuration, IHCS is able to find the next promising configuration, with a slightly modified backward rule (the *alternative* rule).

Alternative rule

$$\frac{AS \not\vdash_X \bot \quad \mathcal{R}elax \subseteq AS \quad \mathcal{A}ctivate \subseteq \mathcal{R}S \quad \mathcal{R}eset \subseteq (AS \setminus \mathcal{R}elax) \quad PC(\Phi)}{\langle AS \bullet \mathcal{R}S \bullet \emptyset \rangle \to \Phi}$$

where $\Phi = \langle AS \setminus (\mathcal{R}elax \cup \mathcal{R}eset) \bullet \mathcal{R}S \setminus \mathcal{A}ctivate \cup \mathcal{R}elax \bullet \mathcal{R}eset \cup \mathcal{A}ctivate \rangle$

This rule is implemented using the backward algorithm with slight modifications in Steps 1 and 2 in order to find an alternative to a best configuration rather than to a conflicting one. In Step 1 all active constraints must be considered instead of only the supporters of a failing constraint as in the normal backward rule, i.e. $\Phi_{conf} = \Phi$. In Step 2 the computed simplified configuration $\langle AS_{next} \bullet RS_{next} \rangle$ is no better then $\langle AS \bullet RS \rangle$, regarding $\mathcal{LPB}$ comparisons. If it is worse then the search for an alternative fails since the new configuration would also be worse than the known current best configuration.

The promising configuration Φ' determined by the alternative rule will be used by the normal set of rules (the base, forward and backward rules) to find a best configuration. If at any point an intermediate configuration, is worse than the previous one, the search for an alternative best solution fails.

Example 2. An alternative to the solution found in Example 1 is computed by the following transitions:

Configuration	D_X	D_Y	Relaxed @1	@2	Rule
$\langle \{c_1, c_3\} \bullet \{c_2, c_4\} \bullet \emptyset \rangle$	7..10	5..8	1	1	alternative
$\langle \{c_1\} \bullet \{c_2, c_3\} \bullet \{c_4\} \rangle$	5..10	5..10	1	1	forward
$\langle \{c_1, c_4\} \bullet \{c_2, c_3\} \bullet \emptyset \rangle$	5..6	9..10	1	1	base

3.5 Incremental Removal of Constraints

Given a best configuration $\langle AS \bullet RS \bullet \emptyset \rangle$ to a hierarchy $\mathcal{H}$, the removal of a constraint c from $\mathcal{H}$ is straightforward if c is a relaxed constraint, and a best configuration is immediatly obtained by the following rule:

Relaxed Removal rule

$$\frac{AS \not\vdash_X \bot \qquad c \in RS}{\langle AS \bullet RS \bullet \emptyset \rangle \rightarrow \langle AS \bullet RS \setminus \{c\} \bullet \emptyset \rangle}$$

If c is active, a slightly modified backward rule is necessary to obtain a promising configuration:

Active Removal rule

$$\frac{AS \not\vdash_X \bot \quad c \in AS \quad Activate \subseteq RS \quad Reset \subseteq (AS \setminus \{c\}) \quad PC(\Phi)}{\langle AS \bullet RS \bullet \emptyset \rangle \rightarrow \Phi}$$

where $\Phi = \langle AS \setminus (\{c\} \cup Reset) \bullet RS \setminus Activate \bullet Reset \cup Activate \rangle$

This rule is implemented following Steps 3 to 5 of the backward algorithm, provided that $Relax = \{c\}$ and $Activate = RS \cap \bigcup_{\forall i \text{ s.t. } c \in cs_i} CS_i$ and that c is not included in the relaxed store obtained. Feeding Φ to the normal set of transition rules will lead to a best configuration.

Example 3. Removing the active constraint c_4 from the configuration obtained in Example 2 produces the following transitions:

Configuration	D_X	D_Y	Relaxed @1	@2	Rule
$\langle\{c_1,c_4\}\bullet\{c_2,c_3\}\bullet\emptyset\rangle$	5..6	9..10	1	1	active removal
$\langle\{c_1\}\bullet\{c_2\}\bullet\{c_3\}\rangle$	5..10	5..10	1	0	forward
$\langle\{c_1,c_3\}\bullet\{c_2\}\bullet\emptyset\rangle$	7..10	5..8	1	0	base

4   Disjunctive Constraints and Inter-Hierarchies

In logic programming the alternatives to solve a goal are usually specified as different rules for the same literal. This fact raises some problems, since different choices of rules in the logic program may produce solutions from different constraint hierarchies, sometimes producing non-intuitive solutions. In [12] the HCLP scheme is extended with some non-monotonic properties of comparators to cope with inter-hierarchy comparisons.

This problem was dealt with in IHCS by extending it with disjunctive constraints of the form $c = c^1 \bigvee c^2 \bigvee \cdots \bigvee c^n$, where c^i is a normal constraint representing the i-th alternative of c. Constraint c can only be relaxed if $level_c > 0$ and all alternatives have already failed.

This extension enables the specification of more complex constraint hierarchies and we take advantage of the dependency graph to backtrack intelligently to alternative choices.

Disjunctions however complicates the overall IHCS algorithm, as non exhausted disjunctions must be integrated in conflict sets. Since we want to minimize the number of constraints to be relaxed, it is preferable whenever possible to try an alternative choice rather than relaxing extra constraints. As in intelligent backtracking methods, we have to associate an *alternative set* for each disjunction – cf. the $\mathcal{A}lt$ sets of [4] – and to restart from the first alternative disjunctions to be re-inserted – cf. the selective reset of [3].

The use of disjunctive constraints is very useful for the final generation of solutions. After the pruning due to all constraints being treated, some variables may still have several possible values in their domains. If the domain of a variable v is $\{w_1,\ldots,w_n\}$ then adding a constraint $v = w_1 \bigvee \cdots \bigvee v = w_n$ will ensure that a single value will be assigned to v within a best solution. We used such constraint as the basic definition for the built-in value generator - predicate *indomain(v)*.

Some changes in the backward algorithm are required to cope with this extension. In what follows c designates any constraint (disjunctive or not), and c^i designates a disjunctive constraint where i is the current choice.

Step 1) Conflict configuration. With the introduction of disjunctions, conflicts may be solved not only by relaxing non-required constraints, but also by trying alternative choices. A disjunction is *non exhausted* if there are alternative choices yet to try.

For each disjunctive constraint c, an *alternative set* (Alt_c) must be kept. When a conflict is raised and a non exhausted disjunction is chosen to solve the conflict, all the other non exhausted disjunctions pertinent to the conflict are included in the Alt set of the chosen one.

Alt sets allow the recalling of all alternative disjunctions that existed in previous conflicts, when a new conflict occurs before all constraints in the unexplored store are re-activated. Some of those alternatives would not be found by simple analysis of the dependency graph, since some of the arcs originated by unexplored constraints previously activated, are no longer there.

Let c_j be the constraint that failed during the forward phase. We define $Disj$ as the set of all non exhausted disjunctions pertinent to the conflict. First we collect all the disjunctive supporters of c_j ($DisjSup$ set). $Disj$ will be composed by the non exhausted disjunctions from $DisjSup$ plus the constraints in the Alt sets of any constraint from $DisjSup$. If $Disj$ is empty then the conflict may not be resolved by trying an alternative disjunctive branch and the conflict configuration Φ_{conf} is computed as before.

$$DisjSup = \{c_k^i \in AS \mid c_k^i \overset{*}{\hookrightarrow} c_j\}$$
$$Disj = \{c \in DisjSup \mid \text{not exhausted } c\} \cup \bigcup_{c \in DisjSup} Alt_c$$

Step 2) Activate and Relax sets. Since we want to minimize the number of constraints to be relaxed, it is preferable, whenever possible, to try an alternative choice rather than relaxing extra constraints. If $Disj$ is empty, the *Activate* and *Relax* sets will be defined as before. Otherwise, they are calculated as follows, given c_j^i, the last element from $Disj$ that was activated:

$$\mathcal{R}elax = \{c_j^i\} \qquad \mathcal{A}ctivate = \{c_j^{i+1}\} \qquad Alt_{c_j} = Alt_{c_j} \cup (Disj \setminus \{c_j\})$$

Step 3) Reset Set. The reset set is computed as before, provided that special care is taken with disjunctive constraints. If a constraint c^i is to be reset, then c^1 is inserted instead. This will ensure a correct tree search, since backtracking to some early node always implies restarting the search in all subtrees.

Step 4) Untrailing. Unchanged.

Step 5) New configuration. The computation of the new configuration is exactly the same except when an alternative disjunction is tried, in which case the relax store is simply kept unchanged. Note that in this case no constraint is really relaxed nor any relaxed constraint is re-activated. The $\mathcal{R}elax$ set computed in Step 2 will only interfere in the update of the active and unexplored stores (c.f. Step 5 in Sect. 3.3).

5 Applications

We integrated IHCS with prolog to create a HCLP($\mathcal{FD}, \mathcal{LPB}$) language, using pre-processing methods. At present we are employing YAP prolog running on a NeXT Station 68040.

In this section we describe two problems with our HCLP language, namely a set-covering problem and a time-tabling problem, to illustrate the applicability and declarativity of hierarchical constraints and the efficiency of our incremental approach to solve them.

In the set-covering problem, the goal is to minimize the number of services required to cover a set of needs (the problem variables designated by $X_1, \ldots, X_m$). Each variable ranges over the set of services that cover that need. The approach that we took to solve this problem is depicted in the following HCLP program:

$$cover([X_1, \ldots, X_m]) :-$$
$$X_1 = X_m \bigvee \cdots \bigvee X_1 = X_4 \bigvee X_1 = X_3 \bigvee X_1 = X_2 @ 1,$$
$$X_2 = X_m \bigvee \cdots \bigvee X_2 = X_4 \bigvee X_2 = X_3 @ 1,$$
$$X_3 = X_m \bigvee \cdots \bigvee X_3 = X_4 @ 1,$$
$$\vdots$$
$$X_{m-1} = X_m @ 1,$$
$$labeling([X_1, \ldots, X_m]).$$

For m needs, predicate *cover/1* states $m - 1$ disjunctive constraints of level 1. This set of constraints will try to ensure that the service assigned to variable X_i will also be assigned to at least some X_j, $j > i$. Predicate *labeling/1* simply uses the built-in predicate *indomain* to generate values for each variables. A best solution (one that relaxes the minimum of constraints as possible) will correspond to the minimization of services. Table 1 presents results obtained using several real life instances, taken from a Portuguese Bus company. The time presented concerns the first (best) solution found and column *Min* reports the minimum number of services required to cover the needs.

Table 1. Results for the set-covering problem

Needs	Services	Time	Min
13	43	0.33s	6
24	293	3.98s	7
38	67	3.57s	11

The time-tabling problem is taken from the experience in the Computer Science Department of UNL, but it is simplified so that no spatial constraints are considered (it is assumed that there are enough rooms) and each subject is already assigned to a teacher (c.f. [9] for a full description). For this problem we used a multi-level hierarchy to model preferences of different strength regarding the layout of sections of subjects in a time-table. Table 2 presents results for the generation of time-tables for three semesters. The first line reports the results obtained by specifying only required constraints (teachers availability, sections for the same subject at different days, non overlapping of classes for the same semester or given by the same teacher). Each of the other lines shows the effect of adding an extra hierarchical level.

Table 2. Results for the time-tabling problem

Max. level	Number of constraints	Time	Relaxed Constraints @1	@2	@3	@4
0	356	1.80s	(16)	(1)	(7)	(15)
1	+21 = 377	1.86s	2	(4)	(7)	(11)
2	+21 = 398	1.98s	2	1	(5)	(10)
3	+11 = 409	1.98s	2	1	1	(10)
4	+21 = 430	2.33s	2	1	1	0

Constraints in each level are designated to: level 1) avoid consecutive sections of a subject at consecutive days; level 2) avoid consecutive sections of a subject to be apart by more then two days; level 3) disallow any section from a subject with only two sections per week to take place on mondays; 4) place sections of the same subject at the same hour. The *Relaxed Constraints* columns report the number of preferred constraints relaxed in each level (in fact, values inside round brackets do not represent relaxed constraints, since that level was not being used, but rather the number of those that are not satisfied by the solution).

The introduction of the preferred constraints of each level, significantly increases the quality of the solution. The last one satisfies 95% of the preferences against only 47% satisfied by the first one with a mere slowdown penalty of 32%.

6 Conclusion

This paper reports the first formalization of IHCS, and some of its properties are already proven. Further work is still required however to formally prove its more general properties, namely a) soundness (only best solutions are obtained), b) completeness (all such solutions are computed), and c) non redundancy (no repeated solutions). Finally, although the experimental results obtained are quite promising with respect to its performance, the algorithm complexity (both in time and memory requirements) is yet to be fully assessed. On the other hand, we intend to exploit other criteria to specify acceptable solutions, other than the locally-predicate-better, which by removing its optimization nature might require less demanding constraint solvers.

Acknowledgments

This work was started at INRIA/Rocquencourt and at the AI Centre of UNI-NOVA and was funded by Délégation aux Affaires Internationales (DAI) and Junta Nacional de Investigação Científica e Tecnológica (JNICT), as part of a Réseaux-Formation-Recherche Franco-Portugais between the Institute Nationale the Recherche en Informatique et Automatique (INRIA) and the Universidade Nova de Lisboa(UNL). We thank Philippe Codognet for all the helpful suggestions and discussions. At present the work is being supported by JNICT, under project PBIC/C/TIT/1242/92.

References

1. P. Barahona and R. Ribeiro. Building an Expert Decision Support System: The Integration of AI and OR methods. In Martin Schader and Wolfgang Gaul, editors, *Knowledge, Data and Computer-Assisted Decisions*, chapter 3, pages 155–168. Springer-Verlag, Berlin Heidelberg, 1990.

2. A. Borning, M. Maher, A. Martingale, and M. Wilson. Constraints hierarchies and logic programming. In Levi and Martelli, editors, *Logic Programming: Proceedings of the 6th International Conference*, pages 149–164, Lisbon, Portugal, June 1989. The MIT Press.

3. C. Codognet and P. Codognet. Non-deterministic Stream AND-Parallelism based on Intelligent Backtracking. In *Proceedings of 6th ICLP*, Lisbon, 1989. The MIT press.

4. C. Codognet, P. Codognet, and G. Filé. Yet Another Intelligent Backtracking Method. In *Proceedings of 5th ICLP/SLP*, Seattle, 1988.

5. William S. Havens. Intelligent Backtracking in the Echidna Constraint Logic Programming System. Research Report CSS-IS TR 92-12, Simon Fraser University, Canada, 1992.

6. Vipin Kumar. Algorithms for Constraint-Satisfaction-Problems: A Survey. *AI Magazine*, pages 32–44, Spring 1992.

7. Alan K. Mackworth. Consistency in Networks of Relations. *Artificial Intelligence*, 8:99–118, 1977.

8. F. Menezes and P. Barahona. Report on IHCS. Research report, Universidade Nova de Lisboa, 1993.

9. F. Menezes, P. Barahona, and P. Codognet. An Incremental Hierarchical Constraint Solver Applied to a Time-tabling Problem. In *Proceedings of Avignon 93*, May 1993.

10. Luis Moniz Pereira and M. Bruynooghe. Deduction Revision by Intelligent Backtracking. In *Implementations of Prolog*, pages 194–215. J.A. Campbell, 1984.

11. P. Van Hentenryck, Y. Deville, and C.-M. Teng. A Generic Arc Consistency Algorithm and its Specializations. Technical Report RR 91-22, K.U. Leuven, F.S.A., December 1991.

12. M. Wilson and A. Borning. Extending Hierarchical Constraint Logic Programming: Nonmonotonocity and Inter-Hierarchy Comparison. In *Proceedings of the North American Conference 1989*, 1989.

Fast Methods for Solving Linear Diophantine Equations

Miguel Filgueiras and Ana Paula Tomás

LIACC, Universidade do Porto, R. do Campo Alegre 823, 4100 Porto, Portugal
email: mig@ncc.up.pt, apt@ncc.up.pt

Abstract. We present some recent results from our research on methods for finding the minimal solutions to linear Diophantine equations over the naturals. We give an overview of a family of methods we developed and describe two of them, called Slopes algorithm and Rectangles algorithm. From empirical evidence obtained by directly comparing our methods with others, and which is partly presented here, we are convinced that ours are the fastest known to date when the equation coefficients are not too small (ie., greater than 2 or 3).

1 Introduction

We present some recent results from our research on methods for finding the minimal solutions to linear Diophantine equations over the naturals. Such methods will be useful in the implementation of programming languages or systems that solve constraints on the naturals or on finite domains, as well as in term rewriting systems, namely in unification algorithms of terms with associative-commutative function symbols (AC-unification).

We have developed a family of methods all based on the idea that the minimal solutions of an equation may be obtained by using very efficient algorithms that solve equations having a small number of unknowns in combination with an enumeration procedure for the values of the other unknowns. Previously we have reported on methods centered on solving equations on 3 unknowns (Tomás and Filgueiras, 1991a; Tomás and Filgueiras, 1991b; Filgueiras and Tomás, 1992a; Filgueiras and Tomás, 1992b). In this paper we give an overview of the family of methods and describe two of them, called Slopes Algorithm and Rectangles Algorithm. From empirical evidence obtained by directly comparing our methods with others we are convinced that ours are the fastest known to date when the equation coefficients are not too small (ie., greater than 2 or 3).

2 A Family of Methods

Several algorithms have been put forth to find the basis of non-negative solutions to linear Diophantine equations or systems of such equations. The oldest method we know of is due to Elliott (1903) in the context of Number Theory. With the exception of Elliott's and of our methods, all others emerged from work on AC-unification algorithms — see (Domenjoud, 1991) for an overview. The one by Huet (1978) uses lexicographic enumeration (a technique originating from dynamic programming) of values for the unknowns and filters out non-minimal solutions by comparison with the minimal solutions already obtained. Our family of methods may be seen as a refinement of Huet's algorithm: instead of enumerating values for all the unknowns we choose a small number of them (tipically 3 or 4) and use enumeration[1] for the other unknowns. For each valuation of the enumerated unknowns we have to solve an equation in a small number of unknowns and this can be done very efficiently. Moreover, we use some solutions to obtain finer bounds for the unknowns than those proposed by Huet (1978) and Lambert (1987).

In more formal terms let us consider the Equation (1).

$$\sum_i^N a_i \cdot x_i = \sum_j^M b_j \cdot y_j \qquad a_i, b_j, x_i, y_j \in \mathbb{N} \qquad (1)$$

By selecting, for instance, x_1, y_1, and y_2 we get

$$a_1 \cdot x_1 + \sum_2^N a_i \cdot x_i = b_1 \cdot y_1 + b_2 \cdot y_2 + \sum_3^M b_j \cdot y_j$$

which, for each particular valuation of the unknowns in the sums, can be written as

$$a \cdot x = b \cdot y + c \cdot z + v \qquad v \in \mathbb{Z} \qquad (2)$$

to which very fast methods can be applied.

The methods in the family differ in the number of selected unknowns and/or in the algorithms used for solving the reduced equations.

The problem of solving (1) is split into several sub-problems according to the number and pattern of non-null unknowns. We define the *order* of a sub-problem as being the number of non-null unknowns in it. We first solve all order 2 sub-problems, then all the problems with only one non-null unknown in one side of the equation and this in increasing order, and finally all the others in increasing order. In this way and by using a suitable enumeration procedure minimal solutions are generated incrementally: a candidate solution may be accepted as minimal if it is not greater than a minimal solution already obtained. The fact that the solutions of sub-problems of the same order for different patterns of non-null unknowns are never comparable may be used for a highly parallel implementation (although the implementations we have are sequential).

The enumeration of values for the unknowns is controlled by the bounds described in (Huet, 1978; Lambert, 1987), and also by bounds dynamically determined from *quasi-Boolean* solutions, ie., solutions whose non-null unknowns all but one have value 1. On the other hand, solutions whose non-null unknowns are all 1 (*Boolean* solutions) are used to avoid dealing with sub-problems for which no minimal solution will be generated. Furthermore, in the Rectangles

---

[1] Not a lexicographic enumeration, see Section 5.

Algorithm not only Boolean and quasi-Boolean solutions but all the solutions computed so far are used to dynamically derive bounds.

In the next sections the basic algorithms that are at the core of the Slopes Algorithm and the Rectangles Algorithm are presented.

3 The Basic Slopes Algorithm

The Basic Slopes Algorithm, which solves directly Equation (2) for $v \geq 0$, is an improvement of the basic Congruence-Based Algorithm — CBA for short (Tomás and Filgueiras, 1991a). It results from the identification of all possible *minimal spacings*[2] which is a consequence of the following theorem.

Theorem 1. *Let $s_2 = (y_k, z_k)$ and $s_1 = (y_k + dy_k, z_k - dz_k)$ be two minimal solutions of (2), with $v = 0$, such that $0 < y_k < dy_k$ and there is no minimal solution with y-component in $]y_k, y_k + dy_k[$. Then, taking $F_k = \lceil dy_k/y_k \rceil$, the minimal solution with maximum y-component less than y_k is*

$$(y', z') = (F_k \cdot y_k - dy_k, F_k \cdot z_k + dz_k)$$

No superfluous (ie., non-minimal) candidate solution is generated. The algorithm starts from the two minimal solutions $(y_{max}, 0)$, $(y_{max} - dy_1, dz_1)$, where (Tomás and Filgueiras, 1991b) $y_{max} = a/\gcd(a, b)$, the *minimum spacing* (which depends only on a, b, and c) is

$$dy_1 = (m_b \cdot \frac{c}{\gcd(a, b, c)}) \bmod y_{max} \qquad dz_1 = \frac{\gcd(a, b)}{\gcd(a, b, c)}$$

and m_b is an integer such that $\gcd(a, b) = m_a \cdot a + m_b \cdot b$. The minimum slope line is followed until there is a (minimal) solution (y_1, z_1) with $y_1 < dy_1$. Theorem 1 can then be applied resulting a new minimal solution (y'_1, z'_1) which, together with (y_1, z_1), defines a new spacing for minimal solutions and a new slope. The same procedure is used for this pair and the new spacing. The algorithm stops when a minimal solution with null y-component is found.

When $v > 0$ the starting solution is given by the following formula[3]

$$z_0 = \frac{-v \cdot M_c}{\gcd(a, b, c)} \bmod dz_1 \qquad y_0 = \frac{(-v - z_0 \cdot c) \cdot m_b}{\gcd(a, b)} \bmod y_{max}$$

where $b \cdot M_b + c \cdot M_c + a \cdot M_a = \gcd(a, b, c)$ and y_{max} and m_b are defined as above (Tomás and Filgueiras, 1991b). Now the problem is to find the minimal spacing to be applied next.

From CBA we have that any minimal spacing is of the form

$$(dy_1 \cdot k - y_{max} \cdot t, k \cdot dz_1)$$

----

[2] A minimal spacing is the difference between two consecutive (in y-decreasing order) minimal solutions of (2), $v \geq 0$.

[3] $\gcd(a, b, c)$ divides v, otherwise no solution exists.

with minimum k. So, when starting from a minimal solution with $y = y_s$ the minimal spacing is the solution of the *inequality problem*: minimize k, subject to $0 < k \leq y_{max}$, $0 < y_s < y_{max}$, and

$$dy_1 \cdot k < y_s \quad (\text{mod } y_{max}) \tag{3}$$

in the sense of $0 \leq dy_1 \cdot k - y_{max} \cdot t < y_s$, for some $t \geq 0$ with $k > 0$, $y_s > 0$ and *min* t, k. This can be written as $y_{max} \cdot t \leq dy_1 \cdot k < y_s + y_{max} \cdot t$. The question turns out to be that of finding just one multiple of dy_1 in the interval. The problem may be solved by using congruences: find the set of minimal solutions of

$$(y_{max} \bmod dy_1) \cdot t + y_s \equiv 0 \quad (\text{mod } dy_1)$$

or, equivalently, find the set of minimal solutions of

$$dy_1 \cdot k - y_s \equiv 0 \quad (\text{mod } y_{max}) \tag{4}$$

Equation (4) is equivalent to $dy_1 \cdot k + (y_{max} - 1) \cdot y_s \equiv 0 \quad (\text{mod } y_{max})$, and its solution set can be obtained by Theorem 1 in decreasing y-component order. If (k_i, y_i) is the ith solution in the set, then k_i solves (3) for $y_i < y_s \leq y_{i-1}$.

Since $dy_1 \cdot k_i \equiv y_i \quad (\text{mod } y_{max})$, the spacing sought is $(-y_i, dz_1 \cdot k_i)$. An implementation detail that is worth noting is that we are interested in solving a family of problems like that of Equation (2) only differing in v. They determine the same inequality problem, which we solve only once.

The method for solving Equation (2) with $v < 0$ is the same as in CBA until a minimal solution with $y < y_{max}$ is found, after what the above method is applied.

4 The Basic Rectangles Algorithm

This new algorithm results from an effort to speed up the enumeration procedure and the tests for minimality. The idea is to solve (5)

$$a \cdot x = b \cdot y + c \cdot z + d \cdot w + v, \quad v \geq 0 \tag{5}$$

by taking x and w as dependent unknowns and selecting dynamically either y or z as a free unknown to have its values enumerated. Which of y or z is selected depends on a worst-case estimation of the number of values remaining to be given.

Suppose that z was the one selected, and that the search space was

$$]y_0, y_M[\times]z_0, z_M[\times]w_0, w_M[\ .$$

For a given value z_1 an equation in 3 unknowns is solved as in the Slopes Algorithm and minimal solutions are computed in w-decreasing order, with $y_0 < y < y_M$. Any solution (not minimal) with $w \leq w_0$ establishes a new proper upper bound y_M^1 for y, and may narrow substantially the search space rectangle. In this case, the choice of the free variable is reviewed, but now for a smaller rectangle $]y_0, y_{\mathrm{M}}^1[\times]z_1, z_{\mathrm{M}}[$.

In order to shorten the search, this new algorithm makes a better use of the minimal solutions computed at each step, and takes advantage of the empirical evidence that minimal solutions occur close to the axes. One of the main ideas has been that of identifying what minimal solutions are relevant in rejecting candidate solutions, and what upper bounds, for the values of y, z, and w, they introduce.

Relevant solutions are kept in an ordered list, so-called *filter*, that is updated whenever a minimal solution is found. Actually, not one but two filters are kept because of the possible selection of either y or z as free variables. During the process, filters are adjusted to the current rectangle, providing a dynamical upper bound for w. When this upper bound becomes w_0 or less, the search is stopped. Also, as filters are kept ordered, only a small segment of the active filter must actually be used to test each candidate.

The Rectangles Algorithm generates much less candidate solutions that are not minimal, and is to some extent less sensitive to the order of coefficients than the Slopes Algorithm. Obviously, it is not symmetric since dynamic selection of the free variable only applies to z and y. Proof of completeness of this method follows trivially from the completeness of the Slopes Algorithm.

5 Implementation

For a fast access to the information concerning Boolean solutions and for speeding up the comparison between minimal solutions and candidates, we attach to each configuration of non-zero components a bit mask. Each minimal solution is stored along with the mask for the current subproblem. We keep track (in a lazy way) of the minimal solutions having a mask compatible with the current one, in order not to loose time searching for them.

The enumeration algorithm implemented is iterative and increases the value of one unknown at a time, until this value reaches its upper bound. Components are incremented from right to left, and the algorithm ensures that the values of the unknowns placed to the right of the one being incremented are 1.

In the current implementation, the Rectangles Algorithm applies to Equation (1), when $N = 1$. The values of all but three unknowns in the right-hand side are enumerated. Bounds for this enumeration are derived from minimal solutions already computed. For each valuation, bounds for the other three unknowns are also derived and used in solving the subproblem of the type (5) associated to it. How to speed-up the derivation of bounds and the construction of filters has been a major concern of our research. We have tried out several approaches with distinct levels of lazy evaluation of bounds and filters. This was motivated by empirical evidence that many candidates are filtered out just by the bounds of the search space, and that normally, when changing a valuation by increasing the value of one unknown, a decrease in these bounds does not happen.

6 Comparisons

When presenting CBA (Tomás and Filgueiras, 1991a) we noted that it compared favourably, in terms of speed, with the algorithms of Huet and of Fortenbacher — described in (Guckenbiehl and Herold, 1985).

In this section we give some results of an extensive comparison of our new algorithms with CBA[4] and the algorithms by Elliott (1903) and by Clausen and Fortenbacher (1989). The latter was generally believed to be the fastest method available, according to the results of comparisons[5] in (Clausen and Fortenbacher, 1989). The results below show clearly that our methods are faster than the other two, and therefore, for the moment being, the fastest available when the problems to solve are not too small.

All the algorithms under comparison were implemented in the same language (C, using the standard Unix cc with optimization flag $-O$) and the same machine (an old Sun 3/60). Execution times in the Tables below are CPU-times obtained by making calls to the appropriate Unix system routines. For problems that take less than 1/100 of a minute, the computation of the solutions was repeated 100 times and the average CPU-time spent is given. The values shown are the lowest CPU-times obtained in at least 3 runs.

We have adopted a sample of about 45 equations for comparisons, and we choose for presentation an illustrative subset of that sample (cf. Table 1). The first seven equations were taken from (Guckenbiehl and Herold, 1985), while the last four show the behaviour of the algorithms when the coefficients are larger. Note that the size of the problems was kept relatively small because of the inefficiency of the algorithms we are running. Larger problems will be treated when comparing our own algorithms between them.

Table 1. Equations used in the benchmarks.

	Coefficients	Min. sols.
E1	(2 1)(1 1 1 2 2)	13
E2	(2 1)(1 1 2 10)	13
E3	(9 5 2)(3 7 8)	65
E4	(9 5 2)(1 2 3 7 8)	119
E5	(3 3 3 2 2 2)(2 2 2 3 3 3)	138
E6	(8 7 3 2 1)(1 2 2 5 9)	345
E7	(10 2 1)(1 1 1 2 2)	349
E8	(653)(235 784 212)	37
E9	(29 13 8)(42 15 22)	133
E10	(29 13 8)(44 14 23)	216
E11	(23 21 15)(19 17 12 11)	303

---

[4] More specifically, CBA-V5, Slopes-V5i, Rect-LS1, and Rect-LG.

[5] With algorithms by Huet (but improved with the bounds of Lambert), by Fortenbacher, and by Lankford.

We start by comparing the Slopes algorithm with the algorithm by Elliott which we implemented from scratch[6]. From the basic implementation an enhanced one was made by introducing filtering by Boolean solutions and taking advantage of the fact (noticed by Eric Domenjoud — personal communication, 1992) that about one third of the work done by the algorithm is superfluous. The results of the comparison are in Table 2. We have also implemented the version for solving systems of equations and compared it with recent methods for solving systems of equations — those of (Domenjoud, 1991; Boudet *et al.*, 1990) — with favourable results for the latter. The details of these comparisons may be found in (Filgueiras and Tomás, 1992c).

Table 2. Timing (ms) Slopes and Elliott algorithms.

Eq.	Slopes	Elliott basic	Elliott enhanced	Ell.(enh.) /Slopes
E1	3.5	18.7	1.7	0.5
E2	2.8	34.8	6.5	2.3
E3	17.7	1216.7	350.0	19.8
E4	44.3	8.4e3	1.6e3	36.1
E5	133.3	36.2e3	7.0e3	52.5
E6	200.0	431.8e3	60.7e3	303.5
E7	166.7	247.2e3	54.6e3	327.5
E8	16.7	19.7e3	1.5e3	89.8
E9	50.0	14.7e3	2.6e3	52.0
E10	533.3	75.3e3	15.9e3	29.8
E11	450.0	0.50e6	0.11e6	244.4

In order to compare the algorithm of Clausen and Fortenbacher we translated the Pascal program given in their paper to C and changed the graph initialization procedure so that the maximum coefficient in the equation being solved is taken into account. The results of a direct comparison with the Slopes algorithm are illustrated in Table 3. The conclusion is that our method is faster when the maximum coefficient is greater than about 3.

Finally we compare our algorithms between them. For the Rectangles algorithm we present the results for two of its implementations named Rect-LS1 and Rect-LG, the latter determining finer bounds for all unknowns. For the previous set of equations we get the results in Table 4. We may conclude that there is no major difference for small problems, although Slopes is faster than CBA when the coefficients increase, and the Rectangles algorithm beats by large the other two when solving equation E8, for obvious reasons.

---

[6] Using the descriptions in (Elliott, 1903; MacMahon, 1918; Stanley, 1973) — the latter however has some errors in its description and a wrong termination proof; see (Filgueiras and Tomás, 1992c).

Table 3. Timing (ms) Slopes and Clausen & Fortenbacher algorithms.

Eq.	Slopes	CF	CF/Slopes
E1	3.5	2.5	0.7
E2	2.8	11.0	3.9
E3	17.7	49.0	2.8
E4	44.3	300.0	6.8
E5	133.3	50.0	0.4
E6	200.0	1.55e3	7.8
E7	166.7	516.7	3.1
E8	16.7	1.75e3	104.8
E9	50.0	500.0	10.0
E10	533.3	1.02e3	1.9
E11	450.0	2.13e3	4.7

Table 4. Timing (ms) CBA, Slopes, Rect-LS1 and Rect-LG.

Eq.	CBA	Slopes	R-LS1	R-LG
E1	3.7	3.5	3.5	3.7
E2	2.7	2.8	3.0	3.0
E3	17.2	17.7	16.7	16.7
E4	42.5	44.3	33.3	33.3
E5	133.3	133.3	133.3	150.0
E6	233.3	200.0	233.3	283.3
E7	216.7	166.7	133.3	150.0
E8	33.3	16.7	7.0	7.0
E9	66.7	50.0	66.7	33.3
E10	583.3	533.3	550.0	766.7
E11	516.7	450.0	466.7	433.3

The differences between the algorithms become more visible for larger problems, as those in Table 5 for which we obtained the results in Table 6.

When there are many coefficients not too different (first two examples) Slopes appears to be faster than the other methods. In the next three examples one of the coefficients is much larger than the others, and the Rectangles algorithm is faster. The last three examples (equations with a single left-hand side coefficient and three on the left-hand) show the behaviour of the algorithms when the size of the left-hand side coefficient increases. The Rectangles algorithm is clearly better.

7 Conclusions

The results presented in the previous section clearly show that our methods are faster than the other methods available. This claim may be not true however when the coefficients are too small (2 or 3).

Table 5. A set of larger problems.

	Coefficients	Min. sols.
L1	(15 14 13 12 11)(11 11 12 13 14)	1093
L2	(25 24 23 21)(21 21 22 23)	3167
L3	(5021)(9 13 19)	5759
L4	(3229 95)(9 13 19)	2473
L5	(753 57)(9 11 13 19)	3337
L6	(653)(122 200 235)	53
L7	(1653)(122 200 235)	75
L8	(11653)(122 200 235)	151

Table 6. Timing (ms) the larger problems.

Eq.	CBA	Slopes	R-LS1	R-LG
L1	2.97e3	1.52e3	1.65e3	1.80e3
L2	27.72e3	17.85e3	19.62e3	32.00e3
L3	0.56e6	0.48e6	950.0	950.0
L4	49.78e3	42.42e3	1.78e3	516.7
L5	49.28e3	43.83e3	12.56e3	11.65e3
L6	33.3	16.7	10.2	10.5
L7	133.3	66.7	17.2	17.3
L8	12.38e3	1.87e3	33.3	33.3

From the work done so far there are some directions of research that appear as promising. One of them has to do with introducing more laziness in the evaluation of bounds. Another concerns extensions of the basic Rectangles algorithm for equations with two unknowns in each side and with more than four unknowns.

Other points that we will address in the near future are:

1. the possible application of the ideas underlying our methods in obtaining methods for solving systems. A method for solving systems under particular forms has been already designed and will be implemented soon,
2. further study of the Elliott algorithm which has a simple formulation and seems to have potentialities not yet explored,
3. integration of our methods in Constraint Logic Programming systems dealing with finite domains and naturals.

References

Boudet, A., Contejean E., and Devie, H.: A new *AC* Unification algorithm with an algorithm for solving systems of Diophantine equations. In Proceedings of the 5th Conference on Logic and Computer Science, IEEE, 289–299, 1990.

Clausen, M., and Fortenbacher, A.: Efficient solution of linear Diophantine equations. *J. Symbolic Computation*, 8, 201–216, 1989.

Domenjoud, E.: *Outils pour la Déduction Automatique dans les Théories Associatives-Commutatives*. Thése de doctorat, Université de Nancy I, 1991.

Elliott, E. B.: On linear homogenous Diophantine equations. *Quart. J. Pure Appl. Math.*, 34, 348–377, 1903.

Filgueiras, M. and Tomás, A. P.: A Congruence-based Method with Slope Information for Solving Linear Constraints over Natural Numbers. Presented at the Workshop on Constraint Logic Programming '92, Marseille. Also as internal report, Centro de Informática da Universidade do Porto, 1992a.

Filgueiras, M. and Tomás, A. P.: Solving Linear Diophantine Equations: The Slopes Algorithm. Centro de Informática da Universidade do Porto, 1992b.

Filgueiras, M. and Tomás, A. P.: A Note on the Implementation of the MacMahon-Elliott Algorithm. Centro de Informática da Universidade do Porto, 1992c.

Guckenbiehl, T. and Herold, A.: Solving Linear Diophantine Equations. Memo SEKI-85-IV-KL, Universität Kaiserslautern, 1985.

Huet, G.: An algorithm to generate the basis of solutions to homogeneous linear Diophantine equations. *Information Processing Letters*, 7(3), 1978.

Lambert, J.-L.: Une borne pour les générateurs des solutions entières positives d'une équation diophantienne linéaire. *Comptes Rendus de l'Académie des Sciences de Paris*, t. 305, série I, 39–40, 1987.

MacMahon, P.: *Combinatory Analysis*, 2. Chelsea Publishing Co., 1918.

Stanley, R.: Linear homogeneous Diophantine equations and magic labelings of graphs. *Duke Math. J.*, 40, 607–632, 1973.

Tomás, A. P. and Filgueiras, M.: A new method for solving linear constraints on the natural numbers. In P. Barahona, L. Moniz Pereira, A. Porto (eds.), *Proceedings of the 5th Portuguese Conference on Artificial Intelligence*, Lecture Notes in Artificial Intelligence 541, Springer-Verlag, 30–44, 1991a.

Tomás, A. P. and Filgueiras, M.: A Congruence-based Method for Finding the Basis of Solutions to Linear Diophantine Equations. Centro de Informática da Universidade do Porto, 1991b.

A Note on Chapman's Modal Truth Criterion

Maria Fox and Derek Long*

Department of Computer Science, University College London, Gower Street, London

Abstract. The formal statement of the Modal Truth Criterion presented by Chapman [1] is shown not to be necessary, in contradiction of Chapman's original claim that the criterion is both necessary and sufficient. This is achieved through the presentation of a counter-example which is a partial plan in which a goal is necessarily true, and yet fails to satisfy Chapman's criterion. A corollary of this result is that the validity-checking problem for partial plans, claimed by Chapman to be polynomially solvable, is now open.

1 Chapman's Modal Truth Criterion for Non-Linear Planners

David Chapman (1987) was the first researcher in planning to make a formal statement of the truth criterion for non-linear planners. The truth criterion is expressed in modal logic to capture the constraint-posting behaviour of non-linear planners.

The English statement of the criterion is complex, and it is tempting when articulating it to move the modalities in a way that makes ambiguous their actual positions in the formal criterion. This can lead to misinterpretations of the criterion. As is demonstrated in this paper, a close examination of the formal statement reveals an interpretation that is not completely consistent with the one Chapman intended.

Given a partial plan P, his criterion states that a proposition p is necessarily asserted in a state s if it was necessarily asserted in a state t necessarily prior to s in P and, considering each step c in P in turn, either c is necessarily too late in the partial order on steps to deny p before s or for any q that c possibly denies q necessarily does not codesignate with p or, if p was denied in a state d between t and s in P, it is reasserted by a "whiteknight" step w necessarily between d and s. This is formally stated by Chapman as follows:

A proposition p is necessarily asserted in a state s iff

$$
\begin{aligned}
&\exists t \cdot \Box t \preceq s \wedge \Box asserted\_in(p, t) \wedge \\
&(\forall c \cdot \Box s \preceq c \vee \\
&\quad (\forall q \cdot \Box \neg denies(c, q) \vee \Box(q \not\approx p) \vee \\
&\quad\quad (\exists w \cdot \Box c \prec w \wedge \\
&\quad\quad\quad \Box w \prec s \wedge \\
&\quad\quad\quad \exists r \cdot asserts(w, r) \wedge (p \approx q \rightarrow p \approx r))))
\end{aligned}
$$

---

[1] The authors are equally responsible for the work described in this paper.

Chapman claims in his 1987 paper that this criterion is necessary and sufficient for determining the validity of an arbitrary partial plan. Furthermore, he claims that since the presence or absence of a constraint in the plan being considered determines whether the plan is necessarily valid, and the constraints can be checked for in polynomial time, the validity of an arbitrary plan can be checked in polynomial time. The identification of the validity-checking problem for plans as polynomially solvable has been hailed as one of the significant contributions of Chapman's paper.

The complexity argument presented by Chapman depends on the positioning of the modalities in his criterion. Chapman's paper does not provide any framework for the interpretation of the modalities, so the following assumptions are used in this paper:

1. Possible worlds in the context of planning are totally ordered and instantiated sequences of actions. These are referred to as *completions*. They are accessible via sequences of constraint additions. Given a partial plan P, a proposition p is *necessarily* asserted in a state s if p is asserted in s in every completion of P and *possibly* asserted in s if p is asserted in s in some completion of P.
2. Chapman intended his criterion to be interpreted in the framework of K modal logic. This is the minimal modal extension to classical logic.

On the basis of these assumptions the criterion as stated is read in the following way:

The proposition p is necessarily asserted in s iff there is some state t that can be identified in the current plan (because the existential is outside the scope of the modality) such that, in all completions t has p asserted in it and t is before s and, considering each step c in the plan in turn, either :

1. c is after s in every completion, or
2. c does not deny any q in any completion, or
3. no q that c denies codesignates with p in any completion,

or there is a whiteknight to reachieve p between c and s.

Considering points 1-3 which express the first three disjuncts of the third conjunct of the criterion (these three disjuncts can be referred to as the "clobberer clause" of the criterion), it is seen that, because of the positioning of the modalities, one or other condition must be true in all completions of the current plan (ie: either c is out of range in all completions or c denies no q in all completions or q is bound to be distinct from p in all completions) if there is to be no denying step before s. This condition is too strong since provided that, in all completions, either c is out of range or does not deny any q that could codesignate with p, there is no clobbering step.

In placing the modalities as he has, Chapman has treated as equivalent the modal sentences $\Box a \vee \Box b \vee \Box c$ and $\Box(a \vee b \vee c)$. Since they are not equivalent the criterion does not express what Chapman intended.

2   A Counter-Example

The effect of the incorrect placing of the modalities is that Chapman's criterion rejects as invalid plans that are actually valid. All the plans it accepts as valid are indeed valid, so the criterion is sufficient. However, it is not necessary as claimed. The following counter-example demonstrates this.

Consider the following operators:

Puton(X,Y)
Pre: clear(Y)
     holding(X)
Add:on(X,Y)
     handempty
Del: clear(Y)
     holding(X)

Pickup(X)
Pre: clear(X)
     handempty
     on(X,Y)
Add:holding(X)
     clear(Y)
Del: on(X,Y)
     handempty

and the partial plan:

$$pickup(Z) \rightarrow puton(a, X) \rightarrow pickup(Y)$$

where $\rightarrow$ indicates a total ordering on the four operators. Assume there is a binding constraint $(clear(X) \not\approx clear(Y))$ and that a further binding constraint ensures that Z is on Y at the start of the plan so that $clear(Y)$ is asserted after application of the first operator. If the plan consisting of these operators and constraints is presented to the criterion it will reject the plan as invalid because the criterion cannot recognise that $clear(Y)$ is necessarily asserted at $pickup(Y)$.

In the above partial plan there is a state, the output state of $pickup(Z)$, in which $clear(Y)$ is asserted and this state is before the input state of $pickup(Y)$. Considering each other operator in the plan, either it must be after $pickup(Y)$ in every completion (no operator can come between the input state of a step and that step) or it must deny no proposition q in any completion or no q that it denies can codesignate with $clear(Y)$ in any completion. If some operator fails to meet any of these conditions then there must be a whiteknight to reachieve $clear(Y)$ before $pickup(Y)$.

In this plan $puton(a, X)$ is necessarily before $pickup(Y)$. The clobberer clause quantifies over all conditions q, so conditions 2 and 3 must be true for $q = clear(b)$ (for some constant b) in particular. The clause states that either $puton(a, X)$ does not deny $clear(b)$ in any completion or $clear(b)$ does not codesignate with $clear(Y)$ in any completion. The whiteknight clause can be ignored since there is no operator between $puton(a, X)$ and $pickup(Y)$ that could serve. Although the criterion requires that one of the remaining two conditions (2 or 3) be true there are some completions in which $puton(a, X)$ does deny $clear(b)$, where X is bound to b and Y is bound to some other constant and some in which $puton(a, X)$ does not deny $clear(b)$, where Y is bound to b and X is bound to some other constant. So $clear(Y)$ is asserted at $pickup(Y)$ in every completion (so necessarily asserted at $pickup(Y)$) but Chapman's criterion rejects the plan as invalid.

The problem is that the modalities in the disjunct:

$$\Box(\neg denies(puton(a, X), clear(b))) \vee \Box(clear(b) \not\approx clear(Y))$$

require that one or other condition be true in all completions. The modality can be moved outside the disjunction to weaken and therefore correct the clobberer clause.

The modalities in Chapman's original criterion can be rearranged to yield a necessary and sufficient criterion (the proofs are all provided in [2]). However, since Chapman's complexity argument rests on the positioning of the modalities in his statement their repositioning leaves open the status of the validity-checking problem for partial plans.

References

1. Chapman, D.: Planning for conjunctive goals. Artificial Intelligence **29** (1987) 333–377
2. Fox, M., Long, D.: A re-examination of the modal truth criterion for non-linear planners. Research Note, University College London, (1992).

Learning Operators While Planning

José L. S. Ferreira
zeluis@alma.uc.pt

Ernesto J. F. Costa
ernesto@mercurio.uc.pt

Laboratório de Informática e Sistemas, Univ. Coimbra
Quinta da Boavista, Lote 1, 1º
3000 Coimbra
Tel: + (351) 39 701775
fax: + (351) 39 701266

Abstract. Machine Learning has been used by a number of planning systems, allowing to learn macro operators and plan schemata. Most previous research, however, has not addressed the aspect of learning the operators for the planners to apply. We present a first version of PLOP, Planning and Learning OPerators, a system that acquires operators by interacting with a user while planning. Empirical results seem to suggest that this is a promising and useful use of learning systems in the context of planning. We present the first results of our work and discuss future goals of this research.

Keywords: Learning, Planning.

1 Introduction

Machine Learning systems have been built that learn macro operators [Korf 85, Laird et al 86, Mooney 88, Shell et al 89], plan schemata [Minton 85], i.e. general combinations of actions that when executed will achieve a pre-defined goal, or a domain theory [Gil 91].

The purpose of our research is to learn in the context of planning, but in a rather different way. To build a plan, any system needs to know what actions can be executed. This knowledge is described by means of operators, which are assumed to be known for any planning system.

Acquiring the operators is however, as for any knowledge intensive system, a complex and time consuming task. The purpose of our system is to learn the operators while planning, by an intelligent interaction with the user.

This paper describes a first version of PLOP, a system that learns operators while planning.

This is a very early version, but we are interested in pursuing this research, considering the satisfactory results we have already achieved.

In the following section, we describe some aspects of our approach that have to be taken in consideration to describe the system's operation. Next, we describe the algorithm used by PLOP. We then present some considerations on the learning phase. We conclude with a session with our system and some comments about the results and the future trends in this research.

2 The Learning Task

Planning systems are based on the capabilities of predicting the result of acting over a given environment. In order to deal with the execution of an action and predict its effects, actions are described by means of operators. Operators contain the action description and knowledge about how the action is performed and how it interacts with the world. The preconditions that have to hold so that the action can be executed, and the effects of executing it in a given state of the world are some of the knowledge an operator has to include.

When planning, it is assumed that the operators are known and error free, and that the system will find a plan, if such exists. Most planning systems also assume that any changes in the world are due to the application of the operators.

In our approach, we suppose that there are not enough operators and the known ones may be incorrectly defined. We maintain the assumption that any changes occuring in the world are only due to the execution of the actions known by the planner.

Our purpose is to learn correct descriptions of the needed operators, based in the interaction with an expert that supervises the execution of a plan. The user defines the initial and desired states of the world and he then guides the system, supervising the plan proposed by the system and proposing whatever actions have to be performed at each moment in order to achieve the final state.

For the moment, learning is explanation-based [Mitchell et al 86, Dejong et al 86] and inductive. It is our purpose to add analogy-based learning soon.

3 Representation

3.1 State Description

A world description, normally referred to as state, is a conjunction of predicates that are true in the world. We do not have negated predicates describing a state, such as BlockA is NOT FREE. The initial and intermediate states have to be completely described. The final state may be described by just what is really important to be achieved. For example, in the description of a final state it is accepted that (ON BlockA BlockB)(ON BlockB BlockC) can be a description of a three blocks stack. (FREE BlockA) is true, but it is not necessarily stated.

3.2 Operator's Description

We have tried to establish a description for the operators that could contain context dependent information, to guarantee that all changes in the world could be predicted by the operator's description. As a result, we divide the operator's conditions and effects into two separate sets.

There are two kinds of conditions:

-Those that have to be true in order to apply the operator, called conditions;
-Those that don't have to be true when applying one operator, but if verified, will reflect on the operator's results, called side-conditions.

Accordingly, there are two types of effects in the operator's description:

- Those that always occur when the operator applies, resulting from the operator's conditions, and known as post-conditions;
- Those that can occur when the operator applies, resulting from the side-conditions, provided they are verified and hereafter referred to as side-effects.

Let us think of the operator STACK. To stack one block on top of another, both have to be free (nothing on top of them). As a result, only one of them remains free, and they will be stacked. If, and only if, the block to be moved is on top of another just before it is moved, the one under it will become free as a result. Otherwise, nothing happens, but the operator is still applicable. Being on top of another block is context information when applying the operator.

Therefore, one operator will be described as:

ACTION: (action-name $\{obj\}^+$)
CONDITIONS: $\{(attr \{obj\}^+)\}^+$
SIDE-CONDITIONS: $\{(attr \{obj\}^+)\}^*$
POST-CONDITIONS: $\{(attr \{obj\}^+) \mid (NOT (attr \{obj\}^+))\}^+$
SIDE-EFFECTS: $\{(attr \{obj\}^+) \mid (NOT (attr \{obj\}^+))\}^*$

Where $\{X\}^*$ means any occurrence of X, $\{X\}^+$ means at least one occurrence of X, $\{X \mid Y\}$ means that X or Y can occur, attr is any attribute descriptor and obj is any object descriptor.

Negation is used to describe the changes in the world made by an operator. If the application of a given operator will make an attribute Ai of the world untrue, we state it by adding (NOT Ai) to the operator's post conditions. This is a different way of representing the ADD and DELETE lists of STRIPS [Fikes et al 72] like operators.

The operator STACK, for example, can be described as:

ACTION: (STACK x y)
CONDITIONS:
      (FREE x)
      (FREE y)
SIDE-CONDITIONS:
      (ON x z)
POST-CONDITIONS:
      (ON x y)
      (NOT (FREE y))
SIDE-EFFECTS:
      (NOT (ON x z))
      (FREE z)

It is assumed that the variables appearing in the description of one operator are universally quantified.

4. System Description

4.1 The Learning Algorithm

The learning algorithm is as follows:

```
PLOP (ACTUAL_ST, FINAL_ST)
begin
loop
   FIND_A_PLAN(ACTUAL_ST,FINAL_ST)
   if  there is a plan for this problem
      then propose it step by step;
          if the user accepts the whole plan
             then exitloop
             else ACTUAL_ST becomes the last accepted state;
                  ACTUAL_OP becomes the first one rejected;
                  specialize ACTUAL_OP so that it is not applicable to ACTUAL_ST
          endif
      else if there are any partial plans
          then propose them one by one and step by step, until one of
               them is accepted or there are no more partial plans;
             if some steps of a partial plan have been accepted
                then ACTUAL_ST becomes the state achieved at the end
                     of the accepted steps of this partial plan;
             endif endif endif
   ask for the action to be executed next;
   if an operator exists that should have been applied
      then ACTUAL_OP becomes the existing operator;
           generalize ACTUAL_OP so that it is applicable to ACTUAL_ST
      else initialize ACTUAL_OP with the action description;
           explain, why and what for, is this action applied;
           if such an explanation can not be found
              then ask for the effects of the action    ;;'what for' explanation
                   build an explanation with them;
           endif endif
   actualize ACTUAL_OP with this explanation;
   loop
      ACTUAL_ST is actualized by applying
      ACTUAL_OP to the current state;
      propose the resulting state to the user;
      if ACTUAL_ST is correctly defined
         then exitloop
         else ask for corrections to ACTUAL_ST;
              actualize ACTUAL_OP accordingly
      endif
   endloop
   save ACTUAL_OP
endloop
end
```

4.2 The Planner

We have implemented a simple planner, that essentially moves through a search space in a breadth first manner. Points in this search space are state descriptions of the world.

One must tell why this search is made blindly. This is due to several constraints imposed by the fact that we want to learn operators. First, we consider already known operators as potentially erroneous. This means that we can not trust in their correct application, which implies that any attempt to partially order the search space does not make sense.

Second, one may have insufficient knowledge to build the plan, only partial plans or, in the worst case, nothing at all. This can happen when there are not enough operators. What we can know at any moment is that some operators are applicable to some states, but we can't know if any of them is more promising than any other, since we don't know what operators are missing and their applicability conditions. For this reason, we do not consider ordering the search space. Of course, some ordering techniques, for example based in means ends analysis could be worthwhile try. For the moment, however, as we rely heavily on the teacher's capabilities of classifying the partial plans achieved, we do not have this kind of verification in progress.

5. Explanations

Step 2 of our algorithm involves finding explanations for the applicability of one particular operator whose action is known, but whose applicability conditions and effects are not. We have not mentioned the use of a domain theory, so one may ask whether there can be any explanation.

There may be situations in which some partial causal explanations can be found.

Let us look at one example. Suppose we are presented with the next very simple problem, described by one initial and one final state, and we are trying to find a plan that solves the problem.

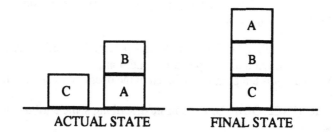

ACTUAL STATE   FINAL STATE

Let us also suppose that PLOP's knowledge base is empty. The user is asked for the action to be executed towards the goal. In this example, the first action in the plan is to stack block B on block C.

The system then knows that the operator STACK refers two objects, in this particular case B and C. Remind that we rely on the assumption that any changes occurring in the world when applying an operator are due to the operator's action.

What can there be in the desired final state that can justify the application of this operator? The fact that B is on top of C in the final situation, and that we are applying an operator that will make changes involving these two objects seems a promising explanation to its use.

Therefore, we will consider (ON B C) an explanation to the need of the operator's application and will include it in the post-conditions of the operator. The fact that both B and C have nothing on top, stated as being free, is also considered a cause or possibility condition for the applicability of the operator. These facts are included in the conditions of the operator. With this first partial description of our operator, PLOP presents the state that will be achieved if it is applied. It is then up to the user to correct the resulting proposed state. The system will then refine the operator, until the resulting state is accepted as correct. This interaction will hopefully also lead to the correct description of the operator.

An explanation is, therefore, a set of world descriptors that justify the execution of an action. This set of terms is included both in the operator's conditions and post-conditions.

Side-conditions are the world descriptors involving the objects not referred in the action description whose attributes are changed by the execution of the action. The refinement process will reorganize the conditions and post-conditions. Side-effects are always acquired by interaction with the user.

The following heuristic establishes what can be an explanation and how is it used in the operator's description:

Explanation Heuristic:

Let (ACTION OBJA) be the description of the operator's action, where ACTION is the action's name (e.g., MOVE, CLIMB), and OBJA is the non empty set of entities the action involves.

1- Let (PRED OBJP) be a predicate describing some attribute of the current state of the world, where PRED is the predicate's name and OBJP the non empty set of entities related by the predicate.

If OBJP $\cap$ OBJA $\neq \emptyset$, (PRED OBJP) is a potential cause, therefore condition, for the applicability of the operator;

-If OBJP $\subseteq$ OBJA, (PRED OBJP) is a potential condition for the action to be applied, so it is included in the operator's conditions;
-Otherwise it is temporarily included in the operator's side-conditions.

2- Likewise, let (PRED OBJP) be a predicate describing some attribute of the desired or final state.

-If OBJP $\subseteq$ OBJA, then (PRED OBJP), will be considered a potential post-condition;

Side-effects are not acquired by looking into the world's actual and final state.

This heuristic is the basis of finding explanations. Nevertheless, since the operator's initial description is most times incomplete, it will be revised whenever the interaction with the user indicates that the actual one is not correct or complete. It happens normally that some of the considered side-conditions will become conditions, others will be ignored. It can also happen that at the end of a session, there are no conditions in the operator's description, only side conditions. For the moment, in such cases all side conditions will be "promoted" to conditions. This will have to be further investigated. It is important to notice that the easiness of learning operators is strongly influenced by the description of actions, regarding the objects involved. However, the final description of the operator is hopefully the same. The less complete the action description is, more the learning depends on the user's answers. For example, suppose that one has to solve the problem described above, but there is a robot's hand to manipulate blocks. If picking block A with the robot's hand is written as (PICK A), that refers only the action's object, instead of (PICK H A), which is better described, since it contains the action's agent and object, the final operator will be the same, as described next, but the learning phase will be longer and more dependent on the user.

```
OPERATOR PICK:
ACTION: (PICK X)        ;; could be (PICK X H)
CONDITIONS:
        ((EMPTY H)
         (FREE X))
SIDE-CONDITIONS:
        ((ON X Y) )
POST-CONDITIONS:
        ((NOT (FREE X))
         (HOLDS H X)
         (NOT (EMPTY H)))
SIDE-EFFECTS:
        ((NOT (ON X Y))
         (FREE Y))
```

6 One Session with PLOP

A commented session with PLOP follows. In bold typeface we have put the answers given by the user to the system's questions. In italics, we have put our comments.
DESCRIBE THE INITIAL STATE:
((free a)(free c)(on a b)(empty h))
DESCRIBE THE FINAL STATE:
((on a b)(on b c)(free a)(empty h))
ACTUAL STATE: ((FREE A) (FREE C) (ON A B) (EMPTY H))
DESIRED STATE: ((ON A B) (ON B C) (FREE A) (EMPTY H))
WHAT MUST BE DONE NOW? **(pick a h)**

The first action to execute is to pick block A with the hand H.

I CAN'T EXPLAIN WHAT TO ACHIEVE WITH (PICK A H).
WHAT IS IT? **(holds h a)**

From the description of the problem, its initial and final state, it is be possible to derive the purpose of picking block A. Notice that, following the explanation

*heuristic, (EMPTY H) would be the only candidate, that is eliminated because it is
already true in the initial state. The actual conditions of the operator are (FREE A)
and (EMPTY H). As side-conditions, the operator now has (ON A B).*

AFTER APPLYING (PICK A H), WE ACHIEVE:
    (HOLDS H A)
    (FREE A)
    (FREE C)
    (ON A B)
    (EMPTY H)

IS IT CORRECT?   (Y or N): **n**

*Having no knowledge about the domain and no explanations, the resulting proposed
state is necessarily incorrect. The user has to correct the system, by telling what has
to be changed, so that the state becomes correct.*

DESCRIBE THE CHANGES TO THE PROPOSED STATE
((free b)(not (empty h))(not (on a b))(not (free a)))

AFTER APPLYING (PICK A H), WE ACHIEVE:
    (FREE B)
    (HOLDS H A)
    (FREE C)

IS IT CORRECT?   (Y or N): **y**

*The system confirms the state is now correctly described. It could have been the case
that the user forgot something or incorrectly gave some erroneous information. We
must tell that the user is considered an expert, so his statements are considered true,
unless contradicted by himself. In such cases, the latter statement is true, therefore
overcoming any former contradicting one.*
*At this point, the operator PICK is completely described. Its description is the one
shown at the end of this session, the only difference being the names of the variables.*

ACTUAL STATE: ((FREE B) (HOLDS H A) (FREE C))
DESIRED STATE: ((ON A B) (ON B C) (FREE A) (EMPTY H))
WHAT ACTION MUST BE DONE NOW?
(putdown h a)

AFTER APPLYING (PUTDOWN H A), WE ACHIEVE:
    (FREE A)
    (EMPTY H)
    (FREE B)
    (HOLDS H A)
    (FREE C)

IS IT CORRECT?   (Y or N): **n**
DESCRIBE THE CHANGES TO THE PROPOSED STATE
((not (holds h a)))

Observe that, in this case, the proposed state is almost correct. This is because some explanations for the necessity of applying the operator were found and they are correct. The referred explanations are (EMPTY H) and (FREE A). If they were not correct, the state would have been corrected and so would the operator.

AFTER APPLYING (PUTDOWN H A), WE ACHIEVE:
    (FREE A)
    (EMPTY H)
    (FREE B)
    (FREE C)

IS IT CORRECT? (Y or N): **y**

At this moment, the system already knows two operators. Therefore, regarding their conditions and the actual state, some partial plans can be built. Each of them will be proposed, step by step. The user has to reject those that do not belong to the simpler plan.

I CAN APPLY (PICK A H), AND ACHIEVE
    ((HOLDS H A) (FREE B) (FREE C))
IS IT CORRECT FOR THE PLAN (Y or N): **n**
I CAN APPLY (PICK B H), AND ACHIEVE
    ((HOLDS H B) (FREE A) (FREE C))
IS IT CORRECT FOR THE PLAN (Y or N): **y**
I CAN APPLY (PUTDOWN H B), AND ACHIEVE
    ((FREE B) (EMPTY H) (FREE A) (FREE C))

This should not have been proposed. It makes a cycle in the plan. This is being corrected.

IS IT CORRECT FOR THE PLAN (Y or N): **n**
ACTUAL STATE: ((HOLDS H B) (FREE A) (FREE C))
DESIRED STATE: ((ON A B) (ON B C) (FREE A) (EMPTY H))

The actual state corresponds to having accepted (PICK B H). Since the known operators seem to be insufficient, the user is asked to give more information.

WHAT ACTION MUST BE DONE NOW?
(stack b c)

AFTER APPLYING (STACK B C), WE ACHIEVE:
    (ON B C)
    (HOLDS H B)
    (FREE A)
    (FREE C)

IS IT CORRECT? (Y or N): **n**

Again, a domain theory could simplify the work. C can not be free if B is ON it, for example. The corrections made by the user will again correct the operator.

DESCRIBE THE CHANGES TO THE PROPOSED STATE
((not (free c))(not (holds h b))(empty h))

AFTER APPLYING (STACK B C), WE ACHIEVE:
  (EMPTY H)
  (ON B C)
  (FREE A)

IS IT CORRECT? (Y or N): **n**

Corrections can be made one by one.

DESCRIBE THE CHANGES TO THE PROPOSED STATE
((free b))

AFTER APPLYING (STACK B C), WE ACHIEVE:
  (FREE B)
  (EMPTY H)
  (ON B C)
  (FREE A)

IS IT CORRECT? (Y or N): **y**

Now, there seems to be enough operators to build the plan. Even so, it is proposed to the user. If it was not accepted, it would mean the operators were incorrectly described. They would have to be corrected. It is not the case, here.

SOLUTION:

APPLY	ACHIEVE
(PICK A H)	((HOLDS H A) (FREE B) (ON B C))
IS IT CORRECT? (Y or N): **y**	
(STACK A B)	((EMPTY H) (ON A B) (FREE A) (ON B C))
IS IT CORRECT? (Y or N): **y**	
OK	

At the end of this session, the learned operators were:

OPERATOR PUTDOWN:
ACTION: (PUTDOWN x9 x10)
CONDITIONS:
  (HOLDS x9 x10)
POST-CONDITIONS:
  (NOT (HOLDS x9 x10))
  (EMPTY x9)
  (FREE x10)

```
OPERATOR STACK:
ACTION: (STACK  x13 x11)
CONDITIONS:
       (FREE x11)
       (HOLDS x12 x13)
POST-CONDITIONS:
       (FREE x13)
       (NOT (FREE x11))
       (ON x13 x11)
       (EMPTY x12)
       (NOT (HOLDS x12 x13))


OPERATOR PICK:
ACTION: (PICK x7 x6)
CONDITIONS:
       (EMPTY x6)
       (FREE x7)
SIDE-CONDITIONS:
       (ON x7 x8)
POST-CONDITIONS:
       (NOT (FREE x7))
       (NOT (EMPTY x6))
       (HOLDS x6 x7)
SIDE-EFFECTS:
       (NOT (ON x7 x8))
       (FREE x8)
```

7 Related Work

As said in the beginning, most learning systems applied to planning are used to learn macro operators or general plan schemata. Systems like LEX [Mitchell et al 83], Robo-Soar [Laird et al 90] or PRODIGY [Carbonell et al 90] are used to learn in the context of planning, but not to learn operators.

Only Diffy-S [Kadie 88] is concerned with the same aspect of learning operators. However, the approach followed there is very different from ours. In Diffy-S, operators are not learned while planning. Instead, some examples of application situations are given, by means of an independent description (before the operator's application) and a dependent description (after application). Using a background knowledge containing, among other things, primitive function schemata, constructive induction functions and a heuristic evaluation function, the system finds a set of explanations that covers the examples. It then uses concept learning to build a set of conditions that specify when each explanation is applied. The outcome is a hypothesis operator schema that puts together the conditions and the explanation functions and performs as intended by the given examples.

The problem with this approach is that it relies on a set of good examples, which are eventually dificult to define, since they have to consider all the application contexts. This is not possible if the environment is not completely predictable. In reactive situations, this type of learning can not be used. Learning while planning is a good strategy for learning in reactiveworlds. The ability to acquire and maintain context dependent information also helps this kind of learning.

8 Conclusions and Future Work

We have presented a first version of a system that learns operator descriptions while planning, based on the user's help and on its own capabilities of finding partial causal explanations from the description of the world that justify or explain the execution of particular actions in particular states. We know the system is still very limited and primary, but we have achieved
quite satisfactory results in the blocks world, as in some simple robot domains. We have tried to learn the operators described in the example given in [Sacerdoti 74]. Most of them have been correctly acquired.
The approach followed is different from any other seen in the literature. We intend to continue with this line of research, by adding other capabilities to the system.
Our immediate concern is to add a domain theory to the system, that can make the system less dependent of the interaction with the user. We also intend to be able to incrementally acquire this domain theory.
A more efficient planner will have to be implemented, especially for when many operators are known. When there are not enough operators, we think that an exhaustive space search has to be carried out.
The main objective of our work is to learn in reactive or unpredictable worlds.

9 References

Carbonnel, J. G & Gill, Y. (1987). Learning by Experimentation, Proceedings of the Fourth International Machine Learning Workshop.

Carbonnel, J. G & Gill, Y. (1990). Learning by Experimentation: the Operator Refinement Method, Machine Learning: An Artificial Intelligence Approach, Volume III, Morgan Kaufmann, Irvine 1990.

DeJong, G. F. & Mooney, R. J. (1986). Explanation-Based Learning: An Alternative View, Machine Learning 1, pp 145-176.

Drummond, M. & Currie, K. (1989). Goal Ordering in Partially Ordered Plans, Proceedings of the Nineth International Joint Conference on Artificial Intelligence, pp 960-965.

Fikes, R. E. & Nilsson, N. J. (1972). Learning and Executing Generalized Robot Plans, Artificial Intelligence 3, pp 251-288.

Gil, Y. (1991) A Domain Independent Framework for Effective Experimentation in Planning, Proceedings of th Eighth International Workshop on Machine Learning, pp 13-17.

Kadie, Carl M. (1988). Diffy-S: Learning Robot Operator Schemata from Examples, Proceedings of the Fifth International Conference on Machine Learning, pp 430-436.

Korf, R. E. (1985), Macro-Operators: A weak Method for Learning, Artificial Intelligence 26, pp 35-77.

Laird, J.E., Rosenbloom, P. S. & Newell, A.(1986). Chunking in SOAR: The Anatomy of a General Learning Mechanism, Machine Learning 1, pp 11-46.

Mitchell, T. M., Keller, R. & Kedar-Cabelli, S. (1986). Explanation-Based Generalization: A Unifying View, Machine Learning 1, pp 47-80.

Mitchell, T., Utgoff, P. & Banerji, R. (1983). Learning by Experimentation: Acquiring and Refining Problem Solving Heuristics, Machine Learning: An Artificial Intelligence Approach, Volume I, Tioga, Palo Alto 1983.

Mooney, R. J. (1988). Generalizing the Order of Operators in Macro-Operators, Proceedings of th Fifth International Workshop on Machine Learning, pp 270-283.

Sacerdoti, E. D. (1974). Planning in a Hierarchy of Abstraction Spaces, Artificial Intelligence 4, pp 115-135.

Shell, P. & Carbonnel, J. (1989). Towards a General Framework for Composing Disjunctive and Iterative Macro-operators, Proceedings of the Nineth International Joint Conference on Artificial Intelligence, pp 596-602.

Evaluating Evidence for Motivated Discovery

Michael M. Luck*

Department of Computer Science
University College London
Gower St, London, WC1E 6BT, UK
mikeluck@cs.ucl.ac.uk

Abstract. Inductive discovery can be said to proceed through the accumulation of evidence in attempts to refute the current theory. Typically, this has involved a straight choice between the falsification of a theory and its continued use, with little or no consideration given to the possibility of error. This paper addresses the problems of error and evidence evaluation. It considers a variety of different kinds of error and uncertainty that arise through interaction with an external world, in both scientific discovery and other inductive reasoning. In response, it proposes a generally applicable model for the evaluation of evidence under differing motivations, and describes its implementation in the MID system for motivated discovery.

Keywords: discovery, motivation, error, knowledge acquisition.

1 Introduction

Discovery is an interactive reasoning process which relies heavily on feedback from experiments in detecting and correcting inconsistencies and inadequacies in current theories and views of the world. In providing a foundation for work to proceed, a six-stage framework for inductive discovery has been developed encompassing prediction, experimentation, observation, evaluation, revision and selection [9]. In short, the framework involves the generation of predictions, subjecting these to experimentation, and observing and evaluating the results. If the observations are not consistent with the predictions, then the theory used to generate the predictions must be revised and a suitable revision selected for subsequent use.

This paper addresses issues in the evaluation of evidence relevant not only to discovery, but also to a range of other reasoning and learning paradigms. It begins by introducing a framework for discovery and describing the role of evaluation within that framework. The next section considers error and the different kinds of uncertainty that can arise in evidence, and continues with a discussion of the notion of acceptability of evidence. Then a model for the evaluation of evidence is presented, specifying the relationship between the relevant factors. Finally, the implementation of the model in a system for motivated inductive discovery is described, showing how motivations are used to control the degree of acceptability required of the evidence.

---

* This work was carried out under a SERC studentship award.

1.1 A Six Stage Framework for Inductive Discovery

The framework is cyclical, repeating over and over until stability is achieved with a consistent domain theory. It begins with *prediction* which entails generating predictions for a given scenario, and then subjecting these to some kind of *experimentation*. Through *observation* and *evaluation*, the results of the experiment are evaluated with respect both to the motivations of the reasoning agent and to the predictions. In the event that they are adequate and consistent with the predictions, no action is necessary. If the observations and predictions are anomalous, however, the domain theory must be *revised*, and a suitable revision *selected* to be passed through to the beginning of the cycle for use in generating new predictions. Even when no prediction failure occurs, the domain theory is still liable to provide anomalies at a later stage.

The framework is shown in Figure 1. Theories are represented by small thick-edged boxes. The original domain theory in the top left-hand corner is the input to the framework which may be a null theory if the domain is new. Shown in the figure are the different kinds of information that the framework requires in addition to the domain theory. In order to be able to design and carry out experiments, for example, substantial amounts of domain background knowledge as well as domain independent knowledge are required. Thin arrows indicate the flow of knowledge and information involved in each stage. Thick black arrows indicate the direction of the cycle.

1.2 Motivated Inductive Discovery

In considering inductive discovery, we are concerned with finding out new knowledge, and correcting any errors in existing knowledge. However, the need for which the knowledge must be acquired is also important. Normally this need is for knowledge for its own sake in much the same way as other knowledge acquisition systems. At other times, though, there is a need for knowledge in order to take a particular action or achieve a certain result. The difference lies in the motivation of the system, in what motivates this goal of acquiring knowledge.

The motivations of independent reasoners are of particular relevance and significance to reasoning in general [7]. In inductive discovery, we assert that motivations can be used to control the basic reasoning strategy in order that it may apply to a large variety of domains and contexts. Some psychological research in particular has recognised the role of motivations in reasoning in a similar way to that suggested here. Kunda [5] informally defines motivation to be, "any wish, desire, or preference that concerns the outcome of a given reasoning task" and suggests that motivation affects reasoning in a variety of ways including the accessing, constructing and evaluating of beliefs and evidence, and decision making. In this paper, we will see how motivations can control the evaluation of evidence in the six-stage framework.

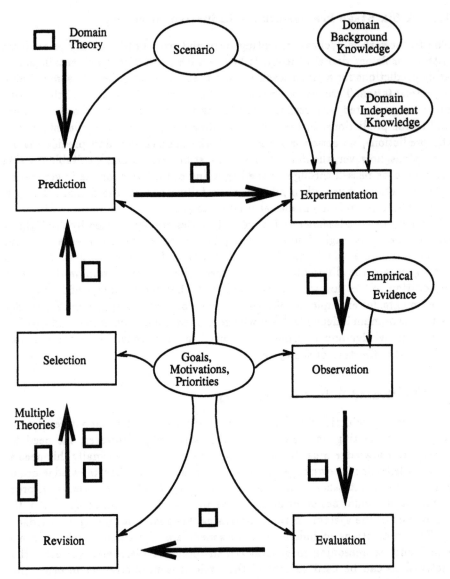

Fig. 1. The progress of theories under the six-stage framework of inductive discovery

1.3 Evaluating Evidence

The role of the evaluation stage in the framework is to determine if the current theory or hypothesis under consideration is refuted by the observed evidence. At the most basic level, the choice is simple: if the evidence supports the theory, then there is no refutation; if the evidence contradicts the the theory, then the theory is refuted. In the vast majority of existing computational models of scientific discovery, this is the norm. Yet this notion of evaluation, with a straight choice between the falsification of a theory and its continued use, is naive. The need for the possibility of the rejection of evidence is undeniable. It can be seen in the common practice of experimenters who often need to reject some of their data because of unreliability. In any real situation, the possibility of error in a variety of forms arises, and has important consequences for the rest of the inductive programme. Only very recently, however, has the problem of error in discovery begun to be taken seriously [15]. Moreover, if work on scientific discovery is to be applied in a more general inductive context, then a stronger and more extensive notion of error and uncertainty is demanded.

2 Error and Uncertainty

The six stages of the framework described above can be divided up into two parts: external stages entailing experimentation and observation; and internal stages entailing prediction, evaluation, revision and selection. *Experimentation* involves the manipulation of real world scenarios through the design and construction of controlled experiments in a suitable environment. *Observation*, though somewhat more passive, is also involved in interacting with the external world and serves as an entry point for evidence into the system. Any interaction with real-world scenarios must admit the inherent *uncertainty* (in a broad sense) that pervades experimentation and observation to some degree. Hon [3] locates four sources of error: laying down the theoretical framework of the experiment; constructing the apparatus and making it work; taking observations or readings; and processing the recorded data and interpreting them. Some of the problems associated with the theoretical framework are outside the scope of the current work. The remaining kinds of error, however, can be reduced from the broad classification of *experimental* and *observational error*, to more definite dimensions which are examined below.

Reliability Evidence must be observed (or perceived in some way), and it must be observed (or perceived) by a *source*. *Reliability* is a measure of the ability of a particular source of evidence as the interpreter and recorder of that evidence to provide correct observation statements. Any source of observations, be it a human observer or a machine, is necessarily imperfect, resulting in some degree of variation in the *reliability* of that source. Reliability here is used in a very specific sense, referring only to the ability of a named source in a particular situation to provide accurate observation statements of the phenomenon under investigation. The reliability of a source is in question for many reasons at different levels. A human observer, for example, may have poor eyesight which could result in the introduction of doubt into observations. In the case of a machine observer, analogous difficulties arise with considerations of the equipment used, such as the quality of lenses, and so on. The raw data of observation must also be interpreted and recorded to produce comprehensible evidence, and this conversion from sense perceptions to observation statements is another process susceptible to unreliability. Reliability is thus related to the *objective* abilities of a particular source independent of the status of the observed evidence.

Trustworthiness *Trustworthiness* can be defined as a measure of malicious intent on the part of the information source. A source of information, even if it is absolutely reliable in terms of its ability to observe, might still provide uncertain evidence because of an intention to mislead. An independent agent acting as observer and providing input to a system in the form of observation statements has its own goals and motivations which do not necessarily correspond to those of the reasoner. Garigliano et al. [2], for example, use the case of buying a second-hand motor-bike to illustrate this. A used-bike dealer has a definite financial advantage in selling a bike and will therefore present it as favourably as possible. He might try to sell it without taking on any responsibilities but alternatively, if he is concerned for his reputation, he might give a guarantee. The evidence that he provides in attempting to sell a bike thus comes into question given his aim of getting a good deal. Buyers would only accept his evidence if confident that the dealer does not intend to cheat them. The problem of judging the dealer's *trustworthiness* is independent of problems of his reliability, since one might believe that he is fully aware of the true state of a particular bike, but is not inclined to share that knowledge. This is related to and also provides a way of dealing with the notion of *bluff* [8] which is prevalent in domains of game-playing and military strategy where agents also intentionally mislead others. Trustworthiness is thus an evaluation of the motives of an observing agent which are not necessarily the same as one's own.

Accuracy *Accuracy* is a measure of the uncertainty arising through the evidence itself or in the method of obtaining that evidence, independent of any problems associated with an observer. In addition to the difficulties arising from the abilities and the nature of the observer, we can consider the phenomenon itself under investigation through experimentation in some form. Direct sense-perception in many instances is inadequate, especially in scientific domains, and phenomena must be observed and quantities measured using a variety of instruments and devices of varying *accuracy*. Microscopes, telescopes, rulers and other such tools are commonplace and provide the basis for observation, yet they all have limits to their accuracy. A microscope for example, has a finite degree of magnification beyond which things cannot be observed, and it also admits the possibility of inaccuracy due to faults in the lenses and so on. This kind of error occurs at a different conceptual level to that described above to illustrate the *reliability* of a machine observer.

Here, the lens contributes to the *accuracy* of the data itself. As an alternative example, consider standing at a bus-stop and looking at the front of a bus as it approaches to see what number it is. While the observer may be perfectly reliable and trustworthy, the number of the bus may be partially obscured so that only the top part of it is showing. It then becomes very difficult to distinguish between a number 19 or a number 18 or a number 10, for example. Here again, the evidence that is available is itself insufficient. Accuracy is the traditional dimension of uncertainty that is considered in evaluating evidence, and is most usually addressed by the provision of simple error tolerances.

Credibility *Credibility* is a measure of the uncertainty that arises through conflict with established constraints and prior beliefs. Although the observer may be reliable and trustworthy, and the data accurate, this does not deal with the case of exceptional circumstances when the evidence violates normal constraints. These violations include problems caused by such things as hallucinations, mirages, optical illusions and so on. What is needed is a measure of the degree of *credibility* associated with such observations. For example, the degree of credibility associated with the observation that John is flying around his office is very low (since this is more likely to be an hallucination). Alternatively, when watching a magician, the observation that a lady has been sawn in half is also not very credible. To some extent, credibility is dependent on the expectations that are derived from existing theories, and acts as a form of conservatism. The degree of credibility will also depend on the strength with which these theories are held. Strongly held theories which conflict with observations will produce low credibility, while weak conflicting theories (including the current theory) will not affect credibility as greatly. In this respect, it reflects concerns with the theoretical framework noted earlier. Measures of credibility thus reduce the value of evidence that is highly suspect through tricks of nature.

Simple numerical measures of accuracy alone provide no information as to the circumstances in which error has originated. Our concern is with the acquisition of knowledge. As such, it is important to locate sources of error so that confidence in those sources in future situations may be adjusted in the light of the results of the current reasoning process, as well as coping with the uncertainty that currently exists. This contrasts with the use of simple error tolerances which assume a Gaussian distribution of results, an assumption which may not be justified, and which provides no useful information about the uncertainty itself.

3 Acceptable Evidence

Because of the different kinds of error and uncertainty that can arise, evidence cannot simply be accepted and used to refute or support a theory. An evaluation of observations received as evidence is necessary in order that the character of the evidence can be assessed and accepted or rejected as the situation demands.

The following section addresses the issue of how to use these four dimensions to determine whether or not a theory or hypothesis is refuted by the observations.

3.1 Confidence

The notion of the acceptance of evidence leads to a two-way split of evidence into that which is sufficiently good to be used, and that which must be rejected. Suppose that the four dimensions described above can be combined in some way to form a single measure for evidence, *confidence*. Now it can be said that if we have sufficient *confidence* in some evidence then that evidence is acceptable and may be admitted. If not, then the evidence must be rejected outright and re-observed (possibly involving a new or repeated experimental set-up). This means that there is a point of commitment to evidence beyond which observations are accepted in full and before which they are rejected outright so that the need to maintain large amounts of data on the certainty of propositions (theories and data) throughout the reasoning process is avoided.

We define $C(e)$, the confidence in a piece of evidence, e, to be a function on reliability, r, trustworthiness, t, accuracy, a and credibility, c, as follows:

$$C(e) = f(r, t, a, c)$$

3.2 Acceptance Thresholds

Now, in order that a piece of evidence, e, may be considered acceptable, the confidence in it, $C(e)$, must exceed some limit, the *acceptance threshold*, C_{accept}, which marks the degree of confidence that is required for acceptance. However, this threshold value cannot be an objective quantity since the degree of confidence required in any given situation is clearly dependent on the motivations of a reasoner with reference to possible consequences of incorrect decisions based on the acceptance of faulty evidence. Consider taking a train to Scotland today for a business meeting. Since the meeting is very important, a high degree of confidence in the acquired evidence is necessary in order not to be late. This might mean rejecting the evidence provided by a co-worker, but accepting the evidence provided by the railway authorities about the times of trains. Alternatively, if there is a party rather than a business meeting, it is more reasonable to accept the evidence of a friend, since even if that evidence is incorrect, being late for a party is not very important. These examples illustrate the relation between the importance of the situation and the degree of confidence required. Consideration of motivations can provide a simple measure of the importance of any given situation which can then be used to determine the appropriate acceptance threshold value.

3.3 Action Points

Although the upper confidence limit above prevents a paralysis of action in situations of high importance, this fails to consider issues of *urgency*. Time is often a factor in critical situations of importance, and it may not be reasonable to reject evidence that falls short of the threshold with such time constraints. Examples might include the systems in a nuclear power plant, or in an aeroplane which has experienced some sort of failure, and so on. In these cases, importance is high, but time is also severely limited, and the acceptance threshold may still be too high for the available evidence. To deal with this, there must be an *action point* which is determined by the *urgency* of the situation, and which allows reasoning to be based on evidence with a low degree of confidence — lower than the acceptance threshold for confidence. This action point is usually the same as the acceptance threshold because if there is no (or low) urgency, then there is no need to accept suitably uncertain evidence. As urgency increases and approaches a critical level, the action point decreases so that less and less confident evidence may be accepted in order to act. Note that a (high) degree of urgency implies that the reasoning is motivated for action. In fact there will always be urgency to a greater or lesser extent when reasoning to satisfy action motivations.

(The roles of importance and urgency have also been recognised by Sloman [14] in developing a computational theory of mind, but they are more thoroughly developed below.)

Whenever evidence is accepted, the manner of its acceptance is relevant to determining how it may be used. If poor evidence is accepted when reasoning for action, then it is used to provide a *local* update to the domain theory for the current situation only. It is used for *temporary* revision rather than permanent revision so that the need for action can be satisfied, but without compromising the need to maintain a correct and consistent domain theory. Further or better evidence may subsequently be obtained for use in generating a permanent revision [10].

4 A Model of Evaluation

The requirements of a system for evaluation have been discussed in general terms above. This section provides a more formal model of evaluation. First, it is necessary to specify the four parameters of uncertainty: reliability, trustworthiness, accuracy and credibility.

Reliability, r, and trustworthiness, t, are defined to take values in the interval between 0 and 1: $r \in [0, 1]$ and trustworthiness, $t \in [0, 1]$. The upper limit of 1 denotes perfect evidence without any possibility of error, while the lower limit of 0 denotes evidence that is perfectly incorrect. 0.5 indicates evidence which there is no reason to believe or disbelieve in terms of its reliability or trustworthiness. Thus values ranging from 0.5 to 1 indicate increasing degrees of support for the evidence, while values ranging from 0.5 to 0 indicate increasing degrees of support against the evidence. These lower values provide strong reasons for the rejection of evidence since the evidence is judged to be not merely uncertain, but misleading.

Reliability and trustworthiness are both attributes of a source of observations, and allow the possibility not only of uncertainty of their correctness, but also of uncertainty in their incorrectness. In other words, the observations provided may not merely be approximate, but deliberately misleading as discussed earlier. It is easy to see this in the case of trustworthiness, for it might be expected that a source will attempt to mislead, in which case the parameter value will be below 0.5. With reliability, however, this is less obvious, since it is a measure of the ability of a source. Consider, though, an observer who has no malicious intent (so that trustworthiness takes a high value), but who provides evidence with no basis in observation. Instances of this will be rare, but are nevertheless plausible. For example, in response to requests for information (such as the time of the last train to Scotland), people often guess answers. Mostly, there is some basis in experience for this, but sometimes there is none, or the experience may be so far removed and irrelevant that the evidence may be judged to be not so much approximate as incorrect. This is exacerbated in extreme cases, such as mental disorder, for example, where sources are trustworthy (in the sense of no malicious intent), but are unreliable to the point of providing totally false information.

Thus in evaluating *binary* evidence, very low values for trustworthiness and reliability may also provide a basis for acceptance, since the opposing evidence may be assumed to hold. This work does not consider binary evidence, however, and the issue is not addressed further.

Accuracy, a, and credibility, c, as attributes of the phenomenon itself take values from the interval between 0 and 1: accuracy, $a \in [0, 1]$ and credibility, $c \in [0, 1]$. The upper limit of 1 denotes perfectly accurate or credible evidence, while the lower limit of 0 denotes no degree of accuracy or credibility at all. Note that these are attributes of the phenomenon, not of its manner of observation.

Note that the meaning of the values for each of the parameters of uncertainty is relative and lies in its comparison with other values. Thus a value of 0.5 for accuracy, for example, means only that it is more accurate than a value of 0.4, and less accurate than a value of 0.6. It is possible however, to use a particular interpretation of these values, and treat them as probabilities, say, so that a value of 0.5 for accuracy would take on the meaning of a 0.5 probability of perfect accuracy. In the current work, however, no such interpretation is used. The only significance of the values is in the ordering they impose on the associated evidence.

Given values for each of the four parameters of uncertainty, we can define confidence by some function which combines them. The confidence, C, in a piece of evidence, e, is defined below, where f is a function that combines positive values into a single measure for confidence. Note that if reliability or trustworthiness have values less than 0.5, then the confidence is zero.

$$C(e) = \begin{cases} 0, & \text{if } r < 0.5 \text{ or } t < 0.5 \\ f(r, t, a, c), & \text{otherwise} \end{cases}$$

In the implementation of this model in the MID system, a simple product function for f is used: $f(r, t, a, c) = r \times t \times a \times c$. This admits the significance of each of the dimensions of uncertainty, but allows their relative strength to be balanced, providing a measure less sensitive to fluctuations in the assessment of the values. By leaving the function f unspecified, however, different ways of combining the values of uncertainty are possible.

Now we can define an *acceptance threshold*, C_{accept}, which is the amount of confidence required for acceptance of the evidence in order to be able to act on it. This is proportional to the importance of the current situation, denoted by the *importance index*, $\mathcal{I}$. However, with high importance, confidence will not increase proportionately. Similarly, with very low importance, some minimum degree of confidence is necessary. Thus we have:

$$C_{accept} = \begin{cases} C_{max}, & \mathcal{I} > C_{max} \\ C_{min}, & \mathcal{I} < C_{min} \\ \mathcal{I}, & \text{otherwise} \end{cases}$$

The importance index, $\mathcal{I}$, is drawn from the interval 0 to 1: $\mathcal{I} \in [0,1]$. The upper limit of 1 denotes supreme importance, while 0 denotes no importance at all. Particular values used derive their significance from comparison with other values of importance in the same way as for the dimensions of uncertainty. Thus a value of 0.5 indicates greater importance than a value of 0.4, but less importance than a value of 0.6. Importance is calibrated by reference to confidence and the dimensions of uncertainty. The value of the importance index is significant in the level of confidence demanded, and by extension in the degree of uncertainty permitted.

Finally, an action point can be defined by introducing the urgency $\mathcal{U}$ associated with the scenario which is also drawn from the interval 0 to 1. $\mathcal{U} \in [0,1]$. The upper limit of 1 denotes maximum urgency, and demands immediate attention, while the lower limit of 0 denotes minimum or no urgency. $\mathcal{U}_{lim}$ is a limiting value for urgency below which no reduction to the acceptance threshold is necessary.

$$C_{action} = \begin{cases} C_{accept}, & \text{if } \mathcal{U} < \mathcal{U}_{lim} \\ C_{accept} \cdot (1 - \mathcal{U}), & \text{otherwise} \end{cases}$$

Acceptance thresholds and action points bear some similarity to Marsh's cooperation thresholds which also use importance in deciding when an agent should cooperate with another in order to achieve its goals [12]. However, it is not clear how measures of importance in his model are derived. In the discussion of an implementation below, the origin of importance is addressed through the use of motivations in the reasoning agent.

5 Motivated Inductive Discovery

The model presented here has been implemented in the MID system for Motivated Inductive Discovery. MID is a program based on the framework introduced earlier which reasons about simple physical processes in a manner similar to Rajamoney's COAST system [13]. An important point to note about MID is that it acts as a particular reasoning agent defined by a set of internal motivations. It uses a representation of the motivations of the agent to control and direct the reasoning process [9].

MID possesses a theory concerning the domain under investigation comprising its knowledge about physical processes in that domain. When presented with a new scenario, MID generates predictions and compares these against recorded observations resulting from external experimentation. If there is an anomaly, then MID revises its domain theory, otherwise MID operates normally. Before MID compares the observations with the predictions, however, MID evaluates the observations themselves to determine if they are acceptable in accordance with the model specified above. The parameters of uncertainty in the system are associated with and derived from a number of different elements in MID. Values for accuracy and reliability originate with the scenario (description) since they are factors of the scenario and do not vary within that scenario. Reliability and trustworthiness, however, are associated with the observations themselves. (In MID, observations are grouped in sets under observers, since it is the observer that is inadequate.) The confidence and urgency limits are factors of the domain, defining the practical limits of the acceptability of evidence. Urgency itself is also associated with the current scenario, while importance is derived from the motivations of the reasoning agent. This is discussed below.

5.1 Importance and Motivation

Importance, responsible for determining the required level of confidence for the acceptance of evidence, is a subjective factor. What is very important to one person is not as important to another in the same situation. In the train timetable example given earlier, it was clearly less important to the co-worker to catch the train on time. At the same time, there is an independent factor which affects such considerations, namely *urgency*, which can be considered as a parameter of the scenario itself. Although variable, importance is strongly related to the goals that demand action and reasoning, and by extension, to the motivations that specify goals. Regardless of the kind of situation (the domain theory, scenario, etc.), the importance is a function of the strength of motivation to act (or reason) in that situation. Thus the stronger the motivation, the greater the importance, and the more confidence is necessary for acceptance of evidence.

Using a model of motivations similar to that of Maes [11], motivations in MID are represented as an array of motivational strength values for a fixed set of motivations or desires (such as hunger, curiosity, and safety, for example). The importance index, $\mathcal{I}$, is thus defined to be kv_{max} where k is a proportionality constant, and v_{max} is the value of the *salient* motivation of the reasoning agent, the motivation with the highest strength value. The reasoning agent can be said to be reasoning *under* this motivation and, consequently, its strength is representative of the importance attached to the reasoning undertaken in order to satisfy that motivation. The stronger the motivation, the more the motivation needs to be satisfied (for unsatisfied motivations grow stronger and will subsequently demand stronger and possibly greater action) and the more important it is that the reasoning process should be successful. This requires greater effort in terms of time and resources to be spent on evaluation in order to avoid the

Table 1. Summary of rejection of evidence behaviour

Importance	Urgency	C_{action}	$C(e) < C_{\text{action}}$
high	high	mid-range	reject observations
high	low	high	reject observations and scenario
low	high	low	not possible
low	low	low	reject observations

consequences of an undesirable failure. Thus motivation determines importance, and importance determines the acceptance threshold.

Urgency, on the other hand, is related to the situation itself, regardless of the importance that any individual attaches to it. In situations that demand immediate attention, the need to act is very strong. This is not unrelated to importance, because urgent situations will increase the importance through heightened motivations. Urgency and importance each provide a complement to the other, one deriving its significance from the motivations of the reasoning agent in a particular situation, the other from the situation itself. This notion of importance and urgency is similar to the idea of Maes [11] in which the behaviour of a creature is determined both by motivations and goals on the one hand and by external observation on the other. It provides for the ability to respond based on both internal and external considerations.

5.2 Rejecting Evidence

If MID finds that the evidence is not acceptable under the circumstances, then some element of it may be rejected. The rejection of evidence is strongly dependent upon importance and urgency. In situations with some urgency, only observations can be rejected, since the urgency of the situation demands that that particular situation be addressed. If urgency is not high, then with high importance, the scenario itself can be rejected if necessary. Rejection of the scenario is not usual, and is only allowed if there is no sufficiently reliable and trustworthy observer in the original scenario. MID's behaviour is summarized in Table 1. Note that when rejecting a scenario, the observations are also rejected. Note also that in the case of low importance and high urgency (higher than the limit for action thresholds), the confidence level cannot be lower than the action threshold value. Once MID finds that the evidence is acceptable, it is used to reason about the current phenomenon.

6 An Example

Suppose we have a domain with values for C_{max} and C_{min} of 0.9 and 0.1 respectively, and U_{lim} of 0.7. Now, given a scenario in which relatively accurate evidence can be observed, which has no special features reducing its credibility, and which has low urgency (accuracy is 0.8, credibility is 0.9 and urgency is 0.4), and an observer who is relatively reliable but less trustworthy (values for reliability and trustworthiness of 0.9 and 0.8), we can calculate the confidence in the evidence. Using the simple multiplication function in MID, this is $(0.9 \times 0.8 \times 0.8 \times 0.9) = 0.52$.

The urgency of the situation (0.4) is below the limit for the domain (0.7), so the action point reduces to the acceptance threshold. Now, suppose that the salient motivation in MID has a moderately high strength value of 0.6 which determines the importance index. This lies between the confidence limits, so the acceptance threshold is simply the importance index which is 0.6. At this point, we know that the observations are not acceptable since the confidence (0.52) is below the acceptance threshold.

New observations are needed, and we can specify a requirement on the acceptable level of uncertainty that is introduced because of the observer. We know that accuracy and credibility are 0.8 and 0.9, and the acceptance threshold is 0.6, so we can require a combined value of not less than $0.6/(0.8 \times 0.9) = 0.83$ for the uncertainty due to the observer. Subsequent evidence is provided by a completely trusted observer with values of 0.9 for reliability and 1.0 for trustworthiness, giving a value of 0.9 for observer uncertainty, and 0.65 for combined confidence. (Note that the value of 1.0 for trustworthiness may be unlikely, though possible with oneself as the observer, for example.) The observations are therefore accepted. If it was not possible to exceed the threshold, then the scenario would have to be rejected and replaced with one whose values for accuracy and credibility would allow acceptance.

This example shows how poor evidence which may lead to an incorrect conclusion can be rejected in favour of better evidence. This is important because poor evidence can seriously affect the reasoning process in the subsequent stages of discovery by introducing inconsistencies and errors that may be propagated through the domain theory. Furthermore, the acceptability of evidence is not fixed, but is instead related to the importance of the situation with respect to the reasoning agent, and to the urgency of the situation itself so that a flexible response can be achieved. For example, if time was short, then the urgency might increase so that the acceptance threshold would be reduced and the original evidence could be accepted despite being of relatively poor quality.

7 Discussion

If an inductive reasoning system is to be of value, then it must be able to cope with both experimental and observational error, and must be able to evaluate them in an appropriate context. It is, however, insufficient to address the presence of error by introducing simple tolerance levels. Experimental evidence must be evaluated relative to the current motivations of a system, taking into account the implications of success or failure. In medical domains, for example, even a small degree of error may be unacceptable if it would lead to the loss of a patient's life, while weather prediction systems may, in certain circumstances, allow a far greater error tolerance.

In evaluating evidence, we want to be able to judge not only the accuracy of data, but also the validity of such data. Criticisms of the naive falsificationist approach to scientific discovery include precisely this point — that the evidence may be inadequate, insufficient or even plainly wrong. Consider the example of testing the hypothesis that all swans are white. If a black swan is found, then the hypothesis can be refuted. However, it might be the case that the swan was really white and the black swan was a hallucination, or that the light was bad and what appeared to be a black swan was in fact white, or that it wasn't a swan at all, but a duck. This common example is somewhat contrived, but there are real instances. Karp[4], for example, notes that biologists studying attenuation often modified the initial conditions of an experiment because of the uncertainty of their knowledge of these conditions. Indeed, the ability to recognise and reject inadequate evidence is necessary for a full account of reasoning.

The rejection or acceptance of evidence is tied intimately to the motivation that guides the reasoning process. Highly motivated reasoning implies that a successful outcome is strongly desired, and that the consequences of failure would be severe given such a high strength of motivation. Clearly, in order to achieve a successful result, the evidence must be sufficiently good to enable accurate and effective reasoning, and thus the validity of the evidence used for the reasoning process acquires greater importance. Alternatively, if the reasoning is not strongly motivated, then the consequences of an inappropriate result are less severe, perhaps negligible, and less effort is demanded in evaluating evidence. Evidence must be evaluated to some degree to determine whether it is acceptable for the purposes and motivations of the reasoning agent. Motivations determine what this level of acceptability should be.

An example relevant to discovery is Crick and Watson's discovery of the double helix of DNA. In attempting to become the first to discover the structure of DNA, they used 'quick and dirty' rather than the most reliable methods. Their first attempt at a model was a fiasco, according to Crick [1], partly because of "ignorance" on his part, and "misunderstanding" on Watson's. By contrast, work by Wilkes and Franklin was progressing slowly as they concentrated on using their experimental data as fully as possible, and avoided resorting to guessing the structure by trying various models. Crick states that Franklin's experimental work was first class and could not be bettered, while Watson simply wanted to get at the answer as quickly as possible by sound methods or flashy ones. While the actual motivations of the individual researchers cannot be known, the distinction between their different motivations has been noted [1], and we can see a corresponding distinction in their evaluation of evidence.

8 Conclusion

Most work on discovery has considered the evaluation of evidence with regard to error only implicitly if at all. BACON [6], for example, uses a single fixed error tolerance parameter which is inadequate for most non-trivial purposes. This is particularly so when considering cases of scientific discovery, for it ignores the real issues in science of locating and analysing the source of the error. Recently, some effort has been directed at actively determining error, and reducing it as far as possible, but it has concentrated on numerical discovery [15]. Moreover, the kind of error considered is limited to only one of the parameters of uncertainty discussed earlier, *accuracy*. Effective reasoning systems must be able not only to reason on the basis of supplied evidence, but also to reject that evidence if it is inadequate. This is an important requirement, but one which has been neglected in the past.

This paper has described a model for evaluation which uses four parameters of uncertainty: accuracy, credibility, reliability and trustworthiness. The question of when evidence is acceptable has also been addressed, not in the form of a static, fixed rating of evidence, but by considering the evidence in light of the motivations of the reasoning agent, and defining a variable measure for acceptability. The distinction between the model itself and its use in the MID system is deliberate, allowing other interactions with different implementations. Although the question of how importance may be defined is open, the role of importance is fixed. The decision to use a single salient motivation to determine importance rather than combining the complete set of motivations was for the sake of simplicity. Enhancements of this work may subsequently investigate other possibilities, but the model holds regardless. Further work might extend the model by specifying the way in which the parameters of uncertainty can be updated based on the results of the reasoning or action that arises out of the use of accepted evidence.

The model provides a means of addressing the problem of evidence evaluation, which applies to reasoning in both centralized and distributed domains, and in both scientific and everyday contexts. In this respect, it also relates to the problems associated with distributed sources of information which are increasingly being used in a variety of areas, and also to the modelling of autonomous agents in multi-agent environments. This is already the subject of investigation [12], and it seems that there is much benefit to be gained in attempting to combine the various approaches. The important point is that all evidence is susceptible to error and uncertainty. It must be evaluated in relation to the need for which it is obtained, and in such a way that allows a complete rejection of that evidence if necessary.

Acknowledgements
Thanks to Derek Long for commenting on earlier drafts of this paper.

References

1. F. Crick. *What Mad Pursuit: A Personal View of Scientific Discovery*. Basic Books, New York, NY, 1988.

2. R. Garigliano, A. Bokma, and D. Long. A model for learning by source control. In B. Bouchon, L. Saitta, and R. R. Yager, editors, *Lecture Notes in Computer Science, 313*. Springer-Verlag, 1988.

3. G. Hon. Towards a typology of errors: An epistemological view. *Studies in History and Philosophy of Science*, 20(4):469–504, 1989.

4. P. D. Karp. Hypothesis formation as design. In J. Shrager and P. Langley, editors, *Computational Models of Scientific Discovery and Theory Formation*, pages 275–317. Morgan Kaufmann, San Mateo, CA, 1990.

5. Z. Kunda. The case for motivated reasoning. *Psychological Bulletin*, 108(3):480–498, 1990.

6. P. Langley, H. A. Simon, G. L. Bradshaw, and J. M. Zytkow. *Scientific Discovery: Computational Explorations of the Creative Processes*. MIT Press, Cambridge, Mass., 1987.

7. D. Leake and A. Ram. Goal-drivern learning: Fundamental issues and symposium report. Technical Report 85, Cognitive Science Program, Indiana University, Bloomington, Indiana, 1993.

8. R. Lelouche and S. Doublait. Qualitative reasoning with bluff and beliefs in a multi-actor environment. *International Journal of Man-Machine Studies*, 36:149–165, 1992.

9. M. M. Luck. Motivations in inductive discovery: Reasoning for knowledge and action. Research Note RN/92/80, Department of Computer Science, University College London, 1992.

10. M. M. Luck. *Motivated Inductive Discovery*. PhD thesis, University College London, In preparation.

11. P. Maes. A bottom-up mechanism for behaviour selection in an artificial creature. In J. A. Meyer and S.W. Wilson, editors, *Proceedings of the First International Conference on Simulation of Adaptive Behaviour: From Animals to Animats*, pages 238–246. MIT Press/Bradford Books, 1991.

12. S. Marsh. Trust and reliance in multi-agent systems: A preliminary report. In *Pre-Proceedings of the Fourth European Workshop on Modelling Autonomous Agents in a Multi-Agent World*, 1992.

13. S. A. Rajamoney. *Explanation-based Theory Revision: An Approach to the Problems of Incomplete and Incorrect Theories*. PhD thesis, Department of Computer Science, University of Illinois, Urbana, Illinois, 1989.

14. A. Sloman. Motives, mechanisms, and emotions. *Cognition and Emotion*, 1(3):217–233, 1987.

15. J. Zytkow, J. Zhu, and R. Zembowicz. The first phase of real-world discovery: Determining repeatability and error of experiments. In *Proceedings of the Ninth International Conference on Machine Learning*, pages 480–485, Aberdeen, 1992.

How to Learn in an Incomplete Knowledge Environment: Structured Objects for a Modal Approach

Eric Auriol

University of Kaiserslautern, Department of Computer Science
P.O. Box 3049, D-W-6750 Kaiserslautern, Germany

INRIA, Projet CLOREC
Domaine de Voluceau-Rocquencourt B.P. 105, 78153 Le Chesnay Cedex, France

Abstract. We present a formalism and a method that allow to learn structured representations in a noisy knowledge base. The formalism fills the gap between Artificial Intelligence and Data Analysis research's domains. It describes a kind of structured modal object called "hoard", that can express various semantics as probability, possibility and belief. The method aims at growing and refining a knowledge base, composed of hoards, by the incremental use of a data base, composed of hoards subparts. Two levels of knowledge are involved: structured hoards represent classes, and non structured individuals represent data. The main goals of the method are to match quickly both levels by automatic rules generation, and to acquire new knowledge in the structured level, by using the flat data base. Some applications are, for example, situation understanding, image analysis, adaptation to temporal variable process, negotiation.

1 Introduction

In many cases, a specialist is confronted to two contradictory tasks. First, he wants to increase as much as possible his knowledge, by taking new experiences into account. Second, he is often required to express his knowledge as simplest as possible, so that, for example, an automatic decision support system can use it efficiently.

The approach we are proposing tries to fulfill these two requirements. The method deals with *different level of abstraction between the data and the knowledge*. The set of data is composed of individual objects, called *elementary assertions*, while the knowledge focuses on combinations of two, three or more of these objects, called *intensional hoards* [5]. A hoard appears when we need to express relations between different parts of a structured object. For instance, a certain kind of mushroom is made of two distinct parts: a hat and a stem, where the size of the hat is always bigger than the size of the stem. We are using a modal knowledge: a *modal hoard* is a mapping which takes its values in an ordered set [7], for instance the interval [0, 1], instead of in a boolean set.

The problems we attempt to solve are: how an iterating presentation of examples can allow to increase and to improve a knowledge base composed of such objects? And how this knowledge can be expressed in an easy and usable way?

Two classical phases are processed to answer the problem: generalization and specialization [17]. For each hoard of the knowledge base, the generalization phase allows to produce a discriminating rule and then to extract the corresponding vectors of examples of the data set. In the specialization phase, the knowledge base is updated, taking into account the results of the former phase. Hence, two goals are conducted together: the creation of an efficient set of rules to identify a complex structure in a data base (identification); and the incremental refinement of the knowledge base (learning).

The identification phase follows the MINSET algorithm [24]: we define a method that minimizes the number of characteristic descriptors of a hoard, so that the complexity of the matching decreases strongly. A "minimal" (in some sense) rule is deduced. A quality measure is computed on the rules; the rules of highest quality are then applied on the data set, forming the *extension* of the hoard. Because of the main concept of the formalism (i.e. a hoard is a mapping in an ordered interval), a membership degree of each element of the extension of the hoard can be computed, according to the definition of the hoard.

The learning step is based upon the notion of completeness [3, 5]. A hoard is complete if it describes exactly its extension. To achieve the completeness we define a modal learning function, which depends on the semantic of the domain (boolean, probabilistic, possibilistic). The process is incremental "by packs": a single event does not modify the knowledge base, as it does in direct concept formation [10]. It needs a set of data available at a date t, and a knowledge base on these data, to go on.

The first section of the paper presents the symbolic objects, the second recalls the intended problem, and the third one exposes the theoretical grounds of the method. To make the things clearer, the forth section illustrates the technique on a toy-example: the recognition and learning of two types of mushroom, with a set of stems and hats. We discuss the results and we compare the method to other approaches in the fifth section. The conclusion give an overview of the future work to be done.

1 Basic Concepts

Symbolic objects [5] have been studied with a growing interest in the past five years. These objects generalize the classical attribute-value paradigm of the traditional data analysis and build a bridge towards the Artificial Intelligence scientific community. Their main features are: representation of multivalued data; links between data or/and attributes; expression of semantics as probability, possibility and belief; use of the couple intension-extension to handle the generalization-specialization classical techniques used in Artificial Intelligence. For instance, a symbolic object "assertion" a_1 = [weight = [60, 90]] $\wedge$ [size = [150, 190]] $\wedge$ [size $\geq$ 175 $\Rightarrow$ weight $\geq$ 80] represents a class of human with some general properties (their weight is between 60 and 90, etc.). a_1 is an application in the boolean set {true, false}: for a given human John, a_1(John) = true if John fulfils the above conditions. Else a_1(John) = false.

1.1 Boolean Objects

As a general meaning, a symbolic object is defined as a *conjunction of events* pointing on the *descriptions* of the values of some attributes. Each attribute can take several values for a same object. For instance an assertion a = [color = {blue, green}] $\wedge$ [size = [5, 10]] is a symbolic object which describes a type of mushroom's stem. Symbolic objects constitute a subset of the first order predicates' logic. We keep here the formalism coming from the data analysis: we think it is easier and more adequate to express semantics and to highlight the role of the variables and their activity domain (for a deeper discussion, see [3] pp. 42-43). Several definitions are useful:

Definition 1: Individuals, Attributes

Let Ω_t be the set of individuals or objects given at a date t (let us call it Ω), $\Omega = \{\omega_1, ..., \omega_n\} \subseteq \Pi$, where Π is the set of all possible objects. Each object is described by attributes y_i (also called "descriptors" or "variables"):

$$y_i : \Pi \to O_i, \ i = 1, ..., p$$

$$\omega \to y_i(\omega) \in V_i \subseteq O_i$$

The point $(y_1(\omega), ... , y_p(\omega)) \in O = O_1 \ x \ ... \ x \ O_p$ is called the "description of ω"; O is the space of descriptions.

A basic kind of symbolic objects are *events*. An event denoted $e_i = [y_i = V_i]$ where $V_i \subseteq O_i$ is a mapping from Ω in {true, false} (or [0, 1], etc.) so that $e_i(\omega) = $ true $\Leftrightarrow$ $y_i(\omega) \in V_i$. When $y_i(\omega)$ is meaningless $V_i = \emptyset$, and when its value has a meaning but is unknown $V_i = O_i$. The extension of e_i in Ω denoted $\text{Ext}_\Omega e_i$ is the set of elements of Ω such that $e_i(\omega) = $ true.

An assertion is a conjunction of events : $a = \bigwedge_i [y_i = V_i]$. Each object ω of Ω is described by an elementary assertion ω^s:

Definition 2: Elementary Assertion

Let φ be the mapping from Ω in S, the set of symbolic objects defined on Ω by the attributes y_i. Each $\omega \in \Omega$ is described by an elementary assertion $\varphi(\omega) = \omega^s = [y_1 = y_1(\omega)] \wedge ... \wedge [y_p = y_p(\omega)]$.

A hoard is a conjunction of q assertions based on q distinct objects. It allows to express properties and relations denoted R between the objects and their values :

Definition 3: Hoard

$$h = \bigwedge_i \bigwedge_j [y_i(u_j) = V_i^j] \bigwedge_{ijkl} [y_i(u_j) \ R_{ijkl} \ y_k(u_l)] \text{ where } V_i^j \subseteq O_i,$$

$$h(\omega_1, ..., \omega_q) = \text{true} \Leftrightarrow \forall \ i, j, k, l, \ y_i(\omega_j) \in V_i^j \text{ and } y_i(\omega_j) \ R_{ijkl} \ y_k(\omega_l).$$

$y_i(u_j) = V_i^j$ is called an *elementary event* of h.

Example of a hoard

A type of mushroom composed of a stem and a hat can be described by a hoard *h*

$$h = [\text{color(hat)} = \{\text{blue, green}\}] \wedge [\text{size(stem)} = [5, 10]]$$

An assertion focuses only on a single individual (let us say, a hat)

$$a = [\text{color} = \{\text{blue, green}\}] \wedge [\text{circumference} = [3, 4]]$$

1.2 Modal Objects

In some fields of applications, a boolean representation of the knowledge is not sufficient. We need to include uncertainty to represent the real world with more accuracy. The determinist aspect may be altered by using *modal* objects [6]. A symbolic object is called modal if it expresses variation, doubt, or other kinds of uncertainty. Varying semantics (probabilistic, possibilistic, belief) give a precise meaning to some words such as "probable", "plausible", "necessary", etc. [9]. An example of a probabilistic modal assertion is a_2 = [hair_color = (0.5)grey, (0.5)white]. The meaning of the numbers 0.5 is: it exists a class of humans which can have a grey hair or a white hair, with an equal probability (evaluated, for example, by the frequency). For a given *old_man*, a_2(*old_man*) measures a kind of similarity between *old_man* and the elements of this class. The result is no more a "yes" or "no" answer, but instead is a value belonging to the continuous interval [0, 1]. The problem is, how to compute this value for a given *old_man* described for instance by the elementary assertion *old_man*^{s} = [hair_color = (0.8)grey, (0.2)white]? (on the particular individual *old_man*, the numbers 0.8 and 0.2 represents a doubt: is the hair really grey or may be white?). The following formal definitions [8] allow to do it:

Definition 4: Modal Assertion
- M_x is a set of modes: M_x = [0, 1], M_x = {never, often, always}, etc. x denotes the semantic of the domain: boolean, probability, possibility, belief.
- Q_i = $\{q_i^j\}_j$ is a set of mappings q_i^j from O_i in M_x.
- y_i is a descriptor, mapping from Ω in Q_i.
- OP_x = $\{\cup_x, \cap_x, C_x\}$ is a set of operators, $\cup_x$ and $\cap_x$ express a kind of union and intersection within subsets of Q_i and $C_x(q_i)$ is the complementary of q_i in Q_i.
- g_x is a "comparison" function from $Q_i \times Q_i$ in an ordered space L_x (for instance, L_x = [0, 1]).
- f_x is an "aggregation" function from $P(L_x)$, the product set of L_x, in L_x.

Given OP_x, f_x and g_x, a modal assertion a_m is a mapping from Ω in the ordered space L_x, denoted $a_m = \bigwedge_i [y_i = \{q_i^j\}_j]$ so that if $\omega \in \Omega$ is described $\forall$ i=1, ..., p by $y_i = \{r_i^j\}_j$ (where $\forall$ i, j, $r_i^j \in M_x$), then:

$$a_m(\omega) = f_x(g_x(\cup_x^j q_i^j, \cup_x^j r_i^j))_i \qquad (1)$$

We extend the former definition in the case of modal hoards. An example of a probabilistic modal hoard is:

$$h = [color(hat)=(0.9)blue,(0.1)green] \wedge [size(stem)=(0.2)[5,10],(0.8)]10,15]]$$

It represents a class of mushrooms where the color of the hat is very often blue and rarely green, etc.

Definition 5: Modal Hoard
- Q_i = $\{q_{i,k}^j\}_j$ is a set of mappings $q_{i,k}^j$ from O_i in M_x, relative to an individual u_k.
- y_i is an attribute, mapping from Ω in Q_i for each u_k.
- h_x is an aggregation function from $P(L_x)$ to L_x.

Given OP_x, f_x, g_x and h_x, a modal hoard is a mapping h_m from Ω^q in L_x, denoted $h_m = \bigwedge_k \bigwedge_i [y_i(u_k) = \{q_{i,k}^j\}_j]$ so that if $(\omega_1, ..., \omega_q) \in \Omega^q$ is described $\forall$ k=1, ..., q and $\forall$ i=1, ..., p by $y_i(\omega_k) = \{r_{i,k}^j\}_j$ (where $\forall$ i, j, k, $r_{i,k}^j \in M_x$) and $\forall$ i, j, k, l, $y_i(\omega_j)$ R_{ijkl} $y_k(\omega_l)$, then :

$$h(\omega_1, ..., \omega_q) = h_x(f_x(g_x(\cup_x^j q_{i,k}^j , \cup_x^j r_{i,k}^j))i)k \qquad (2)$$

h computes the similarity between a q-uplet $(\omega_1,...,\omega_q)$ of the data set Ω, described by the modes $\{r_{i,k}^j\}_j$, and the intensional hoard h of the knowledge set, described by the modes $\{q_{i,k}^j\}_j$ [1]. The example given in the fourth part of this paper provides concrete details on this somewhat theoretical definition.

2 The Problem

Let us recall the problem. A knowledge base of modal structured objects called hoards is given at a date t. For example, an expert can describe a type of mushroom by a couple (stem, hat), where the stem has often an annulus and the hat is often red, sometimes blue, and the foot's size is always bigger than the hat's circumference: *mushroom* = [presence of annulus(stem) = (*often*)true] ∧ [color(hat) = (*often*)red, (*sometimes*)blue] ∧ [(*always*)(size(stem) ≤ circumference(hat))]. *Often, sometimes* and *always* are modes, corresponding to a well-defined semantic. Given a set Ω of elementary objects (in this example, hats and stems), we want first identify the structured objects contained in Ω^q; and then improve the knowledge base H by completing missing information and by modifying the modes of the elementary events of the hoards in H.

The following method separates the identifying phase from the learning phase. The identifying phase splits in two steps:

- minimal characterization of a hoard, with respect to the other hoards of the knowledge base. For instance, if the first type of mushroom *mushroom*[1] is clearly different from the others because it has always a green hat, then a rule should be: *rule*[1] = ([type_of(u) = hat] ∧ [color(u) = green] ⇒ *mushroom*[1]);
- application of the rules on Ω.

The main goal of this phase is clearly to reduce the matching complexity of the mechanism. Instead of looking at all the combinations of a vector of q individuals in a set of size n, we wish to find a simpler characterization of the vector, so that only a subpart of all the available information is used. Afterward the vector is completed with the remaining information.

The learning phase uses the output of the identification phase. It is the heart of the knowledge refinement's procedure. This task is achieved in two steps:

- completeness of the hoards belonging to the knowledge base;
- statistical modification of the modes.

We present first a theoretical overview of the method. In the forth section, a toy-example allows the different steps of the algorithm to be detailed in a more concrete way.

3 Theoretical Approach

Let H_t be a set of modal hoards at date t. For t = 0, the knowledge base may be

---

[1] One may consider that the property $h(\omega_1, ..., \omega_q) \geq \alpha$ leads to a fuzzy filter on the data [23]. Converted to the symbolic data analysis' language, this set is called the extension of *h* to level α [7].

provided by an expert of the domain. Let Ω be a set of data, each of them described by an elementary assertion.

3.1 Identification Phase

How to Produce a Characteristic Rule of a Hoard?
The goal of this step is to simplify the matching between a hoard and its extension: there are $C_n^q = \frac{n!}{q! \, (n-q)!}$ ways of getting a subset of size q in a set of size n. We want to decrease the number of possibilities, by minimizing the number of characteristic individuals in the hoard (i.e. by increasing the simplicity of the definition), and then the number of the attributes involved.

Algorithm
Let h be a hoard of H_t. The following method allows to determine a "minimal" rule r (in the way explained higher) associated to h: the premise p of the rule may be a hoard, or simply an assertion, and its conclusion is the hoard h.

> ❶ $p = \varnothing$. Let E be the set of elementary events $e_i = [y_i(u_k) = \{q_{i,k}^j\}_j]$ specific to h (i.e. that do not appear in the other hoards of H). If Card(E) = 1, then $p = \{E\}$. End of the procedure.
> ❷ Add in p the elementary event e of E of "maximal" mode (the space of modes is ordered !).
> ❸ Compute the quality of r (see below).
> ❹ If Quality(r) < α (threshold given by the user), go to ❷ else go to ❶ for another hoard of H.

Fig. 1. Minimal rule creation algorithm

Evaluation of the Quality of a Rule
The quality index measures the representativeness of the premise p of a rule r according to its conclusion h. Each elementary event of p is written: $y_i(\omega_k) = q_{i,k}^j$ (we give the same notation to the mapping $q_{i,k}^j$ and to the values it takes on different attributes). Let I (resp. K) be the set of indexes i of the attributes (resp. of indexes k of individuals) used in p. The quality Q of the rule r is computed by:

$$Q(r) = \frac{1}{Card(h)} \sum_{i \in I, k \in K} \cup_x^j q_{i,k}^j \tag{3}$$

Intuitively $Q(r) > \alpha$ means that r is supposed to express at least α percents of the knowledge contained in h. Q is a numerical measure. It supposes that the set L_x is numerical. In this paper *we restrict the meaning of the modes to a probabilistic or a possibilistic semantic* (therefore, $L_x = [0, 1]$ is convenient).

How Rules are Applied onto Ω?
Let r be a rule associated to a hoard h. Let n_K be the cardinal of the forming set K of individuals used in the premise of this rule. We associate to each index $k \in K$, a set I_k of elementary events $y_i(u_k) = q_{i,k}^j$, $i \in I_k$. For k = 1 to n_K, we look for an individual ω_k satisfying the definition $y_i(\omega_k) = q_{i,k}^j$ for ever $i \in I_k$. If several solutions are possible, we retain the one which produces the biggest sum on its modes.

The application of a rule r on Ω leads to determine the extension of the premise p of r in Ω^{nK}. Therefore, after this phase, only n_K individuals are taken into account by p. As we want to find the extension of the conclusion of r (namely h) in Ω^q, we have to look for the missing $(q - n_K)$ individuals in Ω. We use the properties and relations defined in h on these missing individuals, to decrease the size of the search field[2]. The individual objects used in the process are removed from the data base. The set of vectors found in Ω^q constitutes the extension ext_h of h on Ω^q.

Use of the Mapping h to Compare h with its Extension ext_h

Let us recall that h is a mapping from Ω^q in an ordered set L_x. Therefore, it is possible to verify the real adequacy between ext_h and h, and then to reject elements providing a too poor adequacy. If $c = (\omega_1, \dots, \omega_q)$ is an element of ext_h we can compute:

$$Ad(h, c) = h(c) = h_x (f_x (g_x (\cup_x^j q_{i,k}^j , \cup_x^j r_{i,k}^j))_i)_k \qquad (4)$$

Hence c is rejected if $h(c) < \beta$, where β is a threshold given by the user. h acts as a filter at level β on the elements of its extension. One can retain more or less elements simply by modifying the threshold β.

3.2 Learning Phase

The learning paradigm consists in refining h by completeness, with respect to its extension found through the identification step. A symbolic object is complete if it describes exactly the elements of its extension [5]. It appears to be an impossible task when we deal with complex objects such as modal hoards. We need to redefine the completeness.

Definition: Completeness

A modal hoard h is complete if :

① Each elementary event appearing in at least an element of its extension, appears in the definition of h;

② Each mode $q_{i,k}^j$ applied to an elementary event e_i of h is the result of a mapping

τ from $L_x^{n_h}$ to L_x (where n_h is the number of elements of ext_h that contain the

event e_i), so that τ keeps the right semantic in the hoard. For instance τ may be the mean for a probabilistic semantic, or the maximum for a possibilistic semantic.

The function τ is required to "trend" towards the completeness. This goal is achieved in two steps. First the modes of the missing elementary events are computed (to encompass the ① of the former definition). Next the modes of the previous existing elementary events are refined to match as best as possible with the new data.

---

2 As a result of this, instead of directly looking for a subset of q individuals in a set of size n, we split the problem in two parts: first the discovery of a subset of n_K individuals (n_K < q), then the research of the $(q - n_K)$ missing. The complexity of the matching problem decreases strongly: $C_n^{nK} + C_n^{q-nK} << C_n^q$ in the worst case. Moreover, the application of the domain theory limits the search space of these missing individuals.

Completeness of Elementary Events

Let $e_i = [y_i = r^j_{i,k}]$ be a kind of elementary event appearing in a subset S of the elements of the extension of h, but not appearing in the definition of h itself; we have called n_h the cardinal of such an event in ext_h (see the former definition). When adding to h the event: $e_i = [y_i = q^j_{i,k}]$, $q^j_{i,k}$ is defined by :

$$q^j_{i,k} = \tau(\{r^j_{i,k}\}_s), s \in S \tag{5}$$

If the semantic $x = pr$ is probabilistic, τ is the mean of the modes:

$$\tau(\{r^j_{i,k}\}_s) = \frac{1}{n_h} \sum_{s \in S} (\cup^j_{pr} \{r^j_{i,k}\}) \tag{6}$$

If the semantic is possibilistic, τ is the maximum of all the modes :

$$\tau(\{r^j_{i,k}\}_s) = \max_{s \in S} \{\cup^j_{pr} \{r^j_{i,k}\}\} \tag{7}$$

Refinement of the Modes of Known Events

Let $e_i = [y_i = r^j_{i,k}]$ be a kind of elementary event appearing in a subset S of the elements of the extension of h, that appears also in h; let n_h be the cardinal of such an event in ext_h. Let q^{old}_i be the "old" mode of e_i for the attribute i in the hoard h. The problem is to refine q^{old}_i according to the actual modes $r^j_{i,k}$ of e_i. We define a *transfer function* T such that the new mode q^{new}_i is refined by:

$$q^{new}_i = T(q^{old}_i) = (1 - \gamma) q^{old}_i + \gamma\, q_i, \; q_i = \tau(\{r^j_{i,k}\}_s), s \in S \tag{8}$$

where $q_i = \tau(\{r^j_{i,k}\}_s), s \in S$.

The parameter γ, provided by the user, determines the learning intensity. It gives the relative weights between the past and actual knowledge - the experience and the data. Note that the transfer function keeps the right probabilistic or possibilistic semantics.

3.3 General Outline of the Method

Two sources of knowledge are involved: the expert knowledge, supposed poor and imprecise at the beginning of the process (it may be for instance a ill-defined model on the data); and the implicit and new knowledge coming from the new data (they adapt the current knowledge to the new reality). The process tries to adjust, by an incremental way, the two sources to each other.

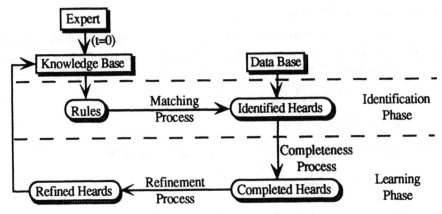

Fig. 2. Summary of the method

4 Applications and Example

The learning paradigm presented here supports a wide field of applications. Let us recall the following examples: image analysis, where only subparts of a scene are observed; intelligent handling of objects by a multi-armed robot; adaptation to a variable process, etc.

Two applications have been further studied in Thomson-CSF RCC/SES. They both deal with data fusion. The first one uses individual radar registrations and strategically knowledge on the foe's global radar deployment; the goal is to recognize subsets of radar. The second one deals with planes operations; one tries to detect as soon as possible, a well-defined foe operation (for instance by observing the number and the type of planes, their radio exchanges, etc.), and to adapt the knowledge to some tactical variations.

We present the algorithm's mechanism on a toy-example. Let us suppose that we are looking for two types of mushroom. An expert has described them by some attributes attached to the hat and the stem. Unfortunately the mushrooms are no more intact, but instead all the hats and the stems are mixed together in a basket. Therefore, we have two hoards (the couples stem/hat) described by the expert; and we have a lot of individual data, hats and stems. The task consists in putting together hats and stems, in recognizing the type of mushroom, and eventually in increasing the expert knowledge by refining the values of attributes given previously.

4.1 Domain Knowledge

Let $H = \{mushroom_1, mushroom_2\}$ be two types of mushroom described by a couple (stem, hat). Ω is the set of individual objects (stems and hat mixed in the basket). Let us set that $x = pr$ is a probabilistic semantic. We extend the definition of probabilistic assertions [8] by setting: $\forall\ k, h_{pr}(\{L_k\}) = \text{mean}\{L_k\}$.

Attributes

There are five attributes: *part, size, circum, color* and *annulus*:

$$y_1 = \text{"parts of mushroom"}: \quad \Omega \qquad \to O_1 = \{\text{stem, hat, other}\}$$

$$y_2 = \text{"size"}: \quad y_1^{-1}(\text{stem}) \qquad \to O_2 = [0, 10] \cup\ ]10, 20]$$

y_3 = "circumference": $\quad y_1^{-1}$(hat) $\quad \rightarrow O_3 = [0, 5] \cup {]}5, 10] \cup {]}10,15]$

y_4 = "color": $\quad y_1^{-1}$(hat) $\quad \rightarrow O_4 = \{$blue, red, green, other$\}$

y_5 = "presence of annulus": $\quad y_1^{-1}$(stem) $\quad \rightarrow O_5 = \{$true, false$\}$

Note that *part* is not a discriminating attribute, but only an informative one. We assume that each mushroom is normally well composed of a stem and a hat. The elementary events involving *part* do not help in the identification process, therefore they do not occur in the forthcoming computations.

Basic Knowledge of the Mushrooms Expert: the Hoards

• *mushroom*$_1$ = $[part(X) = $ foot$] \wedge [size(X) = (0.75)[0, 10], (0.25)[10, 20]] \wedge$
$[part(Y) = $ hat$] \wedge [color(Y) = $ red$]$

mushroom$_1$ describes a type of mushroom which has a stem of size between 0 and 10 inches three times on four and between 10 and 20 inches one time on four, and a red hat. The modes are defined by:

$q_{1,1}^1$(stem) = 1; $q_{1,1}^1$(hat) = 0; $q_{1,1}^1$(other) = 0; $q_{2,1}^1$([0,10]) = 0.75;

$q_{2,1}^1$(]10,20]) = 0.25; $q_{1,2}^1$(stem) = 0; $q_{1,2}^1$(hat) = 1; $q_{1,2}^1$(other) = 0;

$q_{4,2}^1$(blue) = 0; $q_{4,2}^1$(red) = 1; $q_{4,2}^1$(green) = 0; $q_{4,2}^1$(other) = 0.

Note that there is no disjunction of values in the description (j = 1 for each descriptor). In other words, we will not use the operators $\cup_{pr}$, $\cap_{pr}$, and C_{pr} of OP_{pr} in this example. For the end of this paper, we can simplify the notation by using q_{ik} instead of $\{q_{i,k}^j\}_j$.

• *mushroom*$_2$ = $[part(X) = $ foot$] \wedge$
$[part(Y) = $ hat$] \wedge [color(Y) = (0.5)$blue, (0.5)green$] \wedge [circum(Y) \le size(X)]$

mushroom$_2$ describes a type of mushroom which has a blue or a green hat (with equal probabilities) and its hat's circumference is smaller than its foot's size.

The Data

For the sake of simplicity in this toy-example we deal only with the case where the modes $r_{i,k}^j$ are 0 or 1 $\forall$ i, j, k (we can also simplify the notation by r_{ik}). We have 14 individuals (7 hats and 7 stems) described by five attributes.

In this table the examples covered by the expert knowledge on the first kind of mushroom (*mushroom*$_1$) are shadowed (cf. figure 3, next page).

ind \ var	part	size	circum	color	annulus
ex_1	stem	8	nil	nil	true
ex_2	stem	8	nil	nil	true
ex_3	stem	7	nil	nil	false
ex_4	stem	6	nil	nil	true
ex_5	stem	15	nil	nil	false
ex_6	stem	8	nil	nil	false
ex_7	hat	nil	8	blue	nil
ex_8	hat	nil	9	blue	nil
ex_9	hat	nil	5	red	nil
ex_{10}	hat	nil	8	red	nil
ex_{11}	hat	nil	15	red	nil
ex_{12}	hat	nil	11	red	nil
ex_{13}	hat	nil	12	other	nil
ex_{14}	stem	15	nil	nil	false

Fig. 3. Set of data Ω

4.2 Application of the Algorithm

We detail all the phases of the algorithm, in the same order as in the theoretical presentation.

Identification Phase

Determination of Identification Rules
Rules are computed onto the definitions of $mushroom_1$ and $mushroom_2$, and then applied onto the data set. The quality rates are $\alpha = \beta = 0.5$. The set of elementary events characterizing $mushroom_1$ against $mushroom_2$ is:
$E = \{[size(X) = (0.75)[0, 10]]; \ size(X) = (0.25)]10, 20]]; \ [color(Y) = (1)red]\}$
The event of maximum mode is $[color(Y) = (1)red]$, therefore the first proposed rule is:
$rule_1 = ([part(X) = \{hat\}] \wedge [color(X) = \{red\}] \Rightarrow mushroom_1)$. The rule's quality is $Q(rule_1) = 0.5$, (let us recall that *part* is not a discriminating attribute), which is coherent with the threshold α^3. In the same way we find:
$rule_2 = ([part(X) = \{hat\}] \wedge [color(X) = \{blue, green\}] \Rightarrow mushroom_2)$, of quality $Q(rule_2) = 0.5$.
One may note that, in this case, the rules are firing on a single individual, instead of

---

3 Note that if the threshold was higher (for instance $\alpha = 0.7$), we should have to add another item to the rule's premiss: $[type(Y) = \{stem\}] \wedge [size(Y) = (0.75)[0, 10]]$.
Then the rule should be: $[rule_1 = [type(X) = \{hat\}] \wedge [y_4(X) = \{red\}] \wedge [type(Y) = \{stem\}]$
$\wedge [size(Y) = [0, 10]] \Rightarrow mushroom_1]$, of quality $Q(rule_1) = \dfrac{1 + 0.75}{2} = 0.875$.

on a couple. For each hoard, the number of matching to be tested decreases from 91 $(= \frac{n(n-1)}{2})$ to $n = 14$ (where n is the cardinal of Ω).

Firing the Rules onto Ω^2

The first rule $rule_1$ is true for ex_9. Therefore, an element of the extension of $mushroom_1$ in Ω^2 is composed of ex_9. We have to look for the second part of $mushroom_1$, described by $[part(X) = \{stem\}] \wedge [size(X) = (0.75)[0, 10], (0.25)[10, 20]]$ in $mushroom_1$. Here every ex_i such that $part(ex_i) = \{stem\}$ is possible, but it is better to choose an example with the size of the stem being between 0 and 10 inches: we can choose between ex_1, ex_2, ex_3, and ex_4. For example, the couple (ex_1, ex_9) matches well with the description of $mushroom_1$. We extract ex_1 and ex_9 of the data set Ω, and the rule $rule_1$ is iterated on the remain of Ω's data.

Eventually, the following couples are found: (ex_1, ex_9), (ex_2, ex_{10}), (ex_3, ex_{11}) and (ex_4, ex_{12}). They are the extension of $mushroom_1$ in Ω^2.

By the same way, we obtain using $rule_2$: $Ext_{\Omega^2}mushroom_2 = \{(ex_5, ex_7), (ex_{14}, ex_8)\}$.The property $[circum(Y) \le size(X)]$ allows to avoid the possible matching (ex_6, ex_8), because the size of ex_6 is smaller than the circumference of ex_8.

Adequacy Between a Hoard and its Extension

Let us compute $mushroom_1(ex_1, ex_9)$: $mushroom_1(ex_1, ex_9) = h_{pr}(f_{pr}(g_{pr}(q_{i,k}, r_{i,k}))_{i=1,5})_{k=1,2}$. Only two attributes are relevant for this calculus: *size* and *color* (*part* is not discriminant). Using the probabilistic definitions of h_{pr} and f_{pr} (mean) and g_{pr} (scalar product), we obtain: $mushroom_1(ex_1, ex_9) = \frac{1}{2} [(0.75 \times 1) + (1 \times 1)] = \frac{7}{8}$, which is above threshold β. The other computations also give: $mushroom_1(ex_2, ex_{10}) = \frac{7}{8}$; $mushroom_1(ex_3, ex_{11}) = \frac{7}{8}$; $mushroom_1(ex_4, ex_{12}) = \frac{7}{8}$.

For $mushroom_2$, only *color* is used for the calculus (*part* is not discriminant and the property is only used to verify the legality of the matching). The computation give: $mushroom_2(ex_5, ex_7) = \frac{1}{2}$; and $mushroom_2(ex_{14}, ex_8) = \frac{1}{2}$.

Learning Phase

Completeness of Elementary Events

Let us consider the couple (ex_1, ex_9). ex_1 is described by three attributes: *part, size* and *annulus*. However in $mushroom_1$, X is described by only two attributes: *part* and *size*. Then $mushroom_1$ has to be completed by the elementary event: $[annulus(X) = q_{5,1}(true), q_{5,1}(false)]$, where $q_{i,k}(mode) = \tau(\{r_{i,k}(mode)\}_s)$, $s \in S$. Let us recall that S denotes the set of events of the extension of $mushroom_1$ where the attribute *annulus* appears: ex_1, ex_2, ex_3, ex_4 (Card(S) = 4). $q_{i,k}(true) = \frac{1}{4}(1+1+0+1) = 0.75$; $q_{i,k}(false) = \frac{1}{4}(0+0+1+0) = 0.25$. Hence $mushroom_1$ is completed by the event $[annulus(X) = 0.75(true), 0.25(false)]$.

$mushroom_1$ is also completed by: $[circum(Y) = (0.5)]5, 10], (0.5))]10, 15]]$, and $mushroom_2$ by: $[circum(Y) =]5, 10]]$ and $[size(X) =]10, 20]]$.

Refinement of Previous Modes

When there is no previous definition of an event in the hoard, its modes are computed from nothing. But if such a definition occurs, the event's modes have to be refined if the past knowledge expressed in the hoard and the current knowledge presented in the data are different. For instance in $mushroom_2$, the color of the hat is green or blue: $q_{4,2}(green) = 0.5$ and $q_{4,2}(blue) = 0.5$, but the corresponding hats in the extension of $mushroom_2$ in Ω^2 are always blue ($r_{4,2}(blue) = 1$ and $r_{4,2}(green) = 0$ for every hat). The function T allows the modes' refinement:

$$T(q^{new}) = (1 - \gamma)\, q^{old} + \gamma\, T(\{r_{i,k}(m)\}_s),\ s \in S$$

Let be $\gamma = 0.5$; T is the mean. The refined modes are :

$$q_{4,2}(blue) = (1 - 0.5) \times 0.5 + 0.5 \times (\tfrac{1}{2}\,(1 + 1)) = 0.75 \quad \text{and}$$

$$q_{4,2}(green) = (1 - 0.5) \times 0.5 + 0.5 \times (\tfrac{1}{2}\,(0 + 0)) = 0.25.$$

In this toy-example, one can verify that only another mode is changing. It concerns the *size* in $mushroom_1$. In the definition of $mushroom_1$, the *size* of the foot is between 0 and 10 with a probability of 0.75 and between 10 and 20 with a probability of 0.25. Therefore, all of the four feet of the extension of $mushroom_1$ have a *size* between 0 and 10 inches. The refinement of *size* in $mushroom_1$ is computed by:

$$q_{2,1}([0, 10]) = (1 - 0.5) \times 0.75 + 0.5 \times (\tfrac{1}{4}\,(1 + 1 + 1 + 1)) = 0.875 \quad \text{and}$$

$$q_{2,1}(]10, 20]) = (1 - 0.5) \times 0.25 + 0.5 \times (\tfrac{1}{4}\,(0 + 0 + 0 + 0)) = 0.125.$$

4.3 Result of the Process: Comparison Between old and new Hoards

- $mushroom_1^t = [part(X) = \text{foot}] \wedge [size(X) = (0.75)[0, 10], (0.25)]10, 20]] \wedge$

  $[part(Y) = \text{hat}] \wedge [color(Y) = \text{red}]$

- $mushroom_1^{t+1} = [part(X) = \text{foot}] \wedge [size(X) = (0.875)[0,10], (0.125)]10,20]] \wedge$

  $[annulus(X) = (0.75)\text{true}, (0.25)\text{false}] \wedge$

  $[part(Y) = \text{hat}] \wedge [circum(Y) = (0.5)]5, 10], (0.5)]10, 15]] \wedge [color(Y) = \text{red}]$

$mushroom_1$ describes a type of mushroom which has a stem of size between 0 and 10 inches ($pr = 0.75$) or between 10 and 20 inches ($pr = 0.25$), an annulus ($pr = 0.75$), and a red hat of circumference between 5 and 10 inches ($pr = 0.5$), or between 10 and 15 inches ($pr = 0.5$) (compare with the description of § 4.1 about the domain knowledge).

In the same way, we observe a refinement in the definition of $mushroom_2$:

- $mushroom_2^t = [part(X) = \text{foot}] \wedge$

  $[part(Y) = \text{hat}] \wedge [color(Y) = (0.5)\text{blue}, (0.5)\text{green}] \wedge$

  $[circum(Y) \le size(X)]$

- $mushroom_2^{t+1} = [part(X) = \text{foot}] \wedge [size(X) =]10, 20]] \wedge [annulus(X) = \text{false}] \wedge$

  $[part(Y) = \text{hat}] \wedge [circum(Y) =]5, 10]] \wedge [color(Y) = (0.75)\text{blue}, (0.25)\text{green}] \wedge$

  $[circum(Y) \le size(X)]$

5 Discussion and evaluation

According to [19], learning consists in building and in modifying representations on the basis of a set of experiences. In this definition appears the basic notion of *representation*. The representation language we are using, coming from the symbolic objects, allows to express abstractions by using variables, and relations between these variables. Quantitative as well as relational information can be used. This kind of information has been successfully used to build pyramidal representations [2] and key identification graphs [15], in factorial axis representation [12], with histograms [4], and many others in the symbolic data analysis field of research.

The close subject dealing with concept formation has been also widely pointed up, as part as an incremental process in COBWEB [10] or not [18]. The systems deal usually with an aggregation (or a generalization) phase on the objects, followed by a characterization (or a specialization) phase of the classes (see, for instance, GLAUBER, RUMMAGE and DISCON in the domain of scientific discovery [14]; CLUSTER/2 [18] is one of the earlier example).

Learning methods of complex or structured objects are also well known in the Artificial Intelligence community. Systems are using commonly a First Order Logic, where objects are predicates [13], or defined by examples as in KBG [1] or graphs as in CHARADE [11]. The semantic is expressed *outside* of the objects and is used for instance in an induction engine, as for example in KATE [16].

Eventually, a lot of works is coming from the Inductive Logic Programming approach. The representation and the structure of the knowledge are direct consequences of the use of this knowledge. Therefore, most of the systems are incremental, can use a background knowledge, and are able to learn recursive concepts (see, for example, FOIL [21] or ITOU [22]).

In our method, it is impossible to learn these kinds of recursive concepts because the rules are directly extracted from the knowledge base which has an acyclic structure. Our formalism allows us to redefine the dual notion of specialization-generalization found in most algorithms [20], by the couple intension-extension. It may be seen as a subset of the first order logic representation, where the semantic and the domain knowledge are declared *inside* the objects. This formalism makes the statistical aspect of the method clearer, by highlighting the role of the attributes as in symbolic data analysis.

The results well correspond to a learning process, where new representations are built and some other are refined on the basis of a set of data. The originality of this learning comes from that different levels of abstraction are used between the data and the domain knowledge. It is too early to have a full evaluation of the impact of the method on various application fields. Thus, as shown on the example of section 4, the two goals defined at the beginning of the paper (increasing the knowledge by using new experiences and expressing this knowledge in an easy way) can be fulfilled on a specific application.

6 Conclusion

We have presented a method dealing with a new kind of problem: how to recognize and to learn structured objects, when only an incomplete knowledge is available, and subparts of the objects are observed. To answer the problem, we have defined a special kind of objects: the modal hoards, based upon a formalism coming from the symbolic data analysis. New properties defined on the hoards lead towards an original learning process, that uses strongly the modal approach. Thus, some crucial points have to be improved: the automatic calculus of thresholds, according to the used index quality; the expression of the transfer function for belief objects; the evolution of the learning intensity during time; the learning of modes on properties; the formulation of new hypothesis with the individuals not used in the process. An extension of the process to a hierarchical model would be useful, so that we could use complex objects at different levels of knowledge. The next steps we are trying to develop are: how to create a structure as a lattice on the set of modal hoards, and how to use such a structure to build a visual representation of the hoards.

This work has been supported by the Thomson-CSF RCC company to which the author is greatly indebted, especially to Mr Gilbert Milhem, for the fruitful discussion about the problem. In the same way to Pr Edwin Diday from INRIA and to the CLOREC team, for their theoretical support on symbolic objects and their constant encouragement during this work. Thanks to Dr. Michel Manago and to the Research Group on Artificial Intelligence of the University of Kaiserslautern, especially Prof. Dr. Michael M. Richter, who are allowing me to continue my thesis work in a very good environment during my National Duty.

7 References

1. Bisson G. "Learning of rule systems by combining clustering and generalization", in Proc. of Symbolic-Numeric Data Analysis and Learning, eds. E. Diday, Y. Lechevallier, Nova Science Publishers, New York, pp. 399-415.

2. Brito P., Diday E. "Pyramidal representation of symbolic objects", in *Proc. of the NATO advanced Workshop on data and computed-assisted decisions*, Hamburg 3-5 Sep. 1989, eds. M. Schader, W. Gaul, Springer-Verlag.

3. Brito P. *Analyse de données symboliques. Pyramides d'héritage*, Thèse de l'Université Paris IX Dauphine, 1991.

4. De Carvalho F.A.T. "Histogrammes de variables d'objets assertion booléens", in *Traitement des connaissances Symboliques-Numériques*, Paris 14-15 Mai 1992, pp. 65-81, ed. LISE - CEREMADE, Université Paris IX Dauphine.

5. Diday E. "Introduction à l'approche symbolique en analyse des données", in *Actes des journées Symboliques-Numériques pour l'apprentissage de connaissances à partir des données*, eds. E. Diday, Y. Kodratoff, CEREMADE - Université Paris IX Dauphine, 1987, pp. 21-56.

6. Diday E. "Introduction à l'analyse des données symboliques: objets symboliques modaux et implicite", in *Actes des 2èmes journées Symboliques-Numériques pour l'apprentissage de connaissances à partir d'observations*, eds. E. Diday, Y. Kodratoff, LRI - Université de Paris-Sud, Orsay, 1988, pp. 1-30.

7. Diday E. "Towards a statistical theory of intensions for knowledge analysis", Rapport de Recherche INRIA N° 1494, 1991.

8. Diday E. "Des objets de l'analyse des données à ceux de l'analyse des connaissances", in *Induction Symbolique et Numérique à partir de données*, CEPADUES-EDITION, pp. 9-75, 1991.

9. Dubois D., Prade H. *Théorie des possibilités*, ed. Masson, 1985.

10. Fisher D. "Conceptual clustering, Learning from examples and Inference", in *Proc. of the 4th International Workshop on Machine Learning*, Irvine, California, 1987.

11. Ganascia J.B. "Improvement and refinement of the learning bias semantic", in *Proc. of the 8th ECAI*, pp. 238-270, 1988.

12. Gettler-Summa M. "Factorial axis representation by symbolic objects", in *Traitement des connaissances Symboliques-Numériques*, Paris 14-15 Mai 1992, pp. 53-64, ed. LISE - CEREMADE, Université Paris IX Dauphine.

13. Kodratoff Y. *Leçons d'apprentissage symbolique automatique*, CEPADUES-EDITIONS, 1986.

14. Langley P., Fisher D. "Approaches to conceptual clustering", in *Proc. of the 9th IJCAI*, Morgan Kaufman Publishers, pp. 691-697, 1991.

15. Lebbe J., Vignes R. "Un système générateur de graphes d'identification d'objets symboliques", in *Induction Symbolique et Numérique à partir de Données*, CEPADUES-EDITIONS, 1991.

16. Manago M. *Intégration de techniques numériques et symboliques en apprentissage*, Thèse de l'Université Paris-Sud, Orsay, 1988.

17. Michalski R. S. "Pattern recognition as rule-guided inductive inference", in *IEEE Transactions on pattern analysis and machine intelligence*, Vol. PAMI-2, n° 4, 1980.

18. Michalski R. S., Stepp R. "An application of AI techniques to structuring objects into an optimal conceptual hierarchy", in *Proc. of the 7th IJCAI*, Vancouver, Canada, 1981.

19. Michalski R.S., Carbonell J., Mitchell T. "Understanding the nature of learning", in *Machine Learning 2 - An artificial Intelligence Approach*, Tioga, pp. 3-25, 1986.

20. Mitchell T. "Generalization as search", in *Artificial Intelligence*, Vol. 18, pp. 243-250, 1982.

21. Quinlan J.R. "Learning logical definitions from relations", in *Machine Learning Journal 5*, pp. 239-266, 1990.

22. Rouveirol C. *ITOU: induction de théorie en ordre un*, Thèse de l'Université Paris-Sud, Orsay, 1991.

23. Vignard P. *Représentation des connaissances. Mécanismes d'exploitation et d'apprentissage*, INRIA, 1991.

24. Vignes R. *Caractérisation automatique de groupes biologiques*, Thèse de l'Université Paris VI, 1991.

The Semantics of Rational Contractions

Jürgen Giesl[1] and Ingrid Neumann[2]

[1] Dept. of Computer Science, Technical University Darmstadt, Alexanderstr. 10,
64283 Darmstadt, Germany, Email: giesl@inferenssysteme.informatik.th-darmstadt.de
[2] Dept. of Computer Science, University of Karlsruhe, Kaiserstr. 12,
76128 Karlsruhe, Germany, Email: neumann@ira.uka.de

Abstract

The *Logic of Theory Change* developed by Alchourrón, Gärdenfors and Makinson is concerned with the revision of beliefs in the face of new and possibly contradicting information. This nonmonotonic process consists of a contraction and an expansion transforming one belief into another. Beliefs are represented by consistent deductively closed sets of formulas. To achieve minimal change Alchourrón, Gärdenfors and Makinson suggested widely accepted postulates that rational contractions have to fulfill.

In practical applications, e.g. knowledge representation, deductively closed sets of formulas have to be representable in a finite way. Therefore our main interest is in *rational finite contractions*, i.e. rational contractions that transform sets of formulas possessing a finite base into finitely representable sets again.

We have formulated a semantical characterization of rational finite contractions which provides an insight into the true nature of these operations and shows all possibilities to define concrete functions of this kind.

Semantically, the rational finite contraction of a set Φ by a formula φ means extending the models M of Φ by some set of models of $\neg\varphi$. This set has to be uniquely determined by its restriction to a finite subsignature.

By means of this characterization we have examined the relationship of the concrete contractions known from literature and have found that they are all defined according to the same semantical strategy. Its aim is to extend the former set of models M by those models of $\neg\varphi$ that can be obtained by a *"small"* change of M.

This strategy results in maintaining those formulas of Φ which belong to the subsignature not affected by the change of M. But as the number of "important" formulas in Φ is not equal for different subsignatures of the same size we argue that this strategy leads to a contraintuitive behaviour[3].

We have discovered that the syntactical goal of keeping as many important formulas as possible in the contracted set corresponds to the following semantical strategy: M has to be extended by some models I of $\neg\varphi$ such that the *number of "big" changes* of M which result in I is *as large as possible*. Using our characterization we suggest a new rational finite contraction defined according to this strategy.

---

[3] When restricting ourselves to clauses instead of formulas a clause is the more important the less literals it consists of. If Φ is the deductive closure of $\{a, b \lor c\}$ the subsignatures $\{a, c\}$ and $\{b, c\}$ have the same size, but the most important clause of Φ does not belong to the latter one.

A Uniform Framework for Deductive Database Derivation Strategies

Robert DEMOLOMBE[1]

ONERA/CERT
2 av. Edouard Belin, B.P. 4025
31055 Toulouse,
FRANCE
demolomb@tls-cs.cert.fr

A uniform framework is presented to describe the most typical strategies that are used to compute answers to Deductive Databases. The framework is based on the definition of a general Least Fixpoint operator that operates on meta rules. Each set of meta rules represents a different strategy, and the forward evaluation of these meta rules generates the same set of consequences as it is generated by each strategy. This allows an easy qualitative comparison of their efficiency.

An original feature of this presentation is that answers are sets of clauses and not just sets of substitutions, another one is that the operator operates on an extended Herbrand base which is a set of ground clauses, and not just a set of ground atoms.

We first consider Deductive Databases with Horn clauses and we present strategies based on the general ideas of Forward chaining, Backward chaining, and parallel or sequential evaluation of antecedents in the rules. We show that strategies, like Magic Sets, can also be represented with limited modifications. The modification is essentially to define an abstract interpretation where derivations that differ only by constant names are considered as the "same" derivation. Additional meta rules simulates compilation of object rules for a given type of query.

Then we consider non Horn clauses, and we present strategies to compute Intensional answers and Conditional answers. These answers are sets of clauses that contain an instance of the literal that represents the query. These answers can be used for finding missing hypothesis, and then for Abductive reasoning.

Though the paper presents new strategies for the computation of Intensional and Conditional answers, its main purpose is didactic, and we think that the presented framework will allow to design more easily new strategies.

Keywords: Deductive Databases, Automated Deduction

Assumption Set Semantics
(The Procedures)

Joaquim Nunes Aparício

DCS, U. Nova de Lisboa
2825 Monte da Caparica, Portugal
jna@fct.unl.pt

Abstract. Our purpose is to extend logic programming semantics for programs with some form of denial statements [2] specifying that some sets of literals cannot all belong to the meaning of a program. Denials represent an intuitive form of knowledge representation extending the capabilities of logic programming as a tool for knowledge representation and reasoning. In [2] we defined the intended meaning of a program with a set of denials, and show that a set of denials is isomorphic to sets of assumption based denials. The model theory we introduce there is clearly general in the sense it does not rely on any particular semantics. A consequence is that satisfaction of (denials) may be seen as satisfaction w.r.t. to a smaller class of models (revised models) which are also stable under a suitable operator. Operationally, satisfaction of denials is equivalent to membership of the set of assumption based denials, thus avoiding the need for general consistency checking, which are more suitable (in some sense) for logic programming based implementations.

In [1] we introduce $WFS_\perp$ and show an application of the use of denial rules to add a second form of negation in the spirit of [3] when the logic programming semantics being used is well founded semantics [4] and define the conditional meaning of the program. Here we present procedures [1] which are sound and complete (for ground programs) w.r.t. $WFS_\perp$ and the conditional meaning of the program.

References

1. Joaquim N. Aparício. Declarative belief revision (poster). In *LPNMR93 workshop*, July 1993.
2. Joaquim N. Aparício. *Logic Programming: A Tool for Reasoning*. PhD thesis, Faculdade Ciências e Tecnologia, 1993. In preparation.
3. L. M. Pereira and J. J. Alferes. Well founded semantics for logic programs with explicit negation. In B. Neumann, editor, *10th European Conference on Artificial Intelligence*, pages 102–106. John Wiley & Sons, Ltd, 1992.
4. A. Van Gelder, K. A. Ross, and J. S. Schlipf. The well-founded semantics for general logic programs. *Journal of the ACM*, 38(3):620–650, 1991.

---

[1] Code is available electronically from the author.

Bargaining Agents

Stefan Bussmann and Jürgen Müller

German Research Center for Artificial Intelligence (DFKI)
Stuhlsatzenhausweg 3 D-6600 Saarbrücken 11 Germany
E-mail: mueller@dfki.uni-sb-de Tel.: ++49 681 302 5322 Fax: ++49 681 302 5341

Abstract. The following extended abstract will give a brief overview of a multi agent game domain and our agent architecture.

Bargaining for Letters

The scenario consists of a group of agents that have to construct words from letters. Each agent has a certain set of letters and he is looking for additional ones to succeed in building one word out of a given list. An agent does neither know the other agents' words, nor does he know that the other agents want to build words at all. Since we are dealing with a bargaining scenario, the agents only know that the other agents have letters which they are willing to trade. It is the agents' task to find out which letters the others trade and which letters they may accept in return.

The Agent Architecture

A bargaining agent consists of three components, the *communicator*, the *knowledge base*, and the *planner*, that all run in parallel.

1. **The Communicator**: This component is the interface of the agent. It receives and performs speech acts. Received speech acts are translated into the internal format and inserted into the knowledge base. Simultaneously, the communicator retranslates internal formats to speech acts.
2. **The Knowledge Base**: It holds the data structures of the *discourse model*, e.g. the history of the speech acts, and the *domain knowledge*, which includes knowledge about what the bargainer has, e.g. his letters, and how he behaved in the past, e.g. the denial of proposals.
   As soon as a speech act is inserted, the knowledge base does the *semantic forwarding* with the help of rules that fire on certain types of speech acts. Besides, it does part of the agent's reasoning.
3. **The Planner**: The planner executes the problem solving algorithm. The planning is not done in the classical sense, but it pursues a special scheme of a bargaining problem solving.

The full paper describes the different components in detail and it presents a selected run of the bargaining process.

A Constraint Maintenance Algorithm Based on Value Propagation

Gilles Trombettoni

Secoia Project, INRIA – CERMICS, 2004 route des Lucioles,
B.P. 93, 06902 Sophia-Antipolis Cedex, FRANCE
email: trombe@sophia.inria.fr

Abstract. Constraint problems are usually solved by specific satisfaction methods. Another way for solving constraints, called solution maintenance, is to try to recover the consistency from an existing solution, disturbed by the addition of new constraints and/or the update of some variables. We present in this paper a solution maintenance algorithm based on value propagation in the constraint network. This algorithm is specially appropriate to interactive applications like spreadsheets, several different kinds of programs for incremental manipulation of geometrical figures, and also in case-based reasoning. Although the method is efficient and incremental, it may not be able to find a solution even when the constraint problem has one.

The basic principle of the algorithm is the following. The user gives in an incremental manner computation methods $m(C, V)$ which compute a new value for the set of variables V in order to satisfy the constraints C. Perturbations introduced into a solution involve a solving phase divided into two steps: the *planning step* and the *runtime step*. During the planning step, the algorithm builds a directed acyclic graph (DAG) yielding a partial order between methods, according to the topology of the constraint network and the available methods. The roots of this DAG correspond to the initial perturbations. In the runtime step, the algorithm follows the DAG from the roots to the leaves and applies a method at each node. If this step succeeds, we get a new solution. Note that the variables can be modified only once during the solving phase.

The *Constraints* system manages both another propagation algorithm and a reasoning maintenance system in order to obtain solution maintenance. The resulting algorithm is quite inefficient.

The main influence on the design of our value propagation has been the *Prose* system by Pierre Berlandier (INRIA). Our algorithm improves the one used in Prose on the following points:

- several distinct methods associated to the same constraint can be applied during a solving phase,
- the computation methods are general and may satisfy several constraints by altering the value of several variables,
- the basic principle of the *runtime step* presented above is extended in order to take into account methods yielding several values for a variable (in the case of inequations for example), and
- our algorithm can avoid some kinds of failures due to cycles in the constraint network.

A Text-to-Phoneme Translator for the Portuguese Language

Geraldo Lino de Campos

Dimas Trevisan Chbane

Departamento de Engenharia de Computação e Sistemas Digitais
Escola Politécnica da Universidade de São Paulo -São Paulo 01065-970
Caixa postal 8174 - BRASIL - e-mail: RTC@FPSP.FAPESP.BR

A system for text-to-speech conversion for the Portuguese language is described. The system includes a 320,000 words vocabulary, encompassing all valid Portuguese words. Using information in this vocabulary and a set of rules, the system is able to translate a general text in the corresponding phoneme sequence.

Ain73Ainsworth, W. A., A system for Converting English Text into Speech. IEEE Trans. on Audio and Electroacoustics, **21(3)**:288-240, June 1973.

All87Allen, J., Synthesis of Speech from unrestricted text, Proc. of the IEEE, **64(4)**:433-422, April 1987.

Coi89

Van Coile, B. M., The DEPES Development system for Text-to Speech Synthesis, in Proc. of the Inter. Conf. on Acoustics, Speech and Signal Processing, 250-253, 1989.

Elo76Elovitz, H. S. et al, Letter-to-sound Rules for Automatic Translation of English text to Phonetics, IEEE Trans. on Acoustics, Speech and Signal Processing, ASSP **24(6)**:446-459, Dec. 1976

Fre60Fredkin, E., Trie Memory, Comm. of the ACM, **3(9)**:490-500, Sept 1960.

Gro89Gross, M., The Use of Finite Automata in the Lexical Representation of Natural Language, in M. Gross and D. Perrin, editors, Electronic Dictionaries and Automata in Computational Linguistics, 34-50, Springer-Verlag, Berlin, 1989. Lecture Notes in Computer Science, vol 377.

Her87Hertz, S. R. et al, The Delta Rule Development System for Speech Synthesis from Text. Proc. of the IEEE, **73(3)**:737-793, Sept. 1987

Kla87Klatt, D. H., Review of test-to-Speech Conversion for English, Journal of the Acoustical Society of America, **82(3)**:737-793, Sept 1987

Luc93Lucchesi, C. L., and Kowaltowsky, T., Applications of Finite Automata Representing Large Vocabularies, submitted for publication

Sam78Samburg, M.R. et al, On reducing the buzz in LPC synthesis, J. Acoust. Soc. Am. **63(3)**, Mar 1978

Learning probabilistic models by conceptual pyramidal clustering

E. Diday (*) , P. Brito (**) , E. Mfoumoune (*)

(*) INRIA, Rocquencourt, 78153 Le Chesnay Cedex France & Univ. Paris-IX Dauphine, France

(**) Universidade de Aveiro, Secção Autónoma de Matemática, Campus Universitário de Santiago, 3800 Aveiro, Portugal

Abstract

Symbolic objects (Diday (1987, 1992), Brito, Diday (1990), Brito (1991)) allow to model data on the form of descriptions by intension, thus generalizing the usual tabular model of data analysis. This modelisation allows to take into account variability within a set. The formalism of symbolic objects has some notions in common with VL1, proposed by Michalski (1980) ; however VL1 is mainly based on propositional and predicate calculus, while the formalism of symbolic objects allows for an explicit interpretation within its framework, by considering the duality intension-extension. That is, given a set of observations, we consider the couple (symbolic object - extension in the given set). This results from the wish to keep a statistics point of view. The need to represent non-deterministic knowledge, that is, data for which the values for the different variables are assigned a weight, led to considering an extension of assertion objects to probabilist objects (Diday 1992). In this case, data are represented by probability distributions on the variables observation sets. The notions previously defined for assertion objects are the generalized to this new kind of symbolic objects. Other extensions can be found in Diday (1992).

In order to obtain a clustering structure on the data, we propose a pyramidal symbolic clustering method. Methods of conceptual clustering have known a great improvement in the last years. These methods aim at obtaining a system of interpreted clusters. In the eighties a large number of conceptual clustering methods have been developed, mention should be made to Michalski (1980), Michalski, Diday and Stepp (1982), Fisher (1987). The pyramidal model (Diday (1984, 1986), Bertrand (1986)) generalizes hierarchical clustering by presenting an overlapping instead of a partition at each level ; pyramidal clustering produces a structure which is nevertheless much simpler than the lattice structure, since each cluster should be an interval of a total order θ (as a consequence, pyramids present no crossing in the graphic representation). So, the pyramidal model supplies a structure which is richer than hierarchical trees (in that it keeps more information), and that, compared to lattices, are easily interpretable.

The method we present builds a pyramid by an agglomerative algorithm. Each cluster is represented by a symbolic object whose extension - that is the set of elements verifying it - is the cluster itself. Hence a cluster is represented by a couple extension - intension.

An application on textual data modelled by probabilist objects (texts described by frequency of key-words) allowed to obtain a pyramid whose clusters (representing though groups of texts) are themselves represented by probabilist objects, we thus identify groups of texts refering to close subjects.

Springer-Verlag
and the Environment

We at Springer-Verlag firmly believe that an international science publisher has a special obligation to the environment, and our corporate policies consistently reflect this conviction.

We also expect our business partners – paper mills, printers, packaging manufacturers, etc. – to commit themselves to using environmentally friendly materials and production processes.

The paper in this book is made from low- or no-chlorine pulp and is acid free, in conformance with international standards for paper permanency.

Lecture Notes in Artificial Intelligence (LNAI)

Lecture Notes in Computer Science